RATIONALISING CONSTRUCTIVE TRUSTS

Constructive trusts significantly interfere with the rights of an apparent legal owner of property. This makes it necessary for their imposition to be properly explained and justified. Unfortunately, attempts to rationalise constructive trusts as a whole—as opposed to specific doctrines or particular aspects of constructive trusts—have been few and far between.

Rationalising Constructive Trusts proposes a new structure for a coherent understanding of constructive trusts. By using a combination of conceptual tools, it provides answers to a number of crucial questions, for example: What are the ingredients of a constructive trust claim? What are the limits of constructive trusts? How can we rationalise the imposition of constructive trusts in particular situations? Why do judges exercise varying degrees of remedial discretion in different doctrines?

From a wider perspective, the structured understanding helps us to appreciate the precise ambit and role of express, constructive, and resulting trusts.

Volume 25 in the series Hart Studies in Private Law

Rationalising Constructive Trusts

Dr Ying Khai Liew

•HART•
OXFORD • LONDON • NEW YORK • NEW DELHI • SYDNEY

HART PUBLISHING
Bloomsbury Publishing Plc
Kemp House, Chawley Park, Cumnor Hill, Oxford, OX2 9PH, UK

HART PUBLISHING, the Hart/Stag logo, BLOOMSBURY and the Diana logo are trademarks of Bloomsbury Publishing Plc

First published in Great Britain 2017
Paperback edition, 2020

A catalogue record for this book is available from the British Library.

Library of Congress Cataloging-in-Publication Data

Names: Liew, Ying Khai, author.

Title: Rationalising constructive trusts / Dr. Ying Khai Liew.

Description: Portland, Oregon : Hart Publishing, 2017. | Series: Hart studies in private law ; volume 25 | Includes bibliographical references and index.

Identifiers: LCCN 2017018593 (print) | LCCN 2017022549 (ebook) | ISBN 9781509917075 (Epub) | ISBN 9781849465960 (hardback)

Subjects: LCSH: Constructive trusts—Great Britain. | Constructive trusts.
Classification: LCC KD1925 (ebook) | LCC KD1925 .L54 2017 (print) | DDC 346.4105/9—dc23

LC record available at https://lccn.loc.gov/2017018593

ISBN: HB: 978-1-84946-596-0
PB: 978-1-50993-516-1
ePDF: 978-1-50991-708-2
ePub: 978-1-50991-707-5

Typeset by Compuscript Ltd, Shannon

For Debbie and Callum (as his bedtime story)

PREFACE

In the long and decorated history of equity, there is perhaps no other area more fundamentally misunderstood, and yet widely utilised, than constructive trusts. This is not to say that constructive trusts are under-studied: to the contrary, the literature is voluminous. However, attempts to rationalise constructive trusts *as a whole*—as opposed to specific doctrines or particular aspects of constructive trusts—have been few and far between. This has resulted in a fragmented and unstructured law of constructive trusts, where each doctrine is treated in isolation and with little regard being paid to how they relate to one another. One of the consequences of this state of affairs is that the outcomes dictated by the operation of each doctrine, while more or less predictable, cannot properly be explained and justified.

This state of affairs is, however, not inevitable. *Rationalising Constructive Trusts* develops a structured approach to the law of constructive trusts using a combination of conceptual tools. These conceptual tools have never been put to use for the purposes of analysing constructive trusts, whether individually or in combination. When used in combination, however, they help form a clear structure of the law of constructive trusts. This structure not only allows us to explain the outcomes of cases which have hitherto eluded justification; they also make addressing difficult areas of the law easier, and the practical application of the law more straightforward.

This book proposes a structure of the law of constructive trusts and provides an in-depth discussion of 13 constructive trust doctrines, demonstrating their places within the proposed structure. These 13 doctrines cover the full range of major constructive trust doctrines as they are currently found, not only in English law, but also in other Commonwealth jurisdictions. One may quibble about whether the law of constructive trusts covers a wider (or narrower) range of doctrines, and the reasons for including these 13 doctrines (and excluding others) will certainly be explored. Ultimately, however, this book is not so much concerned simply with explaining cases and doctrines which have been identified by the label 'constructive trust', but with the rationales and justifications which underpin them. It is only by exploring the cases and doctrines from the perspective of their underlying rationales that we can attain a proper understanding of the law.

I have endeavoured to state the law as at 2 March 2017, in the hope that what comes afterwards will reflect a more structured understanding of the law of constructive trusts.

Ying Khai Liew
London
World Book Day 2017

ACKNOWLEDGEMENTS

This book has been ten years in the making. A decade ago as an eager undergraduate at King's College London, I turned up uninvited at Charles Mitchell's office, intimating that I wanted to undertake a doctorate, but that I hadn't the faintest idea of which area of law to research in. Instead of turning me away in view of the fact that I wasn't even halfway through the LLB course, he demonstrated characteristic kindness and patience, suggesting constructive trusts as a potential area of research. I am indebted to him not only for my fascination with constructive trusts, but also for his unwavering support for my academic pursuits ever since.

This book grew out of my PhD thesis written under the supervision of Craig Rotherham, whose support extended significantly beyond his call of duty as my supervisor. I am grateful for his guidance and friendship which has persisted long after the completion of my thesis.

I would also like to thank many others who contributed to the completion of this book along the way: Ben McFarlane for his invaluable advice and support throughout the writing process; Adam Doyle, Ori Herstein, Paul Matthews, Nick McBride, Lionel Smith, Sandy Steel, Leslie Turano, and Ian Williams for insightful discussions which have helped shape my thoughts; Simone Degeling, Simon Gardner, Jamie Glister, Weng Tchung Low, Magda Raczynska, Philip Sales LJ, Charlie Webb, Man Yip, and Rafal Zakrzewski for their helpful comments on various parts of the manuscript; Julius Grower and E-Jin Lee for excellent research assistance at different stages of the writing process.

I owe a debt of gratitude to my parents for their wisdom and support throughout. Finally, I thank my wife Debbie for her continuing love and trust, and Jesus Christ for perfecting the law with grace.

I acknowledge the School of Law at the University of Nottingham which provided me a scholarship to pursue my PhD, and the Society of Legal Scholars (SLS) for providing funding for research assistance from the 2016 Research Activities Fund.

CONTENTS

PART C

TABLE OF CASES

TABLE OF LEGISLATION

1

Introduction

Constructive trusts have been the source of much controversy. Since the middle of the twentieth century, courts and academics have made determined efforts to understand why they are imposed. Yet, even today, there is no universal agreement, save for the fact that they arise 'by operation of law', that is, they arise for some reason other than simply in response to the intention of the parties. This is unfortunate, because the application of legal rules must be underpinned by a logically consistent body of norms, in order that proper justifications can be given for legal decisions.

The imposition of a constructive trust has significant consequences. A constructive trust obliges an apparent legal owner to hold 'his' property as trustee in favour of another. This drastically affects the trustee's position. The property does not form part of his estate and he retains no right to benefit from it. It will not devolve with his other assets upon his death; and where he is insolvent, his creditors have no claim over property which is subject to the trust. From the beneficiary's perspective, the constructive trust is advantageous: he obtains important equitable rights under the trust.

Constructive trusts are imposed in a wide variety of circumstances. The diverse contexts in which they arise makes it difficult, and perhaps impossible, to explain all constructive trusts by reference to a single rationale. However, this should not deter attempts to distil common rationales for categories of constructive trusts which, at first sight, may seem unrelated. Such attempts are important to avoid the law being a 'chaos of unsorted information', where contradictory approaches are taken towards a single case as a result of the law being understood merely in terms of 'lists of more or less familiar topics.'[1] Yet, this is what we find in the present law of constructive trusts, where individual cases are typically determined according to the accepted wisdom of the category into which it falls, with little regard to how they relate to other categories of constructive trusts.

1.1. Aim and Reasons

The aim of this book is to make sense of the law by proposing a structured understanding of constructive trusts. The reasons for undertaking this project are threefold. First, it allows us to understand precisely the requirements and rationales of any given constructive trust doctrine. Often judges and commentators come to grips only with the core situations in which

[1] Peter Birks, 'Equity in the Modern Law: An Exercise in Taxonomy' (1996) 26 *University of Western Australia Law Review* 1, 3, 5.

a doctrine applies, without appreciating the limits of a doctrine or its underlying rationales. Such a limited understanding of the law is detrimental to its rational development.

Secondly, attempting to make sense of constructive trusts allows us to identify and appreciate common themes which run through seemingly distinct doctrines. The operation of constructive trust doctrines is often thought to be confined within certain factual ambits. Looking beyond the factual constraints provides a wider appreciation of why, precisely, constructive trusts arise in different situations.

Thirdly, it encourages a better appreciation of the unique role of constructive trusts. In this regard, important questions arise as to how constructive trusts relate to express and resulting trusts, the answers to which are crucial for a proper understanding of the law of trusts as a whole. Issues also arise as to how constructive trusts relate to formality statutes, contractual principles, and other equitable maxims. Resolving these important matters will help us to understand the crucial role played by constructive trusts in the law and the ambit within which they operate.

1.2. Scope and Definition Trusts

Underlying this book is a vision of trusts law which views each type of trust—express, constructive, and resulting[2]—as having a unique role to play in the law.[3] Indeed, it is on the basis of this vision that the 13 substantive doctrines discussed in this book have been selected. Despite the fact that these constructive trust doctrines are not united by a single rationale, as explained in Chapter 3, they are chosen because they fill a conceptual space distinct from those occupied by express and resulting trusts. In some cases, the distinct conceptual space of the doctrine is easily appreciated, because the factual contexts in which the doctrines operate cannot be explained by way of an express or resulting trust analysis. But it may also be the case that an express or resulting trust might provide a plausible alternative analysis of some doctrines; and where such a possibility arises, the discussion in the relevant chapters will explain the reasons for which the constructive trust analysis is to be preferred.

In order appreciate the proper scope within which constructive trusts operates, it is necessary to explain the conceptions of express and resulting trusts adopted in this book.

1.2.1. Express Trusts

Express trusts are commonly defined in contradistinction to constructive and resulting trusts. The latter trusts are said to arise 'by operation of law', whereas express trusts arise

[2] There are also statutory trusts, eg trusts arising in the context of co-owned legal estates under ss 34 and 36 of the Law of Property Act 1925 (as amended by the Trusts of Land and Appointment of Trustees Act 1996)—but we are not concerned with these.

[3] Hence, 'the bewildering English preoccupation with the proper taxonomy of trusts' (Paul Finn, 'Common Law Divergences' [2013] *Melbourne Law Review* 509, 513 fn 24) is not so bewildering after all, particularly where the concern is not with taxonomy as an end in itself.

due to a settlor's successful exercise of his power to set up a trust.[4] A number of conditions must be met. The settlor must be capable of declaring an express trust. The settlor can only declare a trust of property which he owns. The 'three certainties' propounded in *Knight v Knight*[5]—certainty of intention, subject-matter, and objects—must also be met.

In addition, and most importantly for the present purposes, the settlor's intention to create a trust must be *properly manifested*.[6] This involves complying with any relevant formality requirement where appropriate, such as those required for the enforcement of inter vivos express trusts concerning land[7] and the validity of testamentary express trusts.[8]

The requirement for a proper manifestation of intention is best understood in relation to the facilitative nature of the express trust device.[9] When a settlor properly creates an express trust, he can legitimately expect that his manifested intention to create a trust will be given legal effect. However, in order for the arrangement to be enforced *qua* an express trust it is necessary for the settlor first to comply with any relevant formality requirement in order successfully to make use of the express trust facility. Where the settlor's intention is properly manifested, his intention 'creates and defines the express trust'.[10] Thus, a settlor may unilaterally create an express trust,[11] even if the trust property is transferred to the intended trustee who has no knowledge of the transfer or the trust.[12]

The foregoing should not be taken to mean that the consent of others is always irrelevant: for instance, the full range of rights and duties intended to be created by the settlor will not come into existence if the intended beneficiaries disclaim the gift, or so long as there are no trustees who accept office;[13] moreover, once a trust is up and running there are a number of ways by which trustees and beneficiaries may collude to alter the rights and duties existing under the trust.[14] Nevertheless, it remains the case that a trust is *created* through the settlor's unilateral act of properly declaring a trust. This explains why an express trust will not fail for want of a trustee,[15] and provided that there are trustees

[4] Ben McFarlane and Charles Mitchell, *Hayton and Mitchell: Text, Cases and Materials on the Law of Trusts and Equitable Remedies*, 14th edn (London, Sweet & Maxwell, 2015) [1-046].

[5] *Knight v Knight* (1840) 3 Beav 148, 49 ER 58.

[6] Robert Chambers, 'Constructive Trusts in Canada' (1999) 37 *Alberta Law Review* 173, 183. See also Robert Chambers, *Resulting Trusts* (Oxford, OUP, 1997) 220ff; Peter Birks, *An Introduction to the Law of Restitution*, revised edn (Oxford, OUP, 1989) 65; Simon Gardner, *An Introduction to the Law of Trusts*, Clarendon Law Series, 3rd edn (Oxford, OUP, 2011) 97.

[7] The Law of Property Act 1925, s 53(1)(b) provides that 'all declarations … of trusts or confidences of any lands … shall be manifested and proved by some writing signed by the party who is by law enabled to declare such trust'.

[8] The Wills Act 1897, s 9 (as amended by the Administration of Justice Act 1982, s 17) provides that a valid will must be made 'in writing and signed by the testator, in the presence of two or more attesting witnesses present at the same time.'

[9] See, eg, Gardner, *Law of Trusts* (n 6) 28ff; Charlie Webb, 'The Myth of the Remedial Constructive Trust' (2016) 69 *Current Legal Problems* 353, 353.

[10] Chambers, *Resulting Trusts* (n 6) 224.

[11] *Fletcher v Fletcher* (1844) 4 Hare 67, 67 ER 564; *Mallott v Wilson* [1903] 2 Ch 494 (Ch); *Re Kayford Ltd* [1975] 1 All ER 604 (Ch) 607; *Re Goldcorp Exchange Ltd* [1995] 1 AC 74 (PC) 100.

[12] David Hayton, Paul Matthews and Charles Mitchell, *Underhill and Hayton: Law Relating to Trusts and Trustees*, 19th edn (London, LexisNexis Butterworths, 2016) [12.70].

[13] Ying Khai Liew and Charles Mitchell, 'The Creation of Express Trusts' (forthcoming 2018).

[14] Ying Khai Liew and Charles Mitchell, 'Beneficiaries' Consent to Trustees' Unauthorised Acts' in Paul Davies, Simon Douglas, and James Goudkamp (eds), *Defences in Equity* (Oxford, Hart Publishing, 2018).

[15] See *Underhill and Hayton* (n 12) [8.8].

who take office the beneficiaries have rights under the trust until and unless they expressly choose to disclaim.[16] Moreover, at the outset trustees only have the choice of taking up office or not at all; they are not permitted to cherry pick specific terms of the trust while rejecting others.[17] Hence, at least when a trust is first created,[18] the existence and terms of the trust are sourced in the settlor's unilateral creative intention.

1.2.2. Resulting Trusts

In contrast to express trusts, resulting and constructive trusts do not respond to a settlor's properly manifested intention to create a trust. They arise 'by operation of law', and since compliance with any relevant formality requirement is necessary only for the enforcement of express trusts, the informality of an arrangement is no bar to the imposition of resulting and constructive trusts. It might be thought that there is no further meaningful distinction to be drawn between resulting and constructive trusts.[19] However, the distinction is useful since it sheds light upon the reasons for why a trust arises.[20]

The term 'resulting' originates from the Latin word '*resalire*', which means 'to jump back'. According to Peter Birks, this may mean one of two things. It may either refer to the mere fact that 'the interest arising under [the trust] is carried back to the settlor', or it may refer 'to the mode in which the trust originates'.[21] Birks labelled these conceptions 'resulting in pattern' and 'resulting in origin' respectively.[22] Solely focusing on the former is liable to cause more confusion than it cures. For example, suppose A transfers property to B and properly manifests his intention to create a trust for his own benefit. While this trust would undoubtedly be enforced as an express trust, it would likewise fit the description of a 'resulting trust', since the interest in the property originally owned by A is 'carried back' to A under the trust. But describing the trust as an 'express resulting trust' is confusing, and is not a term commonly employed to explain such a trust.[23]

Take another example. *Goff & Jones* defines a 'constructive trust' as arising in cases where 'the law deems one party to have conferred the same proprietary rights on another party as he would have acquired, had an express trust been declared in his favour—although in fact no valid declaration of trust has been made.'[24] It follows that it is possible for a constructive trust to arise where A transfers property to B intending B to hold on trust for A, but fails

[16] See, eg, *Re Stratton's Disclaimer* [1958] Ch 42 (CA) 54.

[17] *Re Lysaght* [1966] 1 Ch 191 (Ch) 206–07.

[18] That is to say, prior to any later modification of the terms of the trust as the result of an agreement between trustees and beneficiaries.

[19] This might be thought to be the implication of the following words found in *Cook v Fountain* (1676) 3 Swan 585, 591: 'All trusts are either, first, express trusts, which are raised and created by act of the parties, or implied trusts, which are raised or created by act or construction of law'.

[20] Robert Chambers, 'Trust and Theft' in Elise Bant and Matthew Harding, *Exploring Private Law* (Cambridge, CUP, 2010) 237.

[21] Birks, *Law of Restitution* (n 6) 60.

[22] ibid 60–61.

[23] Charles Mitchell, Paul Mitchell, and Stephen Watterson, *Goff & Jones: The Law of Unjust Enrichment*, 9th edn (London, Sweet & Maxwell, 2016) [38-07].

[24] ibid [38-06].

to comply with the relevant formality requirement.[25] Since such a trust is also 'resulting in pattern', it could be described as a 'constructive resulting trust'. On this view, '[c]onstructive trusts are either resulting trusts … or non-resulting trusts.'[26] However, this understanding masks important differences relating to why constructive and resulting trusts arise. To obtain a proper understanding of the law, the focus must be on the 'origin' aspect of resulting trusts, since this involves considering the substance of the parties' rights and duties and the reasons for which the trusts arise.

From this perspective, there are two possible analyses of resulting trusts. One focuses on a positive intention—a creative intent to bring a trust into existence; the other on negative intention—a lack of intention to benefit another.

1.2.2.1. Positive Intention

It is often thought that resulting trusts turn on showing, by way of presumption or actual evidence,[27] that there is some positive intention to create a trust. The positive intention conception is often attributed to Lord Browne-Wilkinson's judgment in *Westdeutsche Landesbank Girozentrale v Islington LBC*.[28] The relevant passage in *Westdeutsche* is not at all free from difficulty. His Lordship said that resulting trusts give effect 'to [the trustee's] presumed intention' and 'to the common intention of the parties'.[29] It is unclear whose intention is thought to be relevant. Whichever it may be, however, both formulations are inaccurate. Since they rely—either wholly or partly—on the trustee's intention, one would have thought that, were there objective evidence that the trustee positively did not intend to hold the property on trust for the transferor, a resulting trust would not arise. After all, '[p]resumptions may be looked on as the bats of the law flitting in the twilight but disappearing in the sunshine of actual facts',[30] and the trustee's actual intention would be sufficient to rebut any presumption of resulting trust. But this is not how resulting trusts work:[31] they have been imposed on a transferee where there is clear evidence that the transferee was unaware of the transfer of property from the transferor.[32] Therefore, if resulting trusts respond to a positive intention, it must be that of the transferor's.

There are two variations to this view which require examination.

[25] This is reflected in many cases relating to the doctrine in *Rochefoucauld v Boustead*, discussed in Chapter 4.

[26] *Re Llanover Settled Estates* [1926] Ch 626 (Ch) 637, Citing *Underhill on Trusts*, 8th edn (London, Sweet & Maxwell, 1926) 147.

[27] See *Vandervell v IRC* [1967] 2 AC 291 (HL) 313, 315; Robert Chambers, 'Is There a Presumption of Resulting Trust?' in Charles Mitchell (ed), *Constructive and Resulting Trusts* (Oxford, Hart Publishing, 2010).

[28] *Westdeutsche Landesbank Girozentrale v Islington LBC* [1996] AC 669 (HL) 708. This is certainly the way in which William Swaddling reads the case: see William Swaddling, 'Explaining Resulting Trusts' (2008) 124 *LQR* 72, 72. However, it is noted that Lord Browne-Wilkinson also spoke of resulting trusts as arising where the transferor 'did not intend to make a gift to [the transferee]': see *Westdeutsche* (n 28) 708.

[29] *Westdeutsche* (n 28) 708.

[30] *Mackowik v Kansas City* 94 SW 256 (1906).

[31] Specifically in relation to the 'common intention' formulation, Cromwell J has said in *Kerr v Baranow* [2011] 1 SCR 269 that 'the common intention resulting trust is doctrinally unsound. It is inconsistent with the underlying principles of resulting trust law. Where the issue of intention is relevant to the finding of resulting trust, it is the intention of the grantor or contributor alone that counts.'

[32] See, eg, *Re Vinogradoff* [1935] WN 68 (Ch).

1.2.2.1.1. Declaration of Trust

According to William Swadling, 'presumed' resulting trusts[33]—those that arise in the context of voluntary transfers of property and the provision of purchase money for the purchase of property in another's name—respond to a *declaration* of trust by the transferor or provider of money.[34] There are numerous difficulties with this view. It entails that the rationale for these resulting trusts are the same as those underpinning express trusts, since they both respond to one's successful exercise of a power to create a trust.[35] However, it is misleading and wrong to think that resulting trusts—which, it is emphasised, arise by operation of law—are facilitative in nature. Moreover, if declarations of (express) trusts may simply be presumed, then this significantly limits the scope of operation and justification of the statutory formality requirements for the creation or enforcement of express trusts. In addition, if Swadling's view is correct, then no resulting trusts would arise in cases where there is positive evidence that the transferor or provider of purchase money did not declare a trust, but this is clearly not what we find in the case law.[36]

1.2.2.1.2. Intention to Create a Trust

An alternative thesis is that resulting trusts arise in response simply to the transferor's or money-provider's objective positive intention, proved either by positive evidence or alternatively though a presumption. In recent years this thesis has been given significant exposition by John Mee. It requires careful consideration, since it is inconsistent with the negative intention approach which, as we will see, is ultimately adopted in this book.

According to Mee, in presumed resulting trusts cases the positive intention approach is consistent with the historical development of resulting trusts.[37] He also suggests that there is an 'equivalence'[38] in the statements that 'A did not intend to make a gift to B', and that 'A intended to create a trust for himself'; therefore, judicial statements to the former effect necessarily entail the latter. Mee gives a different explanation in relation to 'automatic' resulting trusts—that is, cases 'where the transfer to B is made on trusts which leave some or all of the beneficial interest undisposed of'.[39] In these cases, because A transfers property to B in whom A reposes trust,[40] equity 'fill[s] any gap in the beneficial interest under a trust' in A's favour.[41] This rule 'can be seen as one of the background rules which are triggered when

[33] As opposed to 'failed trust resulting trusts' which arise where properly declared trusts 'lack objects, offend the rule against perpetuities, or both': William Swadling, 'Explaining Resulting Trusts' (2008) 124 *LQR* 72, 73. According to Swadling, these trusts 'def[y] legal analysis': Swadling, 'Explaining Resulting Trusts' (n 33) 102.

[34] ibid 80ff.

[35] See *Hayton and Mitchell* (n 4) [14-092].

[36] See, eg, *Vandervell* (n 27) and *Re Vinogradoff* (n 32) where resulting trusts arose despite the fact that there was evidence that the transferor positively did not intend for the transferee to act as trustee, and therefore clearly did not declare a trust.

For other criticisms of Swadling's view, see John Mee, 'Presumed Resulting Trusts, Intention and Declaration' [2014] *CLJ* 86, 90ff.

[37] Mee, 'Presumed Resulting Trusts' (n 36) 94ff.

[38] ibid 103.

[39] *Re Vandervell's Trustees Ltd (No. 2)* [1974] Ch 269 (CA) 294.

[40] John Mee, '"Automatic" Resulting Trusts: Retention, Restitution, or Reposing Trust?' in Mitchell, *Constructive and Resulting Trusts* (n 27) 230ff.

[41] ibid 234.

a person chooses to create a trust. It is part of a package of rules which cover matters which the settlor may not have consciously considered'.[42]

It is situations of voluntary transfers which may potentially overlap with many of the constructive trust doctrines examined in this book, and so the viability of Mee's approach to presumed resulting trusts must be considered. However, there are two subsets of situations concerning voluntary transfers which may also overlap with Mee's approach to automatic resulting trusts. First, where A transfers property to B without having decided what will happen to the beneficial interest of the property, a presumption of resulting trust arises on the facts in A's favour. Mee says that this presumption cannot be rebutted by positive evidence of A's indecision; but the trust can also be explained as an 'automatic' resulting trust which arises due to the fact that A reposes trust in B.[43] Secondly, in a presumed resulting trust case where A transfers property to B pursuant to an express trust which turns out to be unenforceable due to A's lack of compliance with a relevant statutory formality requirement, Mee's 'reposing trust' thesis would also be relevant since it applies where 'some or all of the trusts specified by the settlor might infringe a legal rule',[44] and its operation does not hinge on A having first made a proper declaration of trust.[45] Since A reposes trust in B but A's express intention cannot be enforced due to non-compliance with a formality requirement, a gap in the beneficial interest arises which is filled by an 'automatic' resulting trust.

Mee certainly provides a plausible historical account of resulting trusts.[46] However, he also suggests that, 'whatever the position before the Statute of Frauds, the voluntary transfer resulting trust in respect of land did not actually survive that statute'.[47] Because such resulting trusts nevertheless remain part of the modern law, it is necessary for us to grapple with the relationship between resulting trusts and express trusts (which require compliance with any relevant statutory formality requirement to be enforceable),[48] the explanation of which may well be different from the rationale underpinning the historical cases.

As a starting point, it can be observed that the law reflects 'a liberal vision of the institution of property'.[49] As Simon Gardner explains:[50]

> To give an owner maximal freedom in the disposition of his assets, it is necessary maximally to treat them as for him alone to dispose of ... [This insight] operates ... where the legal title has effectively been transferred; but its previous owner has neither (intentionally and successfully) conferred beneficial ownership on the transferee nor (likewise) alienated it in some other direction. The logic of the insight is that in such a situation the previous owner should be treated as himself retaining[51] beneficial ownership.

[42] ibid.
[43] Mee, 'Presumed Resulting Trusts' (n 36) 97.
[44] Mee, '"Automatic" Resulting Trusts' (n 40) 209.
[45] ibid 232.
[46] See further John Mee, 'Resulting Trusts and Voluntary Conveyances of Land, 1674–1925' (2011) 32 *Journal of Legal History* 215.
[47] Mee, 'Presumed Resulting Trusts' (n 36) 105–06.
[48] See S 1.2.1.
[49] Gardner, *Law of Trusts* (n 6) 296.
[50] ibid.
[51] Gardner probably means that the transferor 'is to have' the beneficial ownership, rather than *retaining* (strictly speaking) the beneficial interest, since '[u]nless and until there is a separation of the legal and equitable estates, there is no separate equitable title': *Westdeutsche* (n 28) 706.

Mee certainly subscribes to the liberal vision of resulting trusts. Observing the historical position—which, he argues, still applies today—he writes:[52]

> The transferor's will might have been made clear by an express statement that the transferee was intended to take beneficially, which would settle the use in him. Alternatively, there might have been a declaration that the transferee was to hold on trust, which would also be decisive. In the absence of any expression of intention, an explanation for the voluntary conveyance might be found in the fact that it was made to a close family relation. If, however, there was no other explanation, it was assumed that the intention was that the transferee would be a trustee.

However, if we take seriously the liberal vision of the institution of property, there are three crucial reasons why Mee's historical account may not be relevant in the modern law. First, in certain cases Mee's thesis obscures the distinction between express and resulting trusts. Consider an oral declaration of trust of some personalty by A, constituting B as trustee for A's benefit. Ordinarily, A's positive intention to create a trust would be taken to have effectively created an express trust. However, the very same positive intention would confirm the presumption of resulting trust on Mee's thesis, leading to the conclusion that the trust is also resulting in nature. This poses a problem for the liberal vision because it fails to distinguish between trusts arising as a result of A's successful exercise of his freedom to create a trust, and trusts arising because the reason for A's transfer of property to B *cannot be explained*. The same problem arises in relation to the 'reposing trust' explanation of the informal, voluntary transfer cases: there is a failure to make an important distinction between the different means by which A may repose trust in B.

Secondly, Mee's thesis obscures the distinction between resulting and constructive trusts. Consider a secret trust[53] case where A leaves property by will to B based on B's informal promise to A that B will hold the property for C's benefit. When A dies, B does not hold the property on an express trust due to A's non-compliance of the Wills Act 1837, s 9.[54] On Mee's thesis, 'a conclusion that the transferor did not intend a gift (or, to use the language of retention, did not intend to pass the beneficial interest to the transferee) is equivalent to a conclusion that the transferor did intend to create a trust'.[55] However, despite the fact that A did not intend a gift to B—and the fact that A had reposed trust in B—it is manifestly clear from the secret trusts cases that a constructive trust arises upon A's death for *C's* benefit: the property is not simply held on a resulting trust for A's estate. Mee's thesis does not account for why the law sometimes chooses to give effect to A's informally manifested positive intention to create a trust for C instead of responding to the fact that A reposes trust in B or that A does not intend to make a gift to B.

Thirdly, Mee's thesis does not provide a convincing reason for the fact that a resulting trust arises where A transfers property to B without having decided on the fate of its beneficial interest.[56] If the content of the presumption of resulting trust is that A positively intends

[52] Mee, 'Presumed Resulting Trusts' (n 36) 96.

[53] The secret trusts doctrine is discussed in Chapter 5.

[54] As discussed in Chapter 5, S 5.1.

[55] Mee, 'Presumed Resulting Trusts' (n 36) 102–03. The fact that A did not intend a gift does not simply give rise to a *presumption* that A intended to create a trust because presumptions 'apply where there is no evidence "of the intention with which a transfer is made"': Mee, 'Presumed Resulting Trusts' (n 36) 99, quoting *Lavelle v Lavelle* [2004] EWCA Civ 223, [2004] 2 FCR 418 [13].

[56] There is certainly historical force in Mee's thesis in relation to this point (Mee, 'Presumed Resulting Trusts' (n 36) 97); but in the modern law the historical reason seems unconvincing.

to create a trust for himself, as Mee contends, then positive evidence of A's indecision ought properly to rebut the presumption, since it provides evidence that A did *not* intend to create a trust for himself. To say that such evidence does not rebut the presumption entails forcing upon A an intention which A clearly did not have. Such an analysis unnecessarily deprives A of his autonomy, which in turn runs contrary to the liberal vision of the institution of property. The same criticism can be made on the 'reposing trust' conception: ambiguity as to A's intentions concerning the fate of the beneficial interest in the property transferred to B entails ambiguity as to whether A in fact reposes any trust in B at all; and to insist that A does so is to deprive A of his autonomy.

1.2.2.2. Negative Intention

On a different approach propounded by Robert Chambers, resulting trusts 'do not depend on an implied intention to create a trust'; instead, they 'come into being because the [transferor] did not intend to benefit the [transferee].'[57] This book adopts Chambers' negative intention approach for a number of reasons.

Apart from the fact that this view finds much judicial support,[58] it also has the distinct advantage of explaining all resulting trusts cases.[59] In particular, it accounts for cases such as *Vandervell v IRC*[60] and *Re Vinogradoff*[61] where resulting trusts arose despite the fact that there was evidence that A positively did not intend for B to act as trustee.[62] Such evidence is consistent with an absence of intention to benefit B.

Most importantly, however, the negative intention approach best advances the liberal vision of the institution of property. As Chambers observes, '[i]t is almost always preferable to give effect to the parties' intentions, but when that is impossible, the resulting trust fulfils the … function of ensuring that unintended benefits are returned.'[63] By responding to A's negative intention, resulting trusts act as a 'default' legal response whereby the beneficial interest in property which A transfers to B is returned to A if and only if the law is unable to give effect to A's positive intention in some way.[64] Hence, if A properly creates an express trust which is enforceable, the trust will not be taken to be a resulting trust despite the fact that A does not intend to benefit B (the trustee) with A's property. Similarly, in the context of some doctrines discussed in this book (including secret trusts) where A and B come to an informal agreement that B will hold A's property for C, constructive trusts may arise in C's

[57] Chambers, *Resulting Trusts* (n 6) 2. Chambers' thesis is built on the work of Peter Birks. See, eg, Peter Birks, 'Restitution and Resulting Trusts' in Stephen R Goldstein (ed), *Equity: Contemporary Legal Developments* (Jerusalem, Hebrew University of Jerusalem, 1992).

[58] See, eg, *Air Jamaica Ltd v Charlton* [1999] 1 WLR 1399 (PC) 1411; *Lavelle v Lavelle* (n 55) [13]–[14]; *Twinsectra v Yardley* [2002] UKHL 12, [2002] 2 AC 164 [92]; *Patel v Mirza* [2016] UKSC 42, [2016] 3 WLR 399 [238]. See also PJ Millett, 'Restitution and Constructive Trusts' (1998) 114 *LQR* 399, 401.

[59] Chambers, *Resulting Trusts* (n 6) 21.

[60] *Vandervell* (n 27).

[61] *Re Vinogradoff* (n 32).

[62] See discussion in *Underhill and Hayton* (n 12) [22.9].

[63] Chambers, 'Is There a Presumption of Resulting Trust?' (n 27) 286. See also *Underhill and Hayton* (n 12) [22.13]. A similar point is made in Charles Rickett, 'The Classification of Trusts' (1999) 18 *New Zealand Universities Law Review* 305, 317–8.

[64] These ideas are discussed in more detail in relation to the doctrine in *Rochefoucauld v Boustead* in Chapter 4 at S 4.5.1.2.2.

favour despite the fact that A does not intend to benefit B. The negative intention approach also explains why a resulting trust arises where A transfers property to B where A is undecided on the fate of its beneficial interest. The lack of any relevant positive intention on A's part entails that the 'default' position ought to apply: a resulting trust arises in response to the fact that A does not intend to benefit B with the property.

An important point concerning the negative intention thesis requires observation. In his monograph *Resulting Trusts*,[65] Chambers suggests that the negative intention thesis entails not only that resulting trusts are restitutionary in nature, but that they 'reverse unjust enrichment'.[66] As *Goff & Jones* explains, unjust enrichment is an event, while restitution is a legal response; moreover, while unjust enrichment may trigger a restitutionary response, restitution is not the only possible response to unjust enrichment, and unjust enrichment is not the only event which may trigger a restitutionary response.[67] This book endorses the view that resulting trusts are restitutionary in nature: they always restore to A an interest transferred by him to B. However, this book stops short from adopting the position that the event triggering resulting trusts is unjust enrichment. Such an analysis gives rise to difficult questions which are beyond the scope of this book. For example, Chambers suggests that a resulting trust would arise 'in every case in which the provider is entitled to restitution on the basis of non-voluntary transfer'.[68] It is highly debatable whether proprietary restitution is or should generally be available as a response to unjust enrichment;[69] and it is unnecessary to resolve these debates in order to accept that resulting trusts arise in response to the transferor's lack of intention to benefit the transferee.

1.2.3. Constructive Trusts

One of the main points made in this book is that constructive trusts may arise in the context of an informally manifested positive intention to create a trust (or to make a gift), or in response to the commission of a wrong. It can immediately be observed that this accords constructive trusts a conceptual space distinct from express and resulting trusts. It is clear that express and resulting trusts do not respond to any wrongdoing at all. Moreover, '[t]here is a fine but important distinction between [positive] intent conceived as creative of rights [for express trusts] … and [positive] intent conceived as a fact which, along with others, calls for the creation of rights [through a constructive trust].'[70] It is one of the central tasks of this book to identify the 'other' facts which, along with positive intention, trigger constructive trusts, as well as to identify what types of wrongdoing give rise to them.

[65] Chambers, *Resulting Trusts* (n 6) Ch 4.
[66] ibid 104. Other events apart from unjust enrichment—such as a wrong—may trigger restitution, but these events have nothing to do with resulting trusts.
[67] *Goff & Jones* (n 23) [1-02].
[68] Chambers, *Resulting Trusts* (n 6) 113.
[69] See, eg, *Goff & Jones* (n 23) [38-33]–[38-34].
[70] Birks, *Law of Restitution* (n 6) 65.

1.3. Methodology

The primary methodology which will be employed is that first propounded by Peter Birks,[71] which analyses legal rights as responses triggered by legally significant real-world events. On this approach, constructive trusts are taken to be legal responses, and the identification of the real-world events which are deemed legally significant enough to trigger them is crucial for a structured understanding of the law of constructive trusts.

The event/response methodology often brings to mind Birks' scheme which categorises legal responses according to four categories of events: consent, wrongs, unjust enrichment, and miscellaneous others.[72] Focusing on trusts as legal responses to these events provides important insights. Where the event of an unjust enrichment triggers a trust, the best analysis is that the trust is a resulting trust. This is because unjust enrichment triggers restitution, and resulting trusts are always restitutionary.[73] As for the event of consent, Birks cited as an example an 'express declaration of trust',[74] which suggests that it is the proper manifestation of intention of the settlor whose 'consent' is legally significant, and which triggers an express trust response. What remains, therefore, are the events of 'wrongs' and 'miscellaneous others', which may potentially trigger constructive trusts. It is crucial to identify what rights are breached which trigger constructive trusts, and the particular events within the 'miscellaneous' category which likewise trigger constructive trusts. This enables different constructive trust doctrines to be grouped together according to their triggering events in order to make sense of this area of law.

There are two other related methodologies employed in this book. The first is a normative inquiry. For each distinct category of constructive trusts, an attempt will be made to identify the rationale underpinning their imposition. Doing so not only reveals how constructive trusts relate to express and resulting trusts as well as contractual principles, but also provides a meaningful way of understanding the limits of constructive trusts. The second examines constructive trusts in relation to the rights and duties of the parties involved. It will be seen that some constructive trusts give effect to the parties' primary rights and duties, others give effect to secondary rights and duties, and yet others have little to do with substantive rights and duties at all. A significant advantage of this methodology is that it reveals much about the extent to which courts are afforded remedial discretion; it also sheds light on how remedial discretion relates to the doctrine of precedent.

[71] Birks, 'Equity in the Modern Law'; Peter Birks, 'Equity, Conscience, and Unjust Enrichment' (1999) 23 *Melbourne University Law Review* 1.

[72] See: Peter Birks, 'Property and Unjust Enrichment: Categorical Truths' [1997] *New Zealand Law Review* 623, 628; Peter Birks 'Rights, Wrongs, and Remedies' (2000) 20 *OJLS* 1, 37; Peter Birks, 'The Concept of a Civil Wrong' in David G Owen (ed), *The Philosophical Foundations of Tort Law* (Oxford, OUP, 1997) 34; Birks, 'Equity in the Modern Law' 8–11; Peter Birks 'Misnomer' in WR Cornish, Richard Nolan, Janet O'Sullivan et al (eds) *Restitution: Past, Present and Future* (Oxford, Hart Publishing, 1998) 1; Peter Birks, 'The Law of Restitution at the End of an Epoch' (1999) 28 *University of Western Australia Law Review* 13.

[73] See discussion above in the main text following n 65 and further in Chapter 16, SS 16.1.2.1. and 16.1.2.2.

[74] Birks, 'Categorical Truths' (n 72) 628.

1.4. The Structure of the Book

This book has 14 chapters, excluding the introductory and concluding chapters. They are divided into three parts.

Part A provides an overview of the analysis proposed in this book. It consists of two chapters. Chapter 2 lays the groundwork by establishing a number of building blocks upon which the analysis is built. Chapter 3 sets out and explains the structure of the law of constructive trusts.

Part B explores nine constructive trust doctrines which make up the 'core' doctrines within the structure. Each of Chapters 4 to 11 examines one of these doctrines, except Chapter 8 which looks at two of them (with the argument being made that they ought to be treated as one). They are 'core' doctrines because they most clearly explain a particular category within the structure of the law of constructive trusts.

In Part C, each of Chapters 12 to 15 examines one of four 'non-core' doctrines. The appropriate analysis of these doctrines is far from straightforward because their underlying rationales are as yet under-explored and therefore ambiguous. A central theme of Part C is that each of these doctrines can be analysed by way of 'orthodox' constructive trust principles such that they can easily be placed within one or more categories within the structure of constructive trusts.

PART A

2

Building Blocks

This chapter introduces four building blocks upon which the analysis in this book rests. Each building block is presented in the form of a distinction. The first is a factual distinction between 'qualified interest' (QI) and 'absolute interest' (AI) situations. The second is a distinction between primary and secondary rights. The third relates to a distinction between decisions which require the pleading and proving of breach, causation, remoteness, and mitigation, and those which do not. The fourth is a distinction between different types of remedies and the factors courts take into account when awarding them. These building blocks are simply introduced in this chapter; in Chapter 3 these building blocks will be applied to construct a structure of the law of constructive trusts.

2.1. 'Qualified Interest' and 'Absolute Interest' Situations

There are two distinct and mutually exclusive situations in which constructive trusts arise. The first is where the property in question is at the outset owned *absolutely* by B, the person against whom the trust obligation arises. Here, one of the causative events to which the constructive trust responds is an act of B in relation to *his own* property. The second relates to property which B does not previously own. Here, one of the material events is an act of B in relation to property he has yet to acquire, and the result is that, when B later obtains title to the property in question, a constructive trust arises with the effect that he ever only takes a *qualified* interest in that property. These cases can respectively be referred to as AI and QI situations.

A comparison between proprietary estoppel[1] and the doctrine in *Rochefoucauld v Boustead*[2] illustrates this distinction. A claim in proprietary estoppel lies where B promises or assures A that B will cede to A an interest in property B owns, and A acts in detrimental reliance on B's promise. Where a constructive trust is imposed, it reflects an AI situation: it arises in relation to property which was owned absolutely by B at the outset. In contrast, the doctrine in *Rochefoucauld* typically applies where B informally promises to hold A's land on trust for A or C. When A relies on B's promise and transfers the legal title of the land to B, a constructive trust arises to compel B to carry out his promise. This reflects a QI situation: the constructive trust arises in relation to property not previously belonging to B, and has the effect of qualifying B's interest in the property acquired from A.

The historical enforcement of trust (originally, use) arrangements also illustrates the distinction between QI and AI situations. When use arrangements were first enforced

[1] This doctrine is discussed in Chapter 7.
[2] This doctrine is discussed in Chapter 4.

in English law, the Court of Chancery was willing to enforce such arrangements only in QI situations. As George Spence notes, '[u]ses or trusts originally were created by an actual transfer of the legal estate in property from [A] to [B]; or, as it was afterwards called, by *transmutation of possession*.'[3] In other words, the enforcement of the first use arrangements had the effect of qualifying the interest B acquired in property which he did not previously own. Because A had effectively parted with his legal title at common law, the Court of Chancery was willing to enforce such arrangements although consideration may not have been provided for the enforcement of the arrangement.[4]

In contrast, the Court of Chancery initially declined to act in AI situations. Where B constituted himself as *feoffee* over property he owned absolutely, 'the person who declared the trust still retained the legal interest, so that to effectuate the trust, the court must have deprived him, in effect, of his legal rights; and if there were no consideration, there was nothing to call on the Court of Chancery to interfere.'[5] Certainly, it was eventually accepted that B could use the trust as a facilitative device to declare himself express trustee over his own property. Nevertheless, the historical context indicates that the tendency to draw a distinction between QI and AI situations existed from the earliest days of the law of trusts.

2.2. Primary and Secondary Rights

The second building block is the distinction between primary and secondary[6] rights.[7] The first appearance in English jurisprudence of this distinction can be found in John Austin's lectures. According to Austin, primary rights are rights which exist '*in* and *per se*', while secondary rights 'arise out of violations of primary rights'.[8] Where A has a primary right against B, B owes a primary duty towards A which does not arise from a wrong. That is to say, the primary right and duty constitute a legal *relationship* between A and B which does not hinge on B committing a breach of a duty. On the other hand, when B commits a civil *wrong* by breaching a primary duty,[9] A obtains a secondary right against B that the consequences of B's beach is corrected.

The distinction between primary and secondary rights can be illustrated by observing the doctrine of proprietary estoppel.[10] When B promises A that A will obtain an interest

[3] See George Spence, *The Equitable Jurisdiction of the Court of Chancery* (Pennsylvania, Lea and Blanchard, 1846) 447.

[4] ibid 449.

[5] ibid 449–50.

[6] Or, as Diplock LJ labelled these, 'original' and 'substitutive' rights: *Hardwick Game Farm v Suffolk Agricultural Poultry Producers Association* [1966] 1 WLR 287 (CA) 341.

[7] Where A has a right against B, B has a correlative or equivalent duty towards A: Wesley Newcomb Hohfeld, Walter Wheeler Cook (ed), *Fundamental Legal Conceptions as Applied in Judicial Reasoning*, (New Jersey, The Lawbook Exchange, 2010) 36, 38. We can therefore speak of rights and duties interchangeably.

[8] John Austin, R Campbell (ed), *Lectures on Jurisprudence*, 5th edn (London, John Murray, 1885) 762. Hohfeld, too, was of the view that, quite apart from a primary right/duty relationship, a new, secondary right/duty relation arises when a primary right is infringed: see discussion in Donal Nolan and Andrew Robertson, 'Rights and Private Law' in Donal Nolan and Andrew Robertson (eds), *Rights and Private Law* (Oxford, Hart Publishing, 2014) 19.

[9] See generally James Edelman, *Gain-Based Damages: Contract, Tort, Equity and Intellectual Property* (Oxford, Hart Publishing, 2002) 32–63.

[10] The following points are discussed in detail in Chapter 7.

in B's property, A obtains a primary right—and B incurs a corresponding primary duty—that B will ensure the reliability of his induced assumptions. This primary right-duty relationship does not depend on B breaching a duty: the relationship comes into existence simply because B makes a relevant promise or assurance. If B informs A of B's intention to renege on his promise before A acts in reliance, B discharges his primary duty and the matter rests there. Similarly, if B does not so inform A before A acts in reliance but B goes on to perform his promise, B's primary duty is discharged. However, if B does neither of these, B commits a breach of his primary duty. This gives A a secondary right to compensation—and B incurs a corresponding secondary duty to compensate A—in relation to any net detriment suffered through A's reliance on B's promise.

2.3. Breach, Causation, Remoteness, and Mitigation

The third building block is the distinction between claims which require the pleading and proving of breach, causation, remoteness, and mitigation, and those which do not. Where the claim is that the defendant should perform his primary duty, it is not necessary for the claimant to plead and prove those elements.[11] All that needs to be shown is that the defendant is under such a primary duty, and that a non-performance of that duty can be enforced by compelling performance *in specie* or by providing a monetary substitute. In contrast, a claim for the enforcement of the claimant's secondary right requires the pleading and proving of those elements. As Lionel Smith explains:[12]

> [A]s soon as a claim is framed [as a claim for loss or gain caused], issues of causation must be brought in, because the only relevant loss [or gain] is the loss [or gain] that the defendant caused. And as soon as that is raised, issues of remoteness arise, because there are limits to the responsibility that we can rightly impose on someone for the causal outcomes of a breach of duty.

To illustrate this distinction, compare again proprietary estoppel and the doctrine in *Rochefoucauld*. A claim by way of the doctrine in *Rochefoucauld* that B holds property on constructive trust for A is a claim for the enforcement of A's primary right. So, in general terms, A must show that '[B] [did] not receive the trust property in his own right but by a transaction by which both parties intend to create a trust from the outset ...'.[13] Importantly, it is unnecessary further to show that B has committed a breach of trust which has caused A to suffer a loss and which is not too remote. In contrast, a claim by way of proprietary estoppel is for the enforcement of A's secondary right. Therefore, it is necessary to plead and prove a breach, causation of loss, and remoteness. Thus, A must show that A has suffered detrimental reliance as a result of B's failure to carry out the promise, 'detrimental reliance' being shorthand for 'loss caused by B's breach'; moreover, compensation will not be provided for loss which is too remote by virtue of rule that the court will only provide the 'minimum equity to do justice to the plaintiff'.[14]

[11] See Charles Mitchell, 'Equitable Rights and Wrongs' (2006) 59 *Current Legal Problems* 267, 279, 283.

[12] Lionel Smith, 'The Measurement of Compensation Claims against Trustees and Fiduciaries' in Elise Bant and Matthew Harding (eds), *Exploring Private Law* (Cambridge, CUP, 2010) 373.

[13] *Paragon Finance plc v DB Thakerar & Co* [1999] 1 All ER 400 (CA) 409.

[14] These points are discussed in Chapter 7, S 7.1.

2.4. Types of Remedies

The fourth building block is the distinction between different types of remedies. By 'remedies' it is meant an order of the court,[15] this being 'the core meaning of the term ... most commonly expressly adopted by those who write on remedies'.[16]

While there are various ways in which private law remedies may be analysed,[17] one particularly powerful method is to distinguish different types of remedies viz-a-viz the parties' rights and duties. More specifically, an important distinction can be drawn between 'replicative', 'reflective', and 'transformative' remedies. It is necessary to pause and explain what these terms mean, and how each type of remedy relates to remedial discretion.

2.4.1. Zakrzewski's Scheme

It is helpful to start with the analysis propounded by Rafal Zakrzewski in his monograph *Remedies Reclassified*.[18] On Zakrzewski's scheme, a distinction is drawn between replicative and transformative remedies.

Replicative remedies simply restate primary or secondary rights.[19] To take an example from the law of contracts, an award of a sum due under a contract and an award of damages for breach of contract are both replicative remedies: they respectively restate the claimant's primary right to the contractual sum and his secondary right to compensation due to the other party's non-performance. Likewise, an order for a common account against an express trustee and an order for an account on the basis of wilful default against a breaching trustee respectively replicate the beneficiary's primary and secondary rights.

Transformative remedies are different: they bear little resemblance to, and substantially alter, the claimant's pre-trial substantive rights.[20] Asking whether these remedies replicate primary or secondary rights 'does not provide us with meaningful categories', since they *transform* the claimant's pre-trial rights, resulting in 'a legal relation that significantly differs from any legal relation that existed before the court order was made'.[21] Examples of such remedies are an order giving guidance to trustees[22] and a court's ability to allow the recovery

[15] An 'order' includes 'judgments, decrees, orders, and pronouncements': Rafal Zakrzewski, *Remedies Reclassified* (Oxford, OUP, 2005) 44.

[16] ibid 17. See, eg, William Blackstone, *Commentaries on the Laws of England*, 1st edn (Oxford, Clarendon Press, 1768) vol 3, 396; Peter Birks, 'Three Kinds of Objection to Discretionary Remedialism' (2000) 29 *University of Western Australia Law Review* 1, 5; and the cases and commentators cited in Zakrzewski, *Remedies Reclassified* (n 15) 17 and 44. Zakrzewski's in-depth analysis of the meaning of 'remedy' also leads him to this meaning of the term (Zakrzewski, *Remedies Reclassified* (n 15) Chs 2–4). In particular, the term 'remedies' is conceptually distinct from substantive (primary or secondary) rights (see Zakrzewski, *Remedies Reclassified* (n 15) Chapter 4). *cf* Austin, *Lectures on Jurisprudence* (n 8) 761, who used the term to refer to secondary rights.

[17] For an overview of the different analyses commonly made, see Nolan and Robertson, 'Rights and Private Law' (n 8) 18–21.

[18] Zakrzewski, *Remedies Reclassified* (n 15).

[19] ibid 55.

[20] ibid 102.

[21] ibid 203.

[22] *Chapman v Chapman* [1954] AC 429 (HL) 446.

of incurred expenses where a contract is discharged due to frustration 'if it considers it just to do so having regard to all the circumstances of the case'.[23] One can hardly say that beneficiaries have a substantive *right to* the particular guidance given to their trustees, or that a contracting party has a substantive *right to* the recovery of incurred expenses where the contract is frustrated. Another recent example in English law is the award of damages in lieu of injunction, at least in the context of the tort of nuisance where the defendant obtains a planning permission for his actions. The Supreme Court has suggested that such an award 'involves a classic exercise of discretion, which should not, as a matter of principle, be fettered',[24] in particular by the restrictive criteria set out for the exercise of such discretion in *Shelfer v City of London Electric Lighting Co*.[25] This is because the award may have the goal either, or a combination, of public law and private law aims, which has to be determined on a case-by-case basis.[26] Thus, it is difficult to say that claimants have a *right to* an award of damages in lieu of injunction in any particular case,[27] since 'the outcome should depend on all the evidence and arguments' without 'any inclination either way'.[28]

One important consequence of distinguishing between replicative and transformative remedies is that it indicates the different ways in which courts exercise discretion in relation to different remedies. According to Zakrzewski, in relation to replicative remedies, the content of the remedy is selected at an institutional level 'by the law',[29] with judges having only the discretion to determine whether certain 'bars' operate on the facts of the case before them.[30] Here, judges are provided with 'a choice *not* to order something[,] [t]hat something [being] clearly defined by the law relating to [the claimant's] substantive rights.'[31] In contrast, when awarding transformative remedies, 'the court has a choice to create an entirely new remedy that does not replicate any of the claimant's substantive rights. This is a choice to order something. But that something is generally not defined by the substantive law. Further choices are required as to what is to be ordered. The creation of an entirely new right with new content requires a wide gamut of considerations to be taken into account.'[32] Here, discretion as to the content of the remedy is exercised at the instance-specific level 'by the court'.[33]

2.4.2. The Adopted Scheme

The remedial scheme adopted for the purposes of this book is a modification of Zakrzewski's scheme. While his 'transformative' category is retained and adopted, remedies which

[23] Law Reform (Frustrated Contracts) Act 1943, s 1(2).
[24] *Lawrence v Fen Tigers Ltd* [2014] UKSC 13, [2014] AC 822 [120]. See too [170].
[25] *Shelfer v City of London Electric Lighting Co* [1895] 1 Ch 287 (CA).
[26] *Lawrence* (n 24) [157].
[27] Indeed, the obiter statements in the Supreme Court leave much ambiguity as to whether claimants start out having a right to an injunction or to damages.
[28] *Lawrence* (n 24) [122].
[29] Zakrzewski, *Remedies Reclassified* (n 15) 100–01.
[30] ibid 92, 97.
[31] ibid 98.
[32] ibid.
[33] ibid 100–01.

Zakrzewski categorises as 'replicative' consist, upon closer inspection, of two distinct types of remedies—'replicative' and 'reflective'. These three types of remedies will be examined in turn.

2.4.2.1. *Replicative Remedies*

It is unobjectionable to label remedies which give effect to primary rights as 'replicative'. The reason for this is best understood by observing that courts exercise little to no discretion as to both the *goal* and *content* of replicative remedies. Discretion as to goal involves the making of policy choices which dictate the purpose or object of the remedy in question; discretion as to content relates to the determination of the manner of realising the goal of the remedy.[34] It is inherent in the nature of replicative remedies that they are logically restricted to compelling B to carry out his primary duty; and in doing so they give A 'the very thing to which he or she is entitled',[35] such remedies being 'peculiar to [their] own nature as derived from the event which gives [them] birth'.[36] The fact that the law deems the parties' primary relationship—which consists of their primary rights and duties—as worthy of being enforced negates the need for courts to exercise discretion as to the goal of the awarded remedy; and the content of such a remedy is determined by direct reference to the parties' primary rights and duties. This is why Peter Birks has written that 'a primary event implies a very narrowly defined response'.[37] Thus, for example, following a successful action for a contractual debt due[38] or to hold a trustee to account for trust property,[39] the awarded remedy restates and enforces the parties' rights and duties as revealed in their contract or trust instrument. Since the goal and content of the remedy simply replicates the primary contractual or trust relationship between the parties, there is little scope for the exercise of remedial discretion.

2.4.2.2. *Reflective Remedies*

Some circumspection is necessary when dealing with remedies which give effect to secondary rights. This is because there is an unfortunate tendency to over- or to under-emphasise the differences between such remedies and transformative remedies, in particular when discussing damages awards. It is necessary to reject these tendencies in order to obtain a proper analysis, which is that damages awards—and, to the same extent, other remedies which are awarded in relation to breaches of primary duties—constitute a remedial category distinct from replicative and transformative remedies.

Take first the tendency to over-emphasise the difference. This tendency is reflected in Zakrzewski's work, which leads him to categorise as 'replicative' those remedies which

[34] Paul Finn, 'Equitable Doctrine and Discretion in Remedies' in WR Cornish, Richard Nolan, Janet O'Sullivan et al (eds), *Restitution Past, Present and Future* (Oxford, Hart Publishing, 1998) 268–70. So, for example, discretion as to goal may relate to the question of whether a particular remedy ought to be compensatory, punitive, restitutionary, etc; discretion as to content may relate to the precise sum to be awarded to further a particular remedial goal.

[35] Nolan and Robertson, 'Rights and Private Law' (n 8) 20.

[36] Peter Birks, 'Equity in the Modern Law: An Exercise in Taxonomy' (1996) 26 *University of Western Australia Law Review* 1, 41.

[37] ibid 14.

[38] *White and Carte (Councils) Ltd v McGregor* [1962] AC 413 (HL).

[39] *AIB Group (UK) plc v Mark Redler & Co Solicitors* [2014] UKSC 58, [2015] AC 1503 [116]; Sir P Millett, 'Equity's Place in the Law of Commerce' (1998) 114 *LQR* 214, 225–27.

give effect to secondary rights. In attempting to avoid damages from being classified as a transformative remedy,[40] Zakrzewski says that an award of damages 'redresses the *non-performance* of a secondary right to the payment of damages arising from a wrong'.[41] However, it is doubtful whether one can ever fully perform his secondary duty to pay damages to another prior to a court order, since the duty-bound party would not normally be in a position to determine what the appropriate content of the damages ought to be. Even if performance were attempted, this would not discharge the duty, since 'pre-payment is no defence to a claim in damages'.[42]

The tendency to under-emphasise the difference can be seen in Stephen Smith's writing. Smith suggests that awards of damages do not confirm or affirm an existing duty to pay damages, but are *created* by court orders.[43] By this he means that A does not obtain a secondary *right* to compensation from the moment B infringes A's primary right; rights to compensation arise only at the remedial stage. However, as Allan Beever has noted, the secondary 'duty to repair' reflects a fundamental *right*: '[t]here is surely no remedy more basic than the repair of a wrong',[44] and such a right surely arises at the moment the wrong is committed. Moreover, a remedy awarded pursuant to an exercise of discretion as to both goal and content, which provides the claimant a right against the defendant where none existed before, needs to be distinguished from cases where the claimant already has a right in existence, the courts' role being simply to ascertain its content—the appropriate means of realising that right.

Ultimately, a proper analysis calls for a nuanced approach by taking a middle ground between the two exaggerated views. The fact that a secondary right is *created* when B breaches A's primary right is not inconsistent with the view that that right already in existence allows for[45] some discretion as to *content*[46] to be exercised by the court in relation to the awarded remedy. As John Gardner writes, 'the secondary obligation is a rational echo of the primary obligation, for it exists to serve, so far as may still be done, the reasons for the primary obligation that was not performed when its performance was due.'[47] Making the same point differently, Arthur Ripstein, in explaining the Kantian view of wrongs and remedies, observes that compensatory damages—and, to the same extent, any remedy which gives effect to secondary rights:

> simply gives [the right-holder] back what [he] had all along, because [his] right to what [he] had survives any wrongs committed against it ... That is just to say that [the right-holder] ha[s] a right to cancel the consequences of [the wrongdoer's] wrong, and so a right to compel [the wrongdoer] to compensate [the right-holder] by giving [him] back what [he] had before ... Damages [and, to the same extent, any remedy giving effect to secondary rights] make that right effective in space and

[40] Zakrzewski, *Remedies Reclassified* (n 15) 79.

[41] ibid 166–67 (emphasis added).

[42] Stephen Smith, 'Why Courts make Orders (And What This Tells us About Damages)' (2011) 64 *Current Legal Problems* 51, 74. See *Edmunds v Lloyds Italico & l'Ancora Compagnia di Assicurazione e Riassicurazione SpA* [1986] 1 WLR 492 (CA) 496.

[43] See, eg, Stephen A Smith, 'Duties, Liabilities, and Damages' (2011–2012) 125 *Harvard Law Review* 1727.

[44] Allan Beever, 'Our Most Fundamental Rights' in Nolan and Robertson, *Rights and Private Law* (n 8) 81.

[45] As is the case with transformative remedies (see n 60 below), although reflective remedies allow for discretion as to content to be exercised, such discretion is not exercised in every case in which these remedies are awarded.

[46] It does not provide for the exercise of discretion to re-evaluate the *goal* of the remedy on a case-by-case basis.

[47] John Gardner, 'What is Tort Law For? Part 1: The Place of Corrective Justice' (2011) 30 *Law & Philosophy* 1, 40.

> time, precisely because the object of the right was [the right-holder's] power to determine the use of that thing in time and space.[48]

So, as Paul Finn notes, there are doctrines which 'suggest what is the goal of the remedy but leave it to the "appropriateness" principle to determine the manner of that goal's realisation'.[49] Hence, although remedies which give effect to secondary rights provide for a wider remedial potential than replicative remedies, the 'remedy is not at large.'[50]

In order to reflect the fact that remedies which give effect to secondary rights differ from replicative and transformative remedies, they can be labelled as 'reflective' remedies.

2.4.2.2.1. Discretion as to Content

An important point concerning the exercise of discretion as to content requires clarification at this juncture. It might be thought that such discretion arises not only in relation to reflective remedies, but also in relation to *replicative* remedies. Take, for example, a contractual indemnity clause which provides that one party has an obligation to pay 'a reasonable sum' on the occurrence of certain events. A failure to pay would allow the aggrieved party to make a debt claim, which is a claim for a replicative remedy.[51] Here, just as in the case of a claim for damages for loss caused (a reflective remedy), 'the amount to be paid may … require quantification pursuant to an order for the assessment of the sum due.'[52] The exercise of quantification or liquidation might be thought to indicate that discretion as to content can also be exercised in relation to the award of replicative remedies.

This is, however, an erroneous view. Discretion as to content is not exercised simply because the court is required to quantify or ascertain the appropriate sum to be awarded. When quantifying a replicative remedy, courts simply give direct effect to the right in question 'in so far as is practically possible given the imprecise nature of the substantive right'[53] without creating new content or amending the content of the claimant's primary right. In particular, the court does not have room to exercise discretion as to the extent to which the defendant is to be liable, which is pre-determined by the primary relationship between the parties; the court's task is simply to render certain the uncertain term.

In contrast, the award of a reflective remedy requires the court to grapple with the issue of remoteness,[54] and this allows for[55] discretion as to content to be exercised. Such discretion may affect the *extent* or *type* of remedy awarded. The award of damages for breach of

[48] Arthur Ripstein, *Force and Freedom: Kant's Legal and Political Philosophy* (Cambridge MA, Harvard University Press, 2009) 304–05. See too Robert Stevens, 'Rights Restricting Remedies' in Andrew Robertson and Michael Tilbury (eds), *Divergences in Private Law* (Oxford, Hart Publishing, 2016) 160–61.

[49] Finn, 'Equitable Doctrine' (n 34) 269.

[50] ibid 270.

[51] Rafal Zakrzewski, 'The Nature of a Claim on an Indemnity' (2006) 22 *Journal of Contract Law* 54, 62–63.

[52] ibid 63. Another example of a replicative remedy which may involve the exercise of liquidation can be found in the Sale of Goods Act 1979, s 8, which provides that, where the price of a contract of sale is not fixed by the contract, fixed in a manner agreed by the contract, or determined by the course of dealing between the parties, the buyer must pay a 'reasonable price'. A court awarding the seller a replicative remedy for a sum due under a contract of sale must therefore determine what amounts to a 'reasonable price'.

[53] Zakrzewski, *Remedies Reclassified* (n 15) 79.

[54] The same may be said of mitigation (see David Wright, 'Discretion with Common Law Remedies' (2002) 23 *Adelaide Law Review* 243, 273); but the focus is on remoteness because this has the greater impact on the discussion in this book.

[55] But see n 60 below.

contract serves as an example of discretion as to content affecting the *extent* of the remedy, where judges have 'considerable latitude … in determining issues such as mitigation and remoteness of damages'.[56] So, for instance, *Chitty on Contracts*[57] notes that, since remoteness requires only that a particular type of loss was contemplated by the parties instead of the extent of that loss, '[t]he application of the test for remoteness to a particular set of facts therefore depends largely on the judicial discretion to categorise losses into broad categories'. An example of discretion as to content affecting the *type* of the remedy is found in proprietary estoppel, where a personal or proprietary remedy may be awarded according to the facts of a case. When awarding reflective remedies, courts are not merely making the imprecise precise, but often also make judgment calls on a case-by-case basis to arrive at the appropriate content of the awarded remedy.

2.4.2.3. *Transformative Remedies*

Finally, in relation to transformative remedies, these provide for the widest remedial potential. Their award *creates* 'a legal relation that significantly differs from any legal relation that existed before the court order was made'.[58] They transform and substantially alter A's substantive rights.[59] The transformative nature of these remedies is brought to bear in their provision for the exercise of discretion as to both the goal and content of the appropriate remedy. Instead of merely replicating or reflecting A's pre-trial rights, the award of a transformative remedy allows for[60] 'many of the policy choices that are entrenched in the law relating to substantive rights … to be reopened.'[61] It may therefore be difficult to predict in advance whether a transformative remedy will be awarded in a particular case, and—if it is awarded—what its content would be. On the other hand, it is inherent in the nature of transformative remedies that they allow courts the greatest degree of flexibility to respond to the sensitivities of the facts of a particular case.

2.4.3. The Doctrine of Precedent

A final, crucial point needs to be made in relation to the fourth building block. In the earlier discussion of reflective and transformative remedies, it was noted that these remedies respectively *allow for* discretion as to content, and discretion as to goal and content, to be exercised by the courts. The italicised words emphasis the fact that, in principle, discretion *may* be exercised in the award of these remedies. However, it does not entail that such

[56] John McGhee (ed), Snell's Equity, 33rd edn (London, Sweet & Maxwell, 2016) [17-004]. See too Wright, 'Discretion' (n 54); Sir Robin Cooke, 'Remoteness of Damages and Judicial Discretion' [1978] 37 *CLJ* 288.

[57] Hugh Beale (ed), *Chitty on Contracts: Vol 1 General Principles*, 32nd edn (London, Sweet & Maxwell, 2016) [26-116].

[58] Zakrzewski, *Remedies Reclassified* (n 15) 203.

[59] ibid 102.

[60] Note that although transformative remedies allow for such discretion to be exercised, it is not necessarily exercised in every case where transformative remedies are awarded: some transformative remedies can be obtained as a matter of course (see Zakrzewski, *Remedies Reclassified* (n 15) 207). It will be suggested below (see S 2.4.3.) that this has nothing to do with the inherent nature of the remedy in question, but is simply an effect of the doctrine of precedent.

[61] ibid 98.

discretion is invariably exercised in practice on a case-by-case basis. So, in some contexts, reflective or transformative remedies appear to be awarded as a matter of course. However, it is important to resist the temptation to analyse these remedies as simply replicative in nature.

In common law systems where the doctrine of precedent applies, the way in which discretion operates in practice is necessarily more qualified than the way it arises in civil law systems. Like cases are to be treated alike, and the ability to reconsider an established precedent is significantly diminished where the precedent was set by a higher court. Therefore, even if a court ostensibly has the ability to exercise remedial discretion on a case-by-case basis, it is unlikely to decide it differently from a previous case with materially identical facts. It follows that it is necessary to distinguish between two plausible explanations for why, in any particular case, remedial discretion is not exercised in practice. On the one hand, the lack of discretion may be due to the inherent nature of the remedy awarded; on the other hand, it may be due to the operation of the doctrine of precedent.

There are at least four reasons why this distinction matters. First, because the doctrine of precedent operates indiscriminately regardless of the type of remedy in question, merely exploring whether discretion is actually exercised in practice is unhelpful for understanding why the court imposes the particular remedy.

Secondly, the distinction allows us to determine what elements are necessary to be pleaded and proved in order to obtain a particular type of remedy. For example, it is impossible accurately to assess whether it is necessary for a claimant to establish the elements of breach, causation, and remoteness simply by observing whether remedial discretion is or is not exercised in practice in a particular type of case. Instead, it is necessary further to investigate what type of remedy is in question, and whether the particular remedy sought is one which replicates, reflects, or transforms the claimant's substantive rights.

Thirdly, the distinction has practical implications when a court is faced with a novel case where, by definition, the doctrine of precedent has no application. In these cases, it remains necessary for the court to determine whether it has the ability to exercise remedial discretion, and (if so) to what extent such discretion may be exercised. Without the benefit of precedent to determine its outcome, everything turns on the nature of the specific remedy in question.

Fourthly, the distinction allows for a precise articulation of the rights of a claimant. It makes clear that a claimant not only has rights *against the defendant*, but also rights *against the court*. Quite apart from the fact that the claimant has rights against the defendant which create in the defendant corresponding duties towards the claimant, the claimant also has a right 'to create an obligation in the court to adjudicate [his] matter in the light of [his] rights'.[62] The claimant's right against the defendant determines the nature of the remedy in question; the claimant's right against the court compels the court to comply with the doctrine of precedent. That these rights are distinct is reinforced by the fact that they are triggered by different events: rights against the defendant are triggered by the relevant causative real-world events; rights against the court 'arise at the discretion of plaintiffs, who … are privileged to decide whether or not to exercise their legal power to initiate court proceedings.'[63] It is the rights and duties between the parties which has bearing upon the type of remedy sought.

[62] Ori J Herstein, 'How Tort Law Empowers' (2015) 65 *University of Toronto Law Journal* 99, 109, 121.
[63] ibid 120.

3

The Structure of the Law of Constructive Trusts

This chapter applies the building blocks introduced in Chapter 2 to construct a structure of the law of constructive trusts.

3.1. Categories of Causative Events: Bilateral, Unilateral, and Court-Based

	BILATERAL		UNILATERAL	COURT-BASED
	NON-CONTRACT-BASED	CONTRACT-BASED		
Replicative Constructive Trusts	***The Doctrine in Rochefoucauld v Boustead*** ***Secret Trusts*** ***The Doctrine in Pallant v Morgan***	***Specifically Enforceable Contracts for Sale*** ***Future Property***	***The Rule in Re Rose***	—
Reflective Constructive Trusts	***Proprietary Estoppel***	—	***Gains Made in Breach of Fiduciary Duty***	
Transformative Constructive Trusts	—			***Remedial Constructive Trusts***

Figure 1: The structure of the law of constructive trusts: 'core' doctrines

Constructive trusts can be divided into three broad categories, distinguished according to their material causative events. These categories are: bilateral events, unilateral events, and court-based events. In the 'bilateral events' category are cases where constructive trusts are triggered by the acts of two parties. The 'unilateral events' category concerns cases where constructive trusts are triggered by acts involving one party only. And cases involving 'court-based events' are those where constructive trusts owe their existence primarily to a court's decision that they should arise. This latter category does not imply that one or both parties' pre-trial acts are utterly irrelevant to the imposition of these constructive trusts, or that a court order is not needed for constructive trusts to be awarded in the former two categories. Rather, in the 'court-based' category the central role of the court in awarding constructive trusts is emphasised, since the remedy bears little resemblance to the parties' pre-trial rights and duties arising from their acts.

We will now look at each category in turn to construct an analytical structure of the law of constructive trusts. A schematic summary of the structure can be found in Figure 1 above.

3.2. Bilateral Events

The doctrines which come under the 'bilateral events' category fall within one of two sub-categories: 'contract-based' and 'non-contract-based'. The former consists of doctrines where it is a prerequisite for the imposition of a constructive trust that the parties are in a contractual relationship. The latter consists of doctrines where neither a legal contract between the parties nor compliance with any formality provision is required. Within each sub-category, the distinction between QI and AI situations is analytically significant.

3.2.1. Non-Contract-Based Subcategory

Within the non-contract-based subcategory, a number of core constructive trust doctrines can be identified. The doctrines which reflect QI situations are the doctrine in *Rochefoucauld v Boustead*, secret trusts, and the doctrine in *Pallant v Morgan*. The core doctrine reflecting AI situations is proprietary estoppel.

3.2.1.1. QI Situations

In the typical case[1] relating to the doctrine in *Rochefoucauld*, A and B enter into an informal agreement by which B agrees to hold A's land on trust for A, and in reliance A transfers the legal title of the land to B. In the typical secret trusts case, B informally promises a testator, A, that B will hold any property he receives under A's will on trust for C. A leaves property

[1] It is important to stress that these are merely typical scenarios in which the doctrines arise. Variations of the typical scenarios may still trigger the operation of the doctrines. These variations are discussed in the chapters dedicated to each of the doctrines.

in his will to B and the will is left unchanged until his death in reliance on B's promise to fulfil A's wishes. In the typical case relating to the doctrine in *Pallant*, one bidding party (B) at an auction informally agrees to cede some part of the property yet to be acquired to another bidding party (A) if B succeeds in acquiring the property. In reliance A refrains from attempting to procure the property, thereby conferring an advantage in relation to B's acquisition of the property. In all three cases, B's promise and A's reliance triggers the imposition of a constructive trust which compels B to fulfil his promise.

It is observable that B's promise is always to the effect that he will take only a qualified interest in property yet to be acquired, and that A's reliance arises in the form of the provision of an advantage to B in relation to B's acquisition of that property. More specifically, the 'advantage' is an *opportunity* to acquire the property in question. In relation to the doctrine in *Rochefoucauld* and secret trusts, this occurs when A transfers the property directly to B; in relation to the doctrine in *Pallant*, this occurs when A acts in such a way that B's chances of acquiring the property are increased.[2] Understood in these terms, it can be observed that these QI doctrines are 'advantage-based': they are concerned with holding B to his promise to qualify the interest he acquires in property acquired with the benefit of an advantage conferred by A in reliance on that promise.

In response to B's promise and A's reliance, A acquires a primary right, and B is subject to a corresponding primary duty, from the moment of B's acquisition. This primary right and duty constitute a constructive trust relationship between the parties. Following a successful claim by way of one of these doctrines, courts impose a constructive trust remedy which replicates the parties' primary right and duty. As a replicative remedy, the constructive trust award is not conditional upon pleading and proving that B had committed a wrong: '[B's] trusteeship is independent of and precede[s] [any] breach of trust'.[3] Neither do issues of causation, remoteness, and mitigation arise. Thus, B incurs custodial duties[4] and a duty to account[5] *from the moment* of acquisition, since B's 'assumption to act … itself'[6] gives rise to his duties in relation to the trust property. As Millett LJ (as he then was) observed of such cases, B 'does not receive the trust property in his own right but by a transaction by which both parties intend to create a trust from the outset … His possession of the property is coloured from the first by the trust and confidence by means of which he obtained it'.[7]

3.2.1.2. AI Situations

The doctrine of proprietary estoppel is made up of 'three separate, irreducibly dissimilar, strands'.[8] The promise-based strand applies where B promises that B will cede an interest

[2] This is all that is required for A to fulfil the element of reliance in relation to the doctrine in *Pallant v Morgan*: see Chapter 6, S 6.2.1.2.5.

[3] *Paragon Finance plc v DB Thakerar & Co* [1999] 1 All ER 400 (CA) 408. Millett LJ was here referring to the doctrine in *Rochefoucauld v Boustead*, secret trusts, and the doctrine in *Pallant v Morgan*.

[4] *Banner Homes Group plc v Luff Developments Ltd* [2000] Ch 372 (CA) 399, a case reflecting the doctrine in *Pallant v Morgan*.

[5] *Rochefoucauld v Boustead* [1897] 1 Ch 196 (CA) 212.

[6] *Selangor United Rubber Estates Ltd v Cradock (No. 3)* [1968] 1 WLR 1555 (Ch) 1579.

[7] *Paragon Finance* (n 3) 409.

[8] Ben McFarlane, *The Law of Proprietary Estoppel* (Oxford, OUP, 2014) [1-05]. See McFarlane (ibid) Chapter 1 generally for the distinctions between these strands.

in his property to A, and A detrimentally relies on B's promise. The acquiescence-based strand applies where A detrimentally relies on a mistaken belief as to A's current rights, and B who knows of A's mistaken belief fails to assert B's right against A. The representation-based strand applies where B makes a representation to A in relation to a fact, or mixed fact and law, on which it is intended that A would rely, and A relies in such a way such that he would suffer a detriment if B denies the representation. For the purposes of this book, 'proprietary estoppel' will generally refer to the promise-based strand.

It is easy to explain why the representation-based strand is not discussed: it does not fall within the ambit of the law of constructive trusts at all. Its effect is merely preclusive; its operation 'depends on the broader doctrine of estoppel by representation, which is "really a rule of evidence".'[9] The reason for not focusing on the acquiescence-based strand is more subtle. Ben McFarlane suggests that the key distinction between this strand and the promise-based strand lies in the fact that, unlike the latter strand which requires 'a positive representation or assurance by [B]', the former strand can apply 'even if [A] is unaware of [B]'s failure to assert [B]'s right'.[10] It follows that, unlike the promise-based strand which is concerned with compensating A for a loss he suffers, the acquiescence-based strand is concerned with preventing B's fraudulent or dishonest action.[11]

Although both strands are capable of imposing a duty on B towards A[12] by way of a constructive trust,[13] there are a number of reasons for focusing on the promise-based strand. The first is that this strand is 'the most practically important of the three strands of the doctrine'.[14] Secondly, the elements required to trigger the promise-based strand most closely approximate to those which trigger the QI doctrines, and therefore observing the differences between this strand and the QI doctrines provides valuable lessons for the purposes of making sense of constructive trusts. Thirdly, the promise-based strand and the acquiescence-based strand are united in a number of crucial aspects, and therefore the lessons learnt from a survey of one of the strands would apply equally to the other. These aspects are that both strands reflect AI situations since, where a constructive trust is awarded, it arises in relation to property owned by B from the outset; that both strands reflect the same remedial approach[15] whereby the remedy awarded is commensurate with the level of detrimental reliance A suffers; and that in contrast to the QI doctrines which are 'advantage-based', both strands are 'detriment-based'.

It can be observed that B's promise commonly relates to property which B owns absolutely at the outset, and therefore A's reliance never increases B's opportunity of acquiring property to which B's promise relates. When B promises that A will obtain an

[9] ibid [7-32].

[10] Hence, unlike in relation to the promise-based strand, '[B]'s failure to assert a right against [A] is one of the ingredients of [A]'s cause of action' in relation to the acquiescence-based strand: Ben McFarlane, 'Proprietary Estoppel: The Importance of Looking Back' in Paul S Davies and Justine Pila (eds), *The Jurisprudence of Lord Hoffmann: A Festschrift in Honour of Lord Leonard Hoffmann* (Oxford, Hart Publishing, 2015) 342.

[11] McFarlane, *The Law of Proprietary Estoppel* (n 8) [1-07].

[12] ibid [9-23].

[13] ibid [10-39].

[14] ibid [1-15].

[15] ibid [7-14].

interest in B's property, B is under a primary duty to ensure the reliability of his induced assumptions. B may discharge this duty by informing A of B's intention to renege on his promise before A acts in reliance, or by performing his promise where A has acted in reliance. But if B does neither of these, then B commits a breach of his primary duty which gives A a secondary right to compensation in relation to any net detriment suffered through acting in reliance on B's promise. Depending on the *degree* of detriment suffered, the court may impose a constructive trust remedy, or it may award compensatory damages (or 'equitable compensation'). These remedies are imposed as reflective remedies. Therefore, A must plead and prove that B's breach of duty has caused A to suffer loss, and that the extent of the loss claimed is not too remote.

3.2.2. Contract-Based Subcategory

For a constructive trust to arise in the contract-based subcategory, it is a prerequisite that the parties must first have entered into a legally binding contract. Two doctrines fall within this subcategory. The first relates to specifically enforceable contracts of sale. These are contracts for valuable consideration that B will transfer *property B owns* to A, and therefore represents an AI situation. The second relates to constructive trusts arising in the context of contracts for value to assign or transfer future property. This represents a QI situation: B's contractual promise relates to property yet to be acquired, and 'immediately on the acquisition of the property described [B] would hold it in trust for [A], according to the terms of the contract',[16] 'without any further act on the part of [B]'.[17]

It might be thought that the distinction between AI and QI situations within this subcategory has implications both for the events which trigger these constructive trusts and the extent to which remedial discretion is exercised. In relation to triggering events, it is said that a merely executory contract for value for the transfer of property presently owned by B is sufficient to give rise to a constructive trust, whereas in relation to future property A must also have performed his part of the contract by providing consideration before a constructive trust would arise.[18] It is also suggested that 'considerations applicable to cases of specific performance' which affect whether a constructive trust is imposed in the context of specifically enforceable contracts of sale do not constrain the imposition of constructive trusts in cases involving future property.[19] This presumably means that, unlike in the context of contracts of sale, constructive trusts can be triggered in future property cases despite the fact that damages is not shown to be inadequate on the facts of the case.[20] It has also been claimed that the applicability of specific performance in one

[16] *Holroyd v Marshall* (1862) 10 H L Cas 191, 211; 11 ER 999, 1007.

[17] *Re Lind* [1915] 2 Ch 345 (CA) 360.

[18] See, eg, *Holroyd* (n 16) 10 H L Cas 209, 211; 11 ER 1006, 1007; *Re Clarke* [1887] Ch D 348 (CA) 352; *Tailby v Official Receiver* (1888) 13 App Cas 523 (HL) 547.

[19] *Tailby* (n 18) 547. Cf *Holroyd* (n 16) 10 H L Cas 211, 11 ER 1007; *Re Clarke* (n 18) 352.

[20] See, eg, *Re Clarke* (n 18) 352.

doctrine and not to the other reflects a difference as to remedial discretion.[21] In relation to contracts of sale it is thought that specific performance allows courts to exercise discretion, but such discretion has no role to play in relation to cases where future property is concerned.

Notwithstanding these apparent distinctions, it will be seen in Chapter 8 that there are no meaningful distinctions to be drawn between both doctrines. The reason for this conclusion is not simply that both doctrines have been said to reflect an application of the maxim 'equity considers as done that which ought to be done'.[22] Rather, a careful consideration of the requirements of the doctrines indicates that they in fact respond to the same material events. It will also be seen that inadequacy of damages is in fact a prerequisite for a constructive trust to arise in relation to both doctrines. A unified analysis suggests that both doctrines give rise to constructive trusts which are imposed are replicative remedies: they arise to enforce the primary contractual relationship between A and B. Courts do not in fact exercise discretion as to goal or content of the remedy in both doctrines, which confirms the replicative nature of these constructive trusts.

3.3. Unilateral Events

Within the 'unilateral events' category falls two core doctrines: the rule in *Re Rose* and the rule concerning gains made in breach of fiduciary duty. On the face of it, there may seem to be little in common between these doctrines, each operating within its own sphere with its own requirements and rationales. However, these doctrines can also be distinguished according whether they reflect an QI or AI situation, and whether they provide for the imposition constructive trusts as replicative or reflective remedies.

3.3.1. AI Situation

The rule in *Re Rose* operates where B has done everything in his power to effectuate a voluntary transfer of his property to A. Pending the vesting of the legal title to the property in A, a constructive trust arises to compel B to hold the property for the benefit of A. This doctrine reflects an AI situation, since the constructive trust is imposed on property which B owns at the outset.

The rule in *Re Rose* gives rise to constructive trusts imposed as replicative remedies. When B unilaterally fulfils the requirements of the doctrine, A acquires a primary right,

[21] JD Heydon, MJ Leeming and PG Turner, *Meagher, Gummow & Lehane's Equity: Doctrines & Remedies*, 5th edn (NSW, LexisNexis Butterworths, 2015) [6-270]; Sarah Worthington, 'Proprietary Remedies: The Nexus between Specific Performance and Constructive Trusts' (1996) 11 *Journal of Contract Law* 1, 8.

[22] In relation to specifically enforceable contracts of sale, see, eg, *HR Trustees Limited v Wembley plc* [2011] EWHC 2974 (Ch) [65]; Worthington, 'Proprietary Remedies' (n 21) 3. In relation to future property, see, eg, *Tailby* (n 18) 546, *Palette Shoes Pty Ltd v Krohn* (1937) 58 CLR 1, 16.

and B is subject to a corresponding primary duty. This primary right and duty make up a constructive trust relationship between the parties. Following a successful claim by A, a constructive trust remedy is imposed which replicates the parties' primary right and duty. It is therefore not necessary for A to plead or prove that B has committed a wrong by breaching his voluntary promise to transfer his property to A, that the wrong has caused A to suffer a loss, or that the loss is not too remote to be the subject of a constructive trust remedy.

3.3.2. QI Situation

The rule concerning gains made in breach of fiduciary duty reflects a QI situation. This rule arises where a fiduciary (B) makes a gain, such as a bribe or secret commission, in breach of his fiduciary duty towards his principal (A). Because a constructive trust arises, B never becomes the absolute owner of the gain from the moment it is acquired. Thus, B ever only takes a qualified interest in the property representing the gain.

A's claim is a wrong-based claim. The claim is that B's breach of his primary fiduciary duty caused B to make a gain for which he ought to account. Pursuant to this, a constructive trust is imposed, which has the effect of qualifying B's interest in the property representing the gain from the moment the gain is made, so long as the gain is not too remote. As such, constructive trust remedies which are imposed in relation to such gains in B's hands are imposed as reflective remedies.

3.4. Court-Based Events

The 'court-based' category consists of one doctrine: the 'remedial constructive trust'. In particular, it is the remedial constructive trust device as utilised in many Commonwealth jurisdictions such as Australia, Canada, New Zealand, Singapore, and Malaysia.

As transformative remedies, these constructive trusts arise pursuant to a court's exercise of discretion both as to the goal and content of the appropriate remedy to be imposed on a case-by-case basis. The wide-ranging ability to exercise remedial discretion is reflected in the label 'court-based', which highlights the central role of the court in awarding these trusts, and de-emphasises the relationship between the remedy and the parties' pre-trial rights and duties.

Therefore, it is unnecessary and unhelpful to ask whether transformative remedies transform primary or secondary rights. Instead, it is necessary to focus on the difficult questions raised by these trusts, such as: how much liberty do Commonwealth courts have in awarding these trusts; do they provide for an unbridled exercise of discretion; how does the award of remedial constructive trusts relate to the doctrine of precedent; is there any justification for allowing for their imposition? These and other matters are discussed in Chapter 11.

3.5. 'Non-Core' Doctrines

	BILATERAL		UNILATERAL	COURT-BASED
	NON-CONTRACT-BASED	CONTRACT-BASED		
Replicative Constructive Trusts	***The Doctrine in Rochefoucauld v Boustead*** ***Secret Trusts*** ***The Doctrine in Pallant v Morgan*** ***Mutual Wills (A)*** ***(part of) The Quistclose Doctrine*** ***Donatio Mortis Causa (A)***	***Specifically Enforceable Contracts for Sale*** ***Future Property***	***The Rule in Re Rose*** ***Donatio Mortis Causa (B)***	—
Reflective Constructive Trusts	***Proprietary Estoppel*** ***Mutual Wills (B)*** ***The 'Common Intention Constructive Trust'***	—	***Gains Made in Breach of Fiduciary Duty***	
Transformative Constructive Trusts		—		***Remedial Constructive Trusts***

Figure 2: The structure of the law of constructive trusts: 'core' doctrines and 'non-core' doctrines

The foregoing sections have explained how the core doctrines make up the structure of the law of constructive trusts. The core doctrines are discussed in Part B of this book. Part C addresses four 'non-core' doctrines: mutual wills, the *Quistclose* doctrine, the 'common intention constructive trust', and *donatio mortis causa*. As explained in Chapter 1,[23]

[23] See Chapter 1, S 1.4.

the underlying rationales of these doctrines have not been sufficiently explored to date, and a renewed analysis will be proposed for each of these doctrines in Chapters 12 to 15. These chapters demonstrate that the 'non-core' doctrines can easily be placed within one or more categories within the proposed structure of constructive trusts. A summary of their respective places within the structure is set out in Figure 2 above, with the 'non-core' doctrines underlined. It might be thought that their categorisation is unconventional, either because they do not accord with a 'mainstream' understanding of these doctrines, or because (in the case of mutual wills and *donatio mortis causa*) they cut across two different categories within the structure. It is the task of the chapters in Part C to explain and justify their places within the structure of the law of constructive trusts.

PART B

4

The Doctrine in *Rochefoucauld v Boustead*

By virtue of the Law of Property Act 1925, s 53(1)(b), 'a declaration of trust respecting any land ... must be manifested and proved by some writing signed by some person who is able to declare such a trust'.[1] In certain circumstances, however, a constructive trust may arise to enforce an agreement which does not comply with this formality requirement. The enforcement of such a trust has come to be known as an application of 'the doctrine in *Rochefoucauld v Boustead*'.[2]

The essence of the doctrine in *Rochefoucauld v Boustead* is found in the words of Lindley LJ in the Court of Appeal:[3]

> [T]he Statute of Frauds does not prevent the proof of a fraud; and ... it is a fraud on the part of a person to whom land is conveyed as a trustee, and who knows it was so conveyed, to deny the trust and claim the land himself. Consequently, notwithstanding the statute, it is competent for a person claiming land conveyed to another to prove by parol evidence that it was so conveyed upon trust for the claimant, and that the grantee, knowing the facts, is denying the trust and relying upon the form of conveyance and statute, in order to keep the land himself.

As his Lordship indicates, the transferee must have taken a conveyance of land 'as a trustee' before the doctrine in *Rochefoucauld v Boustead* can come into play. In most cases, this occurs where A transfers his land to B pursuant to an informal agreement that B will hold some interest in the land on trust for A. For instance, in *Bannister v Bannister*,[4] A, an elderly woman, conveyed two cottages to B, her brother-in-law, on the understanding that A would be allowed to live rent-free in one of them for as long as she desired. The case of *Rochefoucauld* provided authority for the Court of Appeal's ruling that a constructive trust arose for A's benefit.[5]

[1] This more succinctly replaced the Statute of Frauds 1677, s 7, which provided that 'all declarations ... of trusts or confidences of any lands ... shall be manifested and proved by some writing signed by the party who is by law enabled to declare such trust'. References in this Chapter to s 7 instead of s 53(1)(b) are merely contextual, and can otherwise be read interchangeably.

[2] *Rochefoucauld v Boustead* [1897] 1 Ch 196 (CA). In the course of discussion, many cases which were decided prior to *Rochefoucauld* will be referred to as applying 'the doctrine in *Rochefoucauld v Boustead*'. This is not a cause for concern. The label 'the doctrine in *Rochefoucauld v Boustead*' indicates that the Court of Appeal's decision in *Rochefoucauld* provided the first clear enunciation of the doctrine. It does not imply that the doctrine arose for the first time in the case of *Rochefoucauld*.

[3] ibid 206 (emphases added). His Lordship delivered the joint judgment of the Court of Appeal which also included Lord Halsbury LC and AL Smith LJ.

[4] *Bannister v Bannister* [1948] 2 All ER 133 (CA).

[5] ibid 136. In *Singh v Anand* [2007] EWHC 3346 (Ch), HHJ Norris QC thought that the doctrine in *Rochefoucauld v Boustead* was distinct from the doctrine at play in *Bannister* (n 4) (compare *Singh* [144](h) and *Singh* [144](m)). The distinction is illusory and uncalled for.

However, the doctrine can also arise in relation to a rarer fact-pattern, where A has only a less-than-absolute right in the land—for instance, an equity of redemption. Rather than transferring his land outright, here A *allows* the land in question to be transferred to B. The doctrine is equally applicable in this situation. Indeed, this fact-pattern was present in the case of *Rochefoucauld* itself, as will be discussed below.[6]

4.1. The Nature of the Trust

The doctrine in *Rochefoucauld v Boustead* was traditionally thought simply to represent an application of the maxim 'equity will not allow a statute to be used as an instrument of fraud' in the context of s 53(1)(b). Thus, courts were willing to enforce B's informal promise for A's benefit simply on the basis that the statute might be used by B in a manner which would perpetrate a 'fraud'.[7] It is therefore only relatively recently that courts and commentators have addressed the question of the nature of the trust enforced through an application of the doctrine. Although a spate of recent cases has classified the trust as being constructive in nature,[8] commentators are divided as to whether the trust enforced is constructive[9] or express.[10]

[6] See S 4.1.2.1.

[7] See, eg, *Mestaer v Gillespie* (1805) 11 Ves Jun 621, 627–28; 32 ER 1230, 1232; *Lincoln v Wright* (1859) 4 De G & J 16, 22; 45 ER 6, 9; *Haigh v Kaye* (1872) LR 7 Ch App 469 (CA) 474; *Booth v Turle* (1873) LR 16 Eq 182 (Ch) 187; *Re Duke of Marlborough* [1894] 2 Ch 133 (Ch) 141; *Rochefoucauld* (n 2) 206.

[8] See, eg, *Taylor v Davies* [1920] AC 636 (PC) 650–51; *Bannister* (n 4) 136; *Re Densham (A Bankrupt)* [1975] 3 All ER 726 (Ch) 732; *Chattey v Farndale Holdings Inc* (1998) 75 P & CR 298 (CA) 316; *Paragon Finance plc v DB Thakerar & Co* [1999] 1 All ER 400 (CA) 409; *Banner Homes Group plc v Luff Developments Ltd* [2000] Ch 372 (CA) 383–84; *JJ Harrison (Properties) Ltd v Harrison* [2001] EWCA Civ 1467, [2002] BCC 729 [36]; *Samad v Thompson* [2008] EWHC 2809 (Ch), [2008] NPC 125 [128]; *Staden v Jones* [2008] EWCA Civ 936, [2008] 2 FLR 1931 [31]; *De Bruyne v De Bruyne* [2010] EWCA Civ 519, [2010] 2 FLR 1240 [51]; *Crossco No 4 Unlimited v Jolan Ltd* [2011] EWCA Civ 1619, [2012] 2 All ER 754 [94]; *Groveholt Ltd v Hughes* [2012] EWHC 3351 (Ch), [2013] 1 P & CR 20 [14].

[9] See, eg, George P Costigan Jr, 'The Classification of Trusts as Express, Resulting, and Constructive' (1913–14) 27 *Harvard Law Review* 437; TG Youdan, 'Formalities for Trusts of Land, and the Doctrine in *Rochefoucauld v Boustead*' (1984) 43 *CLJ* 306; MP Thompson, 'Using Statutes as Instruments of Fraud' (1985) 36 *Northern Ireland Legal Quarterly* 358; Gbolahan Elias, *Explaining Constructive Trusts* (Oxford, OUP, 1990) 108; Patricia Critchley, 'Instruments of Fraud, Testamentary Dispositions, and the Doctrine of Secret Trusts' (1999) 115 *LQR* 631; Ben McFarlane, 'Constructive Trusts Arising on a Receipt of Property *Sub Conditione*' (2004) 120 *LQR* 667; AJ Oakley, *Parker and Mellows: The Modern Law of Trusts*, 9th edn (London, Sweet & Maxwell, 2008) [10-273]; Simon Gardner, 'Reliance-Based Constructive Trusts' in Charles Mitchell (ed), *Constructive and Resulting Trusts* (Oxford, Hart Publishing, 2010) 68.

[10] See, eg, William Swadling, 'The Proprietary Effect of a Hire of Goods' in Norman Palmer and Ewan McKendrick (eds), *Interests in Goods*, 2nd edn (London, LLP, 1998); William Swadling, 'A Hard Look at *Hodgson v Marks*' in Peter Birks and Francis Rose (eds), *Restitution and Equity (Vol 1): Resulting Trusts and Equitable Compensation* (London, LLP, 2000); Philip H Pettit, *Equity and the Law of Trusts* (12th edn, OUP 2012) 98; JE Penner, *The Law of Trusts*, Core Text Series, 10th edn (Oxford, OUP, 2016) [6.10]; Robert Pearce and Warren Barr, *The Law of Trusts and Equitable Obligations*, 6th edn (Oxford, OUP, 2015) 196; William Swadling, 'The Nature of the Trust in *Rochefoucauld v Boustead*' in Mitchell, *Constructive and Resulting Trusts* (n 9); Paul Matthews, 'The Words which are Not There: A Partial History of the Constructive Trust' in Mitchell, *Constructive and Resulting Trusts* (n 9).

4.1.1. Express Trust Arguments

Three arguments have been advanced to support the view that the doctrine in *Rochefoucauld v Boustead* entails the enforcement of express trusts.

4.1.1.1. The Literal Argument

The most straightforward argument is based on the judgment in *Rochefoucauld v Boustead.* The relevant words of Lindley LJ are as follows:[11]

> The trust which [A] has established is clearly an express trust within the meaning of that expression as explained in *Soar v Ashwell.*[12] The trust is one which both [A] and [B] intended to create. This case is not one in which an equitable obligation arises although there may have been no intention to create a trust. The intention to create a trust existed from the first.

It has been argued that the words used in the judgment conclusively indicate that the trust enforced by way of the doctrine is an express trust.[13]

There is no shortage of discussion as to whether this interpretation of Lindley LJ's words is justified. Those who disagree with the express trust categorisation suggest that this argument takes Lindley LJ's words too literally at the expense of the spirit of the judgment as a whole.[14] They suggest that Lindley LJ's statement 'may possibly be explained as amounting only to a statement that the trust is an express trust for the purpose of the limitation Acts'[15] in order to avoid the conclusion that A's case was time-barred. This view has been approved both in the Court of Appeal[16] and in the Privy Council.[17]

Conversely, William Swadling suggests that, although *Soar v Ashwell* 'included in [the] definition of express trusts things which are better classified as constructive trusts … it does not therefore follow that all trusts falling within the category "express" were to be seen as constructive'.[18] He argues that *Soar* was itself a case concerned with 'a conventional express trust, not one so named purely for limitation purposes', and therefore that the reference to *Soar v Ashwell* in *Rochefoucauld* is at best 'ambiguous.'[19]

[11] *Rochefoucauld* (n 2) 208.

[12] *Soar v Ashwell* [1893] 2 QB 390 (CA).

[13] See, eg, Pettit, *Equity and the Law of Trusts* (n 10) 97–98; Pearce and Barr, *The Law of Trusts* (n 10) 196; Swadling, '*Rochefoucauld v Boustead*' (n 10) 99.

[14] See, eg, Youdan, '*Rochefoucauld v Boustead*' (n 9) 331; AJ Oakley, *Constructive Trusts*, 3rd edn (London, Sweet & Maxwell, 1997) 30; McFarlane, '*Sub Conditione*' (n 9) 675–76; Gardner, 'Reliance-Based Constructive Trusts' (n 9) 68–69.

[15] Youdan, '*Rochefoucauld v Boustead*' (n 9) 331. As Oakley observes, 'until the enactment of the Limitation Act 1939, express trustees were unable to rely on the Statutes of Limitation as against the beneficiaries whereas the limitation period ran in favour of potential constructive trustees. This encouraged the courts to classify as express trusts certain trusts which were clearly nothing of the sort (*Soar v Ashwell* itself was a case of this kind and contains a very full review of the situations in which the courts were prepared to do this)': Oakley, *Constructive Trusts* (n 14) 30.

[16] *Paragon Finance* (n 8) 409–10; *JJ Harrison* (n 8) [36].

[17] *Taylar v Davies* (n 8) 650–51.

[18] Swadling, '*Rochefoucauld v Boustead*' (n 10) 101.

[19] ibid 103.

4.1.1.2. *The Disapplication Thesis*

The phrase 'manifested and proved by some writing' in s 53(1)(b) is usually taken to mean that a declaration of trust must be 'evidenced by a signed writing … and in the absence of such writing the trust is valid although unenforceable.'[20] Since a *properly manifested* intention is necessary to give rise to an enforceable express trust,[21] and because the doctrine in *Rochefoucauld v Boustead* usually relates to informal agreements, it might be thought to be obvious that the agreement cannot be enforced *qua* an express trust. Instead, the trust can only be a constructive trust, the operation of which is exempted from the requirement for written evidence by s 53(2).[22]

A different view has been suggested by William Swadling, which may be referred to as the 'disapplication thesis'. He suggests that s 53(1)(b) is not a rule of enforceability but one of 'proof': it is a rule of evidence.[23] This evidential rule is 'disapplied' on a finding of 'fraud', 'with the result that there would be nothing standing in the way of an (informal) express trust's "validity".'[24] Disapplying the requirement for writing allows A to prove the oral express trust;[25] 'and so whatever [the statute says], it [does] not [stand] in the way … of the express trust.'[26] This thesis is endorsed by Matthews, who remarks:[27]

> It is a complication that in some cases the judges who rely on the principle that equity will not allow the statute to be used as an instrument of fraud sometimes go on also to rely on s 53(2) of the Law of Property Act 1925, on the basis that this is a 'constructive' trust … However, that is just inconsistent and wrong. It is one or the other [i.e. an (oral) express trust or a constructive trust]; it cannot be both simultaneously.

4.1.1.3. *The Definitional Argument*

According to one school of thought, '[a] constructive trust is one which arises by operation of law, and not by reason of the intention of the parties, express or implied.'[28] The focus is sometimes on A's intention: if A clearly intends to create a trust relationship, then 'as a

[20] Youdan, '*Rochefoucauld v Boustead*' (n 9) 320–21, citing *Forster v Hale* (1798) 3 Ves Jun 696, 707; 30 ER 1226, 1231; *Harper v Paterson* (1864) 14 UCCP 538, 545; *Wilde v Wilde* (1873) 20 Gr 521, 531–53; *Rochefoucauld* 206–07; *Owchar v Owchar* [1949] 2 DLR 432; *Gardner v Rowe* (1828) 5 Russ 258, 38 ER 1024.

[21] See, eg, Robert Chambers, 'Constructive Trusts in Canada' (1999) 37 *Alberta Law Review* 173, 183; Robert Chambers, *Resulting Trusts* (Oxford, OUP, 1997) 220ff; Peter Birks, *An Introduction to the Law of Restitution*, revised edn (Oxford, OUP, 1989) 65; Simon Gardner, *An Introduction to the Law of Trusts*, Clarendon Law Series, 3rd edn (Oxford, OUP, 2011) 97.

[22] This provides that 'This section does not affect the creation or operation of resulting, implied or constructive trusts.' This more succinctly replaced the Statute of Frauds 1677, s 8, which provided that, '[w]here any conveyance … shall or may arise or result by the implication or construction of law … then and in every such case such trust or confidence shall be of the like force and effect as the same would have been if this statute had not been made'.

[23] Swadling, '*Rochefoucauld v Boustead*' (n 10) 107, 108, 113.

[24] ibid 105.

[25] ibid 113.

[26] ibid 107. See also Swadling, 'Hire of Goods' (n 10) 511–12; Swadling, '*Hodgson v Marks*' (n 10) 66.

[27] Matthews, 'The Words which are Not There' (n 10) 21 fn 89. See too Penner, *The Law of Trusts* (n 10) [6.10]; Pettit, *Equity and the Law of Trusts* (n 10) 99.

[28] Jamie Glister and James Lee, *Hanbury and Martin: Modern Equity*, 20th edn (London, Sweet & Maxwell, 2015) [12-001]. A similar view to the effect that an express trust and not a constructive trust responds to the 'intention of the parties' is found in Swadling, '*Rochefoucauld v Boustead*' (n 10) 101, text to fn 29.

matter of definition, [the] trusts should be classified as express trusts.'[29] At other times B's intention is emphasised: a constructive trust is 'imposed by law against the intentions of the trustee'.[30]

One who subscribes to this view would naturally argue that the trust enforced through an application of the doctrine in *Rochefoucauld v Boustead* is express in nature. The cases which reflect the doctrine invariably involve an (informal) agreement between the parties and always reflects an intention to create a trust on the facts. Therefore, on this view, the trust which enforces that intention cannot be a constructive trust, and can only be express in nature.

4.1.2. An Analysis of *Rochefoucauld v Boustead*[31]

One way in which the express trust categorisation can be refuted is by analysing the facts of *Rochefoucauld* in order to determine the nature of the trust which was enforced in that case. It is unfortunate that *Rochefoucauld* has eluded the searching analysis it deserves, since the unusual facts of the case reveals that an express trust could not possibly have arisen.

4.1.2.1. Facts

In 1868, the Comtesse de la Rochefoucauld (A) was the registered owner of certain coffee estates in Ceylon known as the Delmar estates. The estates were subject to a mortgage vested in a Dutch company. This was most likely a mortgage in the classical sense where the legal title to the land was transferred to the mortgagee, leaving the mortgagor with nothing more than an equity of redemption,[32] that is, an equitable right for the return of the title when the mortgage is paid off. The mortgagee wanted to seek repayment of the mortgage, but A was unable to repay the mortgage debt. To avoid foreclosure, A entered an agreement with John Boustead (B) and another man, Duff, under which they agreed to purchase the estates from the Dutch company and to hold these on trust for A, subject to A's repayment of their outlay.[33] Duff later pulled out of the arrangement, but B went ahead. It was agreed that he would bid at the Dutch company's auction of the estates. If and when he won the bidding, A would not insist on her equity of redemption for the repayment of the balance of the sale price after the discharge of the mortgage held by the Dutch company. The result of this arrangement was that B would only have to pay the Dutch company the price sufficient to cover A's mortgage debt and expenses.[34]

The reports do not disclose why A wanted the estates to be sold by auction instead of securing an agreement with the company to the same effect from the beginning,[35] since the

[29] *Parker and Mellows* (n 9) [4-107].

[30] *Westdeutsche Landesbank Girozentrale v Islington LBC* [1996] AC 669 (HL) 708.

[31] The report commonly cited is *Rochefoucauld* (n 2). However, various other reports—which are largely consistent between themselves—supplement this main report with vital information for the purposes of this Chapter. At the Court of Appeal level, these are: (1896) 13 TLR 118, (1896) 45 WR 272, (1897) 75 LT 502 and (1897) 66 LJ Ch 74. Only the Law Times report will be cited where it is necessary to depart from the Official Report.

[32] Kevin Gray and Susan Francis Gray, *Elements of Land Law*, 5th edn (Oxford, OUP, 2008) [6.1.6] fn 2.

[33] We will refer to this agreement as the 'initial agreement'.

[34] *Rochefoucauld* (n 2) 197–98.

[35] The headnote of the Official Report merely states that the arrangement involving the auction was made '[t]o obviate some difficulties which arose': *Rochefoucauld* (n 2).

classic context of an auction of a mortgaged property is a forced sale. In recounting the facts, Lindley LJ observed that the parties' arrangement was designed to avoid the Comtesse's recently-divorced husband, Mr Cavendish, from enforcing the interest he acquired in the estates under the decree of the Divorce Court.[36] It is thus a plausible explanation that the sale by auction was to give an appearance to Mr Cavendish that the estates were being sold absolutely to Mr Boustead, with the Comtesse retaining no interest in the estates. Whatever the reason, it is clear that the Dutch company was not a party to the initial agreement, although it did later sign an agreement to sell the estates at the agreed price.[37]

The arrangement was carried out and B became the registered owner of the estates in 1873,[38] financing the bulk of his payment by an immediate remortgage of the estates to the Dutch company.[39] Without A's knowledge, B then repeatedly mortgaged—and eventually sold—the estates.[40] A considerable surplus remained from the sale on which A sought an account.[41] The Court of Appeal held that B could not invoke the Statute of Frauds 1677, s 7, to deny A's beneficial interest, for that would be to use the statute as an 'instrument of fraud'.[42]

4.1.2.2. Analysis

What was the nature of the trust enforced in *Rochefoucauld*? Applying his 'disapplication thesis'[43] to the facts of the case, Swadling concludes that the Court enforced the oral express trust directly.[44] On closer examination, however, this conclusion does not withstand scrutiny: there was not even an (informal) express trust on the facts of the case which the Court could have enforced. An express trust requires a settlor who declares the trust, regardless of whether it is declared orally or in written form. It is trite law that a settlor can only declare a trust over an interest which he owns; he cannot declare a trust over an interest in property which that he does not have. The outcome in *Rochefoucauld* was that A was declared as the absolute owner of the beneficial interest in the estates.[45] If A was a beneficiary under an informal *express* trust, this implies that there was a capable settlor—one who owned the absolute interest in the estates at the outset who declared that trust. However, there was no such settlor on the facts of the case.

4.1.2.2.1. A as Settlor?

The first possibility is that the Comtesse (A) was the settlor of the informal express trust. She would have been capable of expressly setting up the trust had she been the transferor

[36] *Rochefoucauld* (n 31) 75 LT 502 (CA) 504–05.
[37] ibid 505.
[38] *Rochefoucauld* (n 2) 205–06.
[39] ibid 198.
[40] ibid 204.
[41] ibid.
[42] ibid 206.
[43] See S 4.1.1.2.
[44] See too Penner, *The Law of Trusts* (n 10) [6.10].
[45] *Rochefoucauld* (n 2) 212. Of course, the Court also held that the Comtesse was subject to a lien in Boustead's favour for his expenditures and expenses; but this does not mean that her interest was subject to the Dutch company's interest obtained through Boustead's remortgaging of the estates.

of the estates to B. But the facts indicate that A was not capable of transferring—let alone settling—the estates. At first sight, the reports of the appellate decision say little concerning A's initial rights in the estates. However, the reports of the first-instance decision not only reveal that the Dutch company was 'in possession as mortgagees',[46] but also confirm that the company sold the estates B using its 'power of sale as mortgagees'.[47] The inevitable inference from this is that A's interest at the outset was limited to an equity of redemption. This made it impossible for her to have transferred to B what he obtained in 1873—the absolute beneficial interest in the estates, free from the mortgage. This remains the case even though A had consented to—and, indeed, initiated—the arrangement.

4.1.2.2.2. The Dutch Company as Settlor?

A second possibility is that the Dutch company was the settlor of the informal express trust. This might seem to follow from the Court of Appeal's statement that the land was 'conveyed' to B 'as a trustee',[48] and it was the Dutch company which made the conveyance. This would be a plausible analysis if 'the transferor (the Dutch company) *intended* the transferee (Boustead) to hold the property on trust for the Comtesse de la Rochefoucauld'.[49]

It is trite that a settlor of an express trust must have a sufficiently certain intention to create the trust.[50] Such an intention cannot be found on the part of the Dutch company. On the facts as recounted by Lindley LJ,[51] the initial agreement between A and B was reached sometime between 1868, when the Dutch company wished to call in the mortgage, and 1871, when B and the Dutch company signed an agreement for sale to effectuate the initial agreement. This timeline indicates that the Dutch company's involvement in 1871 was separate from, subsequent to, and subject to the initial agreement between A and B: it was certainly not a party to the initial agreement. In fact, the Dutch company appears to have been a disinterested party vis-à-vis the trust arrangement. This is seen from the fact that it sold the estates by auction, whereby B had to submit the winning bid before he could 'enter into an agreement with the company to purchase the estates … at a price sufficient to cover their mortgage debt and expenses'.[52] The Dutch company was only interested in recouping its mortgage debt, and did not intend to create a trust at all.

It might be argued that it does not matter what the Dutch company actually wanted, provided that it *agreed*—as it did—to give effect to the initial agreement by selling the estates to B for the sum owing on A's security.

This argument does not withstand scrutiny. It is trite law that a settlor may only declare a trust over property up to the extent of his own initial interest in that property; one cannot give more than what one owns. In *Rochefoucauld* the Court ultimately concluded that A owned the absolute equitable interest in the Delmar estates: she was 'the defendant's

[46] *Rochefoucauld* (n 31) 65 LJ Ch 794 (Ch).

[47] *Rochefoucauld* 74 LT 783 (Ch).

[48] *Rochefoucauld* (n 2) 206. The phrase 'as a trustee' surely leaves open the prior question of the *nature* of the trust which makes the defendant a trustee; but for the sake of argument we shall proceed as if this referred to an express trust.

[49] Gardner, 'Reliance-Based Constructive Trusts' (n 9) 68 (emphasis added).

[50] *Knight v Knight* (1840) 3 Beav 148, 49 ER 58.

[51] *Rochefoucauld* (n 31) 75 LT 502 (CA) 505.

[52] *Rochefoucauld* (n 2) 197.

cestui que trust'.[53] It was also held that the account of B's dealings with the estates was to 'be an account as between a trustee and his cestui que trust, not an account as between mortgagor and mortgagee'.[54] It follows that, for the Dutch company to have been the settlor, it must first have been the absolute beneficial owner of the estates. But the facts reveal that the estates were sold through the exercise of the Dutch company's power of sale[55] and not pursuant to an order of foreclosure. An order of foreclosure would have 'vest[ed] the ownership of, and the *beneficial title* to, the land, *for the first time*, in the [mortgagee]',[56] paving the way for analysing the Dutch company as the capable settlor. But such an order was not obtained. Moreover, A's equity of redemption subsisted all along in the estates, even up to the point when the estates were transferred to B. Unless a mortgagor's equity of redemption is foreclosed, '[t]he interest of the land … remain[s] in the mortgagor'.[57] Furthermore, '[a]n equity of redemption has always been considered as an estate in the land … and therefore cannot be considered as a mere right only'.[58] As Bowen LJ observed in *Marquess of Northampton v Pollock*,[59] 'equity regards the mortgaged property as security only for money, and will permit of no attempt to clog, fetter, or impede the borrower's right to redeem and to rescue what was, and still remains in equity his own.' Therefore, the Dutch company could not have expressly settled the estates even though it possessed the legal title as mortgagee. It was obliged to respect A's equity of redemption, the obligation of which remained binding throughout, even though A gave up that equity pursuant to her agreement with B.

4.1.2.2.3. B as Settlor?

A third possibility is that B was the settlor of the trust, declaring himself trustee for A's benefit after[60] the estates were transferred to him from the Dutch company. This is the interpretation James Penner takes, who analyses *Rochefoucauld* as 'a self-declaration case' in which '[B] … was the settlor of the trust'.[61] Likewise, Swadling writes that there was 'a declaration of trust *by the defendant* in [A's] favour'.[62]

If one simply read the Official Reports of the Court's decision, this analysis might seem promising. Thus, relying solely on the headnotes of the Official Reports,[63] Swadling notes simply that B bought the estates in 1873, and subsequently mortgaged the estates 'in 1876, 1877 and 1879, without the knowledge of the claimant'.[64] But this fails to note that B had 'immediately remortgaged the estates to the Dutch company for £53,000, so that his actual payment out of pocket was under £5,000'.[65] The immediacy of the remortgaging would

[53] ibid 209.
[54] ibid 212.
[55] See main text to n 47 above.
[56] *Heath v Pugh* (1881) 6 QBD 345 (CA) 360 (emphases added), affd (1882) LR 7 App Cas 235 (HL).
[57] *Casborne v Scarfe* (1737) 1 Atk 603, 605–06; 26 ER 377, 380.
[58] ibid.
[59] *Marquess of Northampton v Pollock* (1890) 45 Ch D 190 (CA) 215.
[60] It is not possible to endorse an express trust analysis if we say that the relevant declaration occurred *prior to* B's obtaining the transfer of the estates, since an express declaration of trust of future property is void: *Holroyd v Marshall* (1862) 10 H L Cas 191, 11 ER 999; *Re Tilt* (1896) 40 Sol Jo 224 (Ch). See Chapter 8, S 8.2.
[61] Penner, *The Law of Trusts* (n 10) [6.12]. However, he says little else to justify this view.
[62] Swadling, '*Rochefoucauld v Boustead*' (n10) 113 (emphasis added).
[63] *Rochefoucauld* (n 2) 198.
[64] Swadling, '*Rochefoucauld v Boustead*' (n 10) 97.
[65] *Rochefoucauld* (n 31) 75 LT 502 (CA) 505.

have made it impossible for B to have declared a trust over the unencumbered beneficial interest of the estates.

There are two possible replies to this. The first is based on the fact that '[t]he estates were sold … many years ago' and A claimed to be entitled only to the 'considerable surplus [which] remained [from the proceeds of sale]'.[66] This may appear to indicate that A had admitted that her beneficial rights were held subject to the Dutch company's rights under the remortgage, leaving open the possibility of concluding that B had declared the trust *after* remortgaging the estates to the Dutch company. However, the Court clearly held that A was an absolute beneficiary of the estates, and also that B's trusteeship commenced from the moment the estates were conveyed to him.[67] These entail that there is no possibility based on the timing of events that B could have expressly declared a trust of the full beneficial interest of the estates.

Secondly, it might be asked whether B had, for a *scintilla temporis*, the unencumbered title to the estates. If he did, then there exists a moment in time wherein B may be said to have owned the unencumbered fee simple of the estate, making it theoretically possible for B to have declared an oral express trust during that slice of time. The cases which have dealt with this issue have emerged from a similar fact pattern where property is purchased with the aid of a charge or mortgage from the outset. The only case deciding the point before *Rochefoucauld* was *Meux v Smith*,[68] which held that no *scintilla temporis* exists. *Meux* was followed by the Court of Appeal in *Re Connolly Bros (No. 2)*.[69] In *Church of England BS v Piskor*,[70] Evershed MR distinguished *Re Connolly Bros* and *Meux* and came to the opposite conclusion. However, the House of Lords in *Abbey National Building Society v Cann*[71] held this ground of distinction to be invalid, preferring instead to view the purchaser as never having acquired anything more than an equity of redemption.[72] Ultimately, therefore, the second possible reply also fails.

The possibility that B declared the trust is also inconsistent with the Court's judgment, which did not refer to any occurrence after the transfer which could have been interpreted to be a declaration of the trust. Instead, it was held to be 'quite clear that the conveyance to [B] grew out of the arrangement which he … [was] to have carried out, and was made for precisely the same purpose'.[73] The emphasis was on the initial agreement between A and B, and not on any subsequent act or declaration by B after receiving the estates. Moreover, the Court referred to B as having taken the conveyance 'as a trustee',[74] and in its final order

[66] *Rochefoucauld* (n 2) 204.

[67] ibid 206.

[68] *Meux v Smith* (1843) 11 Sim 410, 59 ER 931.

[69] *Re Connolly Bros (No. 2)* [1912] 2 Ch 25 (CA). Although *Re Connolly Bros (No. 2)* did not explicitly rely on *Meux*, the effect of this was noted by Evershed MR in *Church of England BS v Piskor* [1954] Ch 553 (CA) 564.

[70] *Piskor* (n 69) 564.

[71] *Abbey National Building Society v Cann* [1991] 1 AC 56 (HL). In coming to this conclusion, the House of Lords approved *Re Connolly Bros (No. 2)* (n 69), *Coventry Permanent Economic Building Society v Jones* [1951] 1 All ER 901 (Ch) and *Security Trust Co v Royal Bank of Canada* [1976] AC 503 (PC), and overruled *Piskor* (n 68).

[72] And in *Southern Pacific Mortgages Ltd v Scott* [2014] UKSC 52, [2015] AC 385 [114], the Supreme Court refused to 'bury' the decision in *Cann*, and held that 'at least in the standard case where completion and mortgage take place virtually simultaneously and the mortgage is granted to secure borrowings without which the purchase would not have taken place, completion and mortgage are one indivisible transaction and there is no *scintilla temporis* between them'.

[73] *Rochefoucauld* (n 31) 75 LT 502 (CA) 505.

[74] *Rochefoucauld* (n 2) 206.

'declared that the defendant purchased the Delmar estates as a trustee for the plaintiff'.[75] Clearly, the Court was not enforcing a trust self-declared by B; otherwise he would not have been said to have acquired the estates *as a trustee*.

In fact, the way in which the doctrine has developed since *Rochefoucauld* was decided reinforces the conclusion that B was not the settlor of an express trust. It is commonly agreed that A cannot rely on the doctrine where B, an owner of land, informally declares himself as trustee for A.[76] Although there appears to be only one English decision on this point,[77] a host of Commonwealth decisions[78] adopt this position.[79] This approach is based on sound principle. As Timothy Youdan points out, 'the general statements of the doctrine, including that of Lindley LJ in the *Rochefoucauld* case, refer to the trustee acquiring the property subject to a trust';[80] and 'to hold otherwise would wholly frustrate the functions carried out by section 7',[81] leaving no room for that provision to apply.

4.1.3. A Constructive Trust

Given the division of interests in the estates at the outset, it was impossible that the trust which was enforced was express in nature. This conclusion allows us to reject two express trust arguments which were set out above,[82] paving the way for a constructive trust analysis.[83]

Consider first the literal argument. Because on the facts of *Rochefoucauld* there could not have been an informal express trust at all, it is misleading to take Lindley LJ literally when his Lordship labelled the trust as 'express'. Rather, as Millett LJ explained in *Paragon Finance plc v DB Thakerar & Co*,[84] it was common for constructive trusts such as that which arose in *Rochefoucauld* to be 'treated in the same way as express trusts and were often confusingly described as such' for limitation purposes. Unlike an express trust which is created by the trustee being 'named as such in the instrument of trust', B 'had assumed the position of a trustee for [A] or had taken possession or control of property on [A's] behalf'.[85] Nevertheless, because B's possession of the estates was 'treated … as the possession of his *cestuis que trustent*',[86] *Soar v Ashwell*[87] makes clear that such constructive trusts are liable to

[75] ibid 212.

[76] See, eg, JD Feltham, 'Informal Trusts and Third Parties' [1987] *Conveyancer and Property Lawyer* 246, 247; Youdan, '*Rochefoucauld v Boustead*' (n 9) 325; *Hanbury and Martin* (n 28) [6-007]; Mark Pawlowski and Kim Everett, 'Declarations of Trust and Unmarried Couples' (1999) 29 *Family Law* 721, 723; Pearce and Barr, *The Law of Trusts* (n 10) 195; David Hayton, Paul Matthews and Charles Mitchell, *Underhill and Hayton: Law Relating to Trusts and Trustees*, 19th edn (London, LexisNexis Butterworths, 2016) [12.75].

[77] *Smith v Matthews* (1861) 3 De G F & J 139, 45 ER 831.

[78] *Morris v Whiting* (1913) 15 DLR 254; *Organ v Sandwell* [1921] VLR 622, 630; *Permanent Trustee Co v Scales* (1930) 30 SR (NSW) 391 Eq; *Beemer v Brownridge* [1934] 1 WWR 545, 555–56 and 567; *Last v Rosenfeld* [1972] 2 NSWLR 923, 928, 933; *Wratten v Hunter* [1978] 2 NSWLR 367.

[79] The cases cited in nn 77–78 come from Youdan, '*Rochefoucauld v Boustead*' (n 9) 325, fn 2, and Feltham, 'Informal Trusts' (n 76) 247, fn 6.

[80] Youdan, '*Rochefoucauld v Boustead*' (n 9) 325.

[81] ibid 325–26.

[82] See S 4.1.1. The third—the definitional argument—will be dealt with in S 4.2.1.1.

[83] As to why the trust is not—and ought not to be—a resulting trust, see S 4.5.1.

[84] *Paragon Finance* (n 8) 409.

[85] *Taylor v Davies* (n 8) 651.

[86] ibid 650–51.

[87] *Soar v Ashwell* (n 12).

be treated *as* express trusts for limitation purposes. This means that, outside the limitation context, there is no justification for analysing the trust as an express trust.

Consider next the disapplication thesis. Given that there was no express trust which arose on the facts of *Rochefoucauld*, whether orally declared or otherwise, there was no (express) declaration of trust of land' that had to be 'manifested and proved by some writing'. Even assuming that s 7 could be disapplied in the way in which Swadling and Matthews suggest, its 'disapplication' in *Rochefoucauld* would have been of no effect, since there was no (oral) express trust which could be enforced anyway.

4.2. Promise and Reliance

In Chapter 3,[88] it was observed in relation to the QI doctrines that B's promise and A's reliance trigger the imposition of a constructive trust which compels B to fulfil his promise. The elements of promise and reliance arise in a specific way: B's promise is always to the effect that he will take only a qualified interest in property yet to be acquired, and A's reliance arises in the form of the provision of an advantage to B in relation to B's acquisition of that property. These elements are reflected in the doctrine in *Rochefoucauld v Boustead.*

It is easy to see how the elements of promise and reliance arise on the facts of *Rochefoucauld.* Prior to B's acquisition of the estates, he had made a promise to A that he would not take the absolute ownership of the estates, but that he would do as A wished. In reliance on that promise, A allowed the estates to be transferred to B: rather than arranging for the valuable estates to be subjected to a re-mortgage, A relied on B to carry out their agreement. Furthermore, A did not insist on her equity of redemption, and this conferred on B the advantage of acquiring the unencumbered legal title to the estates without having to pay the full sale price for them. The Court of Appeal held that B was subject to a constructive trust from the moment of acquisition,[89] which indicates that he ever only received a qualified interest in the estates.

The same analysis also applies to other cases which have applied the doctrine in *Rochefoucauld v Boustead.* Where B informally agrees to hold A's land on trust for A, and A transfers or allows his land to be transferred to B in reliance on B's promise, a constructive trust arises to ensure that B takes only a qualified interest once he acquires A's land.

This section explores how precisely the elements of promise and reliance arise in the doctrine in *Rochefoucauld v Boustead.*

4.2.1. Promise

In every case which has applied the doctrine,[90] the parties always reach an informal pre-acquisition agreement whereby B promises to hold an interest in the acquired property

[88] See Chapter 3, S 3.2.1.1.
[89] *Rochefoucauld* (n 2) 212.
[90] See, eg, *Lincoln v Wright* (n 7); *Davies v Otty (No. 2)* (1865) 35 Beav 208, 55 ER 875; *Haigh v Kaye* (n 7); *Booth v Turle* (n 7); *Re Duke of Marlborough* (n 7); *Bannister* (n 4); *De Bruyne v De Bruyne* (n 8).

on trust. This indicates that B agrees only to take a qualified interest in the acquired property. As Millett LJ observed in *Paragon Finance plc v DB Thakerar & Co*,[91] citing the case of *Rochefoucauld v Boustead* as an example, some constructive trusts arise where '[B] does not receive the trust property in his own right but by a transaction by which both parties intend to create a trust from the outset and which is not impugned by [A].'

There are at least four key roles which the element of promise plays in the doctrine in *Rochefoucauld*,[92] and likewise in the other doctrines which reflect QI situations within the non-contract-based, bilateral events category of constructive trusts. First, requiring B to make a promise ensures B communicates his intention. It has been said that 'the thought of man is not triable, for the devil knows not the thought of man'.[93] Only by B manifesting or 'stipulating'[94] his intention to take a qualified interest in the property can the law ensure that B is actually committed to carrying out his promise. Otherwise, an uncommunicated intention or an intention which is not properly communicated will certainly not be sufficient to subject B to a constructive trust.

Secondly, B's promise determines the content of the remedy imposed. The courts have consistently bound B to carry out his promise to the fullest extent possible. Thus, where A transfers property to B upon B's promise to re-convey the whole of the property to A, B is bound by a constructive trust to do as promised, regardless of whether the transaction was for the benefit of B[95] or A,[96] or for no apparent reason at all.[97] Where B promises to hold a lesser interest in the conveyed property on trust for A, a constructive trust arises over that interest, even though B may have given consideration for the transfer.[98] Indeed, where B promises to purchase the property and hold it on trust for A subject to the repayment of B's expenses, a constructive trust arises over the whole property for A's benefit, although A's interest will be subject to a lien in B's favour.[99] And as will be discussed below,[100] where B promises to hold the property on trust for C instead of A, the law also gives effect to B's promise by declaring that he holds the property on a constructive trust for C's benefit.[101]

Thirdly, the focus on B's promise justifies why a constructive trust arises despite the informality of the parties' agreement. In all the relevant cases, A fails properly to declare an express trust, usually due to his non-compliance with the Law of Property Act 1925, s 53(1)(b).[102] This means that the imposed trust cannot be analysed as responding to A's unilateral intention, since this would be at odds with the statutory formality requirement.

[91] *Paragon Finance* (n 8) 409.

[92] And, likewise, in the other doctrines which reflect QI situations within the bilateral events non-contract-based category.

[93] Year-Book 17 Edw IV I (1478) (Brian CJ).

[94] *Bannister* (n 4) 136.

[95] *Re Duke of Marlborough* (n 7). A conveyed property to B to enable B to mortgage it in his own name.

[96] *Davies v Otty (No. 2)* (n 89). A, fearing he would be prosecuted for bigamy (it turned out he was not liable), conveyed property to B in order to protect the property.

[97] *Haigh v Kaye* (n 7). No reason for the conveyance from A to B appears from the report, although B admitted that he was obliged to re-convey the property to A when A called for it.

[98] *Booth v Turle* (n 7); *Bannister* (n 4).

[99] *Lincoln v Wright* (n 7); *Rochefoucauld* (n 2).

[100] See S 4.5.2.3.

[101] It is therefore mistaken to think that constructive trusts 'always result in a bare trust': (Paul Matthews, 'All About Bare Trusts: Part 1' [2005] PCB 266, 270), since the terms of the trust depend on the content of B's promise, at least in the context of the doctrine in *Rochefoucauld v Boustead*.

[102] Or its predecessor, the Statute of Frauds 1677, s 7.

Nevertheless, by responding to B's promise, the doctrine gives effect to the parties' intention that B should take only a qualified interest in the acquired property.

Fourthly, the focus on B's promise is also significant because it takes B's original intention to be relevant—that is, B's intention as determined at the time when he made his promise as opposed to his current intention, whatever that may be. This explains why it is a common mistake to assume that these trusts respond to B's wrongdoing. It is sometimes thought that equity has to intervene only when B changes his mind and therefore, as Lord Browne-Wilkinson suggested, constructive trusts are 'imposed by law against the intentions of the trustee'.[103] However, his Lordship's statement cannot account for cases where these constructive trusts are imposed even though B has not changed his mind.[104] Thus, the better view is that these doctrines always take into account B's *original* intention, as objectively manifested through his promise, ignoring any later change of heart.

4.2.1.1. Rejecting the Definitional Argument

The importance of B's promise allows us to reject the definitional argument,[105] which suggests that the trusts enforced in the doctrine are express in nature because constructive trusts are only imposed against the intentions of the parties. Rather, it is necessary to qualify the various statements[106] commentators have made in arguing for the express trust categorisation. Simply because A intends to create a trust relationship does not necessarily mean that 'as a matter of definition, [any trust arising] should be classified as express trusts':[107] this holds true only where the settlor unilaterally and properly manifests an intention to create a trust. It is also accurate to say that 'a constructive trust ... arises for a reason other than a declaration of trust on the part of a right-holder [ie the settlor]'[108] only if this is taken to mean that a declaration by the settlor is *itself* insufficient to give rise to a constructive trust. Conversely, it is a logical flaw to conclude that a constructive trust 'based on an intention to create a trust ... is something of a misnomer',[109] or that it will never arise 'by reason of the intention of the parties, express or implied.'[110] Although an express trust responds to the settlor's intention, it does not follow that the trust is always express when one of the events to which the trust responds is the parties' positive intention. The trust may be express or constructive, depending on whether B's intention is coincidental. If A *properly* manifests his intention to create a trust, then B's intention is merely coincidental: the express trust does not rise or fall with it. On the other hand, if A's intention is not properly manifested, a constructive trust will only arise under the doctrine in *Rochefoucauld*

[103] *Westdeutsche* (n 30) 708.

[104] See, eg, *Re Duke of Marlborough* (n 7).

[105] This argument was explained in S 4.1.1.3. The other two express trust arguments, the literal argument and the disapplication thesis, were set out in SS 4.1.1.1. and 4.1.1.2. respectively, and rejected in S 4.1.3.

[106] These statements are found in S 4.1.1.3.

[107] *Parker and Mellows* (n 9) [4-107].

[108] James Penner and William Swadling, *Law of Trusts* (London, University of London Press, 2007) [7.1.4].

[109] ibid [7.1.5].

[110] *Hanbury and Martin* (n 28) [12-001]. For a similar view, see Swadling, '*Rochefoucauld v Boustead*' (n 10) 101, text to fn 29.

v Boustead if B also shares that intention, as manifested through his promise to A.[111] In this situation, B's intention is not coincidental but crucial. This is confirmed by the observation that B must have 'knowledge'[112] of the trust reposed in him in order for the doctrine to arise.

4.2.2. Reliance

The cases also clearly indicate that A relies on B's promise by conferring an advantage on B, such reliance being induced by B's promise. By his act of reliance, A fulfils his part of the agreement, which makes it necessary at that point to enforce B's promise,[113] the outstanding act, to bring the agreement to completion. The cases reflect two alternative ways in which reliance can be satisfied. The most straightforward cases are those where A, the absolute owner of the property at the outset, conveys the property to B. But the requirement is also satisfied where A does not have an absolute right in the property at the outset but *allows* the property to be transferred to B.[114] In both groups of cases, A's act of reliance results in the transfer of the property to B, therefore leading B to obtain an advantage—the legal title—in relation to the acquisition of the property.

4.2.2.1. Control

In relation to the cases where A is not initially the absolute owner of the property, but only has some controlling power in it, the question arises as to how much control A must have in the property in question for the doctrine to operate. In the only two decided cases which reflect this fact-pattern, *Rochefoucauld v Boustead*[115] and *Lincoln v Wright*,[116] A was the holder of an equity of redemption. Due to the considerable substance of this right, there is no objection in saying that, by not insisting on A's equity of redemption, A conferred on B a clear opportunity to acquire his property in reliance on B's promise. Moreover, given that mortgagees are only legally entitled to recoup their advances, A in such a situation would also have a 'controlling' right in the property in the sense that, short of the mortgagee obtaining foreclosure, the property is still considered to be A's. However, there are numerous possible ways in which rights in property may be divided, and thus different degrees of 'control' A may assert over the relevant property. This makes it difficult to draw the line

[111] See cases discussed in S 4.5.1.1.2., where the point is made that a constructive trust cannot arise where B is ignorant of A's intention.

[112] See, eg, *Rochefoucauld* (n 2) 206; *Mountain v Styak* [1922] NZLR 131, 140.

Strictly speaking, the element of 'knowledge' is not a *requirement*, but merely a reflection of the state of mind of a transferee who possesses the relevant intention. Any other view would cause unnecessary confusion, such as that which arose in Ungoed-Thomas J's judgment in *Hodgson v Marks* [1971] Ch 892 (CA). He held that the 'fraud' exception was available even against a bona fide purchaser who discovers the trust after the purchase (*Hodgson v Marks* (n 112) 909). The inconsistency of this view is noted in DJ Hayton and C Mitchell, *Hayton and Marshall: Commentary and Cases on the Law of Trusts and Equitable Remedies*, 12th edn (London, Sweet & Maxwell, 2005) [2-27].

[113] The enforcement of B's promise is necessary pursuant to the norm which underlies this doctrine: see discussion in S 4.3.4.

[114] Strictly speaking, A may not be the 'transferor', given that the actual transfer might be made by a third party, such as a mortgagee; however, the term 'transferor' will be used to include persons in such a position.

[115] *Rochefoucauld* (n 2).

[116] *Lincoln v Wright* (n 7).

precisely between cases where A 'allows' property to be transferred and where he does not. Where such ambiguity arises, it is useful to consider whether A's reliance leads B to obtain any opportunity to acquire the property in question. When A's right in the property is too meagre—and his 'control' over it is too little—for him to have 'allowed' the transfer, it is likely that his actions, whatever they may be, would not have conferred any such opportunity on B. Where this is the case, the doctrine in *Rochefoucauld v Boustead* will not apply, since the element of reliance would not be fulfilled.

4.2.2.2. Causal Link

In the cases which have applied the doctrine in *Rochefoucauld v Boustead*, there is no question that A would not have transferred his property—or allowed his property to be transferred—to B had B not promised to qualify his interest in the property. This might suggest that it is necessary to establish a 'but for' causal link between A's act of reliance and B's acquisition of the property. However, as the discussion relating to the doctrine in *Pallant v Morgan* in Chapter 6[117] indicates, it is more accurate to speak of the causal link being that between B's promise and *A's actions*. This fact is brought out in an examination of the doctrine in *Pallant v Morgan* because, unlike in the context of the doctrine in *Rochefoucauld v Boustead*, A's act of reliance is not necessarily a 'but for' cause of B's acquisition. That doctrine indicates that all that is necessary is for B's promise to cause A to act in reliance.

4.2.3. Three Difficult Cases

In examining the case law, there are three cases predating *Rochefoucauld v Boustead* which seem to work against the analysis suggested here. Despite appearing to fit within the ambit of the doctrine, these cases frustrate A's attempt to hold B to his promise. It is necessary to examine the impact of these cases on the general analysis of the doctrine.

4.2.3.1. Bartlett v Pickersgill

In *Bartlett v Pickersgill*,[118] A alleged that B, who purchased an estate with his own money, was bound to perform their oral agreement that the estate was purchased on behalf of A. Lord Keeper Henley refused to allow the admission of parol evidence to prove the agreement between the parties, and so A's attempt to compel a conveyance from B failed. This decision was based mainly on the argument that to allow the parol evidence 'would be to overturn the statute.'[119]

This case can be approached from a number of different perspectives. The first perspective concerns the relationship between s 53(1)(b) and the constructive trust. In *Rochefoucauld v Boustead*, it was observed that A may adduce proof by parol evidence 'notwithstanding the statute'.[120] The language used may appear to indicate that the parol evidence was admitted

[117] See discussion in Chapter 6, S 6.2.1.2.1.
[118] *Bartlett v Pickersgill* (1760) 1 Cox 15, 29 ER 1041.
[119] ibid (n 118).
[120] *Rochefoucauld* (n 2) 206.

in spite of the *entire* Statute of Frauds, which was precisely the concern which arose in *Bartlett*. Such a view is, however, inconsistent with an analysis of the trust as a constructive trust, enforced via the s 53(2) proviso—a section which finds its root in s 8 of the Statute of Frauds. In fact, the use of the word 'statute' in such a context does not refer to the *entire* statute, but to the *formality requirements for express trusts* in the statute. This usage of the term 'statute' can be found in a number of cases predating *Rochefoucauld*. A clear example is seen in *Davies v Otty (No. 2)*[121] where, although Sir John Romilly MR expressed his opinion that 'the Statute of Frauds can have no application to this case',[122] his Lordship nonetheless went on to hold that the case came within s 8 of the Statute of Frauds[123] which excluded trusts which arose by operation of law from formality requirements.[124] As such, the concern raised in *Bartlett* in this context is, at best, exaggerated.

The second perspective concerns the element of reliance. On a close scrutiny of *Bartlett*, the case report mentions only that '[B] bought an estate for [A]'[125] without more. There is no indication that A had any controlling power in—or, indeed, any connection to—the estate. As such, A would not have acted in any way which led to B obtain an advantage in relation to his acquisition; and without having fulfilled the element of reliance, B would have acquired the estate in his own right. Short of any other reliance-based or consideration-based justification in favour of A, then, there would have been no reason why B should have been bound to fulfil his promise.

The third perspective can be dealt with briefly. In the agency context, *Bartlett* essentially held that an agent who had purchased land for his principal was able to rely on the oral nature of the agency and s 53(1)(b) to keep the property for himself. However, this would be manifestly unfair. The case was ultimately overruled in *Rochefoucauld v Boustead*.[126]

4.2.3.2. Leman v Whitley

In *Leman v Whitley*,[127] A wanted to raise a mortgage over his property. Given his financial situation, his lawyer, who was also his father's lawyer, proposed that A should convey his property to his father (B) in order for B, who was in good credit, to raise the mortgage in his own name for A's use. The conveyance was stated to be for £400, although no money was in fact paid. Before the mortgage was completed, B died, leaving a general will that bequeathed all his real property to A's son. Sir John Leach MR held that there was 'no pretence of fraud', and thus 'no trust arising or resulting by the implication or construction of law', since 'to give effect to the trust would be in truth to repeal the statute of frauds.'[128] His Lordship treated B as the purchaser, and awarded A a lien over the land to secure the payment of £400.

[121] *Davies v Otty (No. 2)* (n 90).
[122] ibid 35 Beav 212, 55 ER 876. His Lordship repeated this point again later in his judgment, that 'this is a case in which, in my opinion, the Statute of Frauds does not apply': *Davies v Otty (No. 2)* (ibid) 35 Beav 213, 55 ER 877.
[123] ibid 35 Beav 213, 55 ER 877.
[124] See also *Haigh v Kaye* (n 7) 473–74.
[125] *Bartlett v Pickersgill* (n 118).
[126] *Rochefoucauld* (n 2) 206–07.
[127] *Leman v Whitley* (1828) 4 Russ 423, 38 ER 864.
[128] ibid 4 Russ 426–27, 38 ER 865–866.

At first blush, the decision in this case appears to be wrong. There would hardly be a clearer situation in which the doctrine in *Rochefoucauld v Boustead* should apply. Indeed, it is inconceivable that any court would allow B, had he been alive, to use the statute as a defence to A's claim. However, a closer reading of the case suggests that B may not have made the requisite promise: the reported facts leave open the possibility that A may not have transferred the property on the basis of a promise to that effect by B. It is also notable that the decision in *Leman* was doubted in *Re Duke of Marlborough*,[129] the latter having been considered as the preferred authority on the point. At best, therefore, the decision in *Leman* is of doubtful authority.

4.2.3.3. Lord Irnham v Child

Lord Irnham v Child[130] concerned a grant of an annuity from A to B. Although both parties agreed that the annuity was to be redeemable, the deed which gave effect to the annuity was silent on the issue. It was deliberately left out because both parties thought that the term would be regarded as usurious. Lord Thurlow LC decided against A's attempt to redeem the annuity on the basis that the parties had 'avoided inserting a part of the agreement' instead of having intended to set out the agreement in the deed.[131] In *Marquis v Stangroom*,[132] Eldon LC further explained that, in *Lord Irnham*, inserting the provision to redeem would have been 'directly contrary to [the parties'] intention', and the enforcement of the term would have put the parties in a position 'as if they had been better informed, and consequently had a contrary intention.' There were 'two risks [which] had occurred to the parties: the danger of usury, and the danger of trusting to the honour of the [other] party';[133] and the parties' appreciation and acceptance of the latter risk precluded the enforcement of the term of redemption.

The decision in *Lord Irnham* appears to impose an additional requirement: not only must B promise to qualify his interest in the property, but the parties must also have *unintentionally* avoided reducing that intention to writing. However, the cases reflecting the doctrine have not imposed such a requirement. Indeed, the courts have never deemed it necessary to explore the reasons behind the informal nature of the parties' agreement. On a proper analysis, a constructive trust ought to have arisen in relation to the annuity, since B's promise would have properly qualified his interest in the annuity. As such, this case is best considered as wrongly decided.

4.3. The Rationale

It is necessary at this juncture to consider the rationale that underpins the doctrine in *Rochefoucauld v Boustead*, which dictates that a constructive trust will invariably arise to compel B to perform his promise once the elements of promise and reliance (as explained

[129] *Re Duke of Marlborough* (n 7).
[130] *Lord Irnham v Child* (1781) 1 Bro CC 92, 28 ER 1006.
[131] ibid 1 Bro CC 94, 28 ER 1008.
[132] *Marquis v Stangroom* (1801) 6 Ves Jun 328, 332; 31 ER 1076, 1078.
[133] ibid 6 Ves Jun 332, 31 ER 1078.

above) are fulfilled. This is an important consideration, since the relevant rationale not only underpins the doctrine in *Rochefoucauld v Boustead* but also the other QI doctrines, that is, those which reflect a QI situation within the non-contract-based, bilateral events category of constructive trusts. Since all these doctrines invariably entail the imposition of a constructive trust,[134] it is necessary to explain and justify why this is so.

We will first note three attempts which have been made to rationalise the QI doctrines. Having explained their shortcomings, a different analysis will then be proposed.

4.3.1. The 'Perfection Aim'

In his monograph *Explaining Constructive Trusts*,[135] Gbolahan Elias suggests that the 'inducement rules',[136] which includes the QI doctrines[137] as well as proprietary estoppel,[138] can be explained by way of the 'perfection aim'.[139] Building on Charles Fried's normative account of contracts,[140] Elias suggests that these constructive trusts aim to perfect one's decision to favour another: such a person should be compelled to fulfil his choice to do so.[141] One instance of an exercise of choice is the making of a promise, by which 'one disposes of one's option to act contrarily to the content of the promise.'[142] Once a promisor has made a promise, it does not matter whether he changes his mind:[143] pursuant to the perfection aim, a constructive trust arises to 'give the plaintiff what the defendant chose to confer',[144] thus allowing 'the plaintiff [to] use or enjoy the property basically as the defendant chose.'[145]

It is unclear whose intention is perfected on this conception. In many instances, Elias speaks of the law as perfecting 'the defendant's intention',[146] which indicates that B's intention is paramount. At other times, however, the focus is on A's intention.[147] Certainly, in most cases A is the instigator of the relevant arrangement, and so it might be thought

[134] This can be contrasted with the doctrine of proprietary estoppel where courts may award a lesser remedy: discussed in Chapter 7.

[135] Elias, *Explaining Constructive Trusts* (n 9).

[136] This category of rules comprises the 'secret trust', 'mutual wills', '*Bannister*', '*Gissing*' and 'estoppel' rules: see Elias, *Explaining Constructive Trusts* (ibid) 56–66.

[137] Two points should be noted. First, Elias uses the label 'the *Bannister* rule' instead of 'the doctrine in *Rochefoucauld v Boustead*', but in essence the two are identical. Secondly, writing in 1990, Elias' monograph does not discuss the doctrine in *Pallant v Morgan*, since it was not until the case of *Banner Homes Group plc v Luff Developments Ltd* [2000] Ch 372 (CA) was decided in 2000 that the doctrine was formally recognised as a discrete category of constructive trusts. However, it seems clear that Elias would have considered this doctrine as part of the 'inducement rules' category, which he explains by way of the 'perfection aim'.

[138] See Chapter 7, S 7.3.1. for an evaluation of Elias' thesis in relation to proprietary estoppel.

[139] Elias, *Explaining Constructive Trusts* (n 9) 56–66.

[140] Charles Fried, *Contract as Promise: A Theory of Contractual Obligation* (Cambridge MA, Harvard University Press, 1981).

[141] Elias, *Explaining Constructive Trusts* (n 9) 9.

[142] ibid.

[143] ibid 10.

[144] ibid 59.

[145] ibid.

[146] ibid 10–11, 13, 56, 59, 60.

[147] ibid 10, 13.

that the doctrines are concerned with perfecting A's intention. However, B's intention[148] is also at least equally as important, since B must have *agreed* to carry out the arrangement. In fact, there are good reasons to suppose that Elias cannot have meant that the law perfects A's intention. It is often the case that A could have, but failed to comply with a relevant formality requirement. Such non-compliance entails that A forgoes the opportunity to give express effect to the arrangement he intends. Hence, to enforce the arrangement by reference to A's intention would be to disregard an Act of Parliament without justification. Moreover, it is difficult to justify imposing a constructive trust on B, which significantly limits B's autonomy, *solely* by reference to A's intention where A's intention is not properly manifested.

Instead, Elias must be understood as suggesting that the doctrines aim to perfect B's intention, compelling him to fulfil his promise. When A confers the relevant advantage on B, there is no outstanding intention or promise left on A's part which requires perfecting. But B's promise remains unfulfilled, and it is precisely because he has made such a promise that he is compelled to carry out the arrangement. On this analysis, the constructive trust which deprives B of what appears at law to be *his* property is explained on the basis that he must fulfil what *he* originally intended and promised to do.

This refinement notwithstanding, the 'perfection aim' remains inadequate. It is clear that B is not under a duty to perfect his intention from the moment he makes his promise, but is generally at liberty to renege prior to acquiring the property in question. This means that equity is not perfecting B's intention per se, but is concerned with binding him *in certain circumstances*. Elias does say that B 'will have authority to withdraw until something beyond mere mental choice transpires, the assumed "something beyond" varying with the context.'[149] However, this obscures two distinct ways in which this 'something beyond' may be satisfied. Where an express trust is properly declared and constituted, the settlor's intention may not be withdrawn. By holding the settlor to his intention, the law affirms his autonomy: he has the freedom to dispose of his options and a legitimate expectation that the law will give effect to it.[150] On the other hand, the QI doctrines involve *informal* agreements; therefore, that 'something beyond' is satisfied through different means. The 'perfection aim' fails to give due weight to the importance of A's conferment of the relevant advantage in reliance on B's promise.

4.3.2. Correcting Reliance Losses

Simon Gardner has suggested that the QI doctrines and proprietary estoppel[151] (among other doctrines) can be explained by way of a unified theory: that they all correct reliance

[148] The concern here is with B's objectively ascertained intention; his secret, subjective intention is irrelevant: see, eg, *Re Atkinson* (1911) 80 LJ Ch 370 (CA) 373. See also, in the secret trusts context, *Moss v Cooper* (1861) 1 J & H 352, 366; 70 ER 782, 788: '[i]f you attempt to raise a trust out of some uncommunicated intention, you contravene the express provisions of the statute', since the court would be 'depriv[ing] a legatee of a benefit given to him by will where there is no obligation … accepted by him, and no communication made to him'; and *Addlington v Cann* (1744) 3 Atk 141, 26 ER 885 where no secret trust was enforced because communication to the secret trustee occurred only after the settlor's death.

[149] Elias, *Explaining Constructive Trusts* (n 9) 13.

[150] ibid 9–10.

[151] More specifically, proprietary estoppel cases where a constructive trust is imposed: Gardner, 'Reliance-Based Constructive Trusts' (n 9) 77.

losses. This is 'the loss that someone suffers when, acting in reasonable reliance on another's undertaking, he forgoes his opportunity to achieve the content of the undertaking in some other way.'[152] That is to say, A's reliance on B's promise leads A to lose an opportunity to make alternative arrangements to secure that which he trusts B to do, and this loss cannot be corrected by any other means except through the imposition of a constructive trust to compel B to keep his promise.

One of the difficulties with Gardner's thesis relates to the notion of a 'loss', which, as will be discussed in Chapter 6,[153] proves to be illusory in relation to the doctrine in *Pallant v Morgan*.

A second problem is that Gardner does not sufficiently account for the remedial differences between the QI doctrines and proprietary estoppel. For instance, in writing that the doctrine in *Rochefoucauld v Boustead* allows a third party (C) to enforce the oral arrangement between A and B where B promises to hold A's property for C, Gardner writes that A's detriment is the loss of opportunity '*to establish a trust of the land for [C]*'.[154] This loss can *never* be corrected even if the property is returned to A, presumably because the moment at which that precise opportunity could have been taken has passed. Hence, B is compelled to carry out the original agreement. However, in proprietary estoppel cases A's detriment can sometimes be corrected by a remedy other than a constructive trust, even if the detriment is significant.[155] Furthermore, A's detriment can sometimes be set off by a countervailing gain A receives from B.[156] This significant difference between the two groups of doctrines is left unexplained.

Thirdly, in relation to proprietary estoppel, courts insist that the remedy awarded to A must be proportionate to the detriment A suffers;[157] however, this nuanced approach is not taken in relation to the QI doctrines. This gives rise to the difficulty that, if Gardner's thesis is correct, the imposition of a constructive trust in the QI doctrines may over-compensate A's 'loss'. Take for instance C's ability to enforce an agreement between A and B in the context of the doctrine in *Rochefoucauld v Boustead*. As we have observed, Gardner thinks that a constructive trust must always arise in C's favour in order to correct A's reliance loss. However, it might be asked why the property ought not simply to be returned to A by way of a resulting trust to restore the parties to their status quo and to enable A to re-effectuate the intended arrangement by properly declaring an express trust. To put this in another way, sometimes imposing a resulting trust will suffice to correct the loss A suffers; and in these cases imposing a constructive trust in C's favour would be to over-compensate for A's loss. This is not to suggest that a constructive trust ought not to be imposed in C's favour: we will see[158] that an application of the doctrine in *Rochefoucauld v Boustead* allows for this outcome. The point to be made, however, is that the difficulties explaining the QI doctrines by way of Gardner's thesis indicate that these doctrines have a different aim from proprietary estoppel. Unifying them by way of a single rationale risks masking important differences.

[152] ibid 63.

[153] See Chapter 6, S 6.2.1.2.2.

[154] Gardner, 'Reliance-Based Constructive Trusts' (n 9) 70 (emphasis in original).

[155] See, eg, *Jennings v Rice* [2002] EWCA Civ 159, [2003] 1 FCR 501.

[156] See Sean Wilken QC and Karim Ghaly, *Wilken and Ghaly: The Law of Waiver, Variation, and* Estoppel, 3rd edn (Oxford, OUP, 2012) [11-80].

[157] *Henry v Henry* [2010] UKPC 3, [2010] 1 All ER 988 [65]; *Wilken and Ghaly* (n 155) [11-93].

[158] See S 4.5.2.3.

4.3.3. Conditional Acquisition of Property

Ben McFarlane[159] has also attempted to explain a number of doctrines which include the core QI doctrines and excludes proprietary estoppel. His thesis most closely aligns with that proposed in this book. In his paper 'Constructive Trusts Arising on a Receipt of Property *Sub Conditione*', McFarlane argues that B is bound to fulfil his undertaking if and only if two conditions are met: 'first, that [B] has made an undertaking to confer on another a right relating to the property purchased; secondly, that [B] has, by means of this undertaking, acquired an advantage in relation to the [transfer] of the property.'[160] Where these elements are fulfilled, 'the trust arises to prevent [B]'s reneging on the understanding subject to which he received the property.'[161]

Inasmuch as the idea of 'loss' is central to Gardner's thesis, the concept of 'advantage' is key to McFarlane's analysis. However, McFarlane does not expressly define what an 'advantage' entails, and this causes problems in relation to the doctrine in *Pallant v Morgan.* As will be discussed in Chapter 6,[162] there are two different ways in which 'advantage' can be assessed, and it is crucial to determine which is at play in order properly to understand that doctrine.

McFarlane's thesis also does not address the crucial matter of why the law's remedial approach differs between the QI doctrines and proprietary estoppel. McFarlane contrasts the element of advantage in his thesis with the element of detrimental reliance required in the context of proprietary estoppel, observing that whereas the latter grants a remedy to A which is proportionate to the detriment suffered, the former always results in the enforcement of the parties' arrangement.[163] There is no doubt that the existing law bears out this distinction; however, an explain remains outstanding as to why the fact that B obtains an advantage from A in relation to the acquisition of property should invariably lead to the enforcement of B's promise, instead of engaging the more evaluative approach found in proprietary estoppel cases. Why is it that, in relation to the QI doctrines, courts never ask whether B ought to be compelled simply to pay to A the monetary value of the advantage he obtained from A, which might thereby ensure the proportionality between the advantage B gains and the remedy granted?

McFarlane writes that, where B acts unconscionably 'in reneging on his undertaking',[164] 'the proper response is ... to enforce [the parties'] undertaking as effectively as is possible'.[165] It is unclear whether McFarlane thinks that B must positively renege on the parties' agreement[166] or whether the concern is merely with the possibility of B reneging on his undertaking.[167] Either way, however, it remains necessary to explain the reasons for which it is thought that B ought not to renege on his promise in the first place.

159 McFarlane, '*Sub Conditione*' (n 10).
160 ibid 668.
161 ibid 675.
162 See Chapter 6, S 6.2.1.2.4.
163 McFarlane, '*Sub Conditione*' (n 10) 688–89.
164 ibid 689.
165 ibid.
166 As seems to be suggested at ibid 689.
167 ibid 685.

4.3.4. QI Situations: Norm Against Taking an Advantage

It is suggested that the doctrine in *Rochefoucauld v Boustead*, as well as the other QI doctrines, reflect the 'norm against taking an advantage'.[168]

Suppose that B is given something by A that the parties agree should not be taken by B for his unqualified use. In these circumstances, there exists a well-established norm that B ought not to take that thing for his own enjoyment. This norm is so entrenched that we seldom pause to give it any thought. Yet examples of its application are aplenty. If A lends a book to B, it is clear that B cannot keep the book for himself, but ought to return it within a reasonable time. If A hands over to B a collection of 100 music albums, telling B to pick one for himself, B is surely obliged to return the other 99 albums to A after making his selection. If B agrees to do A a favour by delivering A's coat to C, it is unacceptable for B to take the coat for himself; he is morally obliged to deliver it to C.

The QI doctrines can be explained in a similar vein by way of the 'norm against taking an advantage'. This is that B ought not to retain an advantage or the proceeds of an advantage obtained from an opportunity conferred by A which both parties agree should not be taken by B for his unqualified use. By making a promise to A, B obtains an opportunity from A which leads to B's acquisition of property. Both parties agree that the property should not be taken by B for his own absolute enjoyment. Hence, a constructive trust arises when B acquires the property in question to qualify the interest he obtains in it. The constructive trust recognises and gives effect to the relationship between the parties which they agreed to enter into. It is in view of this relationship that B is compelled to carry out his promise in order to prevent B from taking the property for his own enjoyment contrary to his promise.

For the norm against taking an advantage to apply, it is necessary for four cumulative elements to be present on the facts of a case. The presence of these elements lead to the indubitable conclusion that B ought *never* to take the advantage for himself. First, A must confer on B an advantage. Secondly, both parties must have intended for B not to take the advantage for himself, instead of this being A's unilateral intention. Thirdly, B's promise must have induced A to act: this ensures that B's promise is the basis of A's actions. Finally, B's promise must be to the effect that he will qualify his interest *in the advantage which he obtains*. This ensures that B is never intended to take the unqualified use of that advantage.

It is crucial to note that the norm at play is not simply that B ought not to retain any advantage which he *promises* not to keep for himself. This norm may underlie contracts or express trusts, but cannot explain the QI doctrines where B does not make a formal promise or declaration of trust. Thus, the norm underlying the QI doctrines requires not only an agreement between A and B, but also that an opportunity to acquire the property is obtained by B *from A*.

The norm at play can also be distinguished from a norm which dictates that B ought not to retain an advantage which A transfers to him because *A does not intend* for B to retain it. This norm applies to resulting trusts, which responds to A's lack of intention to benefit B.[169] In contrast, the norm underlying the QI doctrines requires a positive agreement between

[168] This can be contrasted with proprietary estoppel, where the concern is with correcting reliance losses: see Chapter 7, S 7.3.2.

[169] See Chapter 1, S 1.2.2.2.

A and B. Since the norm is triggered by the parties' agreement, it dictates not only that B *ought not to* retain the acquired property, but that B *ought to* carry out his promise to hold the property for the benefit of A or C, as the case may be.

The outcome of an application of the norm against taking an advantage, which is that B is compelled *to carry out his promise* according to the parties' agreement, sometimes faces the objection that it is an excessive legal response. The objection is that B can be prevented from taking an advantage by invariably compelling B to return the acquired property *to A*, or to compel B to compensate A's detrimental reliance. However, it can be observed that it is indeed *necessary* for B to be held to the full extent of his promise. Through the QI doctrines, equity recognises the reality that there is more to the fact that B holds the legal title to the property in question. That reality reveals an agreement whereby B promises to take a qualified interest in the property he acquires. Moreover, B's promise induces A to act in reliance by conferring an opportunity for B to acquire the property to which B's promise relates. Equity therefore compels B to carry out his promise in order to give effect to the reality of the situation. Any other outcome would under-represent the reality of what transpires. Thus, to compel B simply to return the property to A renders the content of B's promise irrelevant to the outcome. Similarly, compelling B merely to make compensation would ignore the fact that B's promise, on the basis of which A conferred the relevant opportunity to acquire the property, was to take only a qualified interest in the property.

4.4. 'Fraud'

It is most commonly thought that the element of 'fraud' lies at the heart of the doctrine in *Rochefoucauld v Boustead*. This section examines whether the idea of 'fraud' has any role to play in this doctrine.

4.4.1. The Disapplication Thesis Again

It is necessary briefly to return to the disapplication thesis, which relies heavily on the idea of 'fraud'.

It will be recalled that the disapplication thesis views s 53(1)(b) as a rule of evidence or proof, which is disapplied where there is 'fraud'.[170] This entails that the analytical sequence for determining whether s 53(1)(b) is 'disapplied' is that 'fraud' must be determined prior to the issue of proof. However, in *Rochefoucauld*, the Court of Appeal said that 'it is a fraud on the part of a person to whom land is conveyed as a trustee … to deny the trust'.[171] This indicates that 'fraud' can only arise if B is already 'a trustee', and surely it is only *after* considering all the relevant evidence that a court can determine whether B is or is not a trustee. But how can such evidence be considered if s 53(1)(b) applies, this provision not having yet been disapplied? This logical fallacy indicates that the disapplication thesis mistakenly treats the existence of 'fraud' as a prerequisite for admitting the relevant evidence: *Rochefoucauld*

[170] See S 4.1.1.2.
[171] *Rochefoucauld* (n 2) 206.

clearly shows that evidence of the alleged trust is admitted, and the existence of the trust duly recognised, before the discussion of 'fraud' becomes relevant at all. In fact, Swadling recognises the circularity of the issue: 'it is only once the evidence which the statute says is inadmissible is admitted that it will be known that a "trustee" is attempting to use the statute as an instrument of fraud;[172] yet, surprisingly, he nevertheless incorporates this circularity within the disapplication thesis.

Another problem with the disapplication thesis is that it does not make clear when a 'fraud' will arise. Swadling acknowledges that 'there is no authoritative statement' for '[w]hat amounts to fraud for the purpose of this doctrine';[173] yet he is content to say that the Court in *Rochefoucauld* 'disapplied [s 7] on perfectly orthodox and long-settled grounds'[174] without explaining what those grounds are. The result is that the disapplication thesis substantially alters s 53(1)(b) by writing into it a word which is not there: that declarations of trusts over land '"*may*" be manifested and proved by some writing'. This, surely, is impermissible.[175]

Another difficulty with making 'fraud' a requirement for the disapplication thesis is the confusion it creates for a party who is reviewing his legal position prior to the initiation of proceedings. Suppose that B who is genuinely in doubt concerning his legal position merely seeks a court's guidance, and does not assert that he is the rightful owner of the property in question. Will the court declare that he is the absolute owner of the property, given that he has not yet actively relied on the statute as an 'instrument of fraud'? Such an outcome is inconceivable. Yet, how will the court justify its declaration otherwise, if the oral express trust is precisely within the ambit of the yet-to-be-'disapplied' s 53(1)(b)? This regrettable confusion also gives cause to reject the role which proponents of the disapplication thesis accord to the idea of 'fraud'.

4.4.2. What is 'Fraud'?

In contrast to the disapplication thesis, the 'norm against taking an advantage' leads to the view that 'fraud' has a merely auxiliary role, since it is not an event to which the doctrine responds. However, it is undeniable that the language of 'fraud' prevails in the doctrine, not least because it was used in the Court of Appeal's statement of the doctrine in the case of *Rochefoucauld* itself. What, then, is the true meaning of 'fraud' in relation to the doctrine?

4.4.2.1. Not Simply Relying on Section 53(1)(b)

The first point of principle to observe is that 'it is not "fraud" to rely on legal rights conferred by Act of Parliament'.[176] Even if we conclude that Swadling is correct to view s 53(1)(b)

[172] William Swadling, 'Property: General Principles' in Andrew Burrows (ed), *English Private Law*, 3rd edn (Oxford, OUP, 2013) [4-208] fn 309.

[173] ibid [4-208].

[174] Swadling, '*Rochefoucauld v Boustead*' (n 10) 113.

[175] Simon Gardner notes that '[t]he judges have no general power to disapply an Act of Parliament on the ground that it does or allows … "fraud" … in individual cases': Gardner, *Law of Trusts* (n 21) 97.

[176] *Midland Bank Trust Co Ltd v Green* [1981] AC 513 (HL) 531.

as a 'rule of evidence', this principle remains valid, given that it is a rule conferred by Parliament.[177] This principle is made clear in the self-declaration cases where an owner of property, B, orally declares a trust over his own property for the benefit of A. As observed earlier,[178] B is able to rely on s 53(1)(b) if he changes his mind, rendering 'fraud' irrelevant in self-declaration cases.[179] Thus, there must be something beyond B's mere reliance on the statute for a 'fraud' to arise.

4.4.2.2. Involves a Conveyance

In *Rochefoucauld*, the Court of Appeal observed that a 'proof of a fraud' will involve proving that 'the grantee … is … relying upon *the form of conveyance and statute*, in order to keep the land himself'.[180] This suggests that, in addition to s 53(1)(b), the existence of a conveyance is central to the meaning of 'fraud'. This explains why 'fraud' never arises in relation to self-declared trusts: they never involve a conveyance because B already owns the property in question, unlike in relation to the doctrine in *Rochefoucauld v Boustead*—in particular the *Bannister*-type cases[181]—where B receives A's land on the informal understanding that B is to hold some beneficial interest in the land on trust for A. In other words, 'fraud' relates to the true nature of the transaction when a *conveyance* takes place, in order to determine the respective rights and obligations of the parties. The true nature of the conveyance varies depending on whether the conveyance is a transfer as a gift, by virtue of a sale, pursuant to a trust arrangement, as a security, etc. In the *Bannister*-type cases, the existence of the conveyance means that the courts must determine whether the true nature of the transaction is an outright transfer to B, or whether there is something more than an absolute conveyance.

4.4.2.3. Cloaks the True Nature of the Conveyance

Another aspect of 'fraud' is the fact that it relates to an attempt to use the absolute form of a conveyance in combination with s 53(1)(b) to cloak the true nature of the transaction. Consider how B might set up his argument in a *Bannister*-type case. B may rely on the wording of s 53(1)(b) in combination with the conveyance deed in his hands in an attempt to defeat A's argument that the conveyance was made on the strength of B's promise. Since it is not a 'fraud' to rely on the statute per se, B's argument is prima facie valid. B is essentially attempting to cloak the discovery of the true nature of the transaction. It is *this* attempt which the law will not permit. And to signify the law's manifest disapproval of such an attempt, it is given the label 'fraud'.

[177] Thus, it is difficult to defend the argument that courts are allowed to 'disapply' s 53(1)(b) despite no provision by Parliament to that effect.

[178] See nn 77–78 above and accompanying main text.

[179] Note, however, that although the *Rochefoucauld* doctrine does not apply, this does not preclude the possibility of A succeeding by way of proprietary estoppel where A detrimentally relies on B's promise.

[180] *Rochefoucauld* (n 2) 206 (emphasis added).

[181] The reference in this section to *Bannister* as the archetype of the *Rochefoucauld* doctrine rather than the case of *Rochefoucauld* itself is due to the fact that there was no informal express trust on the facts of *Rochefoucauld*. This makes it difficult to compare *Rochefoucauld* with the self-declaration cases which involve an informal declaration of express trust.

4.4.2.4. 'Fraud' in Context: A Description

Ultimately, then, there are two ways in which the term 'fraud' may arise in the doctrine. It may act merely as an abridgement of the maxim 'a statute may not be used as an instrument of fraud', or it may take on a meaning independent of the maxim. The difference between the two, although subtle, is of crucial importance.

Where the meaning of 'fraud' is divorced from the maxim, it might be thought that the doctrine is engaged if, and only if, the absolute form of the conveyance is positively *used* to cloak the true nature of the transaction. As Scott LJ held in *Bannister v Bannister*, the fraud which brings the principle into play arises as soon as the absolute character of the conveyance is set up for the purpose of defeating the beneficial interest.[182] A similar view might be taken of the Court of Appeal's words in *Rochefoucauld* that 'it is a fraud on the part of [B] … to deny the trust and claim the land himself':[183] A positive denial of the trust might appear to be a pre-condition for the application of the doctrine.

This is, however, inaccurate. The statement that 'section 53(1)(b) may not be used as an instrument of fraud' remains wholly relevant, even in a case where B has not actively set up the form of the conveyance to deny A's interest. In Scott LJ's terms, the emphasis of the maxim is not on the 'setting up' of the form of the conveyance nor the 'defeating' of the other's interest, but rather on the fact that the statute '*cannot be called in aid*'[184] in such a case. Similarly, the emphasis in *Rochefoucauld* was not on B's active 'denial of the trust', but on the fact that 'the Statute of Frauds *does not prevent* the proof of a fraud'.[185]

Thus, although 'fraud' relates to the attempt to use the absolute form of the conveyance and the statute to cloak the discovery of the true nature of the transaction, the reference to 'fraud' does not presume that B has in fact attempted to do so. Rather, 'fraud' merely *describes* a state of affairs[186]—the cloaking of the true nature of the transaction using the conveyance deed and s 53(1)(b). More specifically, 'fraud' describes the state of affairs which the constructive trust prevents—the 'defeating' or 'denial' of the trust using the conveyance. This is consistent with the analysis of promise and reliance as the causative events of the doctrine, since the causative events are those that would make a denial of the true nature of the transaction a 'fraud', not the occurrence of such an act of denial.

4.4.2.5. Not a Causative Event

One danger of giving 'fraud' a meaning divorced from the maxim is that it encourages the 'defeating' or 'denial' of the trust to be viewed as a causative event triggering application of the doctrine. For instance, Anthony Oakley writes, 'what brings about the intervention of equity is the acquisition of property on the strength of an oral undertaking … followed by an attempt to renege on the undertaking … because of the lack of the necessary statutory formalities.'[187] This sort of understanding is liable to cause fundamental misunderstandings such as that which arose in *Hodgson v Marks* at first instance, where Ungoed-Thomas

[182] *Bannister* (n 4) 136.
[183] *Rochefoucauld* (n 2) 206.
[184] *Bannister* (n 4) 136.
[185] *Rochefoucauld* (n 2) 206 (emphasis added).
[186] 'Fraud' has also been said to be merely 'a conclusion of law' (*Mountain v Styak* (n 112) 140) which 'follows from the facts found' (*Bannister* (n 4) 136).
[187] Oakley, *Constructive Trusts* (n 14) 53–54.

J held that the 'fraud' exception was available even against a bona fide purchaser who only discovers the trust *after* the purchase.[188]

The conceptualisation of 'fraud' as a causative event leads to inexorable analytical difficulties. Consider the period of time between the conveyance of the property and B's reneging on his undertaking. If the act of reneging is a causative event, it follows that, in this period, A has no rights under a constructive trust, since the doctrine has not yet been engaged, nor can B's informal undertaking be enforced, since this is prevented by s 53(1)(b). Not only will this put the parties in a state of deadlock, it may also be that any profits made out of the property, for instance pertaining to rents received from the tenants in the meantime, may be kept by B. This perverse state of affairs does not reflect the law.

Or suppose that A dies immediately after he conveys the property pursuant to B's undertaking. There is no doubt that the doctrine in *Rochefoucauld v Boustead* will enable A's heirs or estate to enforce the undertaking against B, even though B had not reneged on his undertaking to A. Indeed, if it is B who dies instead shortly after the conveyance,[189] it would be impossible for him to renege on his undertaking, and yet A would surely be able to enforce B's promise against B's heirs or estate.

These observations demonstrate that the application of the doctrine in *Rochefoucauld* entails a substantive interest arising prior to and irrespective of any later act of B. The proprietary right arises to bind B from the outset—that is, from the moment the conveyance is completed. As Millett LJ observed in *Paragon Finance plc v DB Thakerar & Co*, B's 'possession of the property is coloured from the first by the trust and confidence by means of which he obtained it'.[190] Such a right, and the corresponding obligation, arises pursuant to a constructive trust which responds to the causative events of promise and reliance, and reflects the norm against taking an advantage. It is therefore unnecessary—and potentially misleading[191]—to couch the emphasis of the doctrine in *Rochefoucauld v Boustead* in terms of a 'fraud doctrine' or a 'fraud exception' to the statutory formality requirement.

4.5. The Outer Limits of the Doctrine

This section considers two issues at the outer limits of the doctrine in *Rochefoucauld v Boustead*. The first concerns the relationship between these constructive trusts and resulting trusts; the second relates to the application of the doctrine in three party cases.

[188] *Hodgson v Marks* (n 112). See discussion at n 112 above.

[189] A less extreme but similar case arose in *Re Duke of Marlborough* (n 7). B died before re-assigning the property—a leasehold—to A, and had not, prior to his death, reneged on the parties' agreement to retransfer the equity of redemption to A. Stirling J held that, 'if [B] had in his lifetime refused to convey … he could not have set up the statute … [and] the Plaintiff, as claiming under him, is in no better position': *Re Duke of Marlborough* (n 7) 146.

[190] *Paragon Finance* (n 8) 409.

[191] In *Singh v Anand* [2007] EWHC 3346 (Ch) [144], HHJ Norris QC attempted to apply 'the pure form of [the 'fraud'] doctrine as applied in *Rochefoucauld v Boustead*' to bind the nominees of the *transferor* of shares, while refusing to impose a constructive trust based on *Bannister v Bannister*, since in that case 'a constructive trust was imposed on the *transferee*' (emphasis added). This is inconsistent, given that the doctrine in *Rochefoucauld* always imposes a constructive trust on the transferee. This confusion illustrates the inconsistencies which may arise if the doctrine is understood simply in terms of 'fraud'.

4.5.1. The Doctrine in *Rochefoucauld v Boustead* and Resulting Trusts

Alongside constructive trusts, the creation and operation of resulting trusts are also not affected by s 53(1)(b) by virtue of s 53(2). Where property is transferred from A to B gratuitously, equity presumes that A does not intend to give the beneficial interest in the property to B.[192] This presumption may be rebutted by evidence to the contrary.[193] But where it is not, either due to a lack of evidence or because it is confirmed by positive evidence that A indeed did not intend to benefit B, a resulting trust arises to compel B to hold the property on trust for A. In most cases relating to the doctrine in *Rochefoucauld v Boustead*, A transfers property outright to B. This makes the resulting trust response potentially relevant, since the informal agreement between A and B will always provide evidence that A does not intend the property to be beneficially owned by B. It might be thought that 'it matters not whether the trusts be resulting or constructive trusts, each being within s 53(2) of the Law of Property Act.'[194] However, inasmuch as it is necessary to distinguish between express and constructive trusts, it is also important to set out the precise relationship between both these trusts to attain a proper understanding of the law. It would also inform the question of whether the doctrine applies in three-party cases.[195]

Before proceeding, it is important to make three clarifications concerning the potential applicability of resulting trusts to cases concerning the doctrine in *Rochefoucauld v Bosutead*. First, the resulting trust analysis is not irrelevant simply because the interest A is awarded after the transfer is made is dissimilar to A's original interest in the property before the transfer. Where a resulting trust arises, A does not 'retain' his equitable interest; rather, A's equitable interest under a resulting trust arises 'for the first time under that trust.'[196] This makes it possible for a resulting trust to confer on A an interest smaller than the interest he initially had in the property.

Secondly, the resulting trust analysis is not irrelevant merely because positive evidence of A's intention is available on the facts of a case. Perhaps owing to the conception of resulting trusts in terms of presumptions, it is commonly thought that 'resulting trusts are imposed only if there is insufficient evidence to ascertain the transferor's intention.'[197] However, the better view is that the presumption is distinct from the resulting trust itself. If evidence is available that A positively intended to benefit himself, presumptions are rendered unnecessary,[198] and yet a resulting trust may still arise in response to the positive evidence that A did not intend to benefit B.[199] This was explicitly the view of Russell LJ in *Hodgson v Marks*.[200] Of course, if the law is able to give effect to A's positive intention as an express

[192] Discussed in Chapter 1, S 1.2.2.2.

[193] Or its effect may be negated if the presumption of advancement applies. This presumption will be abolished if and when the Equality Act 2010, s 199 comes into effect.

[194] *Hayton and Marshall* (n 111) [2-28].

[195] This is discussed in S 4.5.2.3.

[196] *Westdeutsche* (n 30) 706. See also *Commissioner of Stamp Duties (Queensland) v Livingston* [1965] AC 694 (PC).

[197] *Underhill and Hayton* (n 75) [3.3].

[198] 'Presumptions may be looked on as the bats of the law flitting in the twilight but disappearing in the sunshine of actual facts': *Mackowik v Kansas City* 94 SW 256 (1906).

[199] See Chambers, *Resulting Trusts* (n 21) 275.

[200] *Hodgson v Marks* (n 112) 933.

trust, then the trust is better categorised as express in nature,[201] and the resulting trust analysis is irrelevant. But it may be that A's non-compliance with a formality requirement precludes the enforcement of the trust as an express trust, in which case evidence that A positively intended to benefit himself can lead to the imposition of a resulting trust, since it provides evidence that A did not intend to benefit B.

Thirdly, the possibility of adopting a resulting trust analysis is not affected by the view that the Law of Property Act 1925, s 60(3) abolishes the presumption in A's favour where A gratuitously conveys land to B. There have been contrasting views as to whether s 60(3) has the effect of abolishing the presumption.[202] However, even if the presumption is abolished, it does not affect the possibility of a resulting trust arising in the context of the doctrine in *Rochefoucauld v Boustead*. The only effect of that section would be to require positive evidence concerning A's lack of intention to benefit B before a resulting trust would arise.

4.5.1.1. The Cases

There are three distinct groups of cases which are relevant to our discussion. The first is 'pure' constructive trust cases, where the doctrine in *Rochefoucauld v Boustead* applies and the cases cannot be re-analysed as resulting trust cases. The second is 'pure' resulting trust cases. At first sight these cases apply the doctrine in *Rochefoucauld v Boustead* to give rise to constructive trusts, but upon closer inspection they can only be analysed as giving rise to resulting trusts, and therefore fall outside the ambit of the doctrine. Finally, the majority of cases are intersecting cases, where both a constructive trust analysis by way of the doctrine and a resulting trust analysis may potentially explain their outcomes.

4.5.1.1.1. 'Pure' Constructive Trust Cases

Consider first the 'pure' constructive trust cases. It is possible to say with certainty that these cases may only be analysed by way of the doctrine in *Rochefoucauld v Boustead* since, unlike resulting trusts, they do not '[return] beneficial ownership of the trust property to a person who owned the property before it reached the trustee's hands'.[203] If after a conveyance the transferor obtains a beneficial interest in the property *more substantial* than the interest he had prior to the transfer, then the trust being enforced cannot be a resulting trust: it is hardly possible to speak of A's beneficial interest as being 'returned' to him if his interest in the property prior to the conveyance was less than what he obtains afterwards.

Thus, the trusts which arose in *Lincoln v Wright*[204] and *Rochefoucauld v Boustead*[205] could only have been constructive in nature, given that As, who only had an equity of redemption prior to the transfer, were given the absolute beneficial interest in the relevant lands. Similarly, in *De Bruyne v De Bruyne*,[206] the ultimate beneficiaries either had no initial interest in the shares or had, at most, a remote chance of benefitting from the shares under a

[201] This point—concerning the relationship between express and resulting trusts—is discussed in detail in Chapter 13, S 13.2.3.1.

[202] See discussion in Chambers, *Resulting Trusts* (n 21) 18–19; *Underhill and Hayton* (n 75) [25.57]–[25.60].

[203] *Underhill and Hayton* (n 75) [22.4].

[204] *Lincoln v Wright* (n 7).

[205] *Rochefoucauld* (n 2).

[206] *De Bruyne v De Bruyne* (n 8). The facts of this case are set out in the main text from n 271 below.

discretionary trust. Either way, they were ultimately awarded the full beneficial interest in the shares. The result reached in these cases can only be explained on a constructive trust analysis and, therefore, they do not intersect with resulting trusts.

4.5.1.1.2. 'Pure' Resulting Trust Cases

On the other hand are cases which might appear at first sight to reflect the doctrine in *Rochefoucauld v Boustead*, but ultimately fall outside the ambit of the doctrine. These cases involve a conveyance from A to B, however the transfer by A is not made on the basis of a promise by B.

For example, in *Birch v Blagrave*,[207] without his daughter (B)'s knowledge, A transferred his estates to B to avoid being sheriff of London. Lord Hardwicke declared that the property in question was to be held for A based on the fact that '[A's] intention was … not to part with the beneficial interest in the estate.'[208] In *Childers v Childers*,[209] A transferred land to his son (B) because A wanted to enable B to qualify as a bailiff. B died soon after without having heard of the conveyance. Knight Bruce LJ found that B held the land for A because A's intention in executing the deed was not that B should have a beneficial interest.[210] Similarly, in *Cecil v Butcher*,[211] Sir Thomas Plumer MR held that A was the appropriate beneficiary where A had made a conveyance to B to enable B to qualify to kill game, B never having heard of the conveyance.

It has been suggested that the trusts in these cases were enforced as express trusts.[212] However, such a suggestion is clearly wrong. In *Birch* and *Cecil*, A did not comply with the Statute of Frauds 1677, s 7, and so an express trust could not have been enforced. And in all three cases there was no objectively ascertainable positive manifestation of intention to create a trust at the time at which it was alleged that a trust was created.[213] Since the trusts could not have been enforced as express trusts, they could only have been resulting in nature. This analysis is also consistent with the reasoning in these cases: A was the appropriate beneficiary because he did not intend to benefit B absolutely with the interest in the property conveyed to B.

[207] *Birch v Blagrave* (1755) Amb 264, 17 ER 176.

[208] ibid Amb 265, 17 ER 176.

[209] *Childers v Childers* (1857) 1 De G & J 482, 44 ER 810.

[210] ibid 1 De G & J 492, 44 ER 814.

Both *Birch* and *Childers* were cited by Lord Browne-Wilkinson in *Westdeutsche* (n 30) 705 as examples of resulting trusts. His Lordship's explanation was, however, that '[B] or his successors in title have become aware of the facts which gave rise to a resulting trust [by the time action was brought]; his conscience was affected as from the time of such discovery and thereafter he held on a resulting trust'. Upon closer inspection, knowledge by a trustee is only a precondition for the beneficiary to obtain *personal* rights against the trustee (Ying Khai Liew and Charles Mitchell, 'The Creation of Express Trusts' (forthcoming 2018)). B's lack of knowledge does not preclude the fact that a *bare* resulting trust would have arisen immediately the property was transferred to B, as explained in the text.

[211] *Cecil v Butcher* (1821) 2 Jac & W 565, 37 ER 744. A transferred land to his son (B) as a qualification to enable B to kill game. B never knew about it.

[212] William Swadling, 'Property and conscience' (1998) 12 *Trust Law International* 228, 233.

[213] In *Birch* and *Cecil* this state of affairs sustained until after A's death, when A's will had taken effect to divest A of properties including the land in question. In *Childers* A sought a declaration that a trust existed, but after B had died.

4.5.1.1.3. Intersecting Cases

In the majority of cases, the resulting trust provides a realistic alternative analysis to the constructive trust analysis by way of the doctrine in *Rochefoucauld v Boustead*. On the resulting trust recharacterisation, the relief granted to A is analysed as responding to his absence of intention to benefit B with that interest, instead of being based on any positive intention. This technique is made possible in the intersecting cases by the fact that the parties' positive intention that B should hold the property for A corresponds precisely to A's lack of intention to benefit B with that very interest.

It cases where the interest A transfers to B is the very same interest which B ends up being compelled to hold for A, the resulting trust recharacterisation is straightforward. In *Davies v Otty (No. 2)*,[214] A, fearing prosecution for bigamy, conveyed property to B pursuant to B's oral promise to return it to A when the difficulty had passed. It turned out that A was not liable for bigamy, but B reneged on his undertaking. B's promise to hold the beneficial interest for A (to which a constructive trust responds) corresponded precisely to A's lack of intention to benefit B with the property (to which a resulting trust responds). Similar facts arose in *Haigh v Kaye*,[215] where A transferred property to B because A feared an adverse decision in a pending litigation. Again, there was a positive intention because B had promised that A would benefit from the property, as well as the relevant negative intention on A's part.[216] The Canadian case of *Scheuerman v Scheuerman*[217] is another case of this sort. A, a husband, transferred property to B, his wife, to evade execution subject to B's oral agreement to re-convey the property. But for the illegality of the transaction, the facts would have facilitated both a constructive and a resulting trust analysis.

The resulting trust analysis might also apply where the beneficial interest A obtains after the transfer is lesser than the initial interest he had in the property prior to the transfer. In *Booth v Turle*,[218] A conveyed certain premises to B absolutely, and in exchange for B's promise that A would remain beneficiary of a part of the premises (the stables), A reduced the purchase price from £300 to £150. The decision that B held the stables on trust for A could be explained as a constructive trust responding to B's promise to that effect, or alternatively as a resulting trust responding to A's lack of intention to benefit B with the stables. In *Bannister v Bannister*,[219] A, an elderly woman, agreed to sell two cottages which she owned absolutely to B, A's brother-in-law, at an undervalue[220] in reliance on B's promise that she would be allowed to live rent-free in one of them for as long as she desired. The decision that B held one cottage on trust for A for life can either be explained as a constructive trust which responded to B's promise to that effect, or as a resulting trust which responded to A's lack of intention to benefit B with a life interest in that cottage. In *Re Duke of Marlborough*,[221] A, the Duchess of Marlborough, assigned the leasehold of a house to B, the Duke, absolutely

[214] *Davies v Otty (No. 2)* (n 89).
[215] *Haigh v Kaye* (n 7).
[216] This has led Youdan to note of this case that '[t]he court was ... unclear as to the nature of the trust enforced': Youdan, '*Rochefoucauld v Boustead*' (n 9) 332.
[217] *Scheuerman v Scheuerman* (1916) 28 DLR 223.
[218] *Booth v Turle* (n 7).
[219] *Bannister* (n 4).
[220] ibid 135.
[221] *Re Duke of Marlborough* (n 7).

for B to raise a mortgage in his own name. B died before re-conveying the equity of redemption to A according to their agreement. The decision that A, instead of B's creditors, would benefit from the equity of redemption can either be explained as a constructive trust responding to B's promise, or a resulting trust responding to A's lack of intention to benefit B with the equity of redemption.

The strongest case for the resulting trust analysis is *Hodgson v Marks*.[222] A, an elderly widow named Mrs Hodgson, believed that Evans (E), her lodger, was in the insurance business and was well-versed in financial matters. Having knowledge that her nephew might turn E out of the house, A conveyed the property to E on the agreement that the beneficial ownership would remain with A. E sold the house to Marks (B), who became the registered owner subject to a mortgage B incurred for the purchase of the house. B was found not to be in a better position than E, since A had an overriding interest as a person in 'actual occupation'.[223] Based on the clear evidence 'that the transfer was not intended to operate as a gift', Russell LJ[224] saw no reason 'why there was not a resulting trust of the beneficial interest to [A], which would not … be affected by s 53(1).'[225] His Lordship went on to say that 'it matters not whether [B] was or was not debarred from relying upon section 53(1) by the principle that the section is not to be used as an instrument of fraud.'[226] Although the constructive trust analysis was not considered, it would have also yielded the same conclusion. A's transfer of the house in reliance on E's informal promise to hold it on trust for her would have given rise to a constructive trust under the doctrine in *Rochefoucauld v Boustead*; and B, not being in a better position than E, would have been compelled to respect A's right under it.

4.5.1.2. *Justifying the Constructive Trust Analysis*

Despite the fact that the resulting trust presents a plausible alternative analysis in the intersecting cases, these cases ought properly to be analysed by virtue of the doctrine in *Rochefoucauld v Boustead*, giving rise to constructive trusts, and not by virtue of a resulting trust analysis. This section notes a number of reasons for this conclusion. The aim is not to demonstrate that the cases are not *capable of* being analysed as resulting trusts. Rather, the aims are to establish that the constructive trust analysis is *preferable* to the resulting trust analysis, and that it is the former analysis which properly explains the ambit of the doctrine in *Rochefoucauld v Boustead.*

4.5.1.2.1. The Parties' Agreement

The cases within the doctrine invariably place much emphasis on the parties' agreement. Although they often go on to state that B may not rely on the informal nature of the agreement to defeat A's claim, the courts' conclusion that s 53(1)(b) does not prevent proof of parol evidence indicates that the parties' agreement is the source of B's obligation. The focus is on the parties' positive intention which arises through their agreement, and not on

[222] *Hodgson v Marks* (n 112).
[223] Land Registration Act 1925, s 70(1)(g).
[224] With whom Buckley and Cairns LJJ agreed.
[225] *Hodgson v Marks* (n 112) 933.
[226] ibid.

a negative intention on the part of A. The emphasis on the parties' agreement is not merely a coincidence or a convenient method of determining the remedy, but properly reflects the law's preference for analysing the cases using a constructive trust instead of a resulting trust analysis. It is precisely because there was a *positive* agreement between the parties concerning how B is to deal with the property that B is compelled to hold the property consistently with the agreement. As Craig Rotherham notes,[227] '[i]f the parties to a transfer are *sui juris* and not in an intimate relationship, there is much to be said for the view that the law should respond to the transferor's intentions and not to any failure to think about the matter.' It would provide an insufficient explanation of the law and the relevant facts if the resulting trust analysis is preferred, since it would ignore the central role of B's promise in coming to the agreement with A. Indeed, from a practical point of view, why should B's obligation be based on a presumption of A's intention or A's lack of intention to benefit B when there are more compelling reasons to support his claim—the inducement of A's transfer of the property by B's promise to hold the property on trust?

4.5.1.2.2. Roles of the Trusts

Another reason for preferring the constructive trust analysis can be seen from the perspective of the different roles which constructive and resulting trusts play in the law of trusts as a whole.

On a constructive trust analysis, the actions and intentions of both A and B are taken into account. The constructive trust recognises that the transaction was carried out pursuant to an agreement reached between the parties and that A's act of reliance was induced by B's promise to hold an interest in the property for A. B is bound to carry out the entirety of his promise only after the actions and intentions of both parties have been considered.

A resulting trust, on the other hand, acts merely as a 'default' legal response where the law is unable to give effect a positive intention. As Chambers notes, '[i]t is almost always preferable to give effect to the parties' intentions, but when that is impossible, the resulting trust fulfils the … function of ensuring that unintended benefits are returned.'[228] This can be seen in the 'pure' resulting trusts cases[229] where, through ignorance of the transfer, B does not share A's intention as to how B ought to deal with the beneficial interest in the property. Those cases do not warrant the imposition of constructive trusts because a positive intention on B's part was lacking; hence they gave rise to resulting trusts which responded to A's lack of intention to benefit B.

The 'default' nature of the resulting trust is also reflected in the mechanical remedy it provides. Reflecting the default rule that equity abhors gifts, a resulting trust always returns to A the beneficial interest which corresponds precisely to the interest over which A lacks an intention to benefit B. In contrast, a constructive trust strives to give full effect to the content of B's promise. Thus, in the 'intersecting' cases, even though the remedy might appear to be mechanical, this is a red herring. In truth, the remedy responds to the content of B's promise by virtue of a constructive trust. Favouring the resulting trust analysis would fail

[227] Craig Rotherham, *Proprietary Remedies in Context* (Oxford, Hart Publishing, 2012) 135.

[228] Chambers, *Resulting Trusts* (n 21) 286. See also *Underhill and Hayton* (n 76) [22.13]. A similar point is made in Charles Rickett, 'The Classification of Trusts' (1999) 18 *New Zealand Universities Law Review* 305, 317–08.

[229] See S 4.5.1.1.2.

to take into account the true nature of the parties' agreement—and, in particular, the fact and content of B's promise.

The 'default' nature of resulting trusts and the fact that the doctrine in *Rochefoucauld v Boustead* gives effect to positive intentions allow us to understand the various possible remedial responses where A transfers property to B short of creating an enforceable express trust. Where the transfer by A is induced by B's promise to hold that property on trust, then the doctrine in *Rochefoucauld v Boustead* will operate, which leads to the imposition of a constructive trust to bind B to perform the entirety of his promise. Conversely, where there is no evidence of a positive intention or promise on B's part, a resulting trust arises in response to A's negative intention. It follows that, where A transfers property to B despite B having not made the relevant promise, a resulting trust will arise in A's favour regardless of whether A intends to benefit A or C. The same would also be the case if, for some reason, it is impossible for B to carry out his promise, such as where C dies just before the transfer of property from A to B. In such a case, the constructive trust fails, and the next best option is for equity to respond to A's lack of intention to benefit B by way of a resulting trust. The resulting trust may also arise in response to a presumption of a negative intention. Thus, where there is a complete lack of evidence as to A's intention in relation to the beneficial interest in the property transferred to B, either because such intention cannot be proven with certainty or because A had not given thought to it, the presumption of resulting trust will arise to compel B to hold the property for A's benefit.

4.5.1.2.3. Positive and Negative Intention

Another explanation can be found in equity's preference for giving effect to positive as opposed to negative intention. This preference is not merely a coincidence, but is consistent with how equity deals with the element of intention.

It is necessary for equity to intervene at all in these cases because of the need to discover the true reality of the transaction which actually transpired: there is more to the mere fact that B holds the legal title to the property in question. Uncovering that reality reveals an agreement whereby B promises not to take the property for his unqualified use, which induces A to confer an advantage on B to which B's promise relates. Merely to reverse the transaction by way of a resulting trust would be to give effect only to A's negative intention that the property should not be applied for the benefit of B. This would be acting based on a fictitious construct of the circumstances which under-represents the true situation. Instead, equity holds B to his promise because it recognises the reality of what transpires—that B's promise is the basis on which B acquires the property. Hence, a constructive trust arises *precisely* because B promises to qualify his interest in the property; and when A confers the relevant advantage on B and B acquires the property in question, B is held to his promise in order that he does not take the property for his unqualified use.

The case of *Hutchins v Lee*[230] is instructive. There was an assignment of a leasehold estate from A to B which appeared absolute on the face of the conveyance. In reality, the conveyance was effectuated because A was very ill and wished for B to manage the estate on his behalf, and B had promised to hold the property on trust for A. As the headnote of the report accurately states, there was 'no express trust in the deed [of conveyance from

[230] *Hutchins v Lee* (1737) 1 Atk 447, 26 ER 284.

A to B]'.[231] Nevertheless, Lord Hardwicke LC held that evidence of the informal trust arrangement could be admitted. His Lordship explained that this was because B had made the relevant 'declarations … at the time the deed of assignment was executed', and that he had also afterwards made an 'acknowledgment of such a trust as [A] now insisted on'.[232] The crucial point is that A did not succeed simply on the basis that A did not intend to benefit B with his property; rather, through an application of the doctrine in *Rochefoucauld v Boustead*, B was bound by way of a constructive trust because B promised to hold the property on trust.

4.5.1.2.4. *Hodgson v Marks*

What should be made of *Hodgson v Marks*,[233] where a resulting trust analysis was explicitly adopted? It appears that the Court of Appeal inadvertently ignored the constructive trust analysis due to two crucial features of the case. First, counsel for Mrs. Hodgson (A) argued her case solely on the basis that a resulting trust arose. Given that this was sufficient to rule in her favour, it was unnecessary for the court to have gone on to consider whether a constructive trust would have yielded the same result.

Secondly, because the defendant, Marks (B), was a purchaser of the house from Evans (E), the lodger, and was not party to the initial agreement with A, it might have been thought that B had a strong case for arguing that it was not a 'fraud' for B to rely on s 53(1)(b). In relation to this point, B relied on the authorities of *Rochefoucauld v Boustead*[234] and *Bannister v Bannister*[235] to argue that s 53(1)(b) could be relied upon as a defence against A. The feasibility of B's argument perhaps explains why the court sought to avoid determining the point of whether B 'was or was not debarred from relying upon section 53(1) by the principle that the section is not to be used as an instrument for fraud.'[236] This may have led the court to dismiss the doctrine in *Rochefoucauld v Boustead* without any further consideration of its relevance—particularly whether it would also have led to the imposition of a constructive trust.

Nevertheless, the fact that E, not B, was party to the initial agreement would not have hindered a constructive trust analysis. Given that the court had decided that A had an overriding interest against B for being in 'actual occupation',[237] B would have been in no better position than E, and would therefore have been bound to hold the house on trust for A. Moreover, 'fraud' merely provides a description of the state of affairs which the doctrine in *Rochefoucauld v Boustead* prevents, and is not a requirement for the doctrine to operate.[238] Thus, even though the resulting trust analysis in *Hodgson* was plausible on the facts, the bigger picture—the positive intention of the parties as reflected by the agreement between A and E—reveals that an application of the doctrine in *Rochefoucauld v Boustead* would have been the preferable analysis, and the imposition of a constructive trust the better response.

[231] ibid.
[232] ibid 1 Atk 448, 26 ER 284.
[233] *Hodgson v Marks* (n 112).
[234] *Rochefoucauld* (n 2).
[235] *Bannister* (n 4).
[236] *Hodgson v Marks* (n 112) 933.
[237] ibid 932.
[238] See S 4.4.2.4.

Ignoring the bigger picture is liable to mislead the analysis. For example, Chambers writes that, if in *Hodgson* A 'had orally expressed an intention to create a trust for a third person', a resulting trust in A's favour would still have been the appropriate response.[239] Certainly, on a *resulting trust* analysis, A lacks an intention to benefit B, whether B is meant to hold the property for A or for a third party (C). However, on the facts of *Hodgson* as modified by Chambers, this outcome is suspect. In particular, it is unclear why the doctrine in *Rochefoucauld v Boustead* would not apply, which has the effect of giving rise to a constructive trust to compel B to carry out the full extent of his promise. Thus, in *Hodgson*, if the agreement between A and E was for the latter to hold the property on trust for a third party, C, B (who was in no better position than E) would have been compelled to hold the property for C under a constructive trust to carry out the full extent of E's promise.[240]

4.5.2. Three-party Cases

Traditionally, the cases which have applied the doctrine in *Rochefoucauld v Boustead* have involved only two parties: a transferor, A, and a transferee, B. This has resulted in uncertainty as to whether a third party volunteer, C, may rely on the doctrine to enforce the agreement between A and B where B's informal promise is to hold an interest in the property on trust for C.[241] One would have thought that an affirmative answer was obvious, since the constructive trust gives effect to the entirety of B's promise. However, unlike in relation to two-party cases, three-party cases involve the possibility of A changing his mind and demanding the return of the property from B. Furthermore, unlike two-party cases, the intended beneficiary is a volunteer. This raises the question of whether the law should impose a constructive trust in C's favour, or simply a resulting trust to return the property to A.[242]

It is important to note that the potential applicability of the doctrine in *Rochefoucauld v Boustead* to three-party cases does not depend on C fulfilling the element of reliance.[243] Even in two-party cases, the doctrine responds to the reliance of A *qua* settlor and not *qua* beneficiary. This is obvious from the fact that, in two-party cases, A's act of reliance is fulfilled *before* the constructive trust arises, and prior to the trust's arising, he cannot be said to be a 'beneficiary' at all.[244] Thus, in three-party cases, the question is whether C can enforce the content of B's promise to hold on trust for C by pleading B's promise and A's reliance.

[239] Chambers, *Resulting Trusts* (n 21) 34.

[240] The case for enforceability by a third party, C, is discussed in S 4.5.2.3.

[241] Youdan, '*Rochefoucauld v Boustead*' (n 9) 334.

[242] The discussion will not consider James Penner's suggestion that a constructive trust may allow the law to 'impose the result most justified in the circumstances—in some cases the constructive trust should be a bare trust for A … in others it should … [carry] out A's intention': Penner, *The Law of Trusts* (n 10) [6.11]. No attempt has ever been made to explain the basis on which such an unprincipled and inconsistent application of a constructive trust may arise, and thus it is difficult to take Penner's suggestion seriously.

[243] C's acts of detrimental reliance on the agreement between A and B may, however, be relevant for a proprietary estoppel claim (in relation to which see Chapter 7); but this is unrelated to the discussion of the doctrine in *Rochefoucauld v Boustead* where the issue is whether C is able to have a claim without suffering detrimental reliance.

[244] See *De Bruyne v De Bruyne* (n 8) [51]; Gardner (n 21) 329 fn 7.

4.5.2.1. *The Concerns*

The majority of commentators take an extremely circumspect approach to third-party enforceability, citing a number of concerns which would arise if C were able to enforce B's promise.

4.5.2.1.1. The s 53(1)(b) Concern

The first concern is that allowing C to enforce B's promise would leave 'hardly … any scope for the application of s 53(1)(b).'[245] In contrast, returning the property to A if A changes his mind 'entails less interference with the statutory provisions'[246] and 'gives due weight to the statute'.[247] A parallel is drawn with cases where B declares *himself* trustee for C: since the doctrine does not apply in such cases,[248] it is suggested that, for the same reason, C ought not to be allowed to enforce B's promise.[249]

These arguments do not entail that C will never benefit from an informal agreement between A and B. Since an informal declaration of trust is valid but unenforceable, 'B may convey to C unless A has revoked his authority to do so'.[250] The reason A has the right to revoke B's authority is thought to be a result of A's non-compliance with the formality requirement: this 'means that his beneficial entitlement remains with him'.[251]

4.5.2.1.2. The 'Fraud' Concern

Closely related to the first concern is the 'fraud' concern. Underlying the first concern is the idea that s 53(1)(b) should only be sidestepped when it is necessary to prevent 'fraud', and that the law must do no more than that required to prevent such 'fraud' from arising. It is thought that a resulting trust 'is all that is necessary to prevent B's unjust enrichment';[252] and since C is 'not being unjustly deprived of something that he can prove is his',[253] C should not be allowed to enforce the trust because he can 'hardly complain that a *fraud* has been perpetrated against him'.[254] Indeed, one commentator has gone so far as to suggest that 'the Statute of Frauds prevents the courts from enforcing the intention of the parties as such; it does not prevent them from putting the parties *in statu quo*.'[255] As Duff J held *obiter* in *Scheuerman v Scheuerman*,[256] 'to any proceeding by such third person as *cestui que trust* … the 7th section of the Statute of Frauds would have been an effectual answer, but there is no answer to an action … for *restitutio in integrum*'. Such 'restitution of what would otherwise be the unjust enrichment of the recipient' is effected through a resulting trust.[257]

[245] *Underhill and Hayton* (n 76) [12.75].
[246] Youdan, '*Rochefoucauld v Boustead*' (n 9) 335.
[247] Penner, *The Law of Trusts* (n 10) [6.11].
[248] See nn 77–78 above and accompanying main text.
[249] *Underhill and Hayton* (n 76) [12.75].
[250] Jill E Martin, *Hanbury and Martin: Modern Equity*, 18th edn (London, Sweet & Maxwell, 2009) [3-005] fn 27.
[251] *Underhill and Hayton* (n 76) [12.75].
[252] *Hanbury and Martin* (n 28) [6-006].
[253] *Underhill and Hayton* (n 76) [12.75].
[254] Penner, *The Law of Trusts* (n 10) [6.11] (emphasis in original).
[255] Youdan, '*Rochefoucauld v Boustead*' (n 9) 335, noting the view taken by Professor WA Scott.
[256] *Scheuerman v Scheuerman* (n 217) 230.
[257] Chambers, *Resulting Trusts* (n 21) 220.

4.5.2.1.3. The Status Quo Concern

The third concern is based on a distinction drawn between the inter vivos and testamentary contexts. In the latter context, it is impossible to return the parties to their status quo. 'A is dead and is no longer free to give effect to his bounty in a way which complies with the relevant formalities', which leads Feltham to write that 'fraud is interpreted to embrace the disappointment of A's reliance on B to give effect to his bounty in favour of C.'[258] Here, the resulting trust approach is considered to be inappropriate since A 'is necessarily dead and restitution to his estate ... is likely to be the last thing he would have wanted.'[259] In contrast, in the inter vivos context with which the doctrine in *Rochefoucauld v Boustead* is concerned, the fact that A is still alive is thought to be of significance. Thus, 'if [A] still wishes to carry out his intentions, he can declare the trust again'.[260]

4.5.2.2. Rejecting the Concerns

There are a number of analytical difficulties with these concerns against third-party enforceability. The root of these difficulties is that they do not engage with the prior issue of whether B should be bound to carry out his promise given the circumstances of B's acquisition of the property.

4.5.2.2.1. The s 53(1)(b) Concern

In discussing the doctrine in *Rochefoucauld v Boustead*, the phrase 'the statute' is used almost invariably to refer only to s 53(1)(b) instead of the *entire* Law of Property Act 1925 or its predecessor, the Statute of Frauds. Curiously, however, when dealing with third-party enforceability, commentators imply that allowing third-party enforceability contradicts the statute *in its entirety*. Although the preservation of the ambit of s 53(1)(b) is a valid concern, it should not be forgotten that s 53(2), which is in fact part of the statute, does anticipate that the applicable ambit of the formality requirement will be circumvented when a constructive or resulting trust arises.

It is mistaken to argue against third-party enforceability based on the fact that the doctrine does not apply in cases where B declares himself as trustee for C's benefit. Superficially, it might seem consistent to say that, since C cannot invoke the doctrine in self-declaration cases, the same result must follow where A transfers land to B pursuant to an oral trust to hold for C. In reality, however, there is a clear analytical difference. In self-declaration cases, the property starts out as being owned by B absolutely; and in contrast to QI situations, equity is less ready to deprive B of his ownership interest.[261] Thus, unless C has provided consideration or incurred a significant measure of detrimental reliance, it would be difficult to justify the imposition of a constructive trust where B has not declared an express trust. In three-party cases, however, the relevant property is not B's but A's at the outset. In these cases, the applicable norm dictates that B must never take the advantage conferred by

[258] Feltham, 'Informal Trusts' (n 76) 248.
[259] Youdan, '*Rochefoucauld v Boustead*' (n 9) 335.
[260] Penner, *The Law of Trusts* (n 10) [6.11]. See also Youdan, '*Rochefoucauld v Boustead*' (n 9) 335; *Underhill and Hayton* (n 75) [12.75].
[261] See discussion in the main text to n 80 above.

A because B promises to qualify the interest he takes in it;[262] and A's fulfilment of his act of reliance indicates that B's promise is the basis on which B acquires the property. These considerations are absent in the self-declaration cases.

Furthermore, the idea that A 'retains' the beneficial interest of his property due to the lack of compliance with s 53(1)(b) does not square up to the suggestion that B remains free to convey the property to C unless A has revoked his authority to do so. The beneficiary of the arrangement is either A or C; it cannot be both. Consider the matter from B's perspective. Suppose that, upon receiving the property, he honestly and immediately begins to account for the profits to C. Surely it is unacceptable to suggest that B is acting in breach of the resulting trust under which A 'retains' the beneficial interest, given that an oral declaration of trust creates a valid—though unenforceable—trust in C's favour.

Moreover, even if A were to be a beneficiary under a resulting trust, his equitable right cannot be said to have been 'retained' from a time prior to the transfer to B.[263] As Chambers observes,[264] '[t]he resulting trust creates a new equitable property right for the settlor, which is different from the property right he or she had before the transfer to the trustee. As a new right, it cannot be explained as the inertia of a pre-existing beneficial right.'

4.5.2.2.2. The 'Fraud' Concern

In relation to the 'fraud' concern, the discussion concerning the extent to which the law ought to prevent a 'fraud' from arising cannot be divorced from a consideration of the terms on which B acquires the property. If the doctrine in *Rochefoucauld v Boustead* is fundamentally concerned with effecting restitution, then it would be impossible to explain the decision in *Rochefoucauld* itself. Given that the transfer of the Delmar estates was not effectuated by A as absolute owner but by a combination of her consent and the Dutch company's transfer of the legal title, it is difficult to see how a resulting trust could have given A an *absolute* equitable right in the estates. How can A be said to have been 'unjustly deprived' of the *absolute* beneficial right in the estates when all she had was an equity of redemption at the outset?

The idea that the property must be restored to A is based on the suggestion that he has the best claim among the three parties involved, since B will be unjustly enriched if he keeps the property and C is not unjustly deprived because he cannot prove he is entitled to the property. However, if we were to take seriously the idea that the law must do no more than effect restitution to A, the same must also be the case if B has duly conveyed the property to C. Where B has done so, it seems to be thought that the conveyance is valid—and that C has the best claim—since A has not revoked his authority at the time of conveyance.[265] However, three inconsistencies ensue.

First, on what basis does B convey the property to C: under a valid (though unenforceable) trust or a fortuitous effectuation of a mere moral obligation? The latter option, lacking a legal basis, is obviously less preferable. Yet, the former option leaves unexplained why,

[262] This norm is discussed in S 4.3.4.

[263] *Westdeutsche* (n 30) 706. See also *Commissioner of Stamp Duties (Queensland) v Livingston* (n 196) 712; *Vandervell v IRC* [1967] 2 AC 291 (HL) 311; *Re Bond Worth* [1980] Ch 228 (Ch).

[264] Robert Chambers, 'Resulting Trusts in Canada' (2000) 38 *Alberta Law Review* 379, 389. See also Chambers, 'Constructive Trusts in Canada' (n 21).

[265] See main text to n 250 above.

while the property is in B's hands the resulting trust analysis applies, but if it is transferred to C the resulting trust analysis falls away and C is considered to be a beneficiary under an express trust.

Secondly, can A demand the return of the property from C? The answer seems to be in the affirmative if A is taken to be a beneficiary under a resulting trust from the moment he transfers the property to B, given that C is a mere volunteer. Yet, allowing A to do so raises serious concerns over C's security of receipt.[266]

Thirdly, if a conveyance from B to C holds good, this entails that an orally-declared trust has been fully effectuated. This ultimately works against the initial concern of these commentators pertaining to the preservation of the scope of s 53(1)(b). The other alternative, however, is unthinkable: surely, the law will not hold B to have breached a resulting trust in conveying property to C, when it was after all a result of A's failure to provide written evidence of the declaration of trust in the first place.

4.5.2.2.3. The Status Quo Concern

The distinction drawn between inter vivos and testamentary situations is flawed because it plays up non-material differences while playing down material ones. It is of course true that, in the testamentary context, A who has died can no longer change his mind concerning his intention to benefit C. However, this fact is beside the point. What matters is that, *at the moment A's property is transferred to B*, B is intended to hold the property for C's benefit. In the testamentary context, B acquires A's property when A dies; hence if neither party reneges on the agreement prior to that point, a constructive trust arises in C's favour at A's death.[267] Similarly, in the inter vivos context, if the parties intend for B to hold the property on trust for C at the time when A conveys the property to B, then a constructive trust arises in C's favour.

There is ample reason to think that the distinction between 'testamentary' and 'inter vivos' situations in this context is unprincipled and arbitrary. Youdan notes the real possibility that, in what starts off as an inter vivos case, A may well be dead at the date of the proceedings.[268] To quibble about whether such a case is to be considered 'testamentary' or 'inter vivos' is to make the outcome rest on the entirely irrelevant fact of whether A is dead or alive at the date of judgment.[269]

Also beside the point is the argument that, in inter vivos situations, A will have a second chance to create the intended trust for C if a resulting trust is imposed. This argument is fallacious: A will only have a second chance if a constructive trust does not arise to bind B to his promise. Since the doctrine in *Rochefoucauld v Boustead* has the effect of compelling B to carry out his promise, C becomes a beneficiary under a constructive trust from the moment B acquires A's property, and A drops out of the picture. Moreover, it is hardly

[266] It is not possible to work around this problem by suggesting that B holds the property on trust for A with a mandate to transfer to C, analogous to the suggestion in PJ Millett, 'The *Quistclose* Trust: Who Can Enforce It?' (1985) 101 *LQR* 269. This sort of analysis applies only where B is intended to apply A's property exclusively for a specific purpose; it does not apply where A's intention is to benefit C under an outright trust: see Millett, 'The *Quistclose* Trust' (n 266) 290.

[267] See, generally, Chapter 5.

[268] Youdan, '*Rochefoucauld v Boustead*' (n 9) 335.

[269] See TG Youdan, 'Informal Trusts and Third Parties: A Response' [1988] *Conveyancer and Property Lawyer* 267, 269.

convincing to argue in favour of the view that A should be able to renege on the informal agreement by reasoning that a resulting trust would *enable* A to effectuate an express trust for C.

4.5.2.3. The Case for Third-Party Enforceability

Since the cases are ambiguous as to whether C may be able to enforce an informal agreement between A and B,[270] the matter must be approached from first principles. In light of the nature of the constructive trust imposed by virtue of the doctrine in *Rochefoucauld v Boustead*, which is to enforce the full extent of B's promise, the correct position appears to be that C can indeed enforce the agreement where B's promise is to hold the property for C's benefit. Where A relies on B's promise by conferring on B the advantage to which B's promise relates, the relevant causative events are fulfilled and the doctrine in *Rochefoucauld v Boustead* compels B to carry out the content of his promise in C's favour.

The decision in *De Bruyne v De Bruyne*[271] supports this conclusion. The potential beneficiaries of an irrevocable discretionary trust of shares reached an agreement to confer on the defendant, who was one of the beneficiaries, all the shares pursuant to his promise to set up a trust for his five children. In breach of that undertaking, the defendant transferred the shares to his wife as his nominee. Citing *Rochefoucauld v Boustead*[272] and *Bannister v Bannister*,[273] the Court of Appeal held that a constructive trust compelled the defendant to carry out his promise.[274]

The facts indicate that *De Bruyne* was a three-party case, involving a group of potential beneficiaries under a discretionary trust (As), the defendant (B), and the defendant's children (Cs). The Court of Appeal 'concentrate[d] … on the circumstances in which [B] came to acquire the property in order to provide the justification for the imposition of a trust.'[275] The Court's approach rightly considered the fundamental issue of the analysis: did a constructive trust arise upon B's acquisition of the shares? In finding that it did, the Court decided that Cs could enforce the constructive trust. This can be explained on the basis that B's promise to hold the shares on trust for C induced As to rely on B by collectively giving up their rights in the shares in B's favour. A resulting trust analysis would have been inapposite: it would have been impossible to impose a resulting trust because As were potential beneficiaries under a discretionary trust rather than absolute owners at the outset.

One might argue that the result was justified given that Cs were also part of the initial class of potential beneficiaries, thus suffering detriment through the arrangement. However, the complicated terms of the discretionary trust meant that Cs were extremely unlikely to have benefitted under the discretionary trust; and therefore it is not possible to explain the decision as restoring Cs' absolute right to the shares on a resulting trust analysis or as a response to Cs' detriment. Indeed, the judgment does no more than briefly mention Cs'

[270] While Youdan, '*Rochefoucauld v Boustead*' (n 9) 334 suggests that the '[g]eneral statements of the doctrine' indicate a view for C's enforceability, Feltham, 'Informal Trusts' (n 76) 249 thinks that '[t]here is no strong line of authority in C's favour.'

[271] *De Bruyne v De Bruyne* (n 8).

[272] *Rochefoucauld* (n 2).

[273] *Bannister* (n 4).

[274] *De Bruyne v De Bruyne* (n 8) [51], [53].

[275] ibid [51].

initial interests under the discretionary trust,[276] and instead substantially focuses on the agreement between As and B.

Thus, it is a red herring to focus on the possibility of A re-declaring the trust, or on B's potential action or inaction, or C's position, or even on the relevant statutory provisions. Consistent with the two-party cases, B's pre-acquisition promise is enforced where A relies on that promise by transferring the property in question (or allowing the property to be transferred) to B. A constructive trust is imposed for the benefit of A or C, as the case may be; and its enforcement is sanctioned by s 53(2) where the subject-matter of the agreement concerns land. Because a constructive trust arises upon B's acquisition, A cannot change his mind later on. This is not because A is bound by the constructive trust: it is B who is bound to fulfil the agreement. However, A is nevertheless bound to respect the constructive trust in the same way that other interested parties (creditors, etc) cannot establish a better claim to the property than C.

[276] ibid [53].

5

Secret Trusts

The Wills Act 1837, s 9[1] provides that a valid will must be made in signed writing by the testator in the presence of two or more attesting witnesses present at the same time.[2] However, where the secret trusts doctrine applies, the courts nevertheless enforce dispositions by a testator (A) who does not comply with this formality requirement. In fully secret trust cases, the legatee (B) is compelled to hold the property on trust for the secret beneficiary (C) although on the face of A's will the property is left to B absolutely. In half-secret trust cases, A's will refers to the existence of the trust but does not disclose its terms or the intended beneficiaries. B is likewise compelled to hold the property on trust for C. In both instances, the intended dispositions are enforced notwithstanding the non-fulfilment of the formality requirements.

5.1. Nature of the Trust

Two different theories are often proffered in attempts to justify secret trusts in view of the apparent disregard for statute. The first assumes that the doctrine is 'established … with reference to the jurisdiction of Courts of Equity to interpose in all cases of fraud'.[3] This theory is rooted in the maxim that 'equity will not allow a statute to be used as an instrument of fraud', and has been cited as the basis for the secret trusts doctrine in many decided cases.[4] The second, the '*dehors* the will' theory, is based on the view that 'the legislation did not purport to interfere with the exercise of a general equitable jurisdiction, even in connection with secret dispositions of a testator'.[5] On this theory, the Wills Act does not affect secret

[1] As amended by the Administration of Justice Act 1982, s 17.

[2] For a radical alternative view that the Wills Act 1837 has no impact on testamentary trusts, that there is no writing requirement for testamentary trusts concerning personalty, that the Law of Property Act 1925, s 53(1)(b) governs testamentary trusts of land, and that, therefore, the doctrine of secret trusts applies only to testamentary trusts concerning land, see Paul Matthews, 'The Words which are Not There: A Partial History of the Constructive Trust' in Charles Mitchell (ed), *Constructive and Resulting Trusts* (Oxford, Hart Publishing, 2010).

[3] *McCormick v Grogan* (1869) LR 4 HL 82 (HL) 88.

[4] See, eg, *Reech v Kennegal* (1748) 1 Ves 123, 125; 27 ER 932, 933; *Wallgrave v Tebbs* (1855) 2 K & J 312, 322; 69 ER 800, 804; *Jones v Badley* (1868) LR 3 Ch App 362 (CA) 364; *McCormick v Grogan* (n 3) 88, 97; *Re Fleetwood* (1880) LR 15 Ch D 594 (Ch) 607; *Re Pitt Rivers* [1902] 1 Ch 403 (CA) 407; *Re Maddock* [1902] 2 Ch 220 (CA) 227; *Blackwell v Blackwell* [1929] AC 318 (HL) 328–29 (Lord Buckmaster), 335 (Viscount Sumner), 341 (Lord Warrington).

[5] *Blackwell v Blackwell* (n 4) 339.

trusts at all because secret trusts arise outside the will. This theory has been increasingly cited as the justification for secret trusts in the more recent cases.[6]

It is sometimes thought that one's choice of justificatory theory decisively determines the nature of secret trusts. Typically, it is thought that secret trusts are express in nature on the '*dehors* the will' theory, whereas on the 'fraud' theory secret trusts are constructive in nature.[7] Such a tightly-drawn link is unjustified: as will be seen, the nature of the trusts does not necessarily correlate to the justificatory theories in this way. Nevertheless, it is not a straightforward task to establish the nature of secret trusts. As Robert Burgess notes,[8] 'the courts, when discussing secret trusts, have refrained from attempting to put them into any of the recognised categories of express or constructive trusts'; and in their stead, 'academics have stepped in where the courts have feared to tread with an almost inevitable lack of consistency or agreement.'

It is necessary, therefore, to examine the doctrine closely to determine the nature of secret trusts.

5.1.1. The Three Requirements

In every decided case which has enforced a secret trust, three elements always arise on the facts: A's intention to create the trust, communication of that intention to B, and acceptance by B expressly or by acquiescence of the arrangement. The fact that these elements are present is not a matter of coincidence; they are *requirements* in the true sense of the word.[9] Thus, the success of secret trust cases hinges on whether these elements can be established.[10] In relation to the elements of communication and acceptance, English courts have developed specific rules which dictate that, in fully secret trust cases, communication must be made during A's lifetime;[11] while in half-secret trust cases, communication and acceptance must occur before or contemporaneously with the making of the will.[12] This difference is, however, 'simply the result of policy decisions, and does not affect the principle that underlies the enforcement of secret trusts'.[13]

[6] *Cullen v A-G for Ireland* (1866) LR 1 HL 190 (HL) 198; *Blackwell v Blackwell* (n 4) 339 (Viscount Sumner), 342 (Lord Warrington); *Re Young* [1951] Ch 344 (Ch) 350; *Re Snowden (deceased)* [1979] Ch 528 (Ch) 535.

For a view that the '*dehors* the will' theory does not provide a true justification, see JE Penner, *The Law of Trusts*, Core Text Series, 10th edn (Oxford, OUP, 2016) [6.62].

[7] See, eg, Jamie Glister and James Lee, *Hanbury and Martin: Modern Equity*, 20th edn (London, Sweet & Maxwell, 2015) [6-038].

[8] Robert Burgess, 'The Juridical Nature of Secret Trusts' (1972) 23 *Northern Ireland Legal Quarterly* 263, 268.

[9] See, eg, *Blackwell v Blackwell* (n 4) 334; *Ottaway v Norman* [1972] Ch 698 (Ch) 711; *Kasperbauer v Griffith* [2000] 1 WTLR 333 (CA) 343; *Chinn v Hanrieder* [2009] BCSC 635.

A differently enunciated but essentially similar set of requirements can be found in *Wallgrave v Tebbs* (n 4) 2 K & J 321, 69 ER 804, the requirements being that of B's knowledge, A's intention, a promise by B to carry out A's intention, and reliance by A in leaving his property to B.

[10] See, eg, *Re Keen* [1937] Ch 236 (CA); *Re Colin Cooper* [1939] Ch 811 (CA) 815.

[11] *Moss v Cooper* (1861) 1 J & H 352, 36–66; 70 ER 782, 788; *Re Boyes* [1884] LR 26 Ch D 531 (Ch) 536.

[12] *Johnson v Ball* (1851) 5 De G & Sm 85, 64 ER 1029; *Re Hetley* [1902] 2 Ch 866 (Ch); *Re Keen* (n 10); *Re Bateman's Will Trusts* [1970] 1 WLR 1463 (Ch); *Re Freud (deceased)* [2014] EWHC 2577 (Ch), [2014] WTLR 1453 [16]. *cf* the position in Ireland (*Re Browne* [1944] Ir R 90); Australia (*Ledgerwood v Perpetual Trustee Co Ltd* (1997) 41 NSWLR 523); and most American jurisdictions (*Restatement of Trusts* [55(c)(h)]).

[13] See GW Allan, 'The Secret is Out There: Searching for the Legal Justification for the Doctrine of Secret Trusts through Analysis of the Case Law' (2011) 40 *Common Law World Review* 311, 330.

These three requirements distinguish secret trusts from express trusts. A may unilaterally create an express trust even if there has been no communication to and acceptance by B.[14] In contrast, secret trusts invariably require B's consent for the informal agreement to be enforced. As Robert Walker LJ noted in *Gillett v Holt*,[15] an enforceable secret trust arrangement requires 'an agreement between A and B as to conferring a benefit on C because it is the agreement … which would make it unconscionable for B to resile from his agreement.' Fleming also expresses a similar view:[16] 'It is not the unilaterally expressed intention of [A], but the conduct of [B] in inducing the former … to make or revoke his will, which calls the equitable doctrine into operation.' This point is discernible from *Addlington v Cann*,[17] where Lord Hardwicke LC was faced with a case where A's secret intention was expressed in a piece of paper which was only discovered in his closet after his death. His Lordship held that, unless B had induced A to give the property to him, there was not valid trust.[18] Clearly, communication and acceptance were required, since the secret trust could not arise in response to A's unilateral intention.

A point which will be observed below[19] is that some commentators have cited a passage in the judgment in *Wallgrave v Tebbs*[20] for the view that secret trusts are clearly express in nature. That passage in *Wallgrave* was, however, inspired by two cases, one of which was *Addlington*.[21] In view of what was actually decided in *Addlington*, it is difficult to accept the conclusion advanced by those commentators, since express trusts, unlike secret trusts, do not fail for want of communication and acceptance.

An alternative view suggests that the three requirements are merely coincidences, and not in fact *requirements* at all. On this view, to insist on the three elements would be to assume 'a new basis for the enforcement of testamentary dispositions which is wholly inconsistent with the Wills Act, and suggests that a testator could "contract out of" the Wills Act, and create testamentary dispositions by a different method.'[22] This view must be rejected. Simply because the enforcement of secret trusts may appear to give effect to an arrangement which would not otherwise be binding due to a lack of compliance with the Wills Act does not necessarily give rise to any inconsistency. Since the underlying rationale of secret trusts is different from that which underlies the formality requirements in the Wills Act, there is no reason why apparently mutually inconsistent outcomes cannot properly be rationalised and justified. As will be seen below,[23] the fact that the three requirements are necessary for the enforcement of secret trusts indicates that they are enforced as constructive trusts, and that they give effect to the 'norm against taking an advantage'.

[14] *Fletcher v Fletcher* (1844) 4 Hare 67, 67 ER 564; *Mallott v Wilson* [1903] 2 Ch 494 (Ch).

[15] *Gillett v Holt* [2001] Ch 210 (CA) 228.

[16] JG Fleming, 'Secret Trusts' (1947) 12 *Conveyancer and Property Lawyer (New Series)* 28, 29.

[17] *Addlington v Cann* (1744) 3 Atk 141, 26 ER 885.

[18] ibid 3 Atk 151–52, 26 ER 890.

[19] See discussion in the main text following n 83 below.

[20] 'Where a person, knowing that a testator in making a disposition in his favor intends it to be applied for purposes other than his own benefit, either expressly promises, or by silence implies, that he will carry the testator's intention into effect, and the property is left to him upon the faith of that promise or undertaking, it is in effect a case of trust; and, in such a case, the Court will not allow the devisee to set up the Statute of Frauds, or rather the Statute of Wills, by which the Statute of Frauds is now, in this respect, superseded …': *Wallgrave v Tebbs* (n 4) 2 K & J 321, 69 ER 804.

[21] The other being *Muckleston v Brown* (1801) 6 Ves Jun 52, 31 ER 934.

[22] Jill E Martin, *Hanbury and Martin: Modern Equity*, 18th edn (London, Sweet & Maxwell, 2009) [5-013].

[23] See S 5.2.

5.1.2. Section 53(1)(b) of the Law of Property Act 1925

If secret trusts are constructive in nature, it follows that it is unnecessary for A to comply with any formality requirement. It might be thought that the case of *Sellack v Harris*[24] is authority for a contrary position. In that case, A left his real property to his eldest son (B) absolutely in his will, but on A's death-bed A orally informed B that he intended to give the property to his second son (C). B agreed to carry out A's wishes. Lord Keeper Wright and Sir John Trevor MR held that B was free to take A's property absolutely 'because by the Statute of Frauds there ought to have been a Declaration of the Use or Trust in Writing.'[25] The relevant provision these judges had in mind was the Statute of Frauds 1677, s 7 which, in its modernised form as the Law of Property Act 1925, s 53(1)(b) requires a declaration of trust concerning land to be 'manifested and proved' by some signed writing. If secret trusts require compliance with this formality requirement to be enforceable, then it might be argued that secret trusts are express in nature, since express—and not constructive—trusts require a *proper* manifestation of intention by the settlor to be enforceable.[26]

In *Sellack*, however, Cowper LC took a different view and held that B would be perpetrating a 'fraud' if he were allowed to keep the property; thus his Lordship considered that the statute was of no application and no formality requirements stood in the way of C's case.[27] The brevity of the report obscures the precise reasons for the divergence of view between the judges. Nevertheless, Cowper LC's approach has been consistently followed in later cases, with s 53(1)(b) proving to be no bar to the enforcement of secret trusts. Thus, both fully and half-secret trusts have been enforced where trusts over land have been orally declared by A,[28] and where the communication between A and B does not comply with the formality requirement.[29]

Given the strong line of cases post-*Sellack*, one might have thought that the inevitable conclusion is that secret trusts are constructive in nature. As Burgess notes, '[e]xpress trusts require formalities and the essence of a secret trust is … that it operates in spite of the rules as to form.'[30] However, some commentators take a different view, relying on one of two arguments. The first is that case law does not in fact indicate that the formality requirement is dispensed with: s 53(1)(b) remains relevant in secret trust cases. The second is that the courts' non-insistence on the formality requirement proves that secret trusts are express in nature, since s 53(1)(b) is 'disapplied', leading to the enforcement of the underlying oral express trust. These points require examination.

[24] *Sellack v Harris* (1708) 5 Vin Abr 512.

[25] ibid [31].

[26] This point was made in Chapter 1, S 1.2.1.

[27] *Sellack v Harris* (n 24) [31].

[28] In relation to fully secret trusts, see: *Stickland v Aldridge* (1804) 9 Ves 516, 32 ER 703; *Jones v Badley* (n 4); *McCormick v Grogan* (n 3); *Ottaway v Norman* (n 9). In relation to half-secret trusts, see: *Muckleston v Brown* (1801) (n 21); *Re Spencer's Will* (1887) 57 LT 519 (CA).

[29] In relation to fully secret trusts, see: *Wallgrave v Tebbs* (n 4); *Tee v Ferris* (1856) 2 K & J 357, 69 ER 819. In relation to half-secret trusts, see: *Re Fleetwood* (n 4).

[30] Burgess, 'Secret Trusts' (n 8) 269. See also Ben McFarlane and Charles Mitchell, *Hayton and Mitchell: Text, Cases and Materials on the Law of Trusts and Equitable Remedies*, 14th edn (London, Sweet & Maxwell, 2015) [3-161]; David Hayton, Paul Matthews and Charles Mitchell, *Underhill and Hayton: Law Relating to Trusts and Trustees*, 19th edn (London, LexisNexis Butterworths, 2016) [12.81].

5.1.2.1. *Section 53(1)(b) Remains Relevant?*

The argument that the cases do not actually dispense with the need to comply with s 53(1)(b) is based on three authorities, each representing a subtly different rationale. The first is *Re Baillie*,[31] which is taken as authority for the view that half-secret trusts of land must be put in writing to be enforceable.[32] The second is *Cullen v A-G for Ireland*,[33] where Lord Westbury held that 'the title of the party claiming under the secret trust … is a title *dehors* the will, and which cannot be correctly termed testamentary.' Thirdly, *North v Loomes*[34] is used to explain that '[t]he absence of evidentiary writing must be specifically pleaded; if it is not so pleaded, then the absence of the writing will not be a bar to the success of the action.'[35]

5.1.2.1.1. *Re Baillie*

In *Re Baillie*,[36] A gave all his property to his executrix, B, 'upon trust to carry out my verbal wishes'. Before executing the will, he orally said to B: 'if [my relatives] are destitute or if you want you can help them; and if [they] are not going to school you must see that they go to school'.[37] He also intimated that the money would all be B's otherwise. North J held that B received the property on trust as stated in A's will, but felt that he was unable to give effect to A's verbal wishes.[38] Therefore, a resulting trust arose in favour of A's heir-at-law and next-of-kin.

It has been claimed that *Re Baillie* is 'direct authority'[39] that half-secret trusts concerning land require compliance with s 53(1)(b). As Anthony Oakley observes,[40] '[m]ost commentators, on the strength of *Re Baillie* … seem to accept that half-secret trusts are express trusts.'[41] This case is typically distinguished from the fully secret trust case of *Ottoway v Norman*,[42] where 'it was assumed without argument … that a fully secret trust of land need not satisfy s 53(1)(b), presumably because fully secret trusts are clearly constructive trusts imposed to prevent the legatee-trustee taking beneficially.'[43]

Upon closer inspection, however, these views give disproportionate weight to *Re Baillie*, which is 'at best … weak authority for the proposition in support of which it is so often cited.'[44] One problem is that the only report of the case is found in the Times Law Reports in

[31] *Re Baillie* [1886] 2 TLR 660 (Ch).

[32] *Hanbury and Martin* (n 7) [6-038].

[33] *Cullen v A-G for Ireland* (n 6) 198.

[34] *North v Loomes* [1919] 1 Ch 378 (Ch).

[35] AJ Oakley, *Parker and Mellows: The Modern Law of Trusts*, 9th edn (London, Sweet & Maxwell, 2008) [4-104].

[36] *Re Baillie* (n 31) 660.

[37] ibid.

[38] ibid 661.

[39] David Wilde, 'Secret and Semi-Secret Trusts: Justifying the Distinctions between the Two' [1995] *Conveyancer and Property Lawyer* 366, 376. See also Burgess, 'Secret Trusts' (n 8) 271.

[40] His opinions are expressed in substantially similar form in both AJ Oakley, *Constructive Trusts*, 3rd edn (London, Sweet & Maxwell, 1997) 260–63; and *Parker and Mellows* (n 35) [4-103]–[4-107]. For the sake of convenience, the discussion will refer to paragraphs in the latter work unless otherwise required.

[41] *Parker and Mellows* (n 35) [4-105]. The same observation is also made by Burgess, 'Secret Trusts' (n 8) 270. See also *Brown v Pourau* [1995] 1 NZLR 352, 368.

[42] *Ottaway v Norman* (n 9).

[43] *Underhill and Hayton* (n 30) [12.98]. See also *Hanbury and Martin* (n 7) [6-038]; *Parker and Mellows* (n 35) [4-104]; Penner, *The Law of Trusts* (n 6) [6.64]. Sheridan also suggests that fully secret trusts are constructive in nature, whereas half-secret trusts are express trusts: LA Sheridan, 'English and Irish Secret Trusts' (1951) 67 *LQR* 314.

[44] Burgess, 'Secret Trusts' (n 8) 271.

non-verbatim form. From the report, North J appears to have dealt with the formality point simply as an afterthought.[45] Indeed, upon closer inspection, the formality issue could not have formed the *ratio* of the decision. Although the phrase 'upon trust' was used in A's will, his instructions to B were at best precatory and at worst ambiguous. At one point, A had even said to B: 'You have it all in your own hands; you can do as you like'.[46] It can hardly be said that A had the necessary intention to create a secret trust for C, A's relatives. Had B not been identified as taking as trustee on the face of A's will, there is no doubt that B would have been entitled to take A's property absolutely. This would reflect the principle, expressed in *Re Foord*,[47] that 'the Court is prepared to hold that there is a beneficial gift to the first taker on slight expressions and indications of intention.' Given, however, that the property was given to B 'upon trust', the only plausible result was for B to hold the property under a resulting trust for A's heir-at-law and next-of-kin. The formality point was irrelevant to the outcome of the case.

The case of *Re Young*[48] illustrates the point. A husband, A, left all his real and personal property to his wife, B, 'for her lifetime only … it being a condition of this will that after the testator's death', she was to make a new will leaving his estate 'for the purposes she knows he desires it to be used for'.[49] The specific purposes and proportions were orally communicated to her before the execution of A's will, making this a secret trust case as opposed to a case of mutual wills[50] where such proportions will not have been communicated to B. The court held that the secret trust was effective[51] despite the lack of compliance with s 53(1)(b).

In a significant portion of the judgment, Danckwerts J referred to *Re Gardner*.[52] In *Re Gardner*, A left all her property to her husband, B, for his use and benefit during his life, 'knowing that he will carry out my wishes'.[53] Those wishes were that, upon his death, B was to divide A's property equally between certain beneficiaries.[54] These wishes were both expressed in a signed but unattested memorandum and communicated orally to B. Danckwerts J did not consider the trusts which arose in *Re Gardner* as express trusts, but said that they arose 'by operation of law.'[55] Indeed, if Danckwerts J had taken the view that secret trusts are express trusts, the arrangement in *Re Young* itself would not have been enforced, since the lack of compliance with s 53(1)(b) would have been a bar to the enforcement of the secret trust. These cases provide ample reason to doubt, and ultimately reject, *Re Baillie*.

5.1.2.1.2. *Cullen v A-G for Ireland*

Although the '*dehors* the will' theory is often attributed to *Blackwell v Blackwell*,[56] the theory had been referred to much earlier by Lord Westbury in *Cullen v A-G for Ireland*.[57] This theory suggests that secret trusts operate outside A's will, and therefore are not testamentary in nature. Hence, they are not governed by rules of probate but by the law of

[45] ibid.
[46] *Re Baillie* (n 31) 660.
[47] *Re Foord* [1922] 2 Ch 519 (Ch) 521–22.
[48] *Re Young* (n 6).
[49] ibid 345.
[50] The doctrine of mutual wills is discussed in Chapter 12.
[51] *Re Young* (n 6) 349.
[52] *Re Gardner* [1920] 2 Ch 523 (CA).
[53] ibid 527.
[54] ibid 528.
[55] *Re Young* (n 6) 349.
[56] *Blackwell v Blackwell* (n 4).
[57] *Cullen v A-G for Ireland* (n 6). See *Parker and Mellows* (n 35) [4-064].

trusts.[58] Therefore, the argument goes, the formality requirement in the Wills Act is of no application to secret trusts; however, compliance with the Law of Property Act 1925, s 53(1)(b) is required,[59] since that section governs the creation of inter vivos trusts.[60]

Reading the case in context, however, *Cullen* does not propound a general principle for the doctrine of secret trusts. The case was concerned with the applicability of the Irish Stamp Acts to a secret trust arrangement. The relevant legislation exempted from duty any legacy given 'by … will or testamentary instrument' for an exclusively charitable purpose. The House of Lords decided that the secret trust arrangement created by A for an exclusively charitable purpose was not exempted from the tax, since the charitable purpose was not revealed in A's will. As Patricia Critchley notes, this was in fact 'a decision relating to the true construction of tax statutes', and was aimed at preventing the abuse of an exemption from tax.[61] In particular, Lord Westbury was concerned with the meaning of the word 'testamentary' as it was used in the Stamp Acts when his Lordship said that 'the secret trust … cannot be correctly termed *testamentary*';[62] it was not meant to be a general statement of the law.

The fact that the decision in *Cullen* is context-specific is all the more clear from the fact that, not three years after deciding that case, Lord Westbury expressed the view in *McCormick v Grogan*[63] that secret trusts were an application of the principle that 'a statute may not be used as an instrument of fraud' in relation to the Wills Act. As we have noted earlier,[64] the 'fraud' theory provides an entirely different justification for secret trusts than the '*dehors* the will' theory. If in *Cullen* Lord Westbury had meant to propound a general principle applicable to all secret trusts, then his Lordship's later reasoning in *McCormick* would have been contradictory.

More generally, there is a crucial difference between saying that a secret trust arises 'outside the will' and that it arises 'outside the *Wills Act*'. As Critchley astutely observes, '[t]he *dehors* theory … fails … to demonstrate the truth of the latter and too often ends up resting merely upon the former'.[65] Thus, it is difficult to accept that the '*dehors* the will' theory provides a sound basis for justifying secret trusts at all. Instead, it merely provides a factual observation concerning the interrelationship between the secret trust arrangement and the content of A's will. It certainly does not justify the conclusion that s 53(1)(b) must be satisfied for a secret trust arrangement to be enforced.

5.1.2.1.3. *North v Loomes*

North v Loomes[66] is most notably relied on in *Parker and Mellows* and by Robert Pearce and Warren Barr[67] to explain away cases which have enforced orally declared secret trusts of

58 *Blackwell v Blackwell* (n 4) 339; *Parker and Mellows* (n 35) [4-063].

59 See, eg, Sheridan, 'English and Irish Secret Trusts' (n 43) 326; *Parker and Mellows* (n 35) [4-063].

60 The possibility of classifying secret trusts as inter vivos trusts is considered more generally in S 5.1.3.

61 Patricia Critchley, 'Instruments of Fraud, Testamentary Dispositions, and the Doctrine of Secret Trusts' (1999) 115 *LQR* 631, 641.

62 *Cullen v A-G for Ireland* (n 6) 198 (emphasis added).

63 *McCormick v Grogan* (n 3) 97.

64 See S 5.1.

65 Critchley, 'Instruments of Fraud' (n 61) 640.

66 *North v Loomes* (n 34).

67 The argument in *Parker and Mellows* is made at various points: see *Parker and Mellows* (n 35) [4-063]–[4-077], [4-103]–[4-107]. Pearce and Barr run the argument in a single paragraph: Robert Pearce and Warren Barr, *The Law of Trusts and Equitable Obligations*, 6th edn (Oxford, OUP, 2015) 510.

land. It is taken to establish the principle that, '[o]f itself the enforcement of the trusts in such cases fails to prove the point, since a trust will not fail for lack of formalities unless the absence of writing is specifically pleaded as a ground of invalidity.'[68]

It is highly doubtful whether the principle in *North* applies in the context of s 53(1)(b) at all, since that case was specifically concerned with the Statute of Frauds 1677, s 4, which has now been repealed.[69] But even assuming that it does, the principle in *North* is unlikely to provide a sufficient explanation of the cases. One would have expected that, if the enforcement of orally declared secret trusts of land were indeed due to a defective pleading on the part of claimants, this point would have been made explicitly clear in the judgments; otherwise, the courts' silence would tantamount to ignoring the statute without reason. The fact that the principle in *North* is not cited in any of the relevant decisions can only reasonably be taken to indicate that that principle does not explain the cases.

The artificiality of the reliance placed on *North v Loomes* is further demonstrated by exploring what would happen in the event that the lack of writing were pleaded. According to Pearce and Barr, an orally declared secret trust should not fail; instead, '[t]he court should invoke the well established doctrine of *Rochefoucauld v Boustead* ... to prevent [B] denying the trust because of the absence of writing.'[70] They deny that to do so would revert to the 'fraud' theory, since the *Rochefoucauld* doctrine 'would only be employed to prevent the use of s 53(1)(b) ... as an instrument of fraud.'[71] The view in *Parker and Mellows* is more sophisticated. Where the lack of writing is specifically pleaded in half-secret trust cases, it suggests that the authority of *Re Baillie* is decisive.[72] In relation to fully secret trusts, it distinguishes between two scenarios. On the one hand, where B 'rais[es] the absence of the necessary writing as the basis of a claim to take the property beneficially', such 'clearly unconscionable conduct ... would inevitably lead to the imposition of a constructive trust on a quite different ground, namely the principle enunciated in *Bannister v Bannister*.'[73] On the other hand, where B 'admits that he is holding the property [as trustee] ... but cannot point to the writing required by s 53(1)', he 'will find himself confronted by opposing claims from [C] ... and the testator's residuary beneficiary or his statutory next of kin.'[74] In the latter situation, the fraud maxim will not assist him, and the result will depend on 'whether fully secret trusts are constructive trusts ... or express trusts', a decision which 'await[s] definitive resolution by the courts.'[75]

[68] Pearce and Barr, *The Law of Trusts* (n 67) 510.

[69] Oakley nevertheless suggests that s 53(1)(b) is similar to that section as it 'requires only evidentiary writing and is generally thought to be governed by the same principles': *Parker and Mellows* (n 35) [4-104] fn 201, although no further authority is cited.

[70] Pearce and Barr, *The Law of Trusts* (n 67) 510.

[71] ibid.

[72] *Parker and Mellows* (n 35) [4-105]–[4-106].

[73] ibid [4-106]. His cross-reference to an earlier discussion in his work of 'the principle enunciated in *Bannister v Bannister*' (see ibid [4-049]) indicates that this merely refers to the imposition of a constructive trust where the maxim 'equity will not allow a statute to be used as an instrument of fraud' applies—ie an application of the doctrine in *Rochefoucauld v Boustead*.

[74] *Parker and Mellows* (n 35) [4-106].

[75] ibid.

These explanations are untenable. The view proposed by Pearce and Barr in fact concedes that secret trusts are constructive in nature, since, as we have seen in Chapter 4,[76] the doctrine in *Rochefoucauld v Bosutead* leads to the imposition of constructive trusts. Furthermore, it is difficult to see what the distinction is between the 'fraud' theory of secret trusts and the doctrine in *Rochefoucauld v Boustead.* Proponents of the 'fraud' theory have argued that, using the 'instrument of fraud' maxim, 'the Court of Equity has dealt with the Statute of Frauds, and in this manner, also, it deals with the Statute of Wills.'[77] It is also difficult to see why the nature of secret trusts should hinge on what B pleads. Surely the nature of the trust is determined by events which occur up to the time when A's will takes effect and no later.

The suggestion in *Parker and Mellows* is likewise unworkable, given that it endows B with too much control over the ultimate destination of A's property. As Mark Thompson notes, such a suggestion entails that:[78]

> [T]he enforceability of a secret trust concerning land would depend on the integrity of [B]. If he claimed the property beneficially, he would be accounted fraudulent and parol testimony could be admitted, with the result that the trust would be enforced. If he did not make such a claim to the property, there would be no fraud and, consequently, the land would be held for those entitled on intestacy [or the next-of-kin]. The resolution of the competing claims of [C] and the residuary legatees would then depend on a factor outside their control, namely, the probity of [B].

Ultimately, the principle in *North v Loomes* does not lend weight to the argument that secret trusts are express in nature, or that they require compliance with s 53(1)(b) to be enforceable.

5.1.2.2. *Section 53(1)(b) is Disapplied?*

The second argument claims that the courts' non-insistence on s 53(1)(b) proves that secret trusts are express in nature. On this view, when the 'instrument of fraud' maxim is invoked, s 53(1)(b) 'simply [does] not apply … [a]nd with the statutory requirement of writing now removed, no objection could be raised to the validity of the express trust created by the parties.'[79] The main proponent of the 'disapplication thesis' is William Swadling, who makes the case for this view in different works.[80] This thesis is not confined to s 53(1)(b), but is also meant to explain secret trusts in general. Thus, Swadling argues that secret trusts are express in nature because there is no distinction between the courts' approach to s 9 of the Wills Act 1837 and to s 53(1)(b).[81]

[76] See Chapter 4, S 4.1.3.

[77] *McCormick v Grogan* (n 3) 97.

[78] MP Thompson, 'Using Statutes as Instruments of Fraud' (1985) 36 *Northern Ireland Legal Quarterly* 358, 369.

[79] William Swadling, 'The Proprietary Effect of a Hire of Goods' in Norman Palmer and Ewan McKendrick (eds), *Interests in Goods*, 2nd edn (London, LLP, 1998) 512.

[80] Swadling, 'Hire of Goods' (ibid); William Swadling, 'A Hard Look at *Hodgson v Marks*' in Peter Birks and Francis Rose (eds), *Restitution and Equity (Vol 1): Resulting Trusts and Equitable Compensation* (London, LLP, 2000); William Swadling, 'The Nature of the Trust in *Rochefoucauld v Boustead*' in Mitchell, *Constructive and Resulting Trusts* (n 2).

[81] William Swadling, 'The Fiction of the Constructive Trust' (2011) 64 *Current Legal Problems* 399, 417–18.

In Chapter 4,[82] we explored the difficulties presented by the 'disapplication thesis' in the context of the doctrine in *Rochefoucauld v Boustead*. We noted that it fails to explain what 'fraud' means and leads to uncertainty in determining the parties' legal positions. The same criticisms apply to the secret trusts context.

There are three nineteenth-century cases which might appear to lend support to Swadling's theory.[83] In *Wallgrave v Tebbs*, Page Wood V-C in describing a secret trust spoke about how 'the Court will not allow the devisee to set up the Statute of Frauds' and described the Statute as being '*superseded*'.[84] This was approved by Lord Cairns LC in *Jones v Badley*.[85] In *McCormick v Grogan*, Lord Hatherley (as Page Wood V-C had then become) also spoke of 'the jurisdiction of the Courts of Equity to *interpose* in all cases of fraud'; and that a fraudulent secret trustee 'shall have fastened upon his conscience the trust of carrying into full effect' A's instructions.[86] It might be thought that these statements support Swadling's thesis that the Law of Property Act 1925, s 53(1)(b) and the Wills Act 1837, s 9 are 'disapplied' in the face of 'fraud', leading to the direct enforcement of the oral express trust.

Upon closer inspection, however, these cases are inconclusive as to the nature of secret trusts. How do the courts 'supersede' the statutes? How do they admit the oral evidence excluded by the statutes? By what means is the trust fastened on B's conscience? These crucial questions are not addressed in the cases. They yield two potential answers. The first is that the courts are enforcing express trusts by disapplying the statutes; the second is that they are enforcing constructive trusts, and therefore compliance with any formality requirement is unnecessary. The latter analysis is to be preferred, since the imposition of a constructive trust 'avoids the embarrassment of Equity refusing to implement a statute.'[87]

5.1.3. Secret Trusts: Inter Vivos Trusts?

It has been observed that express trusts respond to A's *properly* manifested intention. This means that for an express trust to be enforceable, any relevant formality requirement must first be complied with.[88] The creation of an enforceable testamentary express trust therefore requires the incorporation of the terms of the trust in a validly created will which complies with the Wills Act. In secret trusts cases, there is a complete or partial absence of the material terms of the trust in A's will: in particular, it does not reveal the intended beneficiaries of the arrangement. For this reason, secret trusts are not enforced as express testamentary trusts. For secret trusts to be analysed as express in nature, it seems to follow that they can only be inter vivos express trusts.[89]

[82] See Chapter 4, S 4.4.1.

[83] Noted in *Underhill and Hayton* (n 30) [12.81].

[84] *Wallgrave v Tebbs* (n 4) 2 K & J 321, 69 ER 804 (emphasis added).

[85] *Jones v Badley* (n 4) 364.

[86] *McCormick v Grogan* (n 3) 88–89 (emphasis added).

[87] David Hayton, Paul Matthews and Charles Mitchell, *Underhill and Hayton: Law of Trusts and Trustees*, 18th edn (London, LexisNexis Butterworths, 2010) [12.77]. As noted in *Midland Bank Trust Co Ltd v Green* [1981] AC 513 (HL) 531, 'it is not "fraud" to rely on legal rights conferred by Act of Parliament'. See also Burgess, 'Secret Trusts' (n 8) 269.

[88] See Chapter 1, S 1.2.1.

[89] It might be argued that half-secret trusts are express *testamentary* trusts which are expressly declared in A's will and which takes effect upon his death. However, there are significant differences between words in a will indicating the mere *existence* of a trust, and *creating* an express trust. Indeed, half-secret trusts are 'secret' precisely because the words used in A's will are insufficient to create a testamentary trust on their own due to, among other things, a lack of certainty of objects.

As we have seen above,[90] one of the difficulties with this analysis is that compliance with the Law of Property Act 1925, s 53(1)(b) is not necessary for secret trusts to be enforced, although it is a requirement for arrangements relating to land to be enforceable as inter vivos express trusts. However, this does not rule out the possibility that secret trusts arrangements which do not involve land can be analysed as express inter vivos trusts.

5.1.3.1. Re Gardner (No. 2)

The case of *Re Gardner (No. 2)*[91] appears to give credence to this analysis. A fully secret trust was set up by A for the equal distribution of all her property to three beneficiaries.[92] One of the beneficiaries, C, died in A's lifetime, and the fate of C's share of the trusts fell to be determined. Romer J saw no ground for distinguishing secret trusts from an outright inter vivos express trust. He thought that both cases equally reflected the principle that 'if the owner of property makes a gift of it on faith of a promise by the donee that he will deal with the property in a particular way, an obligation to deal with it is placed upon the donee'.[93] Thus, he held that a one-third share was to be paid to C's personal representative.[94] This result suggests that C had obtained an interest in the property during A's lifetime; only then can it be said that his estate was entitled to the one-third share of A's property.

Romer J's decision has been universally disapproved.[95] Orthodoxy suggests that inter vivos express trusts require constitution during A's lifetime, or else A must have at least done everything that is necessary on A's part to constitute the trust.[96] In the case of secret trusts, constitution occurs only upon A's death: A's will must first take effect for a secret trust arrangement to be enforced;[97] and there have been explicit judicial statements recognising the fact that secret trusts only arise upon A's death.[98] Hence, in *Re Gardner (No. 2)*, A's property would not have been constituted before her death, and it was impossible for a secret trust to have arisen during A's lifetime.

Another implication of *Re Gardner (No. 2)* is that A may not revoke a secret trust arrangement during his lifetime. As William Holdsworth contends, an inter vivos trust is created once B accepts the trust obligation,[99] and since a settlor drops out of the picture once an inter vivos express trust has been properly set up, A may not change his mind.[100] However, this

[90] See S 5.1.2.1.
[91] *Re Gardner (No. 2)* [1923] 2 Ch 230 (Ch).
[92] ibid.
[93] ibid 233.
[94] ibid 235.
[95] For a summary of criticisms expressed before the turn of the 21st century, see Diana Kincaid, 'The Tangled Web: The Relationship between a Secret Trust and the Will' [2000] *Conveyancer and Property Lawyer* 420, 431 fn 94. More recent works that have criticised the decision include: *Parker and Mellows* (n 35) [4-073]; *Hanbury and Martin* (n 7) [6-037]; Pearce and Barr, *The Law of Trusts* (n 67) 508; Penner, *The Law of Trusts* (n 6) [6.65]; *Hayton and Mitchell* (n 30) [3-154]; *Underhill and Hayton* (n 30) [12.104].
[96] *Re Rose (deceased)* [1952] Ch 499 (CA). The rule in *Re Rose* is discussed in Chapter 9.
[97] *Blackwell v Blackwell* (n 4) 334. This approach ensures that the primary of the Wills Act is recognised: see *McCormick v Grogan* (n 3) 89.
[98] See, eg, *Re Young* (n 6) 348; *Kasperbauer v Griffith* (n 9) 343.
[99] WS Holdsworth, 'Secret Trusts' (1937) 53 *LQR* 501. Holdsworth's view is also noted in Bryn Perrins, 'Can You Keep Half a Secret?' (1972) 88 *LQR* 235, 249 and Sheridan, 'English and Irish Secret Trusts' (n 43) 325. See also Ben McFarlane, 'Constructive Trusts Arising on a Receipt of Property *Sub Conditione*' (2004) 120 *LQR* 667, 677.
[100] *Paul v Paul* (1882) 20 Ch D 742 (CA); *Mallott v Wilson* (n 14); *Underhill and Hayton* (n 30) [1.23](d).

is plainly wrong.[101] Since a will is ambulatory and revocable, A may revoke his will, in which case the secret trust will not take effect for lack of constitution.[102] It is also possible for A to revoke the secret trust arrangement without revoking his will.[103] As the Court of Appeal observed in *Kasperbauer v Griffith*,[104] 'the person who makes arrangements which will create a secret trust is able to change his mind and alter his intentions so as to create no trust'. A's ability to revoke the arrangement during his lifetime is manifestly inconsistent with an analysis of secret trusts as an express inter vivos trust.

5.1.3.2. An 'Anticipatory' Inter Vivos Trust?

Pearce and Barr offer an alternative explanation. They suggest that the modern *dehors* the will theory 'postulates two distinguishable stages in the creation of a valid secret trust'.[105] At the first stage where communication and acceptance arises, no trust comes into existence: the property remains A's, and the trust is incompletely constituted.[106] The second stage takes effect when A dies: B's receipt of the property under A's will constitutes the trust.[107] On this view, the trust declared by A is an 'anticipatory'[108] inter vivos express trust.

This analysis is unsustainable. As Simon Gardner notes, the technical sense of the term 'declaration' entails the *creation* of a trust, and in this sense there is no declaration of any trust at all at the first stage.[109] A related issue is that A is unable to declare an express trust at the first stage, since the subject-matter of the trust at that stage would merely be future property.[110] Since there is nothing which amounts to a contract for valuable consideration, A's declaration would be void for uncertainty.[111] Moreover, the simultaneous occurrence of A's death and the coming into effect of his will renders it impossible for A to make a further declaration of his intention when the property vests in B[112] in order to give effect to the trust over future property.

5.1.3.3. B as Settlor?

Another alternative might be to analyse B as the settlor of a secret trust. Since B must be alive at A's death for a secret trust to come into existence it might be argued that B properly

[101] See Burgess, 'Secret Trusts' (n 8) 273; Kincaid, 'The Tangled Web' (n 95) 425–28; Mark Pawlowski and James Brown, 'Constituting a Secret Trust by Estoppel' [2004] *Conveyancer and Property Lawyer* 388, 390–91; Critchley, 'Instruments of Fraud' (n 61) 639–40.

[102] See Kincaid, 'The Tangled Web' (n 95) 426.

[103] *Guest v Webb* [1965] VR 427.

[104] *Kasperbauer v Griffith* (n 9) 346.

[105] Pearce and Barr, *The Law of Trusts* (n 67) 506.

[106] ibid.

[107] ibid.

[108] Fleming, 'Secret Trusts' (n 16) 32, borrowing words from HG Hanbury, *Modern Equity: The Principles of Equity*, 4th edn (London, Stevens & Sons Ltd, 1946) 143 n 50.

[109] Simon Gardner, *An Introduction to the Law of Trusts*, Clarendon Law Series, 3rd edn (Oxford, OUP, 2011) 94–95.

[110] *Re Ellenborough* [1903] 1 Ch 697 (Ch); *Brennan v Morphett* (1908) 6 CLR 22; *Re Northcliffe* [1925] Ch 651 (Ch); *Williams v IRC* [1965] NZLR 395. The future property doctrine is discussed in Chapter 8.

[111] See Chapter 8, S 8.2.

[112] David R Hodge, 'Secret Trusts: the Fraud Theory Revisited' [1980] *Conveyancer and Property Lawyer* 341, 347; noted in Critchley, 'Instruments of Fraud' (n 61) 634.

declares an inter vivos express trust at that point. In *Re Gardner (No.2)*,[113] Romer J thought that the parties to a secret trust arrangement were in 'exactly the same [position] as though [B], after the memorandum had been communicated to him … had executed a declaration of trust binding himself to hold any property that should come to him … upon trust as specified in the memorandum.'

This explanation does not withstand scrutiny. In the first place, it relies on a fiction—that B made a declaration of trust. Moreover, since B may consent through silence to carrying out a secret trust arrangement,[114] sufficiently clear evidence may not be available to establish that B had declared an express trust.[115] In addition, B's consent to act as trustee cannot itself be analysed as the relevant declaration of trust, since the subject-matter of B's declaration would be future property, making the purported trust void for uncertainty. It is also highly unlikely for B to have made a further manifestation of intention at all when he receives the property.[116] Finally, Romer J's view does not explain why the law would compel B to carry out the terms of the secret trust where he has secretly intended to take the property for himself all along, since in this case B cannot in reality or in theory be said to have declared a trust at all.

5.1.4. Further Distinctions

There are three further distinctions between express trusts and secret trusts which indicate that secret trusts are not express in nature.[117]

First, the maxim 'equity will not permit a trust to fail for want of a trustee' which applies to express trusts does not apply to secret trusts.[118] Thus, 'if [B] renounces and disclaims, or dies in the lifetime of [A], [C] can take nothing against the heir-at-law or next-of-kin or residuary devisee or legatee'.[119] The reason for this is that acceptance by B of the trust obligation is an essential requirement for a secret trust arrangement to become binding, the acceptance of which must remain operative when the property is constituted to B at A's death.

It has been suggested that a different result applies to half-secret trusts, where B's predecease will not affect the trust.[120] However, this is disputable, since the point has never been definitively considered by the courts. Moreover, the cases which are usually cited for the conclusion[121]—*Re Smirthwaite's Trusts*,[122] *Sonley v Clock Makers' Company*,[123] *Mallott v Wilson*,[124] and *Re Armitage*[125]—do not concern secret trusts at all, but were cases involving *express* testamentary trusts, since the terms of the trusts were fully disclosed in the will.

113 *Re Gardner (No. 2)* (n 91) 233.
114 *Moss v Cooper* (n 11).
115 Hodge (n 112) 347.
116 ibid.
117 These are discussed generally in Burgess, 'Secret Trusts' (n 8) 269.
118 See, eg, *Re Willis* [1921] 1 Ch 44 (CA); *Re Armitage* [1972] Ch 438 (Ch).
119 *Re Maddock* (n 4) 231.
120 *Parker and Mellows* (n 35) [4-071]; *Underhill and Hayton* (n 30) [12.110].
121 See, eg, *Parker and Mellows* (n 35) [4-071].
122 *Re Smirthwaite's Trusts* (1871) LR 11 Eq 251 (Ch).
123 *Sonley v Clock Makers' Company* (1780) 1 Bro CC 81, 28 ER 998.
124 *Mallott v Wilson* (n 14).
125 *Re Armitage* (n 118).

Secondly, where there are two or more trustees under an express trust, they always hold the legal title to the trust property as joint tenants.[126] In secret trust cases, however, secret trustees may take as tenants in common.[127]

Finally, under an express trust, a trustee can also be one of the beneficiaries under the trust; however, in *Re Rees*,[128] Evershed MR held that this was not possible in a secret trust arrangement.[129] It might be thought that, because in that case Bs were A's solicitors, Evershed MR's point was made in a specific context only, to prevent solicitors from unduly benefitting under a secret trust arrangement.[130] However, there is no public policy concern which prevents settlors from creating express trusts which also benefit their trustee-solicitors.

Given the numerous significant differences between the way in which courts enforce secret trusts and the characteristics of express trusts, it is impossible to escape the conclusion that secret trusts are constructive in nature. Besides having the support of the courts, both explicitly[131] and inexplicitly,[132] this analysis also allows secret trusts to be understood by way of the 'norm against taking an advantage'.

5.2. Rationale

The secret trust doctrine applies where B informally promises to hold property he will receive under A's will on trust for C, and A dies without substantially altering his will, thus allowing the property to be transferred to B, in reliance on B's promise. As a result of his promise, B takes only a qualified interest in the property upon A's death. In Chapter 4,[133] it was explained that doctrines which reflect such QI situations are underpinned by the 'norm against taking an advantage' which applies when a specific type of promise and reliance are present. The secret trust doctrine is also underpinned by this norm. This section establishes the relevance of promise and reliance in secret trusts cases.

5.2.1. Promise

When discussing secret trusts, it is common to speak of the doctrine giving effect to A's, rather than B's, intention. This is unsurprising: after all, it is A who initiates the arrangement in relation to his property. However, B's intention is equally crucial. For a secret trust

[126] Burgess, 'Secret Trusts' (n 8) 269. See also Trustee Act 1925, s 18.
[127] *Re Stead* [1900] 1 Ch 237 (Ch). See also *Tee v Ferris* (n 29).
[128] *Re Rees* [1950] Ch 204 (CA).
[129] Burgess, 'Secret Trusts' (n 8) 269.
[130] See too *Re Freud (deceased)* (n 12) [56].
[131] *Re Cleaver (deceased)* [1981] 1 WLR 939 (Ch) 1024; *Paragon Finance plc v DB Thakerar & Co* [1999] 1 All ER 400 (CA) 409; *Kasperbauer v Griffith* (n 9) 342; *De Bruyne v De Bruyne* [2010] EWCA Civ 519, [2010] 2 FLR 1240 [51].
[132] 'Without creating an express declaration of trust, the law, under the circumstances, implies an obligation of performing the wishes of the testator which the testator had relied upon their performing as the ground for giving the legacy': *Re Spencer's Will* (n 28) 521.
[133] See Chapter 4, S 4.3.4.

arrangement to be enforceable, there must be acceptance by B of the arrangement expressly or by acquiescence.[134] This not only indicates the need for B to have an intention to act as trustee, but also that B must make a pre-acquisition promise, expressly or impliedly, which qualifies his interest in the property he will acquire from A.

The fact that A and B share the same intention in relation to the planned arrangement follows naturally from the fact that secret trusts originate in a pre-acquisition *agreement* between those parties. However, in three situations, it is not suitable to describe the parties as having reached an *agreement* in the usual sense of the word; nevertheless, B can still be said to have made the requisite *promise* to carry out the arrangement.

First, B may respond to A's communication in the form of passive acquiescence or silence.[135] In such cases, since B has knowledge of A's wishes, his subsequent inaction amounts to the making of a promise: it '[encourages A] to bequeath the property in the faith that [A's] intentions will be carried out.'[136] Secondly, in fully secret trust cases, A may communicate his intention to create a secret trust arrangement to B *after* A's will is executed; and this might suggest that it suffices merely for A to *inform* B of A's intention. Even so, it remains necessary to find that B has expressly or impliedly promised to act as trustee during A's lifetime. Thus, acquiescence may amount to a promise; but if it is clear that B refuses to act as trustee, then the arrangement will be of no effect. Thirdly, in *Re Keen*[137] Lord Wright MR stated, obiter, that a secret trust can arise where the terms of the trust are contained in a sealed envelope, handed to B, which remains unopened until after A's death. It might be thought that there is no agreement between the parties in such a case. However, the fact remains that, by accepting the envelope, B promises to carry out A's wishes, *whatever they may be*. As Lord Wright MR explained,[138] '[B] had the means of knowledge available whenever it became necessary and proper to open the envelope.' This can be distinguished from cases where secret trusts are not enforced because the terms of the trust are not put in B's hands until after A's death.[139] In these latter group of cases, the requisite promise would not have been made, since there would have been no means to tell what, precisely, B was agreeing to do.

B's promise is adjudged objectively. Thus, it makes no difference if B harboured a secret, contrary intention while inducing A to leave the property to him, or if B has a change of heart after the property is left to him. Where B makes the relevant promise and A's reliance is complete upon A's death, a constructive trust arises to compel B to perform the entirety of his promise.

The importance of B's promise is fortified by the informal context of secret trusts. Because A does not put the intended trust in writing in line with the Wills Act 1837, s 9, the constructive trust cannot be analysed as giving effect to A's unilateral intention, for this would be to enforce the informal trust as an express trust, thus unjustifiably ignoring the statutory provision. However, because acceptance of the arrangement by B is a necessary

[134] The requirements for a secret trust are set out in S 5.1.1.

[135] See, eg, *Paine v Hall* (1812) 18 Ves 475, 34 ER 397; *Wallgrave v Tebbs* (n 4) 2 K & J 321, 69 ER 804; *Kasperbauer v Griffith* (n 9) 343.

[136] *Blackwell v Blackwell* (n 4) 334.

[137] *Re Keen* (n 10) 242–43.

[138] ibid.

[139] See, eg, *Addlington v Cann* (n 17); *Moss v Cooper* (n 11) 1 J & H 365–66, 70 ER 788.

requirement, secret trusts can be analysed instead as constructive trusts which give effect to B's promise to qualify the interest he obtains in the property left to him by A.

5.2.2. Reliance

In all secret trusts cases, B's promise induces A's reliance, since it is always clear that A would not have left his property to B if B had not agreed to carry out the trust. In the vast majority of cases, reliance occurs when A dies having created a will pursuant to the secret trust arrangement which leaves property to B; but it is also possible for A to rely by leaving his existing will unrevoked[140] or dying intestate,[141] with the result that A's property is transferred to B in reliance on B's promise.

5.2.2.1. A's Reliance, not A's Death

It is worth emphasising that secret trusts are triggered by A's reliance, not A's death. Certainly, the moment at which A's reliance become complete is sometimes precisely the moment of A's death. For instance, this would be so where A dies in a tragic car accident, since it is at that moment, and no earlier, that A can no longer make changes to his testamentary arrangements. However, it is also possible for A's reliance to be complete at a point in time prior to A's death. This may be so, for example, where A becomes incurably insane and remains so for a number of years until he dies,[142] or when A loses consciousness or the ability to communicate just before dying. When it becomes impracticable for A to make any further changes to his testamentary arrangements, A's reliance is complete, which irretrievably leads B to obtain an advantage in relation to the acquisition of A's property. Hence, a constructive trust arises upon A's death, binding B when he acquires the property.

One reason for emphasising that the crucial event is A's reliance not A's death is that commentators often cite A's death as that which justifies allowing C, a volunteer, to enforce the arrangement between A and B in the secret trusts context. This point is often made in connection with an argument that secret trusts and the doctrine in *Rochefoucauld v Boustead* are distinguishable on the basis that, because in the latter doctrine the arrangement is made inter vivos, a constructive trust should not arise in C's favour. In addition to the reasons given in Chapter 4,[143] the fact that secret trusts respond to A's reliance and not A's death gives yet another reason why it is misleading to think that a material distinction between secret trusts and the doctrine in *Rochefoucauld v Boustead* is the fact that the one operates in a testamentary context and the other in an inter vivos context. In both contexts the constructive trusts arise in response to the elements of promise and reliance.

5.2.2.2. Specific Rules

The crucial role of reliance is also reflected in the technical rules of the secret trusts doctrine. Take for instance the rules concerning the timing of communication. In fully secret

[140] *Tharp v Tharp* [1916] 2 Ch 205 (CA).

[141] *Sellack v Harris* (n 24).

[142] See Charles Mitchell, *Hayton and Mitchell: Commentary and Cases on the Law of Trusts and Equitable Remedies*, 13th edn (London, Sweet & Maxwell, 2010) [3-160].

[143] See Chapter 4, S 4.5.2.2.3.

trust cases, A must communicate and secure B's acceptance at any time before A's death.[144] This indicates the need for A to have *relied* on B's promise, since if B discovers A's intention only after A's death, A cannot be said to have left property to B *in reliance on B's promise.*

The corresponding rule in relation to half-secret trusts is not inconsistent with this rationale. In half-secret trusts cases, A's intention must be communicated and B's acceptance secured before or contemporaneously with the execution of A's will.[145] This rule can be seen simply as a product of the particular context in which the secret trusts doctrine operates. Because the testamentary transfer of property from A to B is necessarily effectuated by way of A's will, courts have held that the will must 'first [operate] according to its terms'[146] for a secret trust arrangement to take effect. Taking this a step further, courts have also indicated a desire not to allow the doctrine of secret trusts to detract from the general requirement that testamentary dispositions must generally comply with the Wills Act 1837, s 9. The half-secret trusts communication rule is a product of this desire: thus, it is said that '[A] cannot reserve to himself a power of making future unwitnessed dispositions by merely naming a trustee and leaving the purposes of the trust to be supplied afterwards'.[147] It is unlikely that this logic withstands scrutiny,[148] in particular in view of the fact that it is inherent in the enforcement of secret trust arrangements that courts are giving effect to dispositions which do not comply with s 9. Ultimately, however, this debate concerns the appropriate timing at which A must secure B's promise. It does not detract from the fact that it remains necessary for A to have *relied* on B's promise by leaving his will unchanged until his death.

Another technical rule is that if B disclaims or dies during A's lifetime, a secret trust will not come into existence.[149] It is clear that this rule operates only where A is aware of B's renunciation, disclaimer, or death and has the opportunity to alter his will.[150] This rule indicates the clear need for reliance, for if A is aware of B's renunciation, disclaimer, or death but does not do anything to alter his will, the subsequent transfer of A's property to B at A's death can no longer be said to constitute an act of reliance on B's promise to carry out the arrangement. Hence, a constructive trust would not arise.

[144] *Moss v Cooper* (n 11) 1 J & H 365–66, 70 ER 788; *Re Boyes* (n 11) 536.
[145] *Johnson v Ball* (n 12); *Re Hetley* (n 12); *Re Keen* (n 10); *Re Bateman's Will Trusts* (n 12).
[146] *Blackwell v Blackwell* (n 4) 334.
[147] ibid 339. See too *Johnson v Ball* (n 12) 5 De G & Sm 91, 64 ER 1032.
[148] See, eg, Holdsworth (n 99).
[149] *Re Maddock* (n 4) 231.
[150] This can be deduced from the fact that, if B attempts to renounce the legacy after A has died, he will not be permitted to do so: *Blackwell v Blackwell* (n 4) 328. The reason for this is that A will no longer have the opportunity to alter his will. See also Jamie Glister, 'Disclaimer and Secret Trusts' [2014] *Conveyancer and Property Lawyer* 11.

6

The Doctrine in *Pallant v Morgan*

The doctrine in *Pallant v Morgan*[1] is a relatively new constructive trust doctrine. Although the essence of the doctrine can be traced to the decision of Harman J in *Pallant v Morgan*,[2] it was not until the Court of Appeal's decision in *Banner Homes Group plc v Luff Developments Ltd*[3] that the doctrine in *Pallant v Morgan* was identified as a discrete doctrine giving rise to constructive trusts.[4]

In *Pallant v Morgan*,[5] A and B, via their agents, were potential bidders for a plot of land. The agents reached an agreement whereby A would refrain from bidding, and B would sell part of the land to A if he succeeded in purchasing it. Having submitted the winning bid, B attempted to take the entire land for himself. It later came to light that A's agent had authority to bid up to £2,000 and B's agent could have bid up to £3,000. As a result of A staying out of the bidding, B acquired the land for £1,000. Harman J held that B was trustee of the land for himself and A jointly, subject to A's repayment of B's outlay in relation to A's share.

In *Banner Homes*,[6] two companies, A and B, agreed to acquire and develop a site through a joint-venture company. B purchased the site through the joint-venture company and then sought to exclude A from the joint venture. It emerged that A had not considered acquiring the site for itself, but that B had kept A on board because it thought that A might emerge as a rival for the acquisition of the site.[7] Chadwick LJ found that B held the shares in the joint-venture company jointly for B and A.

According to Chadwick LJ, there are five features of the doctrine in *Pallant v Morgan*.[8] First, the parties' agreement[9] must precede the acquisition of the land; secondly, the agreement does not need to be contractually enforceable; thirdly, it must contemplate that, if the acquiring party (B) succeeded in securing the land, the non-acquiring party (A) would

[1] Although the phrase 'the *Pallant v Morgan* equity' has crept into modern vocabulary, it seems better to refer to the subject as 'the doctrine in *Pallant v Morgan*'. The term 'doctrine' indicates more precisely the subject-matter of the present discussion—a set of norms—instead of a type of interest as connoted by the term 'equity'. In the following discussion, the phrase '*Pallant v Morgan* equity' will be used only when quoting verbatim from other sources.

[2] *Pallant v Morgan* [1953] Ch 43 (Ch).

[3] *Banner Homes Group plc v Luff Developments Ltd* [2000] Ch 372 (CA).

[4] See observations in MP Thompson, 'Constructive Trusts and Non-binding Agreements' [2001] *Conveyancer and Property Lawyer* 265, 270; Nicholas Hopkins, 'The *Pallant v Morgan* "Equity"?' (2002) 66 *Conveyancer and Property Lawyer* 35, 39; Ben McFarlane and Charles Mitchell, *Hayton and Mitchell: Text, Cases and Materials on the Law of Trusts and Equitable Remedies*, 14th edn (London, Sweet & Maxwell, 2015) [15-156].

[5] *Pallant v Morgan* (n 2).

[6] *Banner Homes* (n 3).

[7] ibid 400.

[8] ibid 397–99.

[9] While judges have variously used the terms 'agreement', 'arrangement', and 'understanding', for the sake of simplicity this chapter will use the term 'agreement'.

obtain some interest in it; fourthly, A must have, in reliance on B, conferred an advantage on B in relation to the acquisition, or have suffered a detriment to A's own ability to acquire it on equal terms; and finally, A's reliance need not arise by keeping out of the market, although the circumstances must make it 'inequitable' for B to ignore the agreement and keep the land. Where the subject-matter concerns land[10] and the parties do not comply with the Law of Property (Miscellaneous Provisions) Act 1989, s 2(1)[11] a constructive trust may still arise, which is exempted from the formality requirement by s 2(5)[12] of that Act.

6.1. A Discrete Doctrine

It is not disputed that an application of the doctrine in *Pallant v Morgan* gives rise to constructive trusts, which oblige B to fulfil the pre-acquisition agreement made with A.[13] Often, however, the facts of a case falling within the doctrine may also be explained on the basis of another doctrine. Therefore, it is necessary to explore whether the doctrine in *Pallant v Morgan* is a discrete doctrine of constructive trust, or whether it should be analysed as a specific example of a different doctrine.

6.1.1. Specific Performance?

At a high level of generality, it might be thought that the doctrine in *Pallant v Morgan* is an instance-specific application of the law on specific performance. In *Banner Homes*,[14] Chadwick LJ surveyed various first instance decisions and traced the origins of the doctrine to the nineteenth-century case of *Chattock v Muller*.[15] In *Chattock*, there was a pre-acquisition agreement that B would purchase land on behalf of A and B. In reliance on the agreement, A had refrained from competing with B for the property and thereby lost the opportunity to bid for the land himself. While the ratio of the judgment indicates that *Chattock* was a case relating to specific performance,[16] its obiter statements provided the basis for the development of the doctrine in *Pallant v Morgan*.

There are two distinct parts to the judgment in *Chattock*. The first is Sir Richard Malins V-C's unreserved judgment, reported in non-verbatim form, where he held that B became a trustee of the property for A. Malins V-C then reserved his judgment 'on the defence that the agreement did not point out accurately the boundary of the portion which was to belong to [A]'.[17] This reserved judgment was fully reported in the case report.

[10] Although rarely so, the subject-matter may not concern land. In such cases, there are no formality requirements; however, where the agreement does not justify specific performance, the doctrine in *Pallant v Morgan* may nevertheless apply.

[11] This provides that '[a] contract for the sale or other disposition of an interest in land can only be made in writing and only by incorporating all the terms which the parties have expressly agreed in one document.'

[12] This provides that 'nothing in this section affects the creation or operation of resulting, implied or constructive trusts.'

[13] *Banner Homes* (n 3) 397; *Cox v Jones* [2004] EWHC 1486 (Ch), [2004] 2 FLR 1010 [46].

[14] *Banner Homes* (n 3) 385–96.

[15] *Chattock v Muller* (1878) LR 8 Ch D 177 (Ch).

[16] This was noted by Chadwick LJ in *Banner Homes* (n 3) 398 and by Megarry J in interlocutory proceedings in *Holiday Inns Inc v Broadhead* (Ch, 19 December 1969), as reported in *Banner Homes* (n 3) 389–93, 390.

[17] *Chattock v Muller* (n 15) 181.

In his unreserved judgment, the Vice-Chancellor noted that '[B] had lulled [A] into not making an offer for the estate', and that '[B] was all the time leading [A] to believe that if he bought the property [A] should have the part he wanted'.[18] Therefore, he held that '[B] was … no longer at liberty to change his mind'.[19] Later, in his reserved judgment, the Vice-Chancellor held that '[i]n a case like this, where [B] has acquired the estate or part of it by a fraud on [A] … the Court would be bound, if possible, to overcome all technical difficulties in order to defeat the unfair course of dealing of [B]'[20] and to 'do its best to ascertain what the agreement leaves uncertain.'[21] Although the Vice-Chancellor was prepared to compel B 'to give the *whole* estate to [A] at the price given for it' in view of the uncertainty, he was ultimately satisfied that the uncertainty could be resolved by reference to a memorandum and plan prepared by B in the course of the parties' negotiations.[22]

In *Pallant v Morgan*, Harman J held that *Chattock* formed the basis for the principle that '[t]he same *certainty* will not be required in cases where there is any *element of fraud*, as in simple cases of specific performance of a contract.'[23] The 'elements of fraud' arose in *Chattock* when B lulled A into not making an offer by leading him to believe that he would obtain the part of the property he wanted.[24] To prevent B from taking the property and reneging on his promise, *Chattock* decided that the 'certainty bar' may be lowered either to give effect to other documents which formed part of the parties' negotiations (according to the ratio of the case) or to overlook the absence of agreement concerning the apportionment of the property (according to the obiter statements in Malins V-C's reserved judgment). In such cases, 'specific performance will be decreed, despite a lesser degree of certainty.'[25]

In *Pallant*, an element of 'fraud' similar to that in *Chattock* arose, and Harman J held that '[t]o allow the [B] to retain [the land in question] under these circumstances would be tantamount to sanctioning a fraud on his part'.[26] However, he ruled that A could not rely on ordinary principles of specific performance, given that the parties' agreement left too many terms undecided.[27] This is a crucial point which bears emphasising. On the facts in *Pallant*, the parties' agreement was so uncertain that it could not even be cured by lowering the 'certainty bar' in line with the principle in *Chattock*.[28] Nevertheless, Harman J found that the 'fraud' in *Pallant* '[was] if anything stronger than [*Chattock*]'.[29] Therefore, he ordered B to hold the property for himself and A jointly pending an agreement as to its division, failing which it was to be sold and the proceeds equally divided.[30] This indicates that *Pallant* was not decided simply through an application of the principle in *Chattock*, but was based on a substantively different principle. This different principle gave A a right not explicitly afforded by the law on such facts before *Pallant* was decided.

[18] ibid 180.
[19] ibid.
[20] ibid 181–82.
[21] ibid 182. This point was based on the case of *Gregory v Mighell* (1811) 18 Ves 328, 34 ER 341.
[22] *Chattock v Muller* (n 15) 181–82 (emphasis added).
[23] *Pallant v Morgan* (n 2) 48 (emphases added). Harman J was quoting from George Russell Northcote (ed), *Fry on Specific Performance*, 6th edn (London, Stevens & Sons, 1921) 184 [386].
[24] *Chattock v Muller* (n 15) 180.
[25] *Holiday Inns Inc v Broadhead* (n 16) 390 (Megarry J).
[26] *Pallant v Morgan* (n 2) 48.
[27] ibid.
[28] See *Time Products Ltd v Combined English Stores Group Ltd* (Ch, 2 December 1974), as reported in *Banner Homes* (n 3) 393–95, 394.
[29] *Pallant v Morgan* (n 2) 50.
[30] ibid.

In *Banner Homes*, Chadwick LJ appears to have misinterpreted the ratio of *Chattock*. According to his Lordship, 'it was not the existence of the memorandum which led [Malins V-C] to treat [B] as a trustee of the property'.[31] Instead, his Lordship said that it was B's actions and A's reliance—elements which Harman J in *Pallant* summarised as 'elements of fraud'[32]—which made it 'unconscionable' for B to have acted inconsistently with their understanding.[33]

While it is true that such 'fraud' was part of Malins V-C's reasoning, it was not the reason for the enforcement of the parties' agreement. Specific performance was ordered in *Chattock* only because there remained a sufficiently high level of certainty in the parties' agreement: apart from failing to incorporate the terms of apportionment, the agreement was otherwise certain enough to be specifically performed. Without the parties' agreement meeting this level of certainty, specific performance would not have been ordered, even if the elements of 'fraud' were present on the facts. Indeed, such was the case in *Pallant*: even the 'stronger'[34] element of 'fraud' which arose on the facts in *Pallant* (as compared to *Chattock*) was not sufficient to give rise to specific performance. Thus, the trust in *Chattock* fell within the *contract-based*, bilateral events category of constructive trusts, where a constructive trust is imposed pursuant to a specifically enforceable agreement to secure the interest under it.[35] This doctrine was engaged because the court thought that there was a specific enough contract between the parties which 'ought to [have been] performed';[36] the constructive trust did not arise solely on the basis of A's and B's actions, as Chadwick LJ suggested.

Despite his Lordship's misreading of *Chattock*, the five features of the doctrine which Chadwick LJ identified in *Banner Homes* remain sound. Much of this can be credited to the clarity with which Harman J decided *Pallant*, as well as other first instance decisions which have acknowledged the distinction between the doctrine in *Pallant v Morgan* and specific performance. Take for instance the decision handed down pursuant to interlocutory proceedings in *Holiday Inns Inc v Broadhead*.[37] In that case, Megarry J explicitly recognised that *Chattock* 'represents the requirements of specific performance being modified in the case of fraud', this being distinct from the doctrine in *Pallant v Morgan* which 'represents the substitution of an alternative remedy for specific performance', and which in contrast to specific performance is 'an innominate equity of an entirely different nature.'[38] Indeed, as Chadwick LJ ultimately observed, '[i]t is unnecessary that the arrangement or understanding should be contractually enforceable', since 'if there is an agreement which is enforceable as a contract, there is unlikely to be any need to invoke the *Pallant v Morgan* equity; equity can act through the remedy of specific performance and will recognise the existence of a corresponding trust.'[39]

Analytically, therefore, an order for specific performance will be granted only where the pre-acquisition agreement is at least as certain as the agreement in *Chattock*. Furthermore,

[31] *Banner Homes* (n 3) 387.
[32] *Pallant v Morgan* (n 2) 48.
[33] *Banner Homes* (n 3) 387. See discussion at main text to nn 23–24 above.
[34] See main text to n 29 above.
[35] See, eg, *Lysaght v Edwdards* (1876) LR 2 Ch D 499 (Ch); *Walsh v Lonsdale* (1882) LR 21 Ch D 9 (CA). This doctrine is discussed in Chapter 8.
[36] *Banner Homes* (n 3) 397–99.
[37] *Holiday Inns Inc v Broadhead* (n 16) 389–93.
[38] ibid 390.
[39] *Banner Homes* (n 3) 398.

compliance with the Law of Property (Miscellaneous Provisions) Act 1989, s 2(1) remains necessary where the property is land. But where these requirements are not fulfilled and specific performance is unavailable, the doctrine in *Pallant v Morgan* may still have a role to play.[40]

6.1.2. Proprietary Estoppel?

The relationship between the doctrine in *Pallant v Morgan* and proprietary estoppel[41] is the subject of some controversy. Some judges have emphasised the similarities between these doctrines. For example, in *Yaxley v Gotts*,[42] Robert Walker LJ commented that, 'in the area of a joint enterprise for the acquisition of land (which may be, but is not necessarily, the matrimonial home) the two concepts coincide.' Similarly, in *Banner Homes*, Chadwick LJ noted that, in *Holiday Inns Inc v Broadhead*,[43] Megarry J had 'express[ed] the view … that the *Pallant v Morgan* equity had much in common with proprietary estoppel'.[44] Judges have also failed to agree upon whether the *Holiday Inns* judgment was, on a proper understanding, an application of the doctrine in *Pallant v Morgan* or proprietary estoppel.[45] On the other hand, in *Cobbe v Yeoman's Row Management Ltd*,[46] Lord Scott stated unequivocally that the application of the doctrine in *Pallant v Morgan* 'is not one that requires or depends upon any estoppel.'

There are important differences between the two doctrines which justify regarding the doctrine in *Pallant v Morgan* as conceptually distinct from proprietary estoppel. According to Lord Walker in *Thorner v Major*,[47] 'most scholars agree that the doctrine [of proprietary estoppel] is based on three main elements, although they express them in slightly different terms: a representation or assurance made to the claimant; reliance on it by the claimant; and detriment to the claimant in consequence of his (reasonable) reliance'. In contrast, the doctrine in *Pallant v Morgan* may apply where A's reliance confers on B an advantage to which A suffers no corresponding detriment.[48] Indeed, in both *Pallant v Morgan*[49] and *Banner Homes*,[50] A was adjudged not to have incurred any detrimental reliance at all, but nevertheless succeeded based on the fact that A's act of reliance had conferred an advantage on B.

A second difference is that the doctrine in *Pallant v Morgan* applies only where the agreement is made before the acquisition of the property: '[i]t is the pre-acquisition arrangement which colours the subsequent acquisition by [B] and leads to his being treated as a trustee if he seeks to act inconsistently with it.'[51] In contrast, proprietary estoppel generally concerns situations where an assurance or promise is given in relation to property which the

40 *Holiday Inns Inc v Broadhead* (n 16) 390.
41 This doctrine is discussed in Chapter 7.
42 *Yaxley v Gotts* [2000] Ch 162 (CA) 176.
43 *Holiday Inns Inc v Broadhead* (n 16) 389–93.
44 *Banner Homes* (n 3) 391.
45 It is suggested in S 6.2.1.3. that *Holiday Inns* is best analysed as an application of proprietary estoppel.
46 *Cobbe v Yeoman's Row Management Ltd* [2008] UKHL 55, [2008] 1 WLR 1752 [15].
47 *Thorner v Major* [2009] UKHL 18, [2009] 1 WLR 776 [29].
48 *Banner Homes* (n 3) 399.
49 *Pallant v Morgan* (n 2).
50 *Banner Homes* (n 3).
51 ibid 397. See also *Cobbe* (n 46) [33].

promisor already owns absolutely. As Morgan J observed at first instance in *Crossco No. 4 Unlimited v Jolan Ltd*,[52] 'there [is] an important difference between a case of a pre-acquisition arrangement and a post-acquisition arrangement.'

A third difference flows from the detailed discussion of proprietary estoppel undertaken in Chapter 7. One important conclusion reached in that chapter is that proprietary estoppel is a wrong-based doctrine, and any remedy arising through an application of that doctrine is a reflective remedy. In contrast, constructive trusts which arise through an application of the doctrine in *Pallant v Morgan* are replicative remedies, since they arise as soon as B acquires the property in question without requiring any breach of duty on B's part.

6.1.3. Agency and Fiduciary Law?

It has been directly or indirectly suggested on various occasions that the doctrine in *Pallant v Morgan* will arise only if the parties are in a fiduciary or agency relationship. It is undeniable that, in many cases, the parties can properly be described as being in either or both of these relationships. However, it is a different matter altogether to suggest that the doctrine in *Pallant v Morgan* is simply a fact-specific application of fiduciary or agency law. It is necessary to consider whether such an analysis is justified. Because not all agency relationships are fiduciary relationships,[53] and vice versa,[54] it is necessary to consider both doctrines in turn.

6.1.3.1. Agency Law

The idea that the doctrine in *Pallant v Morgan* applies only where the parties are in an agency relationship has been mooted by both judges and commentators. For instance, in *Hooper v Gorvin*,[55] Kevin Garnett QC, sitting as a Deputy High Court judge, said that *Chattock* and *Pallant* 'were decided … on the basis that [B] was acting both for himself and as agent for [A] when bidding for the property'. On Nicholas Hopkins' view, although 'the elements of a *Pallant v Morgan* equity, as identified by Chadwick LJ in *Banner Homes*, were present on the facts [in *Pallant v Morgan*]', he thinks that Harman J 'did not base his intervention on the existence of these factors … [but] on agency.'[56] He also suggests that the authorities prior to *Banner Homes* were based on a finding of agency.[57] *Bowstead and Reynolds on Agency* also cites *Pallant v Morgan* as an illustration of the rule that an agent becomes a trustee for his principal if the agent acquires land for his principal in his (the agent's) own name.[58]

[52] *Crossco No. 4 Unlimited v Jolan Ltd* [2011] EWHC 803 (Ch), [2011] NPC 38 [363]–[364].

[53] See JE Penner, 'Distinguishing Fiduciary, Trust, and Accounting Relationships' (2014) 8 *Journal of Equity* 202, 216–218, discussing *Paragon Finance plc v DB Thakerar & Co* [1999] 1 All ER 400 (CA) 416. *cf* Julius AW Grower, 'Explaining the "*Pallant v Morgan* Equity"' (2016) 80 *Conveyancer and Property Lawyer* 434, 436.

[54] *Crossco No. 4 Unlimited v Jolan Ltd* [2011] EWCA Civ 1619, 14 ITELR 615 [88].

[55] *Hooper v Gorvin* [2001] WTLR 575 (Ch) [46].

[56] Hopkins, 'The *Pallant v Morgan* "Equity"?' (n 4) 38–39.

[57] ibid 40.

[58] Peter G Watts, *Bowstead and Reynolds on Agency*, 20th edn (London, Sweet & Maxwell, 2016) [6-083].

A more radical view that the doctrine in *Pallant v Morgan* should be abolished in favour of an agency analysis is proposed in Jessica Uguccioni, 'Buyer Beware: Failed Joint Venture Negotiations and Involuntary Business Partnerships' [2011] *Journal of Business Law* 160. See too Man Yip, 'The *Pallant v Morgan* Equity Reconsidered' (2013) 33 *Legal Studies* 549; *Pallant v Morgan* (n 2) 50.

6.1.3.1.1. Authority

From the point of view of authority, it is difficult to accept that the doctrine in *Pallant v Morgan* was considered simply to be an application of agency law, since the seminal judgments in both *Pallant v Morgan* and *Banner Homes* do not once refer to B as A's agent.[59] If agency law were the basis of these decisions, one would have expected to find explicit references to the agency relationship between the parties.

Julius Grower has suggested that Harman J's judgment in *Pallant* 'was predicated on his finding that the parties' agreement ... had the effect of rendering [B] an agent of [A] in respect of [B's] acquisition of land.'[60] He cites Harman J's judgment which held that 'the proper inference from the facts [was] that [B] ... was bidding for both parties.'[61] It is doubtful that this analysis is correct. To quote the passage more fully, Harman J said that B 'was bidding for both parties on an agreement that there should be an arrangement between the parties on the division of the lot if he were successful.'[62] In saying this, Harman J was making a contradistinction with a suggestion, sourced in *Chattock*,[63] 'that [B] could become bound to hand over the whole property to [A] at the price he gave for it.'[64] Read in context, the judge was dealing simply with the *remedial* aspect of the case, rather than addressing the *doctrinal basis* upon which A's claim would succeed.

One might attempt to argue that the case of *Pallant* indirectly propounds an agency analysis, since Harman J based his decision on *Chattock v Muller* and the judgment in *Chattock* had explicitly identified B as A's agent.[65] However, this argument is unconvincing. Before referring to *Chattock*, Harman J observed that '[t]o allow [B] to retain [the land] under [the circumstances of the case before him] would be *tantamount to sanctioning a fraud* on his part'.[66] After briefly discussing the facts of *Chattock* and quoting a passage from that case, Harman J then observed that '[t]he present case is if anything *stronger than that one*', before handing down his final order.[67] It is clear that *Chattock* was cited simply to indicate that 'fraud' would allow the court 'to *overcome all technical difficulties* in order to defeat the unfair course of dealing of [B]':[68] Harman J certainly did not refer to *Chattock* in order to suggest that the technical difficulties would be overcome by an application of the agency analysis suggested in *Chattock*.

6.1.3.1.2. Remedy

In spite of authority, a different sort of argument might be advanced—one which suggests that cases which reflect the doctrine in *Pallant v Morgan* *should* be understood as a specific application of agency law.[69]

[59] In *Pallant*, the term 'agent' arises solely in the context of referring to the fact that A and B had acted through their agents; there was no suggestion that A and B were in an agency relationship. *cf* Yip, 'The *Pallant v Morgan* Equity Reconsidered' (n 58) 565.

[60] Grower, 'Explaining the "*Pallant v Morgan* Equity"' (n 53) 436.

[61] *Pallant v Morgan* (n 2) 50.

[62] ibid.

[63] *Chattock v Muller* (n 15).

[64] *Pallant v Morgan* (n 2) 50.

[65] *Chattock v Muller* (n 15) 181. See Hopkins, 'The *Pallant v Morgan* "Equity"?' (n 4) 39.

[66] *Pallant v Morgan* (n 2) 48 (emphasis added).

[67] ibid 50 (emphasis added).

[68] ibid 49 (emphasis in the original), citing *Chattock v Muller* (n 15) 181.

[69] See Yip, 'The *Pallant v Morgan* Equity Reconsidered' (n 58) 565ff; Grower, 'Explaining the "*Pallant v Morgan* Equity"' (n 53). *cf Crossco* (CA) (n 54) [88], where Etherton LJ suggests (albeit without elaboration) that the doctrine in *Pallant v Morgan* can arise in the absence of an agency relationship.

The fit between an agency relationship and the facts which engage the doctrine in *Pallant v Morgan* is not an easy one. Take for instance the facts of *Pallant*: because B would have bid for the property regardless of whether he had entered into a pre-acquisition agreement with A, it is difficult to say that B had acted 'in circumstances indicating that his acts arise from [A]'s manifestation [to the agent that he is willing for the agent to act]'.[70]

But even if this objection could be overcome, the agency analysis is unable to account for the remedial aspects of the doctrine in *Pallant v Morgan*. For instance, it is significant that *Pallant* propounded a different default rule of apportionment from that applied in *Chattock*. In *Chattock*, Malins V-C was prepared to compel B to sell the *entire* estate to A had there been any uncertainty as to the proportion A was to take.[71] This is consistent with an agency analysis since, by default, an agent who purchases property for his principal holds the entire property on trust for his principal.[72] But in *Pallant*, a different default rule of apportionment was applied. Given the absence of an agreement as to apportionment, Harman J declared that the property was to be held for the parties in equal shares 'on the basis that equality is equity.'[73] This difference cannot be explained simply by way of an agency analysis; rather, it is indicative of a different rationale underpinning the doctrine in *Pallant v Morgan*.[74]

Even more compelling is the fact that an agency analysis cannot explain the constructive trust remedy without incorporating an inordinate number of fictions. The starting point is that an agency relationship is not necessarily a *trust* relationship.[75] Whether receipts by an agent of property from his principal or from a third party on behalf of his principal are held on trust or simply by way of a personal capacity depends on the express or implied agreement between the parties. Thus, '[t]he essence of an [agency] agreement in [the] context [of the doctrine in *Pallant v Morgan*] is *consent*';[76] therefore, it needs to be shown that the parties not only consented to an agency agreement but also expressly or impliedly consented to the fact that B would hold any receipts on trust for A. This may be demonstrated if B 'is bound to keep the trust property separate from his own and apply it exclusively for the benefit of [A]', since if B can 'mix the money which he received with his own and use it for his own cash flow[, this] would be inconsistent with the existence of a trust.'[77] However, the pre-acquisition agreement between the parties in the context of the doctrine in *Pallant v Morgan* is characteristically vague. Thus, it is fictitious to suggest that the parties had come to any agreement at all concerning whether B would hold the acquired property on trust or is bound to keep it separate from his own. After all, the parties' agreement is commonly to the effect that B would simply sell a portion of the property to A, and an arrangement of sale is prima facie inconsistent with an express agreement that the seller would hold on trust as agent for the buyer.

In addition, an agent is generally not allowed to retain a benefit for himself while acting as agent unless the consent of his principal is sought. Because most cases applying the doctrine

[70] *Bowstead & Reynolds* (n 58) [1-006].
[71] *Chattock v Muller* (n 15) 181–82.
[72] *FHR European Ventures LLP v Cedar Capital Partners LLC* [2014] UKSC 45, [2015] AC 250 [33].
[73] *Holiday Inns Inc v Broadhead* (n 16) 390.
[74] See discussion in S 6.2.1.1.2.
[75] See Penner, 'Distinguishing' (n 53).
[76] Yip, 'The *Pallant v Morgan* Equity Reconsidered' (n 58) (emphasis in the original).
[77] *Paragon Finance* (n 53) 416.

in *Pallant v Morgan* ultimately result in the parties each obtaining a half-share interest in the property, it is necessary to rely on yet another fiction—that A had, through the parties' informal agreement, consented to B retaining a half-share for himself even though the parties had not considered the matter at all. The better view, therefore, is that the doctrine in *Pallant v Morgan* cannot fully be explained simply as an application of agency law.

6.1.3.2. *Fiduciary Law*

There have been suggestions that the doctrine in *Pallant v Morgan* can be explained by way of a fiduciary analysis. Writing extra-judicially, Sir Terence Etherton observes that '[t]he decision in *Banner Homes* can be justified on the narrow and purely conventional basis that [B] owed fiduciary obligations to [A] and, in acting as it did, was in breach of those obligations.'[78] Sitting in the Court of Appeal, Etherton LJ made the same point in his Lordship's dissenting judgment in *Crossco No. 4 Unlimited v Jolan Ltd*:[79] 'the cases in which the *Pallant v Morgan* equity has been applied can be explained in a wholly conventional way as examples of breach of an existing fiduciary duty.' Similarly, Simon Gardner[80] cites *Banner Homes* to show that '[fiduciary] relationships or duties [can] properly [be] found as between parties dealing with one another on a commercial basis'. Gardner has also written[81] that the doctrine 'may be capable of explanation in another way: on the basis that when the buyer acquires the property, he does so as (pro tanto) a fiduciary for the other.' These statements do not simply suggest that fiduciary duties may arise *after* B becomes a trustee under a constructive trust; they mean that a constructive trust arises upon B's acquisition because the parties are or were in a fiduciary relationship.

6.1.3.2.1. Authority

By way of authority, it is notable that the term 'fiduciary' does not arise at all in the judgments in *Pallant v Morgan* or *Banner Homes*. In the latter case, Chadwick LJ explored previous first instance decisions at length in order to explain the features of what he labelled the '*Pallant v Morgan* equity'. This effort would not have been necessary if his Lordship were purporting simply to apply established principles of fiduciary law.

Indeed, where both the doctrine in *Pallant v Morgan* and fiduciary law have been relied on as alternative grounds of pleading by counsel, courts have analysed both grounds as distinct, unrelated doctrines.[82] Consider for example the case of *Hooper v Gorvin*.[83] B was part of an action group formed by tenants dissatisfied with the landlord's service charge. He acted as spokesperson and intermediary for the negotiation for the sale of the freehold

[78] Terence Etherton, 'Constructive Trusts and Proprietary Estoppel: The Search for Clarity and Principle' [2009] *Conveyancer and Property Lawyer* 104, 122–23.

[79] *Crossco* (CA) (n 54) [94].

[80] Simon Gardner, *An Introduction to the Law of Trusts*, Clarendon Law Series, 2nd edn (Oxford, OUP, 2003) 145 fn 30.

[81] Simon Gardner, 'Reliance-Based Constructive Trusts' in Charles Mitchell (ed), *Constructive and Resulting Trusts* (Hart Publishing 2010) 72. See too Sarah Nield, 'Constructive Trusts and Estoppel' (2003) 23 *Legal Studies* 311, 317, 325; Grower, 'Explaining the "*Pallant v Morgan* Equity"' (n 53) 437.

[82] See, eg, *Du Boulay v Raggett* (1989) 58 P & CR 138 (Ch); *Thames Cruises Ltd v George Wheeler Launches Ltd* [2003] EWHC 3093 (Ch); *Button v Phelps* [2006] EWHC 53 (Ch).

[83] *Hooper v Gorvin* (n 55).

to the tenants, who planned to contribute in equal proportions to the purchase price. When the landlord refused to sell the land in pieces, B acquired the entire land on his own accord. Kevin Garnett QC, sitting as a Deputy Judge of the High Court, refused to apply the doctrine in *Pallant v Morgan*,[84] but nevertheless found B to be liable as a fiduciary to the other tenants.[85] This indicates that the doctrine in *Pallant v Morgan* is not simply an application of fiduciary law.

6.1.3.2.2. Vulnerability

It is a feature of fiduciary relationships that the fiduciary has the power to affect the principal's legal position and therefore the principal's position is vulnerable and capable of being abused by his fiduciary.[86] In the context of the doctrine in *Pallant v Morgan*, the element of vulnerability can be seen in cases where A's reliance is in the form of an omission, the classic example being where he refrains from bidding in competition with B. By relying on B, A is put in a vulnerable position. However, according to Chadwick LJ in *Banner Homes*, B's reliance may also arise by way of a positive act.[87] Thus, the doctrine in *Pallant v Morgan* may apply where, for example, there is an agreement between the parties where in view of forming a joint venture, B's role is to purchase land and A is to persuade the third party vendor to sell the land to B. Instead of passively allowing B to 'act on his behalf', A plays an active role for their common benefit. The fact that A is not in a position of 'vulnerability' is immaterial: the agreement is simply that each party is to contribute in his own way to the achievement of a common goal.

It is also difficult to analyse the parties' pre-acquisition agreement as sufficient to create a fiduciary relationship at all. In *JP Morgan Chase Bank v Springwell Navigation Corporation*,[88] Gloster J (as her ladyship then was) said:

> the mere fact that one party to a commercial relationship 'trusts' the other does not predicate a fiduciary relationship. The word 'trust' like the word 'advice' has a variety of meanings. In a broad sense, trust is an important element in many commercial dealings … [What is needed is for A to have a] legitimate expectation that, in its commercial dealings with [B], [B] would subordinate its interests to those of [A].

And as *Underhill and Hayton* notes, cases where courts have found that commercial joint venturers were in a fiduciary relationship have been those where 'the parties' contract ha[d] spelt out very clearly that one party will act in the exclusive interest of the other'.[89] In relation to the doctrine in *Pallant v Morgan*, the *pre*-contractual context in which the doctrine applies not only indicates a lack of a contractual relationship between the parties, but also a lack of an agreement that B would subordinate his interests to A's. Instead, the parties'

[84] ibid [46].

[85] ibid [51].

[86] See David Hayton, Paul Matthews and Charles Mitchell, *Underhill and Hayton: Law Relating to Trusts and Trustees*, 19th edn (London, LexisNexis Butterworths, 2016) [1.52].

[87] *Banner Homes* (n 3) 398.

[88] *JP Morgan Chase Bank v Springwell Navigation Corporation* [2008] EWHC 1186 (Comm) [574]. This passage was quoted with approval in *Barclays Bank plc v Svizera Holdings BV* [2014] EWHC 1020 (Comm), [2015] 1 All ER (Comm) 788 [8] and *Bailey v Barclays Bank plc* [2014] EWHC 2882 (QB) [88].

[89] *Underhill and Hayton* (n 86) [30.80].

agreement is commonly predicated simply on an *eventuality: if* B succeeds in acquiring the property in question, A will be given a share in it. Such an agreement does not itself indicate that B takes on a duty to act in A's best interest, particularly where both parties are commercial parties dealing at arms' length.

6.1.3.2.3. Joint Venture

There have been a number of suggestions that the doctrine in *Pallant v Morgan* is a doctrine relating to joint ventures. For example, in *Herbert v Doyle*,[90] Arden LJ identified *Pallant v Morgan* as 'a "joint venture" case where parties agree that one of them should acquire property for their joint benefit'. In *Cobbe*,[91] Lord Scott suggested that the doctrine gives rise to constructive trusts where 'a joint venture … involves the acquisition of an identified piece of land'. And in *Benedetti v Sawiris*,[92] Patten J said that the cases applying the doctrine in *Pallant v Morgan* 'concern what might be described as joint ventures where an agreement short of a contract has been reached in relation to the acquisition of property and one of the parties acquires the property but then subsequently refuses to implement the terms of that agreement.' If it is true that the doctrine in *Pallant v Morgan* only relates to joint ventures, it might further be argued that a fiduciary analysis becomes relevant. For instance, Simon Gardner has suggested that the 'real question' in order to determine whether a fiduciary relationship arose in *Banner Homes* 'is not whether the relationship is commercial, but whether it amounts to a joint venture.'[93] And, in *Thames Cruises Ltd v George Wheeler Launches Ltd*,[94] Peter Smith J cited *Banner Homes* as an example of the proposition that the fiduciary analysis 'has been held to apply where a property is acquired for a joint project or money is paid by one joint venturer to another'.

The first question which arises for consideration is whether the doctrine in *Pallant v Morgan* applies only to joint ventures. Since the phrase 'joint venture' 'is not a technical one with a settled common law meaning',[95] it might be the case that the phrase is not used in this context to connote any specific *requirement* for the application of the doctrine. On this view, the use of the phrase is no more than a reference to the parties' agreement, whatever its content may be. This view is not inconsistent with an analysis of the doctrine in *Pallant v Morgan* as a discrete doctrine of constructive trusts. As McIntyre and Sopinka JJ observed in *Lac Minerals Ltd v International Corona Resources Ltd*,[96] '[i]n every commercial venture, one of the parties approaches the other … This is not an *indicium* of a fiduciary relationship.'

On the other hand, the technical meaning of the phrase implies that there is 'an association of persons … with a view to mutual profit'.[97] Yet, even on this reading, parties working

[90] *Herbert v Doyle* [2010] EWCA Civ 1095, [2010] NPC 100.

[91] *Cobbe* (n 46) [30]. See also *Benedetti v Sawiris* [2009] EWHC 1330 (Ch) [505]; *National Trust for Places of Historical Interest v Birden* [2009] EWHC 2023 (Ch) [132].

[92] *Benedetti v Sawiris* (n 91) [505].

[93] Gardner, *Law of Trusts*, 2nd edn (n 80) 145 fn 30.

[94] *Thames Cruises Ltd* (n 82) [66].

[95] *United Dominions Corporation Ltd v Brian Proprietary Ltd* (1984) 157 CLR 1, 10.

[96] *Lac Minerals Ltd v International Corona Resources Ltd* [1989] 2 SCR 574, 603.

[97] *United Dominions Corporation Ltd* (n 95) 10.

towards a joint venture (in the technical sense of the phrase) are not necessarily in a fiduciary relationship, as the majority of the Canadian Supreme Court[98] held in *Lac Minerals Ltd v International Corona Resources Ltd.*[99] Moreover, it is not obvious that the cases relating to the doctrine in *Pallant v Morgan* can all be understood as giving rise to a joint venture in the technical sense. Certainly, the relationship between the parties in cases such as *Banner Homes*[100] can properly be understood as a joint venture. However, it fails to explain cases such as *Pallant v Morgan* where the parties did not contemplate sharing any profits generated from the land. Indeed, in *Banner Homes*[101] Chadwick LJ did not think that it was a requirement that the interest acquired by B must arise out of the parties' joint effort in developing the land. Instead, what seems to be crucial for the finding of a fiduciary relationship is that the joint venture should take the form of a partnership.[102] As Peter Smith J observed in *Thames Cruises,*[103] the 'the existence of a joint venture of itself will not invoke quasi-partnership obligations.' Clearly, however, the doctrine in *Pallant v Morgan* does not apply only to partnerships or quasi-partnerships. Indeed, the applicability of the doctrine does not depend on the precise *characterisation* of the parties' relationship, but focuses on their *actions* which make it 'inequitable or unconscionable to allow the acquiring party to retain the property for himself'.[104]

6.1.3.2.4. Acquisition

An alternative argument in favour of the fiduciary analysis might be that the fact of B's acquisition of the property itself gives rise to a fiduciary relationship between the parties—that a constructive trust arises *in order to* prevent B from taking the whole property for his own gain. This view also does not withstand scrutiny, since 'the presence of conduct that incurs the censure of a court of equity in the context of a fiduciary duty cannot itself create the duty.'[105] The words of Megarry V-C in *Tito v Waddell (No. 2)*[106] in the context of the self-dealing rule are apposite:

> If there is a fiduciary duty, the equitable rules about self-dealing apply: but self-dealing does not impose the duty. Equity bases its rules about self-dealing upon some pre-existing fiduciary duty: it is a disregard of this preexisting duty that subjects the self-dealer to the consequences of the self-dealing rules. I do not think that one can take a person who is subject to no pre-existing fiduciary duty and then say that because he self-deals he is thereupon subjected to a fiduciary duty.

So it is with the doctrine in *Pallant v Morgan*: it is analytically inconsistent to say that B is subjected to a fiduciary duty simply because he is attempting (or may attempt) to make a profit by keeping the acquired property for himself absolutely. It is necessary to identify some agreement prior to the acquisition which gives rise to a fiduciary relationship between the parties in relation to the property acquired. And as the discussions in the previous

[98] With Lamer, McIntyre and Sopinka JJ in the majority and La Forest and Wilson JJ in the minority on the fiduciary point.
[99] *Lac Minerals Ltd* (n 96).
[100] *Banner Homes* (n 3).
[101] ibid 398.
[102] *United Dominions Corporation Ltd* (n 95) 11.
[103] *Thames Cruises Ltd* (n 82) [66].
[104] *Banner Homes* (n 3) 398.
[105] *Lac Minerals Ltd* (n 96) 600.
[106] *Tito v Waddell (No. 2)* [1977] Ch 106 (Ch) 230.

sections have indicated, it is difficult to identify such an agreement on the facts of many of the cases which have applied the doctrine in *Pallant v Morgan*.

6.1.3.2.5. Nature of the Remedy

A final reason why the doctrine in *Pallant v Morgan* cannot simply be analysed as a specific application of fiduciary law is based on the discussion in Chapter 10. One of the conclusions which will be reached in that Chapter is that constructive trusts imposed over gains made by a fiduciary in breach of his duty can only logically be analysed as reflective remedies, which respond to B's breach of a primary duty of loyalty.[107] In the doctrine in *Pallant v Morgan*, a constructive trust arises at the moment of B's acquisition. However, that constructive trust cannot be said to arise from any event which constitutes a breach of a primary duty. In particular, the fact that B acquires the property cannot itself be said to be a breach of a primary duty of loyalty, since B's acquisition of property is precisely what the parties hoped for. For this reason, too, the cases which have applied the doctrine in *Pallant v Morgan* cannot simply be analysed as an application of fiduciary law.

6.1.4. 'Common Intention Constructive Trust'?

In *Crossco No. 4 Unlimited v Jolan Ltd*,[108] Arden[109] and McFarlane[110] LJJ suggested that the doctrine in *Pallant v Morgan* is 'firmly based on a common intention constructive trust'. According to Arden LJ[111] who provided an elaboration on this point, the reasoning proffered in *Banner Homes*[112] 'makes it clear that the ratio of that case is firmly based on the kind [of trust] enunciated in *Gissing v Gissing*.'[113] This observation is surprising. In the first place, the relevant passages in *Banner Homes* to which her Ladyship refers do not once mention either the common intention constructive trust (CICT) or the case of *Gissing*. Instead, in those passages, Chadwick LJ was clearly elaborating on the features of a unique doctrine. Furthermore, in *Banner Homes*,[114] Chadwick LJ also held that the doctrine in *Pallant v Morgan* might be triggered either by advantage or by detriment. This is impossible to square with the fact that a CICT requires A to act to his detriment, as clearly set out in *Gissing v Gissing*.[115] The doctrines are also different in other ways. For example, unlike the doctrine in *Pallant v Morgan*, the CICT may arise even where there is no express agreement or understanding,[116] and where the relevant agreement is made post-acquisition.[117] These differences indicate that the two doctrines are distinct and cannot be conflated.

107 See Chapter 10, S 10.2.3.
108 *Crossco* (CA) (n 54).
109 ibid [129].
110 ibid [120].
111 ibid [129].
112 *Banner Homes* (n 3) 397–99. The points that Chadwick LJ made, and to which Arden LJ referred, are summarised in the main text following n 8 above.
113 *Gissing v Gissing* [1971] AC 886 (HL).
114 *Banner Homes* (n 3) 399.
115 *Gissing v Gissing* (n 113) 905.
116 See, eg, *Midland Bank plc v Cooke* [1995] 4 All ER 652 (CA).
117 In considering the CICT, Lord Bridge in *Lloyds Bank plc v Rosset* [1991] 1 AC 107 (HL) 132 said that the courts would see if 'there has at any time prior to acquisition, or exceptionally *at some later date*, been any agreement, arrangement or understanding reached between them that the property is to be shared beneficially' (emphasis added).

There is, however, admittedly an overlap between the doctrines in certain cases, namely where there is an express pre-acquisition agreement between the parties, and where A's reliance is detrimental in nature. Might it be said that both doctrines are equally plausible alternatives in such cases—that, at least in these cases, the doctrine in *Pallant v Morgan* is but an unusual application of the CICT in a commercial context?[118]

The answer is firmly in the negative. The CICT has been developed in the domestic shared homes context, which reflects the core policy aim of addressing the social realities which arise in intimate relationships.[119] A clear example is seen from the judgment in *Stack v Dowden*,[120] where it was held that the law in this area 'has ... moved on in response to changing social and economic conditions.' It is necessary to restrict the policy-influenced development of the CICT from having any application beyond its proper ambit.

From this policy perspective, a number of central differences between the doctrines can be appreciated. First, the courts take a very generous approach to the evidence in determining whether a 'common intention' can be established. For instance, in *Grant v Edwards*,[121] the fact that B had obtained sole legal title to the house by giving an *excuse* to A provided the basis for the inference of an *express* common intention. An even clearer example is seen in *Midland Bank plc v Cooke*,[122] where despite A's honest admission that the parties 'never gave ownership a thought or reached any agreement about it', the court nevertheless inferred the existence of a common intention. It can be seen that judges are willing to 'strain the concept of common intention' in their attempt to do justice on particular facts.[123] In contrast, the doctrine in *Pallant v Morgan*, which is unaffected by such policy considerations, responds only to 'a clear and common intention'.[124]

Another difference is that, in CICT cases where the parties have reached an express agreement concerning their respective shares in the property, the court may nevertheless depart from it where there is 'very good reason for doing so'.[125] *Underhill and Hayton* suggests that an example of such an occasion is where one party only does half of what he agrees to: in such a situation, it is suggested that A's 'scale of detriment' will affect his share in the property.[126] On the other hand, where the parties have agreed on the issue of apportionment, an application of the doctrine in *Pallant v Morgan* will always give rise to a constructive trust which reflects the agreed proportion even in the absence of detriment.[127] It is certainly clear that the policy considerations relating to the family homes cases should not

[118] Thompson, 'Constructive Trusts' (n 4) 266.

[119] A detailed discussion of this doctrine is found in Chapter 14.

[120] *Stack v Dowden* [2007] UKHL 17, [2002] 2 AC 432 [60]. *Underhill and Hayton* (n 86) suggests that the reason for this rule is that the resulting trust 'discriminates against women by focusing too narrowly on one type of contribution to the parties' relationship, viz financial contributions, to the exclusion of other types, eg home-making, child-care, etc.'

[121] *Grant v Edwards* [1986] Ch 638 (CA).

[122] *Midland Bank plc v Cooke* (n 116) 575.

[123] Nield, 'Constructive Trusts and Estoppel' (n 81) 320. See also discussion in Simon Gardner, *An Introduction to the Law of Trusts*, Clarendon Law Series, 3rd edn (Oxford, OUP, 2011) 335–36; Grower, 'Explaining the "*Pallant v Morgan* Equity"' (n 53) 441–42.

[124] Nield, 'Constructive Trusts and Estoppel' (n 81) 320. See also the judgment of Etherton LJ in *Crossco* (CA) (n 54) [85] to this effect.

[125] *Mortgage Corporation Ltd v Shaire* [2001] Ch 743 (Ch) 750; *Crossley v Crossley* [2005] EWCA Civ 1581, [2006] WTLR 225 [32].

[126] *Underhill and Hayton* (n 86) [30.32]–[30.33].

[127] See, eg, *Pallant v Morgan* (n 2); *Holiday Inns Inc v Broadhead* (n 16) 391; *Banner Homes* (n 3).

be transposed to the doctrine in *Pallant v Morgan*. As Etherton LJ astutely noted in *Crossco No 4 Unlimited v Jolan Ltd:*[128]

> In a commercial context, it is to be expected that the parties will normally take legal advice about their respective rights and interests and will normally reduce their agreements to writing and will not expect to be bound until a contract has been made … They do not expect their rights to be determined in an 'ambulatory' manner by retrospective examination of their conduct and words over the entire period of their relationship. They do not expect the court to determine their respective property rights and interests by the imputation of intentions which they did not have but which the court considers they would have had if they had acted justly and reasonably and thought about the point.

Therefore, assimilating the CICT and the doctrine in *Pallant v Morgan* in any manner or form is inaccurate and unhelpful, and liable to mislead a proper analysis.

6.2. Rationale

The doctrine in *Pallant v Morgan* arises where B informally promises that, if he successfully acquires property from a third party, he will cede some interest in the property to A, and A acts in reliance on B's promise in such a way that provides B an advantage by increasing B's opportunity of successfully acquiring the property. As a result of his promise, B takes only a qualified interest in the property upon acquiring it. In Chapter 4,[129] it was observed that doctrines which reflect such QI situations are underpinned by the 'norm against taking an advantage'. The doctrine in *Pallant v Morgan* is also underpinned by this norm.

This categorisation places the doctrine within the same conceptual space as the doctrine in *Rochefoucauld v Boustead* and secret trusts. The close link between these doctrines has been noted by judges and commentators. For example, in *Paragon Finance plc v DB Thakerar & Co*[130] Millett LJ treated the constructive trusts which arose in all three doctrines as cases of the same class. Similarly, Sarah Nield notes that the root of the doctrine in *Pallant v Morgan* is found in *Rochefoucauld v Boustead.*[131] Her view is based on an analysis by Timothy Youdan[132] that one strand of the doctrine in *Rochefoucauld* 'relates to situations where [B] purchases property from a third party pursuant to some agreement or arrangement between A and B that [B] will hold the property for [A] (or jointly with [A]) or that he will dispose of all or part of the property to A, and [this] provides the basis for the *Pallant v Morgan* equity.'[133]

Despite sharing the same conceptual space, a significant factual difference between the doctrines is that, unlike the doctrine in *Rochefoucauld v Boustead* and secret trusts, the doctrine in *Pallant v Morgan* arises in situations where A does not own any prior interest in the property which B acquires. As Lewison J noted in *Kilcarne Holdings Ltd v Targetfollow*

[128] *Crossco* (CA) (n 54) [87].
[129] See Chapter 4, S 4.3.4.
[130] *Paragon Finance* (n 53) 408–09.
[131] Nield, 'Constructive Trusts and Estoppel' (n 81) 315.
[132] TG Youdan, 'Formalities for Trusts of Land and the Doctrine in *Rochefoucauld v Boustead*' (1984) 43 *CLJ* 306.
[133] Nield, 'Constructive Trusts and Estoppel' (n 81) 315.

(Birmingham) Ltd,[134] in the 'paradigm *Pallant v Morgan* case [A] has no entitlement at law. If equity does not intervene, he is left with nothing.' This fact raises important issues relating to the elements of promise and reliance.

In relation to the element of reliance, it is more difficult in the context of the doctrine in *Pallant v Morgan* to determine whether A acts in reliance on B's promise, since A's actions do not involve a straightforward transfer of property from A to B. The variety of possible ways in which A may rely on B's promise necessitates identifying a rule which distinguishes between acts sufficient to bind B to his promise and those that do not. In relation to the element of promise, it is notable that the doctrine in *Pallant v Morgan* commonly (though not necessarily) involves commercial parties locked in pre-acquisition negotiations. As a result, the content of B's promise may not reflect a high degree of certainty or conclusiveness. In particular, B might clearly promise to qualify his interest in the acquired property without having decided on the precise proportion he intends to cede to A. The question arises as to whether this should militate against an application of the doctrine, or whether there is an analytically consistent manner to deal with the issue of apportionment.

The resolution of these matters is crucial, not only for a proper appreciation of the doctrine in *Pallant v Morgan*, but also for understanding the QI situations within the non-contract-based, bilateral events category of constructive trusts. This is because the ways in which the elements of promise and reliance are fulfilled in the doctrine in *Pallant v Morgan* indicate that the doctrine is a peripheral application of the QI doctrines. Being situated at the outer limit of the conceptual space, it is no surprise that the doctrine in *Pallant v Morgan* is crucial for indicating the boundaries of the QI doctrines.

6.2.1. Promise and Reliance

The fact that B's promise and A's reliance are necessary to give rise to the doctrine is neatly demonstrated by the cases of *Kilcarne Holdings Ltd v Targetfollow (Birmingham) Ltd*[135] and *Clarke v Corless*.[136]

In *Kilcarne*, A's case could not be made out because A did not make the requisite promise. B acquired a 250-year lease of Baskerville House with £1 million borrowed from A in exchange for loan notes. The Court of Appeal held that the doctrine could not apply because '[t]here was never any agreement, arrangement or understanding between [the parties] that the lease should be acquired for their joint benefit or that [A] would obtain some interest in it.'[137]

In *Clarke*, the claimants (A) could not rely on the doctrine in *Pallant v Morgan* because the requisite element of reliance was missing. In that case, the parties were purchasers and tenants of houses in an estate previously owned by a property development company, Allum Estates Ltd. Allum retained the communal areas which were eventually purchased by B. A brought a claim based on the parties' pre-acquisition discussions, claiming that the

[134] *Kilcarne Holdings Ltd v Targetfollow (Birmingham) Ltd* [2004] EWHC 2547 (Ch) [232].
[135] ibid.
[136] *Clarke v Corless* [2010] EWCA Civ 338, [2010] WTLR 751.
[137] *Kilcarne Holdings Ltd* (n 134) [22].

land purchased by B was held on constructive trust for A. The Court of Appeal affirmed Proudman J's first instance finding that 'the agreement reached was sufficient to found the necessary equity if it was in fact relied upon up to and including the date on which [B] acquired the retained land'.[138] However, the Court accepted the judge's conclusion that, on the evidence, 'there had never been any effective reliance by [A] on the … agreement'.[139] This was because A had done nothing in reliance on B's promise such that B obtained an advantage in relation to the acquisition of the land: their actions had always indicated 'a lack of interest or reliance on the original proposal to acquire the retained land for the residents through some form of common ownership.'[140]

6.2.1.1. Promise

Three issues arise for consideration in relation to the element of promise. First, how firm need B's promise be? Secondly, what are the consequences, if any, of the fact that B's promise often reveals that B (and A) had given no thought to the precise way in which the property is to be apportioned? Thirdly, is there an inconsistency in the way in which the element of promise arises in the context of the doctrine in *Rochefoucauld v Boustead* and the doctrine in *Pallant v Morgan*?

6.2.1.1.1. Firmness

In the context of the doctrine in *Rochefoucauld v Boustead* and secret trusts, it is often easy to conclude that B makes a firm promise to qualify his interest in the property: A would not normally permit B to acquire A's property unless A has extracted a firm promise from B concerning B's dealing with the property.[141] In relation to the doctrine in *Pallant v Morgan*, however, A often has no power directly to compel a third party to transfer the property to B. Moreover, the parties are commonly locked in pre-acquisition negotiations, and in this context B's promise may not necessarily be a firm one. Stated from A's perspective, it may be the case that A acts in a way which confers on B an advantage in relation to acquiring the property simply pursuant to a mere hope, speculation, or rumour from someone else that B intends to share the property with A, rather than on the basis of an unequivocal promise. The question arises as to what degree of firmness is required of B's promise to invoke the doctrine.

In *Banner Homes Group plc v Luff Developments Ltd*,[142] it was said to be enough for the arrangement to have been 'contemplated' by the parties. But mere 'contemplation' is surely not a precise enough threshold, especially in view of the fact that B must have induced A's reliance. In particular, B's *contemplation* of a state of affairs does not require *communication* of that intention to A; and, as we have seen,[143] B's uncommunicated intention is

[138] *Clarke v Corless* (n 136) [50].
[139] ibid [61].
[140] ibid [63].
[141] If A, not intending to make a gift to B, transfers his property to B without securing a promise at all, then a resulting trust will arise to compel B to return the property to A: see discussion in Chapter 4, S 4.5.1.1.2.
[142] *Banner Homes* (n 3) 398.
[143] See Chapter 4, S 4.2.1.

insufficient to engage the doctrine. The better view is that, through his promise, B must have indicated his *commitment* or provided a *guarantee* that he would qualify his interest in the property.[144] This degree of firmness helps to distinguish between cases where B extends merely 'a friendly gesture' from cases where B gives 'an assurance' to A.[145] As Harman J observed in *Pallant*, this distinction is 'crucial', and said that he was 'bound to choose between these two versions'.[146] The yardstick of a 'commitment' or 'guarantee', as opposed to mere 'contemplation', is more helpful in determining which version arises on the facts of a particular case.

In some cases, B may expressly indicate that his promise is a contingent one, this being stated verbally or through written correspondences which are 'subject to contract'[147] or 'binding in honour'[148] only. In the usual case where the parties are commercial actors who '[understand] the significance of the expression'[149] and 'the meaning and effect of the words',[150] B is, in fact, indicating that he does *not* intend to qualify his interest in the property to be acquired before entering into a binding legal contract. Where A then purports to rely on such a promise, A acts in 'premature reliance',[151] and the doctrine in *Pallant v Morgan* will not apply. Thus, if and when B acquires the property, he takes it free from any obligation. But it is important to note that equity looks to substance and not form, and the doctrine is not precluded simply because the phrase 'subject to contract' is used.[152] In all cases it is necessary to determine the substance of B's promise.

6.2.1.1.2. Apportionment

There is no question that, where the parties have agreed upon a method of apportioning the property or the specific portions each party will obtain, effect will be given to this.[153] This is because the constructive trust enforces the full extent of B's promise,[154] and in this situation B would have promised to apportion the property in the manner the parties have agreed upon. For example, in *Time Products Ltd v Combined English Stores Group Ltd*,[155] where the parties' agreement contemplated that a company called Collingwoods would be 'acquired

[144] JA Simpson and ESC Weiner (eds), *The Oxford English Dictionary*, 2nd edn (Oxford, OUP, 1989) Vol XII, 614 defines the word 'promise' as '[a] declaration or assurance made to another person, with respect to the future, stating that one will do, or refrain from, some specified act, or that one will give or bestow some specified thing. (Usually in good sense, implying something to the advantage or pleasure of the person concerned).'

[145] *Pallant v Morgan* (n 2) 46.

[146] ibid.

[147] *London & Regional Investments Ltd v TBI plc* [2002] EWCA Civ 355. Note, though, that the doctrine in *Pallant v Morgan* would not have applied in this case anyway because the agreement was a post-acquisition one: B had always been the owner of the property which was the subject-matter of the agreement.

[148] *Cobbe* (n 46) [37].

[149] *Generator Developments LLP v Lidl (UK) GmbH* [2016] EWHC 816 (Ch) [45].

[150] ibid [195].

[151] *Cobbe* (n 46) [34].

[152] *Generator Developments LLP* (n 149) [192].

[153] *Banner Homes* (n 3) 391.

[154] This is also the reason why, where the agreement is that B will sell some part of the property to A, this becomes a term of the constructive trust, so A must make payment to obtain his share in the property. Thus, in *Banner Homes*, this was effected by the property being 'charged for payment by [Banner Homes] for half of the purchase price of the shares': Hopkins, 'The *Pallant v Morgan* "Equity"?' (n 4) 37.

[155] *Time Products Ltd* (n 28) 393–95.

at the lowest possible price as a joint venture in equal shares', Oliver J duly declared that Collingwoods was held upon trust for both parties in equal shares from the date of acquisition. Similarly, in *Cox v Jones*,[156] B was compelled to hold the purchased flat on a constructive trust for A absolutely in accordance with the parties' agreed method of apportionment. In this way, an agreement as to apportionment makes 'equity's job slightly easier ... in terms of quantification of interest.'[157]

Often, however, the parties would not have given any thought to the issue of apportionment. Yet, this does not prevent the application of the doctrine, which simply requires a 'minimum threshold'—that B promises to cede *some* (undefined) interest in the property to A. Thus, where the parties have not decided on how precisely to apportion the property, 'the property [will be] held for the parties in equal shares, presumably on the basis that equality is equity'.[158]

The question arises as to whether this feature of the doctrine is justified. It might[159] be objected to on the basis that ordering an equal division of the property in such cases imposes on B an obligation he had never agreed to carry out, since an equal division may not have been intended or contemplated. Moreover, in *Banner Homes*,[160] Chadwick LJ said that the doctrine in *Pallant v Morgan* 'does not seek to ... make for [the parties] some bargain which they have not themselves made'.[161] Might this feature of the doctrine be said unjustifiably to impute an intention '[w]here a reasonable certainty as to the fractions is unattainable' or 'in the absence of valuation evidence as to the values of the respective interests'?[162]

It seems not: the courts remain committed to giving effect to B's promise. A close examination reveals that it is not entirely accurate to say that courts automatically order an *equal division* whenever the parties have not agreed on the issue of apportionment. In *Pallant v Morgan*, Harman J first declared that B held the property *jointly* for himself and A, before going on to hold that 'if [the parties] still fail to agree on a division the property must be resold ... and the proceeds of sale divided equally'.[163] Similarly, in *Banner Homes*, Chadwick LJ encouraged the parties to 'agree on the appropriate form of order in the light of the decision of this court', failing which further submissions would be made before he would reach a final order.[164]

From these cases it can be seen that the parties are held to be *joint tenants* of the property so that they may decide amongst themselves how best to apportion the property. This indicates that courts do not actively impute a term of apportionment into the parties'

[156] *Cox v Jones* (n 13).
[157] ibid [45].
[158] *Holiday Inns Inc v Broadhead* (n 16) 390 (Megarry J).
[159] See, eg, *Pallant v Morgan* (n 2) 50.
[160] *Banner Homes* (n 3) 400.
[161] In the context of his Lordship's judgment, the use of the word 'bargain' refers to an 'enforceable contract'. This is clear from the fact that Chadwick LJ was rejecting the first instance decision to refuse relief on the ground that it 'turn[s] a common arrangement or understanding, which is implicitly qualified by the right of either side to withdraw, into an unqualified arrangement or undertaking which denied any such right': *Banner Homes* (n 3) 400. However, that statement also holds true where 'bargain' means 'arrangement' in a looser sense: a constructive trust will not compel B to perform that which he did not promise.
[162] ibid 391.
[163] *Pallant v Morgan* (n 2) 50.
[164] *Banner Homes* (n 3) 401.

agreement where none exists. Instead, they strive to give full effect to the content of B's promise by encouraging the parties to come to an agreement. However, when the parties fail to reach an agreement—and this will usually be the case due to the acrimony between the parties by the time the case is litigated—there are only three possible outcomes. Either B is allowed to take the property absolutely, or B holds the property on trust absolutely for A, or an equal division of the property is ordered. Clearly, the latter response more accurately reflects B's pre-acquisition promise to qualify his interest in the acquired property. Hence the equal division of property in such cases.

The case of *Island Holdings Ltd v Birchington Engineering Co Ltd*[165] is illustrative. The parties had agreed to tender for a long lease of land owned by the local authority in apparent competition, with the intention that B would submit the higher tender and acquire the lease. They agreed in writing that B would then sell a defined portion of land to A at three-fifths of the purchase price. B's tender was accepted in due course; but before being granted the lease, the local authority indicated its willingness to offer the freehold at a slightly higher price. B accepted this offer. In return, B offered to sell the freehold of the previously agreed portion of land to A at a corresponding extra cost. This second agreement was accepted 'subject to contract'. B later reneged on the second agreement when they could not agree on particular terms. A's contractual claim failed because 'the original agreement had been discharged and replaced by a new agreement which was subject to contract and so unenforceable.'[166] However, applying the doctrine in *Pallant v Morgan*,[167] Goulding J decided that B held the land for both parties in equal shares.[168]

It is important to understand why the court did not give effect to the initial arrangement directly but held that the parties were to share the land equally. In the first place, if the parties had not made the original agreement, the second agreement alone would not have been binding because of the conditional nature of the agreement: being an agreement 'subject to contract', B would not have firmly promised to cede the property.[169] However, in the original agreement B had clearly promised to take a qualified interest in the property, and A had effectively relied on this promise.[170] This meant that the property was subject to a constructive trust immediately upon B's acquisition by reference to the first agreement. The existence of this constructive trust would not have been affected by the second agreement which was entered 'subject to contract'. Nevertheless, given that B acquired a larger interest than that which was contemplated in the first agreement, the initial method of apportionment was no longer applicable: the second agreement negated the initial term of apportionment with a view to renegotiating that term. When the parties eventually failed to agree on the matter, equal division was the only way in which the court could have given effect to the original agreement.

[165] *Island Holdings Ltd v Birchington Engineering Ltd* (Ch, 7 July 1981), as reported in *Banner Homes* (n 3) 396, 396.

[166] ibid.

[167] Although the judge's attention was not brought to *Pallant v Morgan* itself, it has been observed that 'the principle which he applied is familiar': the judge did, after all, apply the principles which make up the doctrine in *Pallant v Morgan*. See *Banner Homes* (n 3) 396.

[168] *Island Holdings Ltd* (n 165) 396.

[169] Another reason why the doctrine would not have applied is that the agreement would have been made post-acquisition: B had already accepted the local authority's offer for the freehold of the land.

[170] *Island Holdings Ltd* (n 165) 397.

6.2.1.1.3. The Doctrine in *Pallant v Morgan* and the Doctrine in *Rochefoucauld v Boustead*

It might be thought that there is an inconsistency in the way in which the element of promise arises in the doctrine in *Rochefoucauld v Boustead* and the doctrine in *Pallant v Morgan*. In the former doctrine, 'the bargain should have included a stipulation under which some *sufficiently defined beneficial interest* in the property was to be taken by another';[171] in the latter doctrine the proportion to be ceded need not be defined. However, this distinction is simply a reflection of the different contexts in which both doctrines arise, and does not affect the fundamental analyses of these doctrines.

In the context of the doctrine in *Rochefoucauld v Boustead*, it is only ever possible to say that B has made a promise to qualify his interest in the property he will acquire where he makes clear the extent of the interest in the property to which his promise relates. It is usually the case that A owns the property at the outset, and so it is unlikely for A to deprive himself of his own property on the basis of a vague promise by B to hold some undefined part of the property on trust without reaching a prior agreement concerning the specific interest to be held on trust. If it is indeed shown that A allowed the transfer to be made on such a vague promise, a constructive trust would not arise; instead, all that has been shown is that A did not intend for B to take the property for B's own benefit, and a resulting trust would arise.

In relation to the doctrine in *Pallant v Morgan*, however, the agreement is always contingent on B's success in obtaining the property from a third-party: B may acquire the property while the parties are still engaged in negotiations. In addition, the mere fact that A does not intend for B to take the property for himself cannot give rise to a resulting trust since A is not the transferor. As a result, it is *necessary* for a constructive trust to be imposed although the precise term of apportionment may be unclear. Otherwise, B would be allowed to keep the property contrary to the 'norm against taking an advantage'.[172]

There are, however, cases relating to the doctrine in *Rochefoucauld v Boustead* where A, who has a less-than-full ownership right in the property, *allows* the property to be transferred to B absolutely. For instance, in *Lincoln v Wright*[173] and *Rochefoucauld v Boustead*,[174] A only had an equity of redemption prior to the transfer, but allowed the property to be transferred to B absolutely. In these cases, just as in the context of the doctrine in *Pallant v Morgan*, a resulting trust would not explain the result because A did not own the full ownership interest of the property prior to the transfer but ends up with the full beneficial interest in the property at the end of the story. In these cases, might it be said that a 'sufficiently defined beneficial interest' is unnecessary for a constructive trust to arise?

It depends. In most cases, if A has a significant controlling power in the property, he would not consent to the transfer if B vaguely promises to hold an undefined portion on trust. If A allows the transfer anyway, it would usually indicate that A did not act *in reliance on* B's promise, and a constructive trust would not arise. However, if it can be shown that A did in fact rely on B's vague promise, B's receipt of the property would probably be evidence

[171] *Bannister v Bannister* [1948] 2 All ER 133 (CA) 136 (emphasis added).
[172] This norm was explained in Chapter 4, S 4.3.4.
[173] *Lincoln v Wright* (1859) 4 De G & J 16, 45 ER 6.
[174] *Rochefoucauld v Boustead* [1897] 1 Ch 196 (CA).

that B had in fact promised to hold the *entire* property on trust for A, since B would have known that A's reliance had given him an advantage in relation to the acquisition of the property. Short of a clear agreement that B would be allowed to keep an agreed portion of the property for himself, the parties would probably have agreed that B was not meant to enjoy any unqualified benefit in the property.

In cases where A does not have a significant enough amount of control of the property in order for A to have any say as to whether it is transferred to B,[175] then A's situation falls to be considered by way of the doctrine in *Pallant v Morgan*. The question becomes whether A has conferred any advantage in relation to B's acquisition of the property in reliance on B's promise to qualify his interest in the property. If so, a constructive trust will be imposed even if the parties have not decided how they will subsequently apportion the property.

6.2.1.2. *Reliance*

A must *rely* on B's promise in order for the doctrine in *Pallant v Morgan* to operate. Reliance indicates that B's promise is the basis on which A acts, and that B's promise is the basis on which he obtains an advantage from A in relation to the acquired property, thus justifying the enforcement of B's promise.

In the typical cases concerning the doctrine in *Rochefoucauld v Boustead* and secret trusts, A is the transferor of the property B acquires. There, it is seemingly easy to conclude that B's promise induces A to rely on B by transferring the property to B. In truth, however, the simplicity of these facts masks a number of vital points in relation to the element of reliance, which are unravelled in the context of the doctrine in *Pallant v Morgan*. These points will be addressed in turn.

6.2.1.2.1. Inducement

B's promise must induce A's act of reliance. If A would have acted exactly as he did whether or not B had made a promise, it is difficult to see how B's promise forms the basis on which B acquires the property such that a constructive trust is justified. If a constructive trust were imposed, it would surely be an unjustifiable windfall for A, who would have done nothing to deserve the benefit of B's promise. After all, a mere promise is unenforceable,[176] and 'equity will not assist a volunteer'.[177] To avoid this unacceptable outcome, it is necessary for A's reliance to be induced by B's promise by way of a 'but for' causal link. Where this is satisfied, then 'the circumstances make it inequitable for [B] to retain the property for himself in a manner inconsistent with the arrangement or understanding on which [A] has acted.'[178]

[175] See discussion in Chapter 4, S 4.2.2.1.

[176] 'The breaking of a promise, without more, is morally reprehensible, but not unconscionable in the sense that equity will necessarily prevent its occurrence or remedy the consequent loss': *Commonwealth of Australia v Verwayen* (1990) 170 CLR 394, 416 (Mason CJ). See also *Cobbe* (n 46) [92]; *Walton v Walton* (CA, 14 April 1994): 'if there had been nothing more than the promise, [the defendant] would have been free to change her mind'.

[177] *Milroy v Lord* (1862) 4 De GF & J 264, 45 ER 1185; Jeffrey Hackney, *Understanding Equity and Trusts* (London, Fontana Press, 1987) 118.

[178] *Banner Homes* (n 3) 399. Note that the term 'inequitableness' is used in a conclusory way to describe the situation where A has relied on B's promise in the requisite way; it is not a separate requirement for the doctrine to apply. The same observation was made in relation to the term 'fraud' in Chapter 4, S 4.4.2.4.

A further question arises for consideration. Because in the context of the doctrine in *Pallant v Morgan* A is not the transferor of the property B acquires, is there an additional requirement that A's actions (and B's promise)[179] must be a 'but for' cause *of B's acquisition of the property*?

There are two categories of cases where A's actions are a 'but for' cause of B's acquisition. One category involves A forgoing a clear opportunity to acquire the property for himself in favour of B. The facts of *Pallant v Morgan*[180] would have been an example had A been authorised to bid on a sum more substantial than B, and had stayed out of the bidding in order to allow B to acquire the land. A's staying out of the bidding would have directly led B to acquire the property. This corresponds to Chadwick LJ's suggestion that A's reliance may be '*detrimental* to the ability of [A] to acquire the property *on equal terms*'.[181]

In another category, A's actions may also be a 'but for' cause of B acquisition without having to give up an opportunity to acquire the property for himself on equal terms. An example would be where A convinces X, A's close friend, to sell X's land to B in reliance on B's promise to share the land with A, in circumstances where A is not previously interested in acquiring the land outright for himself and does not have the means of doing so. Without suffering any 'detriment', A's actions would nevertheless be a 'but for' cause of B's acquisition of the property, since A would have conferred on B an outright opportunity to acquire the land which B would not otherwise have had.

These examples notwithstanding, there is good reason to think that it is unnecessary to establish a 'but for' causal link between A's actions and B's acquisition. Once the courts recognise that informal agreements reached in the context of pre-acquisition negotiations can lead to the imposition of a constructive trust, this necessarily entails eschewing the need for such a causal link. Pre-acquisition negotiations are inherently contingent in nature: they are characterised by uncertainty and involve probabilities which may not materialise. Various other factors which are out of the parties' control may also be significant variables which contribute to—or frustrate—B's acquisition. If B succeeds in acquiring the property, it would be unjust to allow B to argue, with the benefit of hindsight, that A's actions had a lesser causal relationship to his acquisition than the parties had predicted, and so to allow B to retain the property for himself absolutely.

Consider again the earlier example where A convinces X, A's close friend, to sell X's land to B in reliance on B's promise to share the land with A, in circumstances where A was not interested or able to acquire the land outright for himself. In principle, it ought not make a difference to the outcome if it can be shown that X had planned to sell the property on the open market anyway, and that there was a reasonable possibility that B might have (for instance) responded to an advertisement placed by X in a local newspaper which B reads every morning and might have acquired the property that way. Such facts might indicate that A's actions was not a 'but for' cause of B's acquisition; yet, by ensuring that the property *was* sold to B, A's actions would have conferred on B an advantage in relation to his acquisition. By focusing on the parties' pre-acquisition agreement, therefore, the courts are

[179] Because B's promise must be a but-for cause of A's actions, these elements can be used interchangeably in the enquiry. Thus, the question whether B's promise must be a but-for cause of B's acquisition of the property yields the same answer as the question whether A's actions must be a but-for cause of B's acquisition.

[180] *Pallant v Morgan* (n 2).

[181] *Banner Homes* (n 3) 398 (emphases added).

more interested in the fact that A had contributed *in some way* to B's acquisition, instead of requiring that A's actions are a 'but for' cause of B's acquisition.

This analysis is reflected in *Pallant*[182] and *Banner Homes.*[183] In *Pallant*, had A not stayed out of the biding, B would still have succeeded in acquiring the land, albeit at a price of at least £2,001. In *Banner Homes*, it was shown that A did not consider acquiring the site for itself, and so had B not kept A on board, B would still have succeeded in acquiring the site. In both cases, therefore, A's actions were not a 'but for' cause of B's acquisition. Nevertheless, in both cases, B was compelled to give effect to his promise: it was sufficient that B's promise was a 'but for' cause of *A's acts of reliance.*

6.2.1.2.2. Advantage or Detriment?

What is the minimum effect which A's reliance must have on B's acquisition? It was said in *Banner Homes* that '[A] should do (or omit to do) something which confers an advantage on [B] in relation to the acquisition of the property; or is detrimental to the ability of [A] to acquire the property on equal terms'.[184] It might have been thought to be obvious why detriment is not insisted upon in every case: 'detriment' arises only where A forgoes an outright opportunity to acquire the property for himself; and we have seen[185] that the doctrine is not confined to such cases.

However, it has been suggested that B's advantage in every case can be re-characterised as a detriment on A's part in the form of '[a] loss that [A] suffers when, acting in reasonable reliance on [B]'s undertaking, he forgoes his opportunity to achieve the content of the undertaking in some other way'.[186] In Chapter 4,[187] it was explained that Simon Gardner suggests that this re-characterisation is capable of explaining a number of constructive trust doctrines including the doctrine in *Pallant v Morgan.* In spite of Chadwick LJ's statement in *Banner Homes* that detriment is unnecessary, Gardner suggests that A does lose the opportunity of securing 'a binding joint venture agreement with [B] (or perhaps, though this may have been only a theoretical possibility, someone else), and so to take an interest in the property that way.'[188] This loss arises because A refrains from 'playing a bargaining chip that might otherwise have helped him demand a proper contract before the start of bidding.'[189]

There are two main difficulties with this analysis. First, it is not always the case that A has the opportunity to demand a pre-acquisition binding contract. Suppose B receives instructions from its parent company specifically prohibiting B from entering into a formal joint venture arrangement with A. B nevertheless enters an informal agreement with A to share the property, simply to keep A out of the bidding process in order to increase B's opportunity of acquiring the property for itself. It is clear that A would not have lost any opportunity of securing 'a *binding* joint venture agreement' with B, since B did not have authority to enter into such an agreement; but the doctrine would surely operate to bind B to his promise.

182 *Pallant v Morgan* (n 2), the facts of which were set out in the main text following n 5 above.
183 *Banner Homes* (n 3), the facts of which were set out in the main text following n 6 above.
184 ibid 398.
185 See S 6.2.1.2.1.
186 Gardner, 'Reliance-Based Constructive Trusts' (n 81) 63.
187 See Chapter 4, S 4.3.2.
188 Gardner, 'Reliance-Based Constructive Trusts' (n 81) 73.
189 ibid 74.

Secondly, if it is sufficient that A had lost a 'theoretical' opportunity to secure a binding agreement with someone else, this entails that it would be unnecessary to produce concrete evidence of A having such an opportunity—for instance, through identifying another party who would, on the balance of probabilities, have entered into a similar agreement with A. However, this is inconsistent with the approach taken by judges, who are not prepared to find that A has suffered detriment where it is shown that A's opportunity to acquire the property was 'a merely fanciful possibility'.[190] Indeed, in general, the courts are reluctant to impose a remedy on the basis of a theoretical loss of opportunity: at a minimum, courts tend either to provide that a claimant can establish a loss based on evidential presumptions or, alternatively, to treat the advantage which the defendant obtains as the basis for relief.[191]

6.2.1.2.3. Acquisition-Related Advantage

The context in which the doctrine in *Pallant v Morgan* operates makes clear that A's reliance does not need to involve a transfer of property: it may arise through a variety of different acts. This is consistent with the 'norm against taking an advantage',[192] since this norm does not limit the form of actions which may lead to B obtaining an advantage in relation to his acquisition of the property. For the same reason, in *Banner Homes* Chadwick LJ observed that A need not act by staying out of the market:[193] this indicates that A's act of reliance is not restricted to any particular form.

However, it would be a mistake to think that it follows from this, and from the fact that A's actions need not be a 'but for' cause of B's acquisition, that *any* action induced by B's promise would fulfil the element of reliance for the purposes of the doctrine in *Pallant v Morgan*. As discussed in Chapter 3,[194] A must have conferred on B an advantage in relation to B's acquisition of the property to which his promise relates. This means that, at a minimum, A's actions must relate to B's acquisition of the property. Otherwise, B will be deemed to have acquired the property for himself absolutely, since A would not have conferred any relevant advantage in relation to B's acquisition to justify A having any claim to the property.

Take again the facts of *Pallant v Morgan*.[195] There were in fact two plots of land being auctioned, lots 15 and 16, both of which B successfully acquired. A constructive trust arose through an application of the doctrine in *Pallant v Morgan* in relation to lot 16, but it did not arise in relation to lot 15. This was so despite the fact that B's pre-acquisition promise had been to the effect that B would sell a portion of *both* lots to A if B successfully acquired them. This can be explained on the basis that A's reliance did not relate to B's acquisition of lot 15 at all. The negotiations were entered into by the parties' agents, and A had not given his agent the authority to bid for lot 15.[196] By staying out of the bidding for lot 16,

[190] *Cox v Jones* (n 13) [46]. See also Sean Wilken QC and Karim Ghaly, *Wilken and Ghaly: The Law of Waiver, Variation, and Estoppel*, 3rd edn (Oxford, OUP, 2012) [11-73].

[191] See *Strand Electric & Engineering Co Ltd v Brisfords Entertainments Ltd* [1952] 2 QB 246 (CA) 257, where Romer LJ analysed the relief on the basis of a presumed loss, and Denning LJ (ibid 255) analysed the relief on the basis of an advantage gained. See too Craig Rotherham, '"*Wrotham Park* Damages" and Accounts of Profits: Compensation or Restitution?' [2008] *Lloyd's Maritime and Commercial Law Quarterly* 25, 34–35.

[192] Explained in Chapter 4, S 4.3.4.

[193] *Banner Homes* (n 3) 399.

[194] See Chapter 3, S 3.2.1.1.

[195] *Pallant v Morgan* (n 2).

[196] ibid 50.

A conferred an advantage in relation to B's acquisition of that lot, therefore justifying an application of the doctrine; but that act did not relate in any way to B's acquisition of lot 15, therefore no constructive trust arose in relation to lot 15.

For the same reason, it would be insufficient for the purposes of the doctrine in *Pallant v Morgan* for A to rely, for example, by conferring an advantage on B in the form of looking after B's ailing grandmother or mowing B's lawn in return for B's promise, even though A acts pursuant to a pre-agreed course of action.[197]

6.2.1.2.4. Prospective Advantage

In explaining the element of advantage, Chadwick LJ observed that, in *Pallant*, '[A]'s agreement … to keep out of the bidding gave an advantage to [B]—in that he was able to obtain the property for a lower price than would otherwise have been possible'.[198] This approach assesses the element of advantage from the standpoint of what ultimately transpires to be the gain made by B, with the benefit of hindsight—that is, after all the factual eventualities are revealed. In other words, this approach focuses on an *ultimate* or *net* advantage B gains in relation his acquisition of the property.

This 'net advantage' approach gives rise to difficulties. Consider an act of reliance arising through omission,[199] the classic case being where A refrains from bidding in competition with B.[200] On an assessment made with the benefit of hindsight, suppose that it transpires that A's reliance had in fact led B to save only a *de minimis* sum in the course of acquiring the property—£1, for example. Or suppose that a third-party's intervening bid had increased the ultimate purchase price so that it negated the net effect of A's reliance. In the former case, there is certainly a 'net advantage', but would the imposition of a constructive trust be justified? In the latter case, ought the fact that there is no 'net advantage' lead to A being left without a remedy?

Consider also acts of reliance arising through commission. In the case law, A's contribution is usually substantial, arising for instance through committing to a joint venture[201] or performing services in favour of B.[202] However, if the net market value of A's contribution turned out to be *de minimis*, would this suffice? Certainly, A would have conferred on B a 'net advantage',[203] but it is not immediately obvious that this would justify the imposition of a constructive trust.

There are three possible solutions. The first is simply to accept Chadwick LJ's 'net advantage' approach without more. However, as the hypothetical examples cited in the two preceding paragraphs show, this may lead to arbitrary results in certain cases. In turn, serious

[197] As Chadwick LJ observed in *Banner Homes* (n 3) 400, the doctrine 'does not seek to give effect to the parties' bargain'. It would, however, be possible for A to make a claim based on proprietary estoppel, to the effect that A should be compensated for the detriment suffered in reliance on B's induced assumptions that A would obtain an interest in B's property: see discussion in Chapter 7.

[198] ibid 398.

[199] Chadwick LJ held that A's act of reliance may arise through acts of omission or commission: *Banner Homes* (n 3) 398.

[200] *Pallant v Morgan* (n 2).

[201] *Banner Homes* (n 3) 401.

[202] *Time Products Ltd* (n 28) 395.

[203] There would probably not be any material detriment, since the A's contribution would not itself indicate that he had given up the ability to acquire the property on equal terms.

doubts would be raised as to the legitimacy of imposing constructive trusts through the doctrine in *Pallant v Morgan*, leading to the possible conclusion that the doctrine is 'anything but equitable in its operation'.[204] The second possibility is to postulate a minimum sum below which B will not be considered as having gained any 'material advantage'. However, this will always be an arbitrary exercise. The third possibility is to recognise that, in reality, the courts are not after all concerned with the 'net advantage' B obtains.

It is submitted that the third solution best explains the doctrine in *Pallant v Morgan*. Rather than being concerned with a 'net advantage', courts assess and respond to a 'prospective advantage'. This entails assessing advantage at a point in time *prior* to B acquiring the property. Consider the way in which Chadwick LJ evaluated B's position in *Banner Homes* itself.[205] It was held that A did not suffer any detriment by entering into the arrangement with B, since A did not 'consider the site as a potential acquisition for its own commercial portfolio';[206] however, B kept A 'on board' because, 'if dropped, [B thought that A] might emerge as a rival for the site.'[207] Notice how the element of advantage was assessed: it was enough that '[B] saw it as an advantage that [A's] belief that the site was out of play should be maintained'.[208] Prospectively, B had obtained an advantage by keeping A on board; it was irrelevant that B's belief turned out to be misplaced from a 'net advantage' point of view. Indeed, on the facts, B had not obtained a 'net advantage': a retrospective evaluation revealed that A 'had, itself, known of and been interested in the site ... but that interest had not been pursued at that time in the light of actual or perceived planning constraints.'[209] All that mattered was that B 'obtained the advantage which it sought'[210] from A's reliance. The element of advantage is judged prospectively.

One might object that this analysis is unacceptable from A's point of view: without a net advantage (or detriment), the award of a constructive trust in A's favour is not justified. This is because (the argument goes) the lack of a net advantage (or detriment) would not even be sufficient to engage the other more commonly pleaded claims: the lack of detriment would rule out a proprietary estoppel claim; the lack of net advantage would rule out an unjust enrichment claim; the absence of an enforceable contract would rule out any contractual claim. However, these other claims do not tell us anything about a claim by way of the doctrine in *Pallant v Morgan*, which can be justified on the basis of the 'norm against taking an advantage'.[211] When A's actions are calculated to increase B's chances of acquiring the property, B obtains an advantage. The advantage is conferred on the basis that B will carry out his promise. If it materialises in the acquisition of property but B is then allowed to take the whole property for himself, B would be retaining the proceeds of the advantage which he obtained from A. This remains so whether or not it survives in the form of a 'net advantage'. It is therefore necessary for equity to impose a constructive trust to bind B to his promise which was the basis on which the advantage was conferred in the first place.

[204] Hopkins, 'The *Pallant v Morgan* "Equity"?' (n 4) 49.
[205] The facts of *Banner Homes* were set out in the main text following n 6 above.
[206] *Banner Homes* (n 3) 400.
[207] ibid.
[208] ibid.
[209] ibid 377.
[210] ibid 400.
[211] This norm was explained in Chapter 4, S 4.3.4.

The same point can be made in another way. It would only be necessary for A's reliance to produce a net advantage (or detriment) if the rationale of the doctrine in *Pallant v Morgan* were concerned with stripping B's gains (or correcting A's reliance loss). Understood by way of the present analysis, however, the position is different: it is B's promise, given prior to the acquisition, and A's reliance, completed prior to B's acquisition, which determines whether B will be bound to fulfil his promise. Once the elements of promise and reliance are fulfilled, it would be unjust to allow B to escape the consequences of qualifying his interest in the property merely because B can show that the opportunity A conferred does not survive by way of a 'net advantage', determined with the benefit of hindsight.

6.2.1.2.5. Calculated Opportunity as Advantage

Since the relevant advantage arises and is assessed prior to the acquisition, an 'advantage' does not consist solely of B's acquisition of the property itself or savings B makes in the purchase price. Instead, the advantage is an *opportunity* to acquire the property, as measured at the time it is conferred by A. Because the acquisition is prospective when the parties enter into their agreement, all the factual eventualities of the acquisition are not yet known. If A acts in an agreed way which aims to increase the chances of B acquiring the property, and A's acts are taken by B to provide such an opportunity, then A confers on B the relevant advantage which fulfils the element of reliance. In short, such an opportunity is conferred whenever A's agreed actions are *calculated to* increase B's chances of acquiring the property.

It might be thought that there is a significant difference between the doctrine in *Pallant v Morgan* as compared to the doctrine in *Rochefoucauld v Boustead* and secret trusts. In the latter two doctrines, the property in question is often transferred to B from A, whereas in the doctrine in *Pallant v Morgan* B acquires the property from a third-party vendor. Upon closer inspection, these doctrines are united in their approach to reliance. In all three doctrines, B always obtains an *opportunity* to acquire the property in question from A, which corresponds to A's contribution in some way to the occasion of B's acquisition. In cases where A is the transferor, the opportunity B obtains is simultaneous with its materialisation in the form of the acquisition of the property, and so the courts do not deal with the opportunity as a distinct element from the fact of acquisition. Nevertheless, it remains the case that B always obtains an opportunity because he is given the occasion of acquiring A's property. Hence, the only relevant difference between cases where A is the transferor and cases where B acquires property from a third-party relates to the relative length of time between opportunity and acquisition: it is simultaneous in most of the former cases,[212] whereas in the latter cases the acquisition is prospective.[213] Thus, at a more fundamental level, B always obtains an advantage in the form of an opportunity to acquire the property from A or a third-party vendor to which his promise relates. If and when the opportunity materialises, equity binds B to fulfil his promise in relation to the property.

[212] See Chapter 5, S 5.2.2.1. for examples in relation to the secret trusts doctrine where A's reliance is complete—and therefore B obtains the relevant opportunity—before B actually acquires A's property.

[213] It might be thought that another difference is that acquisition is guaranteed where A is the transferor and not guaranteed in relation to the doctrine in *Pallant v Morgan*. However, because B must acquire the property before any constructive trust can be imposed, this is not a material difference insofar as the imposition of constructive trusts is concerned.

6.2.1.2.6. Timing and Acquisition

It is necessary for A's reliance to be fulfilled before—and be effective until—the time of B's acquisition. As Patten LJ observed in *Clarke v Corless*,[214] 'the agreement reached [is] sufficient to found the necessary equity if it was in fact relied upon up to and including the date on which [B] acquired the retained land so as to make their retention of it unconscionable.' If A's actions arise only after B acquires the property, they clearly do not confer any advantage in relation to B's acquisition. There would then be no reason why a constructive trust would arise immediately upon B's acquisition of the property. Hence, such a case would fall to be considered as an AI situation, with B being taken to have acquired the property in his own right.[215] This explains why the doctrine in *Pallant v Morgan* has been said to apply only where the parties reach a *pre-acquisition* agreement, and not where the agreement concerns property B owns all along.[216]

Given that A's reliance must be completed prior to B's acquisition, it is important to consider what counts as an 'acquisition'. In most cases, an 'acquisition' occurs when B obtains title to the property. However, certain situations call for a more precise analysis, for instance where B attempts to renege on a promise during the acquisition process. It seems that, at a minimum, an 'acquisition' requires for B to gain some substantive interest in the property.

Take for instance the Northern Irish case of *Gilmurray v Corr*.[217] B agreed to purchase the freehold interest in certain lands and to cede the driving range which was part of those lands to A. The material events were that 'from 13 November the vendors held the lands as trustees for [B]', and that '[B] had tried on 20 November to introduce a covenant restricting [A] in the enjoyment of the driving range'.[218] B was held to be bound to his promise. It did not matter that the agreement to purchase was only signed by B on 26 November, because he had already obtained an interest in the property as beneficiary under a trust from 13 November.[219] Having 'acquired' a qualified interest in the equitable title, B could not have reneged on his original intention to sell the driving range to A. A similar analysis also explains the case of *Holiday Inns Inc v Broadhead*,[220] discussed below, where the securing of an option to purchase the relevant land was considered an 'acquisition' for the purposes of the doctrine.

Presumably an 'acquisition' would also occur where the third party transferor acts in such a way which fulfils the requirements for the rule in *Re Rose* to apply.[221] So, where the third party has done everything in his power to transfer the property to B,[222] B obtains a substantive and unrevocable interest in the property by way of a constructive trust sufficient to count as an 'acquisition' for the purposes of the doctrine in *Pallant v Morgan*.

[214] *Clarke v Corless* (n 136) [50].

[215] The doctrine of proprietary estoppel may therefore be potentially relevant.

[216] This feature was first identified by Chadwick LJ in *Banner Homes* (n 3) 400, and was subsequently approved by Lord Scott in *Cobbe* (n 46) [33]. See also *Benedetti v Sawiris* [2009] EWHC 1330 (Ch) [520]. As Morgan J observed in *Crossco* (Ch) (n 52) [364], 'there can be an important difference between a case of a pre-acquisition agreement and a post-acquisition agreement.'

[217] *Gilmurray v Corr* [1978] NI 99.

[218] ibid 104.

[219] That beneficial interest was not negated by the fact that, between 13 and 26 November, 'the evidence required by the Statute of Frauds would have been lacking if the defendant had occasion to insist on his rights': ibid 104.

[220] *Holiday Inns Inc v Broadhead* (n 16).

[221] This doctrine is discussed in Chapter 9.

[222] The precise requirements of the doctrine are found in Chapter 9, S 9.1.

6.2.1.2.7. Limits

Although a wide range of actions by A is capable of fulfilling the element of reliance, there are three important ways in which A's reliance may limit the application of the doctrine.

First, the objective significance of A's reliance may have a bearing on whether the doctrine in *Pallant v Morgan* applies. For instance, where the agreement is that A will contribute merely a small sum of money to the acquisition, this may well be evidence that the parties intended merely to treat A's money as a personal loan, rather than for A to acquire a beneficial interest in the acquired property. As the Court of Appeal observed in *Ashburn Anstalt v WJ Arnold & Co*,[223] a mere loan of money from A to B to assist in B's acquisition of property does not confer on A a right by way of a constructive trust. Where A's reliance is objectively and relatively insignificant, the implication is that B may well have not made the requisite promise to hold the property on trust for A in order for the doctrine to apply.

Secondly, where A's reliance consists of a financial contribution to B's acquisition, and where the parties have not reached an agreement concerning how the property is to be apportioned, a 'purchase money resulting trust' may provide an alternative solution if B had not made the requisite pre-acquisition promise to engage the doctrine in *Pallant v Morgan*.

Thirdly, if A is to be remunerated by B for A's actions, this may count against an operation of the doctrine. So, for instance, if A acts as B's solicitor or agent, A may act pursuant to B's request in such a way that helps B to acquire the property; but because A is remunerated, it is likely that A would not have been induced to act by a promise by B to cede an interest in the property to A.

6.2.1.3. Holiday Inns Inc v Broadhead

The case of *Holiday Inns Inc v Broadhead*[224] requires special consideration. It has proven to be a difficult case to rationalise, causing disagreement among judges concerning whether the case represents an application of proprietary estoppel or the doctrine in *Pallant v Morgan*. According to Chadwick LJ in *Banner Homes*,[225] Megarry J who heard the claim for interlocutory relief in *Holiday Inns* 'express[ed] the view … that the *Pallant v Morgan* equity had much in common with proprietary estoppel, as exemplified in *Ramsden v Dyson* and the other cases in that line of authority.'[226] Chadwick LJ also noted that Goff J in the final hearing of *Holiday Inns*[227] 'adopted the analogy with proprietary estoppel'.[228] Chadwick LJ himself was in agreement with the proprietary estoppel analysis, although his Lordship was uncomfortable with what he perceived as a pre-acquisition agreement on the facts.[229] On the other hand, in *Cobbe*, Lord Walker analysed the case as 'akin to *Pallant v Morgan*',[230]

[223] *Ashburn Anstalt v WJ Arnold & Co* [1989] Ch 1 (CA) 25. The Court was disagreeing with the contrary conclusion reached by Browne-Wilkinson J in *Re Sharpe (A Bankrupt)* [1980] 1 WLR 219 (Ch).

[224] *Holiday Inns Inc v Broadhead* (n 16).

[225] *Banner Homes* (n 3) 391.

[226] *Ramsden v Dyson* (1866) LR 1 HL 129 (HL).

[227] *Holiday Inns Inc v Broadhead* (1974) 232 EG 951 (Ch).

[228] *Banner Homes* (n 3) 391.

[229] ibid 397–98.

[230] *Cobbe* (n 46) [78].

and Lord Scott thought that it was incorrect to analyse the case under the doctrine of proprietary estoppel.[231]

Using the analysis explained in the previous sections, it is possible to resolve this disagreement. Particular attention needs to be paid to the need for A's reliance to relate to B's acquisition of property.

6.2.1.3.1. Facts

In *Holiday Inns*, a hotel company (A) was interested in entering into a joint venture with B, under which B would cede an interest in his land for A to build a hotel, and they would share the profits made. The parties first made contact through A's representative who arranged for W, the head of A's organisation, to meet with B and to view his five-acre site. During that meeting, W expressed his dissatisfaction with the site and indicated that he would be prepared to settle for that site only if B was unable to secure one of the neighbouring sites. Prompted by this, B acquired an option to purchase an adjacent 15-acre site. Then, A committed much effort and money to acquire a planning permission over the 15-acre site, which ultimately proved to be successful. This increased the value of the land significantly. At this point, B demanded terms more favourable to himself; and although A was willing to meet them, B suddenly broke off negotiations. A sought interlocutory relief before Megarry J, who refused their claim but granted leave to appeal to the Court of Appeal. In order to prevent A's appeal from having any real effect were it to succeed, B exercised the option to purchase and granted a lease over the site to a third party. In the ensuing fresh litigation, Goff J found for A: he ordered an 'equal division, after allowing each party credit in respect of their actual expenditure',[232] subject to the priority of the innocent third-party underlessee.[233]

6.2.1.3.2. Discussion

It is observable that B's promise was made pre-acquisition: before acquiring the option over the 15-acre site,[234] B had already promised to cede to A some interest in any neighbouring land which he might acquire for A to build a hotel. Hence, Chadwick LJ observed in *Banner Homes*[235] that 'it might be said that the arrangement or understanding, made at the time when only the five acre site was owned by [B], did, in fact, precede [B]'s acquisition of the option over the 15-acre site.'

However, it is not immediately obvious when the element of reliance was fulfilled: did A complete its acts of reliance before or after B's acquisition? The answer depends on what counts as an 'acquisition' on the facts—whether it occurred when B obtained the option to purchase over the 15-acre site, or only when B exercised the option. The better view is clearly that it occurred when B obtained the option. By obtaining the option, B acquired 'an

[231] ibid [24], [31].

[232] This is noted in *Banner Homes* (n 3) 393.

[233] This is noted in *Crossco* (Ch) (n 52) [279].

[234] On an alternative view, it might be said that there was insufficient discussion concerning the 15-acre site before B acquired the option over the site. If so, it would be even more obvious that the decision can only be analysed in terms of proprietary estoppel, since on this alternative view, even B's promise would have been made post-acquisition.

[235] *Banner Homes* (n 3) 398.

immediate interest in the land'.[236] Moreover, had the option not been exercised before the case came before Goff J, B would surely have been compelled to exercise it and to hold half the land on trust for A: it would be inconceivable that A's case would hinge on whether B decided to exercise the option. Thus, B's acquisition of the option was the cut-off point for the fulfilment of A's acts of reliance in order for the doctrine in *Pallant v Morgan* to operate.

On the facts, the only action by A in relation to the 15-acre site was its efforts in obtaining the planning permission, which, according to Goff J, began '[s]hortly *after* the option agreement'.[237] He also observed that B 'had no real chance of securing the planning permission himself. He needed the support of an hotelier, and he encouraged [A] to lend him theirs.'[238] The advantage B hoped to gain, and A's conferral of it, arose after B had acquired the option. Furthermore, there is no trace of any act by A which had increased B's opportunity to acquire the 15-acre site. Indeed, A did not become involved in the application for planning permission until after B had acquired the option and instructed a solicitor to prepare a report on the matter.[239] Given that A did nothing which conferred any prospective advantage in the form of an opportunity to acquire the 15-acre site, a constructive trust would not have arisen through an application of the doctrine in *Pallant v Morgan*. Instead, B purchased the site as absolute owner, and A's remedy is best explained as having been imposed through an application of proprietary estoppel.[240]

Unfortunately, Goff J's judgment blurred the line between the doctrine in *Pallant v Morgan* and proprietary estoppel by concluding that 'there is a head of equity under which relief will be given where the owner of property seeks to take an unconscionable advantage of another by allowing or encouraging him to spend money, whether or not on the owner's property, in the belief … that the person expending the money will enjoy some right or benefit over the owner's property which the owner then denies him.'[241] This statement fails to distinguish between QI situations, which concern the pre-acquisition conferral of a prospective advantage, and proprietary estoppel, where the degree of A's detriment determines the appropriate remedy. Ultimately, however, Goff J clearly applied proprietary estoppel principles. Despite speaking of the law as responding to an 'advantage', the degree of detriment A suffered would have justified imposing a constructive trust through the doctrine of proprietary estoppel. Moreover, Goff J undertook an extensive and careful assessment of the range of potentially appropriate remedies before ordering an equal division of the land.[242] This reflects the exercise of remedial discretion in order to determine the appropriate content of the remedy, which is characteristic of a proprietary estoppel analysis. Indeed, as Goff J himself acknowledged, his decision to impose a remedy of equal division was a decision he made '[q]uite apart from the case of *Pallant v Morgan* itself, where this [similar] basis was adopted'.[243]

[236] Charles Harpum, Stuart Bridge and Martin Dixon, *Megarry & Wade: The Law of Real Property*, 8th edn (London, Sweet & Maxwell, 2012) [15-062].
[237] *Holiday Inns Inc v Broadhead* (n 227) 955 (emphasis added).
[238] ibid 1091.
[239] ibid 955.
[240] This doctrine is discussed in Chapter 7.
[241] *Holiday Inns Inc v Broadhead* (n 227) 1087.
[242] ibid 1095–97.
[243] ibid 1095.

If proprietary estoppel provides the better analysis, it appears surprising that, in *Cobbe*, both Lord Scott and Lord Walker attempted to analyse *Holiday Inns* as an application of the doctrine in *Pallant v Morgan*. The basis for Lord Scott's view was that the doctrine arises where 'a joint venture involves the acquisition by one of the joint venturers of the property intended for the purposes of the joint venture'.[244] Framed in this way, it is inevitable that *Holiday Inns* would be analysed as an application of the doctrine in *Pallant v Morgan*. However, as discussed earlier,[245] this statement is inaccurate because the application of the doctrine in *Pallant v Morgan* does not hinge simply on whether property is acquired pursuant to a 'joint venture'.

Lord Walker's reasoning is more sophisticated. His Lordship held that *Holiday Inns* was 'akin to *Pallant v Morgan*' because it was 'a case where one joint venturer *permitted* another to acquire legal rights (in that case, an option to purchase the site) in the belief that the property would be used for the joint venture.'[246] This analysis suggests that A's reliance did, after all, arise *prior* to B's acquisition of the option and, therefore, *conferred* on B an opportunity to acquire the 15-acre site. However, this analysis misrepresents the facts of *Holiday Inns*. There is no indication whatsoever that A was interested in acquiring the 15-acre site (or the option) for itself; in fact, A would have ultimately settled for the existing five-acre site had B not acquired any alternative site.[247] That is to say, in no way did A 'permit' B to acquire the option by stepping aside to facilitate B's acquisition; moreover, B did not require A's permission to acquire the option.

Ultimately, it seems that Lords Walker and Scott were forced to analyse *Holiday Inns* the way they did because of the way in which the principles of proprietary estoppel were interpreted in *Cobbe* itself.[248] As Morgan J observed in *Crossco*,[249] 'if one applied the principles relating to proprietary estoppel as laid down in *Cobbe*, Holiday Inns Inc would not have been able to establish the benefit of a proprietary estoppel because Holiday Inns Inc knew that they did not have the benefit of a legally binding agreement with Mr Broadhead.' In Cobbe, Lord Scott had asserted that proprietary estoppel could only operate to bar B from asserting some fact or a mixture of fact and law which stands in the way of a right claimed by A.[250] In *Holiday Inns*, because A knew that it did not have the benefit of a binding contract with B, there was no fact or a mixture of fact and law which B could be said to have been barred from asserting. Nevertheless, the later decision of the House of Lords in *Thorner v Major*[251] has confirmed that Lord Scott's assertion does not represent the law on proprietary estoppel.[252] Therefore, the characterisation of *Holiday Inns* given by Lords Scott and Walker must be regarded as erroneous.

244 *Cobbe* (n 46) [24].
245 See S 6.1.3.2.3.
246 *Cobbe* (n 46) [78] (emphasis added).
247 *Holiday Inns Inc v Broadhead* (n 227) 953.
248 See, eg, *Cobbe* (n 46) [14]–[16].
249 *Crossco* (Ch) (n 52) [279].
250 *Cobbe* (n 46) [14].
251 *Thorner v Major* (n 47).
252 See Ben McFarlane and Andrew Robertson, 'Apocalypse Averted: Proprietary Estoppel in the House of Lords' (2009) 125 *LQR* 535, 538.

6.3. Three-Party Cases

In the typical case, B promises to cede an interest in the acquired property *to A*. However, because the effect of applying the doctrine in *Pallant v Morgan* is the enforcement of B's promise, nothing in principle prevents C from enforcing the informal agreement between A and B which contains a promise by B to hold some interest in the acquired property for C. Since the doctrine compels B to fulfil his promise, it seems clear that C becomes a beneficiary under a constructive trust from the moment of B's acquisition.

A strong indication of this is found in the case of *Neale v Willis*.[253] Although this case was decided years before *Banner Homes* had formally recognised the doctrine in *Pallant v Morgan* as a discrete category of constructive trusts,[254] the same principle underlying the doctrine in *Pallant v Morgan* can clearly be detected in that case. A husband (B) and wife (C) purchased a council house. They raised the purchase money by way of a mortgage, cash received from the incoming tenant of their former flat and £50 which B borrowed from his mother-in-law (A). A lent the £50 to B in reliance on B's promise that the house would be put in the joint names of B and C. However, B secretly took the conveyance in his own name. The Court of Appeal held that B was bound to carry out his promise to A: a constructive trust was imposed to compel B to hold the house for himself and C jointly.[255]

Apart from the fact that the intended beneficiary was C instead of A, the case is on all fours with the doctrine in *Pallant v Morgan*. B's intention, as objectively deduced from his promise to A, was that C would obtain a joint beneficial interest in the acquired house. It did not matter that A was not party to the proceedings and therefore that a contractual action could not be made out:[256] it was B's promise and A's reliance to which the constructive trust responded. The money A lent to B prior to the acquisition was an act of reliance which was induced by B's promise. It is clear that A had not *simply* made a loan of money to B, but had also conferred on B an advantage in relation to the acquisition of the property. As Lord Denning MR observed, '[B and C] needed the £50 to pay the council, but they had not got it':[257] the parties clearly recognised that A's contribution would provide B an opportunity to acquire the property. It did not matter that B might have been able theoretically to secure a loan from someone else without making such a promise. Furthermore, A would not have acted as she did but for B's promise to hold the property jointly for B and C, this being deduced from the fact that A demanded evidence from B that the application form had included both B's and C's names before she advanced the money to B. Thus, upon B's acquisition of the property,[258] a constructive trust was imposed in C's favour to compel B to carry out the entirety of his promise.

[253] *Neale v Willis* (1968) 19 P & CR 836 (CA).

[254] Furthermore, although *Neale* emerged a number of years after the case of *Pallant v Morgan* (n 2) had been decided, *Pallant* was not referred to in the Court of Appeal's judgment in *Neale*.

[255] *Neale v Willis* (n 253) 839.

[256] ibid.

[257] ibid 838.

[258] ibid 839.

7

Proprietary Estoppel

Although it is commonly recognised that there is a close relationship between constructive trusts and proprietary estoppel, it remains unclear what that relationship precisely entails. Taking as its starting point the remedies awarded in proprietary estoppel, the bulk of the chapter explains how proprietary estoppel can be understood as giving effect to A's secondary right, which arises as a result of a breach of duty B owes towards A. It follows that remedies imposed through the operation of proprietary estoppel, whether personal or proprietary, can be analysed as reflective remedies. As part of this discussion, a number of objections to this analysis will be considered and refuted. Finally, the effects of this analysis will be observed. By comparing proprietary estoppel with the QI doctrines—namely the doctrine in *Rochefoucauld v Boustead*, secret trusts, and the doctrine in *Pallant v Morgan*—two senses of 'constructive trust' can be distinguished. The comparison also reveals the intricacies of how proprietary estoppel and the QI doctrines relate to one another.

For reasons we have observed in Chapter 3,[1] the discussion will be concerned primarily with the promise-based strand of proprietary estoppel, which applies where B promises that B will cede an interest in property he owns absolutely to A, and A detrimentally relies on B's promise.

7.1. The Nature of the Constructive Trust

It is clear that proprietary estoppel falls to be considered within the bilateral events category of constructive trusts: the events which trigger an application of the doctrine involve acts of both parties—a promise by B and reliance by A. The fact that proprietary estoppel is not a contractual claim[2] also easily explains why the doctrine is 'non-contract-based'. A more difficult matter concerns how proprietary estoppel responds to rights. Does the doctrine respond to primary or secondary rights—or, relatedly, are the remedies imposed replicative or reflective in nature?

It might be thought that, because proprietary estoppel *responds* to B's 'unconscionable' conduct, this implies that a wrong has been committed. From this, it might be argued that proprietary estoppel gives effect to A's secondary right. However, this is a superficial

[1] See Chapter 3, S 3.2.1.2.

[2] Ben McFarlane, 'Proprietary Estoppel: The Importance of Looking Back' in Paul S Davies and Justine Pila (eds), *The Jurisprudence of Lord Hoffmann: A Festschrift in Honour of Lord Leonard Hoffmann* (Oxford, Hart Publishing, 2015) 349.

conclusion, since the notion of 'unconscionability'[3] is too imprecise and therefore ill-suited as a causative event. As Tomlinson LJ observed in *Southwell v Blackburn*,[4] 'unconscionability' 'is not a watertight element in the estoppel but rather a feature which permeates all of its elements'.[5] It is more fruitful, instead, to start by observing the remedies which may be awarded by way of proprietary estoppel.

7.1.1. Remedies

When determining the appropriate remedy to be imposed by way of proprietary estoppel, courts exercise remedial discretion, being guided by the notion of the 'minimum equity to do justice to the plaintiff',[6] and aim to achieve proportionality[7] between A's detriment and B's role in inducing it.[8] In cases where parties enter into an arrangement akin to a 'bargain'[9]—that is, where A's reliance arises through the performance of an agreed quid pro quo[10]—courts usually hold B to his promise,[11] often through the imposition of a constructive trust.[12] However, a lesser remedy may also be imposed. For example, in *Campbell v Griffin*,[13] *Jennings v Rice*,[14] *Ottey v Grundy*,[15] *Powell v Benney*,[16] *Henry v Henry*,[17] and

[3] As is the case with 'fraud', see Chapter 4, S 4.4.2.5.

[4] *Southwell v Blackburn* [2014] EWCA Civ 1347, [2015] 2 FLR 1240 [20].

[5] As noted in Ben McFarlane, *The Law of Proprietary Estoppel* (Oxford, OUP, 2014) [5-60], 'B's method of proving a prima facie case of unconscionability consists precisely in establishing each of the three main elements of the doctrine'.

[6] *Crabb v Arun District Council* [1976] 1 Ch 179 (CA) 198.

[7] In Simon Gardner, 'The Remedial Discretion in Proprietary Estoppel—Again' (2006) 122 *LQR* 492, 499, despite arguing that proprietary estoppel does not aim to achieve proportionality but to 'rectify unconscionability ... of a particular kind', Gardner nevertheless recognises that remedial discretion is exercised by the courts, and also concludes that such discretion is necessary: see Gardner, 'Again' (n 7) 507–08.

[8] *Henry v Henry* [2010] UKPC 3, [2010] 1 All ER 988 [65].

[9] The distinction between what can be labelled 'bargain' and 'non-bargain' cases was made by Walker LJ in *Jennings v Rice* [2002] EWCA Civ 159, [2003] 1 FCR 501 [50]; but note that Lord Walker has extrajudicially suggested that it is 'better to refer to a spectrum rather than a dividing line': Lord Walker, 'Which Side 'Ought to Win'?—Discretion and Certainty in Property Law' [2008] *Singapore Journal of Legal Studies* 229, 239.

[10] Susan Bright and Ben McFarlane, 'Proprietary Estoppel and Property Rights' (2005) 64 *CLJ* 449, 458; Ben McFarlane and Sir Philip Sales, 'Promises, Detriment, and Liability: Lessons from Proprietary Estoppel' (2015) 131 *LQR* 610, 619.

[11] This is sometimes expressed as an award for 'expectation relief'. However, since we are primarily concerned with the promise-based strand of proprietary estoppel (see Chapter 3, S 3.2.1.2.), it is more helpful to speak of the objective content of B's promise as opposed to A's expectation (McFarlane, *The Law of Proprietary Estoppel* (n 5) [7-97]). This rightly emphasises the fact that A's expectation may sometimes be completely out of line with what B had promised, and in such cases the difference between A's expectation and the content of B's promise is neglected in the courts' analysis (*Jennings v Rice* (n 9) [50]). After all, B ought not to be made responsible for an expectation which he did not induce. Hence, we will speak of courts 'holding B to his promise' in lieu of 'awarding expectation relief'.

[12] Of course, other remedies are available for the protection of A's expectation interest: see, eg, discussion in McFarlane, 'The Importance of Looking Back' (n 2) 348, and *Parker v Parker* [2003] EWHC 1846 (Ch). However, as this chapter is concerned with achieving a proper taxonomy of constructive trusts, the focus will be on the constructive trust remedy.

[13] *Campbell v Griffin* [2001] EWCA Civ 990, [2001] WTLR 981.

[14] *Jennings v Rice* (n 9).

[15] *Ottey v Grundy* [2003] EWCA Civ 1176, [2003] WTLR 1253.

[16] *Powell v Benney* [2007] EWCA Civ 1283.

[17] *Henry v Henry* (n 8).

Southwell v Blackburn,[18] B was liable only for compensatory damages (or 'equitable compensation'). As Hoffmann LJ (as his Lordship then was) observed in *Walton v Walton*,[19] the remedy:

> … can take various forms. [The court] may order the maker of the promise to pay compensation for the expense which has been incurred. It may make payment of compensation a charge on the property. Or it may require the promise to be kept. The choice of remedy is flexible.

The availability of damages where B's breach causes a loss has been described as a 'sure test'[20] and a 'powerful indicator'[21] that the remedy is wrong-based. After all, '"damages" means nothing more specific than a monetary award given for a wrong.'[22] It follows that *all* proprietary estoppel remedies, whether in the form of a constructive trust or damages, do not give direct effect to A's primary right, but instead reflect A's secondary right.

It might be objected that this analysis overemphasises the availability of compensatory awards in proprietary estoppel. It was certainly once accurate to say that '[t]he presumptive style of relief in proprietary estoppel is the award *in specie* of the interest expected by [A]';[23] and it probably remains true that the number of litigated cases which result in B being held to his promise (including by way of constructive trust) are more numerous than those which do not.[24] However, it would be a mistake to surmise therefrom that compensatory awards are insignificant. A cause of action in proprietary estoppel arises if the elements of assurance or promise, reliance, and detriment flowing as a result of B's wrong are fulfilled.[25] But '[i]t is clear … that these elements are fact sensitive and hugely dependent on the context'.[26] The mere *existence* of these elements says nothing about the *degree* in which they arise, which affects the determination of the awarded remedy. As Simon Gardner observes:[27]

> Proprietary estoppel exists to adjust the prevailing balance of property between [A] and [B] when [A] has formed the relevant kind of expectation, and has acted detrimentally in reliance on it, and these occurrences are ascribable to [B] (via his encouragement of or acquiescence in them), so that it would be unconscionable for him to insist on the *status quo*. It would be inept if this jurisdiction were applicable only to cases in which [A] is precise in his expectation and minutely circumspect in his reliance. The whole point may be that [B] has lulled [A] into an assumption that all will be well, without need for clear particularisation. It is no surprise, therefore, that the law tolerates

[18] *Southwell v Blackburn* (n 4).

[19] *Walton v Walton* (CA, 14 April 1994).

[20] Andrew Burrows, *The Law of Restitution*, 3rd edn (Oxford, OUP, 2010) 622.

[21] James Edelman, 'Equitable Torts' (2002) 10 *Torts Law Journal* 64, 74.

[22] James Edelman, *Gain-Based Damages: Contract Tort Equity and Intellectual Property* (Oxford, Hart Publishing, 2002) 5.

[23] Simon Gardner, 'The Remedial Discretion in Proprietary Estoppel' (1999) 115 *LQR* 438, 466, although this is no longer the case: see Gardner, 'Again' (n 7) 492. It appears that the position in Australia remains that of according primary to expectation relief: see, eg, *Crown Melbourne Limited v Cosmopolitan Hotel (Vic) Pty Ltd* [2016] HCA 26 [39]; *Giumelli v Giumelli* (1999) 196 CLR 101; James Edelman, 'Remedial Certainty or Remedial Discretion in Estoppel after *Giumelli*?' (1999) 15 *Journal of Contract Law* 179, 192.

[24] Donal Nolan, 'Rights, Damage and Loss' (2017) 37 OJLS 255, 269 fn 59; although note that, since 1999, the trend has reversed: see main text to n 113 below.

[25] *Thorner v Major* [2009] UKHL 18, [2009] 1 WLR 776 [29].

[26] *Aspden v Elvy* [2012] EWHC 1387 (Ch), [2012] 2 FLR 807 [99].

[27] Gardner, 'Again' (n 7) 508.

inexactitude over these matters. To complete its work, this tolerance has to be carried forward into the apparatus for quantifying relief.[28]

Although cases are usually litigated only when B's assurance is reasonably firm and A's detrimental reliance is substantial, this does not accurately reflect the range of possible proprietary estoppel claims which may be brought on less certain facts. Indeed, it is arguably the case that, in theory, there are numerically more successful proprietary estoppel cases where the remedy does not hold B to his promise as compared to those which do. This is because a proprietary estoppel claim will be successful whenever the three elements of assurance or promise, reliance, and detriment arise; but B will not be compelled to carry out his promise *unless* the case is finely tuned—that is, only where a sufficient threshold is reached in relation to the firmness of B's assurance or promise, the degree of A's detriment, the proportionality between these elements, etc. Thus, as Lord Walker remarked in *Clarke v Swaby*,[29] '[o]ften the equity can best be satisfied by a monetary award.'

7.1.2. Causation and Remoteness

While it may not be immediately obvious, it is necessary for A to establish that B's breach of duty caused him the loss complained of, and that the loss is not too remote. The need for a causal link between B's promise and A's detriment[30] is established when A demonstrates the element of reliance.[31] As Robert Walker LJ (as his Lordship then was) observed in *Campbell v Griffin*,[32] 'the question of reliance ... is really an issue of causation'.

Because it is necessary for B to have induced A's reliance, it must be shown that B's promise was a 'but for' cause of A's actions. To this extent, the causation test to be applied is similar to the QI doctrines.[33] However, because proprietary estoppel is concerned with correcting the net detriment A suffers, all things considered,[34] it is also necessary to show that B's breach was a 'but for' cause of the net detriment A suffers. As HHJ Mackie QC observed in *Magrath v Parkside Hotels Ltd*,[35] unless such reliance is established, '[a] claim is bound to fail because no detriment having a causal link to the assurances relied upon has been pleaded'. And as Ben McFarlane notes,[36] '[B] should not be made to bear responsibility for [A]'s detriment if, even in the absence of the conduct of [B] on which [A]'s claim depends, [A] would in any case have acted in such a way as to suffer that detriment.'

[28] See also Sean Wilken QC and Karim Ghaly, *Wilken and Ghaly: The Law of Waiver, Variation, and Estoppel*, 3rd edn (Oxford, OUP, 2012) [11-84]; McFarlane and Sales, 'Promises, Detriment, and Liability' (n 10) 632.

[29] Clarke v Swaby [2007] UKPC 1, [2007] 2 P & CR 2 [18].

[30] Andrew Robertson, 'Estoppels and Rights-Creating Events: Beyond Wrongs and Promises' in Jason W Neyers, Richard Bronaugh and Stephen GA Pitel (eds), *Exploring Contract Law* (Oxford, Hart Publishing, 2009) 219; *Wilken and Ghaly* (n 28) [11-53].

[31] *Gillett v Holt* [2001] Ch 210 (CA) 232; *Jennings v Rice* (n 9) [21].

[32] *Campbell v Griffin* (n 19) [19].

[33] See, in particular, the discussion in Chapter 6, S 6.2.1.2.1.

[34] The concept of a 'net detriment' or 'harm' can be contrasted with detriment as referring simply to the inherent costs of A's act of reliance: see discussion at S 7.1.6.

[35] *Magrath v Parkside Hotels Ltd* [2011] EWHC 143 (Ch) [30]. See too the Singapore Court of Appeal's decision in *V Nithia (co-administratrix of the estate of Ponnusamy Sivapakiam, deceased) v Buthmanaban s/o Vaithilingam* [2015] 5 SLR 1422, [2015] SGCA 56 [44]: 'proprietary estoppel should be pleaded expressly and the facts relevant to each element should be pleaded specifically.'

[36] McFarlane, *The Law of Proprietary Estoppel* (n 5) [3-175].

Remoteness comes into play through the application of the 'minimum equity to do justice to the plaintiff'[37] concept, which prevents B from being liable for any detriment A suffers which is too remote. In addition, the requirements of causation and remoteness can also be seen from the fact that any benefit A receives from B may be taken into account when determining the extent of A's detriment.[38]

The fact that causation and remoteness are relevant to a proprietary estoppel claim supports the secondary-rights analysis of the doctrine. It is only because proprietary estoppel is concerned with A's loss that 'issues of causation must be brought in, because the only relevant loss is the loss that [B] caused. And as soon as that is raised, issues of remoteness arise, because there are limits to the responsibility that we can rightly impose on someone for the causal outcomes of a breach of duty.'[39] By taking into account issues of causation and remoteness, courts are able to tailor the content of the awarded remedy according to the circumstances of the case.

7.1.3. The Primary Duty

What is the primary duty B breaches? Three possibilities can be dismissed immediately. The first is that B's primary duty arises from an express declaration of trust. In proprietary estoppel cases, B does not comply with the formality requirements of the Law of Property Act 1925, s 53(1)(b) to create an enforceable express trust, and an oral self-declaration of trust over an interest in land is unenforceable.[40] Moreover, an express trustee's inconsistent dealing with trust property results in the direct enforcement of his primary duty, and not in the award of a remedy which responds to his secondary duty.[41]

The second is that B has a primary duty to fulfil his promise to A. Such a duty underlies the law of contracts, but it does not explain proprietary estoppel because it underrepresents its crucial elements, in particular the requirement that A must have suffered detrimental reliance. That requirement indicates that B does not have a duty to fulfil his promise as such: B may renege on his promise until and unless A has acted in reliance on B's promise such that A suffers detriment.[42] As Hoffmann LJ observed in *Walton v Walton*,[43] the doctrine 'does not look forward into the future and guess what might happen. It looks backwards from the moment when the promise falls due to be performed [viz the time of B's breach][44] and asks whether, in the circumstances which have actually happened, it would be unconscionable for the promise not to be kept.'

[37] *Crabb v Arun District Council* (n 6) 198.

[38] See *Wilken and Ghaly* (n 28) [11-80] and cases cited therein.

[39] Lionel Smith, 'The Measurement of Compensation Claims against Trustees and Fiduciaries' in Elise Bant and Matthew Harding (eds), *Exploring Private Law* (Cambridge, CUP, 2010) 373.

[40] *Smith v Matthews* (1861) 3 De G F & J 139, 45 ER 831; *Morris v Whiting* (1913) 15 DLR 254; *Organ v Sandwell* [1921] VLR 622, 630; *Permanent Trustee Co v Scales* (1930) 30 SR (NSW) 391 Eq; *Beemer v Brownridge* [1934] 1 WWR 545, 555–56, 567; *Last v Rosenfeld* [1972] 2 NSWLR 923, 928, 933; *Wratten v Hunter* [1978] 2 NSWLR 367.

[41] See Charles Mitchell, 'Equitable Rights and Wrongs' (2006) 59 *Current Legal Problems* 267, 276–77. Apparently, a different approach is taken in relation to cases involving bare commercial trusts: *AIB Group (UK) plc v Mark Redler & Co Solicitors* [2014] UKSC 58, [2015] AC 1503 [70], [106].

[42] See also Robertson, 'Estoppels and Rights-Creating Events' (n 30) 209–24; Nolan, 'Rights, Damage and Loss' (n 24) 15.

[43] *Walton v Walton* (n 19).

[44] See discussion in S 7.1.5.

The third is that the primary duty is a duty to reverse an unjust enrichment. It is clear that English courts have never used proprietary estoppel in such a way.[45] The focus of proprietary estoppel is not on a gain B makes but on the detriment A suffers by acting in reliance.[46]

What, then, is the primary duty, the breach of which gives rise to rights and duties in proprietary estoppel? In his monograph *Protecting Reliance*, Michael Spence suggests that the primary duty B breaches is a 'duty to ensure the reliability of induced assumptions'.[47] This provides a useful definition of B's primary duty, and explains why the elements of assurance or promise, reliance, and detriment are required. When B promises A that A will obtain an interest in B's property, B incurs a primary duty to act reliably in relation to A's assumptions which he has induced. There are two means by which this duty may be discharged. Either B must inform A of B's intention to renege on his promise before A acts in reliance, or else B must perform his promise: in either case, B acts reliably and A has no cause of complaint. If, however, B does neither, he commits a breach which causes A to suffer detriment. At this point, A obtains an 'equity by estoppel' against B, giving A a cause of action in proprietary estoppel. This 'equity' requires liquidation by a court to 'quantify the measure of the prejudice to [A] by [B]'s failure to honour his promise.'[48] Pursuant to this, a proprietary or personal remedy may be awarded. The aim of the remedy is to ensure that '[B] does not leave [A] to suffer a detriment as a result of [A]'s reasonable reliance on [B]'s promise.'[49]

7.1.3.1. Not Preventing Loss

A closer inspection of Spence's monograph would reveal that the phrase 'duty to ensure the reliability of induced assumptions' is not used as an exhaustive formulation of the primary duty. Rather, Spence uses that phrase simply as a shorthand for a more specific idea. In expanded form, Spence writes:[50]

> The primary obligation is that [B] must, in so far as he is reasonably able, prevent harm to [A]. 'Harm' consists in the extent to which [A] is worse off because the assumption has proved unjustified than he would have been had it never been induced. The secondary obligation is that, if [A] does suffer harm of the relevant type, and [B] might reasonably have prevented it, then [B] must compensate [A] for the harm he has suffered.

Similarly, others have also identified the primary duty in proprietary estoppel as being to 'protect against harm resulting from reliance on inconsistent conduct',[51] or to prevent detrimental reliance on a promise'.[52]

[45] Burrows (n 20) 678. *cf* Tang Hang Wu, 'An Unjust Enrichment Claim for the Mistaken Improver of Land' (2011) 1 *Conveyancer and Property Lawyer* 8, which comes to a different conclusion, but only in relation to very specific facts.

[46] See, eg, McFarlane and Sales, 'Promises, Detriment, and Liability' (n 10) 614.

[47] Michael Spence, *Protecting Reliance: The Emergent Doctrine of Equitable Estoppel* (Oxford, Hart Publishing, 1999) 2.

[48] *Southwell v Blackburn* (n 4) [14].

[49] McFarlane, 'The Importance of Looking Back' (n 2) 347.

[50] Spence, *Protecting Reliance* (n 47) 2.

[51] Andrew Robertson, 'The Reliance Basis of Proprietary Estoppel Remedies' (2008) 4 *Conveyancer and Property Lawyer* 295, 301. See too Robertson, 'Estoppels and Rights-Creating Events' (n 30) 210: 'A has a 'right not to be harmed by [B]'s inconsistent conduct'.

[52] Nicholas J McBride, 'A Fifth Common Law Obligation' (1994) 14 *Legal Studies* 35, 45.

In a number of previous publications[53] I adopted a similar approach, couching B's primary duty in terms of a duty to prevent harm. However, Donal Nolan has recently argued that 'a [primary] right not to suffer loss is conceptually impossible',[54] 'loss' being taken to mean 'becoming worse off', a state of affairs which amounts to a 'detrimental difference' to A.[55] The reason for this, he argues, is that 'it is never possible to say at any particular moment in time that [B]'s conduct has left [A] worse off, because we can never know whether later events will affect the impact that [B]'s conduct had on [A]'s welfare.'[56] In the context of proprietary estoppel, this means that detrimental reliance on an assumption cannot be a right-creating event, given the impossibility of determining whether detriment has been suffered at any given point in time.[57]

It may well be that Nolan's argument is incorrect.[58] But if it is a valid argument, then B's primary duty cannot be couched in terms of 'prevention of harm'. Nevertheless, this does not affect the possibility of couching B's primary duty *simply* in terms of a 'duty to ensure the reliability of induced assumptions', which is the conception adopted in this chapter.

On this conception, when B induces A's assumptions through promising to give A an interest in B's property, there are two courses of action by which B can act reliably and thereby discharge his primary duty. He may either *inform A of his intention to renege before A has acted in reliance on B's promise*,[59] or he may *fulfil his promise*. Crucially, B's duty is to be *reliable*; the duty need not be couched in terms of a duty to *prevent harm*, even though being reliable would have that very effect. However, where B does not act reliably, then B breaches his primary duty, which gives A a cause of action in proprietary estoppel. It is certainly necessary for A to prove net harm in order successfully to establish a proprietary estoppel claim;[60] but the relevance of harm in relation to a claim based on A's secondary right is not controversial. As Nolan writes, 'there is nothing to stop the law from making the *actionability* of a wrong depend on whether at a given moment it looks as if the wrong has caused the claimant loss'.[61]

7.1.4. Goal

Remedies awarded pursuant to successful proprietary estoppel claims are reflective in nature. This entails that courts have and do exercise remedial discretion to determine the

[53] Ying Khai Liew, 'The Secondary-rights Approach to the "Common Intention Constructive Trust"' [2015] *Conveyancer and Property Lawyer* 210, 213; Ying Khai Liew, 'Explaining the Mutual Wills Doctrine' in Birke Häcker and Charles Mitchell (eds), *Current Issues in Succession Law* (Oxford, Hart Publishing, 2016) 123; Ying Khai Liew, 'Reanalysing Institutional and Remedial Constructive Trusts' [2016] *CLJ* 528, 540.

[54] Nolan, 'Rights, Damage and Loss' (n 24) 8.

[55] ibid 2.

[56] ibid 9.

[57] ibid 15 fn 57.

[58] *cf*, eg, NJ McBride, 'Rights and the Basis of Tort Law' in Nolan and Robertson (eds), *Rights and Private Law* (Oxford, Hart Publishing, 2012); Sandy Steel, 'Book Review' [2014] *CLJ* 466, 468. It is unnecessary to take a view on the matter for the purposes of the present enquiry.

[59] This supports the view that proprietary estoppel does not simply impose a duty on B to fulfil his promise to A: see discussion in S 7.1.3.

[60] See S 7.1.6.

[61] Nolan, 'Rights, Damage and Loss' (n 24) 12.

appropriate content of the awarded remedy on a case-by-case basis to attain a specific remedial goal.[62] This goal in the context of proprietary estoppel is compensation of A's loss.

7.1.4.1. Language of Expectation

The compensatory goal of proprietary estoppel might be thought to be contentious for two reasons. First, it is undeniable that, when dealing with proprietary estoppel, courts do not frame their analysis in terms of A's detriment alone, but also focus on A's 'expectation'. For example, in *Jennings v Rice*,[63] Robert Walker LJ observed that '[t]he equity [in proprietary estoppel] arises … from the combination of expectations, detrimental reliance, and the unconscionableness of allowing [B] to go back on the assurances.' The focus on A's expectation might be thought to be inconsistent with a compensatory goal.

In reply, it should first be observed that the aim of proprietary estoppel is not *simply* to fulfil A's expectation, either by holding B to his promise or by awarding the expectation measure of damages. It was noted earlier[64] that proprietary estoppel was once conceptualised as presumptively concerned with awarding expectation relief,[65] but that there has been an increasing willingness to provide a lesser remedy since the turn of the twenty-first century. This trend indicates that, unlike a contracting party's duty, the primary duty in relation to proprietary estoppel is not simply that B should fulfil his promise. Although an expectation on A's part may be created by B making a promise, it remains possible for B to act reliably by informing A of his intention to renege prior to A's reliance on that expectation. So the aim of proprietary estoppel is to compensate A for the loss A suffers where he acts in reliance on B's promise and where B fails to ensure that A obtains the promised interest.

It might be tempting therefrom to conclude that the language of 'expectation' is simply an historical relic which still filters through in the modern law for no good reason. But this would also be a mistake. It is observable that B is responsible for creating the state of affairs which gives rise to his primary duty: B's promise is that which induces A's assumptions, creating a duty on B's part to be reliable. Where B fails to act reliably, the goal of the remedy is to compensate A; but in view of B's role in creating the primary duty in the first place, it is unsurprising that, in some situations—where the response is proportionate, in view of the firmness of B's promise and the degree of detriment A suffers—compensating A entails giving effect to A's expectation by compelling B to fulfil his promise. After all, as we observed in Chapter 2,[66] 'the secondary obligation is a rational echo of the primary obligation, for it exists to serve, so far as may still be done, the reasons for the primary obligation that was not performed when its performance was due.'[67] This is why the maximum remedy which may be imposed in proprietary estoppel is the expectation measure.[68] Hence, there is no difficulty in analysing the goal of the remedy as being compensatory, despite the fact that judges often refer to A's 'expectation'.

[62] See Chapter 2, S 2.4.2.2.1.
[63] *Jennings v Rice* (n 9) [49].
[64] See n 23 above and accompanying main text.
[65] More precisely, the holding of B to his promise: see n 11 above.
[66] See Chapter 2, S 2.4.2.2.
[67] John Gardner, 'What is Tort Law For? Part 1: The Place of Corrective Justice' (2011) 30 *Law & Philosophy* 1, 40.
[68] McFarlane, *The Law of Proprietary Estoppel* (n 5) [7-95]ff.

7.1.4.2. Availability of Proprietary Remedies

Secondly, it is notable that proprietary remedies are seldom, if ever, imposed as compensatory remedies outside the proprietary estoppel context. Is there any justification for treating proprietary estoppel differently?

Andrew Robertson's work provides inspiration for a possible answer.[69] There are a great number of potential cases where the detriment A suffers by acting in reliance on B's assurance or promise can be fully compensated by an order for compensatory damages.[70] This is because there is a large range of possible acts by A which would result in such a remedy being imposed as a proportionate response vis-a-vis B's promise. However, at a certain point, the magnitude of detriment A suffers is so substantial, measured vis-a-vis B's promise, that two other factors becomes relevant to the court's exercise of its remedial discretion in determining the content of the appropriate remedy.[71]

First, there may be certain aspects of A's acts of reliance which make it difficult to quantify the detriment A suffers.[72] Robertson cites a number of examples, such as the performance of services in the expectation of benefit, emotional investments in a home, loss of opportunity to make a financial gain or avoid a financial loss, and personal life changing decisions. Courts tend to shy away from quantifying such non-financial detriment because mis-quantifying the loss would risk under-compensating A. Where A's detrimental reliance is substantial enough that such a risk becomes a probable eventuality, courts are more likely to compel B to carry out his promise.

Secondly, B's promise is also likely to be enforced in view of B's role in creating the state of affairs. It can be said that '[w]henever [B] harms [A], there is a stronger reason to let the cost fall on the party who had a better opportunity to avoid the risk.'[73] Thus, Gardner writes that '[B] is responsible, by his encouragement or acquiescence, for an expectation on the part of [A], and for the reliance that [A] has placed on that expectation, to his detriment.'[74] But the extent of B's responsibility does not stop there: he is also responsible for failing to carrying out his primary duty to act reliably, and as a result he is also responsible for the detriment A suffers and for causing any difficulties in quantifying that detriment. Where A's detrimental reliance is substantial, the wrongful effect of B's unreliability becomes more pronounced. As a result, courts are more likely to compel B to carry out his promise.

Susan Bright and Ben McFarlane also suggest three other factors which justify the award of a proprietary remedy in proprietary estoppel.[75] The first is where there is a need to

[69] Although it must be emphasised that what follows merely takes *inspiration* from Robertson's ideas expressed in Robertson, 'The Reliance Basis' (n 51) and does not adopt his more general views in that paper. Thus, Robertson does not view the goal of proprietary estoppel simply as that of compensation, but that it 'prevents harm' where expectation relief is granted, and 'compensates harm' in other cases: Robertson, 'The Reliance Basis' (n 51) 315ff. Such an analysis, which entails understanding some remedies as replicative in nature and others as reflective in nature, is undesirable: see discussion in S 7.2.4. Note also that Robertson's analysis is that expectation relief *in specie* should be awarded *unless* it is not possible or practical to do so.

[70] See main text following n 28 above.

[71] Hence, 'the purpose of proprietary estoppel is not … [simply] to reverse the detriment which [A] has suffered, but to grant an appropriate remedy in respect of the unconscionable conduct': *Ottey v Grundy* (n 15) [61].

[72] Robertson, 'The Reliance Basis' (n 51) 303ff.

[73] Adam Slavny, 'Nonreciprocity and the Moral Basis of Liability to Compensate' (2014) 34 *OJLS* 417, 435.

[74] Gardner, 'Again' (n 7) 500.

[75] See Bright and McFarlane, 'Proprietary Estoppel and Property Rights' (n 10) 468ff.

support the use of a land in which A has an interest. For example, if B promises A a right of way over B's land and A sells part of his land and what remains is inaccessible without access over B's land, then a proprietary remedy which enforces B's promise is likely to be awarded, since a personal remedy would be insufficient to support A's use of his land.[76] The second is where there is a need to protect A's current occupation of B's land. Finally, a proprietary remedy is also likely to be awarded where A's reliance takes the form of giving up an opportunity to acquire a property right.

7.1.5. Breach

In *Lloyd v MGL (Rugby) Ltd*,[77] Wilson LJ observed in relation to proprietary estoppel:

> Equity intervenes to make the promise unable to be revoked (and able to be enforced) not at the time when it is made but only at a significantly later stage, namely in the events both that [A] should have acted to his detriment in reliance upon it and that [B] should have sought unconscionably to withdraw from it.

This observation is consistent with the analysis of proprietary estoppel remedies as reflective in nature, which entails that B's breach of duty must be pleaded and proved. Thus, A has no claim in proprietary estoppel if B acts reliably by informing A of his intention to renege before A has relied, or where B fulfils his promise: only where B breaches his primary duty will a proprietary estoppel claim become relevant. Similarly, A will have no claim if the agreed event (such as B's death where B promises to leave property to A in B's will) has not yet occurred, since the moment at which B's reliability is to be measured has not yet come to pass.[78] So prior to any breach, B could, for example, charge the property in question and the chargee would take priority over A.[79] However, once B breaches his primary duty by acting unreliably, A suffers detriment which gives him a cause of action in proprietary estoppel.

In practice, three scenarios can be distinguished. First, B may promise to cede an interest to A at an expressly defined moment during B's lifetime—for instance a particular date in the near future. Here, B would breach his primary right only if A has acted in reliance by that date and B does not then fulfil his promise by securing A's interest in the property. However, because of the informality which surrounds the making of promises in the context of proprietary estoppel, it is uncommon for B expressly to state when precisely performance of his promise would be due.

Secondly, B's promise may be ambiguous as to when performance of his promise can be expected. For instance, B may promise that A will have a 'home for life',[80] that a hotel will 'all be [A's] one day',[81] or that a farm is 'going to be [A's]'.[82] If B does not inform A of his

[76] *Crabb v Arun District Council* (n 6).

[77] *Lloyd v MGL (Rugby) Ltd* [2007] EWCA Civ 153 [38].

[78] Note, though, that if the agreed event has not yet occurred, a breach may be committed if it becomes clear that B will no longer fulfil his promise, for instance where B promises to leave property to A by will but later executes a new will to the contrary: see *Bradbury v Taylor* [2012] EWCA Civ 1208.

[79] The decision in *Campbell v Griffin* (n 19) is not inconsistent with this: see S 7.1.5.1.

[80] *Campbell v Griffin* (n 19).

[81] *Wayling v Jones* (1995) 69 P & CR 170 (CA).

[82] *Gillett v Holt* (n 31).

intention to renege on the promise before A acts in reliance, the most obvious way for B to avoid breaching his primary duty would be to secure A's interest in the promised property *as soon as practicable.* If B fails to do so, that failure constitutes a breach.

Thirdly, B may promise to leave to A an interest in the property at B's death.[83] Take for instance the case of *Thorner v Major*, where B's promise[84] was that '[A] would be [B]'s successor to [the farm]'.[85] Given the contingent nature of B's promise—giving rise to 'an odd sort of estoppel that is produced by representations that are, in a sense, conditional'[86]—no breach occurs in B's lifetime so long as it remains possible for B to carry out his promise at his death.[87] So, for instance, in *Thorner* it was held that 'changes in the character or extent of the property [during B's lifetime] ... do not exclude [a proprietary estoppel] remedy where there is still an identifiable property'.[88] The same would be the case if B became ill during his lifetime and needed to sell a part of the farm to fund the costs of his medical expenses:[89] the subject-matter remains in existence and fulfilment of the promise—that A would take over the farm—remains possible. However, if B sold the farm entirely during his lifetime, this would be a breach; and this explains Lord Scott's suggestion in *Thorner* that in this case A might 'succeed in establishing a proprietary claim in equity and to consequential relief'.[90]

In all cases, A obtains a secondary right—an 'equity by estoppel'—against B during B's lifetime. This is so even where B promises to leave property to A at B's death: if he fails to do so, B breaches his primary duty when, in B's lifetime, it becomes impracticable for B to ensure that A will so benefit. Where B dies after committing a breach, A's subsisting cause of action against B survives against B's estate by virtue of the Law Reform (Miscellaneous Provisions) Act 1934, s 1.

7.1.5.1. Campbell v Griffin

It might be thought that the case of *Campbell v Griffin*[91] contradicts the foregoing analysis, but upon closer inspection it does not.

In 1985, an elderly couple, B1 and B2, made wills leaving their estates to Xs. From 1987, B1 and B2 repeatedly assured a lodger, A, that A would have a 'home for life'[92] if A cared for them. In 1993, B1 made a codicil to that effect, giving A a life interest in their house.

[83] See, eg, *Wayling v Jones* (n 81); *Gillett v Holt* (n 31); *Jennings v Rice* (n 9).

[84] Although the judges used the term 'assurance', this term was taken to be synonymous with 'promise': see McFarlane, *The Law of Proprietary Estoppel* (n 5) [2-86].

[85] See, eg, *Thorner v Major* (n 25) [40], [42].

[86] ibid [19].

[87] This analysis avoids the need to rely on the slippery concept of 'unconscionably' as having a 'residuary role in allowing a court to take account of the specific factual circumstances ... such as a significant change of circumstances, which may have occurred after the time of B's reliance', as suggested in McFarlane and Sales, 'Promises, Detriment, and Liability' (n 10) 616.

[88] *Thorner v Major* (n 25) [9], [18]. So, in *Thorner*, the fact that B sold part of the land which made up the relevant farm and acquired other land which added to the totality of the farm did not affect A's claim.

[89] ibid [19].

[90] ibid [18]. At *Thorner v Major* (n 25) [20] his Lordship suggested that if B was forced to sell his *entire* farm to fund his medical expenses, a court would not prevent B's realisation of the farm. This is not inconsistent with the analysis proposed in the main text: the sale would still constitute a breach. But because B's promise is to make a testamentary disposition to A, which implies that the parties understand that vicissitudes of life may well impact on the performance of the promise, a proportionate response in such a case is likely to be compensatory damages.

[91] *Campbell v Griffin* (n 19).

[92] ibid [10].

At some point after 1995, the County Council took out a statutory charge on the house for the recoupment of the costs B1 and B2 incurred by being taken into residential care. In the event, B1's codicil did not take effect: because B1 predeceased B2, the latter took the house by virtue of survivorship.[93] Later, A sought an interest in the house against B2's executor. The Court of Appeal held that A had obtained an equity by estoppel, and awarded compensatory damages of £35,000 secured by a charge on the house.[94]

Of relevance to the present discussion is Robert Walker LJ's observation that:[95]

> In these circumstances it is almost certainly unnecessary to decide the issue of priority as between [A] and the County Council. But in my view [A]'s claim has priority, being based on his actual occupation and on his equity having arisen before [B1 and B2] first went [into residential care] …

At first sight, this might be thought to suggest that A had an equity by estoppel before a breach was committed by B1 and/or B2. However, this view is misplaced. The assurances given by B1 and B2 were neither that A would be named as *legatee* in their will, nor that A would *inherit* the house, but that A would have a '*home for life*'. In order to discharge their primary duty to ensure the reliability of their induced assumption, they ought to have secured A's interest in the house as soon as practicable, for example, by declaring a trust to that effect or securing a transfer of the legal title. Indeed, they had ample opportunity to do so before the County Council's charge took effect. Due to their failure to do so between 1987 and 1995, B1 and B2 clearly committed a breach of their primary duty. This would have given A a secondary right—an equity by estoppel—before the County Council took out its charge. Therefore, A's claim would have had priority over the County Council's claim, in line with the analysis proposed in this section.

7.1.6. Detriment-as-Harm

It can be observed that the word 'detriment' can mean two different things. When it is used as an adjective in the phrase 'detrimental reliance', it describes the event of reliance. This can be labelled 'detriment-as-event'. For instance, if A's reliance involves caring for B, the event of A's caring *in itself* can be described as 'detrimental', insofar as it refers to A's *costs* in terms of time, money, and effort.[96] The characterisation of A's acts as 'detrimental' in this sense focuses wholly on A: it does not involve evaluating A's position vis-à-vis B.

This can be contrasted with the second sense of the word 'detriment', which involves a more global appreciation of the facts. Here, 'detriment' describes the *net harm* A suffers from the whole course of events. This can be labelled 'detriment-as-harm'. If B fulfils his promise, A suffers no detriment: even though A may have acted in reliance and thereby expended time, money, and effort, the fact that B fulfils his primary duty to be reliable means that no harm has befallen A. Conversely, where B fails to act reliably, then A would

93 ibid [13].

94 ibid [34]–[36].

95 ibid [37].

96 See, eg, Siôn Hudson and Brian Sloan, 'Testamentary Freedom: Mutual Wills Might Let You Down' in Warren Barr (ed), *Modern Studies in Property Law, Vol 8* (Oxford, Hart Publishing, 2015) 168: 'Detriment is the easiest aspect of a proprietary estoppel claim for a carer to prove, because the very act of caring usually means that some detriment has been incurred.'

suffer detriment: he would be left worse off as a result of B's breach. Detriment-as-harm requires B to have committed a breach; detriment-as-event does not.

A number of factors suggest that proprietary estoppel is not concerned with detriment-as-event but detriment-as-harm. First, the positive law reflects a usage of the term in the latter sense. In *Grundt v Great Boulder Pty Gold Mines Ltd*, Dixon J noted:[97]

> [T]he real detriment or harm from which the law seeks to give protection is that which would flow from the change of position [that is, reliance] if the assumption were deserted that led to it. So long as the assumption is adhered to, [A] cannot complain. His complaint is that when afterwards [B] makes a different state of affairs the basis of an assertion of rights against him, then if it is allowed, his own original change of position will operate as a detriment.

Indeed, B's reliance 'need not be immediately, or intrinsically, detrimental',[98] nor need it be 'onerous, unpleasant or damaging'.[99] This point is fortified by the fact that courts are willing to weigh the disadvantages A suffers against the countervailing benefits he enjoys from acting in reliance.[100] Such an exercise would only be necessary if courts are concerned with the net harm A suffers; otherwise, any subsequent advantage A obtains would not reduce the costs A has already incurred in terms of detriment-as-event.

Secondly, detriment-as-harm prevents proprietary estoppel from intruding upon the territory of contract law. On the detriment-as-event analysis, B's promise can be enforced merely because A relies on the promise in a costly way. But mere reliance on B's promise would not normally suffice as consideration to render B's promise contractually binding. Furthermore, even if A's reliance suffices as consideration, it does not explain why the parties' lack of compliance with the Law of Property (Miscellaneous Provisions) Act 1989, s 2(1)[101] can lead to the enforcement of B's promise via proprietary estoppel.[102] Conversely, by focusing on detriment-as-harm, proprietary estoppel can be seen to play a different role from contract law, in that the goal is to compensate A for reliance caused by B's acting unreliably in relation to assumptions he induced. By distinguishing proprietary estoppel from the law of contracts, both areas of law can be understood as having distinct roles to play. Hence, proprietary estoppel can operate even where various contractual requirements are absent, or where B's promise is not certain enough to be contractually binding.[103]

Thirdly, detriment-as-event is not compensatable, but detriment-as-harm is. Suppose that B promises to transfer land to A if A cares for B. By duly undertaking those acts, A would have incurred detriment-as-event. If B then fulfils his promise and conveys his land to A, the costs A incurs in terms of time, money, and effort would still be an outstanding 'detriment'. Such 'detriment' would not be sufficient for A to sustain a proprietary estoppel claim against B where B fulfils his promise. Instead, courts are concerned with compensating

[97] *Grundt v Great Boulder Pty Gold Mines Ltd* [1937] 59 CLR 641, 674.
[98] McFarlane, 'The Importance of Looking Back' (n 2) 335.
[99] *Wilken and Ghaly* (n 28) [11-64].
[100] See, eg, *Henry v Henry* (n 8) [51]; *Southwell v Blackburn* (n 4) [14].
[101] This provides that 'A contract for the sale or other disposition of an interest in land can only be made in writing and only by incorporating all the terms which the parties have expressly agreed in one document or, where contracts are exchanged, in each.'
[102] *Yaxley v Gotts* [2000] Ch 162 (CA).
[103] Observed in McFarlane and Sales, 'Promises, Detriment, and Liability' (n 10) 629.

A for the detriment-as-harm he incurs as a result of B's failure to ensure the reliability of his induced assumptions. This is why in the foregoing example, if B fulfils his primary duty, A has no claim in proprietary estoppel against B. A suffers no net harm.

It might be suggested that it is possible to adopt an analysis whereby it is not necessary to establish detriment-as-harm to obtain a remedy, so long as detriment-as-event is established and it can be shown that A *would* suffer detriment-as-harm *if* B does not fulfil his promise.[104] There are two difficulties with this analysis. First, it would suggest that proprietary estoppel always enforces A's primary right by invariably holding B to his promise to ensure he acts reliably once A has relied on his promise. However, it is clear that courts may also award compensatory damages; and where they do so, B is in effect allowed to breach his primary duty, subject to making good any harm the breach may cause.

Secondly, such an analysis suggests that proprietary estoppel remedies are available although A does not actually suffer any detriment-as-harm. The difficulty with this can be appreciated by considering a case where B promises to leave a testamentary gift of his land to A if A takes care of B. Does A have an action in proprietary estoppel against B after having looked after B for only a week if B does not renege or threaten to renege on his promise? On the detriment-as-harm analysis, the answer would be 'no' since B has not committed a breach. But on the detriment-as-event analysis, the answer would be 'yes': A would have incurred detriment-as-event, even if only for a week, and it certainly can be said that he would suffer detriment-as-harm *if* B does not fulfil his promise. Yet, if A takes B to court, it is not easy to see how the appropriate remedy would be assessed. The court would surely not compel B to fulfil his promise, since this would not be a proportionate response to the week's worth of detriment incurred by A, but neither would A be awarded compensatory damages, since it is not yet clear that B would not make a will in A's favour.

Ultimately, the better view is that proprietary estoppel is concerned with detriment-as-harm and not detriment-as-event. As Robert Walker LJ observed in *Gillett v Holt*,[105] 'detriment must be judged at the moment when [B] seeks to go back on it.'[106] Where B fails to ensure the reliability of his induced assumptions, he breaches his primary duty, which generates a secondary right in A's favour for B to repair, so far as possible, the detriment-as-harm caused to A.

7.2. Objections

There are a number of potential objections to the secondary-rights analysis of proprietary estoppel. These objections either take issue with a particular aspect of the analysis, or propose a different analysis altogether. This section addresses these potential objections.

[104] See, eg, Robertson, 'Estoppels and Rights-Creating Events' (n 30) 210; *Wilken and Ghaly* (n 28) [11-64].
[105] *Gillett v Holt* (n 31) 232.
[106] Although McFarlane takes this to mean that potential detriment suffices (see, eg, McFarlane, *The Law of Proprietary Estoppel* (n 5) [4-48]), it can also be taken to mean that B is free to renege on his promise if A has not begun relying, consistent with the analysis proposed in this chapter.

7.2.1. Transformative Remedies?

The first objection is the claim that remedies awarded by way of proprietary estoppel are transformative in nature. On this view, a constructive trust award bears little resemblance to A's pre-trial substantive right, and so 'it [is] never … possible to say in estoppel cases that [A] comes under a duty to do a particular act before an order of the court is made.'[107]

This view reflects two inaccurate assumptions commonly made about transformative remedies: that a remedy which exists for the first time from the time of a court order can only be transformative in nature,[108] and that a remedy which allows for remedial discretion to be exercised can only be transformative in nature.[109] The problems with these exaggerated assumptions have been discussed in Chapter 2.[110] In particular, that discussion demonstrated that many reflective remedies—such as the right to a payment of a sum of money following a breach of trust—also take effect from the time the court order is made, since the content of such remedies remain unascertained until a court decides on the matter. Furthermore, determining the appropriate *content* of reflective remedies often requires the exercise of remedial discretion. Crucially, however, unlike transformative remedies, the *goal* of reflective remedies, including those imposed by way of proprietary estoppel, is never open to judicial discretion. As HHJ Behrens rightly noted in *Aspden v Elvy*:[111]

> The Court has a discretion as to how the equity is to be satisfied in any particular case … however … the court must take a principled approach and cannot exercise a completely unfettered discretion according to the individual judge's notion of what is fair in any particular case.

In proprietary estoppel, that goal is always to provide compensation: the awarded remedy invariably aims to compensate A for the harm caused by B's unreliability.

7.2.2. Primary Rights?

The second objection is the claim that proprietary estoppel remedies give direct effect to A's primary right once the necessary elements of promise, reliance, and detriment are fulfilled.

The most obvious problem with this view is that it fails to account for the availability of compensatory awards in proprietary estoppel. Such awards are characteristically awarded in response to a wrong; they do not enforce primary rights directly. Indeed, if proprietary estoppel remedies replicated the parties' primary rights and duties, the enforcement of B's promise would be more commonplace than in the present law.

In response, one might say that the law is in a process of settling down, where those awards are becoming less discretionary and more rule-based.[112] However, this response is unconvincing, given that proprietary estoppel cases—at least since 1999—have taken the law away from giving primacy to expectation relief.[113]

[107] Rafal Zakrzewski, *Remedies Reclassified* (Oxford, OUP, 2005) 132–33.
[108] ibid 210.
[109] ibid 97–101.
[110] See Chapter 2, S 2.4.2.2.
[111] *Aspden v Elvy* (n 26) [100].
[112] Zakrzewski (n 107) 132.
[113] Gardner, 'Again' (n 7) 492. See also McFarlane and Sales, 'Promises, Detriment, and Liability' (n 10) 618: 'there is no need to assume that enforcing [A]'s claim must involve protecting [A]'s expectation.'

7.2.2.1. Not Fault-Based

Those who subscribe to the primary rights analysis might take issue with the fact that proprietary estoppel does not depend on B departing or threatening to depart from the assumption he induced.[114] On this contention, it can hardly be said that B commits a 'wrong' if, for instance, B dies suddenly due to the onslaught of a sudden illness after A has incurred reliance but before B can fulfil the promise, or if B duly leaves the property to A in his will but it later turns out that the intended effect is not achieved due to some reason out of B's control.[115]

Instead of undermining the presently proposed analysis, however, this contention simply highlights the fact that a civil wrong can be committed without fault or blameworthiness. All that is required is for B to have breached a primary duty owed to A.[116] In proprietary estoppel, B's primary duty arises when he induces A's assumptions. Where A's assumption is induced through B's making of a promise which is 'of a character which is seriously meant, which invites reliance by [A] and which, on a reasonable interpretation, carries normative promissory weight',[117] this gives B fair warning that something may happen which might result in a significant claim by A against B. Since the making of a promise is a conscious act of free will on B's part, it is hardly objectionable to say that the risk that A would be harmed ought properly to lie with B and B alone. So, for instance, if B promises that A will have a 'home for life', a failure to secure A's interest in the promised property as soon as practicable[118] constitutes a breach of B's primary duty despite the fact that B may not have acted in a blameworthy manner.

It might be pointed out that torts which impose strict liability where the breach consists of an omission instead of a positive act, and where the breach can be committed without intention or negligence, are rare. However, unlike many strict liability torts, the fact that B incurs a primary duty is the result of B's own decision to make a promise in the first place. Having created the occasion for A to act in reliance, B is not in complete ignorance of the state of affairs he created; therefore, it is no cause for complaint if B is held liable for failing to ensure he acts reliably, thereby causing A harm, even though he may not be at fault for doing so.

7.2.3. Not Wrongs-Based?

A third objection, suggested by Robertson, is that proprietary estoppel is not part of the law of wrongs. He argues that if 'it is possible to identify an event, or series of events, that creates primary rights recognised by the law prior to and independently of any infringement of those rights',[119] then the doctrine under examination is not part of the law of wrongs on Peter Birks' fourfold classification of rights-creating events.[120] This is because 'an obligation

[114] Robertson, 'Estoppels and Rights-Creating Events' (n 30) 206.

[115] eg *Campbell v Griffin* (n 19), discussed in S 7.1.5.1.

[116] Peter Birks, 'Rights, Wrongs, and Remedies' (2000) 20 *OJLS* 1, 31.

[117] McFarlane and Sales, 'Promises, Detriment, and Liability' (n 10) 613-4. See too main text to n 73 above.

[118] Discussed in main text following n 82 above.

[119] Robertson, 'Estoppels and Rights-Creating Events' (n 30) 203.

[120] Namely: consent (contracts), wrongs (torts), unjust enrichment, and other events: P Birks, 'The Concept of a Civil Wrong' in DG Owen (ed), *Philosophical Foundations of Tort Law* (Oxford, OUP, 1995) 31, 33.

should be regarded as falling within the category of wrongs only if it cannot properly be understood as falling within one of the other categories.'[121] He concludes that proprietary estoppel is not a wrong-based doctrine because one can identify a series of rights-creating events, namely: '(i) the inducement by [B] of an assumption which is adopted by [A], and (ii) such action on the faith of that assumption by [A] that [A] would suffer detriment if [B] did not adhere to it.'[122]

Robertson appears to remain of the view that remedies awarded by way of proprietary estoppel are reflective and not replicative in nature where he writes: 'a wrong is committed when [B] behaves inconsistently without taking steps to ensure that this does not cause harm to [A]. [B] commits a wrong by infringing [A]'s right not to be harmed by [B]'s inconsistent conduct.'[123] His argument, however, is that B's commission of a wrong is not part of the events which create A's rights in proprietary estoppel.

It is difficult to see the utility in categorising proprietary estoppel as a 'non-wrong' if no award can be obtained under the doctrine without first establishing a breach of a primary duty. The same can be seen in relation to other doctrines. For example, contracts fall to be considered within Birks' 'consent' instead of 'wrongs' category because A's primary right can be enforced directly through the award of certain remedies such as specific performance, even though remedies such as damages may also be awarded in response to a breach of contract. But in relation to the tort of battery, even though it is possible to identify the event of 'birth' which gives rise to primary rights and duties,[124] the tort falls to be considered within Birks' 'wrongs' category. This is because an action based on the tort of battery does not give rise to remedies which directly enforce A's primary right to bodily safety but compensates for harm caused by B's intrusion on his bodily integrity.

Two responses might be made. First, it might be said that proprietary estoppel is not wrongs-based because, upon the occurrence of the relevant events—the inducement of an assumption and detrimental reliance—and prior to and independently of any breach, B's freedom of action is immediately constrained.[125] However, the same can also be said of areas of law which fall properly to be considered as wrongs-based on Birks' scheme. A 'wrong' is a breach of a primary duty, and by definition a primary duty imposes a constraint on B's freedom of action prior to and independently of a breach. So, in the previous example relating to the tort of battery, it can similarly be said that one's freedom of action is constrained in relation to another's bodily safety prior to the tort being committed. This does not mean that the tort falls outside Birks' 'wrongs' category.

Secondly, it might be said that a distinction ought to be drawn between cases where effect *can no longer be given* to A's primary right due to the nature of B's breach,[126] and cases where, despite this being a possibility, *the law chooses* to give effect to A's secondary right instead. It might be argued that only the former, and not the latter, should properly fall to be considered as wrongs-based. From the perspective of understanding remedies imposed

[121] Robertson, 'Estoppels and Rights-Creating Events' (n 30) 202.
[122] ibid 210.
[123] ibid.
[124] Robert Stevens, *Torts and Rights* (Oxford, OUP, 2007) 287.
[125] See Robertson, 'Estoppels and Rights-Creating Events' (n 30) 207, 210, 224.
[126] eg in relation to the tort of battery, B's infringement of A's bodily integrity has already occurred and the violation cannot be undone.

by courts, this distinction is unhelpful. If for whatever reason a particular doctrine leads only to the imposition of remedies which respond to B's wrong, then treating the doctrine as wrongs-based helps us to understand why a claim based on that doctrine requires claimants to demonstrate breach, causation, and remoteness. Otherwise, it would be necessary to draw a practically sterile distinction between cases where the lack of detriment caused by B's wrong prevents a claim from arising, and cases where a claim is made out but no remedy should be awarded.[127]

7.2.4. A Hybrid Approach?

The analysis proposed in this chapter entails that *all* proprietary estoppel remedies give effect to A's secondary right. Even if B is compelled to fulfil his promise, this is not analysed as an enforcement of B's primary duty to be reliable; instead, it is understood as the best way to achieve the goal of compensation on the facts of the particular case. The fourth objection to the proposed analysis takes a contrary view. It suggests that courts take a hybrid approach to proprietary estoppel, namely that courts enforce B's primary duty where he is compelled to make good his promise, but enforce B's secondary duty where compensatory damages are awarded.

Although not explicitly so stated, the hybrid analysis may be gleaned from the suggestion by Ben McFarlane and Philip Sales that '[t]he relief afforded to [A] under the promise-detriment principle is protection in respect of [A]'s detrimental reliance, unless and until any performance he or she has rendered under a reciprocal arrangement with [B] of which [B]'s promise forms part amounts to substantial performance by [A] of the return [B] wished to secure by making that promise'.[128]

Such a hybrid approach is misleading. Assume that the parties enter into a bad bargain where B promises to transfer his house worth £10 million to A in return for A agreeing to mow B's lawn. The 'minimum equity to do justice' and 'proportionality' notions would surely limit A's remedy to compensatory damages. This example shows that proprietary estoppel is not after all concerned with enforcing bargains, although it can be said that the existence of a 'bargain' would make it *more likely* that B is compelled to perform his promise since bad bargains are not commonplace: it is more probable that the promised interest and acts of reliance are objectively worth what the parties think they are.

Alternatively, the hybrid analysis may also be gleaned from Robertson's writing. He suggests that, where the court cannot prevent harm by granting expectation relief *in specie*, then compensation will be granted.[129] This approach suggests according primacy to expectation relief and reducing the award to compensatory damages where appropriate. While this may be the approach taken in Australia,[130] it does not represent the position taken in English law. There are two reasons why such an approach ought to be avoided in principle.

[127] See *Appleby v Cowley* (*The Times*, 14 April 1982).

[128] McFarlane and Sales, 'Promises, Detriment, and Liability' (n 10) 620.

[129] Robertson, 'The Reliance Basis' (n 51) 316. Note, though, that the view Robertson puts forward in this work has been superseded by his renewed analysis contained in Robertson, 'Estoppels and Rights-Creating Events' (n 30).

[130] See n 23 above.

First, prospective parties to a proprietary estoppel claim need to know in advance whether it is necessary to establish breach, causation, and remoteness; and the need (or absence thereof) to establish these elements cannot logically be determined by the choice of remedy—a consideration which arises only *after* a claim has been made out. Secondly, to avoid turning the 'minimum equity to do justice' concept into an empty catchphrase, courts ought always to start out by considering whether compensatory damages would do justice in a particular case, and then to increase this to an award which binds B to his promise only where justified. As Aldous LJ observed in *Jennings v Rice*:[131]

> once the elements of proprietary estoppel are established an equity arises. The value of that equity will depend upon all the circumstances including the expectation and the detriment. The task of the court is to do justice. The most essential requirement [in determining the value of the equity] is that there must be proportionality between the expectation and the detriment.

7.2.5. Section 116(a) of the Land Registration Act 2002

The fifth objection concerns the timing of the remedies. The Land Registration Act 2002, s 116(a) provides that an 'equity by estoppel … has effect from the time the equity arises as an interest capable of binding successors in title'.[132] The practical effect of this provision is that, if the court imposes a constructive trust,[133] A obtains priority in the property as from the time B breaches his primary duty.[134] This may appear to be inconsistent with the analysis of proprietary estoppel proposed in this chapter, which suggests that A does not have a right to a constructive trust until and unless such an order is made by the court.

7.2.5.1. The Nature of A's Secondary Right

One issue this objection raises concerns the nature of A's secondary right.[135] When B breaches his primary duty, does A obtain a proprietary or personal secondary right? On one view ('the first view'), A gains a personal right against B from the moment of B's breach, which can be increased at the remedial stage to a proprietary right at the court's discretion. On another view ('the second view'), A gains a proprietary right from the moment of B's breach, which may diminish over time according to the extent of detriment A suffers. If A's right is proprietary in nature, then it may be possible to say that, where a constructive trust is ultimately awarded by the court, the constructive trust always had proprietary effect from the date of B's breach. But if A's right is personal in nature, then a different explanation is required in relation to s 116(a).

[131] *Jennings v Rice* (n 9) [36].

[132] This section did not aim to create a new rule, but meant merely to confirm the existing state of the law: see Law Commission, *Land Registration for the Twenty-First Century: A Conveyancing Revolution* (Law Com No. 271, 2001) [5-30]–[5-31].

[133] Or another lesser proprietary interest, for instance an award for compensatory damages secured by a charge: see *Campbell v Griffin* (n 19).

[134] If, however, B sells the property to a purchaser with a defence, a constructive trust cannot arise, but A will still have a personal claim against B in proprietary estoppel: see Susan Bright and Ben McFarlane, 'Personal Liability in Proprietary Estoppel' [2005] *Conveyancer and Property Lawyer* 14.

[135] As distinct from the remedy ultimately awarded by the court.

The second view must be rejected for a number of reasons. First, it does not square with the cases. Take for instance *Jennings v Rice*.[136] B promised but failed to leave her house by will to A in return for A's caring for B. A sued B's administrator successfully in proprietary estoppel, and was awarded compensatory damages. It is difficult to analyse the award as responding to A's varying level of detriment over time. The level of detriment A suffered—in carrying out actions requested by B—remained fixed from the moment of B's breach when B died without leaving the property to A. Pressing the declaratory theory into action, one might even say that B was 'only ever entitled' to a personal remedy.[137]

Secondly, quite apart from the possible inconsistency inherent in the idea of a secondary proprietary right,[138] it is difficult to see how A can be said to have a secondary proprietary right when A may bring a proprietary estoppel claim against B even though the extent of the detriment A suffers at the time of B's breach is not substantial.[139] If A's secondary right is proprietary in nature, a proprietary remedy would normally follow; but where the detriment A suffers is not substantial, there is no doubt that a personal remedy would be awarded. Instead, it is better to say that A's secondary right is a personal right, since this would ordinarily lead to a personal remedy being imposed, with a proprietary remedy arising only where justified. As Susan Bright and Ben McFarlane have demonstrated, proprietary estoppel will generate a proprietary right only where it is shown that 'a personal right against [B] is inadequate to protect [A]'s reliance'—that '[A]'s reliance is not adequately protected if he has a right enforceable against [B] only.'[140]

Thirdly, there are three features of the rules concerning damages awards identified by Stephen Smith[141] which help explain why it is necessary for a court to liquidate B's secondary duty in proprietary estoppel before performance falls due. The first is that there is 'no damages on damages': A cannot obtain compensation for detriment which is attributable merely to B's failure to pay damages from the moment of B's breach of duty.[142] Thus, detriment which results from the mere fact that B breaks his promise is, in itself, insufficient to grant A a remedy.[143]

Smith's second point is that 'pre-payment is no defence to a claim in damages'.[144] Although this rule is untested in relation to proprietary estoppel, it appears logically consistent. If B pays A a sum of money when he commits the relevant breach of duty, this would not prevent A from bringing an action in proprietary estoppel against B,[145] since—and this is Smith's third point—'the existence and content of a duty to pay damages cannot reasonably

[136] *Jennings v Rice* (n 9).

[137] *cf* Ben McFarlane, 'Proprietary Estoppel and Third Parties after the Land Registration Act 2002' (2003) 62 *CLJ* 661, 663.

[138] Discussed in Chapter 10, S 10.3.3.1.

[139] See main text following n 28 above.

[140] Bright and McFarlane (n 49) 466.

[141] Stephen Smith, 'Why Courts make Orders (And What This Tells us About Damages)' (2011) 64 *Current Legal Problems* 51. Note, though, that this is not to endorse the 'liability model' (discussed in S 7.2.6. below) propounded by Smith, at least in relation to proprietary estoppel.

[142] ibid 71.

[143] See *Wilken and Ghaly* (n 28) [11.64]; *Commonwealth v Verwayen* [1990] 170 CLR 394, 429.

[144] Smith (n 141) 74. See *Edmunds v Lloyds Italico & l'Ancora Compagnia di Assicurazione e Riassicurazione SpA* [1986] 1 WLR 492 (CA) 496.

[145] Although the courts would allow a set-off between the pre-paid amount and the ultimate court order: Smith (n 141) 74.

be determined in advance of an order'.[146] In relation to proprietary estoppel, A can never be sure whether the money paid over by B would correspond to the amount a court would award after having the benefit of examining all the facts of the case. Indeed, it may yet be the case that a court would impose a constructive trust.[147] In this regard, it is necessary to treat with caution McFarlane's suggestion that '[t]he prospect of [A]'s suffering a detriment is a crucial part of [A]'s cause of action and, if [B] can remove that detriment, then, it seems, [B] cannot be said to have acted unconscionably, even if [A] has not been placed in the position [A] would have occupied had the promise been performed'.[148] Except in the case where B 'removes' A's detriment by fulfilling his promise,[149] it is the court, and not the parties, who is in the position to judge whether A's detriment has been fully compensated by B; assessing this requires the court to take into account issues of causation and remoteness; and a court will only undertake such an assessment if A establishes a proprietary estoppel claim in the first place.

Ultimately, the second view must be rejected, and the first view adopted. The question then arises: how can this be reconciled with s 116(a) (and the common law which it purports to confirm), which deems that any proprietary award will take effect from the moment of B's breach?

7.2.5.2. *Doctrine of 'Relation Back'*

One plausible answer is that the remedial effect of a constructive trust remedy is backdated 'by virtue of some doctrine of relation back'[150] to the time of B's breach. On this analysis, an 'equity by estoppel' is not a proprietary right, but is '*capable* of'[151] binding successors in title.

The employment of the 'doctrine of relation back' appears justified where it is impossible to be certain whether a constructive trust arises until a later event (the court order) occurs; but the trust's purpose is to enforce the parties' rights and duties which arose at an earlier point in time—that is, at the date of B's breach. As Rotherham notes, '[c]onstructive trusts are not natural phenomena; it is in our power to determine whether they ... pre-[exist] any judicial recognition. The decision should be made with a view to its practical implications.'[152] In relation to proprietary estoppel, the awarded remedy aims to correct A's loss caused by B's breach of duty. If a court determines that a constructive trust (or other proprietary) remedy would only take effect from the date of the court order, then A may be left with an unremedied loss in the period between B's breach and the date of judgment. Furthermore, backdating the effect of a constructive trust remedy is justified on the basis that the law ought to prevent B—and anyone deriving a right from him other than a purchaser with a defence—from profiting from his wrong.

[146] ibid 75.

[147] Of course, if the 'pre-payment' by B is the granting of the promised interest in his property to A, then A will have no claim in proprietary estoppel. The carrying out of B's promise entails that B discharges his primary duty (see discussion in main text from n 59 above), and so A will have no enforceable secondary rights (see *Grundt v Great Boulder Pty Gold Mines Ltd* (n 97) 674).

[148] McFarlane, 'The Importance of Looking Back' (n 2) 346.

[149] As to which see n 147 above.

[150] Kevin Gray and Susan Francis Gray, *Elements of Land Law*, 5th edn (Oxford, OUP, 2009) [9.2.89].

[151] Land Registration Act 2002, s 116 (emphasis added).

[152] Craig Rotherham, *Proprietary Remedies in Context* (Oxford, Hart Publishing, 2012) 27.

If this analysis is correct, it can also be predicted that, where a constructive trust is awarded, it is only the *proprietary* effects of the trust which are backdated to the time of B's breach: A would never succeed in holding B personally liable to account for the property for any period before the court order. This follows from the rule that B will not be held liable to account until and unless he has knowledge of the trust;[153] and such knowledge would arise for the first time only if and when the court decides to award a constructive trust on the date of judgment.

7.2.6. Liability?

The final objection requires extensive treatment. Instead of conceptualising proprietary estoppel as giving rise to *rights* and *duties*, Ben McFarlane has suggested that the doctrine gives rise to a *liability*. McFarlane's liability model is built on the writings of Stephen Smith, and so it is useful to begin by observing what Smith says of liabilities.

Duties and liabilities are fundamentally different in nature. Smith writes:

> duty-imposing rules and liability-imposing rules have different forms: duty-imposing rules tell citizens how to act (and how others should act towards them), whereas liability-imposing rules (or more strictly 'liability to orders imposing rules') tell citizens what the state may do to them (and what they may cause the state to do to others).[154]

In Ori Herstein's words, 'liability is the state of exposure to the exercise of power' by the court, which has 'the ability to change and create law; that is, a capacity to modify, annul, and create legal relations, rights, immunities, obligations, statuses, powers, and entitlements.'[155]

Duties and liabilities constrain defendants' actions in different ways. Smith explains:

> [t]o say that individuals have legal obligations to do X means that, from the law's perspective, they must do X. In contrast to say that someone has incurred a legal liability to Y means that the liable person may have Y done or imposed upon her if another person (or institution, etc) exercises a legal power.[156]

Putting it differently, Nolan and Robertson write, in relation to liabilities: 'the defendant is not susceptible to legal action because he or she has violated a right of the claimant, but simply because the law has laid down that in circumstance *x*, *y* has a claim against *z*.'[157]

As is the case with primary and secondary rights, a distinction can be drawn between primary and secondary liabilities. Smith's work, which has primarily been concerned with the liability to pay damages, relates to secondary liabilities. These liabilities arise where there is a prior breach, for example a breach of contract. In contrast, a primary liability arises without the need of a prior breach.

[153] *Westdeutsche Landesbank Girozentrale v Islington LBC* [1996] AC 669 (HL) 707.

[154] Stephen A Smith, 'A Duty to Make Restitution' (2013) 26 *Canadian Journal of Law and Jurisprudence* 157, 162.

[155] Ori J Herstein, 'How Tort Law Empowers' (2015) 65 *University of Toronto Law Journal* 99, 107.

[156] Stephen A Smith, 'The Restatement of Liabilities in Restitution' in Charles Mitchell and William Swadling (eds), *The Restatement Third, Restitution and Unjust Enrichment: Comparative and Critical Essays* (Oxford, Hart Publishing, 2013) 233. See too Smith, 'A Duty to Make Restitution' (n 154) 161.

[157] Donal Nolan and Andrew Robertson, 'Rights and Private Law' in Nolan and Robertson, *Rights and Private Law* (n 58) 16.

On McFarlane's view, proprietary estoppel gives rise to a primary liability.[158] He explains:[159]

> the occurrence of the triggering facts does not, by itself, give [A] a vested claim-right against [B].[160] Instead, when facts sufficient to support [A]'s claim have occurred, [B] comes under an initial liability to [A], and that liability is translated into a duty to [A] if and when a court order is made in [A]'s favour.

As to what those 'triggering facts' are, McFarlane writes:[161]

> [The promise-based strand of proprietary estoppel] applies where [B] makes a promise that [A] has or will acquire a right in relation to [B]'s property and [A], reasonably believing that [B]'s promise was seriously intended as a promise on which [A] could rely, adopts a particular course of conduct in reasonable reliance on [B]'s promise. If, as a result of that course of conduct, [A] would then suffer a detriment were [B] to be wholly free to renege on that promise, [B] comes under a liability to ensure that [A] suffers no such detriment.

7.2.6.1. Assessment

A major factor for rejecting the duty model in relation to proprietary estoppel appears to be the desire to incorporate two ideas in the analysis: on the one hand, the idea that B's freedom of action is constrained from the moment the elements of the doctrine are satisfied, and on the other hand, the idea that it is not mandatory for B to perform any actions until the date of judgment. Presumably, this is owed to the fact that, prior to the court order, 'it would normally be impossible for [B] to satisfy [the] duty … because the duty's content could not be determined prior to a judicial decision':[162] B will not know whether he is bound to fulfil his promise or to pay compensatory damages. On the analysis proposed in this chapter, proprietary estoppel is conceptualised differently. B's primary duty is to act reliably, having induced A's assumptions. B can discharge this duty either by informing A of his intention to renege before A has relied, or by carrying out his promise otherwise. B's duty is certainly mandatory,[163] the breach of which gives rise to a secondary duty to compensate. And as discussed in Chapter 2,[164] the existence of a duty to compensate is not incompatible with the fact that performance of that duty is contingent upon liquidation of that duty by a court.

There are a number of reasons why the liability analysis of proprietary estoppel ought to be rejected. Not only are there some general explanatory difficulties with reconceptualising a defendant's duty as a liability, there are also specific difficulties with applying the liability

[158] See Ben McFarlane, 'Equitable Estoppel as a Cause of Action: Neither One Thing Nor One Other' in Simone Degeling, James Edelman, and James Goudkamp (eds), *Contract in Commercial Law* (Sydney, Thomson Reuters, 2016) 376.

[159] McFarlane, *The Law of Proprietary Estoppel* (n 5) [9-23].

[160] McFarlane and Sales, 'Promises, Detriment, and Liability' (n 10) 633.

[161] McFarlane, *The Law of Proprietary Estoppel* (n 5) [1-15].

[162] Stephen A Smith, 'Duties, Liabilities, and Damages' (2011–2012) 125 *Harvard Law Review* 1727, 1743. This is written in relation to the argument that there is no duty to pay damages, but presumably the same idea underpins the liability model of proprietary estoppel.

[163] By 'mandatory', it is meant that B has no choice but to act reliably, otherwise he will breach that duty.

[164] See Chapter 2, S 2.4.2.2.1.

model to proprietary estoppel, in particular in relation to explaining the elements of detriment, causation, and remoteness, as well as the relationship between the doctrine and remedial constructive trusts.

7.2.6.1.1. General Conceptual Problems

Although it is unnecessary for the purposes of the present discussion to assert that reconceptualising a defendant's private law duty as a liability is *never* analytically sound, it can be observed that there are a number of inherent difficulties with the liability conception which potentially apply beyond proprietary estoppel.

First, unlike duties which govern the relationship between private actors, liabilities concern the relationship between private actors and the court. The liability model claims that a legal relationship arises between A and B when (and only when) a court makes an order. Prior to a court order, A has no relationship with B, but only 'a power to create an obligation in the court toward the litigants for the lawful adjudication of their matters.'[165] However, *all* subjects of the law within the legal system have a power to create such an obligation in the court, and a liability to comply with a court's pronouncement. Hence, the liability model does not provide an explanation for why the cases tell us that A has a claim *against B*, and in specific relation to proprietary estoppel it does not tell us why a court order will direct B *to compensate A*. In McFarlane's terms, it is difficult to see why 'when facts sufficient to support [A]'s claim have occurred, [B] comes under an initial liability *to [A]*,[166] when liability rules are 'fundamentally directed at judges'.[167]

Secondly, to say that B is subjected to the authority of the state—ie the court—does not explain why the state ought to interfere with private ordering at all. In specific relation to proprietary estoppel, on one view at least, it is not immediately obvious why the doctrine should provide relief at all, given that the parties could have, but did not, enter into a formal contract express trust relationship to give effect to the intended arrangement.

Thirdly, on Smith's view,[168] a strong pointer that the law is concerned with a liability and not a duty is where an alleged 'duty' cannot be discharged prior to a court order due to its content being otherwise unascertainable. But the assumption that a duty can only exist where its content is *immediately ascertainable* and *immediately dischargeable* is demonstrably false. For instance, a trustee with a duty to invest trust assets certainly has a 'duty' properly so-called, but it surely does not compel him to make investments *immediately* he takes on the role of trusteeship: he is entitled, for example, to wait for more favourable market conditions before investing. Similarly, a trustee with a duty to distribute trust assets among a large class of discretionary beneficiaries certainly has a 'duty' properly so-called, but he may take his time to ascertain the precise individuals who fall within the class and to whom he ought to make distribution before discharging the duty.

Fourthly, the liability conception is, in a sense, unhelpfully reductionist. A defendant upon whom a court imposes *any* remedy can be said to be subject to a liability, since he is exposed to the exercise of the court's power to impose remedies. However, to say that he is subject to a liability does not even begin to distinguish between the different types of

[165] Herstein, 'How Tort Law Empowers' (n 155) 120.
[166] McFarlane, *The Law of Proprietary Estoppel* (n 5) [9-23] (emphasis added).
[167] Smith 'Duties, Liabilities, and Damages' (n 162) 1749.
[168] See main text to n 162 above.

remedies, since the liability model tells us only that *a* remedy may be imposed against B through the court's exercise of its power to make such awards. In turn, the liability model does not explain how different remedies relate to the exercise of judicial discretion. In specific relation to proprietary estoppel, this perpetuates the existing problem of identifying and justifying the exercise of remedial discretion which courts exercise.

7.2.6.1.2. Detriment

One effect of adopting the liability model in relation to proprietary estoppel is that it involves conceptualising detriment in the form of a 'prospect'. In order for B to be subject to a liability, A must rely in such a way that '[A] *would* suffer a detriment *if* [B] were wholly free to act as [B] wishes.'[169]

Two difficulties with this conception of detriment have been noted in an earlier discussion.[170] An additional difficulty is that it does not tell us the means by which courts remove the prospect of detriment. Since B's reneging on his promise is that which would cause A's prospective detriment to become a reality, the most obvious way to remove the prospective detriment would be to compel B to perform his promise. But, as we have seen,[171] the enforcement of B's promise is not, and ought not to be, the default remedial approach in proprietary estoppel.

In reply, it might be said that 'the answer to the question of how best to enforce and protect [A]'s right is not affected by the fact that [A]'s right has arisen by proprietary estoppel, rather than by some other means. In any particular case, a court must decide how, given the situation at the time of its order, it can give best practical effect to [A]'s right.'[172] This analysis is based on a distinction drawn by Scarman LJ in *Crabb v Arun DC* between the questions of 'what is the extent of the equity?' and 'what is the relief appropriate to satisfy the equity?'[173] But this analysis is also unjustifiably reductionist: for example, it does not explain why courts might take into account considerations of 'practical justice' when determining the remedy in proprietary estoppel but not when awarding remedies when dealing with the QI doctrines.[174] The analysis also does not clearly identify what the goal of the imposed remedy ought to be in any particular case, which gives rise to difficulties in identifying the limits on the exercise of judicial discretion.

7.2.6.1.3. Causation and Remoteness

Consider a proprietary estoppel case involving an 'intervening cause', for example, where A's reliance consists of working for B, and A is injured in a car accident when driving to his place of work.[175] There seems to be no doubt that B will not be compelled to compensate for A's injury.[176] On the duty model, causation and remoteness rules can easily be mobilised

[169] McFarlane, *The Law of Proprietary Estoppel* (n 5) [3-26] (emphases added).
[170] See main text to and following n 104.
[171] See S 7.1.3.
[172] McFarlane, *The Law of Proprietary Estoppel* (n 5) [9-24].
[173] *Crabb v Arun District Council* (n 6) 193.
[174] *cf* the 'remedial constructive trust', which can be imposed to achieve 'practical justice': See Chapter 11, S 11.2.2.2.1.
[175] This example is drawn from McFarlane, *The Law of Proprietary Estoppel* (n 5) [4-63].
[176] Although, as McFarlane notes, 'case law ... seems to offer no clear examples of such a set of facts': McFarlane, *The Law of Proprietary Estoppel* (n 5) [4-68].

to explain this outcome. On the liability model, McFarlane also says that this result can be achieved[177] in the following way:[178]

> an analogy can be drawn with the causal concepts of *novus actus interveniens*, or of reasonable foreseeability. The detriment suffered by [A] is to be regarded as too remote, or 'collateral' even though it can be factually linked to the course of conduct through which [A] satisfied the reliance element of a proprietary estoppel claim.

However, because on the liability model the doctrine gives rise to a primary (as opposed to a secondary) liability, the question arises: how are concepts of causation and remoteness of loss accounted for? The suggested answer seems to be that courts take into consideration only 'reasonable reliance' or 'relevant detriment':[179] that '[B] [is] not ... held responsible for detriment arising from conduct of [A] that [B] could not reasonably have expected to result from [B]'s ... promise.'[180] Yet, it is difficult to see where in the liability model the ideas of 'responsibility' and 'reasonableness' fit, since that model dictates simply that in a particular situation the court must ensure that A suffers no detriment. Neither is it wholly satisfactory simply to draw 'analogies ... to principles adopted by the courts when assessing damages payable as a result of loss caused by a breach of contract or tort',[181] since if the applicable principles are those which relate to remedies which give effect to secondary rights, then there is good reason to think that, after all, proprietary estoppel is better understood by way of the duty model.

But even if we accept those analogies as purely analogies, their usefulness runs out at some point. McFarlane notes that the question of what amounts to 'reasonable reliance' or 'relevant detriment' is not simply concerned with the 'purely factual [question] of whether [B] could reasonably have foreseen [A]'s reliance'; instead, it 'includes a normative element'.[182] However, as Charles Mitchell has written, issues relating to intervening causes 'are more *obviously* in point when the question is framed in terms of remoteness, because it will then explicitly require the court to assess whether or not imposing liability is fair and in accordance with the principles underlying the rules that give the claimant her cause of action'.[183] Such normative considerations are context-specific, and so considerations which arise in relation to breaches of contract or tort are not immediately in point in relation to proprietary estoppel. Moreover, the lack of an obvious means by which the liability model takes into account such normative considerations is troubling. Again, in relation to intervening causes, Mitchell notes that 'such rules have the potential to produce drastic consequences for [B], and it would be reassuring to think that the courts have consciously adopted them because they have made a deliberate policy choice and have not merely blundered into them and then rationalized their position afterwards.'[184]

[177] ibid [4-63].
[178] ibid [4-64].
[179] ibid [4-67].
[180] ibid [4-68]. McFarlane also thinks that this explains a 'duty to mitigate': if A does not take easily available options to limit his losses, the additional losses are simply those which could not reasonably have been expected to result from B's promise (ibid [4-74]–[4-75]). But the criticisms provided in the text apply equally to this aspect of his analysis.
[181] ibid [4-68].
[182] ibid [4-72].
[183] Charles Mitchell, 'Causation, Remoteness, and Fiduciary Gains' (2006) 17 *King's College Law Journal* 325, 337, drawing on Jane Stapleton, 'Cause-in-Fact and the Scope of Liability for Consequences' (2003) 119 *LQR* 388, 421.
[184] Mitchell, 'Equitable Rights and Wrongs' (n 41) 332.

7.2.6.1.4. Remedial Constructive Trusts

Might Smith's secondary liability analysis provide an alternative approach to proprietary estoppel? On this view, proprietary estoppel does not give rise to a primary liability, which is the view McFarlane takes. Rather, when B breaches his primary duty to ensure the reliability of induced assumptions, B is subjected to a secondary liability which 'crystallises' into a duty only at the date of the court order.

This analysis also does not withstand scrutiny. On this analysis, court orders *create*, rather than *confirm*, B's legal duty.[185] This entails that, where constructive trusts are awarded by way of proprietary estoppel, they exists for the first time when they are imposed, and the property rights arising under those trusts are created by judges on a case-by-case basis. However, English judges have repeatedly emphasised that such 'remedial constructive trusts', 'with [the] critical features of judicial discretion and retrospectivity',[186] are not part of English law.[187]

In Chapter 11, it will be seen that the position in English law has in fact been greatly exaggerated, owing to a poor definition of what the phrase 'remedial constructive trusts' entails. It will also be seen that constructive trusts might be labelled 'remedial' when they are used as transformative *or* reflective remedies; and it is the former usage, and not the latter, which is rejected in English law. But the liability model of proprietary estoppel takes the view that constructive trusts can be imposed as transformative remedies, since on that model, their imposition has nothing to do with the parties' pre-trial rights and duties.[188] This difficulty is avoided on the duty model, which entails the imposition of constructive trusts as reflective remedies.

In summary, given that the liability model of proprietary estoppel does not withstand scrutiny, it does not pose a serious objection to the secondary-rights analysis proposed in this chapter.

7.3. The Rationale

It is necessary to pause to make explicit the rationale or norm which underpins proprietary estoppel. This consideration is particularly important for distinguishing between the QI doctrines and proprietary estoppel. While both groups of doctrines might appear to be united in the fact that they respond to the elements of B's promise and A's reliance, there are significant differences. In Chapter 3,[189] it was seen that B's promise in an AI situation relates to property which B owns absolutely at the outset, and that A's reliance never increases B's opportunity of acquiring property to which his promise relates. This stands in contrast to

[185] See, eg, Smith 'Duties, Liabilities, and Damages' (n 162) 1727; Smith, 'A Duty to Make Restitution' (n 154) 161.

[186] *Crossco No. 4 Unlimited v Jolan Ltd* [2011] EWCA Civ 1619, 14 ITELR 615 [84].

[187] See also *Turner v Jacob* [2006] EWHC 1317 (Ch) at [85]; *Westdeutsche* (n 153) 714; *Re Polly Peck International plc (in administration) No. 2* [1998] 3 All ER 812 (CA) 830; *Re Sharpe (a bankrupt)* [1980] 1 WLR 219 (Ch) 225; *Bailey v Angove's PTY Ltd* [2016] UKSC 47, [2016] 1 WLR 3179 [27].

[188] See the definition of 'transformative remedies' given in Chapter 2, S 2.4.2.3.

[189] See Chapter 3, S 3.2.1.2.

the QI doctrines, where B's promise is always to the effect that he will take only a qualified interest in property yet to be acquired, and A's reliance arises in the form of the provision of an advantage to B in relation to B's acquisition of that property. Moreover, while the QI doctrines invariably provide for the imposition of constructive trusts, in proprietary estoppel a lesser remedy may be imposed. A discussion of the rationale underpinning proprietary estoppel explains and justifies why the differences exist.

7.3.1. Perfection and Reparation?

It is first necessary to say something about Gbolahan Elias's attempt at explaining proprietary estoppel. As we saw in Chapter 4,[190] Elias suggests that the 'inducement rules', which includes the QI doctrines as well as proprietary estoppel, can be explained by way of the 'perfection aim'. However, the 'perfection aim' does not provide an exhaustive explanation of proprietary estoppel. According to Elias, where 'induced losses' are involved,[191] they 'offer the plaintiff the option of getting reparation or restitution'.[192] Thus, 'under the proprietary estoppel rule the plaintiff may sue for reparation for his loss'.[193] This reflects 'notions of responsibility that one who causes loss to another should, in principle, have to repair that loss.'[194]

Elias' explanation of proprietary estoppel is unsatisfactory. To say that proprietary estoppel has a 'perfectionary aim' gives the false impression that no meaningful distinctions can be drawn between QI and AI situations. Elias attempts to account for the obvious difference in remedial approach between the two situations by suggesting that, in relation to proprietary estoppel, reparation may also be sought. He elaborates that '[i]t is important to grasp that … proprietary estoppel … may offer such non-perfectionary options as well as perfectionary ones. We distort the two rules if we begin to suggest that they are either "only perfectionary" or "not perfectionary at all".'[195] However, no explanation is given as to *why* the law pursues these two distinct aims only in the case of proprietary estoppel. It can be observed that A also suffers reliance loss in many cases relating to the QI doctrines, and yet there is no suggestion that courts ever award mere compensation pursuant to the aim of reparation in those doctrines. There is also a lack of explanation as to what guides the courts in choosing among the two aims.

7.3.2. AI Situations: Correcting Reliance Losses

It is suggested that there are two sets of norms at play in relation to proprietary estoppel. Because proprietary estoppel gives effect to secondary rights, it follows that there is one norm which underpins the primary duty owed by B to A, and another which underlies equity's response to B's secondary duty.

[190] See Chapter 4, S 4.3.1.
[191] Gbolahan Elias, *Explaining Constructive Trusts* (Oxford, OUP, 1990) 61.
[192] ibid 63.
[193] ibid.
[194] ibid 26.
[195] ibid 64.

It was seen earlier[196] that the primary duty which B breaches in proprietary estoppel cases is a duty to ensure the reliability of induced assumptions. Therefore, the norm underpinning the primary duty is the norm that one ought to ensure that he acts reliably in relation to induced assumptions. Thus, B ought to act reliably by informing A of B's intention to renege on his promise before A acts in reliance, or else B ought to perform his promise. Where B discharges his primary duty, A has no cause of action in proprietary estoppel at all because A does not suffer any detriment.[197] But where B fails to act as he ought to, A suffers harm which triggers B's secondary duty to compensate for the harm caused. At this stage, proprietary estoppel becomes relevant. The operative norm at the secondary duty level—and therefore the norm which underpins proprietary estoppel—is that 'the law ought to correct reliance losses'.[198]

It can be observed at once that, unlike in relation to the QI doctrines, the applicable norm in relation to proprietary estoppel allow for more flexibility. One aspect of that flexibility relates to the facts which a court may take into account when deciding on the appropriate remedy. As Simon Gardner observes:[199]

> Proprietary estoppel exists to adjust the prevailing balance of property between claimant and defendant when the claimant has formed the relevant kind of expectation, and has acted detrimentally in reliance on it, and these occurrences are ascribable to the defendant (via his encouragement of or acquiescence in them), so that it would be unconscionable for him to insist on the status quo. It would be inept if this jurisdiction were applicable only to cases in which the claimant is precise in his expectation and minutely circumspect in his reliance ... It is no surprise, therefore, that the law tolerates inexactitude over these matters.

Thus, unlike the QI doctrines where A's reliance must be in the form of providing an advantage to B in relation to B's acquisition of the property to which B's promise relates, in proprietary estoppel *any* act of reliance by A may potentially be relevant. This is because the operative norms dictate that B must generally compensate for *any* loss A suffers when B acts unreliably. Hence, the focus is on the detriment A suffers from acting in reliance on B's promise.

The norm at play also explains the remedial flexibility found in proprietary estoppel. Unlike the QI doctrines where B ought never to take the property he acquires for his unqualified use, it is not obvious in relation to proprietary estoppel that B ought to carry out the entirety of his promise whenever A suffers detrimental reliance of any kind. This is particularly so given that there can be different kinds of expectation which A may form various degrees of detriment which he may suffer. By 'seek[ing] to react to multiple considerations',[200] therefore, it is unsurprising that proprietary estoppel allows for the exercise of remedial discretion in order to grant a remedy proportionate to A's detriment.[201] Such flexibility is necessary in order to ensure that A's reliance losses are adequately corrected.

[196] See main text to n 47 above.

[197] See discussion in S 7.1.6.

[198] Simon Gardner, 'Reliance-Based Constructive Trusts' in Charles Mitchell (ed), *Constructive and Resulting Trusts* (Oxford, Hart Publishing, 2010) 79. See also *Wilken and Ghaly* (n 28) [11-94]: 'The prime aim of the discretion [in proprietary estoppel] should be to prevent detriment.'

[199] Gardner, 'Again' (n 7) 508.

[200] ibid 507.

[201] Bright and McFarlane, 'Proprietary Estoppel and Property Rights' (n 10) 453–54; *Wilken and Ghaly* (n 28) [11-94].

Hence, applying the notion of doing the 'minimum equity to do justice to the plaintiff',[202] the awarded remedy ensures that B is compelled to do no more and no less than needed to compensate A for harm caused by B.

7.4. Lessons

The proposed analysis of proprietary estoppel helpfully identifies the doctrine's unique place within the structure of constructive trusts, as an AI situation within the non-contract-based, bilateral events category. Not only does this analysis reveal the reasons behind and limits to the remedial discretion afforded in the doctrine, it also explains the respective roles of the requirements for a successful proprietary estoppel claim. In addition to these, there are three further lessons to be gained, which impacts our understanding of the relationship between proprietary estoppel and the QI doctrines, and of constructive trusts as a whole. These lessons are discussed in this section.

Before proceeding, it needs to be noted that this section does not discuss the 'common intention constructive trust' (CICT). Certainly, most suggestions to the effect that proprietary estoppel and constructive trusts should be assimilated arise in the context of the CICT.[203] However, because the CICT has been developed wholly in the context of resolving disputes where couples purchase property jointly occupied as a family home,[204] the development of the CICT has been affected by policy concerns specific to that context.[205] These unique policy concerns have led courts to an unprecedented willingness to stretch conventional constructive trust concepts to do justice on particular facts,[206] with the unfortunate result of blurring the clear distinction between doctrines which impose constructive trusts as replicative remedies on the one hand and reflective remedies on the other. These and other related matters are discussed in Chapter 14, where the argument is made that the CICT doctrine ought properly to be considered as a specific application of proprietary estoppel. The present discussion is concerned with the relationship between proprietary estoppel and the QI doctrines.

7.4.1. Two Senses of 'Constructive Trust'

The analysis in this chapter indicates that there are two senses in which the phrase 'constructive trust' is used. On the one hand, a 'constructive trust' describes a relationship between A and B which is triggered by a set of real-world events. On the other hand, a 'constructive trust' is a remedy, the subject-matter of a court order.

[202] *Crabb v Arun District Council* (n 6) 198.

[203] See, eg, *Christian v Christian* (1981) 131 NLJ 43 (CA); *Yaxley v Gotts* (n 102) 176–80; *Oxley v Hiscock* [2005] Fam 211 (CA) [66].

[204] *Crossco* (CA) (n 186) [85].

[205] See, eg, *Stack v Dowden* [2007] UKHL 17, [2002] 2 AC 432 [42]; *Jones v Kernott* [2011] UKSC 53, [2011] 3 WLR 1121 [56]–[57], [78].

[206] Simon Gardner, *An Introduction to the Law of Trusts*, Clarendon Law Series, 3rd edn (Oxford, OUP, 2011) 335–36.

The first sense of 'constructive trust' can be seen in relation to the QI doctrines. Where the elements of promise and reliance are fulfilled in the relevant way, primary rights and duties immediately arise. These rights and duties make up a constructive trust relationship, the existence of which does not depend on a court order. In this sense, 'constructive trusts' line alongside express trusts and resulting trusts as being terms which describe a primary right-duty relationship which arise between the parties when they are triggered by predetermined events. This sense of 'constructive trust' is not relevant to proprietary estoppel: the primary relationship between the parties in proprietary estoppel is not a *trust* relationship at all, but one which gives rise to a duty on B's part (and a corresponding right on A's part) to act reliably in relation to induced assumptions.[207]

The second sense of 'constructive trust' is relevant both in relation to the QI doctrines and proprietary estoppel, although they are imposed through different means. In relation to the QI doctrines, a constructive trust is imposed as a replicative remedy, whereby the remedy simply 'declares' and enforces the parties' primary constructive trust relationship. Hence the remedy invariably compels B to carry out the full extent of his promise. Conversely, proprietary estoppel provides for the imposition of reflective remedies, and a constructive trust is one remedy among others which might be imposed by courts through an exercise of discretion as to content in order to achieve the goal of compensation. Where a constructive trust is imposed, it originates from the court order, but gives effect to A's secondary right and is backdated to take effect from the moment of B's breach.

7.4.2. Pre-Acquisition and Post-Acquisition Agreements

In recent years, there have been a number of judicial observations which suggest that important lessons can be drawn from the distinction between pre- and post-acquisition agreements. These have largely arisen in the context of the doctrine in *Pallant v Morgan*. For example, in *Banner Homes Group plc v Luff Developments Ltd*, Chadwick LJ observed of the doctrine in *Pallant v Morgan*: '[i]t is the pre-acquisition arrangement which colours the subsequent acquisition by the defendant and leads to his being treated as a trustee if he seeks to act inconsistently with it.'[208] Affirming this observation in *Cobbe v Yeoman's Row Management Ltd*,[209] Lord Scott saw no basis for imposing a constructive trust under that doctrine where 'the property … is owned by one of the parties before the joint venture has been embarked upon'. This view was echoed by Morgan J in *Crossco No. 4 Unlimited v Jolan Ltd*,[210] who suggested that 'there can be an important difference between a case of a pre-acquisition arrangement and a post-acquisition arrangement.'

[207] The distinction between 'constructive trusts' and 'proprietary estoppel' *in this sense* seems to underlie Lord Walker's statement in *Stack v Dowden* (n 205) [37] that 'I am now rather less enthusiastic about the notion that proprietary estoppel and "common interest" constructive trusts can or should be completely assimilated. Proprietary estoppel typically consists of asserting an equitable claim against the conscience of the "true" owner. The claim is a "mere equity". It is to be satisfied by the minimum award necessary to do justice … which may sometimes lead to no more than a monetary award. A "common intention" constructive trust, by contrast, is identifying the true beneficial owner or owners, and the size of their beneficial interests.' However, as explained in Chapter 14, although courts claim that the CICT simply reflects the parties' agreement, upon closer inspection this is untrue.

[208] *Banner Homes Group plc v Luff Developments Ltd* [2000] Ch 372 (CA) 397.

[209] *Cobbe v Yeoman's Row Management Ltd* [2008] UKHL 55, [2008] 1 WLR 1752 [33].

[210] *Crossco No. 4 Unlimited v Jolan Ltd* [2011] EWHC 803 (Ch), [2011] NPC 38 [363]–[364].

It is submitted that the pre-acquisition and post-acquisition distinction is vital for appreciating the differences between the QI doctrines and proprietary estoppel. The QI doctrines always relate to pre-acquisition agreements. The property in question is never B's to begin with; hence, for a constructive trust to arise, B must promise to take merely a qualified interest in the property to be acquired, and A must rely in such a way as to provide an advantage in relation to B's acquisition. In contrast, proprietary estoppel cases concern property B already owns absolutely. Hence, agreements which give rise to this doctrine are 'post-acquisition' agreements.

There are two 'in-between' cases which merit consideration. The first is where A relies on B's post-acquisition promise in a way which confers on B an advantage. Suppose B promises to give A an interest in B's own property, and A relies on this promise by conferring on B an advantage such as caring for B,[211] working for B,[212] or improving B's property.[213] Even though it might be said that B receives an 'advantage', this is not a relevant advantage similar to that required to trigger the QI doctrines. The 'advantage' is not related to B's acquisition of a property to which his promise relates; moreover, B also does not promise to take a qualified interest *in any property which materialises from the advantage* which he obtains from A. Indeed, in contrast to the QI doctrines, the advantage which B obtains from A *is* after all intended for B's unqualified enjoyment, the hope or expectation being only that B will in turn fulfil his promise to grant A an interest in B's property. Thus, these cases are not ultimately 'advantage-based'; rather, the focus is on the detriment A suffers in yielding up the aforementioned advantage to B, and fall to be considered by way of proprietary estoppel.

The second is cases where A relies on B's pre-acquisition promise in a way which does not confer on B a relevant advantage. It is obviously possible to conceive of cases where B promises to cede an interest in property yet to be acquired to A, the promise of which induces A to act in reliance, but not in a way which contributes to B's opportunity of acquiring the property to which his promise relates.[214] It might be said that B has made a 'pre-acquisition' promise. However, because A does not rely on the promise in a manner which increases B's opportunity of acquiring the property to which his promise relates, they ultimately fall to be considered by way of proprietary estoppel, with B being treated as the absolute owner of the property upon acquisition. To paraphrase Millett LJ in *Paragon Finance plc v DB Thakerar & Co*,[215] B receives the trust property 'in his own right', since his possession of the property is not coloured from the first by the trust and confidence by means of which he obtained it. Again, such cases are not ultimately 'advantage-based'; instead, the focus is on the detriment A suffers.

It is crucial to note that what matters is whether the elements of promise and reliance are fulfilled before B has acquired the property in question, or whether they relate to property B already owns. Nothing turns on whether A is promised an immediate, unconditional interest or an inheritance or future interest. The latter distinction was drawn by Lord Scott in *Thorner v Major*, where his Lordship suggested that proprietary estoppel should be applied where A is promised an immediate, unconditional interest, whereas 'the principles

[211] See, eg, *Jennings v Rice* (n 9).
[212] See, eg, *Gillett v Holt* (n 31).
[213] See, eg, *Voyce v Voyce* (1991) 62 P & CR 290 (CA).
[214] One such case is *Holiday Inns Inc v Broadhead* (Ch, 19 December 1969), as reported in *Banner Homes* (n 208) 389–93, which was discussed in Chapter 6, S 6.2.1.3.
[215] *Paragon Finance plc v DB Thakerar & Co* [1999] 1 All ER 400 (CA) 409.

of remedial constructive trusts' should be applied where A is promised an inheritance or future interest.[216] This distinction is superfluous. As the discussion in Chapter 11[217] will demonstrate, the phrase 'remedial constructive trusts' can refer either to constructive trusts imposed as reflective remedies or as transformative remedies, and that English law does not recognise transformative constructive trusts. Assuming (as we should) that Lord Scott was aware of this, the distinction his Lordship attempted to draw turns out to be illusory. On a proper analysis, whatever the nature of A's promised interest, immediate or future, a reflective constructive trust may be imposed; and proprietary estoppel is the only existing doctrine in English law which allows such constructive trusts to be imposed.

7.4.3. Alternative Causes of Action

It is not uncommon for claimants to plead one of the QI doctrines and proprietary estoppel as alternative grounds of claim on a particular set of facts. It might be thought that claimants will prefer to rely on one of the QI doctrines over proprietary estoppel where possible for the simple reason that the former doctrines guarantee the enforcement of B's promise.[218] However, there is a deeper reason for this preference, which relates to the inherent nature of these doctrines. If a court holds that the primary legal relationship between A and B is a constructive trust, then B's primary duty is enforceable 'from the first':[219] B is under a duty to account for the property from the moment of acquisition. Because B is *never* treated as the absolute owner of the property, B is incapable of causing harm to A through denying A the promised interest and keeping the property for himself. This renders proprietary estoppel irrelevant. On the other hand, if there is no primary trust relationship between A and B, then B is taken to be the absolute owner of the property: the property is not subject to any trust. Only then does it become relevant to speak of B causing harm to A by acting unreliably through inducing A's assumptions concerning what B will do with his property. This brings proprietary estoppel into the picture.

This analysis indicates an inherent analytical logic in the interplay between the two sets of doctrines. There are two limbs to this logic. First, if the parties reach an agreement concerning property B owns absolutely (a post-acquisition agreement), only a proprietary estoppel claim can be substantiated; secondly, if the agreement is reached *before* B acquires the property in question (a pre-acquisition agreement), and that A relies in the relevant way before B acquires the property, then A might succeed on the basis of either one of the QI doctrines *or* proprietary estoppel, subject to the proviso that the QI doctrines must be considered first.

The truth of the first limb is reflected by the fact that the QI doctrines—specifically the doctrine in *Rochefoucauld v Boustead*—has always been held not to be relevant where B makes an informal self-declaration of trust over an interest in land he owns absolutely.[220] The reason commonly cited for this is that B does not perpetrate a 'fraud'; but 'fraud' does not provide a sufficient reason for the imposition of constructive trusts.[221] The real reason is that, if B owns the property absolutely, it is not subject to a primary constructive trust

[216] *Thorner v Major* (n 25) [19]–[20].
[217] See, in particular, Chapter 11, S 11.2.2.1.
[218] See, eg, McFarlane (n 60) 689.
[219] *Paragon Finance* (n 215) 409.
[220] See n 40 above.
[221] See discussion in Chapter 4, S 4.4.

relationship which exists 'from the first'. Hence it is necessary for courts to consider the degree of detrimental reliance A suffers and thence to impose a proportionate remedy.

As for the second limb, it is observable that there are cases which could have been resolved using one of the QI doctrines which, however, have been decided by way of proprietary estoppel. For example, consider the case of *Baker v Baker and Baker*.[222] The defendants (Bs) were A's son and daughter-in-law. A, the claimant, and Bs reached an agreement whereby A would contribute £33,950 to the purchase of a house in Bs' names; and in return A would be given the right to reside in a 'granny room' in the house rent free for the rest of his life.[223] This was carried into effect. Eight months in, Bs accused A of sexually molesting Bs' young daughter; but upon investigation, this allegation was held to be unfounded.[224] A left the house, being 'deeply hurt, highly offended and furious'.[225] He claimed a beneficial interest in the house by way of a resulting trust, and alternatively an entitlement to compensation by way of proprietary estoppel. At first instance, HHJ Hywel Moseley QC dismissed A's resulting trust claim,[226] presumably because the facts suggested that A had provided the money as a gift to Bs, hence there was not the requisite lack of intention to benefit Bs. However, the judge allowed A's proprietary estoppel claim, and this was upheld in the Court of Appeal.[227]

On the facts, it would have been possible for A to argue, based on the doctrine in *Pallant v Morgan*, that Bs should be held to their promise from the moment Bs acquired the house, given that Bs had made a pre-acquisition promise to qualify the interest they would obtain in the house, and A had provided an advantage in the form of an opportunity in relation to Bs' acquisition of it.[228] However, this was clearly not what A desired, given the reasons for his leaving, and hence was not pleaded. By making a proprietary estoppel claim, therefore, A was in essence giving up his right to argue that a primary trust relationship arose when Bs acquired the house. As a result, Bs were treated as absolute owners of the house. On this basis, Bs' denial of A's promised interest indicated that B had acted unreliably in relation to induced assumptions, and this breach caused A to suffer detriment. Therefore, A was able to receive compensatory damages from Bs for the detriment he suffered.[229]

7.4.3.1. The Extent of Proprietary Estoppel

Since proprietary estoppel can, in principle, provide an alternative claim to the QI doctrines in cases involving pre-acquisition agreements, it needs to be considered whether the *extent* of proprietary estoppel enables it to play such a role. In general the answer is 'yes'. However, there are two aspects which may potentially cause concern.

The first relates to the subject-matter of the claim. Because the QI doctrines can apply to any property, realty or personalty,[230] the question arises as to whether proprietary estoppel

[222] *Baker v Baker and Baker* (1993) 25 HLR 408 (CA). The case of *Watson v Goldsbrough* [1986] 1 EGLR 265 P (CA) is probably another example.

[223] *Baker v Baker* (n 222) 410.

[224] ibid 411.

[225] ibid.

[226] ibid.

[227] The Court agreed with the applicability of proprietary estoppel to the facts of the case—this was not a ground of appeal—but disagreed with the extent of the remedy and remitted the matter to the judge for re-assessment.

[228] For a detailed discussion, see Chapter 6, S 6.2.

[229] See *Baker v Baker* (n 222) 411–12.

[230] See, eg, *De Bruyne v De Bruyne* [2010] EWCA Civ 519, [2010] 2 FLR 1240.

can equally apply to promises which do not relate to an interest in land. It is difficult to say for certain, given that most decided cases have concerned land. However, it would be arbitrary if the success of such a claim rises and falls with the subject-matter of B's promise.

In fact, the decision in *Re Basham*[231] suggests that the claim is not confined to real property.[232] In that case, A successfully claimed by way of proprietary estoppel where B promised to leave his residuary estate to her (A). Crucially, B's residuary estate did not only include real property—a cottage[233]—but also cash, furniture and other chattels.[234] The applicability of proprietary estoppel to personalty was not held to be objectionable by the judge in that case; and later cases which have considered[235] *Re Basham*, including one in the House of Lords,[236] have not taken issue with this aspect of the case. It has also been held that a promise that A will share in the *profits* arising out of the development of land[237] or a promise to *purchase* land,[238] as opposed to a promise relating to an interest *in* land, can invoke the doctrine as well. Indeed, there have also been judicial suggestions that proprietary estoppel can apply to beneficial interests under a trust[239] and patents.[240] And in *Motivate Publishing FZ LLC v Hello Ltd*,[241] Birss J, in considering a case relating to publishing licence, held:

> I can think of no reason in principle why a proprietary estoppel should not be available to the claimants in this case to prevent the defendant from denying the existence of a licence of this kind. It would be a right enforceable by the claimants against the defendant. The fact that the licence is a licence of intellectual property rights rather than an interest in land makes no difference. No case has been drawn to my attention in which a proprietary estoppel has been refused on that ground. I hold it is available to the claimants.[242]

It is reasonable to conclude, therefore, that a proprietary estoppel claim may extend to personalty. This is particularly relevant in the testamentary context, where testators who do not comply with the Wills Act 1837, s 9 are unable to create express testamentary trusts over any property, including personalty. In such cases, it may be possible for claimants to rely on the secret trusts doctrine, or alternatively proprietary estoppel, even where the subject-matter is personalty.

231 *Re Basham (deceased)* [1986] 1 WLR 1498 (Ch).

232 See *Wilken and Ghaly* (n 28) [11-127] and cases cited therein for a strong case for this proposition. See too McFarlane and Sales, 'Promises, Detriment, and Liability' (n 10) 621–25; McFarlane, *The Law of Proprietary Estoppel* (n 5) [10-59]ff.

233 In fact, the cottage made up only less than half the total value of the residuary estate which was granted to A by way of a trust pursuant to her proprietary estoppel claim.

234 *Re Basham* (n 231) 1500.

235 See, eg, *Jiggins v Brisley* [2003] EWHC 841 (Ch), [2003] WTLR 1141 [80]; *Shovelar v Lane* [2011] EWCA Civ 802, [2012] 1 WLR 637 [38]. The decision in *MacDonald v Frost* [2009] EWHC 2276 (Ch), [2009] WTLR 1815 [13]–[16], which doubted *Re Basham*, says nothing about the applicability of the claim to personalty.

236 *Thorner v Major* (n 25) [20], [63].

But *cf* Christine Davis, 'Estoppel: An Adequate Substitute for Part Performance?' (1993) 13 *OJLS* 99, 103–04, where it is suggested that proprietary estoppel can indeed extend to property other than land, but cannot cover cases where the subject-matter is purely money.

237 *Sutcliffe v Lloyd* [2007] EWCA Civ 153.

238 *Salvation Army Trustee Co Ltd v West Yorkshire Metropolitan CC* (1981) 41 P & CR 179 (QB).

239 *Strover v Strover* [2005] EWHC 860 (Ch).

240 *Yeda Research and Development Co Ltd v Rhone-Poulenc Rorer International Holdings Inc* [2007] UKHL 43, [2008] 1 All ER 425 [22].

241 *Motivate Publishing FZ LLC v Hello Ltd* [2015] EWHC 1554 (Ch) [61].

242 Note, though, that proprietary estoppel did not apply on the facts because the licensor had not made the necessary representations to invoke the doctrine.

The second relates to the potential claimant in proprietary estoppel. Suppose B promises A that he will leave the property he will acquire to C. This three-party scenario would not hinder the QI doctrines from arising, and C would be able to enforce B's promise.[243] The question arises whether C can bring a claim by way of proprietary estoppel, to make the argument that A's reliance on B's promise justifies compelling B to carry out his promise in favour of C. In the decided cases, the claimant has never been C: it has always been A who *personally* incurs detrimental reliance. Yet, no judicial statement has conclusively ruled out the possibility that C may bring such a claim. Furthermore, there seems to be nothing in principle which prevents C (as opposed to A where, for instance, A has died) from attempting to establish that A's detrimental reliance *on B's promise to grant C an interest* justifies holding B to his promise,[244] thereby giving rise to a constructive trust remedy in C's favour. After all, one way in which B may discharge his primary duty to be reliable is to carry out his promise, and in reference to his failure to do so after A has incurred detrimental reliance it may be appropriate in certain cases to compensate A by compelling B to hold the promised interest on constructive trust for C.

In reply, one might cite *Lloyd v Dugdale*[245] as authority for the requirement that a claimant in proprietary estoppel must have suffered personal detriment. One question which arose for consideration in that case was whether A had a proprietary estoppel claim where B's promise to A that A would personally acquire[246] B's property was detrimentally relied on, not by A personally, but by C.[247] The Court of Appeal gave a negative answer, stating that 'it remained necessary for [A] to show some detriment incurred by him personally as a result of [B]'s representations.'[248] However, it is crucial to note that B did not promise to benefit C but *A*. Hence the case indicates only that the *promisee*, A, must personally incur detrimental reliance; it says nothing about the possibility that *C* may rely on proprietary estoppel where B's promise to A was that B would grant C a benefit, and where A, as promisee, had personally suffered detrimental reliance. Thus, it is submitted that neither case law nor principle rules out C's ability to plead proprietary estoppel where C is the object of B's promise or assurance.[249]

243 Discussed in detail in Chapter 4, S 4.5.2.

244 It may be, however, that the level of A's detrimental reliance would not justify holding B to his promise, in which case compensatory damages would only be awarded to A's estate, and C would obtain nothing.

245 *Lloyd v Dugdale* [2001] EWCA Civ 1754, [2002] 2 P & CR 13 [35].

246 ibid [29]–[30].

247 Although C was a company owned by A, it was held that C was a separate and distinct legal entity from A: *Lloyd v Dugdale* (n 245) [48], [58].

248 ibid [35].

249 Alternatively, of course, one could say that C's right to enforce B's promise based on A's detrimental reliance gives rise to a *sui generis* claim that is akin, but not identical, to proprietary estoppel. However, this seems unnecessary, given that the variable factors affecting such a case—B's promise, A's detrimental reliance and A's expectation—are identical to claims by way of proprietary estoppel.

8

Specifically Enforceable Contracts of Sale and Future Property

Within the bilateral events category of constructive trusts fall two contract-based doctrines: constructive trusts arising in the context of specifically enforceable contracts of sale, and those arising in the context of contracts for value to assign or transfer future property. Unlike the other doctrines discussed in this book, the doctrines discussed in this chapter require A and B to have entered into a legally binding contract for constructive trusts to be imposed. This includes complying with the Law of Property (Miscellaneous Provisions) Act 1989, s 2 where necessary.[1] These doctrines fall within the bilateral events category, since the participation of both parties is necessary to trigger the constructive trusts.

8.1. Specifically Enforceable Contracts of Sale

Where A and B enter into a specifically enforceable contract of sale, the seller, B, holds the property on constructive trust for A until the property is conveyed. The core case involves the sale of land, but the doctrine is not so limited. Thus, for example, contracts relating to security interests over machinery[2] and securities,[3] subsisting equitable interests,[4] and a 'virtual assignment'[5] have been said to be capable of engaging the doctrine. However, in cases which do not involve land, judges commonly draw analogies with contracts relating to the sale of land.[6]

[1] In particular, s 2(1) of the 1989 Act provides: 'A contract for the sale or other disposition of an interest in land can only be made in writing and only by incorporating all the terms which the parties have expressly agreed in one document or, where contracts are exchanged, in each.' Note, however, that it remains unnecessary for the parties to comply with the formality requirements for the creation and enforcement of express trusts found in s 53 of the LPA 1925, since s 53(2) holds that that section has no application to constructive trusts: see PG Turner, 'Understanding the Constructive Trust between Vendor and Purchaser' (2012) 128 *LQR* 582, 598.

[2] *Holroyd v Marshall* (1862) 10 H L Cas 191, 11 ER 999.

[3] *Swiss Bank Corp v Lloyds Bank Ltd* [1982] AC 584 (HL) 595.

[4] *Re Holt's Settlement* [1969] 1 Ch 100 (Ch).

[5] *Clarence House Ltd v National Westminster Bank* [2009] EWCA Civ 1311, [2010] 1 WLR 1216; defined in the main text following n 34 below.

[6] See, eg, *Re Holt's* (n 4) 116, *Clarence House Ltd* (n 5) [45].

The reason why contracts relating to land are taken as the reference point relates to the requirement for the contract to be specifically enforceable. As *Snell's Equity* explains:[7]

> Land is treated very differently from goods, because no two pieces of land are identical and may have a particular value to the purchaser or lessee. Where the necessary conditions are satisfied, the court will therefore almost invariably decree specific performance of a contract regarding land ...

Land is therefore the most common subject-matter in relation to which specific performance is awarded, since damages would usually be an inadequate remedy.[8]

8.1.1. A 'Trust'?

It is commonly agreed that the trust which arises under this doctrine is constructive in nature.[9] It is clearly not a resulting trust, since the trust does not arise to *return* an interest in the property to A. Neither is the trust an express trust. B does not have an intention to create a trust, but an intention to enter into a contract; and it is *in spite of* the lack of an intention to create a trust that a constructive trust arises pursuant to the maxim that 'equity considers as done that which ought to be done'.[10] For the same reason, these constructive trusts are substantively different from those which arise in the non-contract-based doctrines within the bilateral events category, since in those doctrines one of the material events is B's intention—manifested in the form of a promise—to hold property on trust.[11]

However, there have been disagreements as to whether it is appropriate to say that a *trust* arises at all from the moment the parties enter into the contract. The orthodox position is that it does: 'the moment you have a valid contract for sale the vendor becomes in equity a trustee for the purchaser of the [property] sold'.[12] However, it is patently the case that the parties' rights and duties arising at that point in time differ from those which trustees and beneficiaries commonly have. As Lord Walker explained in *Jerome v Kelly* in relation to a contract for the sale of land:[13]

> It would ... be wrong to treat an uncompleted contract for the sale of land as equivalent to an immediate, irrevocable declaration of trust (or assignment of beneficial interest) in the land. Neither [B] nor [A] has unqualified beneficial ownership. Beneficial ownership of the land is in a sense split between [B] and [A] on the provisional assumptions that specific performance is available and that the contract will in due course be completed, if necessary by the court ordering specific performance. In the meantime, [B] is entitled to enjoyment of the land or its rental income. The provisional assumptions may be falsified by events, such as rescission of the contract (either

[7] John McGhee (ed), *Snell's Equity*, 33rd edn (London, Sweet & Maxwell, 2016) [17-008]. See too [24-004].

[8] ibid [17-007].

[9] See, eg, *Shaw v Foster* (1871–72) LR 5 HL 321, 356; *Snell's Equity* (n 7) [24-004].

[10] See, eg, *HR Trustees Limited v Wembley plc* [2011] EWHC 2974 (Ch) [65]; Sarah Worthington, 'Proprietary Remedies: The Nexus between Specific Performance and Constructive Trusts' (1996) 11 *Journal of Contract Law* 1.

[11] See, eg, Chapter 4, S 4.2.1.

[12] *Lysaght v Edwards* (1875–76) LR 2 Ch D 499 (Ch) 506. See too *Paine v Meller* (1801) 6 Ves Jr 349, 352; 31 ER 1088, 1089; *Broome v Monck* (1805) 10 Ves Jr 597, 606; 32 ER 976, 980; *Central Trust and Safe Deposit Co v Snider* [1916] 1 AC 266 (PC) 272.

[13] *Jerome v Kelly (Inspector of Taxes)* [2004] UKHL 25, [2004] 1 WLR 1409 [32]. See too *Lysaght v Edwards* (n 12) 506.

under a contractual term or on breach). If the contract proceeds to completion the equitable interest can be viewed as passing to [A] in stages, as title is made and accepted and as the purchase price is paid in full.

Because A does not become the outright 'equitable owner' or 'beneficial owner' of a 'proprietary interest' when the contract is made, it is sometimes argued that the relationship between A and B at that point cannot be described as a trust.[14] In specific relation to contracts for the sale of land, alternative views have been suggested: that a trust arises when A pays the first part of the purchase money,[15] or at the agreed completion date,[16] or when A pays all the purchase money.[17]

The better view, however, is that a constructive trust does arise when the parties first enter into a specifically enforceable contract of sale, notwithstanding the fact that there are obvious differences between the trust arising in this context and the rights and duties which arise under a typical trust. Upon entering the contract, A does in fact acquire an equitable right which is enforceable against third parties, the right of which can be protected by caveat or registration.[18]

In support of this view, it can be noted that ownership is not an absolute concept. Honoré has famously explained that there are 'eleven leading incidents' of ownership, namely 'the right to possess, the right to use, the right to manage, the right to the income of the thing, the right to the capital, the right to security, the rights or incidents of transmissibility and absence of term, the prohibition of harmful use, liability to execution, and the incident of residuarity'.[19] In relation to specifically enforceable contracts of sale, Robert Chambers observes that, at the moment the parties enter into the contract, '[B] still has the rights to possess, use, manage, and receive income from the land until the transaction is complete, but [A] has the right to the capital and the incidents of transmissibility, absence of term, and residuarity.'[20] As the parties proceed through the stages of performing the contract—as consideration passes from A to B, and as the agreed time for completion and date of transfer come to pass—the incidents of B's ownership pass to A 'in stages',[21] this being secured by distinct equities which operate in A's favour, arising and capable of being enforced at these different stages.[22] Nevertheless, this does not detract from the conclusion that, at the moment the contract is made, '[A] immediately acquires an equitable interest in the [property], sharing beneficial ownership with [B]';[23] and since '[t]he essential feature common to all trusts is that the trustees are required by the rules of equity to use the trust

[14] See, eg, *Kern Corp Ltd v Walter Reid Trading Pty Ltd* (1987) 163 CLR 154, 191–92; *Stern v McArthur* (1988) 165 CLR 489, 521–22; Worthington, 'Proprietary Remedies' (n 10) 11–12.

[15] Charles Harpum, Stuart Bridge and Martin Dixon, *Megarry & Wade: The Law of Real Property*, 8th edn (London, Sweet & Maxwell, 2012) [15-056].

[16] *Dowson v Solomon* (1859) 1 Dr & Sm 1, 9; 62 ER 278, 281.

[17] *Shaw v Foster* (n 9) 357, as interpreted by Mason J in *Chang v Registrar of Titles* (1976) 137 CLR 177, 184; Worthington, 'Proprietary Remedies' (n 10) 11–12; Jamie Glister and James Lee, *Hanbury & Martin: Modern Equity*, 20th edn (London, Sweet & Maxwell, 2015) [12-016].

[18] *Jerome v Kelly* (n 13) [29]; Robert Chambers, 'The Importance of Specific Performance' in Simone Degeling and James Edelman (eds), *Equity in Commercial Law* (Sydney, Lawbook Co, 2005) 451; Turner, 'Understanding the Constructive Trust' (n 1) 585–86. A's interest can also be insured: *Kern Corp Ltd* (n 14) 172.

[19] AM Honoré, 'Ownership' in AG Guest (ed), *Oxford Essays in Jurisprudence* (Oxford, OUP, 1961) 107.

[20] Chambers, 'The Importance of Specific Performance' (n 18) 452–53.

[21] *Jerome v Kelly* (n 13) [32].

[22] For a fuller account of these distinct equities, see Turner, 'Understanding the Constructive Trust' (n 1) 585ff.

[23] Chambers, 'The Importance of Specific Performance' (n 18) 454.

assets at least partly for the benefit of others',[24] it is wholly appropriate to describe the parties as being in a constructive *trust* relationship.[25]

There are also a number of advantages for the general law of constructive trusts in taking the view that a constructive trust arises from the moment A and B enter into the contract.[26] In the context of this book, the most pertinent of these advantages is described by Turner in the following terms:[27]

> [Refusing to recognise that a trust arises when the contract is made] could encourage the making of factually incorrect statements about the nature and evolution of trusts. It would become easier, for example, to argue that what are currently 'constructive' trusts have nothing to do with trusts. That would be a disadvantage: it would obscure the historical fact that constructive trusts were generated by the realisations that certain concerns addressed by the law on express trusts can arise where there is no express trust, and that these concerns call for solutions analogous to those provided by the law on express trusts.

It is little surprise, then, that those who take the view that specifically enforceable contracts of sale[28] have nothing to do with constructive trusts[29] also argue that many of the doctrines discussed in this book are not constructive trust doctrines at all;[30] or that 'there ... [is] no such thing as a ... constructive trust'[31]—'that the constructive trust is not a genuine trust, only a misleading label to describe certain court orders'.[32] The fact that this book does not subscribe to such views provides affirmation of the wider advantage which accompanies the view that a constructive trust arises at the very moment a specifically enforceable contract of sale is entered into.

8.1.2. Requirements

For most parts, the requirements which have to be fulfilled for a constructive trust to arise are settled, and are neatly summarised in the proposition that there must be a 'specifically enforceable contract of sale'.

First, the parties must have entered into a contract. It is most common for a contract to be entered into expressly, although it is also possible for such a contract to be construed out of a different arrangement. For example, in *Clarence House Ltd v National Westminster Bank plc*[33] the parties entered into a 'virtual assignment'. This arrangement was described in the judgment[34] as:

> an arrangement under which all the economic benefits and burdens of the relevant lease (including any management responsibilities) are transferred to a third party, but without any actual

[24] ibid 455.

[25] See also Turner, 'Understanding the Constructive Trust' (n 1) 597, where it is observed that, '[a]s soon as the contract is formed, vendor-purchaser relations display features shared by all trusts of property', namely 'that they keep the property available for the performance of an obligation.'

[26] ibid 599–600.

[27] ibid.

[28] In particular, the vendor-purchaser constructive trust: William Swadling, 'The Vendor-Purchaser Constructive Trust' in Degeling and Edelman, *Equity in Commercial Law* (n 18).

[29] Swadling, 'The Vendor-Purchaser Constructive Trust' (n 28) 474–85.

[30] See, eg, Chapter 4, S 4.1.1. and Chapter 5, S 5.1.

[31] William Swadling, 'The Fiction of the Constructive Trust' (2011) 64 *Current Legal Problems* 399, 432.

[32] ibid 431.

[33] *Clarence House Ltd* (n 5).

[34] ibid [2].

assignment of the leasehold interest or any change in the actual occupancy of the premises in question. It is typically employed where the relevant lease contains covenants against assigning or parting with the possession of the demised property without the consent of the landlord, and there are concerns either that the landlord may be unwilling to consent to a legal assignment of the lease because of perceived concerns about the financial standing of the assignee, or that the landlord's consent may not be available in advance of the scheduled date for completion of the transaction.

Although the arrangement was not expressly entered into as a contract of sale, the Court of Appeal was willing to construe the arrangement as a contractual arrangement. Thus, as Ward LJ held, in somewhat colourful language, 'I recognise that virtual assignments are strange new beasts in the forest; that one must circle around them suspiciously and cautiously; but the moment one gets close and has a good sniff, the overwhelming smell is of contract'.[35]

Secondly, the contract must be a contract *of sale*. This simply reflects a requirement that the transfer or assignment of property from B must be made for 'valuable consideration',[36] although consideration does not need to have actually passed for the doctrine to apply. It is crucial to note that 'consideration' is used in the contractual sense of the term. That is to say, the consideration provided by B must result in 'a benefit to [B] or a detriment to [A]',[37] and must be provided as an agreed quid pro quo in return for B's promise to assign or transfer the property in question.[38] Losing sight of this may cause the erroneous view that A's consideration is but 'detrimental reliance' which may potentially engage a proprietary estoppel analysis.[39] There are significant differences between these doctrines: reliance in proprietary estoppel need not be an agreed quid pro quo to B's promise,[40] but must have been performed by A before any right can arise against B; moreover, unlike in relation to specifically enforceable contracts of sale, the incurrence of detrimental reliance merely engages the courts' remedial discretion to determine the appropriate remedy to compensate A, and does not guarantee that a constructive trust will arise.[41]

Thirdly, it is implicit in the need for a contract that the parties must satisfy any formality requirement for the validity of a contract. Specifically, where the contract relates to 'the sale or other disposition of an interest in land', the parties must comply with the Law of Property (Miscellaneous Provisions) Act 1989, s 2.[42] Although no case has yet turned on

[35] ibid [47].

[36] See, eg, *Re Holt's* (n 4) 116, *Palmer v Carey* [1926] AC 703 (PC) 706–07. Note that the Sale of Goods Act 1979, s 2(1) provides that *money* consideration is required for the Act to apply. Note, however, that the doctrine 'almost never operates in relation to a contract for the sale of goods', because '[s]uch a contract can, by itself, transfer [B]'s ownership of goods to [A], without the need for a deed or delivery … There is hence no point at which [A] can have a right [under a constructive trust]': Ben McFarlane and Robert Stevens, 'The Nature of Equitable Property' (2010) 4 *Journal of Equity* 1, 16. See also *Re Wait* [1927] 1 Ch 606 (CA) 638.

[37] *Edgeware Highway Board v Harrow Gas Co* (1874) LR 10 QB 92 (QB) 95.

[38] Hugh Beale (ed), *Chitty on Contracts: Vol 1 General Principles*, 32nd edn (London, Sweet & Maxwell, 2016) [3-002] 'The doctrine of consideration is based on the idea of reciprocity'.

[39] This doctrine is discussed in Chapter 7.

[40] Detrimental reliance is insufficient, which may be incurred even though there is a 'lack [of] consideration because the party relying on the estoppel made no counter-promise and so incurred no obligation': *Chitty on Contracts* (n 38) [4-145].

[41] For other reasons why proprietary estoppel cannot be analysed by way of a contractual analysis, see *Chitty on Contracts* (n 38) [4-145].

[42] See n 1 above.

Note that it is not possible to argue that compliance with s 2(1) is unnecessary in view of the fact that a specifically enforceable contract of sale gives rise to a constructive trust and that 'nothing in this section affects the

this point, it is clearly assumed in the cases. As will be discussed below, the contract must be specifically enforceable in order for a constructive trust to arise; and it has been observed by Lord Diplock in *Gibson v Manchester City Council*[43] that a 'contract of which specific performance is sought to be enforced[, where it] is a contract for the sale of land … is … subject to the requirements as to writing laid down in section 40 of the Law of Property Act 1925', this section being the predecessor of s 2 of the 1989 Act. Indeed, the decision in *Gibson* stands for the proposition that '[t]here can be no specific performance unless there is a valid and binding concluded contract';[44] and as *Snell's Equity* notes, such contracts must be 'supported by consideration and [comply] with any relevant requirements of form.'[45] It is therefore clear that compliance with s 2 of the 1989 Act is a prerequisite where the subject-matter of the contract is land.[46]

Finally, a constructive trust arises only if 'a Court of Equity would under all the circumstances of the case grant specific performance of the contract.'[47] The need for the contract to be specifically enforceable is inextricably linked to the constructive trust. As Lord Parker observed in *Central Trust and Safe Deposit Co v Snider*,[48] that the fact that a constructive trust arises is 'the logical consequence of the power of a Court of Equity to grant, and its practice in granting, specific performance of a contract to convey or settle [property].' The logical connection appears to be that it is only in relation to contracts which are specifically enforceable that the maxim 'equity considers as done that which ought to be done'[49] can be applied; and one way in which that maxim finds expression is through the imposition of a constructive trust which secures the performance of the contract. Thus, for instance, in *Clarence House* the doctrine was held not to apply because the 'virtual assignment'[50] could not be specifically enforced: A could not compel the transfer of the legal title of the lease from B without the consent of B's landlord, the consent of which neither A nor the court could compel.[51] Another example relates to an agreement for security. Where the contract is purely executory, the contract is not specifically enforceable,[52] and therefore no trust arises when the contract is entered into. However, once the creditor (A) advances money to the debtor (B), the contract is specifically

creation or operation of … constructive trusts' (s 2(5)). As Ben McFarlane explains, s 2(1) relates to a contract—a means of acquiring rights—whereas s 2(5) refers to particular types of right. 'Like any type of right, those rights either arise by virtue of a contract or they do not. If they do not, then they are not in any case caught by s 2, which applies only to a particular type of contract. But if, like the constructive trust which arises where there is a specifically enforceable contract of sale, the rights do arise by virtue of a contract, then they will only arise if the formal requirements of s 2 are satisfied': Ben McFarlane, 'Proprietary Estoppel and Failed Contractual Negotiations' [2005] *Conveyancer and Property Lawyer* 501, 520–21.

43 *Gibson v Manchester City Council* [1979] 1 WLR 294 (HL) 296.

44 *Snell's Equity* (n 7) [17-006].

45 ibid. See also *Snell's Equity* (n 7) [24-004] fn 20.

46 The importance of this requirement will be seen in S 8.3.2.

47 *Howard v Miller* [1915] AC 318 (PC) 326. See also *Palmer v Carey* (n 36) 706–07; *Re Holt's* (n 4) 116; *Chang v Registrar of Titles* (n 17) 184. *cf* Simon Gardner, 'Equity, Estate Contracts and the Judicature Acts: *Walsh v Lonsdale* Revisited' (1987) 7 *OJLS* 60, where the requirement of specific enforceability is doubted, albeit from a historical perspective, in relation to cases falling within the doctrine in *Walsh v Lonsdale* (1882) 21 Ch D 9 (CA).

48 *Central Trust and Safe Deposit Co* (n 12) 272.

49 See n 10 above.

50 Defined in the main text following n 34 above.

51 *Clarence House Ltd* (n 5) [45]–[46].

52 *Rogers v Challis* (1859) 27 Beav 175, 179–80; 54 ER 68, 70.

enforceable, and A obtains a proprietary right to B's asset which forms the subject-matter of the security[53] by way of a constructive trust.[54]

It is necessary to pause to consider the precise relationship between an order of specific performance and the constructive trust doctrine under consideration. It logically follows from the fact that a constructive trust arises from the moment the parties enter into a contractual relationship that the constructive trust's existence does not depend on A *obtaining* an order of specific performance.[55] If so, what is the role of specific performance in the doctrine? Judges appear to speak of specific performance in anticipatory terms. For example, in *Jerome v Kelly*, Lord Walker spoke of the doctrine as arising 'on the *provisional assumptions* that specific performance is available and that the contract will in due course be completed, if necessary by the court ordering specific performance.'[56] Similarly, in *Central Trust* Lord Parker observed that 'it is tacitly *assumed* that the contract would in a Court of Equity be enforced specifically'; and '[if] for some reason equity would not enforce specific performance, or if the right to specific performance has been lost by the subsequent conduct of the party in whose favour specific performance *might* originally have been granted, the vendor or covenantor either never was, or has ceased to be, a trustee in any sense at all.'[57]

Turner helpfully explains the mechanics of this anticipatory approach in the following terms:[58]

> Facts that will be provable once the contract's performance is underway may be completely uncertain at an earlier stage. Unprovable facts are therefore ignored when testing whether the purchaser acquires an interest in land upon formation of the contract, or whether any of the various other equities arises.

If, at a later date, A fails to prove facts which need to be proved to obtain an order of specific performance, or if there are factors which would preclude such an order from being made, 'then the interest that vested in [A] when the contract was formed will prove to be of no further use. It will be extinguished in the same way as the interest of the purchaser who loses a priority contest or by rescission ab initio.'[59]

8.1.3. Right and Remedy

The constructive trust which arises in this doctrine is a replicative remedy: it gives effect to the parties' primary rights and duties under the contract, and does not arise pursuant to the exercise of remedial discretion as to the goal and content of the remedy.

[53] Louise Gullifer, *Goode on Legal Problems of Credit and Security*, 5th edn (London, Sweet & Maxwell, 2013) [2-11]; JF Keeler, 'Some Reflections on *Holroyd v Marshall*' (1967–70) 3 *Adelaide Law Review* 360, 373.

[54] The right which A obtains has retrospective effect from the date of the agreement (see Gullifer, *Goode on Legal Problems of Credit and Security* (n 53) [2-11]), as is the case in relation to the doctrine of 'relation back' which applies to future property cases: see discussion in main text following n 126 below.

[55] See too *McLaughlin v Duffill* [2008] EWCA Civ 1627 [25]–[26].

[56] *Jerome v Kelly* (n 13) [32] (emphasis added).

[57] *Central Trust and Safe Deposit Co* (n 12) 272 (emphases added).

[58] Turner, 'Understanding the Constructive Trust' (n 1) 591.

[59] ibid.

This proposition might be thought to be inconsistent with the commonly held belief that specific performance is a discretionary remedy.[60] Since it is a precondition for the constructive trust to arise that the contract of sale is specifically enforceable, the argument goes, the constructive trust can be said to be subject to the exercise of judicial discretion insofar as this is necessary to determine the specific enforceability of the contract.

There are two possible responses to this argument. First, in relation to specific performance, the discretion involved is 'not an arbitrary or capricious discretion, but one to be governed as far as possible by fixed rules and principles.'[61] One way of understanding such discretion is that they relate only to whether certain 'bars' to the remedy operate in particular circumstances.[62] Courts are merely engaged in an exercise of 'ascribing weight to the relevant bars and the competing considerations and balancing them against each other to reach a decision … The discretion is narrow in the sense that it involves a choice between only two options: whether the bars operate to prevent the remedy being granted or not.'[63] Crucially, this does not detract from the fact that the remedy is replicative in nature.[64] As *Snell's Equity* aptly notes, an order of specific performance can be contrasted with damages for breach of contract in that, unlike damages awards, specific performance does not involve 'considerable latitude for judges in determining issues such as mitigation and remoteness of damages.'[65] In other words, unlike reflective remedies, an order of specific performance does not involve discretion as to content.[66]

Secondly, even if it is conceded that specific performance does involve a significant enough amount of discretion such that a comparison with an order of damages is appropriate, it remains the case that we are here concerned with a constructive trust remedy, and not with an order for specific performance. As has been noted above,[67] while it is a precondition for the doctrine to apply that the parties enter into a specifically enforceable contract of sale, it is not necessary for A first to have obtained an order of specific performance. Moreover, we have also seen[68] that courts take an anticipatory approach to the question of specific enforceability: the courts require only that A should prove facts which can be proved at the specific point in time in relation to the specific enforceability of the contract; facts which are unprovable are ignored. From these analyses, it can be seen that a constructive trust invariably arises whenever a contract of sale is found to be specifically enforceable in the anticipatory sense; the exercise of remedial discretion is not involved.

From the perspective of the parties' rights and duties, then, the *constructive trust* is a replicative remedy which gives effect to the parties' primary relationship, namely a specifically

[60] See, eg, *Re Scott and Alvarez's Contract* [1895] 2 Ch 603 (CA) 612, 614, 615; *Stickney v Keeble* [1915] AC 386 (HL) 419; *Co-Operative Insurance Society Ltd v Argyll Stores (Holdings) Ltd* [1998] AC 1 (HL) 9, 11, 16.

[61] *Lamare v Dixon* (1873) LR 6 HL 414 (HL) 423. See too *Co-Operative Insurance Society Ltd* (n 60) 16.

[62] Rafal Zakrzewski, *Remedies Reclassified* (Oxford, OUP, 2005) 92. See also Stephen A Smith, 'Form and Substance in Equitable Remedies' in Andrew Robertson and Michael Tilbury (eds), *Divergences in Private Law* (Oxford, Hart Publishing, 2016) 334.

[63] Zakrzewski, *Remedies Reclassified* (n 62) 93. See also Andrew Burrows, *Remedies for Torts and Breach of Contract* (Oxford, OUP, 2004) 457. Moreover, 'they play a small role in the law governing specific relief and are rarely relevant in litigation': Smith, 'Form and Substance' (n 62) 334.

[64] Zakrzewski, *Remedies Reclassified* (n 62) 92.

[65] *Snell's Equity* (n 7) [17-004].

[66] As to the distinction between discretion as to goal and content, see Chapter 2, S 2.4.2.1.

[67] See main text to n 55 above.

[68] See main text following n 55 above.

enforceable contractual relationship. Identifying this primary relationship is crucial for a number of reasons. First, it allows us to appreciate why it can be said that a constructive trust arises in relation to specifically enforceable contracts, while maintaining that remedial discretion is not exercised. Primary contractual relationships can be divided into those which are specifically enforceable—assessed on the basis of the facts available at any given time—and those which are not; and a constructive trust invariably arises in relation only to the former relationships. If in the light of later facts a contract which was once deemed specifically enforceable turns out no longer to be so, then A's right under a constructive trust is likewise extinguished, with no remedial discretion having been exercised.

A second reason is that it reveals why a binding legal contract—which includes compliance with any relevant formality requirement—is a necessary precondition for the doctrine to apply.[69] Where there is no binding legal contract, the parties would not be in the relevant primary relationship, and so a constructive trust will not be imposed.

A third reason is that it explains why the requirement of form is a necessary precondition for this doctrine to apply, but not for the non-contract-based doctrines. For example, it might seem strange that the doctrine in *Pallant v Morgan* would invariably give rise to a constructive trust even though the parties are not in a binding contractual relationship, let alone one which is specifically enforceable.[70] The key to understanding this difference is to appreciate that the constructive trusts in both contexts give effect to different types of primary relationships. In the context of the doctrine in *Pallant v Morgan*, the primary relationship is a constructive trust relationship;[71] in the context of the doctrine presently examined it is a specifically enforceable contractual relationship. It is therefore logical that the requirements for establishing one type of primary relationship are not, and ought not to be, transposed to the other.

8.1.4. Rationale

It is generally said that the rationale underlying the constructive trust is the principle that 'equity considers as done that which ought to be done.'[72] However, 'the words of the maxim in fact reveal no functional, normative, or doctrinal explanation of why the … trust operates as it does'.[73] In particular, the maxim does not even begin to explain *when* and *why* equity would consider something which is not yet done as having been done.[74] Instead, a proper rationale must relate to the primary relationship between the parties, since, after all, the constructive trust gives effect and enforces this relationship.

As discussed above,[75] the relevant relationship is a specifically enforceable contractual relationship. Turner's account of the vendor-purchaser constructive trust provides a convincing rationale for constructive trusts arising in relation to specifically enforceable

[69] See main text to and following n 42 above.
[70] See discussion in Chapter 6, S 6.1.1.
[71] See main text to n 3 in Chapter 3.
[72] See n 10 above.
[73] Turner, 'Understanding the Constructive Trust' (n 1) 600. See too Simon Gardner, *An Introduction to the Law of Trusts*, Clarendon Law Series, 3rd edn (Oxford, OUP, 2011) 326.
[74] For other criticisms, see *Snell's Equity* (n 7) [5-015].
[75] See S 8.1.3.

contracts of sale more generally. His analysis helpfully addresses both parts of the primary relationship, namely the contractual aspect and the specific enforceability aspect.

In relation to the contractual aspect, Turner writes that the constructive trust protects each party's 'performance interest', that is, 'the interest that the vendor and purchaser have in the due performance of the contract.'[76] The protection offered by the constructive trust goes further than the indirect protection offered by awards of damages for breach of contract, and indeed the direct protection offered by awards of specific performance.[77] Not only does the trust protect the performance interest of A and B against third parties, which reduces the chances of the contract being deprived of its subject-matter,[78] but also puts the parties in as close as possible a position they would have been had the contract been performed by allowing adjustments to be made for (for instance) delay, deterioration, rents, and profits.[79] Turner's explanation in this respect is not dissimilar from the justification which Gardner proposes for this doctrine, namely that it reduces A's vulnerability which arises because these transactions—in particular those relating to land—typically progress slowly.[80] In doing so, this doctrine increases the commercial attractiveness of such transactions.[81]

In relation to the need for the contract to be specifically enforceable, Turner explains that this requirement ensures that the constructive trust arises only where the subject-matter of the contract is 'legally unique'.[82] This ensures that the constructive trust will only be imposed in cases where it is justified, namely where it would be insufficient 'to confine the parties to the common law's protections of the performance interest'.[83]

These explanations reveal *when* and *why* a constructive trust ought to arise, and why the parties' primary specifically enforceable contractual relationship ought to be replicated in the remedy. Equally importantly, these explanations also help us to see why this doctrine is unique. Without the benefit of such explanations, it might be thought that the law is inconsistent. For example, it might be asked why the 'equity sees as done …' maxim applies in the present context, but does not apply in the context of proprietary estoppel where A does provide valuable consideration as a quid pro quo for B's promise to give A an interest in B's property.[84] Such questions fade away once it is appreciated that each doctrine is underpinned by a different rationale. The constructive trust arising in the context of specifically enforceable contracts of sale arises to protect the parties' performance interest of a contract relating to the sale of unique property, while proprietary estoppel compensates A for harm caused by the unreliability of B's induced assumptions.

[76] Turner, 'Understanding the Constructive Trust' (n 1) 601.

[77] ibid.

[78] ibid 602–03. Such third parties includes the successors of A and B, such as their personal representatives: ibid 602.

[79] ibid 602.

[80] Gardner, *Law of Trusts* (n 73) 326–27.

[81] ibid 327.

[82] Turner, 'Understanding the Constructive Trust' (n 1) 604.

[83] ibid.

[84] See main text following n 8 in Chapter 7.

8.2. Future Property

At law, a purported assignment by B of future property to A is wholly void and conveys nothing to A.[85] Similarly, where future property is made the subject-matter of a declaration of trust, the trust is void for uncertainty.[86] But where A gives valuable consideration, equity may treat the assignment or declaration of the future property as a contract to assign the property, which becomes enforceable when B receives the property.[87] A obtains a right against the property to which B holds legal title through a constructive trust[88] which arises when B acquires the property. As Swinfen Eady LJ held in *Re Lind*,[89] '[B], having received the consideration, becomes in equity, on the happening of the event, trustee for [A] of the property devolving upon or acquired by him, and which he had previously sold and been paid for.'

8.2.1. Requirements

It might appear from the cases that the requirements of the future property doctrine are less demanding than those in relation to constructive trusts arising in the context of specifically enforceable contracts of sale.[90]

First, it is necessary for there to be a contract between the parties, which may either be expressly entered into, or construed from the parties' arrangement.[91] The cases say nothing about whether there must be a *valid* contract, that is, whether any relevant formality requirement must be complied with. This issue is discussed below.[92]

In terms of substance, the contract must be a contract for value,[93] for 'equity … will refuse to recognise in favour of a volunteer an assignment of an interest … not yet existing at the date of the assignment, but to arise in the future.'[94] Such consideration must be provided as an agreed quid pro quo.[95]

In addition, the parties must have agreed, either expressly or impliedly, that their rights and duties would arise immediately upon B's acquisition of the property. So, for instance, the older cases draw a distinction between an agreement to grant a security over future property immediately upon the property's acquisition, in which case the doctrine would apply, and an agreement which merely grants a licence to seize future property for the

[85] *Holroyd v Marshall* (n 2); *Re Tilt* (1896) 40 Sol Jo 224.

[86] *Re Ellenborough* [1903] 1 Ch 697 (Ch); *Williams v IRC* [1965] NZLR 395.

[87] *Ellison v Ellison* (1802) 6 Ves Jun 656, 31 ER 1243; *Holroyd v Marshall* (n 2) 10 H L Cas 210, 11 ER 1006; *Tailby v Official Receiver* (1888) 13 App Cas 523 (HL) 530; *Re Lind* [1915] 2 Ch 345 (CA). See also *Williams v IRC* (n 86) 395.

[88] Sarah Worthington, *Proprietary Interests in Commercial Transactions* (Oxford, OUP, 1996) 199; Craig Rotherham, *Proprietary Remedies in Context* (Oxford, Hart Publishing, 2002) 11.

[89] *Re Lind* (n 87) 360.

[90] Although this appearance is deceiving: see discussion in S 8.3.

[91] *Re Lind* (n 87) 364; *Re Clarke* (1887) 36 Ch D 348 (CA) 352.

[92] See S 8.3.2.

[93] *Re Clarke* (n 91) 352; *Bexhill UK Ltd v Razzaq* [2012] EWCA Civ 1376 [42].

[94] *Williams v IRC* (n 86) 399.

[95] As seen in the case of *Re Burton's Settlements* [1955] Ch 82 (Ch).

purposes of selling them and discharging a debt, in which case the doctrine would not apply.[96] In the former case the creditor is said to have an 'immediate interest', whereas the latter case grants only a 'power', which does not give rise to any interest until the power is exercised.[97]

It is also necessary for A to have provided consideration prior to B's acquisition of the property.[98] This requirement is clearly seen from Lord Westbury LC's judgment in *Holroyd v Marshall*.[99] This requirement is thought to be central to the doctrine because, once value has been provided, 'the conscience of [B] is bound when the subject comes into existence.'[100]

Finally, in *Tailby v Official Receiver*,[101] it was held to be necessary for the property acquired by B to 'answer the description in the assignment, or, in other words, that it shall be capable of being identified as the thing, or as one of the very things assigned.'[102]

A point of contention arises as to whether there is a further requirement for the contract to be specifically enforceable before the doctrine would apply. Although the earlier cases are contradictory,[103] the later cases take the view that this is not a requirement of the doctrine.[104] This matter will be discussed in detail below.[105]

8.2.2. Right and Remedy

Constructive trusts which arises under this doctrine are replicative remedies, which give effect to the parties' primary rights and duties. That is to say, where the requirements of the doctrine are fulfilled, 'then immediately on the acquisition of the property described [B] would hold it in trust for [A]'.[106] Crucially, there is no trace of remedial discretion being exercised by the courts either as to the goal or the content of the remedy, which points to the replicative nature of the constructive trusts. The primary relationship to which the constructive trust gives effect appears to be a contractual relationship between the parties, where valuable consideration has been provided prior to B's acquisition of the property.[107]

[96] See, eg, *Reeve v Whitmore* (1863) 4 De GJ & S 1, 46 ER 814; *Thompson v Cohen* (1871–72) LR 7 QB 527.

[97] *Reeve v Whitmore* (n 96) 4 De GJ & S 18, 46 ER 820–21.

[98] *Holroyd v Marshall* (n 2) 10 H L Cas 211, 11 ER 1007; *Tailby v Official Receiver* (n 87) 536; *Snell's Equity* (n 7) [3-030]; AG Guest and Ying Khai Liew, *Guest on the Law of Assignment* (London, Sweet & Maxwell, 2015) [3-24].

[99] *Holroyd v Marshall* (n 2) 10 H L Cas 211, 11 ER 1007. His Lordship twice mentioned the need for B to have received the consideration.

[100] *Palette Shoes Pty Ltd v Krohn* (1937) 58 CLR 127. See too *Re Lind* (n 87) 360.

[101] *Tailby v Official Receiver* (n 87) 533.

[102] Lord Watson prefaced his statement of this requirement by saying that '[t]here is but one condition which must be fulfilled in order to make the assignee's right attach to a future chose in action': *Tailby v Official Receiver* (n 87) 533. In view of the other requirements necessary for the doctrine to apply, this must be considered an unfortunate exaggeration.

[103] *cf*, eg, *Holroyd v Marshall* (n 2) 10 H L Cas 211, 11 ER 1007 and *Tailby v Official Receiver* (n 87) 547.

[104] See, eg, *Re Lind* (n 87) 365.

[105] See S 8.3.3.

[106] *Holroyd v Marshall* (n 2) 10 H L Cas 211, 11 ER 1007. See too *Tailby v Official Receiver* (n 87) 211; *Re Lind* (n 87) 366; *Raiffeisen Zentralbank Österreich AG v Five Star Trading LLC* [2001] EWCA Civ 68, [2001] QB 825 [80]; *Bexhill UK Ltd v Razzaq* (n 93) [42].

[107] As will be explained below, an executory contract for valuable consideration is sufficient to engage this doctrine (see S 8.3.1.) and the specific enforceability of the contract is also a precondition for the future property doctrine to apply (see S 8.3.3.). These point to the fact that, in reality, constructive trusts arising under this doctrine and those which arise in relation to specifically enforceable contracts of sale enforce the same primary relationship.

8.2.3. Rationale

As is the case in relation to specifically enforceable contracts of sale, the rationale of constructive trusts relating to future property is said to be based on the idea that 'equity considers as done that which ought to be done.'[108] As previously noted,[109] however, this maxim does not provide a satisfactory explanation, since its words do not reveal the limits or reason for the constructive trust's arising.

Another sort of explanation suggests that a constructive trust arises because 'the conscience of [B] is bound when the subject comes into existence'.[110] But here we are again left none the wiser as to the reason why B's conscience is bound. After all, as proprietary estoppel indicates, even where A detrimentally relies on B's promise to cede an interest in his property to A, B's conscience is not invariably bound, in the sense that a constructive trust is not imposed in every case; and so from the perspective of B's 'conscience' it is simply not obvious why the law reacts differently in these doctrines.

Foreshadowing somewhat the discussion below,[111] it is suggested that the rationale underpinning this doctrine is in fact precisely the same as that relating to specifically enforceable contracts of sale: the law is protecting each party's 'performance interest' where the subject-matter of the contract is legally 'unique'.[112] The acceptance of this proposition hinges on demonstrating that the requirements of both doctrines are similar, a matter to which the discussion now turns.

8.3. Assimilating the Doctrines

It can be observed that the facts on which constructive trusts arise in relation to specifically enforceable contracts of sale differ from those which arise in relation to future property in one obvious respect: the former reflects an AI situation while the latter reflects a QI situation. In the case of specifically enforceable contracts of sale, B always contracts to sell his property, and the rights and duties which arise under the constructive trust do so in relation to that property which B owns absolutely. In contrast, constructive trusts which arise in the context of future property compel B to take a qualified interest in the property upon its acquisition. Here, B is not considered to be the absolute owner of the property even for a *scintilla temporis*—that is, 'a "spark of time" or … a nanosecond.'[113]

This distinction between AI and QI situations within the contract-based group of doctrines might be thought to explain the degree to which courts are willing to impose

[108] See, eg, *Tailby v Official Receiver* (n 87) 546, *Palette Shoes Pty Ltd* (n 100) 16; David Hayton, Paul Matthews and Charles Mitchell, *Underhill and Hayton: Law Relating to Trusts and Trustees*, 19th edn (London, LexisNexis Butterworths, 2016) [10.8].

[109] See main text to n 74 above.

[110] *Palette Shoes Pty Ltd* (n 100) 27. See too *Re Lind* (n 87) 360; *Re Burton's Settlements* [1955] Ch 82 (Ch).

[111] Discussed in S 8.3.4.

[112] In this regard, it can be noted that the rationale which Gardner proposes in relation to specifically enforceable contracts of sale, namely that it protects A's vulnerability, is also said to apply equally to the future property doctrine: see Gardner, *Law of Trusts* (n 73) 327.

[113] *Kastor Navigation Co Ltdv AXA Global Risks (UK) Ltd (The Kastor Too)* [2004] EWCA Civ 277 [15], the *scintilla temporis* point arising in a different context.

constructive trusts. It is said that consideration need only be executory in relation to specifically enforceable contracts of sale, which indicates that, in this respect, constructive trusts are more readily found in AI situations than in QI situations. On the other hand, the specific enforceability of contracts is said not to be relevant to future property cases, which indicates that, in this respect, constructive trusts more easily arise in QI situations than in AI situations.

Assuming that the law consistently treats like cases alike, however, there are three crucial reasons to suspect that this distinction is illusory. First, the primary rights and duties enforced by constructive trusts in both doctrines are curiously similar. Secondly, the constructive trusts which arise in both doctrines are imposed as replicative remedies. These two reasons point to the fact that, unless there are convincing justifications for treating the 'future-ness' or 'present-ness' of property as materially significant, a distinction ought not to be drawn between the doctrines. The third reason is that many of the so-called requirements of the future property doctrine have been untested in case law, and rest upon various obiter statements which are often phrased in general and wide-ranging terms.[114] For example, in relation to future property, it is said that A must have provided consideration before B's acquisition; but no case has yet determined the position where consideration passes *after* B acquires the property. In addition, the future property cases rarely relate to land, and so it is unclear whether the parties need to comply with any relevant formality requirement for the creation of a contract[115] for the doctrine to apply. Moreover, there has yet to be a case which turns on whether the contract is specifically enforceable,[116] which raises doubts concerning the relevance of this requirement.

There are three aspects of the doctrines which require consideration: the sequence of events, formalities, and specific enforceability. The conclusion which will be reached is that both doctrines can be assimilated, and that they share the same concern of enforcing the parties' primary, specifically enforceable contractual relationship. This conclusion indicates that, within the contract-based subcategory, the distinction between QI and AI situations is, after all, immaterial.

8.3.1. Sequence of Events

In relation to specifically enforceable contracts of sale, an executory contract for valuable consideration is sufficient for a constructive trust to arise. In contrast, for the future property doctrine to apply, it said that consideration must have passed before B acquires the property. These requirements are, however, mutually inconsistent.

Suppose that A and B enter into two contracts for valuable consideration, each concerning a unique subject-matter.[117] In Case 1 the contract relates to future property; in Case 2 it

[114] This is a curious feature of the doctrine, given that it has been part of the law for more than two centuries—for at least as long as constructive trusts arising in relation to specifically enforceable contracts of sale have existed. Thus, in *Holroyd v Marshall* (n 2) 10 H L Cas 209, 11 ER 1006, decided in 1862, Lord Westbury LC spoke of both doctrines as being 'elementary principles long settled in Courts of Equity.' Features of the future property doctrine can be seen to be at play in the 17th century case of *Warmstrey v Tanfield* (1629) Rep Ch 29, 21 ER 498.

[115] Namely the Law of Property (Miscellaneous Provisions) Act 1989, s 2: see n 1 above.

[116] Worthington, 'Proprietary Remedies' (n 10) 7.

[117] Since it will be argued in S 8.3.3. that specific enforceability of the contract is a requirement for the future property doctrine to apply, the present discussion will assume this requirement to be fulfilled.

relates to property B owns. Suppose, then, that in Case 1 the property in question comes into B's hands. Surely the parties are in exactly the same position in Case 1 as in Case 2. Whether an executory contract for valuable consideration is entered into before or after B acquires the property in question appears utterly inconsequential, since the law's concern to protect the parties' performance interest of a contract relating to the sale of unique property[118] is equally pressing in both cases. Indeed, in Case 1, if A provides the contractually agreed consideration after B acquires the property in question, it is difficult to see why A will not obtain a right to the property by way of a (full-blown) constructive trust as would be the case when consideration passes in Case 2.[119] This supports the view that, in Case 1, when B acquires the property and before consideration passes, a constructive trust immediately arises to secure the performance of the contract, although the rights and duties under such trust is less full-blown than when A later provides consideration. If so, then whether or not a constructive trust arises is determined by whether the contract is for value, and not whether consideration has actually passed. So, instead of the two doctrines having separate rules as set out in the preceding paragraph, a single principle can be deduced, which can be stated thusly: a contract for value gives rise to a constructive trust if and when B stands in possession of the subject-matter of the contract. The 'future-ness' or 'present-ness' of the subject-matter of the contract is immaterial.

Two other points support this argument. First, many of the cases concerning future property relate to agreements for security. This provides an important background context for judicial statements to the effect that consideration must have first passed for a constructive trust to arise. This is because purely executory contracts for security are not specifically enforceable.[120] Thus, in *this* context, it is true to say that A must provide consideration prior to B acquiring the property. However, the reason for this is not that it constitutes a general rule which governs future property cases; rather, it is due to the requirement that the contract must be specifically enforceable for a constructive trust to arise, as discussed below.[121]

Secondly, in cases relating to future property, courts have held that A's right under the constructive trust is deemed to have effect from the time the agreement was made, and not merely from the time B acquires the property.[122] In the period between the formation of the contract and B's acquisition of the property, A is said—retrospectively, presumably—to have 'something more than a mere right in contract, something in the nature of an estate or interest'.[123] This curious feature of the doctrine would appear to be baffling if understood in isolation,[124] but the difficulty falls away when the doctrine is viewed alongside specifically

[118] This was seen in S 8.1.4. to be the rationale underpinning constructive trusts arising in relation to specifically enforceable contracts of sale.

[119] See Greg Tolhurst, *The Assignment of Contractual Rights* (Oxford, Hart Publishing, 2006) 378.

[120] See main text following n 51 above.

[121] See S 8.3.3.

[122] *Tailby v Official Receiver* (n 87) 533. See *Guest on the Law of Assignment* (n 98) [3-26].

[123] *Re Lind* (n 87) 364. *cf R v Chester and North Wales Legal Aid Area Office (No. 12)* [1998] 1 WLR 1496 (CA) 1505. Thus, A's priority is unaffected by, for example, B's bankruptcy and discharge prior to acquiring the property: *Re Lind* (n 87) 364.

[124] It is strongly criticised in specific relation to bankruptcy law and agreements for security in Matthews, 'The Effect of Bankruptcy upon Mortgages of Future Property' [1981] *Lloyd's Maritime and Commercial Law Quarterly* 40 (but *cf* Gullifer, *Goode on Legal Problems of Credit and Security* (n 53) [2-14]; Michael Bridge, Louise Gullifer, Gerard McMeel et al, *The Law of Personal Property* (London, Sweet & Maxwell, 2013), [27-013], [29-010]). However, even if an exception is carved out in the bankruptcy context, there remains a need to explain this feature of the doctrine, since its application is not limited to cases where B is bankrupt and/or where the contract is an agreement for security.

enforceable contracts of sale. In relation to the future property doctrine, no constructive trust can arise before B acquires the property for want of subject-matter:[125] 'the means of [performance] are [not yet] obtained'.[126] But once the subject-matter is supplied—that is, when B acquires the property—the arrangement is taken to have the same effect as if it were a case relating to specifically enforceable contracts of sale. That is to say, the parties are taken to have been in a constructive trust relationship from the moment the contract was formed. This is achieved through an application of the doctrine of 'relation back'.

This raises the question as to whether an application of the doctrine of 'relation back' is justified in this context. In Chapter 7,[127] it was observed that a similar device is used in relation to proprietary estoppel: where B breaches his primary duty to act reliably in relation to his induced assumptions, and where a court decides that a constructive trust remedy is appropriate, the trust is taken to have had effect from the time of B's breach. It would appear that the device of 'relation back' is employed where it is impossible for a constructive trust to arise until a later event occurs, but the trust's core purpose is to enforce the rights and duties of the parties which arose at an earlier point in time. So, in relation to proprietary estoppel, a court order is necessary for a constructive trust to arise, and the trust has the aim of giving effect to A's secondary right;[128] hence the need to 'backdate' the effect of the trust to the date of B's breach, when A's secondary right first arose. So it is in relation to the future property doctrine. The core purpose of the trust is to give effect to the parties' primary, contractual relationship, but the trust cannot arise until and unless there is certainty of subject-matter; hence if and when B acquires the property in question, the trust then arises for the first time, but its effect is 'backdated' to the moment when the parties entered into their contract.

8.3.2. Formality

There is no doubt that specifically enforceable contracts of sale must comply with the Law of Property (Miscellaneous Provisions) Act 1989, s 2 for a constructive trust to arise. In contrast, the position in relation to the future property doctrine remains untested, partly because the subject-matter of the contracts arising in relation to this doctrine have not concerned land, and partly because contracts for the sale of land entered into prior to 21 September 1989 were valid but unenforceable. Sporadic judicial statements appear to suggest that compliance with s 2 is unnecessary for the future property doctrine to operate. For instance, in *Re Ellenborough*[129] Buckley suggested, obiter, that 'if value be given, it is immaterial what is the form of assurance by which the disposition is made'. Similarly, in *Tailby*,[130] Lord Macnaghten said that '[t]he mode or form of assignment is absolutely immaterial provided the intention of the parties is clear.'

[125] '[I]n equity a contract which engages to transfer property, which is not in existence, cannot operate as an immediate alienation merely because there is nothing to transfer': *Holroyd v Marshall* (n 2) 10 H L Cas 211, 11 ER 1007.

[126] ibid.

[127] See Chapter 7, S 7.2.5.2.

[128] See Chapter 7, S 7.1.

[129] *Re Ellenborough* (n 86) 700.

[130] *Tailby v Official Receiver* (n 87) 543.

There are a host of reasons for subscribing to the view that compliance with the 1989 Act is crucial for a constructive trust to arise where the future property relates to land. First, nothing in the cases suggest that the doctrine is concerned with enforcing any primary relationship other than a contractual one. Thus, judges emphasise that the arrangement must be capable of being 'construed *as a contract*';[131] it must 'amount to a contract for value';[132] and that the doctrine applies only 'if the is *a contract (for valuable consideration)*'.[133] The courts are clearly looking for a legal contract—one enforceable at common law—as opposed to a merely equitable analogue.[134] This is obvious from the fact that contractual consideration, and not mere reliance, is required for the doctrine to apply.[135] It logically follows that a *valid* contract is required, which requires compliance with the 1989 Act where the contract concerns land.

Secondly, if it is insisted that a valid contract is not required, then it follows that the primary relationship with which the doctrine is concerned is something other than a legal contractual relationship. This would mean that parties are able to collude to oust the effect of the statutory formality requirement. Certainly, as the non-contract-based doctrines indicate, the ability to do so is justifiable if there is a convincing rationale which underlies the law's enforcement of a particular primary relationship. The future property doctrine does not, however, fall to be considered alongside any of the non-contract-based doctrines,[136] nor has there ever been any suggestion that there is a different primary relationship between the parties other than a contractual one which is justifiably protected by way of the future property doctrine.

Thirdly, it would avoid an inconsistency in the law whereby the mere sequence of events dictates whether a valid contract is required. It is hardly consistent if compliance with the 1989 Act is unnecessary if A provides consideration prior to B's acquisition, but compliance is insisted upon where A provides consideration after B's acquisition, that is, where the contract concerns property B owns. The formality requirement surely ought not to turn on the mere sequence of events.

Finally, the need for compliance with the 1989 Act is consistent with judicial statements that the future property doctrine relates to the maxim that 'equity considers as done that which ought to be done'. In *Re Anstis*,[137] Lindley LJ, in relation to a covenant to settle future property, said:

> Equity, no doubt, looks on that as done which ought to be done; but this rule, although usually expressed in general terms, is by no means universally true. Where the obligation to do what ought to be done is not an absolute duty, but only an obligation arising from contract, that which ought to be done is only treated as done *in favour of some person entitled to enforce the contract* as against the person liable to perform it.

[131] *Re Lind* (n 87) 364 (emphasis added).
[132] *Re Clarke* (n 91) 352.
[133] *Bexhill UK Ltd v Razzaq* (n 93) [42] (emphasis added).
[134] An 'equitable analogue' of a contract is found in the mutual wills doctrine when courts speak of requiring a 'contract at law': see Chapter 12, S 12.4.1.
[135] See main text to n 38 above.
[136] See, eg, Ying Khai Liew, '*Rochefoucauld v Boustead* (1897)' in Charles Mitchell and Paul Mitchell (eds), *Landmark Cases in Equity* (Oxford, Hart Publishing, 2012) 436–40.
[137] *Re Anstis* (1886) 31 Ch D 596 (CA) 605–06 (emphasis added).

This passage later formed the basis of Newey J's judgment in *Briggs v Gleeds (Head Office)*,[138] albeit in a different context. The question in *Briggs* was whether pension trustees could be taken to have made certain amendments against the members of the scheme on the basis that the members could have compelled them to do so by way of the 'equity considers as done …' maxim.[139] In this context, Newey J resolved the point in the negative because the members had not complied with s 1 of the 1989 Act, compliance of which was required for the creation of a valid deed. This suggests that only those 'entitled to enforce the contract'—that is, one who has a contractual right, a prerequisite of which is compliance with the 1989 Act where it concerns land—can rely on the 'equity considers as done …' maxim. This surely includes those who claim by way of the future property doctrine.

8.3.3. Specific Enforceability

Perhaps the biggest challenge to the argument that both doctrines rest on the same rationale is the claim that specific enforceability is irrelevant for a constructive trust to arise in relation to contracts concerning future property.

The source of the difficulty lies in the way in which the decision in *Holroyd v Marshall*[140] was interpreted by the House of Lords in *Tailby v Official Receiver*.[141] In the former case Lord Westbury LC, in describing the future property doctrine, said that 'a Court of Equity would compel [B] to perform the contract … assum[ing] that the supposed contract is one of that class of which a Court of Equity would decree the specific performance.'[142] In *Tailby*, however, Lord Watson suggested that Lord Westbury's 'reference … to specific performance [was] an illustration not selected with his usual felicity';[143] and Lord Macnaghten said:[144]

> It is difficult to suppose that Lord Westbury intended to lay down as a rule to guide or perplex the Court, that considerations applicable to cases of specific performance, properly so-called, where the contract is executory, are to be applied to every case of equitable assignment dealing with future property … Greater confusion … would be caused by transferring considerations applicable to suits for specific performance—involving, as they do, some of the nicest distinctions and most difficult questions that come before the Court—to cases of equitable assignment or specific lien where nothing remains to be done in order to define the rights of the parties, but the Court is merely asked to protect rights completely defined as between the parties to the contract … The truth is that cases of equitable assignment or specific lien, where the consideration has passed, depend on the real meaning of the agreement between the parties.

While the question of whether specific performance is relevant to the future property doctrine 'remains an open academic question'[145] because no case has yet turned on this point, it is nevertheless crucial to resolve the matter, since it affects how the doctrine is rationalised. It is submitted that consistency dictates that the future property doctrine, like cases

[138] *Briggs v Gleeds (Head Office) (a firm)* [2014] EWHC 1178 (Ch), [2015] Ch 212.
[139] ibid [80].
[140] *Holroyd v Marshall* (n 2).
[141] *Tailby v Official Receiver* (n 87).
[142] *Holroyd v Marshall* (n 2) 10 H L Cas 211, 11 ER 1007.
[143] *Tailby v Official Receiver* (n 87) 535.
[144] ibid 547.
[145] Tolhurst, *The Assignment of Contractual Rights* (n 119) 378.

relating to specifically enforceable contracts of sale, gives rise to constructive trusts only where the contract is specifically enforceable. Were it otherwise, the consequences would be unacceptable. As Sarah Worthington notes,[146] a constructive trust would not arise if B sells shares in a public company which he presently owns to A even if A provides consideration because such contracts are not normally specifically enforceable; but if B contracts to sell such shares which are future property, then a constructive trust would arise upon B's acquisition of the shares where A has provided consideration.[147] Worthington rightly points out that '[i]t is very difficult to construct a rational argument which justifies this distinction.'[148]

This view is, however, not universally held. For instance, Greg Tolhurst takes a hybrid approach instead: specific performance is relevant where A has not yet provided consideration when B acquires the property, but is irrelevant if A has provided consideration prior to B's acquisition.[149] But it is difficult to see why the mere sequence of events ought to have any impact on the matter. If the time at which A provides consideration is immaterial in cases where the contract of sale relates to property B owns at the outset, it is not obvious why it should matter where the contract relates to future property. After all, the 'uniqueness' of the property, which affects the specific enforceability of the contract, is utterly unaffected by the timing at which A provides consideration.

Others take a more hardline view. *Meagher, Gummow, and Lehane's Equity* suggests that the future property doctrine applies only where consideration has been executed, and therefore that cases relating to executory contracts are irrelevant to a proper understanding of the doctrine.[150] Part of the reason for taking this view is that 'specific performance is a discretionary remedy', and therefore '[f]actors going to the court's discretion to a decree specific performance can hardly be relevant to [the doctrine] which operates without a decree of the court or further act of the parties to vest property in an assignee on the happening of certain events.'[151] This explanation is problematic because, as we have already observed,[152] 'a decree of specific performance' is not a prerequisite to a constructive trust's arising under either the future property doctrine or the doctrine relating to contracts of sale. Moreover, the 'discretion' involved in determining the specific enforceability of contracts for the purposes of these doctrines is not inconsistent with an understanding of these constructive trusts as arising to replicate the parties' primary rights and duties, since it is not an active discretion which is conferred on courts, but merely the ability to determine whether certain 'bars' operate on the facts of the case before them.[153] A rule which dictates that a constructive trust will not arise where the future property is not 'legally unique' hardly involves the exercise of any remedial discretion at all.

[146] Worthington, 'Proprietary Remedies' (n 10) 5.

[147] ibid 5–6.

[148] ibid 6.

Through a careful survey of the decision in *Tailby*, Worthington also explains how the judgments in that case '*assume* [specific enforceability to be] a requirement' (Worthington, 'Proprietary Remedies' (n 10) 6); and this is no less so in relation to Lord Macnaghten's judgment, in which he chose the previous decision of *Bettesworth v Dead and Chapter of St Paul's* (1728) 1 Bro PC 241, 1 ER 541—a case where specific performance was ordered—as an illustration of the future property doctrine (Worthington, 'Proprietary Remedies' (n 10) 7).

[149] Tolhurst, *The Assignment of Contractual Rights* (n 119) 378.

[150] JD Heydon, MJ Leeming and PG Turner, *Meagher, Gummow & Lehane's Equity: Doctrines & Remedies*, 5th edn (NSW, LexisNexis Butterworths, 2015) [6-270].

[151] *Meagher, Gummow & Lehane's Equity* (ibid) [6-270].

[152] See main text to n 55 above.

[153] Zakrzewski, *Remedies Reclassified* (n 62) 92, 97.

On the basis of the decided cases, *Snell's Equity* suggests that '[w]hilst it is sometimes assumed that the [future property doctrine] applies only where A is under a specifically enforceable duty to B, its application to security rights over personal property suggests that, in fact, specific enforceability may not be a requirement.'[154] However, this is a non sequitur. It was earlier observed[155] that a purely executory contract for security[156] is not specifically enforceable, but becomes so once the creditor advances the loan money to the debtor. The reason for this is that, 'where the loan has not yet been made ... the lender can invest his money elsewhere.'[157] However, once the money has been advanced, the 'contract to mortgage property, real or personal, will ... be specifically enforceable, for a mere claim to damages or repayment is obviously less valuable than a security in the event of the debtor's insolvency.'[158] In this latter case, 'it would be unreasonable to treat the agreement to give security as one for which damages would be a sufficient remedy', because 'the point of the security' is that 'a subsequent insolvency or financial difficulties on the part of the borrower may very well render damages an inadequate remedy'.[159] Hence, the fact that the future property doctrine can apply in relation to contracts for security over personal property does not suggest that specific enforceability of the contract is not a requirement for the doctrine to apply.

Indeed, because the vast majority of the cases relating to the future property doctrine have concerned contracts for security, context is crucial. Read in context, statements to the effect that A must provide consideration before B acquires the property are in fact simply indicative of the need for the contract to be specifically enforceable when B acquires the property in order for a constructive trust to arise. Again, read in context, when Lord Macnaghten held that 'considerations applicable to suits for specific performance'[160] are irrelevant to future property cases, his Lordship was making the simple point that issues concerning the 'uniqueness' of the property, as well as 'the requirements of readiness, willingness, and ability to pay the purchase price' are no longer relevant once consideration has been executed.[161] Upon execution of consideration, '[B] is likelier to succeed in obtaining the discretionary remedy of specific performance. The "trust" operating in his favour thus becomes "absolute".'[162] The context of contracts for security does not provide reason for thinking that constructive trusts would arise in relation to contracts for future property where those contracts are not specifically enforceable.

8.3.4. A Common Analysis

If the analysis proposed above is correct, then both doctrines can be assimilated by way of a common analysis. In both contexts, constructive trusts arise to replicate the parties'

154 *Snell's Equity* (n 7) [5-015], citing *Tailby v Official Receiver* (n 87) in relation to this proposition.
155 See main text to n 52 above.
156 In particular those over personal property.
157 Keeler, 'Some Reflections' (n 53).
158 *Swiss Bank Corp* (n 3) 595.
159 Keeler, 'Some Reflections' (n 53) 374.
160 *Tailby v Official Receiver* (n 87) 547, quoted in the main text following n 144 above.
161 Turner, 'Understanding the Constructive Trust' (n 1) 587.
162 ibid.

rights and duties, arising out of their primary contractual relationship, if and when the subject-matter exists in B's hands. It is necessary for there to be a valid legal contract which is specifically enforceable—a contract for valuable consideration is therefore required—but there is no need for consideration to have been executed. Hence, in the future property cases, it does not matter whether A provides consideration before or after B acquires the property. In addition, the 'future-ness' or 'present-ness' of the property—and hence the distinction between QI and AI situations—is of no consequence. The rationale underpinning both doctrines is the protection of the parties' 'performance interest' where the property is 'legally unique'.

This common analysis not only achieves consistency within the contract-based subcategory, but also helpfully highlights why the doctrines within this subcategory are different from the other doctrines discussed in this book. First, it indicates how constructive trusts arise through equity's exercise of its different jurisdictions. In particular, equity's concurrent jurisdiction can be distinguished from equity's exclusive jurisdiction, the former relating to cases where one has a right at common law but nevertheless seeks a remedy in equity which the common law cannot provide, and the latter relating to cases where one's only right is equitable.[163] This distinction is reflected within the bilateral events category of constructive trusts: the contract-based subcategory reflects equity's concurrent jurisdiction, while the non-contract-based subcategory reflects its exclusive jurisdiction. This distinction reveals why it is necessary for the parties to enter into a valid contract where the constructive trusts are contract-based: the reason is that the parties must *first* have a common law relationship in order for equity's concurrent jurisdiction to apply. For the same reason, the specific enforceability of the contract is crucial: only then can it be said that common law damages are an inadequate remedy, thus justifying the imposition of constructive trusts. Again, for the same reason, the distinction between QI and AI situations is inconsequential within the contract-based subcategory: the constructive trusts are not concerned with whether or not the contract relates to property B owns at the outset, but with whether A will obtain an adequate remedy at common law. Since these constructive trusts have a complementary role, courts must ensure that they do not overstep the common law jurisdiction, which explains why there are 'bars' which may prevent contracts from being specifically enforceable,[164] and hence prevent constructive trusts from arising. Such considerations are wholly irrelevant to the non-contract-based doctrines, simply because equity does not need to 'work around' the common law.

The common analysis also indicates why the contract-based doctrines cannot be assimilated with or subsumed within the non-contract-based subcategory. The contract-based doctrines do not require A to have relied in such a way that increases B's opportunity of acquiring the property in question (as is the case with the QI doctrines within the non-contract-based subcategory),[165] nor do they enforce informal promises which have been detrimentally relied upon (as is the case with proprietary estoppel).[166] This explains, for

[163] See Lionel Smith, 'Common Law and Equity in R3RUE' (2011) 68 *Washington and Lee Law Review* 1185, 1194–95. A third jurisdiction is the auxiliary jurisdiction, which refers to pre-trial procedure. See also Mike Macnair, 'Equity and Conscience' (2007) 27 *OJLS* 659, 664–66.

[164] See main text to n 153 above.

[165] See Chapter 3, S 3.2.1.1.

[166] See Chapter 3, S 3.2.1.2.

example, why in relation to the doctrine in *Pallant v Morgan* a full-blown constructive trust arises even though the parties have not entered into a contract at all, or—at any rate—a contract the terms of which are certain enough to be specifically enforceable.[167] It also explains why discretion as to content, which is exercised in relation to proprietary estoppel,[168] does not arise in the relation to the contract-based doctrines.

Finally, the common analysis helpfully distinguishes the contract-based doctrines from the rule in *Re Rose*.[169] Although these doctrines have all been said to be based on the 'equity considers as done …' maxim, they react to different concerns. The contract-based doctrines impose constructive trusts to secure the performance of contractual obligations; those arising in the context of the rule in *Re Rose* support gifts made by 'a person sui juris, acting freely, fairly, and with sufficient knowledge, [who] has it in his power to make … a voluntary gift of any part of his property'.[170] Hence, in the one case a contract *for value* is required, in the other a constructive trust arises in favour of a *volunteer*.

[167] See discussion in Chapter 6, S 6.1.1.
[168] See Chapter 7, S 7.1.4.
[169] Discussed in Chapter 9.
[170] *Kekewich v Manning* (1851) 1 De GM & G 176, 187; 42 ER 519, 524. See discussion in Chapter 9, S 9.3.

9

The Rule in *Re Rose*

The 'rule in *Re Rose*' is the core doctrine which reflects an AI situation within the unilateral events category of constructive trusts. Stated broadly, the rule provides that, where B has done everything in his power to effect a voluntary transfer of property to A, whether by means of a gift to A or for A to hold on trust,[1] a constructive trust arises to give effect to the transfer in equity although the legal title of the property has not yet vested in A. This rule reflects an AI situation because the constructive trust arises in relation to property which B owns absolutely at the outset: obligations under the trust arise due to an act of B in relation to his own property. It falls within the unilateral events category because B's actions alone are enough to trigger the constructive trust: A's participation is not required.

As the label 'the rule in *Re Rose*' indicates, this doctrine is commonly perceived to originate from the two (unrelated) decisions of *Re Rose, Midland Bank Executor and Trustee Co Ltd v Rose*[2] ('*Re Rose 1949*') and *Re Rose, Rose v IRC*[3] ('*Re Rose 1952*'). However, the principles which are embodied in the doctrine can be found in earlier case law.

For instance, in *Fortescue v Barnett*,[4] Sir John Leach MR held that whether an assignment was complete turned on 'whether any act remained to be done by [B] which, to assist a volunteer, this Court would not compel him to do.'[5] In that case there was a voluntary assignment by deed of a policy of assurance to trustees on trust, which was not accompanied by delivery of the policy to the trustees. The trustees did not give notice of the assignment to the assurance office as they ought to have done. Nevertheless, delivery of the policy was held to be unnecessary to perfect the assignment, and the assignment was held to be complete. The reason was because '[n]othing remained to be done by [B]'.[6] Part of the logic of this principle was the fact that the assignor had put it out of his power to renege on the assignment:[7] he could not 'defeat his own grant if the trustees had given notice of the assignment to the assurance office.'[8] The same case also reflects the idea that what constitutes 'doing all that is necessary to be done' depends on the nature of the property. Thus, Sir John Leach MR drew a distinction between an assignment of stock and an assignment of a

[1] *Re Rose, Rose v IRC* [1952] 1 Ch 499 (CA) 505–06.
[2] *Re Rose, Midland Bank Executor and Trustee Co Ltd v Rose* [1949] 1 Ch 78 (Ch).
[3] *Re Rose 1952* (n 1).
[4] *Fortescue v Barnett* (1834) 3 My & K 36, 40 ER 14.
[5] ibid 3 My & K 43, 40 ER 17.
[6] ibid.
[7] See, to the same effect, *Re Griffin* [1899] 1 Ch 408 (Ch) 412.
[8] *Fortescue v Barnett* (n 4) 3 My & K 43, 40 ER 17.

bond: since delivery was essential only in the former case, the lack of delivery in the latter case would not prevent effect from being given to the assignment.[9]

The same principles can also be detected in *Donaldson v Donaldson*,[10] a case involving the voluntary assignment by deed of a beneficial interest under a trust, where notice of this was not given to the trustee. Sir Page Wood V-C held that '[t]he question is in every case … has [B] performed such acts that [A] can take advantage of them without requiring any further act to be done by [B]'; and if so, the 'Court is not called upon to act against [B]', and 'will assist [A] in obtaining the property'.[11] Emphasis was also placed on the nature of the property in question: a deed of assignment was held to be ineffective to pass any stock if the deed was undelivered; but in relation to equitable interest in stock held in the names of trustees a deed of assignment would be effective, since it would enable A to claim the stock as against the trustees.[12]

In both *Fortescue* and *Donaldson* the fact that notice had to be (but was not) given for the effective transfer of the legal title did not prevent the transfer from taking effect in equity. In *Re Griffin*,[13] Byrne J extended this principle by observing that it would not make any difference if it was essential for notice to have been given *by A* and this had not yet been done. This is consistent with the principle that B must have done everything that is necessary *for him* to do to transfer the property.

To be sure, these older cases do not explicitly hold, as the modern cases do, that B would be subject to a *constructive trust* for A's benefit once he has done everything which was necessary to be done to transfer property: they were largely concerned instead with determining whether there was an effective equitable assignment of property.[14] However, on at least one conception, an equitable assignment is indistinguishable from a trust: it does not involve the transfer of rights but the encumbering of the assignor's right with a new equitable right in favour of the assignee.[15] This may explain why the principles developed in these older cases have found their way into the modern iteration of the doctrine, which undoubtedly gives rise to (constructive) trusts.

9.1. Requirements

For the rule in *Re Rose* to apply, B must have to have done everything in his power to effectuate the transfer of property to A, according to the nature of the property in question. But there are also two further requirements which are seldom noticed but are equally important, namely: A must be given the power to attempt to complete the transfer such that B can no longer interfere; and that B must intend to make an immediate transfer of the property.

[9] ibid 3 My & K 42–43, 40 ER 17.
[10] *Donaldson v Donaldson* (1854) Kay 711, 69 ER 303.
[11] ibid Kay 718, 69 ER 306.
[12] ibid Kay 718–19, 69 ER 306–07.
[13] *Re Griffin* (n 7) 412.
[14] See, eg, *Donaldson v Donaldson* (n 10) Kay 719, 69 ER 307; *Re Griffin* (n 7) 412.
[15] See James Edelman and Steven Elliott, 'Two Conceptions of Equitable Assignment' (2015) 131 *LQR* 228, 229.

9.1.1. Doing Everything in B's Power

In *Milroy v Lord*,[16] Turner LJ held that:

> in order to render a voluntary settlement valid and effectual, [B] must have done everything which, according to the nature of the property comprised in the settlement, was necessary to be done in order to transfer the property and render the settlement binding upon him.

This statement is commonly understood[17] as the basis for the rule in *Re Rose*. Thus, in *Re Rose 1949*[18] and *Re Rose 1952*,[19] it was held that a transfer of certificated shares is effective in equity once B executes the appropriate transfer form (as determined by the company's regulations) and delivers the form and the share certificates to A, notwithstanding that A is not yet the legal owner of those shares. Similarly in *Mascall v Mascall*,[20] where B had executed the relevant form for the transfer of registered land and had handed this together with the Land Certificate to A, the Court of Appeal held that the transfer was effective in equity, notwithstanding the fact that A had not yet sent these documents to the Land Registry to register his legal title.

What precisely constitutes 'doing everything necessary to be done' depends on the specific nature of the property in question, since the requirements for constitution differ according to subject-matter.[21] In all cases, it is crucial for B to execute the proper form required for transferring the property in question, otherwise the doctrine will not apply. Thus, in *Milroy v Lord*[22] B's attempt to transfer shares to A was of no effect because the regulations of the company provided that such transfers could only be effectuated through compliance with certain formalities, and B had instead attempted to transfer shares by executing a deed poll.[23] Where a vital document is lost, it is for B to procure a duplicate, in particular where A cannot obtain a duplicate in his own right.[24]

9.1.1.1. *Third-Party Discretion*

In certain cases, whether property is successfully transferred to A hinges on a third party's exercise (or lack thereof) of a discretion to consent (or withhold consent) to A's registration of his legal title. A careful distinction needs to be drawn between cases where third parties have 'negative' discretion, and cases where the discretion is 'positive' in nature.

[16] *Milroy v Lord* (1862) 4 De GF & J 264, 274; 45 ER 1185, 1189.

[17] See, eg, *Mascall v Mascall* (1985) 50 P & CR 119 (CA) 126; AG Guest and Ying Khai Liew, *Guest on the Law of Assignment* (London, Sweet & Maxwell, 2015) [3-50].

[18] *Re Rose 1949* (n 2) 89.

[19] See, eg, *Re Rose 1952* (n 1) 518–19.

[20] *Mascall v Mascall* (n 17).

[21] *cf* Edelman and Elliott, 'Two Conceptions' (n 15) 233–34, where it is suggested that purported statutory assignments which take effect as equitable assignments due to a failure to comply with the requirements of the Law of Property Act 1925, s 136 are constructive trusts which arise 'because the assignor has done all that is necessary to effect the transfer'. This is a misanalysis. The fact that the assignor fails to comply with the requirements of s 136 proves precisely that the assignor has not done all that is required to give rise to a constructive trust.

[22] *Milroy v Lord* (n 16).

[23] See observation in *Re Rose 1952* (n 1) 508–09.

[24] *Zeital v Kaye* [2010] EWCA Civ 159, [2010] 2 BCLC 1 [43].

By 'negative' discretion it is meant that the third party has discretion only to *refuse* to register A's legal title where certain conditions are (or are not) met which are out of B's control. For instance, in relation to shares in private limited companies, the company's regulations commonly grant directors discretion to withhold registration, the discretion of which must be exercised bona fide pursuant to what they consider is in the company's best interest.[25] In contrast, 'positive' discretion means that B must obtain the third party's assent before A's legal title can be registered. For instance, in *Re Fry*,[26] the Defence (Finance) Regulations 1939 imposed restrictions on the transfer of securities, with the result that the consent of the Treasury was a precondition for the transfer of shares. This distinction matters because it is no obstacle to the operation of the rule in *Re Rose* that the third party has negative discretion,[27] but B's failure to obtain consent from a third party who has positive discretion will prevent the doctrine from operating.[28]

In *Re Fry* it was suggested that the reason why the doctrine would not apply where consent was not obtained in a positive discretion case was that the third party 'might … have required further information … and, if so approached, [B] might have refused to concern himself with the matter further, in which case [no one] could have compelled him to do so.'[29] Jonathan Garton has criticised this reasoning by observing that, even in relation to negative discretion, 'it is entirely feasible [that the third party] might ask [B] to supply further details about the transfer and [A].'[30] However, it is submitted that the possibility of a request for further information from B is neither here nor there. In all cases, 'the principle that equity will intervene only where [B] has done everything in his or her power to perfect the gift cannot be literally true because there is almost always something more that [B] could have done.'[31]

A better explanation for the distinction between negative and positive discretion cases can be found in asking what the position would be if the third party does not exercise his discretion. Where the third party has negative discretion and the discretion is not exercised, A will obtain the legal title to the property. Whether or not the third party withholds consent is not something which is within B's power to ensure, but hinges on whether a certain condition outside B's control is (or is not) met; hence B cannot be said not to have done everything in his power to effectuate a transfer to A. In contrast, where consent is not obtained from a third party with positive discretion, the transfer of the legal title to A cannot occur.[32] Since it lies within B's power to obtain consent for the transfer, B's failure to do so entails that he would not have done everything in his power in order to engage the rule in *Re Rose*.

[25] *Re Smith and Fawcett Ltd* [1942] Ch 304 (CA) 306.

[26] *Re Fry (deceased)* [1946] Ch 312 (Ch).

[27] See S 9.2.2.1. for a discussion concerning the position where the third party in fact exercises his discretion to refuse A's registration.

[28] As the result in *Re Fry* (n 26) indicates.

[29] ibid 318.

[30] Jonathan Garton, 'The Role of the Trust Mechanism in the Rule in *Re Rose*' [2003] *Conveyancer and Property Lawyer* 364, 369.

[31] *Pennington v Waine* [2002] EWCA Civ 227, [2002] 1 WLR 2075 [74].

[32] *Re Fry* (n 26) 316.

9.1.2. Giving A the Power to Complete the Transfer

The second requirement is that B must put it in A's power to complete the transfer.[33] This normally involves giving A or A's agent[34] all the relevant documents necessary to complete A's title. The need for A to have the power to complete his title is explained by Browne-Wilkinson LJ in *Mascall v Mascall*:[35]

> The basic principle underlying all the cases is that equity will not come to the aid of a volunteer. Therefore, if [A] needs to get an order from a court of equity in order to complete his title, he will not get it. If, on the other hand, [A] has under his control everything necessary to constitute his title completely without any further assistance from [B], [A] needs no assistance from equity and the gift is complete.

It might be thought that this second requirement is indistinguishable from the first—that B's doing everything necessary to be done to transfer the property to A would *necessarily* include giving A the power to complete the transfer. However, this risks masking important considerations concerning the recipient of the relevant documents. In particular, where the recipient (X) is not A, it is necessary to determine whether X is A's agent; and the outcome may well turn on acts solely within X's control and which has nothing to do with what B does or does not do. For example, in *Hurst v Crampton Bros (Coopers) Ltd*,[36] B intended to transfer shares to A, and pursuant to this delivered an executed share transfer form and the share certificates to X. While it might be said that B had done everything necessary to be done to effectuate the transfer, the rule in *Re Rose* would not yet have applied at this stage, since X was acting merely as *B's* agent. Later, however, X wrote to A informing A of the gift and stated that no further action was required on A's part. Jacob J held that, at this point, X held the documents for A:[37] by writing to A, X had become agent for A, which triggered an application of the doctrine. The same point was made by Lord Hoffmann in *Pehrsson v von Greyerz*[38] where his Lordship observed that the rule in *Re Rose* will apply when X constitutes himself as agent for A. Even if B has done everything in his power to transfer the property, it may not be the case—but it remains necessary—for A or A's agent to have the power to complete the transfer.

Another reason for distinguishing the first and second requirements is that the second requirement provides an important qualification to the first. In *Mascall v Mascall*,[39] it was argued that B had not done everything necessary to be done because he could have done more by asking the Land Registry to register the land in A's favour. Lawton LJ rejected this argument as 'fallacious', observing that '[B] had done everything in his power in the ordinary way of the transfer of registered property'.[40] This indicates that, once A has it in his

[33] Or, where B intends to give property to A to hold on trust for C, B must put it in *A's* or *C's* power to complete the transfer.

[34] *Hurst v Crampton Bros (Coopers) Ltd* [2002] EWHC 1375 (Ch), [2003] BCC 190 [11].

[35] *Mascall v Mascall* (n 17) 126.

[36] *Hurst v Crampton Bros* (n 34). This case and *Pennington v Waine* (n 31) share the same facts, but are concerned with different legal points.

[37] *Hurst v Crampton Bros* (n 34) [11].

[38] *Pehrsson v von Greyerz* [1999] UKPC 26, (1999–2000) 2 ITELR 230 [24].

[39] *Mascall v Mascall* (n 17).

[40] ibid 125–26.

power to complete the transfer, B is considered to have done all that is necessary to be done, despite the fact that it might remain within B's power to do that which A can do to complete the transfer. As Browne-Wilkinson LJ held in *Mascall*, the doctrine applies 'as soon as [A] has within his control all those things necessary to enable him … to complete his title.'[41]

The extent to which A must have it in his power to complete his title is to be measured by B's lack of ability to interfere with A's attempt to perfect his title. It is fulfilled when B is excluded[42] from having any 'right to recover'[43] the relevant documents, such that it is not 'open to [B] to countermand the gift.'[44] Crucially, it is unnecessary that A has the power to complete his title *such that completion would inevitably occur*. Such inevitability may arise, as in the case of land, where the Registrar must register A as the owner 'in the absence of any caveat or the like'.[45] However, the requirement is likewise fulfilled where, as in the case of certificated shares, the company directors have negative discretion to withhold registration.[46] Such discretion is neither inconsistent with B having done all he can to transfer shares to A, nor with A having the power to complete his title.

9.1.3. Intention to Transfer

A third requirement is that B must intend to effectuate an immediate transfer of the property to A when he does all he can to effectuate the transfer. This can be detected in *Donaldson v Donaldson*,[47] where Sir Page Wood V-C commented that a deed of transfer of stock without delivery shows 'an evident intention on the part of [B] to do some further act' and would not invoke the doctrine. Not only did the outstanding act of delivery indicate that B had not done all that was necessary to transfer the stock, it also indicated a lack of intention to make an immediate transfer of the stock to A.[48] Similarly, in *Mascall v Mascall*, in deciding that the rule in *Re Rose* would apply to the facts of the case, Lawton LJ not only observed that '[B] had done everything in his power to transfer the house to [A]', but also that '[B] *had intended* to do it'.[49] This indicates that the third requirement is distinct from the other two requirements.

9.1.3.1. Features of Intention

There are two important features of the element of intention. First, the doctrine is concerned with B's *original* intention, that is, his intention at the time when he does everything in his power to transfer the property to A. This may or may not be consistent with B's *current* intention—that is, B's intention at trial; but the latter intention has no effect on the applicability of the doctrine. Two cases serve as examples. In *Re Rose 1949*, B did everything

[41] ibid 126.
[42] *Re Rose 1952* (n 1) 518.
[43] *Mascall v Mascall* (n 17) 128.
[44] *Pehrsson v von Greyerz* (n 38) [24].
[45] *Mascall v Mascall* (n 17) 123.
[46] See, eg, *Re Rose 1949* (n 2) 89; *Re Rose 1952* (n 1) 518.
[47] *Donaldson v Donaldson* (n 10) Kay 718, 69 ER 307.
[48] See also *Re Williams* [1917] 1 Ch 1 (Ch) 8.
[49] *Mascall v Mascall* (n 17) 125 (emphasis added).

in his power to divest himself of certain preference shares in A's favour. B then made a will which contained certain provisions in A's favour 'if such preference shares have not been transferred to [A] previously to my death'.[50] Jenkins J held that the gift took effect inter vivos and not under B's will. One of the reasons was that B had intended to make an immediate transfer at the time when B did all he could to transfer the shares to A.[51] In *Mascall v Mascall*, B executed a transfer form for the purposes of transferring a house to his son, A. B handed over the form along with the Land Certificate to A. B and A then had a very serious quarrel, after which B did not wish to proceed with the transfer of the house. The Court of Appeal held that B could not recall the gift. One of the reasons was that, when B did all he could to effectuate the transfer to A, B had intended to make an immediate transfer:[52] B's later intention had no bearing on the outcome.

The second feature of the element of intention is that intention is necessary, but not sufficient, for the doctrine to apply. Intending to make an immediate transfer of property will not by itself give rise to a constructive trust; it remains necessary for B to do everything in his power to effectuate the transfer. This point, which may seem obvious, bears emphasising for at least two reasons. On the one hand, it dispels any suggestion that B's intention alone dictates the timing at which the gift takes effect in equity. This very argument was rejected by Lord Hoffmann in *Pehrsson v von Greyerz*,[53] where his Lordship observed of the doctrine that: '[i]f the gift took effect from when the intention to give was manifested, it would have been unnecessary to consider when [A] obtained the power to have himself registered.' On the other hand, it allows us to understand how the doctrine is consistent with the judgment in *Milroy v Lord*,[54] insofar as the law's treatment of the intention of a property owner is concerned. In *Milroy* it was stressed that 'the Court will not give effect to [an intended voluntary settlement by way of actual transfer, or transfer to a trustee, or a declaration of oneself as trustee] by applying another of those modes.'[55] The property owner's intention is at the heart of this rule: the court will avoid 'converting the settlement or the parol declaration to a purpose wholly different from that which was intended to be effected by it, and … creating a perfect trust out of an imperfect transaction.'[56] The fact that the rule in *Re Rose* gives rise to a constructive *trust* despite B's intention to make an immediate *transfer* is not inconsistent with this rule. If B simply intends to make an immediate transfer and does nothing about it, his intention is clearly of no effect; similarly, if B appears to do all that is necessary to transfer property to A but makes clear that he does not intend an immediate transfer, a constructive trust does not arise. But where an intention to make an immediate transfer is coupled with B doing all he can to make that transfer happen, then it is consistent with B's intention to say that he intends to divest himself of the property. The constructive trust gives effect to this very intention.[57]

[50] *Re Rose 1949* (n 2) 90.
[51] ibid.
[52] *Mascall v Mascall* (n 17) 125.
[53] *Pehrsson v von Greyerz* (n 38) [26].
[54] *Milroy v Lord* (n 16).
[55] ibid 4 De GF & J 274, 45 ER 1189.
[56] ibid 4 De GF & J 275, 45 ER 1190.
[57] See further discussion in S 9.3.2.2.

9.1.3.2. Ascertaining Intention

It is often necessary to interpret B's words and/or actions in order to determine whether he objectively intended to make an immediate transfer of property to A since, as with other areas of private law, the rule in *Re Rose* is concerned not with B's subjective intention but with his manifested intention.

The approach taken by the courts is that, if B has done everything necessary to effectuate a transfer of property to A, then B is taken to have the requisite intention unless there is evidence to the contrary. The reason for this is that one will usually only do all that is within his power to effectuate a voluntary transfer of property when he intends an immediate transfer. So, in *Re Rose 1949* where B handed to A the relevant share transfer form and certificates, Jenkins J held that B had intended an immediate transfer: it was not meant 'to depend on whether the act of third parties, namely, the directors, necessary to complete the legal title in [A] by registration should have been performed'.[58] This was so despite the fact that B had executed a later will which made provision for the case where such shares had not been transferred during his lifetime:[59] although B had contemplated that those shares would not have been successfully transferred, this was not taken to be evidence to the contrary. Similarly, in *Re Rose 1952*, B had executed a transfer with the words amounting to 'I transfer the shares' and handed over to A the transfer and share certificates. Evershed MR held that B must have meant to transfer to A 'the shares and all my right title and interest thereunder',[60] there being no evidence that B had meant otherwise.

From these cases, it is also clear that it is *possible* for B to have an intention contrary to that which is prima facie indicated by his actions. So, in *Re Rose 1949*, it would have been possible for B not to have intended to give A any interest in the shares until and unless the transfer was registered;[61] and in *Re Rose 1952*, by 'I transfer the shares' B may have meant to transfer only the legal title to the shares.[62] These contrary intentions would preclude the rule in *Re Rose* from applying; but a contrary intention must be clearly manifested. A contrary intention can also be deduced from the evidence available to the court. One test which can be gleaned from *Re Rose 1952*[63] is to ask whether, at the time B did all in his power to effectuate a transfer, B would have intended to keep any forthcoming income generated by the property for himself. Such intention is inconsistent with an intention to make an immediate transfer, and would prevent the doctrine from applying. Another example can be found in *Smith v Charles Building Services*,[64] where B signed a stock transfer form but did not date it, and handed it to A in the course of business negotiations. When they failed

[58] *Re Rose 1949* (n 2) 90.

[59] See main text to n 50 above.

[60] *Re Rose 1952* (n 1) 513.

[61] See Peter Luxton, 'In Search of Perfection: The *Re Rose* Rule Rationale' [2012] *Conveyancer and Property Lawyer* 70, 74 fn 40. In this situation, B remains the absolute owner of the property until such time as the transfer of the legal title to A is complete, whereupon A becomes its new absolute owner.

[62] In this situation, nothing happens in equity until A obtains the legal title to the property, at which point a resulting trust arises in B's favour in response to B's lack of intention to give A the beneficial interest in the property. As Jenkins J noted in *Re Rose 1949* (n 2) 88, 'a voluntary transfer … intended by [B] to be a transfer by way of gift' can be distinguished from 'a transfer which, when perfected by registration, would give rise to a resulting trust'.

[63] *Re Rose 1952* (n 1) 507.

[64] *Smith v Charles Building Services* [2006] EWCA Civ 14, [2006] BCC 334.

to come to a consensus, B tore up the form. Mann J accepted B's evidence that he did not intend the transfer to have immediate effect: the transfer was intended to be conditional upon the successful outcome of the negotiations.[65] Particular emphasis was placed on the fact that '[b]usinessmen tend to leave dates in such documents blank where they do not intend them to have immediate effect.'[66] As a result, the rule in *Re Rose* did not apply.

The possibility that B may not to make an immediate transfer of property despite seemingly doing everything in his power to do so allays some misgivings which James Edelman has expressed concerning *Re Rose 1952*. Noting that Evershed MR had 'described as "startling" the proposition that [B] could have kept the dividends which had been paid to him prior to the transfer of the shares', Edelman comments: '[i]t is difficult to see why this is startling. It might be the very thing which is expected by a person who is aware that there might be a delay before registration'.[67] However, the point made by Evershed MR is entirely consistent with the finding in that case that B had made 'a voluntary disposition purporting to operate as an immediate gift'.[68] If there was evidence that B had intended to keep the dividends, as Edelman suggests, then such an intention would have precluded the rule in *Re Rose* from applying.

Edelman also asks two other questions concerning *Re Rose 1952*:[69]

> Would the proposition that Mr Rose intended an immediate gift before registration still apply if Mr Rose had returned the share transfer documents immediately before a dividend had been declared, aware of the impending dividend and with the apparent intention that he receive the dividend prior to the registration of transfer? Alternatively, if Mr Rose had made the transfer several days before intending to vote at a general meeting, aware that the transfer would not be registered until after the general meeting? Would Mr Rose have to vote according to the interests of the transferees?

The answer is straightforward in both cases: there would be sufficient evidence that Mr Rose did not intend to make an immediate transfer, and so the doctrine would not have applied. It is therefore difficult to see how these questions reveal any 'problems'[70] with the decision in *Re Rose 1952*.

9.1.4. Unconscionability?

An important question arises as to whether the rule in *Re Rose* can apply by way of an alternative route: that equity will give effect to the intended transaction where it is 'unconscionable' for B to change his mind, even though B has not done everything necessary to effectuate a transfer of property to A. This is often taken to be the effect of the Court of Appeal's judgment in *Pennington v Waine*,[71] which is said to have extended the rule in *Re Rose*.[72] If this is the effect of *Pennington*, then it significantly impacts the scope and analysis of the rule in *Re Rose*.

[65] ibid [69].
[66] ibid.
[67] James Edelman, 'Two Fundamental Questions for the Law of Trusts' (2013) 129 *LQR* 66, 78.
[68] *Re Rose 1952* (n 1) 506–07.
[69] Edelman, 'Two Fundamental Questions' (n 67) 78.
[70] ibid.
[71] *Pennington v Waine* (n 31).
[72] See, eg, John McGhee (ed), *Snell's Equity*, 33rd edn (London, Sweet & Maxwell, 2016) [24-007].

9.1.4.1. Pennington v Waine

In *Pennington v Waine*, Ada Crampon was the majority shareholder and a director of Crampon Bros (Coopers) Ltd. She indicated to her nephew, Harold, that she wanted to give him some of her shares to enable Harold to become a director of the company. She signed a share transfer form and handed this to Pennington, one of the company's auditors. Pennington wrote to Harold, enclosing the relevant form of consent to act as director. Harold was told that he had been appointed as director, and that Ada had arranged for the transfer of shares to him. Pennington also told Harold that no action was required on Harold's part. Harold signed the consent form and Ada countersigned it. No further action was taken in relation to the stock transfer form, and Harold's title remained unregistered when Ada died. The Court of Appeal held that the attempted transfer of shares was nevertheless effective in equity.

On the face of it, the judgment contains three distinct justifications for the decision. For the majority,[73] the main basis of the decision was that in the circumstances it would have been unconscionable for Ada to change her mind and to recall the gift.[74] Arden LJ also gave an alternative explanation, namely that 'the words used by Mr Pennington should be construed as meaning that Ada and, through her, Mr Pennington became agents for Harold for the purpose of submitting the share transfer to the Company. This is an application of the principle of benevolent construction to give effect to Ada's clear wishes.'[75] In the minority, Clarke LJ based his decision on the ground that 'the execution of a stock transfer form can have effect as an equitable assignment without the necessity of a transfer or delivery of the form or the share certificates either to the transferee or to the company.'[76] His Lordship felt that this ruling was justified due to 'the absence of binding authority to the contrary.'[77]

9.1.4.2. Evaluation

Consider Clarke LJ's judgment first. The reasoning gives the superficial appearance that the judgment is based on an application of the rule in *Re Rose*: it holds that Ada had done everything in her power to effectuate an equitable assignment because delivery of the transfer form and share certificate was unnecessary. But it appears that his Lordship's reasoning was made *per incuriam*. It is true that no earlier authority has stated in so many words that an application of the doctrine hinges on B's delivery of the share transfer form and share certificates to A; however, Clarke LJ's judgment cannot be reconciled with Browne-Wilkinson LJ's observation in *Mascall* that the doctrine operates only where A does not require a court order to complete his title.[78] This is a clear indication that delivery is essential, since otherwise A would require a court to compel B to give up these documents to enable A to complete his title.

Consider next the majority's reasoning based on the principle of benevolent construction. It is of course highly doubtful whether even a liberal interpretation of Pennington's

[73] The leading judgment was given by Arden LJ, with Schiemann LJ concurring.
[74] See, eg, *Pennington v Waine* (n 31) [63], [77].
[75] ibid [67].
[76] ibid [81].
[77] ibid.
[78] See main text from n 35 above.

words could be understood as constituting himself as agent for Harold. For an agency relationship to arise, Pennington must have consented to act as Harold's agent, or Harold must have conferred authority on Pennington to so act;[79] however, neither can be deduced from Pennington's words. But even if we assume that such a construction can be justified, this reasoning has nothing to do whatsoever with the rule in *Re Rose*. Although in *Pennington* Arden LJ suggested that the case of *T Choithram International SA v Pagarani*[80]—from which the principle of benevolent construction originates—was an example of a court 'utilising the constructive trust' to mitigate the rigours of the principle that equity will not assist a volunteer,[81] this is misleading. The principle of benevolent construction provides for a liberal *interpretation* of a donor's words in order to reach the conclusion that a trust was in fact *declared* by the donor. In other words, an application of the principle leads to the enforcement of an *express* trust, which responds to the donor's unilateral intention. Applying this to the facts in *Pennington*, the only way in which that principle could have applied was if Pennington's words were interpreted as being an express self-declaration of trust on behalf of Ada, constituting Ada as trustee of the shares for Harold's benefit. This is wholly different from an application of the rule in *Re Rose*, which imposes constructive trusts which do not respond solely to a donor's unilateral intention, but also to his acts of doing everything in his power to effectuate a transfer of property.[82]

The majority's main reasoning based on unconscionability requires a careful analysis, because it is this reasoning which is often taken to provide an alternative inroad to the rule in *Re Rose*. The first point to be made is that, strictly speaking, the Court of Appeal's judgment provides no indication that the unconscionability criterion has anything to do with the rule in *Re Rose*. A major factor which led Arden LJ to apply the unconscionability criterion was the 'policy considerations [which] are evident in *Choithram*';[83] and as noted above,[84] *Choithram* was not a case concerned with the rule in *Re Rose*. Indeed, Arden LJ also recognised that the rule in *Re Rose* does not dispense with the requirement of delivery of the relevant documents to the donee.[85] But even if the trust which arose in Harold's favour was explained as an application of the rule in *Re Rose* with concession being given for the non-delivery of the essential documents, it would fail to explain another aspect of the case. The company's articles of association contained certain pre-emption clauses, with the effect that Ada's shares could not be transferred to Harold without the shares being first offered to the members of the company.[86] Those pre-emption clauses are analogous to third parties having positive discretion[87] insofar as further acts by Ada were necessary before Harold would be put in a position to complete his legal title. The fact that a trust arose in Harold's favour despite Ada's (as well as Pennington's and Harold's) ignorance of

[79] Peter G Watts, *Bowstead and Reynolds on Agency*, 20th edn (London, Sweet & Maxwell, 2016) [2-033].

[80] *T Choithram International SA v Pagarani* [2001] 1 WLR 1 (PC).

[81] *Pennington v Waine* (n 31) [59].

[82] It is curious also to note that although the principle of benevolent construction was not the majority's primary justification of the result reached, Jacob J in *Hurst v Crampton Bros* (n 34) [10]–[11]—the next stage of the *Pennington* litigation—cited this reasoning as the proper basis for the decision in *Pennington v Waine* (n 31).

[83] *Pennington v Waine* (n 31) [63].

[84] See main text from n 80 above.

[85] *Pennington v Waine* (n 31) [66].

[86] ibid [6].

[87] Discussed in S 9.1.1.1. above.

the pre-emption clauses[88] indicates that that trust did not arise through an application of the rule in *Re Rose*.

This analysis leaves us with the question: by virtue of what doctrine did the unconscionability criterion apply to trigger that trust? On Arden LJ's express view, that criterion is to be applied directly: '[t]here can be no comprehensive list of factors which makes it unconscionable for the donor to change his or her mind: it must depend on the court's evaluation of all the relevant considerations.'[89] Such an approach is not only undesirable because it provides courts with unfettered discretion as to whether an incomplete transfer should take effect in equity;[90] it also directly contradicts earlier decisions of highest authority which expressly disapprove the exercise of judicial discretion in relation to the imposition of remedies.[91] One such case is *Royal Brunei Airlines Sdn Bhd v Tan*,[92] where Lord Nicholls said:

> It must be recognised ... that unconscionable is not a word in everyday use by non-lawyers. If it is to be used in [a particular] context, and if it is to be the touchstone for liability ..., it is essential to be clear on what, in this context, unconscionable means. If unconscionable means no more than dishonesty, then dishonesty is the preferable label. If unconscionable means something different, it must be said that it is not clear what that something different is. Either way, therefore, the term is better avoided ...[93]

On another view, which is to be preferred, Arden LJ can be understood as applying the doctrine of proprietary estoppel. This was certainly Briggs J's view in *Curtis v Pulbrook*,[94] where he observed that '[o]n its facts, *Pennington v Waine* appears to have been an example of a sufficient detrimental reliance by the donee, who had agreed to become a director of the subject company upon an assumption that he had received an effective gift of qualifying shares in it'. Unconscionability is not a free-standing element of a cause of action in proprietary estoppel, but is a conclusion which may be drawn when the specific requirements of that doctrine have been fulfilled.[95] From this perspective, the factors which led Arden LJ to her conclusion become clear. Ada had 'told Harold about the gift'[96] and 'her agent [Pennington] also told Harold that he need take no action';[97] these facts amounted to a promise or assurance by Ada that her shares would be transferred to Harold. Because Harold had 'agreed to become a director of the Company [on 1 September] without limit of time, which he could not do without shares being transferred to him',[98] Harold had acted in reliance on Ada's promise.[99] Since it was clear from Pennington's words, and

[88] *Pennington v Waine* (n 31) [7].

[89] ibid [64].

[90] See Margaret Halliwell, 'Perfecting Imperfect Gifts and Trusts: Have We Reached the End of the Chancellor's Foot?' [2003] *Conveyancer and Property Lawyer* 192, 193; Hilary Delany and Desmond Ryan, 'Unconscionability: A Unifying Theme in Equity' [2008] *Conveyancer and Property Lawyer* 401, 433.

[91] And, in specific relation to proprietary remedies, see Chapter 11, S 11.3.1.

[92] *Royal Brunei Airlines Sdn Bhd v Tan* [1995] 2 AC 378 (PC) 392.

[93] See too *Garcia v National Australia Bank Ltd* [1998] HCA 48 [34]; *Australian Competition and Consumer Commission v CG Berbatis* [2003] HCA 18 [43].

[94] *Curtis v Pulbrook* [2011] EWHC 167 (Ch), [2011] 1 BCLC 638 [43]. This analysis 'in effect [regards *Pennington*] as an application of the doctrine of proprietary estoppel': *Hayton and Mitchell* (n 115) [2-116].

[95] Ben McFarlane, *The Law of Proprietary Estoppel* (Oxford, OUP, 2014) [5-60]. See Chapter 7, S 7.1.

[96] *Pennington v Waine* (n 31) [64].

[97] ibid. In a different passage, Arden LJ emphasised that 'Harold was informed of [the gift]' and therefore 'it would have been unconscionable for Ada to recall the gift': ibid [66].

[98] ibid [64].

[99] *cf* Delany and Ryan, 'Unconscionability' (n 90) 433 and Abigail Doggett, 'Explaining *Re Rose*: The Search Goes On?' (2003) 62 *CLJ* 263, 263, 266 who suggest that Harold had not suffered any detrimental reliance. In view of Arden LJ's express finding on this point, these commentators' views must be wrong.

obvious to Harold's knowledge, that the transfer of shares was to enable him to become a director, Ada (through Pennington) breached her primary duty to ensure the reliability of her induced assumptions when those shares were not yet transferred to Harold within two months of Harold's appointment as director—that is, by 30 October[100]—this period being prescribed by the then operative Companies Act 1985, s 291.[101] The constructive trust can therefore be understood as being imposed to compensate Harold for the detriment he suffered as a result of Ada's breach, with the effect of the trust being backdated to the date of the breach.[102] This explains why Arden LJ emphasised that Harold 'could not [continue as director] without shares being transferred to him'; and that 'if Ada had changed her mind on (say) 10 November … the court could properly have concluded that it was too late for her to do this'.[103]

In summary, therefore, the case of *Pennington* is best viewed as having no impact on the rule in *Re Rose*. In particular, it does not stand as authority for the proposition that unconscionability is a criterion for an application of that doctrine.

9.2. The Trust Response

It is undoubtedly the case that a trust arises to bind the property in B's hands once the above-mentioned requirements are fulfilled.[104] Two questions arise for consideration: what is the nature of the trust, and is the trust response in line with the perceived effects of the rule in *Re Rose*?

9.2.1. Nature of the Trust

Although it is commonly said that the trust which arises through an application of the rule in *Re Rose* is constructive in nature,[105] the cases often simply hold that B is a trustee for A's benefit without stating the nature of the trust. Nevertheless, it is clear that the trust is best understood as a constructive trust.

In the first place, there is no doubt that it cannot be a resulting trust. B's intention is often that A should take B's property absolutely, and this intention is inconsistent with resulting trusts which arise when the transferor does not intend the recipient of the property to take the beneficial interest in the transferred property. Thus, in the context of the rule in *Re Rose*, there is 'not a transfer which, when perfected by registration, would give rise to a resulting trust.'[106]

[100] *Pennington v Waine* (n 31) [7].

[101] Subsection (1) of the 1985 Act provided that: 'It is the duty of every director who is by the company's articles required to hold a specified share qualification, and who is not already qualified, to obtain his qualification within 2 months after his appointment'; and subsection (3) provided that: 'The office of director of a company is vacated if the director does not within 2 months from the date of his appointment … obtain the qualification'.

[102] See Chapter 7 in general for a discussion of how the concepts of breach, compensation, and backdating relate to proprietary estoppel.

[103] *Pennington v Waine* (n 31) [64].

[104] See, eg, *Re Rose 1952* (n 1) 511, 518; *Zeital v Kaye* (n 24) [40].

[105] See, eg, *Snell's Equity* (n 72) [22-047].

[106] *Re Rose 1949* (n 2) 88.

The trust is also not an express trust. An express trust requires the settlor to intend to create a trust, and such intention is lacking in cases which reflect the rule in *Re Rose* where the intention is one of making an immediate transfer.[107] As Jessel MR said in *Richards v Delbridge*,[108] 'for a man to make himself a trustee there must be an expression of intention to become a trustee, whereas words of present gift show an intention to give property over to another, and not retain it in the donor's own hands for any purpose'. An express trust analysis also cannot account for cases such as *Mascall v Mascall* which involve land, where compliance with the necessary formality requirement[109] for creating a trust concerning land is lacking.

Instead, analysing the trust which arises through an application of the rule in *Re Rose* as a constructive trust allows the doctrine to be reconciled with Turner LJ's statement in *Milroy v Lord*[110] that '[i]f [a settlement] is intended to take effect by transfer, the Court will not hold the intended transfer to operate as a declaration of trust, for then every imperfect instrument would be made effectual by being converted into a perfect trust.' Although a gift may not be converted 'to a purpose wholly different from that which was intended to be effected by it, and … creating a perfect [express] trust out of an imperfect transaction',[111] it does not violate the autonomy of the donor[112] to giving effect to the transfer by way of a constructive trust through an application of the rule in *Re Rose*.[113] Although the intention to create a trust which is necessary to create an express trust is lacking, this does not prevent a constructive trust from arising in response to B's intention to make an immediate transfer coupled with B doing all that is necessary to effectuate that transfer and granting A the power to perfect the transfer. It is not inconsistent that B's intention may be relevant *either* to the creation of an express trust *or* to the imposition of a constructive trust, since they feature as an element among the triggering events in different ways.[114]

9.2.2. Effects of the Trust

Where the rule in *Re Rose* applies, the following effects ensue. Where B intends to make a gift to A, B holds the property on a constructive trust in A's favour; where B intends to give the property to X to hold on trust for A, the constructive trust compels B to hold the property on trust for A.[115]

Since it is a requirement for the doctrine to apply that A has the relevant documents—and therefore the power—to complete the transfer without being impeded by B, it is normally unnecessary for A to seek an order of a court to compel B to transfer the legal title

[107] *cf* Simon Gardner, *An Introduction to the Law of Trusts*, Clarendon Law Series, 3rd edn (Oxford, OUP, 2011) 70.
[108] *Richards v Delbridge* (1874) LR 18 Eq 11, 14.
[109] Law of Property Act 1925, s 53(1)(b).
[110] *Milroy v Lord* (n 16) 4 De GF & J 274–75, 45 ER 1189–90.
[111] ibid 4 De GF & J 275, 45 ER 1190.
[112] Far from it, it in fact enhances his autonomy: see main text to and following n 173 below.
[113] See, eg, *Re Rose 1952* (n 1) 510.
[114] 'There is a fine but important distinction between [positive] intent conceived as creative of rights [for express trusts] … and [positive] intent conceived as a fact which, along with others, calls for the creation of rights [through a constructive trust]': Peter Birks, *An Introduction to the Law of Restitution*, revised edn (Oxford, OUP, 1989) 65.
[115] Ben McFarlane and Charles Mitchell, *Hayton and Mitchell: Text, Cases and Materials on the Law of Trusts and Equitable Remedies*, 14th edn (London, Sweet & Maxwell, 2015) [2-031].

of the property to A.[116] But to acknowledge that B holds the property on constructive trust for A has other consequences. For instance, B must account to A for profits obtained from being the legal title holder of the property, such as dividends[117] or rental income, while the constructive trust is on foot. It also appears that B may not strive to defeat A's interest in any way. For example, if the company directors seek further information from B in order to come to a decision whether it is in the company's best interest to register A's title to certain shares,[118] B cannot act unreasonably so as to defeat the gift. If A loses the share certificates, B may also be obligated to request for a duplicate copy, since such duplicates are normally only provided to registered shareholders.[119]

As Maitland explained, 'the giver means to get rid of his rights, [in contrast] the man who is intending to make himself a trustee intends to retain his rights but to come under an onerous obligation'.[120] Since B intends to give, and not to come under an onerous obligation, the constructive trust which is imposed on B is simply a bare trust.[121] Thus, while the constructive trust is on foot, B does not owe A any active duties, and need not comply with any other direction except hold the property to A's order and avoid interfering with A's beneficial interest.[122]

9.2.2.1. Shares

Particular questions have arisen concerning the imposition of a constructive trust in specific relation to attempted transfers of certificated shares, which require addressing.

It has been questioned whether the fact that a constructive trust arises may in effect force the company directors to grant A registration.[123] The answer to this is emphatically 'no'. Although shares are properties which are free to be transferred and alienated, their existence is subject to a statutory contract between shareholder and company.[124] If according to the terms of the company's articles of association its directors may legitimately refuse to register a transfer, then their discretion is not circumvented where an existing shareholder, B, does all he can to transfer shares to A, even though a constructive trust arises as between B and A.

What then happens if, after B fulfils all the requirements for the rule in *Re Rose* to apply, the company directors refuse to register A as the new owner of the shares? *Snell's Equity* suggests that this would not negate the efficacy of a gift.[125] It cites *Re Fry* for this proposition;

[116] An exceptional case would be where the authority or body to which A sends the relevant documents in order to complete his title erroneously returns those documents to B, as happened in *Mascall v Mascall* (n 17).

[117] *Re Rose 1952* (n 1) 507.

[118] Garton, 'The Role of the Trust Mechanism' (n 30) 369.

[119] *Zeital v Kaye* (n 24) [43].

[120] FW Maitland, *Equity: A Course of Lectures* (Cambridge, CUP, 1936) 73.

[121] *Snell's Equity* (n 72) [24-008].

[122] In this respect, B is in a similar position to an intended trustee of an express trust who has knowledge of the trust but does not or is yet to consent to acting as trustee: see Ying Khai Liew and Charles Mitchell, 'The Creation of Express Trusts' (forthcoming 2018). Hence, B is under a duty not to disburse the property to anyone other than A, breach of which will render him liable to a claim for substitutive performance, and a duty to take reasonable care of the property, breach of which will render him liable to a reparation claim.

[123] Edelman, 'Two Fundamental Questions' (n 67) 78.

[124] See the Companies Act 2006, s 112.

[125] *Snell's Equity* (n 72) [24-006] fn 31. See too David Hayton, Paul Matthews and Charles Mitchell, *Underhill and Hayton: Law Relating to Trusts and Trustees*, 19th edn (London, LexisNexis Butterworths, 2016) [8.8].

and at the relevant passage of that judgment it refers to,[126] Romer J acknowledged the rule that the validity and effect of an assignment between assignor and assignee of an equitable interest or debt is not affected by the absence of notice to the trustee or debtor.[127] It may be observed that the comparison is not exact: while equitable interests and debts can properly be called choses in action, shares 'form a separate sub-species of chose in action with its own rules.'[128] Moreover, transfers of equitable interests and debts are assignments properly so-called, while the transfer of shares 'resembles more a novation under which the transferee is substituted for the transferor as member of the company, both as regards his rights and his obligations as a shareholder.'[129]

The crucial question therefore is: if the intended transfer from B to A of the legal title to shares cannot be completed due to the directors refusing registration, would the fact that the constructive trust remains afoot force B to accept the onerous—and potentially perpetual—office of trusteeship which he never expressly intended to accept? It seems not. Since a trust will not fail for want of a trustee, it would be entirely appropriate for B (or a court, upon B's or A's application) to find someone else of whom the directors approve, for that person to hold on trust for A.

Another question relates to voting rights of shareholders. It has been suggested that, pending registration of the transfer, A might be able to compel B to vote according to A's interest.[130] Prima facie, this is unconcerning: after all, one aim of the rule in *Re Rose* is to give effect to B's original intention to divest himself of property,[131] so B is deemed not to retain any rights in relation to the shares. However, it has been suggested that A might exert an adverse influence on the company by going further and circumventing the company directors' discretion to refuse to register the transfer by forcing B to vote in a manner which does A's bidding.[132] But this concern is overstated. It is worth reiterating that B who remains the legal title holder of shares—whose name remains on the company register—has a duty to vote in a manner which is 'bona fide for the benefit of the company as a whole.'[133] Since equity follows the law, A cannot compel B to exercise his legal right to the shares in a manner inconsistent with B's attendant duties and obligations as a legal member of the company.

Finally, what are the consequences where, for one reason or other, A holds on to the transfer documents and perpetually refuses to register his title? This did in fact occur in *Hurst v Crampton Bros (Coopers) Ltd*,[134] where A had no intention of seeking registration in order to avoid triggering a pre-emption clause overlooked by B. A's refusal to register his title may perpetuate a trust despite the fact that B never expressly intended to create one.

[126] *Re Fry* (n 26) 317.

[127] Citing as authorities: *Ellison v Ellison* (1802) 6 Ves Jr 656, 31 ER 1243; *Donaldson v Donaldson* (n 10); and *Holt v Heatherfield Trust Ltd* [1942] 2 KB 1 (KBD) 4.

[128] *Macmillan Inc v Bishopsgate Investment Trust plc (No. 3)* [1995] 1 WLR 978 (Ch) 991.

[129] *Guest on the Law of Assignment* (n 17) [1-38]. For a more in-depth discussion of the difference between assignment and novation, see *Guest on the Law of Assignment* (n 17) [1-69]–[1-72].

[130] Edelman, 'Two Fundamental Questions' (n 67) 78.

[131] See S 9.1.3.1.

[132] Garton, 'The Role of the Trust Mechanism' (n 30) 370–71.

[133] *Allen v Gold Reefs of West Africa Ltd* [1900] 1 Ch 656 (CA) 671.

[134] *Hurst v Crampton Bros* (n 34) [11].

This may seem counterintuitive, since the rule in *Re Rose* may, on one view,[135] be understood as a stop-gap measure, granting A an equitable interest *pending* registration.[136] It may be that B intends for the gift to A to be conditional upon the transfer being registered within a reasonable time; or it may be that A expressly disclaims the gift; but if neither of these occur, it appears legitimate for A to refuse to seek registration. Even though B would not have expressly intend to create a trust, the effect of the imposition of a constructive trust is that A gains rights as a beneficiary under that trust. It is therefore within A's rights to keep the trust afoot, although as the owner of merely an equitable right A risks 'a better title to the subject-matter of the gift to arise in a third person.'[137] It remains open to B to transfer his shares to another person who is willing to act as trustee if B does not wish to so act.

9.3. Rationale

In *Kekewich v Manning*,[138] Knight Bruce LJ identified two competing policy considerations which arise in relation to attempted gratuitous transfers. On the one hand, 'a person *sui juris*, acting freely, fairly and with sufficient knowledge, ought to have and has it in his power to make, in a binding and effectual manner, a voluntary gift of any part of his property'; on the other hand, 'a gratuitously expressed intention, a promise merely voluntary, or, to use a familiar phrase, *nudum pactum*, does not (the matter resting there) bind legally or equitably.' Because the rule in *Re Rose* is concerned with B's unilateral actions of transferring his own property to a volunteer,[139] an explanation of the rationale underlying that doctrine must provide a satisfactory middle ground between these two policy considerations. Unfortunately, the current state of understanding reflects the observation that 'the existing rules about the circumstances when equity will and will not perfect an apparently imperfect gift … serve [no] clearly identifiable or rational policy objective.'[140]

This section will observe a number of attempts which have been made to rationalise the rule in *Re Rose* and their shortcomings. It then proposes a new way of rationalising the doctrine.

9.3.1. Difficulties with the Present Understanding

A number of attempts have been made to explain the rule in *Re Rose*, but on reflection they fail to provide a proper explanation of the doctrine.

[135] This is certainly the use to which the doctrine was put in the seminal cases of *Re Rose 1949* (n 2) and *Re Rose 1952* (n 1).

[136] See, eg, *Zeital v Kaye* (n 24) [43]; *Corin v Patton* (1990) 169 CLR 540, 583; Doggett, 'Explaining *Re Rose*' (n 99) 265; Garton, 'The Role of the Trust Mechanism' (n 30) 369.

[137] *Re Griffin* (n 7) 411.

[138] *Kekewich v Manning* (1851) 1 De GM & G 176, 188; 42 ER 519, 524.

[139] Contrast proprietary estoppel, where A must also detrimentally rely on B's promise to transfer an interest in property to A.

[140] *Curtis v Pulbrook* (n 94) [47].

In *Hayton and Mitchell*, it is suggested that the idea underlying the doctrine 'may be that, if, as a result of [B]'s actions, [A] obtains a power, through her own actions, to acquire the relevant property, then a trust arises.'[141] This is certainly an accurate description of an aspect of equity which can be detected in cases which predate *Re Rose 1949 and Re Rose 1952* such as *Fortescue v Barnett*[142] and *Donaldson v Donaldson*,[143] and re-emphasised in *Mascall v Mascall*,[144] that a volunteer (A) who does not require equity's assistance obtains a right against B to complete A's title. But this does not explain why the constructive trust arises when it does: it does not necessarily follow from that aspect of equity that a trust must arise, and only arise, when A has it in his power to complete his title. The explanation for why this is so remains outstanding.

Another suggestion by Jonathan Garton is based on the idea of unconscionability propounded in *Pennington v Waine*. It has been seen that unconscionability is inapt to function as a free-standing criterion for equity's intervention,[145] and Garton largely agrees.[146] However, he goes on to suggest another way in which unconscionability can be used as the underlying basis for the doctrine. Relying on Lord Browne-Wilkinson's statement in *Westdeutsche Landesbank Girozentrale v Islington LBC*[147] that 'the law imposes on [a legal owner a constructive trust] by reason of his unconscionable conduct', Garton suggests:[148]

> by definition, if the circumstances in which the formalities are not completed make it unconscionable for equity to deny the gift, then the conscience of [B] will be affected. On this basis it is entirely acceptable that a constructive trust, along with its attendant liabilities, arises.

He further writes that the rule in *Re Rose* can be explained on the basis that B has 'relinquished the right to stop the legal transfer, and any attempt to prevent its completion would therefore have been unconscionable.'[149] The difficulty, however, is that 'unconscionability' is a conclusion, not a reason for equity's intervention.[150] Surely, a prior logic underlies the imposition of the constructive trust in order for it to be said that any later intervention by B would be unconscionable. It is that prior logic, and not the element of unconscionability, which explains the ambit of, and limits to, the rule in *Re Rose*.

A third suggestion can be gleaned from *Snell's Equity*. Writing about the constructive trust arising by way of the rule in *Re Rose*, it observes: '[i]t gives effect to the fact that [A] is already entitled in equity to seek a specific remedy requiring [B] to fulfil the remaining steps necessary to complete the transfer of the legal title in the property to themselves.'[151] In a footnote,[152] it makes reference to specifically enforceable contracts of sale.[153] This suggests

[141] *Hayton and Mitchell* (n 115) [2-037]. This suggestion is based on Browne-Wilkinson LJ's statement in *Mascall v Mascall* (n 17) 126 that if 'the donee has under his control everything necessary to constitute his title completely without any further assistance from the donor, the donee needs no distance form equity and the gift is complete.'

[142] See main text following n 4 above.

[143] See main text following n 10 above.

[144] See main text following n 35 above.

[145] See discussion in S 9.1.4.

[146] Garton, 'The Role of the Trust Mechanism' (n 30) 373.

[147] *Westdeutsche Landesbank Girozentrale v Islington LBC* [1996] AC 669 (HL) 705.

[148] Garton, 'The Role of the Trust Mechanism' (n 30) 374.

[149] ibid.

[150] This was discussed in the context of the doctrine in *Rochefoucauld v Boustead* in Chapter 4, S 4.4.2.4.

[151] *Snell's Equity* (n 72) [24-008].

[152] ibid [23-008] fn 41.

[153] This doctrine was examined in Chapter 8.

that the same rationale underlies both that doctrine and the rule in *Re Rose*. However, there are clear differences. The constructive trust which arises in relation to specifically enforceable contracts of sale is based on a contract which both B and A have voluntarily entered into, each agreeing to undertake certain obligations in relation to the transfer of property from B to A. In contrast, the rule in *Re Rose* relates to B's unilateral actions: B does not contractually agree to do anything. Furthermore, A neither provides consideration nor detrimentally relies on a promise by B: the gift is entirely voluntary.[154] It is therefore unsatisfactory to rely on specifically enforceable contracts of sale to explain the rationale for the rule in *Re Rose*.

Finally, Gbolahan Elias has written that the rule in *Re Rose* advances the 'perfection aim':[155] it 'compel[s] the defendant to perfect his choice to benefit the plaintiff even if that choice was made gratuitously and without the plaintiff's participation.'[156] It is certainly true that the rule in *Re Rose* can be understood in terms of perfecting B's intention to effectuate a transfer to A. The difficulty, however, is that this does not provide a robust enough rationale for the doctrine. Elias writes that '[a] defendant who has done [all that lies in his power to complete the gift] deserves what he gets [i.e. the imposition of a constructive trust]';[157] but why is this so? A mere promise is certainly not binding, and it remains unclear what it is about A's actions which entail that he ought to be bound. The difficulty is compounded by the fact that the 'perfection aim' is taken to be the basis both of the rule in *Re Rose* and the QI doctrines within the non-contract-based, bilateral events category of constructive trusts. Acting on one's own intention to transfer property is substantively different from the case where one party relies on another's promise to hold on trust. Elias's thesis does not substantively explain what that difference is.

9.3.2. A Counterpart to Resulting Trusts

It is submitted that the best explanation for the rule in *Re Rose* is to understand this doctrine as being a counterpart to resulting trusts, both doctrines being two sides of the same coin.

9.3.2.1. Resulting Trusts

It is necessary to begin with the rationale for resulting trusts on which the present discussion is based. While there is as yet no universally accepted rationale for why resulting trusts arise, Simon Gardner has provided one attractive and intuitively coherent explanation. He writes:[158]

> The transferee of some property should hold it on trust for the transferor, aside from the case where the transferor so stipulates, whenever the transferor has not demonstrably chosen to give his property away and succeeded in doing so. This idea is in turn justified by the insight that whenever

[154] *Milroy v Lord* (n 16) 4 De GF & J 273, 45 ER 1189: 'voluntary as the instrument was, it [did not] contain a contract specifically enforceable against [B]'.

[155] For an explanation of the 'perfection aim', see Chapter 4, S 4.3.1.

[156] Gbolahan Elias, *Explaining Constructive Trusts* (Oxford, OUP, 1990) 49.

[157] ibid.

[158] Gardner, *Law of Trusts* (n 107) 296.

> someone has not demonstrably chosen to give his property away and succeeded in doing so, he should remain its owner ... [This latter insight] is rooted in a liberal vision of the institution of property. To give an owner maximal freedom in the disposition of his assets, it is necessary maximally to treat them as for him alone to dispose of ... [This insight] operates ... where the legal title has effectively been transferred; but its previous owner has neither (intentionally and successfully) conferred beneficial ownership on the transferee nor (likewise) alienated it in some other direction. The logic of the insight is that in such a situation the previous owner should be treated as himself retaining beneficial ownership. The desideratum is achieved in the face of the effective transfer, by ruling that the transferee of the legal title holds it on trust for the previous owner.

Gardner's explanation features three key points. First, equity is seen here to be concerned with a unilateral event—the intention of a property owner; equity is not concerned with the intentions or actions of anyone else. Secondly, it emphasises equity's focus on substance rather than form. That is to say, equity gives effect to the substance of a property owner's intention without being distracted or influenced by the location of the property's legal title. Thirdly, it indicates that resulting trusts are concerned with the freedom of property owners to determine what is to be done with their property. They respond to those owners' intentions, but in a negative sense. As Robert Chambers writes, '[i]t is almost always preferable to give effect to the parties' intentions, but when that is impossible, the resulting trust fulfils the ... function of ensuring that unintended benefits are returned.'[159]

9.3.2.2. The Rule in Re Rose

The flipside of these very same ideas are at play in relation to the rule in *Re Rose*. Adapting Gardner's explanation of resulting trusts, it can be said in relation to the rule in *Re Rose* that B *should* hold property on trust for A, aside from the case where B stipulates otherwise, whenever B *has* demonstrably chosen to give the property away and, in substance, succeeded in doing so—that is, by successfully doing everything in his power to effectuate the transfer and giving A the power to complete the transfer. This can be explained on the basis that whenever someone *has* demonstrably chosen to give his property away and succeeded in doing so, the transferee should be its owner. This, too, advances the liberal vision of the institution of property, giving an owner maximal freedom in the disposition of his assets, maximally treating them as for him alone to dispose of. Thus, where the legal title has not been effectively transferred, but the original owner has intentionally effectuated the transfer, the transferee should be treated as its beneficial owner.

This explanation of the rule in *Re Rose* also reflects the same three key points seen in relation to resulting trusts. First, it has been observed that B's unilateral actions are sufficient to give rise to this doctrine: it reflects the fact that 'the perfection of a gift in equity, or the complete constitution of a trust, must depend solely on the act and will of the donor or settlor.'[160] So, in *Re Rose 1949*, the attempted transfer was held to be effective in equity once B had fulfilled all the requirements for the doctrine to apply because '[t]he position was that, *so far as [B] was concerned*, they had been so transferred.'[161]

Secondly, the doctrine is concerned with the substance of B's intention, and not with form, that is, the location of the legal title. As Mason CJ and McHugh J observed of the

[159] Chambers (n 169) 286. See also *Underhill and Hayton* (n 125) [22.12].
[160] Luxton, 'In Search of Perfection' (n 61) 73.
[161] *Re Rose 1949* (n 2) 90 (emphasis added).

doctrine in *Corin v Patton*,[162] 'it gives effect to the clear intention and actions of the donor rather than insisting upon strict compliance with legal forms. It is a reflection of the maxim "equity looks to the intent rather than the form"'. Inasmuch as resulting trusts relate to cases where legal title to property is transferred in circumstances where there is no indication that the transferor intends for the transferee to benefit from the property, the rule in *Re Rose* arises in relation to cases where B attempts to but does not succeed in transferring legal title to his property but it is clear that B intends for A to benefit from the property. The substance of the transferor's intention is mutually exclusive in these doctrines: either he intends the transferee to benefit from the property or he does not.

Finally, the doctrine is intention-based: it is concerned with B's freedom to determine what is to happen with his own property. B seldom does all that is necessary to effectuate a transfer of property to another unless he intends an immediate transfer to A, and the rule in *Re Rose* applies immediately B completes the necessary acts in order to give effect to such an intention unless there is evidence of a contrary intention on the facts of the case.

It is also notable that this explanation helpfully draws a middle ground between the two competing policy considerations which arise in relation to attempted gratuitous transfers, which were observed earlier.[163] While the doctrine recognises and advances a property owner's freedom to make a voluntary gift of his property, his intention to make an immediate transfer of property is by itself insufficient to give rise to a constructive trust under the doctrine. Otherwise, that freedom afforded to a property owner will work against him by forcing him to hold his property on trust for another despite never expressly intending to do so, and without any other indication that he wished completely to divest himself of the property. Instead, his intention to make an immediate transfer will be given effect only where that intention is coupled with actions which are consistent with such an intention, that is, when he does everything necessary to effectuate such a transfer, giving A the power to complete the transfer.

9.3.3. Consistency and Finality

It remains to be asked *why* an intention to make an immediate transfer coupled with the necessary acts ought to result in B holding the property on constructive trust for A. Relatedly, why is B *deemed* to intend to make an immediate transfer of property when he completes the necessary acts unless a contrary intention is shown; and why is B no longer at liberty to change his mind once the necessary acts are complete? The answer to these questions can be found in the related ideas of consistency and finality.

First, the rule in *Re Rose* reflects the idea that one's actions is taken to be consistent with his intentions, unless a contrary intention is shown. It is obvious that acting consistently with one's intentions is a moral virtue: as the Gospel of Matthew says, '[l]et your "Yes" be "Yes" and your "No", "No"'.[164] This is entirely consistent with equity's practice of giving effect to intention or substance rather than form, such intention or substance being

[162] *Corin v Patton* (n 136) 558.
[163] See main text following n 138 above.
[164] Matthew 5:37 (NKJV).

determined objectively.[165] Since a secret or subjective intention has no effect at law,[166] one's intention must be determined from his words and/or actions.[167] Where express words are used, these ought normally to be given effect: hence, if B does everything necessary to effectuate a transfer to A but expressly states that he does not intend an immediate transfer, the rule in *Re Rose* will not apply. But where such express words are lacking, then B's intention is to be determined from his actions. Doing everything within B's power to effectuate a transfer of property to A, putting it in A's power to complete his title and out of B's power to interfere, is the clearest possible act which indicates an intention to make an immediate transfer of the property to A. This is why Mason CJ and McHugh J commented in *Corin v Patton*:[168]

> The rationale for refusing to complete an incomplete gift is that [B] should not be compelled to make a gift, the decision to give being a personal one for [B] to make. However, that rationale cannot justify continued refusal to recognize any interest in [A] after the point when [B] has done all that is necessary to be done on his part to complete the gift, especially when the instrument of transfer has been delivered to [A]. Just as a manifestation of intention plus sufficient acts of delivery are enough to complete a gift of chattels at common law, so should the doing of all necessary acts by [B] be sufficient to complete a gift in equity. The need for compliance with subsequent procedures such as registration, procedures which [A] is able to satisfy, should not permit [B] to resile from the gift.

Secondly, the rule in *Re Rose* reflects the idea of finality: by completing the relevant acts, B is taken conclusively and irrevocably to intend to effectuate a transfer of property to A and to divest himself of it. Therefore, the doctrine gives effect to the transfer in equity despite the fact that A has not yet become the legal owner of the property.

There are a number of justifications for this. In the first place, it promotes legal and transactional certainty by providing 'a clearly ascertainable point in time at which it can be said that the gift was completed'.[169] This certainty avoids the potential of misleading A concerning B's intentions, thus allowing A the freedom to plan or act according to B's actions which objectively indicate an intention immediately and irrevocably to give property away to A.[170] The certainty is also beneficial to B, who would not be left 'to wait (potentially indefinitely) for an event (registration) beyond his power'.[171] Moreover, in *Hurst v Crampton Bros (Coopers) Lid*,[172] Jacob J observed: 'where a member [gives] a transferee a signed transfer form it [is] rational and businesslike to say that the member had transferred the share to the transferee. Whether the transferee was actually registered in the company's books [is] no longer the transferor's business. The share [is] no longer the transferor's in any meaningful business sense.' The certainty which the rule in *Re Rose* injects into commercial dealings is particularly vital for transactional efficacy.

165 See S 9.1.3.2.

166 See, eg, *Shah v Shah* [2010] EWCA Civ 1408, [2011] WTLR 519 [13].

167 Ying Khai Liew and Charles Mitchell, 'The Creation of Express Trusts' (forthcoming 2018).

168 *Corin v Patton* (n 136) 558.

169 *Pennington v Waine* (n 31) [62].

170 Hence the conclusion can be drawn that, by 'relinquish[ing] the right to stop the legal transfer, … any attempt to prevent its completion would therefore … [be] unconscionable': Garton, 'The Role of the Trust Mechanism' (n 30) 374.

171 Luxton, 'In Search of Perfection' (n 61) 73.

172 *Hurst v Crampton Bros* (n 34) [3].

Certainty aside, the element of finality also affirms B's autonomy, both negatively and positively. Negatively, it does not infringe the policy concerns that the law should ensure that 'donors do not by acting voluntarily act unwisely in a way that they may subsequently regret', or that donors should be permitted 'to change their minds at any time before [the transfer] becomes [complete].'[173] After all, B does not normally take all the necessary steps to effectuate the transfer without intending an immediate transfer to take place unless such a contrary intention is expressed. Therefore, it does not impede B's autonomy to deprive him of the ability to renege on the transfer if, for some reason outside B's control, registration of A's legal title is delayed. Positively, B's autonomy is respected when it is left to him and him alone to determine when his property is transferred. This is reflected in the rule in *Re Rose*, since the transfer is effective at the time B completes the relevant acts which are entirely within his control, as opposed to being dependent on matters outside B's control.

[173] *Pennington v Waine* (n 31) [62].

10

Gains Made In Breach of Fiduciary Duty

Where a fiduciary (B) holds a power on behalf of his principal (A), B comes under a fiduciary duty to exercise that power in what B perceives to be the best interest of A.[1] Where B makes an unauthorised personal gain in breach of his fiduciary duty towards A, the gain (or its traceable proceeds) may be subject to a constructive trust in favour of A. The concern in this chapter is with constructive trusts imposed *through an operation of the fiduciary doctrine*. It is necessary to say something about what the italicised words mean.

In many situations in which a trust is imposed to strip a fiduciary of profits made in breach of fiduciary duty, it is by no means clear that the breach of fiduciary duty is the operative reason for the trust's arising. For example, where a trustee, B, misappropriates trust assets and retains them in their original form, he commits a breach of trust and comes under a duty to restore the assets *in specie*. Where he retains their traceable proceeds, the beneficiary can either assert his equitable ownership of the proceeds or enforce an equitable lien on them to secure the restoration of the trust fund.[2] These are well-accepted remedies for breaches of trust. But if B commits the misappropriation in order to make an impermissible gain for himself, he might also be said to have breached his fiduciary duty. As *Hayton & Mitchell* explains:[3]

> In other words [B] breaches two duties when [he] takes trust property for [himself]. Confusingly, both duties are often described as 'fiduciary duties' ... [when in fact] [o]ne is a 'stewardship' duty to hold the trust property for the beneficiaries and deal with it only in an authorised way ... [T]he other is a duty to act in the beneficiaries' exclusive interest ...

Another set of examples can be seen in cases where B 'either receive[s] property from a third party for the account of [A] or receive[s] for himself that which he ought to have procured for [A]'.[4] Where B attempts to keep the property for himself, he may well do so in breach of his fiduciary duty towards A. However, it is by no means clear that the fiduciary doctrine governs whether a trust arises in these circumstances. B's 'liability to account [arises] from his receipt of [property] in circumstances which made him an accounting party. It [does]

[1] Lionel Smith, 'Fiduciary Relationships: Ensuring the Loyal Exercise of Judgment on Behalf of Another' (2014) 130 *LQR* 608; JE Penner, 'Distinguishing Fiduciary, Trust, and Accounting Relationships' (2014) 8 *Journal of Equity* 202, 203–06.

[2] *Foskett v McKeown* [2001] 1 AC 102 (HL) 130.

[3] Ben McFarlane and Charles Mitchell, *Hayton and Mitchell: Text, Cases and Materials on the Law of Trusts and Equitable Remedies*, 14th edn (London, Sweet & Maxwell, 2015) [12-051] fn 92.

[4] Roy Goode, 'Proprietary Liability for Secret Profits—A Reply' (2011) 127 *LQR* 493, 494.

not arise from any breach of duty, fiduciary or otherwise'.[5] So it is the 'circumstances which made [B] an accounting party' which dictate whether a trust arises. For instance, it is the parties' *contract* which dictates whether an agency relationship[6] compels the agent to hold any property received on A's account on trust. To cite another example, where the parties are in a pre-existing trust relationship, the fact that B receives such property on trust for A is owed to the *trust* relationship—and not the fiduciary relationship—between the parties. Yet another example is seen in cases relating to the doctrine in *Pallant v Morgan*, where a constructive trust arises in A's favour where B promises to hold property acquired from a third-party vendor on trust for A and A relies in such a way which provides an advantage to B in relation to the acquisition of that property. As discussed in Chapter 6,[7] it would be unnecessary—indeed, inaccurate—to explain the constructive trust as arising by virtue of the fiduciary doctrine.

In all these cases, B may or may not have breached his fiduciary duty; however, a trust always arises in relation to a gain in B's hands. In other words, the trust arises because the beneficiary has a 'proprietary base'[8] or a 'pre-existing proprietary right to the profits'.[9] Therefore, these cases are ill-suited for the inquiry pursued in this chapter, since we are here concerned with constructive trusts which are imposed by virtue of the fiduciary doctrine.

Instead, the inquiry is best pursued through examining cases where a constructive trust arises to strip an errant fiduciary of his gains in circumstances where the trust cannot be explained otherwise than through an application of the fiduciary doctrine. There are two categories of such cases. The first concerns B receiving a bribe or secret commission while acting as a fiduciary. Neither these gains nor the opportunity to obtain them can properly be said to belong to A at all: '[B] is not responsible for pursuing those opportunities on behalf of [A]'.[10] The second involves B making secret[11] profits by taking an opportunity which was not open to A to take.[12] Because A does not have a proprietary base or pre-existing proprietary right to the gain in these two categories of cases, the constructive trusts can only be explained as being imposed through an operation of the fiduciary doctrine.

10.1. Fiduciary Relationships: Some General Points

The archetypal fiduciary relationship is that which exists between a trustee and beneficiary.[13] It also arises in other relationships such as those between solicitor and client,

[5] *Paragon Finance plc v DB Thakerar & Co* [1999] 1 All ER 400 (CA) 416.

[6] Which, although normally gives rise to a fiduciary relationship (see *FHR European Ventures LLP v Cedar Capital Partners LLC* [2014] UKSC 45, [2015] AC 250 [13]–[14] and cases cited therein), does not necessarily do so: see, eg, Penner, 'Distinguishing' (n 1) 218. All turns on the parties' contract.

[7] Chapter 6, S 6.1.3.2.

[8] Peter Birks, *An Introduction to the Law of Restitution*, revised edn (Oxford, OUP, 1989) 388.

[9] Goode, 'Proprietary Liability for Secret Profits' (n 4).

[10] Robert Chambers, 'Constructive Trusts and Breach of Fiduciary Duty' [2013] *Conveyancer and Property Lawyer* 73, 78.

[11] This being taken to mean that B had not obtained informed consent from A pursuant to a 'full and frank disclosure of all material facts': *New Zealand Netherlands Society 'Oranje' Inc v Kuys* [1973] 1 WLR 1126 (PC) 1132.

[12] This category covers cases such as *Keech v Sandford* (1726) 2 Eq Cas Abr 741 and *Boardman v Phipps* [1967] 2 AC 46 (HL).

[13] See, eg, *Re West of England & South Wales District Bank, ex parte Dale & Co* (1879) 11 Ch D 772 (Ch) 778.

agent and principal, and director and company. Fiduciary duties are not confined to such established relationships, however, and could potentially arise whenever A and B are in a 'relationship of trust and confidence'. For instance, in *Murad v Al-Saraj*,[14] B was held to be a fiduciary for two sisters (As) in the context of a joint venture to acquire a hotel.

The classic definition of a fiduciary and the duties entailed can be found in Millett LJ's words in *Bristol & West BS v Mothew*:[15]

> A fiduciary is someone who has undertaken to act for or on behalf of another in a particular matter in circumstances which give rise to a relationship of trust and confidence. The distinguishing obligation of a fiduciary is the obligation of loyalty. The principal is entitled to the single-minded loyalty of his fiduciary. This core liability has several facets. A fiduciary must act in good faith; he must not make a profit out of his trust; he must not place himself in a position where his duty and his interest may conflict; he may not act for his own benefit or the benefit of a third person without the informed consent of his principal. This is not intended to be an exhaustive list, but it is sufficient to indicate the nature of fiduciary obligations.

For the purposes of the present discussion, it is unnecessary to explore whether Millett LJ's definition of a fiduciary fares well as a legal test for determining precisely when a fiduciary relationship arises,[16] whether fiduciaries do indeed owe a duty of 'loyalty',[17] the precise relationship between the 'no profit' and 'no conflict' rules,[18] or indeed the broader question of why fiduciary duties are imposed.[19] While these are fascinating issues on which commentators have written extensively, the present enquiry focuses on the remedial choices and decisions which courts are presented with when B makes a gain in breach of his fiduciary duty.

10.1.1. Voluntary

One point which bears emphasising is the voluntary nature of fiduciary duties: a fiduciary relationship arises only if B expressly or impliedly voluntarily undertakes to act as a fiduciary.[20] The duties must be 'freely accepted',[21] and a court will neither impose such duties

[14] *Murad v Al-Saraj* [2005] EWCA Civ 959, [2005] WTLR 1573.

[15] *Bristol & West Building Society v Mothew* [1998] Ch 1 (CA) 18.

[16] It probably does not: see discussion in David Hayton, Paul Matthews and Charles Mitchell, *Underhill and Hayton: Law Relating to Trusts and Trustees*, 19th edn (London, LexisNexis Butterworths, 2016) [27.14].

[17] They probably do not, the term 'loyalty' being shorthand for the constituent facets as enunciated by Millett LJ. See, eg, Matthew Conaglen, *Fiduciary Loyalty: Protecting the Due Performance of Non-Fiduciary Duties* (Oxford, Hart Publishing, 2010) Chapter 3; JE Penner 'Is Loyalty a Virtue, and Even If It Is, Does It Really Help Explain Fiduciary Liability?' in Andrew S Gold and Paul B Miller (eds) *Philosophical Foundations of Fiduciary Law* (Oxford, OUP, 2014); Penner, 'Distinguishing' (n 1) 206–08.

[18] See, eg, *Boardman v Phipps* (n 12) 123; *FHR* (n 6) [5]; Conaglen, *Fiduciary Loyalty* (n 17) 39–40, 113–25. *cf* Smith, 'Fiduciary Relationships' (n 1) 625ff.

[19] On which the literature abounds. See, eg, Paul B Miller, 'Justifying Fiduciary Duties' (2013) 58 *McGill Law Journal* 969; Tamar Frankel, 'Fiduciary Law' (1983) 71 *California Law Review* 795; Robert Flannigan, 'The Fiduciary Obligation' (1989) 9 *OJLS* 285; Matthew Harding, 'Trust and Fiduciary Law' (2013) 33 *OJLS* 81; Irit Samet, 'Guarding the Fiduciary's Conscience—A Justification of a Stringent Profit-Stripping Rule' (2008) 28 *OJLS* 763; Lionel Smith, 'Deterrence, Prophylaxis and Punishment in Fiduciary Obligations' (2013) 7 *Journal of Equity* 87; Smith, 'Fiduciary Relationships' (n 1); Penner, 'Distinguishing' (n 1).

[20] Charles Mitchell, Paul Mitchell, and Stephen Watterson, *Goff & Jones: The Law Of Unjust Enrichment*, 9th edn (London, Sweet & Maxwell, 2016) [38-14]; *Hayton and Mitchell* (n 3) [23-008]; Lionel D Smith, 'Constructive Fiduciaries?' in Peter Birks (ed), *Privacy and Loyalty* (Oxford, OUP, 1997) 263–65; Sir Peter Millett, 'Restitution and Constructive Trusts' in WR Cornish, Richard Nolan, Janet O'Sullivan et al (eds), *Restitution: Past, Present, and Future* (Oxford, Hart Publishing, 1998) 205.

[21] *Ross River Ltd v Waveley Commercial Ltd* [2013] EWCA Civ 910 [2014] 1 BCLC 545 [43].

retrospectively without a voluntary undertaking by B at the time of the relevant events,[22] nor imply that such duties arise simply from the fact that B is a trustee.[23] So, for instance, it is futile to argue that a fiduciary duty arises simply by virtue of the fact that a company (B) appoints subcontractors to do work for another company (A). B does not undertake to act in circumstances of trust and confidence, because it is 'an arms' length relationship between commercial parties, one of whom, with the knowledge and consent of the other, utilise[s] the services of a sub-contractor. Each of the parties [is] entitled to have regard to its own commercial interests in that situation.'[24]

10.1.2. Gain-Based, not Loss-Based

Where B breaches his fiduciary duty, this may result in B making a gain for himself, or in A suffering a loss. Despite a gain-based liability being commonly described as 'a claim for equitable compensation',[25] gain-based and loss-based claims are distinct.[26] '[T]he object of the equitable remedies of an account or the imposition of a constructive trust is to ensure that the defaulting fiduciary does not retain the profit; it is not to compensate the beneficiary for any loss. Accordingly comparison with the remedy in damages is unhelpful.'[27] This chapter concerns gains made by an errant fiduciary, since it is only in relation to gains that a constructive trust might arise in A's favour.

10.2. Categorising the Constructive Trust

Constructive trusts which are imposed through the fiduciary doctrine occupy a category of their own within the structure of the law of constructive trusts. This section establishes that they fall to be considered within the 'unilateral events' category of constructive trusts, being triggered by B's wrongdoing, with the result that B ever only takes a qualified interest in the gain.

10.2.1. 'Unilateral Events' Category

The first issue is to determine whether they fall within the 'bilateral events' or 'unilateral events' category. This requires an examination of the material events which constitute B as fiduciary for A.

[22] *Lonrho plc v Fayed (No. 2)* [1992] 1 WLR 1 (Ch).

[23] Penner, 'Distinguishing' (n 1) 214–16, 219–23.

[24] *Janus Capital Management LLC v Safeguard World International Ltd* [2016] EWHC 1355 (Ch) [247].

[25] *FHR* (n 6) [1]. See also *Sinclair Investments (UK) Ltd v Versailles Trade Finance Ltd (in administration)* [2011] EWCA Civ 347, [2012] Ch 453 [45]ff.

[26] *Barnsley v Noble* [2014] EWHC 2657 (Ch) [300]; *CMS Dolphin Ltd v Simonet* [2001] 2 BCLC 704 (Ch) 733.

[27] *United Pan-Europe Communications NV v Deutsche Bank AG* [2000] 2 BCLC 461 (CA) 484. See too *Target Holdings Ltd v Redferns* [1996] AC 421 (HL) 440; *AIB Group (UK) plc v Mark Redler & Co Solicitors* [2014] UKSC 58, [2015] AC 1503 [120]; *Underhill and Hayton* (n 16) [27.21]ff.

In the vast majority of instances, B's *undertaking* to act in a fiduciary capacity is matched by A's *reposing* of trust and confidence in B. For instance, in *Reading v Attorney-General*,[28] it was said that:

> a "fiduciary relation" exists (a) whenever [A] *entrusts* to [B] property … and relies on [B] to deal with such property for the benefit of [A] or for purposes authorised by him, and not otherwise … and (b) whenever [A] *entrusts* to [B] a job to be performed … and relies on [B] to procure for [A] the best terms available.

However, upon closer examination, it appears unnecessary for A actively to entrust B for B to take on fiduciary duties. In the first place, general judicial statements simply require that B undertakes to act as fiduciary. Thus, recalling Millett LJ's words in *Mothew*, '[a] fiduciary is someone who has *undertaken* to act for or on behalf of another in a particular matter in circumstances which give rise to a relationship of trust and confidence.'[29] Similarly, in the Court of Appeal in *Attorney-General v Blake*,[30] Lord Woolf MR observed that a fiduciary relationship 'arises whenever one party *undertakes* to act in the interests of another or places himself in a position where he is obliged to act in the interests of another.'

The well-known facts of *Boardman v Phipps*[31] are also instructive. Boardman acted as solicitor to the trustees of a family trust. He[32] personally purchased the outstanding shares in a company in which the family trust had a substantial shareholding in order to turn the company around, and in successfully doing so made a profit from which both he and the trust benefitted. Full and frank disclosure of the transaction was not made to all the beneficiaries of the trust,[33] and so the profit Boardman made was a 'secret' profit, in that consent was not given by the beneficiaries for its retention. It can hardly be said that John Phipps, one of the beneficiaries of the trust and the successful claimant in the case, had 'entrusted' Boardman to act as fiduciary in relation to the purchase of the shares, since John Phipps had not approved of Boardman's acts. The trustees of the family trust had decided that the trust would not be in a position to purchase the outstanding shares in the company;[34] moreover, although acting as the personal solicitor to the other beneficiaries of the trust, Boardman did not so act on behalf of John Phipps.[35] So the only reason B was held to be a fiduciary was due to his own undertaking to so act: his fiduciary duties arose because he was a 'self-appointed agent'.[36]

Since the material event giving rise to fiduciary duties is B's own action of undertaking to act as a fiduciary, the doctrine falls to be considered under the unilateral events category. Certainly, once a fiduciary relationship is established, A has 'a legitimate expectation, which equity will recognise, that [B] will not utilise his or her position in such a way which is adverse to the interests of [A]';[37] and moreover, it will 'reasonably entitle [A] to expect

[28] *Reading v Attorney-General* [1949] 2 KB 232 (CA) 236 (emphases added). See too *R v Chester and North Wales Legal Aid Area Office (No. 12)* [1998] 1 WLR 1496 (CA) 1500.
[29] *Mothew* (n 15) 18 (emphasis added).
[30] *Attorney-General v Blake* [1998] Ch 439 (CA) 454 (emphasis added).
[31] *Boardman v Phipps* (n 12).
[32] Along with Tom Phipps, a beneficiary of the trust.
[33] *Boardman v Phipps* (n 12) 93.
[34] ibid 76.
[35] ibid 49.
[36] ibid 108. See too discussion in James Edelman, 'When Do Fiduciary Duties Arise?' (2010) 126 *LQR* 302, 310ff.
[37] *Arklow Investments Ltd v Maclean* [2000] 1 WLR 594 (PC) 598.

that [B] will act in [A]'s interest to the exclusion of [B's] own or a third party's interest.'[38] Nevertheless, it is clear that A's involvement is the result of, and not a necessary ingredient for, the establishment of a fiduciary relationship.

10.2.2. A QI Situation

The constructive trusts imposed through the fiduciary doctrine reflect a QI situation. Unlike AI situations, the constructive trust does not arise in relation to any property which B owns at the outset.[39] Instead, the property which represents the gain is never considered to be B's: a constructive trust arises over the gain from the moment B receives it, with the result that B only ever takes a qualified interest in property.

10.2.3. A Primary-Rights or Secondary-Rights Analysis?

It is not a straightforward matter to determine whether the constructive trusts give effect to primary or secondary rights—whether they are imposed as replicative or reflective remedies. In a series of recent works,[40] Charles Mitchell has demonstrated that there has been a subtle shift over the last two-hundred years in the way in which fiduciary duties are conceptualised. He writes:[41]

> [N]ineteenth century treatise writers consistently stated that [fiduciaries] were 'incapable' of entering legally binding contracts with their principals, or that they could not validly do so because they were subject to an 'equitable disability'. The same language appears in cases throughout the nineteenth and twentieth centuries. It reflects the idea that fiduciary relationships are governed by a set of rules that disable fiduciaries from acting in certain ways, rather than a set of rules that require them to perform certain duties, breaches of which are capable of triggering secondary obligations to disgorge profits or pay compensation … A different way of thinking about fiduciary duty emerged in the case law of the late twentieth century. This envisages that a fiduciary owes a duty 'not to promote his personal interest … in circumstances in which there is a conflict or a real or substantial possibility of a conflict between his personal interests and those of the persons whom he is bound to protect.'[42] Breach of this duty is seen as a civil wrong that triggers a secondary duty to account for unauthorised gains, or to pay compensation for loss.

The 'disability' conception entails a primary-rights analysis which leads to the imposition of constructive trusts as replicative remedies; the 'duty' conception entails a secondary-rights analysis which leads to the imposition of reflective remedies.

Drawing from the increasing availability of claims for compensation for loss against errant fiduciaries, Mitchell predicts that, in the future, 'the disability model [will yield] to the breach of duty model in the context of claims for unauthorised gains.'[43] However, *Snell's*

[38] *Grimaldi v Chameleon Mining NL (No. 2)* [2012] FCAFC 6 [177].

[39] Profits obtained by B prior to becoming a fiduciary cannot be the subject of an account: *Cavendish Bentinck v Fenn* (1887) 12 App Cas 652 (HL).

[40] See, eg, Charles Mitchell, 'Causation, Remoteness, and Fiduciary Gains' (2006) 17 *King's College Law Journal* 325; Charles Mitchell, 'Equitable Compensation for Breach of Fiduciary Duty' (2013) 66 *Current Legal Problems* 307; *Hayton and Mitchell* (n 3) [9-073]ff; *Underhill and Hayton* (n 16) [27.6]–[27.9].

[41] *Underhill and Hayton* (n 16) [27.7]–[27.8] (footnotes omitted).

[42] *Hospital Products Ltd v United States Surgical Corp* (1985) 156 CLR 41,103.

[43] *Underhill and Hayton* (n 16) [27.9] (footnote omitted).

Equity suggests that the appropriate conception varies according to the remedy in question: '[t]he remed[y] of … constructive trusts operate on the basis that [B] was under a disability', but 'where a compensatory remedy is sought, the claim for breach of fiduciary duty takes on the characteristics of a duty-based claim'.[44] This inconsistent approach within the doctrine is not ideal; however, technically '[a] claim for equitable compensation for losses sustained by a claimant is in principle a quite different remedy from a claim for an account of profits made by a defaulting fiduciary.'[45] The essential question, therefore, is whether—history aside, and compensatory claims notwithstanding—there are any reasons based on principle which require constructive trusts imposed over gains made by an errant fiduciary to be categorised one way or the other?

10.2.3.1. Not a Primary-Rights Analysis

A primary-rights analysis entails that the fiduciary doctrine leads to the imposition of constructive trusts as replicative remedies. For this analysis to hold true, two things need to be shown. First, it is necessary to establish that there is something inherent in the fiduciary relationship between A and B which dictates that a trust relationship will always arise immediately the gain is received by B. Secondly, it must be shown that a constructive trust remedy—or any other remedy which might be awarded—is imposed in order to replicate the parties' primary rights and duties.

10.2.3.1.1. Relationship: The 'Agreement' Conception

One way in which the argument can be made that a trust relationship arises in relation to a gain obtained by B is by focusing on the events which create a fiduciary relationship. It was seen earlier that the fiduciary office is voluntarily undertaken.[46] An argument might therefore be made that, through his undertaking, B impliedly also promises to hold any gains obtained while acting in a fiduciary capacity on trust for A.[47] Thus, as David Hayton writes:[48]

> If [A] claim[s] that [B] did no wrong but acted in authorised fiduciary fashion, [B] is precluded or estopped from asserting that he acted wrongfully. 'Equity considers as done that which ought to be done'[49] when [A] claim[s] this as a primary obligation under the completely constituted fiduciary relationship.

And in *Novoship (UK) Ltd v Mikhaylyuk*, the Court of Appeal said that:[50]

> [B's] breach of duty does not consist in the making of a profit … but in the keeping of it for himself. That is not a breach of a personal obligation; it is an abuse of the trust and confidence placed in him by [A] who put him in a position to make the profit because he trusted him not to serve his

[44] John McGhee (ed), *Snell's Equity*, 33rd edn (London, Sweet & Maxwell, 2016) [7-051].
[45] *Barnsley v Noble* (n 26) [300].
[46] See S 10.1.1.
[47] See *Hayton and Mitchell* (n 3) [13-187].
[48] David Hayton, 'The Extent of Equitable Remedies: Privy Council versus Court of Appeal' (2012) 33 *Company Law* 161, 162.
[49] As Lord Templeman said in *Attorney-General for Hong Kong v Reid* [1994] 1 AC 324 (HL) 331.
[50] *Novoship (UK) Ltd v Mikhaylyuk* [2014] EWCA Civ 908, [2015] QB 499 [104], citing Peter Millett, 'Bribes and Secret Commissions Again' (2012) 71 *CLJ* 583, 585. See too Peter Millett, 'Proprietary Restitution' in Simone Degeling and James Edelman (eds), *Equity in Commercial Law* (Sydney, Lawbook Co, 2005) 324.

own interests. Equity's response to the breach of this trust is not to give redress for the breach in the form of equitable compensation but to enforce the duty.

This 'agreement' conception of fiduciary relationships immediately runs into the difficulty that a unilateral promise, without more, never gives rise to a constructive trust.[51] In order to sidestep this problem, it would therefore be necessary to fit these constructive trusts within the bilateral events category within the structure of the law of constructive trusts, more specifically alongside the doctrines which reflect a QI situation.[52] This categorisation entails that a constructive trust arises not simply in response to B's promise, but also because A relies on B's promise in such a way which gives B an advantage in the acquisition of the gain.

The difficulty with this understanding, however, is that it stretches the meaning of 'promise' or 'intention' to breaking point, thereby distorting a proper analysis of the law.[53] In *Sinclair Investments (UK) Ltd v Versailles Trade Finance Ltd*,[54] Lord Neuberger said that 'a bribe paid to [B] could not possibly be said to be an asset which [B] was under a duty to take for [A]'. Any analysis which accepts that receiving a bribe constitutes acting 'in an authorised fiduciary fashion', or that B may expressly or impliedly promise to take a bribe on A's behalf, or that A *relies* on B's promise to hold bribes on trust for A, is surely open to be criticised for encouraging bribery and thus perpetrating 'an evil practice which threatens the foundations of any civilised society.'[55] Moreover, it is also unrealistic to say that, when taking up office, B agrees to hold on trust for A any gain which B makes through taking an opportunity which was not open to A to take.[56] The artificiality of the analysis is all the more pronounced in cases where B is compelled to hold any gains made on trust for A where B acts bona fide for A's benefit and merely happens to make an incidental profit from the endeavour.[57]

Consider also the fact that fiduciary relationships commonly arise out of contractual relationships. In these cases, it is open to the parties contractually to determine whether B should hold any profits made in the course of his duties as debtor or trustee.[58] Where the parties contractually agree that B will account for all profits as a trustee, then a constructive trust which is imposed on gains made by B might be said to replicate the parties' primary contractual/fiduciary relationship. However, it is plainly observable that there are cases of highest authority—in particular *Attorney-General of Hong Kong v Reid* and *FHR European Ventures LLP v Cedar Capital Partners LLC*—where constructive trusts have been imposed on gains made by B despite the fact that the parties had not agreed to enter into a trust relationship.[59] As James Penner explains, on the facts of these cases, the contracts provided 'the only basis upon which [B] has any non-wrong based liability

[51] *Cobbe v Yeoman's Row Management Ltd* [2008] UKHL 55, [2008] 1 WLR 1752 [92]; *Walton v Walton* (CA, 14 April 1994); *Commonwealth of Australia v Verwayen* (1990) 170 CLR 394, 416.

[52] See, generally, Chapter 3, S 3.2.1.1.

[53] A similar problem is identified and discussed in the context of family homes in Chapter 14.

[54] *Sinclair Investments* (n 25) [80].

[55] *Reid* (n 49) 330.

[56] *3464920 Canada Inc v Strother* [2007] 2 SCR 177 [155]. Cases reflecting such a fact-pattern include *Keech v Sandford* (n 12) and *Boardman v Phipps* (n 12).

[57] Such as in *Boardman v Phipps* (n 12).

[58] Penner, 'Distinguishing' (n 1) 219.

[59] See ibid 227–28 for a discussion of this point in relation to *Reid* (n 49) and *FHR* (n 6).

to account at all';[60] hence, because the contracts did not establish a trust relationship, it is difficult to see how the imposed constructive trusts can be said to replicate the parties' primary rights and duties. Indeed, if Hayton is correct that the 'equity sees as done …' maxim applies, then a *personal* accounting relationship would have been replicated in the awarded remedy. Since constructive trusts were ultimately imposed in these cases, and if we accept that these cases represent the current law, then they compel us to reject the primary-rights analysis based on the 'agreement' conception.

10.2.3.1.2. Relationship: The 'Attribution' Conception

An alternative argument for a primary-rights analysis is propounded by Lionel Smith.[61] This argument is not based on B's undertaking or an agreement between the parties,[62] but rather on the very nature of fiduciary relationships. Smith writes:[63]

> The [no-profit] rule is not activated by wrongdoing (although wrongdoing there may be); it is a direct implication of the fact that [B] acts, within a sphere of activity, for and on behalf of [A]. The implication is that whatever may be extracted from that sphere of activity is attributed, as between [B] and [A], as a matter of primary right, to [A]; including that which was extracted without authority, should [A] so choose. It is not necessary to say that opportunities or information 'belong' to [A] in a legal sense; the rule is activated when opportunities or information are used to acquire rights, if they can be said to have been acquired from acting in the fiduciary role. Nor is it necessary to see the result as a remedy for wrongful conduct: profits are attributed to the beneficiary as an implication of the nature of the fiduciary relationship, not as a remedy for a wrong.

There are two main difficulties with this argument. The first relates to justification. Smith says the following in relation to the no-profit rule:[64]

> The fiduciary relationship is characterised by the acquisition by [B] of part of the autonomy—part of the choice-making ability—of [A]. Our autonomy belongs to us, in a non-legal sense. The law seeks, so far as it can, to give effect to this. Thus, when [B], through the use of the levers of control that he holds over [A] beneficiary's autonomy, is able to extract some wealth or value, the law ascribes it to [A] as a matter of primary right.

This explanation does not go far enough to denounce the receipt of bribes and secret commissions by a fiduciary. On a primary-rights analysis, the fact that a trust arises over such gains is a pronouncement that B ought to have done so as part of his fiduciary duties. In Smith's terms, B is taken to have 'exercise[d] the powers held as a fiduciary in *what [B] perceive[s]* to be the best interests of [A]'.[65] There is an obvious contradiction in the suggestion that B's receipt of a bribe or secret commission *is* and *ought to be treated as* a loyal act, particularly where (as is almost always the case) the receipt has not been sanctioned by A or the instrument creating the fiduciary relationship. It is also difficult to see how B is acting 'on behalf of' A in relation to profits which B makes through pursuing opportunities which

[60] ibid 227.

[61] See too similar sentiments expressed in Millett, 'Proprietary Restitution' (n 50) 324; Lord Millett, 'Book Review' (2002) 2 *Oxford University Commonwealth Law Journal* 291, 295. See too *FHR* (n 6) [33].

[62] See Smith, 'Fiduciary Relationships' (n 1) 612–13.

[63] Lionel Smith, 'Constructive Trusts and the No-Profit Rule' (2013) 72 *CLJ* 260, 261-62. See too Smith, 'Fiduciary Relationships' (n 1) 629.

[64] Smith, 'Fiduciary Relationships' (n 1) 628.

[65] ibid 611.

were not open to A to take. B's pursuing of such opportunities do not appear to be detrimental to A's autonomy, since left on his own A would not have been able to take advantage of those opportunities. Nor can it be suggested that B's pursuing of those opportunities is an exercise of his fiduciary power in what he perceives to be in A's best interest: to suggest that fiduciaries ought to pursue opportunities not open to their principals to take imposes an excessive burden on fiduciaries.

The second problem has to do with the constructive trust remedy which, according to Smith,[66] necessarily flows from the 'attribution' conception. He cites in support of his thesis a portion of Lord Russell's judgment in *Regal (Hastings) Ltd v Gulliver*[67] that '[t]he rule of equity which insists on those, who by use of a fiduciary position make a profit, [are] liable to account for that profit … arises from the mere fact of a profit having, in the stated circumstances, been made.' But Lord Russell's statement is neither here nor there in relation to the issue of remedy. As Joe Campbell notes:[68]

> An obligation to account for a profit or benefit can mean several things—it might refer to being obliged to hand it over in specie, it might refer to being obliged to pay its value, or it might refer to being obliged to include it as an item in an overall taking of accounts.

Smith's conclusion that a constructive trust necessarily arises is therefore based on a *non sequitur*: even if it is correct to say that 'whatever may be extracted from [the] sphere of activity is attributed, as between [B] and [A] … to [A]', it does not follow that it is attributed 'as a matter of primary right'. Instead, it is equally possible that such attribution occurs by treating B's receipt of the gain as a breach of his primary right, leading to the imposition of a reflective remedy. Nor does it follow that a constructive trust remedy must invariably arise. It is equally possible for the gain to be 'attributed' to A by way of a lesser remedy.

10.2.3.1.3. Remedy: Lien

In *FHR*, the Supreme Court held that a constructive trust would always arise in relation to bribes and secret commissions received by an errant fiduciary.[69] Upon closer inspection, however, this is an overstatement: it is clearly possible for a lien or a personal remedy to be imposed in relation to such profits, notwithstanding the decision in *FHR*.

Consider first the lien. In the earlier case of *Reid*,[70] Lord Templeman observed that '[B] remains liable for the amount of the bribe if, in the event, the value of the property then recovered by [A] proved to be less than that amount'. Similarly, in *Libertarian Investments Ltd v Hall*,[71] Lord Millett NPJ said:

> [in] an appropriate case [B] will be charged, not merely with the value of the property at the date when it ought to have been acquired or at the date when the account is taken, but at its highest intermediate value. This is on the footing either that [B] was a trustee with power to sell the property or that he was a fiduciary who ought to have kept [A] informed and sought his instructions.

[66] See, eg, Smith, 'No-Profit Rule' (n 63) 262–63.
[67] *Regal (Hastings) Ltd v Gulliver* [1942] 2 AC 134 (HL) 144–45.
[68] Joe Campbell, 'When and Why a Bribe is Held on a Constructive Trust: The Method of Reasoning Towards an Equitable Remedy' (2015) 39 *Australian Bar Review* 320, 332.
[69] *FHR* (n 6) [46]ff.
[70] *Reid* (n 49) 336.
[71] *Libertarian Investments Ltd v Hall* [2013] HKCFA 93 [171].

As Matthew Conaglen notes,[72] the effect is that the court 'effectively permits [A] to elect for a lien over the commission, rather than a constructive trust, where that is beneficial to [A]'.[73]

The trouble with rationalising a lien as a remedy responding to primary rights is that it is difficult to see how this replicates any feature of B's primary duty. Consider first the situation contemplated by Lord Templeman, where a lien is imposed where the value of the property claimed is lower than the value of the gain B initially received. In the context of a tracing claim against a trustee or a knowing recipient,[74] there is no difficulty in understanding the lien as a replicative remedy.[75] Since a trustee and a knowing recipient both have a primary duty to preserve the value of the trust fund initially received,[76] a surviving trust asset or its traceable proceed in their hands can be deemed to be retained or acquired pursuant to that primary duty, which is reflected either in a trust remedy or a lien. But such a 'stewardship'[77] duty is characteristic only of a trust relationship and not a fiduciary relationship, the latter of which is concerned with B's loyalty in exercising his judgment in matters which affect A's legal position. A fiduciary clearly must *avoid* taking a bribe or a secret commission; it is much less obvious why he has a *primary fiduciary duty* to preserve the value of a bribe of secret commission.[78]

Consider next the situation contemplated by Lord Millett, where a lien is imposed to secure the highest intermediate value. The explanation that B 'ought to have kept A informed' is unsatisfactory. Discharging this duty properly surely would entail informing A of B's wayward plan *before* receiving a bribe or secret commission, in which case A would likely have prevented the gain from ever being made. Where the gain has already been made, it is difficult to see how that primary duty can still be carried out. Moreover, to make B liable for the highest intermediate value implies a primary duty to invest property at the most opportune moment. However, unlike trustees, a fiduciary is not under such a primary duty. Therefore, if A can claim the highest intermediate value, then this cannot be on the basis that the remedy is a replicative remedy, unless one is prepared to say that *all* fiduciaries not only have a duty of loyalty but also a duty to invest secret profits, secret commissions, and bribes. This blurring of the line between trustees and fiduciaries ought to be avoided.

[72] Matthew Conaglen, 'Proprietary Remedies for Breach of Fiduciary Duty' (2014) 73 *CLJ* 490, 492. See too *Hayton and Mitchell* (n 3) [13-074].

[73] An equitable lien is 'a cumulative remedy in aid of an equitable *in personam* claim' (*Serious Fraud Office v Lexi Holdings plc (in administration)* [2008] EWCA Crim 1443, [2009] QB 376 [40]) and is 'essentially a positive right to obtain ... an order for sale of the subject property or for actual payment from the subject fund' (*Hewett v Court* (1983) 149 CLR 638, 664).

[74] A tracing claim against an innocent volunteer may result in trust being imposed on the original property or its traceable proceed in his hands, but a lien cannot be asserted against him: *Westdeutsche Landesbank Girozentrale v Islington LBC* [1996] AC 669 (HL) 707.

[75] *Hayton and Mitchell* (n 3) [12-051].

[76] In relation to trustees, see *Low v Bouverie* [1891] 3 Ch 82 (CA) 99. Knowing recipients have a similar duty—'a distinctive, primary, custodial liability, which closely resembles the liability of express trustees to account for the trust property with which they are charged': Charles Mitchell and Stephen Watterson, 'Remedies for Knowing Receipt' in Charles Mitchell (ed), *Constructive and Resulting Trusts* (Oxford, Hart Publishing, 2010) 130.

[77] See main text following n 3 above.

[78] A secondary-rights analysis would, however, avoid this difficulty: one could argue that the gain was made due to B's breach of his duty of loyalty, and therefore the best remedy in the circumstances would be one which preserves the value of the gain in favour of A.

Unhelpfully, the Supreme Court's judgment in *FHR* does not consider whether proprietary remedies other than a constructive trust are relevant to the fiduciary doctrine, and so it is not immediately obvious whether, post-*FHR*, the lien continues to be relevant in cases of bribes and secret commissions. However, logic dictates that it remains of relevance in order to ensure that B does not profit from his breach by keeping any dissipated profits. But once it is accepted that a lien may be imposed as a remedy, it is difficult to explain this by way of a primary-rights analysis.

10.2.3.1.4. Remedy: Personal Remedies

Secondly, consider the fact that even where the gain or its traceable proceed survives in B's hands, A has the option of enforcing a personal remedy[79] instead of a constructive trust.[80] The availability of this option is inconsistent with a primary-rights analysis. On a primary-rights analysis, it is inherent in the nature of A's primary right that he is entitled, by way of a constructive trust, to the very property representing the relevant gain in B's hands. If that property still survives in B's hands but A is able to opt for a personal 'substitutive'[81] remedy, in essence this sanctions a forced sale of the property to B.

An analogous example in relation to express trusts reinforces the point. Suppose a trustee holds a painting on an express trust for a beneficiary. It is manifestly unacceptable if the latter may enforce his primary right under the trust by compelling his trustee to keep the painting and simply pay over its monetary value, since the trustee may not wish to 'purchase' the painting. Hence, where the original trust property survives in the trustee's hands, it is not open to the beneficiaries to elect between a proprietary or personal remedy. The law rightly demands that B should restore the property *in specie* at first instance, and only *where A's proprietary claim to the property in specie is unavailable* will B be subject to a personal obligation to repay the monetary value of the property.

Assuming, therefore, that A may indeed *elect* between a constructive trust and a personal remedy, then it is difficult to accept that the fiduciary doctrine is concerned with giving effect to A's primary right.

10.2.3.2. A Secondary-Rights Analysis

The difficulties encountered by the primary-rights analysis disappear when a secondary-rights analysis is adopted, which entails that remedies imposed through an operation of the fiduciary doctrine are reflective remedies.

First, it is unnecessary artificially to imply that B *agrees* to hold gains—in particular, bribes and secret commissions—on trust for A, or that such a trust arises through the idea

[79] By a 'personal remedy' the courts do not mean that A simply forgoes the proprietary effects of a constructive trust in relation to the property representing the gain in B's hands. Rather, they mean that *in lieu of* asserting a proprietary right to the property in B's hands, A may make a personal *monetary* claim for 'the quantum of that bribe or commission' (*FHR* (n 6) [7]). That is to say, what is contemplated is 'a personal claim to payment of the amount brought out by an account of profits' (*AIB Group (UK) plc* (n 27) [120]).

[80] *FHR* (n 6) [7]; *Underhill and Hayton* (n 16) [27.25].

[81] 'Here the trustee performs by payment of a monetary substitute for the property that he should have been able to distribute or otherwise apply *in specie*': Steven B Elliott and Charles Mitchell, 'Remedies for Dishonest Assistance' (2004) 67 *MLR* 16, 27.

of *attribution*. On the secondary-rights analysis, the constructive trust is understood simply as a remedy which enforces A's secondary right that arises when B commits a breach of his primary fiduciary duty. It also becomes possible to avoid analysing B's receipt of a bribe or secret commission and the making of a profit through pursuing an opportunity not open to A to take as things which B 'ought to have done' in carrying out his office. The secondary-rights analysis takes the view that the receipt of such gains is a *breach* of B's primary fiduciary duty.[82]

Secondly, on the secondary-rights analysis, a constructive trust remedy can arise despite the fact that the parties are not in any pre-existing trust relationship, for the same reason that the trust responds to B's breach and not the parties' primary relationship.

Thirdly, the secondary-rights analysis explains why remedies other than a constructive trust may be available. As discussed in Chapter 2,[83] while the range of potential remedial responses to primary rights is narrow and limited, secondary rights provide a wider remedial potential. In the present context, it is open for A to elect between a constructive trust, a lien, and a personal remedy, either of which can properly be analysed as giving effect to A's secondary right.

10.3. Three Questions

The analysis above indicates that constructive trusts imposed by operation of the fiduciary doctrine fall within the 'unilateral events' category; and as reflective remedies which respond to secondary rights, they occupy a unique space within the structure of the law of constructive trusts.

This analysis raises three questions which require addressing. First, what is the primary duty, the breach of which gives A a secondary right to which the constructive trusts respond? Secondly, how do the elements of breach, causation, and remoteness come into the picture? And thirdly, in principle reflective remedies allow for the exercise of remedial discretion as to content;[84] so, how does the element of discretion arise in relation to the constructive trusts imposed through the fiduciary doctrine?

10.3.1. The Primary Right

In general terms, B's primary duty is that of loyalty. As noted earlier,[85] there are different facets to this overarching duty, including the 'no-profit' and 'no-conflict' rules. The constructive trusts imposed through the fiduciary doctrine are concerned with the 'no-profit' rule, and the duty can be formulated as follows: B has a primary duty to avoid making an unauthorised

[82] Unless A or the instrument creating the fiduciary relationship expressly sanctions B's keeping of bribes and secret commissions—although this is extremely unlikely: see main text from n 65 above.
[83] See Chapter 2, S 2.4.2.2.
[84] See Chapter 2 main text to n 55, n 60, and S 2.4.3.
[85] See main text following n 15 above.

personal gain 'in the course of [B's] execution of [his fiduciary] office'.[86] When such a gain is made, B's primary duty can no longer be enforced. Therefore, A must rely on his secondary right, which arises upon B's breach, to compel B to give up those gains.[87]

It is important to note that it is not necessary for B to be in a position of actual or potential conflict with A for the primary duty to arise. Thus, in *Boardman v Phipps*[88] and *Regal (Hastings) Ltd v Gulliver*,[89] B was held to account for his gains despite the fact that there was no way in which A could have secured the opportunity to make the gain for himself; hence it would be difficult to say that the gains B made were caused by B acting in a way which constituted a conflict of interest. Instead, B's duty is simply to avoid making an unauthorised personal gain while acting as A's fiduciary: it is the fact that B makes the gain when acting as fiduciary which has the potential of causing a conflict of interest. Thus, in *Boardman*,[90] Lord Cohen found against Boardman on the basis that he 'would not have been able to give unprejudiced advice *if* he had been consulted by the trustees'. Although Boardman's purchase of shares did not create an actual or potential conflict of interest since the trustees of the family trust had conclusively decided against purchasing the shares for the trust, he had to account for the profits made on those shares because he undeniably acted 'in the course and execution of' his fiduciary office, and by making those gains he put himself a position of potential conflict of interest.

10.3.2. Breach, Causation, and Remoteness

On a secondary-rights analysis, A must plead and prove that B has breached his primary duty, that this has caused the relevant gain, and that the measure of the gain is not too remote, in order for A to obtain a constructive trust over the gain.

10.3.2.1. Breach

It is sometimes suggested that B's 'breach of duty does not consist in the making of a profit ... but in the keeping of it for himself'.[91] We have seen[92] that this is a suggestion put

[86] *Regal (Hastings) Ltd* (n 67) 147, 149. This was phrased similarly in *Parker v McKenna* (1874) LR 10 Ch App 96 (HL) 118: 'in the course and execution of his [office]'.

[87] It has sometimes been suggested, based on the Privy Council's decision in *Reid* (n 49) 330–31 that the primary duty which B breaches is a duty to uphold 'the foundations of ... civilised society' and 'the administration of justice'. However, the breach of such a duty is a wrong against the state and not against a particular individual, and so it does not explain why A obtains a secondary right against B in equity (see Andrew Burrows, *The Law of Restitution*, 3rd edn (Oxford, OUP, 2010) 641; Penner, 'Distinguishing' (n 1) 227–30). Moreover, such a duty cannot explain why B must account for secret profits made in good faith.

[88] *Boardman v Phipps* (n 12).

[89] *Regal (Hastings) Ltd* (n 67). *Keech v Sandford* (n 12) is not included in this list of cases because 'the opportunity to renew a tenancy, although not strictly a legal right, was effectively recognised as such by the courts in the 18th century'; and so in *Keech*, despite the landlord's refusal to renew the lease in favour of the beneficiary-infant, the fiduciary's renewing of the lease for himself amounted to 'taking advantage of an opportunity ... which [was] really owned by the beneficiary': *Sinclair Investments* (n 25) [58].

[90] *Boardman v Phipps* (n 12) 103 (emphasis added). The facts of *Boardman* are recounted above in the main text following n 31. See Michael Bryan, '*Boardman v Phipps* (1967)' in Charles Mitchell and Paul Mitchell (eds), *Landmark Cases in Equity* (Oxford, Hart Publishing, 2011) for a detailed analysis of the case.

[91] See n 50 above.

[92] See S 10.2.3.1.1.

forward in support of a primary-rights analysis, which does not withstand scrutiny. The suggestion is also problematic because it seems to suggest, contrary to public policy, that *the very receipt* of a bribe or secret commission is sanctionable if, upon receipt, B holds it on trust for A. The secondary-rights analysis takes a different approach: B commits a breach when he *receives* an unauthorised personal gain in the course of acting as a fiduciary.

In establishing B's breach, it is important to ascertain the scope of B's fiduciary office, because this determines whether B's gain was made *in the course of* acting as fiduciary.[93] For instance, any underlying contract between the parties 'can and does modify the extent and nature of the general duty that would otherwise arise',[94] with the result that no breach occurs if a gain is made outside the contracted scope of B's fiduciary office. It is also necessary to determine that scope vis-a-vis the gain made by B. In particular, it needs to be asked whether B's general duty of loyalty extends to the specific 'transaction, or group of transactions'[95] giving rise to the gain, and further, whether it covers the specific property which represents the gain in question.[96]

It is also important to determine whether the gain made by B is *authorised*, since authorisation entails that B has not committed a breach.[97] There are three means by which authorisation may be given. B may seek authorisation from a court;[98] certain gains may be authorised by the instrument which created the fiduciary relationship; or A may consent[99] where B provides full disclosure[100] to A who is (or all As, who are) *sui juris*. In relation to the latter two means, it is possible, though extremely unlikely, that B would be authorised to keep any bribe or secret commission for himself. It is more likely for authorisation to be given to B for the retention of profits made in the course of pursuing opportunities which are not open to A to take in circumstances where those opportunities are pursued bona fide with the aim of making profits for the principal as well. Where authorisation is provided, then there is no reason to hold that B has breached his primary duty, which relates only to *unauthorised* personal gains.

10.3.2.2. Causation

To some extent the issue of causation arises at the 'breach' stage, where it needs to be determined whether B's gain was made 'in the course of' B acting as a fiduciary: if the answer is 'yes', then it can be said that B's gain was caused by his breach of fiduciary duty. But there is a different aspect of causation which also requires attention: can B escape or reduce the extent of his liability by alleging that B could also have made all or part of the same gain through legitimate means? Alternatively, will A's case necessarily fail if B can show 'that,

[93] *Kelly v Cooper* [1993] AC 205 (PC) 215.

[94] *Henderson v Merrett Syndicates Ltd* [1995] 2 AC 145 (HL) 206.

[95] *New Zealand Netherlands Society 'Oranje' Inc* (n 11) 1130.

[96] *Birtchnell v Equity Trustees Executors & Agency Co Ltd* (1929) 42 CLR 384, 408.

[97] The same is the case under express trusts, where beneficiaries authorise their trustees to act in a way which is contrary to the trust deed: see Ying Khai Liew and Charles Mitchell, 'Beneficiaries' Consent to Trustees' Unauthorised Acts' in Paul Davies, Simon Douglas and James Goudkamp (eds), *Defences in Equity* (Oxford, Hart Publishing, 2018).

[98] *Farmer v Dean* (1863) 32 Beav 327, 55 ER 128; Trustee Act 1925, s 42.

[99] *Mothew* (n 15) 18.

[100] *Boardman v Phipps* (n 12) 121.

in any event, the profit could not have been secured by or for A', thereby proving that 'the wrongdoing was not causally related to the gain'?[101]

The case of *Murad v Al-Saraj*[102] is instructive. B and As entered into a joint venture for the acquisition of a hotel. B breached his fiduciary duty by representing that he would contribute a stated sum to the joint venture but in fact never paid any cash to the vendor, who had released him from a legally unenforceable liability. B argued that he ought not to be accountable for all the profits he made. Instead, he argued that the but-for test should be applied to limit his liability to the difference in the amount between As' profits from the venture and the amount for which As would have negotiated had B been forthcoming about his contributions. The majority of the Court of Appeal decided that B should be liable for *all* the profits he had made out of the joint venture. This decision is to the effect that a 'one cause' test is used: causation is satisfied where B fails to show[103] that his breach of fiduciary duty was not one cause of the gain.

The causal test to be applied is succinctly summarised in *Underhill and Hayton*: '[i]n effect, the fiduciary must prove that his breach of duty had no causative effect at all, by showing that he acquired the gain exclusively as a result of activities legitimately undertaken in his own interest.'[104] Therefore, the existence of other legitimate means of obtaining the gains, or the fact that A may not have secured the gain for himself, has no effect on A's case against B. Although the claimant-friendly nature of the test is quite unlike those commonly adopted in the context of many other legal doctrines, it is consistent with 'the courts' general attitude towards breaches of fiduciary duty.'[105]

10.3.2.3. Remoteness

The default remoteness test for gains made by an errant fiduciary appears to be the 'direct consequence test', which is the test applied in relation to claims for compensation in the tort of deceit.[106] On this test, B is liable for all gains flowing directly from his breach of fiduciary duty, regardless of whether the making of those gains is foreseeable or not. This test properly reflects the strict stance taken against errant fiduciaries, and is in line with other rules which hold B to be accountable even though he acted bona fide, that A could not have made the profit for himself, or that B's course of actions was also profitable to A.[107] These rules indicate that, *unless* B makes full and frank disclosure of the planned course of action and obtains consent from A who is *sui juris*, B is taken to have failed 'to resist the temptation to misconduct [himself]'.[108] The desire to deter[109] fiduciaries from acting in breach of duty aligns the default remoteness test with the law's treatment of a tortious defendant who acts fraudulently or deceitfully.

[101] Smith, 'Fiduciary Relationships' (n 1) 630. In suggesting that A's case would fail for this reason, Smith implicitly adopts a 'but for' causation test. But as discussed below, the test adopted by the courts is the 'one cause' test.

[102] *Murad v Al-Saraj* (n 14). See too discussion in Mitchell, 'Fiduciary Gains' (n 40) 332ff.

[103] *Murad v Al-Saraj* (n 14) [77].

[104] *Underhill and Hayton* (n 16) [27.45].

[105] Mitchell, 'Fiduciary Gains' (n 40) 328.

[106] *Smith New Court Securities Ltd v Scrimgeour Vickers (Asset Management) Ltd* [1996] UKHL 3, [1997] AC 254.

[107] See, eg, *Boardman v Phipps* (n 12).

[108] *Murad v Al-Saraj* (n 14) [74].

[109] Although some authors have questioned whether deterrence is a compelling rationale for the strict approach in relation to fiduciaries (see, eg, Lionel Smith, 'The Motive, Not the Deed', in Joshua Getzler (ed), *Rationalizing*

There are, however, at least three situations in which the extent of B's liability may be limited by the element of remoteness. First, in cases where one specific instance of a breach of fiduciary duty results not in a one-off gain but in a stream of income, courts may consider that some gains are too remote. For instance, in *Warman International Ltd v Dwyer*,[110] B was an employee and manager in a company (A) which acted as the distributing agent of gearboxes manufactured in Italy. In breach of fiduciary duty B entered into a joint venture with the Italian manufacturer in competition with A, incorporating a new business for the purpose of the venture. This new business was very profitable. The High Court of Australia, in holding that B would be liable only for the profits made in the first two years of business, said:[111]

> In the case of a business it may well be inappropriate and inequitable to compel [B] to account for the whole of the profit of his conduct of the business or his exploitation of [A]'s goodwill over an indefinite period of time. In such a case, it may be appropriate to allow [B] a proportion of the profits, depending upon the particular circumstances … [T]he stringent rule requiring [B] to account for profits can be carried to extremes and that in cases outside the realm of specific assets, the liability of [B] should not be transformed into a vehicle for the unjust enrichment of [A].

There was a suggestion in the judgment that B's liability would be so limited where 'a significant proportion of an increase in profits has been generated by the skill, efforts, property and resources of [B], the capital which he has introduced and the risks he has taken'.[112] However, it seems that the High Court did not simply wish to provide an allowance for B's skill, efforts, etc in the same way as considered in the third situation below;[113] instead, the judgment reflects a general approach which does 'what is fair and equitable in the circumstances'.[114] This general approach reflects the well-accepted gloss on the 'direct consequence test', which is that 'no element in the consequential position can be regarded as attributable loss and damage [or, in the present context, 'gain'] if it be *too remote* a consequence'.[115]

Secondly, all three judges in *Murad* voiced, obiter,[116] their opinion that in appropriate circumstances a bona fide fiduciary ought not to be liable for all gains made in breach of fiduciary duty. In Arden LJ's words:[117]

> It may be that the time has come when the court should revisit the operation of the inflexible rule of equity in harsh circumstances, as where [B] has acted in perfect good faith and without any deception or concealment, and in the belief that he was acting in the best interests of [A] … [I]t would not be in the least impossible for a court in a future case, to determine as a question of fact whether [A] would not have wanted to exploit the profit himself, or would have wanted [B] to

Property, Equity and Trusts (Oxford, OUP, 2003) 60–61; John H Langbein, 'Questioning the Trust Law Duty of Loyalty: Sole Interest or Best Interest?' (2005) 114 *Yale Law Journal* 929), it is at least clear that the aim of deterrence is attractive to judges, who justify the strict approach on this basis (see, eg, *Murad v Al-Saraj* (n 14) [77]; *Docker v Somes* (1834) 2 My & K 655, 665; 39 ER 1095, 1098–99; *Bray v Ford* [1896] AC 44 (HL) 51; *Guinness plc v Saunders* [1990] 2 AC 663 (HL) 701; *Lindsley v Woodfull* [2004] EWCA Civ 165, [2004] 2 BCLC 131 [30]).

110 *Warman International Ltd v Dwyer* (1995) 182 CLR 544.
111 ibid [33].
112 ibid.
113 Discussed in the main text following n 119 below.
114 *Warman International Ltd* (n 110) [46].
115 *Doyle v Olby (Ironmongers) Ltd* [1969] 2 QB 158 (CA) 168 (emphasis added).
116 *Murad v Al-Saraj* (n 14) [82], [121], [160].
117 ibid [82].

> have acted other than in the way that [B] in fact did act. Moreover, it would not be impossible for a modern court to conclude as a matter of policy that, without losing the deterrent effect of the rule, the harshness of it should be tempered in some circumstances … though I express no view as to the circumstances in which there should be any relaxation of the rule in this jurisdiction. That sort of question must be left to another court.

The occasion to consider this suggestion has yet to arise; but when it does, one way in which it may be addressed is through the element of remoteness.[118] In the same way as different remoteness tests are applied to negligent tortfeasors and those acting deceitfully, it is not impossible for courts to adopt one remoteness rule in relation to bad faith fiduciaries and another where a fiduciary acts bona fide. Instead of the default remoteness rule, it may be appropriate to subject bona fide fiduciaries to the test of 'reasonable foreseeability of that kind of profit', as James Edelman suggests.[119]

Thirdly, where B's actions result not only in a personal gain but also a profit for A, courts have the liberty to limit A's claim by reference to the 'work and skill'[120] expended by B. This can be explained by way of two different analyses. On the one hand, this may reflect an exercise in apportionment, whereby the profits are allocated between A and B according to the source of their respective contributions, for instance 'property or opportunities derived from [A], and time, skill and effort from [B]'.[121] The difficulty with this approach is that it often involves 'a difficult, complex and costly exercise of attribution'.[122] A different analysis involves a consideration of remoteness. As Mitchell explains, 'claims to recover fiduciary gains may also be subject to a discretionary rule that intervening actions by [B] can render some gains too remote to justify ordering [him] to account for them.'[123] While admitting that all the gains in B's hands have been made as a result of a breach of fiduciary duty, this approach allows courts 'to do what is "practically just"[,] [taking into account] [c]onsiderations such as whether [B] has acted honestly or dishonestly; how and for what has [B] been remunerated; would the denial of an allowance leave [A] unjustly enriched; what risk has been borne by [A]; etc'.[124]

10.3.3. Discretion

On a secondary-rights analysis, courts impose reflective remedies in relation to gains made by errant fiduciaries. As seen in Chapter 2,[125] it is inherent in nature of a reflective remedy that discretion can be exercised as to its content (as opposed to the goal of the remedy). However, the Supreme Court in *FHR* has purported to provide an authoritative

118 See Mitchell, 'Fiduciary Gains' (n 40) 339.

119 James Edelman, *Gain-Based Damages: Contract Tort Equity and Intellectual Property* (Oxford, Hart Publishing, 2002) 108.

120 *Boardman v Phipps* (n 12) 104, 112.

121 *Underhill and Hayton* (n 16) [27.35], citing *Docker v Somes* (n 109); *Wedderburn v Wedderburn* (1838) 4 My & C 41, 41 ER 16; *MacDonald v Richardson* (1858) 1 Giff 81, 65 ER 833; *Page v Rattiffe* (1896) 75 LT 371 (CA); *Manley v Sartori* [1927] 1 Ch 157 (Ch); *Re Jarvis* [1958] 1 WLR 815 (Ch); *Warman International Ltd* (n 110); *CMS Dolphin Ltd* (n 26).

122 *Grimaldi v Chameleon Mining* (n 38) [517].

123 Mitchell, 'Fiduciary Gains' (n 40) 337.

124 *Grimaldi v Chameleon Mining* (n 38) [531].

125 See Chapter 2, S 2.4.2.2.

determination that a constructive trust will always be the appropriate remedy; and so it might be thought that (lower) courts will now no longer[126] exercise remedial discretion in relation to gains made by errant fiduciaries. On the face of it, the reflective nature of the remedy appears to be at odds with the lack of ability to exercise discretion post-*FHR*.

10.3.3.1. Secondary Proprietary Rights?

One explanation which might be given for the apparent lack of exercise of discretion is that the constructive trust remedy simply *replicates* a *secondary proprietary right* which A obtains when B breaches his primary duty to avoid making an unauthorised personal gain in the course of his fiduciary office.

The question of whether secondary proprietary rights—as opposed to proprietary *remedies* awarded to give effect to secondary personal rights—exist at all appears only ever to have been addressed once in a bold assertion made by Arianna Pretto that:[127]

> it is not impossible to respond to an acquisitive wrong by raising a trust and hence a proprietary right in the asset thus acquired. The conclusion must be that … there can be such a thing as a secondary … proprietary right.

This is doubtful. According to Hohfeld, a right *in rem*, a 'multital right', is a right which is '*one* of a large *class* of *fundamentally similar* yet separate rights … residing in a *single person* … but availing *respectively* against persons constituting a very large and indefinite class of people.'[128] On the other hand, a right *in personam*, a 'paucital right', 'is either a unique right residing in a person … and availing against a single person …; or else it is one of a *few* fundamentally similar, yet separate, rights availing respectively against a few definite persons.'[129] When B breaches a primary duty owed towards A, B owes a secondary duty to A for the disgorgement of any gains made or for the compensation of any loss caused by the breach. Stating the same from A's perspective, A's secondary right is good against B and B alone, since it was B—and no one else—who committed the wrongful breach. It would therefore seem that A's secondary right can only be a personal right, 'for there are no fundamentally similar rights against persons in general.'[130] This is not to suggest that the courts may not award a reflective remedy which is proprietary in nature. But awarding a proprietary remedy by asserting that it flows inexorably from A having a secondary proprietary right misses a crucial step. It gives the appearance that it is unnecessary to explain what, apart from B's breach of a primary duty, justifies the award of the proprietary remedy, when in truth that explanation is crucial.

[126] See, however, main text following n 166 below for the argument that the decision in *FHR* (n 6) is in fact of a narrower scope than this, given that it does not consider a number of other means by which an errant fiduciary may come to obtain gains.

[127] Arianna Pretto, 'Primary Rights and Rights *in Rem*' in Peter Birks and Arianna Pretto (eds), *Themes in Comparative Law in Honour of Bernard Rudden* (Oxford, OUP, 2002) 77.

[128] Wesley Newcomb Hohfeld, Walter Wheeler Cook (ed), *Fundamental Legal Conceptions as Applied in Judicial Reasoning* (New Jersey, The Lawbook Exchange, 2010) 72 (emphases in the original).

[129] ibid (emphasis in the original).

[130] ibid 102.

10.3.3.1.1. The Cases

In the specific context of gains made in breach of fiduciary duty, the cases bear no indication whatsoever that the nature of the appropriate remedy is dictated by the nature of A's secondary right. Consider *Lister & Co v Stubbs*.[131] B, an employee of A, was in charge of purchasing certain materials used by A in the course of its business. B ordered a large quantity of materials from a firm and received a secret commission. B invested some of the commission in land and other investments, and a portion of the money remained in his hands. The Court of Appeal held that A had no more than a personal right to the secret commission, and thus could not trace into the investments.

The two reasoned judgments handed down in *Lister* indicate that the awarded remedy gave effect to A's secondary *personal* right. Consider first Lindley LJ's judgment. His Lordship affirmed Stirling J's first instance judgment in its entirety, and so it is safe to assume that Lindley LJ was adopting the analysis at first instance that the parties' relationship arose out of B's 'wrongful act … of [receiving] the money in breach of duty'[132]—that is to say, Lindley LJ was concerned with enforcing A's secondary right and not his primary right. On this basis, his Lordship held that 'the relation between [A and B] is that of debtor and creditor'—that is, a personal relationship—and therefore B was 'liable to account for it the moment that he [received the money]'.[133] His Lordship also went on to say that B's 'obligation'—which arose out of B's breach of his primary duty—did not on its own give rise to a relationship 'of trustee and *cestui que trust*'[134]—that is, a proprietary right. In other words, Lindley LJ thought that there was no justification for awarding a proprietary reflective remedy *because* A's secondary right was merely personal in nature.

Cotton LJ's judgment goes further. His Lordship held that 'the moneys which under th[e] corrupt bargain were paid … to [B] cannot be said to be the money of [A] before any judgment or decree in some such action has been made.'[135] On this view, A's secondary right was not even a personal right to the money representing the secret commission, but merely a personal right against B for the disgorgement of the gain. Effect can only be given to the secondary right when the court awards A a reflective remedy.

Consider next *Attorney-General for Hong Kong v Reid*.[136] B accepted bribes in the course of acting as a servant of the Crown. B acquired three freehold properties in New Zealand with the bribe money, to which A, the Attorney-General for Hong Kong, wanted to claim. The Privy Council held that A's claim should succeed, and granted A a proprietary remedy to the bribe money by way of a constructive trust, which allowed A to trace and claim the properties in New Zealand.

There are four distinct steps which led Lord Templeman to award a constructive trust. The starting point was the principle that 'a fiduciary must not be allowed to benefit from his own breach of duty'; secondly, 'the fiduciary should account for the bribe as soon as he receives it'; thirdly, 'equity regards as done that which ought to be done'; and finally, 'it would appear to follow that the bribe … [is] held on a constructive trust'.[137] A close

[131] *Lister & Co v Stubbs* (1890) 45 Ch D 1 (CA).
[132] ibid 11.
[133] ibid 15.
[134] ibid.
[135] ibid 12–13.
[136] *Reid* (n 49).
[137] ibid 336.

examination of these steps indicates that A's secondary right was personal in nature, and that the decision to award a constructive trust was taken through the court's remedial jurisdiction.

First, Lord Templeman's starting point is surprising. In an earlier case in the House of Lords, Lord Goff had observed that '[t]he statement that a man shall not be allowed to profit from his own wrong is in very general terms, and does not of itself provide any sure guidance to the solution of a problem in any particular case.'[138] In particular, it does not explain why a proprietary *remedy* ought to be awarded, let alone why A's secondary right ought to be a proprietary right. As Matthew Conaglen points out, 'it is not apparent that the purpose of … stripping a wrongdoer of their profits … could not be achieved just as adequately through the award of an account of profits.'[139] Taken on its own, the first step in fact indicates that A's secondary right is a personal right: a corresponding personal duty to account is sufficient to prevent B from benefiting from his breach of duty.

In relation to the second step, in a different part of Lord Templeman's judgment it was observed that B 'must pay and account for the bribe to [A]' as 'a debtor in equity' because 'it is unconscionable for a fiduciary to obtain and retain a benefit in breach of duty.'[140] Again, this indicates that, upon B's breach, A obtains a secondary personal right against B: a 'debtor' is, of course, in a personal relationship with his creditor. Admittedly, his Lordship went on to express concern that B would be retaining a benefit if B's bribe 'consists of property which increases in value or … a cash bribe [which] is invested advantageously'.[141] However, because A's secondary right arises at the very moment that B breaches his primary duty—'as soon as [B] receives [the bribe]'—the nature of A's secondary right (as opposed to nature of the remedy) does not depend on events which take place after that breach.

As to the third step, the 'equity considers as done …' maxim 'is only another way of saying that the obligation of the fiduciary to pay the bribe to his principal the moment he receives it is one which equity will enforce.'[142] In particular, it does not turn A's secondary right into a proprietary right. Upon B's breach of his primary duty of loyalty, that which 'ought to be done' is for B to account to A for the bribe as 'a debtor in equity'. At most, an application of that maxim (if, indeed, maxims can be applied directly as such) would mean that the court, in the exercise of its remedial jurisdiction, *considers* or treats B's secondary *personal* duty as having been carried out; it does not indicate that B's breach is itself enough to generate a secondary proprietary right.[143] In any event, the equitable maxim has little justificatory power: its use suggests that the proprietary interest awarded to A was 'manufactured' where none existed prior to the court order.[144]

Because the first three steps indicate that A's secondary right is a personal right, Lord Templeman's conclusion in the final step could not have mysteriously transformed that

[138] *Attorney-General v Observer Ltd* [1990] 1 AC 109 (HL) 286. See too Edelman (n 8) 81.

[139] Matthew Conaglen, 'Thinking about Proprietary Remedies for Breach of Confidence' [2008] *Intellecutal Property Quarterly* 82, 100.

[140] *Reid* (n 49) 331.

[141] ibid.

[142] Millett, 'Bribes and Secret Commissions Again' (n 50) 598.

[143] See also Sarah Worthington, 'Fiduciary Duties and Proprietary Remedies: Addressing the Failure of Equitable Formulae' (2013) 72 *CLJ* 720, 738ff.

[144] See Paul Finn, 'Equitable Doctrine and Discretion in Remedies' in WR Cornish, Richard Nolan, Janet O'Sullivan et al (eds), *Restitution Past, Present and Future* (Oxford, Hart Publishing, 1998) 263.

right into a proprietary right. Instead, the only plausible analysis is that the constructive trust was awarded through the exercise of the court's remedial jurisdiction, where his Lordship took into account events other than B's wrongdoing, namely that B had invested the bribe money in properties which had increased in value.[145] On a proper analysis, then, A's proprietary interest in the proceeds of the bribe arose for the first time when the court awarded the reflective remedy. The proprietary effect of the constructive trust was, however, backdated to the time of B's breach so as to confer on A priority in B's investments.[146]

The same point can also be deduced from the judgment in *FHR*. The Supreme Court grounded its decision on the basis of 'arguments based on principle and practicality',[147] having noted that 'pure legal authority' did not dictate whether bribes or secret commissions made by an errant fiduciary are to be held on trust or in a personal capacity.[148] This was a discussion concerning how best to exercise the Court's remedial discretion to determine the appropriate remedy, as opposed simply to determining the nature of A's secondary right. If the constructive trust remedy simply replicated A's secondary proprietary right, the discussion would surely have concerned the nature of A's right, as opposed to the remedy. As Paul Finn notes, there are doctrines where, 'notwithstanding the interposition of discretion between doctrine and remedy, the appropriate remedial response [may] itself [be] contrived (or else suggested) first and foremost by the policy and purpose of the particular doctrine in question',[149] where 'the doctrine [in question] and its purpose suggests [*sic*] its own natural remedial hierarchy'.[150] The decision in *FHR* dictates that the 'natural remedial hierarchy' of the doctrine is to prefer a constructive trust over a personal remedy unless the former is unavailable due, for instance, to the original asset being destroyed, or unless A opts for a personal remedy.[151] This does not negate the fact that the awarded remedy gives effect to a secondary personal right; and as a reflective remedy, in principle it allows for the exercise of discretion as to content.

10.3.3.1.2. Effects of the Distinction

It might be thought that drawing a distinction between the nature of the right and the nature of the remedy is tenuous and unnecessary because it makes no difference in practice. But this would be a mistake. In particular, a failure to recognise this distinction leads to courts failing properly to justify their decisions, especially where remedial discretion is in fact exercised.

Let us assume, contrary to the discussion above, that A's secondary right may be personal or proprietary in nature. It can be observed that justifications which relate to A's secondary right can only logically be related to B's wrongdoing because secondary rights and duties stem from B's breach. So, for instance, the fact that the imposed remedy corrects the effects

[145] *Reid* (n 49) 331.

[146] As explained in Chapter 7, S 7.2.5.2. and Chapter 8 main text from n 126, backdating the remedial effect of a constructive trust remedy seems justified where it is impossible to be certain whether a constructive trust arises until a later event occurs—a court order, in the present context; but the trust's purpose is to enforce the parties' rights and duties which arose at an earlier point in time—that is, the date of B's breach.

[147] *FHR* (n 6) [33]ff.

[148] ibid [32].

[149] Finn, 'Equitable Doctrine' (n 144) 268.

[150] ibid 269.

[151] *FHR* (n 6) [7].

of B's disloyalty, or that it avoids B from keeping any gains made in breach of his duty owed towards A, might be justifications relevant to a discussion concerning the nature of A's secondary right. But it is clear that courts also take into account other factors in justifying the award of constructive trusts, for example the effects of a proprietary award on B's unsecured creditors in the event of A's insolvency. It is not possible satisfactorily to take into account such a justification unless it is recognised that it relates to the appropriate *remedy* to be awarded, and therefore that it is a factor which influences the court's remedial discretion. This is because the concern for B's unsecured creditors is unrelated to B's wrongdoing.

This explains why the reasoning provided in *Reid* has been criticised as unsatisfactory. According to Lord Templeman, the fact that '[B's] unsecured creditors cannot be in a better position than [A]' was taken to follow as a matter of logic from the principle that 'it is unconscionable for a fiduciary to obtain and retain a benefit in breach of duty.'[152] This has been criticised as giving 'insufficient weight to the potentially unfair consequences to the interests of other creditors',[153] and for 'presuppos[ing] the very point in issue, namely that [A]'s claim is proprietary.'[154] These criticisms arise because Lord Templeman's reasoning relies on a *non sequitur*. The retention of a benefit by B due to his wrongdoing might only be relevant to determining the nature of A's *secondary right*, whereas a discussion of the effects of an award on B's unsecured creditors is a consideration relating to the nature of the appropriate *remedy*.

The distinction between right and remedy can also be used to evaluate the justifications provided in *FHR*. Although the judgment was said to be based on 'legal principle, decided cases, policy considerations, and practicalities',[155] dissatisfaction lingers as to the reasoning employed by the Supreme Court.[156] This may be due to the failure to recognise what was truly at stake: how best to exercise the court's remedial discretion. For instance, it was argued to be 'common sense' that 'the bribe or commission will … [reduce] the benefit from the relevant transaction which the principal will have obtained, and therefore can fairly be said to be his property.'[157] But this reasoning is artificial: it seeks to justify the award of a proprietary remedy by somehow linking this to a pre-existing entitlement or right although it is clear that there is no pre-existing proprietary relationship between the parties which the remedy can replicate. The Supreme Court also dismissed the relevance of B's unsecured creditors on the basis that bribes and secret commissions are 'property which should not be in [B]'s estate at all'.[158] While this reasoning would be appropriate when dealing with remedies which replicate primary duties, such as those attaching to an express trustee, it fails to explain why a *reflective* remedy ought to have proprietary effect. More convincing is the Supreme Court's reasoning that a proprietary remedy would allow A to trace or follow the proceeds of B's gains[159] based on a policy of taking a stringent approach

152 *Reid* (n 49) 331.
153 *Sinclair Investments* (n 25) [83].
154 Goode, 'Proprietary Liability for Secret Profits' (n 4) 494. In *Sinclair Investments* (n 25) [78] Lord Neuberger MR also criticised Lord Templeman's reasoning as 'begging the question' and 'assuming what it asserts'.
155 *FHR* (n 6) [12].
156 The Hon William Gummow AC, 'Bribes and Constructive Trusts' (2015) 131 *LQR* 21, 25; JE Penner, 'Distinguishing Fiduciary, Trust, and Accounting Relationships' (2014) 8 *Journal of Equity* 202.
157 *FHR* (n 6) [37], [43].
158 ibid [43].
159 ibid [44].

towards fiduciaries who receive a bribe or secret commission.[160] This reasoning does not rely merely on the fact of B's breach of duty, but gives a proper justification for why the choice of a proprietary remedy is made.

10.3.3.2. Precedent

It remains undeniable that, as a result of the Supreme Court's decision in *FHR*, later—particularly lower—courts will no longer exercise remedial discretion on a case-by-case basis, at least in relation to bribes and secret commissions received in breach of fiduciary duty.[161]

However, it is crucial to recognise that the constraint placed on the exercise of discretion post-*FHR* is due to an operation of the doctrine of precedent, as opposed to the inherent nature of the imposed remedy. As Charlie Webb writes, '[r]ules may not only confer discretion but also regulate its exercise: having a discretion is consistent with rules determining what sorts of considerations the decision-maker must take account of in making his choice and how those considerations are to be weighted or prioritized.'[162] The fact that (lower) courts are now compelled to treat like cases alike and impose constructive trusts over bribes and secret commissions does not alter the fact that they are imposing reflective remedies, which, in principle, allow for the ability to exercise discretion as to content. It is not the absence of the ability to exercise such discretion, but a (lower) court's consistent application of the authoritative decision of the Supreme Court, which leads to the imposition of a constructive trust. A's 'power to create an obligation in the court to adjudicate [A]'s matter in the light of [A]'s [secondary] rights'[163] consistently with the doctrine of precedent does not entail that courts have no discretion in the award, but simply that the award is constrained by the doctrine of precedent.

10.3.3.2.1. Effects of the Distinction

It might be thought that the imposition of 'reflective remedies constrained by precedent' is practically identical to the imposition of replicative remedies, and therefore that it is unnecessary to distinguish between the reflective nature of the constructive trusts and the constraints placed on their imposition by way of precedent. But this would be a mistake. In Chapter 2,[164] a number of general points were made in favour of maintaining a distinction between the nature of a remedy and the operation of precedent. In addition to those, there are a number of practical reasons why that distinction matters in specific relation to gains made in breach of fiduciary duty. Despite what may have been the intentions of their Lordships sitting in the Supreme Court in *FHR*, there are four categories of cases where that decision is not binding or is at best of persuasive authority. In these situations, everything turns on the distinction between the nature of the remedy and the effect of the doctrine of precedent.

In the first category are cases which necessitate an evaluation of the issue of remoteness on the facts of a particular case. As we have discussed,[165] approaching a breach of fiduciary

[160] ibid [42].

[161] See, eg, *Northampton Regional Livestock Centre Company Ltd v Cowling* [2015] EWCA Civ 651, [2016] 1 BCLC 431 [88].

[162] Charlie Webb, 'The Myth of the Remedial Constructive Trust' (2016) 69 *Current Legal Problems* 353, 361.

[163] Ori J Herstein, 'How Tort Law Empowers' (2015) 65 *University of Toronto Law Journal* 99, 109.

[164] See Chapter 2, S 2.4.3.

[165] See S 10.3.2.3.

duty as a wrong-based claim allows courts—even lower courts—to limit B's liability to consequences of his breach of duty which are not too remote. While *FHR* decides that a constructive trust is the appropriate remedy, it does not—and cannot, in the nature of things—dictate what gains may be too remote in particular cases. Recognising the reflective nature of the remedy allows courts due room to exercise discretion in order properly to assess which gains are too remote, and over which a constructive trust will not arise.

Secondly, there are other means by which gains may be made by an errant fiduciary which were not considered by the Supreme Court. One example which may be cited is *Sinclair Investments (UK) Ltd v Versailles Trade Finance Ltd*,[166] where B's breach of fiduciary duty consisted of misapplying funds by way of a Ponzi scheme in order falsely to inflate the value of shares he held in a personal capacity. Another example, noted by Conaglen, involves B taking a loan from A in breach of B's fiduciary duty and making a profit from his employment of the loan money.[167] It is unclear what the position is in these cases involving indirect gains: either *FHR* applies and the gains are held on a constructive trust, or *Sinclair* applies and B is liable for these gains in a personal capacity. In either case, recognising that the remedy to be imposed is a reflective remedy avoids masking the fact that there is a *choice* to be made as to the content of the appropriate remedy, and that the exercise must be 'convincingly justified by reference to policy and principle'.[168]

Thirdly, it is well-known that the Supreme Court may depart from its own previous decisions in certain situations, most notably 'when it appears right to do so'[169] or where an earlier decision is made *per incuriam*.[170] The unlikeliness of a future Supreme Court departing from the *FHR* decision does not detract from the fact that, if the matter arises for reconsideration, the reflective nature of the remedy will allow courts to exercise discretion as to content. This fact would be overlooked if the distinction between the nature of the remedy and the doctrine of precedent is not maintained.

Finally, there may be room to argue that it remains possible for courts to refuse to award a constructive trust in an appropriate case, notwithstanding the judgment in *FHR*. The fact that reflective remedies in principle allow for the exercise of discretion as to content may provide a residual amount of flexibility to avoid potential injustice on the facts of particular cases.[171]

[166] *Sinclair Investments* (n 25).
[167] Conaglen, 'Proprietary Remedies' (n 72) 492.
[168] *Underhill and Hayton* (n 16) [27.106].
[169] Practice Statement (Judicial Precedent) [1966] 1 WLR 1234 (HL).
[170] See, eg, *Morelle v Wakeling* [1955] 2 QB 379 (CA).
[171] Conaglen, 'Proprietary Remedies' (n 72) 493.

11

Remedial Constructive Trusts

It is often said that English law only recognises institutional constructive trusts, and does not impose remedial constructive trusts. Unlike other Commonwealth jurisdictions, English jurists perceive the imposition of trusts which reflect the 'critical features of judicial discretion and retrospectivity'[1] as manifestly inappropriate and fundamentally unjustified. The fervency with which this view is often asserted gives the impression that 'institutional' and 'remedial' constructive trusts have non-contentious, well-settled meanings. However, upon close inspection, 'many judges and jurists have used the expression "institutional" without explaining its import, while those who have paused to clarify the matter have tended to use the term in quite different ways'.[2] Little time has also been spent to account for the different degrees and dimensions of discretion in relation to remedial constructive trusts, or to investigate whether the timing at which a constructive trust takes effect necessarily determines its nature.

This chapter does three things. First, it explores the present understanding of the phrase 'remedial constructive trusts' in English law and demonstrates its deficiencies. Secondly, it demonstrates how institutional and remedial constructive trusts map on to the distinction between replicative, reflective, and transformative remedies. An important point to be made is that the phrase 'remedial constructive trusts' is capable of referring either to constructive trusts imposed as reflective remedies or as transformative remedies, and it is only the latter which falls to be considered within the 'court-based' category within the structure of the law of constructive trusts. Thirdly, armed with this analysis, it evaluates the status of English law and suggests how English law may be developed in the future.

11.1. The Present Understanding

It is well known that the distinction between institutional and remedial constructive trusts can be traced back to 1922 when Roscoe Pound first distinguished between 'remedial' and 'substantive' constructive trusts,[3] the latter term being substituted for 'institutional' by Ronald Maudsley in 1959.[4] Although the distinction prevails almost a century later, a precise definition of these terms remains elusive.

[1] *London Allied Holdings Ltd v Lee* [2007] EWHC 2061 (Ch) [273]; *Crossco No. 4 Unlimited v Jolan Ltd* [2011] EWCA Civ 1619, 14 ITELR 615 [84].

[2] Craig Rotherham, *Proprietary Remedies in Context* (Oxford, Hart Publishing, 2002) 13.

[3] Roscoe Pound, 'The Progress of the Law 1918–1919' (1920) 33 *Harvard Law Review* 420, 420–21.

[4] RH Maudsley, 'Proprietary Remedies for the Recovery of Money' (1959) 75 *LQR* 234, 237.

11.1.1. Definitions

It is generally thought that two elements distinguish institutional and remedial constructive trusts: the exercise or otherwise of judicial discretion and the timing at which the trusts come into existence.[5]

Consider first institutional constructive trusts. These are commonly understood as trusts which are imposed without the exercise of judicial discretion. Two related points are often cited in support of this view. First, they are created by, and arise from, the occurrence of pre-defined facts or real-world events[6] relating to 'the conduct of the parties'.[7] Secondly, these real-world events are pre-defined in accordance with settled principles, and therefore there is no room for the exercise of judicial discretion.[8] In terms of timing, institutional constructive trusts are said to arise 'automatically'[9] from the occurrence of those pre-defined facts, leaving the court the role merely of declaring that such a trust had arisen in the past.[10] As a result, the consequences which flow from the recognition of an institutional constructive trust, in particular its potentially detrimental effects on third parties, are said to be 'mandatory':[11] they are merely 'side-effects' of the events which trigger the trusts' existence.[12]

In contrast, the imposition of remedial constructive trusts is understood to be at the discretion of the judge, who has liberty to consider whether or not to create new property rights on a case-by-case basis.[13] The exercise of discretion is said to be guided only by whether it is 'just' to impose a constructive trust in a particular case.[14] Hence, it is impossible to predict in advance whether a constructive trust will be awarded, and claimants are said to have 'no rights born of any facts which have happened outside the court'.[15] Since courts can impose these trusts 'without … having to satisfy any established or elucidated rules and requirements',[16] their imposition would reflect the absence of a 'rationale for the availability of proprietary remedies'.[17] In terms of timing, the perceived relevance of discretion means that remedial constructive trusts necessarily exist for the first time when they are imposed by the court.[18] The effects of the trusts are also said to be within the discretion

[5] See, eg, Michael Bryan, 'Constructive Trusts: Understanding Remedialism' in Jamie Glister and Pauline Ridge (eds), *Fault Lines in Equity* (Oxford, Hart Publishing, 2012) 219–24.

[6] *Westdeutsche Landesbank Girozentrale v Islington LBC* [1996] AC 669 (HL) 714. See too Donovan DM Waters, Mark Gillen, and Lionel Smith, *Waters' Law of Trusts in Canada*, 4th edn (Toronto, Carswell, 2012) 508.

[7] The Right Hon Millett LJ, 'Equity—The Road Ahead' (1995–1996) 6 *King's College Law Journal* 1, 18.

[8] Millett, 'The Road Ahead' (n 7) 18, Lord Neuberger, 'The Remedial Constructive Trust—Fact or Fiction', speech at the Banking Services and Finance Law Association Conference, Queenstown, 10 August 2014 www.supremecourt.uk/docs/speech-140810.pdf [27].

[9] Neuberger, 'The Remedial Constructive Trust' (n 8) [7], Millett, 'The Road Ahead' (n 7) 18.

[10] *Westdeutsche* (n 6) 714. See too *Fortex Group Ltd v MacIntosh* [1998] 3 NZLR 171, 172.

[11] *Commonwealth Reserves v Chodar* [2001] 2 NZLR 374 [19].

[12] *Westdeutsche* (n 6) 714.

[13] *Crossco* (n 1) [84]; *Turner v Jacob* [2006] EWHC 1317 (Ch) [85]; *Westdeutsche* (n 6) 714.

[14] Neuberger, 'The Remedial Constructive Trust' (n 8) [28]; Millett, 'The Road Ahead' (n 7) 18; Lynton Tucker, Nicholas le Poidevin, and James Brightwell (eds), *Lewin on Trusts*, 19th edn (London, Sweet & Maxwell, 2015) [7-026].

[15] Peter Birks, 'Three Kinds of Objection to Discretionary Remedialism' (2000) 29 *University of Western Australia Law Review* 1, 6.

[16] Andrew Butler (ed), *Equity and Trusts in New Zealand*, 2nd edn (Wellington, Thomson Reuters, 2009) [13.3.1].

[17] Millett, 'The Road Ahead' (n 7) 19. See too *Re Goldcorp Exchange Ltd (in receivership)* [1995] 1 AC 74 (PC) 104.

[18] *Re Polly Peck International plc (in administration) (No. 2)* [1998] 3 All ER 812 (CA) 830; *Re Sharpe (a bankrupt)* [1980] 1 WLR 219 (Ch) 225. See too *Fortex Group Ltd* (n 10) 175; *Chodar* (n 11) 383.

of the court. Thus, judges have latitude to decide whether the proprietary consequences take effect retrospectively or prospectively.[19]

11.1.2. Deficiencies

Upon close scrutiny, these definitions are deficient in two ways. Not only do they fail fully to account for the distinction between institutional and remedial constructive trusts, they also do not accurately reflect the true state of the law.

Take first the element of discretion. It is difficult to accept the proposition that the exercise of judicial discretion *necessarily* entails that constructive trusts do not have proprietary effect from the occurrence of certain facts. Nor is it necessarily the case that the exercise of such discretion indicates the lack of settled principles and proper rationales. As Etherton J (as he then was) observed in *London Allied Holdings Ltd v Lee*,[20] such a view of judicial discretion may be 'overly emphatic, having regard, for example, to the strong discretion in the Court to decide upon the appropriate form of relief for proprietary estoppel, including whether it should be personal or proprietary and whether it should be to protect the claimant's expectations or compensate for reliance loss.' In the discussion of proprietary estoppel in Chapter 7, it was seen that a claimant (A) obtains an 'equity by estoppel'[21] when B induces A to assume that B will cede an interest in property B owns to A, and A relies on the assumption to A's detriment. This indicates that proprietary estoppel undoubtedly gives effect to A's right born of facts which have happened outside the court. Moreover, courts do not exercise the remedial discretion afforded by proprietary estoppel *simply* on the basis of whether it is 'just' to do so on the facts of a particular case, but proceed on settled and established principles. Thus, the remedy must be proportionate, and courts must impose only the 'minimum equity' to do justice[22] to *compensate* A for his detrimental reliance.[23] Where a constructive trust is awarded, its proprietary consequences 'ha[ve] effect from the time the equity arises' (that is, from the occurrence of the relevant facts) 'as an interest capable of binding successors in title.'[24]

The source of the difficulty lies in using discretion per se as a distinguishing criterion. In a different context, it has been said that '"discretion" is a somewhat protean word. It connotes the exercise of judgment in making choices. In a sense, most decisions involve the exercise of discretion … [T]here can also be discretion even in the hammering of a nail'.[25] Discretion is not a binary, all-or-nothing concept; there are different degrees and shades to it. It is therefore impossible properly to define institutional and remedial constructive trusts merely in terms of whether discretion is or is not exercised.

[19] *Westdeutsche* (n 6) 714–15; *Muschinski v Dodds* (1985) 160 CLR 583, 451.

[20] *London Allied Holdings Ltd* (n 1) [274].

[21] Land Registration Act 2002, s 116(a).

[22] *Henry v Henry* [2010] UKPC 3, [2010] 1 All ER 988 [65]; *Crabb v Arun District Council* [1976] Ch 179, 198.

[23] See, eg, *Campbell v Griffin* [2001] EWCA Civ 990, [2001] WTLR 981; *Jennings v Rice* [2002] EWCA Civ 159, [2003] 1 FCR 501; *Ottey v Grundy* [2003] EWCA Civ 1176, [2003] WTLR 1253; *Henry v Henry* (n 22). These matters are discussed in Chapter 7.

[24] Land Registration Act 2002, s 116(a). This section merely confirms what was already the norm: see Law Commission, *Land Registration for the Twenty-First Century: A Conveyancing Revolution* (Law Com No. 271, 2001) [5-30]–[5-31].

[25] *Carty v London Borough of Croydon* [2005] EWCA Civ 19, [2005] ELR 104 [25].

The element of timing also fares no better. In the first place, it is not an essential characteristic of remedial constructive trusts that they give judges the ability to determine on a case-by-case basis the timing at which proprietary effects first arise. For instance, the Canadian Supreme Court in *Rawluk v Rawluk* held that remedial constructive trusts are 'deemed to have arisen at the time when the unjust enrichment first occurred'.[26] Thus, remedial constructive trusts in Canada remain 'remedial' even though they invariably have retrospective effect. It might then be suggested that remedial constructive trusts should be confined to such 'backdated' trusts, but this view causes even more confusion. Thus, Lord Neuberger has recently suggested that 'remedial' constructive trusts which are of retrospective effect are in reality 'imposed at once as an institutional trust'.[27] Yet, confining 'remedial' constructive trusts only to its prospective effect robs the trusts of much of their content. As Peter Birks has argued, such 'trusts' amount to no more than mere orders for specific delivery of an asset, a jurisdiction already inherent in the common law.[28]

11.1.3. Senses of 'Remedy'

A significant factor which influences one's definition of 'institutional' and 'remedial' constructive trusts is one's understanding of what a remedy entails. This is obvious from various judicial observations. For instance, the oft-quoted observation by Lord Browne-Wilkinson in *Westdeutsche Landesbank Girozentrale v Islington LBC* states that '[a] remedial constructive trust ... is a judicial *remedy* ...';[29] Nourse LJ has defined a remedial constructive trust as 'an order of the court granting, by way of a *remedy*, a proprietary right ...';[30] and Lewison J has observed that remedial constructive trusts are situations where 'the court will impose a constructive trust by way of a *remedy*'.[31]

Given its centrality to the debate, it is curious that the meaning of 'remedy' is left unexplained. Upon closer inspection, it appears that 'remedy' is used in this context simply to refer to the exercise of remedial discretion at the date of judgment, in contradistinction to a mere 'declaration' of the claimant's pre-existing property right. However, this does not overcome the difficulties associated with the element of discretion, as discussed earlier. Moreover, Birks has explained that there are at least five possible meanings of the word 'remedy',[32] and without identifying which of these is at play, it remains impossible properly to distinguish between institutional and remedial constructive trusts. In fact, without first identifying what a 'remedy' means, there is a real possibility that the phrase 'remedial constructive trusts' might even be taken to refer to legal devices that are not *trusts* at all. For example, Bruce Collins QC[33] has

[26] *Rawluk v Rawluk* [1990] 1 SCR 70, 92. See too *Re Polly Peck International* (n 18) 823; *Crossco* (n 1) [84].

[27] Neuberger, 'The Remedial Constructive Trust' (n 8) [15]. This led Lord Neuberger to question whether 'remedial' constructive trusts imposed by the Australian courts are in fact 'institutional' in nature: Neuberger, 'The Remedial Constructive Trust' (n 8) [22].

[28] Peter Birks, 'The End of the Remedial Constructive Trust?' (1998) 4 *Trust Law International* 202, 205–06.

[29] *Westdeutsche* (n 6) 714 (emphasis added).

[30] *Re Polly Peck International* (n 18) 830 (emphasis added).

[31] *Ultraframe (UK) Ltd v Fielding* [2005] EWHC 1638 (Ch), [2006] FSR 17 [1515] (emphasis added).

[32] Birks, 'Three Kinds of Objection' (n 15) 3–6. See too Rafal Zakrzewski, *Remedies Reclassified* (Oxford, OUP, 2009) Chs 2–4.

[33] Bruce Collins QC, 'The Remedial Constructive Trust "Between a Trust and a Catch-Phrase"' (2014) 10 *Trusts & Trustees* 1055, 1058.

used that phrase in connection with a *personal* liability to account in the context of accessory liability, since, on one reading, a 'remedy' is 'nothing more than a formula for equitable relief'.[34] As the Supreme Court has recently confirmed, however, accessory liability makes the defendant liable '*as if he were* a trustee',[35] whereas the subject-matter at hand—constructive trusts—involve making the defendant a *trustee* properly so-called.

11.2. Recharacterisation

In spite of their instability, the elements of discretion and timing are persistently at the heart of the discussion. The tendency to focus on these elements reveals an underlying desire to understand the different *sources* of constructive trusts. This desire can be met if, in line with the approach taken in this book, we understand constructive trusts as remedies—that is, the subject-matter of court orders, no more and no less.[36] This leaves open the questions of *what* rights trigger the trusts and *how* the trusts relate to those rights. On this approach, 'institutional' constructive trusts can be understood as replicative remedies, while 'remedial' constructive trusts can refer either to those imposed as reflective or transformative remedies. This distinction illuminates the debate concerning institutional and remedial constructive trusts.

11.2.1. 'Institutional' Constructive Trusts

Constructive trusts which have traditionally been identified as 'institutional' in nature square easily with constructive trusts imposed as replicative remedies. So, for example, constructive trusts which are imposed in relation to the doctrine in *Rochefoucauld v Boustead* and secret trusts are often described in terms which match those commonly used to identify institutional constructive trusts. Thus, Millett LJ (as he then was) observed of these constructive trusts that B's 'possession of the property is coloured from the first by the trust and confidence by means of which he obtained it'[37]—that is, 'as the result of a transaction by which both parties intend to create a trust from the outset'.[38] There is a clear alignment between these constructive trusts and institutional constructive trusts, which are said to arise 'by operation of law as from the date of the circumstances which give rise to it'.[39]

Moreover, the lack of exercise of remedial discretion in relation to institutional constructive trusts is indicative of the replicative nature of the trusts. Thus, in these doctrines, a constructive trust is invariably imposed, which indicates that the remedial response is narrow and limited. Because the remedy merely replicates the parties' primary rights and duties which have arisen pre-trial, judges never pause to consider whether a lesser remedy would be more appropriate.

[34] *Paragon Finance plc v DB Thakerar & Co* [1999] 1 All ER 400 (CA) 409.
[35] *Williams v Central Bank of Nigeria* [2014] UKSC 10, [2014] AC 1189 [80] (emphasis in original).
[36] See Chapter 2, n 15.
[37] *Paragon Finance* (n 34) 409.
[38] *Coulthard v Disco Mix Club Ltd* [2000] 1 WLR 707 (Ch) 731.
[39] *Westdeutsche* (n 6) 714.

11.2.2. 'Remedial' Constructive Trusts

On the other hand, the present understanding of 'remedial' constructive trusts in terms of discretion and retrospectivity is capable of referring either to constructive trusts imposed as reflective or as transformative remedies.

11.2.2.1. As Reflective Remedies

Proprietary estoppel allows judges to exercise remedial discretion as to the content of the appropriate remedy in a particular case to compensate A for harm caused by B's unreliability in relation to induced assumptions. The exercise of such discretion may lead to the imposition of a constructive trust, the effect of which is backdated to the time of B's breach.[40] These features of the doctrine indicate that, on the present understanding, proprietary estoppel falls within the definition of 'remedial' constructive trusts. As Etherton J (as he then was) observed, proprietary estoppel provides for the imposition of:[41]

> a constructive trust by way of discretionary ... relief, the right to which is a mere equity prior to judgment, but which will have priority over intervening rights of third parties on established principles, such as those relating to notice, volunteers and the unconscionability on the facts of a claim by the third party to priority.

The fact that the phrase 'remedial constructive trusts' can be used to describe constructive trusts which are imposed as reflective remedies is reflected in Lord Scott's judgment in *Thorner v Major*[42] where his Lordship observed (of English law) that '[t]he possibility of a remedial constructive trust over property, created by the common intention or understanding of the parties regarding the property on the basis of which the claimant has acted to his detriment, has been recognised at least since *Gissing v Gissing* [1971] AC 886'. Because English law does not impose constructive trusts as transformative remedies,[43] as will be discussed below,[44] the only plausible explanation of Lord Scott's words is as follows. The reference to *Gissing* points to the 'common intention constructive trust' as applied in the family homes context; and in Chapter 14, we will see that this trust is best explained as a reflective remedy because the trust does not simply give effect to the parties' primary rights and duties. Therefore, by using the phrase 'remedial constructive trust', Lord Scott could only have meant that *reflective constructive trusts* are recognised in English law.

11.2.2.2. As Transformative Remedies

Transformative remedies allow judges to exercise discretion both as to the goal and content of the appropriate remedy in a particular case, and so they provide the widest remedial potential.[45] They also clearly fall within the present understanding of 'remedial' constructive

[40] See discussion in Chapter 7.
[41] *London Allied Holdings Ltd* (n 1).
[42] *Thorner v Major* [2009] UKHL 18, [2009] 1 WLR 776 [20].
[43] And assuming, as we ought to, that Lord Scott was aware of this.
[44] See S 11.3.1.
[45] See Chapter 2, S 2.4.2.3.

trusts. The ability to impose such constructive trusts is most clearly found in jurisdictions outside English law, where a 'remedial constructive trust' can potentially be imposed in any case and whatever the field of private law involved.[46] Their award has little to do with the claimant's pre-existing rights, and instead much to do with the redistribution of property rights to reflect various policy goals which are subject to the courts' discretion. For this reason, these 'remedial constructive trusts' occupy a category of their own within the structure of the law of constructive trusts, falling within the 'court-based' category, since the remedy has more to do with the courts' exercise of discretion and less to do with the parties' pre-trial rights and duties.

11.2.2.2.1. Australia

In Australia, courts are able to make use of a 'remedial constructive trust' to prevent unconscionable conduct in a wide array of cases, such as those involving property acquired in the course of a de facto marriage,[47] estoppel,[48] breach of fiduciary duty,[49] and knowing receipt.[50] The imposition of these trusts unmistakably involves judicial discretion.

It has repeatedly been said that the constructive trust is to be imposed only as a last resort, that is, after other 'lesser'—personal—remedies have been considered and found to be wanting in a particular case.[51] This reflects an exercise of discretion as to the *content* of the appropriate remedy, akin to the 'minimum equity' approach taken by English courts in relation to proprietary estoppel. Such discretion is also reflected in the ability of Australian courts to decide whether the trust will take effect from the date of judgment or from some other earlier point in time.[52]

The extent of discretion does not stop there, however: courts go further by exercising discretion as to the *goal* of the remedy on a case-by-case basis. This is indicated by the open-ended list of potential purposes or objects pursuant to which these trusts may be awarded. For instance, 'unconscionability' has been defined as a situation which the court deems to be 'contrary to justice and good conscience'.[53] This indicates that there is no limit to the potential objects for which the remedy may be awarded, so long as courts do not 'disregard legal and equitable rights and simply do what is fair'.[54] Similarly, while courts are guided by the 'principle of appropriateness' whereby 'the purpose (or imperatives) served by the individual doctrine' informs a judge in the selection of the appropriate remedy, there is also 'the requirement to do "practical justice"',[55] which allows courts to refuse to impose a

[46] Donovan Waters, 'The Constructive Trust: Two Theses—England and Wales, and Canada' http://archive.is/5neoh.

[47] eg *Muschinski v Dodds* (n 19); *Baumgartner v Baumgartner* (1987) 76 ALR 75.

[48] *Giumelli v Giumelli* (1999) 196 CLR 101.

[49] *Grimaldi v Chameleon Mining NL (No. 2)* [2012] FCAFC 6.

[50] *Robins v Incentive Dynamics Pty Ltd (in liquidation)* [2003] NSWCA 71. *cf Wambo Coal Pty Ltd v Ariff* [2007] NSWSC 589 [42], where it was suggested by White J that a constructive trust imposed on a mistaken payment where the recipient knew of the mistake and still retained the money was an 'institutional' trust.

[51] *Bathurst CC v PWC Properties Pty Ltd* (1998) 195 CLR 566 [42]; *Giumelli v Giumelli* (n 48) [4]; *John Alexander's Clubs Pty Ltd v White City Tennis Club Ltd* [2010] HCA 19 [128]; *Farah Constructions Pty Ltd v Say-Dee Pty Ltd* [2007] HCA 22 [200].

[52] *Muschinski v Dodds* (n 19) 451.

[53] *Baumgartner v Baumgartner* (n 46) 83.

[54] *Muschinski v Dodds* (n 19) 436.

[55] *Grimaldi v Chameleon Mining NL* (n 49) [505], [509].

constructive trust for any policy reason. For instance, a judge may be motivated by concerns relating to the proportionality of the remedial response,[56] the protection of third party creditors who are 'materially interested' or 'directly affected' by the award,[57] or the desire to deter the defendant from keeping the proceeds of his wrongdoing.[58] As Deane J observed in *Muschinski v Dodds*,[59] the constructive trust can be 'moulded and adjusted to give effect to the application and inter-play of equitable principles in the circumstances of the particular case.' The clear ability to exercise discretion as to the goal of the appropriate remedy indicates that Australian courts impose constructive trusts as transformative remedies.[60]

This conclusion is fortified by the rule adopted by the High Court in *John Alexander's Clubs Pty Ltd v White City Tennis Club Ltd* that 'where a court is invited to make, or proposes to make, orders directly affecting the rights or liabilities of a non-party [such as a constructive trust], the non-party is a necessary party and ought to be joined.'[61] Such third parties are able not only to make a case against the claimant's 'substantive case', but also to argue that the award of a constructive trust remedy would unfairly prejudice them. In view of this rule, it is hardly possible to say that courts are concerned with replicating or reflecting a claimant's pre-existing right, since the decision whether or not to award a constructive trust hinges on factors which are extraneous to considerations relating to the claimant's rights.

11.2.2.2.2. Canada

In Canada, the 'remedial constructive trust' device is available in two types of claim, namely unjust enrichment and wrongdoing. Unjust enrichment claims are made out when three requirements are satisfied: the defendant received an enrichment, the claimant suffered a corresponding deprivation, and there is an absence of juristic reason for the enrichment which renders the defendant's retention of the enrichment unjust.[62] A wrongdoing claim is made out where the defendant is under an equitable obligation in relation to the activities giving rise to the assets in his hands, and it is shown that the assets were acquired as a result of the defendant's deemed or actual agency activities in breach of that obligation.[63]

[56] ibid [511].

[57] *John Alexander's Clubs* (n 51) [131], [139].

[58] *Robins v Incentive Dynamics* (n 50) [77].

[59] *Muschinski v Dodds* (n 19) 451.

[60] For this reason, Lord Neuberger's suggestion that remedial constructive trusts imposed in Australia are in fact institutional in nature (noted at n 27 above) is misguided.

[61] *John Alexander's Clubs* (n 51) [131]–[132].

[62] *Pettkus v Becker* [1980] 2 SCR 834, 848; *Peter v Beblow* [1993] 1 SCR 980, 987; *Garland v Consumers' Gas Co* [2004] 1 SCR 629 [30]; *Kerr v Baranow* [2011] 1 RCS 269 [36]–[45]. It should be noted, however, that this does not entail a 'pure juristic reasons approach' (see Lionel Smith, 'Demystifying Juristic Reasons' (2007) 45 *Canadian Business Law Journal* 281, 291) but one where there is a mix between 'juristic reasons and reasons for restitution' (Smith, 'Demystifying Juristic Reasons' (n 62) 290). This is obvious from the Supreme Court's decision in *Garland* [44]–[46]. The means by which this element of the claim is to be made out is by reference to a list of established categories of juristic reasons; and although the list was said to be closed, it remains possible to expand that list by adding 'other valid common law, equitable or statutory obligations' (*Garland* [44]), or by the defendant's attempt to rebut the claimant's claim through relying on 'the reasonable expectations of the parties' or 'public policy concerns' (*Garland* [46]).

[63] *Soulos v Korkontzilas* [1997] 2 SCR 217, 241.

Such claims have arisen in cases relating to the acquisition of property by fraud or breach of fiduciary duty.[64]

Once an unjust enrichment or wrongdoing claim is made out, courts have latitude to exercise discretion in order to determine the appropriate remedy. A 'minimum equity'-like approach is detected, which indicates the exercise of discretion as to content. Thus, personal remedies must be deemed inadequate before a constructive trust can be awarded.[65]

In addition, however, courts also exercise discretion as to the *goal* of the appropriate remedy. Consider first the wrongdoing cases. A constructive trust is awarded where the claimant can show a 'legitimate reason for seeking a proprietary remedy', and where there are 'no factors which would render imposition [*sic*] of a constructive trust unjust in all the circumstances of the case'.[66] This indicates a non-exhaustive approach to the potentially relevant purposes or objectives to be achieved by the awarded remedy.

Consider the case of *Soulos v Korkontzilas*,[67] which demonstrates the multifarious policy factors which may be taken into account. B was A's real estate broker, who in breach of his fiduciary duty arranged for his (B's) wife to purchase a property which B was meant to acquire on A's behalf. The majority of the Supreme Court held that a constructive trust was the appropriate remedy. In relation to the requirement to demonstrate a legitimate reason, this was fulfilled by the fact that the property in question held special value to A because the tenant was A's banker, and being the landlord of one's banker was prestigious in his community.[68] The award was also justified by the policy aim of 'ensur[ing] that agents and others in positions of trust remain faithful to their duty of loyalty'.[69] In relation to the requirement to demonstrate that the imposition of a constructive trust was not 'unjust in all the circumstances of the case', the court took into account the fact that undue prejudice would not be caused either to B or to any third party.[70]

The unjust enrichment cases also reveal an open-ended approach to the goal of the awarded remedy, where the constructive trust is used as 'a broad and flexible equitable tool … to determine beneficial entitlement to property'.[71] For a constructive trust to be imposed, it is necessary to show some 'reason to grant to the plaintiff the additional rights that flow from recognition of a right of property';[72] and it appears that any relevant policy factor can be taken into account. Among these are: the appropriateness of granting the claimant priority in bankruptcy, preventing the wrongdoer from retaining any increase in value of the property, the uniqueness of the property in question, the moral quality of the defendant's act,[73] the probability of the defendant paying up a personal award,[74] and the potential 'psychological benefits derived from pride of ownership'.[75] The discretion to

[64] ibid 238.
[65] *Rawluk v Rawluk* (n 26) 107; *Peter v Beblow* (n 62) 988.
[66] *Soulos v Korkontzilas* (n 63) 241. See too *Sun Indalex Finance v United Steelworkers* [2013] 1 SCR 271 [228].
[67] *Soulos v Korkontzilas* (n 63).
[68] ibid [49].
[69] ibid [50].
[70] ibid [51].
[71] *Kerr v Baranow* (n 62) [50].
[72] *LAC Minerals Ltd v Int Corona Resources Ltd* [1989] 2 SCR 574, 678.
[73] All the above-mentioned points are found in *LAC Minerals* (ibid) 678–79.
[74] *Peter v Beblow* (n 62) 999.
[75] *Rawluk v Rawluk* (n 26) 92.

determine the purpose or object of the remedy in a particular case indicates that these constructive trusts are transformative in nature.

11.2.2.2.3. New Zealand

In New Zealand, the award of 'remedial constructive trusts' differs according to whether a case involves property acquired in the course of a de facto marriage or not. In cases that do, the 'heart of the matter' is the claimant's reasonable expectations.[76] In determining the appropriate remedy, both discretion as to goal and content are exercised. Discretion as to content is seen in the 'minimum equity' approach which the courts take: the appropriate remedy depends on the claimant's degree of sacrifice, weighing up the claimant's contributions against benefits received from the defendant, and the length of the parties' union.[77] As for discretion as to goal, although the courts do not treat 'fairness in the round as the ultimate test',[78] a plethora of purposes or objects may be relevant to the selection of the remedy. Thus, it is explicitly acknowledged that the 'reasonable expectations' criterion derives from, and is applied directly in preference to, the Canadian unjust enrichment approach, the Australian approach based on unconscionability, and the English doctrine of proprietary estoppel.[79] These doctrines do not lead to the award of constructive trusts by reference to a single goal: proprietary estoppel concerns compensation for harm, whilst the Canadian and Australian courts take an open-ended approach to the goal of the remedy. To the same extent, the 'reasonable expectations' criterion allows courts to exercise discretion as to goal, which indicates that the 'remedial constructive trusts' are imposed as transformative remedies.

Constructive trusts imposed in cases which do not involve de facto marriages are even more clearly transformative in nature. In these cases, the discretion to grant a remedial constructive trust can be triggered either by unjust enrichment or unconscionability.[80] The former trigger 'is substantially that developed in Canada';[81] and although the latter trigger is not expressly said to be the same as the Australian approach, a high degree of similarity is detected. Thus, in relation to both potential triggers, the New Zealand courts have said that the constructive trust is appropriate only where other remedies are inadequate.[82] Moreover, an open-ended approach as to goal is taken: '[t]he Court must carefully examine the reasons why other forms of relief are inadequate, the interests of any third parties and the other circumstances of the case, and consider whether proprietary relief can be justified'.[83] Potentially relevant factors are the interests and any unconscionable behaviour of third party creditors where the defendant is insolvent,[84] whether a writ of sale and possession would result in the claimant receiving less value than they would from the imposition of a constructive trust,[85] the defendant's behaviour throughout the proceedings,[86] and

[76] *Gillies v Keogh* [1989] 2 NZLR 327, 331. See too *Phillips v Phillips* [1993] 3 NZLR 159.
[77] *Gillies v Keogh* (n 76) 333–34.
[78] ibid 344.
[79] *Phillips v Phillips* (n 76) 167–68.
[80] *Chodar* (n 11) [42]–[44].
[81] ibid [43].
[82] ibid [58].
[83] ibid [47].
[84] *Fortex Group Ltd* (n 10) 175; *Chodar* (n 11) [57].
[85] *Chodar* (n 11) [59].
[86] ibid [60].

whether the court considers that there is some asset or assets belonging to the defendant on which a constructive trust ought to be imposed.[87] The clear exercise of discretion both as to the goal and content of the remedy indicates that the 'remedial constructive trust' is transformative in nature.

11.2.2.2.4. Singapore

In general,[88] Singaporean courts have considered 'remedial constructive trusts' in the context of unjust enrichment claims. The apex court has held that merely establishing an unjust enrichment claim successfully does not lead to the imposition of a 'remedial constructive trust': the trust is founded on fault, which is an additional element required for that remedy to be imposed.[89] The court explained that 'fault' entails a 'state of knowledge which renders it unconscionable for the recipient to keep the moneys'.[90] It requires 'some form or variation of knowing receipt',[91] or 'a particular factor giving rise to unconscionability'.[92]

Because the development of the 'remedial constructive trust' device in Singapore is in its infancy,[93] it is considerably difficult to provide an accurate evaluation of the law. Although the 'fault' requirement is not to be applied in such a way as to turn the device into a 'discretionary tool for fairness and justice',[94] it remains unclear what precise factors the courts are able to take into account in determining the appropriateness of the remedy. It might nevertheless be surmised that the Singaporean courts contemplate the possibility of exercising discretion both as to goal and content in unjust enrichment cases. This can be seen from the fact that, in *Wee Chiaw Sek Anna v Ng Li-Ann Genevieve*, the Court of Appeal took pains to point out that the position taken in Singapore is largely in line with the approach adopted by courts in Canada, Australia, and New Zealand.[95] While not expressly saying so, this impliedly approves and adopts the open-ended approach taken by courts in those jurisdictions in relation to the exercise of discretion.

11.2.2.2.5. Malaysia

Of the jurisdictions surveyed here, Malaysian courts have put in the least effort to explain the rationales and factors to be taken into account in relation to the imposition of constructive trusts. On the rare occasions where something is said, they reveal that the courts' exercise of discretion is wider than those contemplated in the other jurisdictions. For instance, the Court of Appeal and Federal Court have declared that constructive trusts are imposed

[87] *Fortex Group Ltd* (n 10) 175.

[88] An attempt in *Comboni Vincenzo v Shankar's Emporium (Pte) Ltd* [2007] 2 SLR (R) 1020 to apply the remedial constructive trust in the context of a knowing receipt claim was rejected for its failure to distinguish between a personal claim for liability to account and a proprietary claim: *Wee Chiaw Sek Anna v Ng Li-Ann Genevieve* [2013] 3 SLR 801 [138]. The application of the remedial constructive trust in the context of a *donatio mortis causa* claim in *Koh Cheong Heng v Ho Yee Fong* [2011] 3 SLR 125 was held to be confined to its facts and does not affect the general law: *Wee Chiaw Sek Anna* (n 88) [172].

[89] *Wee Chiaw Sek Anna* (n 88) [172], [182].

[90] ibid [172].

[91] ibid [179].

[92] ibid [177].

[93] Man Yip, 'Singapore's Remedial Constructive Trust: Lessons from Australia?' (2014) 8 *Journal of Equity* 1, 2.

[94] *Wee Chiaw Sek Anna* (n 88) [170].

[95] ibid [173]–[184].

whenever 'justice and good conscience' demand it,[96] by which they explicitly adopt the use and meaning of that phrase as explained by Lord Denning in *Hussey v Palmer*.[97] This is in direct contrast to the other jurisdictions surveyed, which have expressly rejected this 'constructive trust of a new model'[98] as the rationale for the imposition of remedial constructive trusts, in favour of an incremental and rationalised approach.

The lack of a more specific rationale for the imposition of constructive trusts can be seen in the case law. Consider two recent Federal Court decisions. In *CIMB Bank Bhd v Maybank Trustees Bhd*,[99] a recipient of trust money was held to be liable for knowing receipt based (curiously) on *dishonest assistance* cases,[100] which then led the court to 'intervene by imputing a constructive trust upon [her] for her role in misapplying the trust monies'. In *RHB Bank Berhad v Travelsight (M) Sdn Bhd*, a case concerning counter-restitution following rescission of a contract due to misrepresentation, the court took the view that, upon rescission, the seller automatically obtained the beneficial title to the property in the buyer's hands, but (curiously) held that a 'remedial constructive trust' had to be imposed for the buyer to obtain the beneficial interest in the money in the seller's hands.[101] These cases leave unexplained the need for, and precise factors leading to, the selection of the constructive trust remedy. Nevertheless, it is at least unquestionable that these cases indicate the exercise of discretion both as to goal and content, which indicates that these 'remedial constructive trusts' are also imposed as transformative remedies.

11.3. Evaluation

11.3.1. The Status of English Law

A few exceptions notwithstanding,[102] judges have repeatedly held that English law recognises only institutional constructive trusts; it does not impose remedial constructive trusts.[103]

[96] *Mayban Trustees Bhd v CIMB Bank Bhd* [2012] 6 MLJ 354 [77]; *CIMB Bank Bhd v Maybank Trustees Bhd* [2014] 3 MLJ 169 [129].

[97] *Hussey v Palmer* [1972] 1 WLR 1286 (CA) 1289. *cf* Low Weng Tchung, *The Law of Restitution and Unjust Enrichment in Malaysia* (Petaling Jaya, LexisNexis, 2015) [14-51], where it is suggested that the cases can be explained as situations of well-established institutional constructive trusts.

[98] This was the expression used by Lord Denning MR to describe such an approach in *Eves v Eves* [1975] 3 All ER 768 (CA) 771.

[99] *CIMB Bank Bhd* (n 96) [128], [129].

[100] Specifically *Royal Brunei Airlines Sdn Bhd v Tan* [1995] 2 AC 378 (PC).
For a fuller criticism of this aspect of the case, see Low, *The Law of Restitution* (n 97) [14-71], [14-77].

[101] *RHB Bank Bhd v Travelsight (M) Sdn Bhd* [2015] 1 AMR 433 [15], [30], www.kehakiman.gov.my/directory/judgment/file/02(f)-36-07-2013(W).pdf 20, 32. The Federal Court was also of the erroneous view that 'the notion of a remedial constructive trust is already part of English law': *RHB Bank Bhd* (n 101) 1 AMR 433 [21], www.kehakiman.gov.my/directory/judgment/file/02(f)-36-07-2013(W).pdf 25.
For a fuller criticism of this case, see Low, *The Law of Restitution* (n 97) [5-120]–[5-122], [14-52]–[14-53].

[102] *Metall Und Rohstoff AG v Donaldson Lufkin & Jenrette Inc* [1990] 1 QB 391 (CA) 479; *Westdeutsche* (n 6) 716; *London Allied Holdings Ltd* (n 1) [273]–[274]; *Clarke v Meadus* [2010] EWHC 3117 (Ch) [82].

[103] *Re Sharpe* (n 18) 225; *Lonrho plc v Fayed (No. 2)* [1992] 1 WLR 1 (Ch) 9; *Re Goldcorp Exchange Ltd* (n 17); *Re Polly Peck International* (n 18) 827, 831; *Ultraframe (UK) Ltd* (n 31) [1515], [1546]; *Turner v Jacob* (n 13) [85]; *De Bruyne v De Bruyne* [2010] EWCA Civ 519, [2010] 2 FLR 1240 [47]–[48]; *Sinclair Investments (UK) Ltd*

By making this observation, these judges are not simply saying that English law approaches the award of constructive trusts differently from other Commonwealth jurisdictions. If this was what was meant, then those statements are accurate: English courts do not impose 'remedial constructive trusts' *as that device is used* in the other jurisdictions. However, those judicial statements reflect a much deeper concern—that it is unthinkable to award proprietary remedies through the exercise of judicial discretion and with retrospective effect.[104] To do so would be unprincipled[105] and 'without recourse to further rationalisation',[106] since only with the authority of Parliament can a court 'grant a proprietary right to A, who has not had one beforehand, without taking some proprietary right away from B'.[107] To borrow the language of La Forest J in *LAC Minerals Ltd v International Corona Resources Ltd*,[108] the English courts' view is that constructive trusts should only 'recognise' and should not 'create' a right of property. This reflects two underlying assumptions concerning the imposition of constructive trusts in English law: they are ever only awarded where judges do not exercise discretion,[109] and that the retrospectivity in their award necessarily creates uncertainty in the law,[110] particularly to the prejudice of third parties.

However, because the present understanding does not take into account the distinction between reflective and transformative constructive trusts, English jurists fall into the error of adopting an exaggerated notion of remedial discretion which fails to recognise that different *degrees* and *dimensions* of discretion are exercised in relation to constructive trusts. It has been explained that reflective remedies provide for the exercise of discretion as to content, while transformative remedies allow for the exercise of discretion as to both content and goal. The former gives effect to secondary rights, while the latter has little to do with pre-existing substantive rights. Once this distinction is appreciated, then it becomes clear that it is *transformative* constructive trusts which are not part of English law.

It is obvious that the imposition of transformative constructive trusts is far more contentious than the imposition of reflective constructive trusts, since the former has the *potential* of leading to the unbridled exercise of judicial discretion.[111] This is not an issue in relation to reflective constructive trusts because the exercise of discretion is constrained in terms of the goal of the remedy. Thus, although proprietary estoppel provides for the exercise of remedial discretion, its exercise is constrained by the goal of compensating A for harm suffered through the unreliability of B's induced assumptions. This is why the exercise of discretion and the retrospective effect of a constructive trust award in this doctrine do not cause any uncertainty: it is precisely because proprietary estoppel remedies give effect to the

v Versailles Trade Finance Ltd (In Administration) [2011] EWCA Civ 347, [2012] Ch 453 [37]; *Crossco* (n 1) [84]; *FHR European Ventures LLP v Cedar Capital Partners LLC* [2014] UKSC 45, [2015] AC 250 [47]; *Angove's Pty Ltd v Bailey* [2016] UKSC 47, [2016] 1 WLR 3179 [27].

104 *London Allied Holdings Ltd* (n 1) [273]; *Crossco* (n 1) [84].

105 *Lonrho plc v Fayed (No. 2)* (n 103) 9; *London Allied Holdings Ltd* (n 1) [273].

106 *Re Goldcorp Exchange Ltd* (n 17) 104.

107 *Re Polly Peck International* (n 18) 831.

108 *LAC Minerals* (n 72) 676.

109 Neuberger, 'The Remedial Constructive Trust' (n 8) [26]: 'property rights are a matter of strict law not discretion.'

110 *London Allied Holdings Ltd* (n 1) [273].

111 This is arguably the case in relation to the way in which Malaysian courts impose constructive trusts: see S 11.2.2.2.5.

claimant's secondary rights that we can confidently state the choices and constraints on the courts' exercise of discretion, as well as predict with reasonable certainty the possible outcome of any particular case. This also explains why it is demonstrably untrue that the ability to vary proprietary rights can only be granted by an Act of Parliament:[112] as proprietary estoppel indicates, English courts are able to do so in a controlled manner, that is, where the exercise of discretion is constrained by the goal of the remedy.

11.3.1.1. Transformative Constructive Trusts: Reflective?

It is necessary to consider and dismiss two types of arguments which might be taken to suggest that transformative constructive trusts have a place in English law. The first is the argument that the 'remedial constructive trust' device as developed in other Commonwealth jurisdictions do not in fact provide judges with the ability to exercise discretion as to goal. This is based on the observations that those jurisdictions apply the 'remedial constructive trust' device pursuant to the fixed object of attaining 'the minimum equity to grant a proprietary remedy',[113] achieving 'fairness or good conscience',[114] or remedying the effects of a defendant's 'fault'.[115] On the basis of these statements, it might be argued that, if either of these serves as the fixed 'goal' of the remedy, then those 'remedial constructive trusts' are in fact imposed as reflective remedies, and are unobjectionable as far as English law is concerned.

Such a view would be erroneous. In the first place, the 'minimum equity' approach, on its own, indicates that discretion is exercised only as to content and not as to goal. It dictates that equity's intervention ought to be the least invasive possible to achieve a particular goal; it says nothing about what goal ought to be achieved. For example, a 'minimum equity' approach might be taken in pursuit of the goal of punishment, or compensation, or equitable redistribution of property rights: the choice of the goal remains at the courts' discretion. Similarly, 'fairness' and 'good conscience' are not precise enough to act as the goal of the appropriate remedy. This is easily demonstrated by the fact that *any* court order aims to do justice, to achieve fairness, and to accord with good conscience; the particular purpose(s) or object(s) for which a transformative constructive trust is imposed remains an open question.

The same can be said in relation to 'fault'. The view that remedial constructive trusts respond to 'fault' supposes that all causative events are 'wrongs giving rise to liability to sanctions or "remedies"'.[116] Even so, there still remains a policy choice to be made in terms of the goal of the remedy imposed in response to the defendant's wrongdoing. As Birks writes, 'if I show that you have committed a wrong, a brand new system with all its choices still before it might think of attaching all sorts of dire remedial consequences'.[117] 'Fault'

[112] See *Re Polly Peck International* (n 18) 831: 'It is not that you need an Act of Parliament to prohibit a variation of proprietary rights. You need one to permit it'.

[113] David Wright, 'Third Parties and the Australian Remedial Constructive Trust' (2013–2014) 37 *University of Western Australia Law Review* 31, 48.

[114] Waters, 'Two Theses' (n 46) 1.

[115] *Wee Chiaw Sek Anna* (n 88) [172].

[116] Peter Birks 'Rights, Wrongs, and Remedies' (2000) 20 *OJLS* 1, 35.

[117] Peter Birks, 'Equity in the Modern Law: An Exercise in Taxonomy' (1996) 26 *University of Western Australia Law Review* 1, 13.

does not indicate whether the remedy ought to be compensatory, restitutionary, punitive, or, indeed, whether the wrong ought to be satisfied further 'by having the wrongdoer's ears cut off.'[118] The goal remains at the court's discretion.

11.3.1.2. Replicative Constructive Trusts: Transformative?

The second argument is that constructive trusts which are part of English law are, upon closer inspection, transformative in nature. On this view, *all* constructive trusts can be deconstructed as transformative constructive trusts. There have been numerous suggestions to this effect.

For example, Donovan Waters writes in relation to Canadian law that it is 'an open issue' whether the 'existing constructive trust situations inherited from English law' 'should be subject to the same *purely remedial* constructive trust process'.[119] In his view, 'logic' dictates an affirmative answer.[120] A similar view is taken by Keith Mason. Writing extra-judicially, he observes that, even where events trigger the availability of (replicative) constructive trusts, 'a stern drill-sergeant roars out "WAIT FOR IT" ... A full-blown proprietary remedy will only be granted if truly necessary and appropriate.'[121] Along the same vein, RP Austin has written that 'a proprietary remedy should not ever be regarded as mandatory. It should be possible for a court to exercise discretion against decreeing proprietary relief if the circumstances suggest that it would be unwise to do so.'[122] Likewise, Michael Bryan suggests that in all cases 'the alternative of ordering personal relief must always be considered, and choice exercised according to flexible but structured criteria.'[123] Similar sentiments are echoed by Joe Campbell,[124] who suggests that claimants in any case merely have 'an equity' which compels courts to decide how best to satisfy that equity on a case-by-case basis.

The view that *all* constructive trusts can be deconstructed is closely connected to the view that there is continuing relevance in the fact that, historically, 'institutional' constructive trusts were 'remedial' in nature. For example, in *Muschinski v Dodds*,[125] Deane J said:

> In a broad sense, the constructive trust is both an institution and a remedy of the law of equity. As a remedy, it can only properly be understood in the context of the history and the persisting distinctness of the principles of equity that enlighten and control the common law. The use or trust of equity, like equity itself, was essentially remedial in its origins ... In time, the relationships which the trust was recognized and enforced to protect actual or presumed intention became standardized and were accepted into conveyancing practice ... [However] the rationale of the constructive trust must still be found essentially in its remedial function which it has predominantly retained.

[118] ibid 12, 14.

[119] Donovan Waters QC, 'Resulting Trusts, and the Canadian Remedial Constructive Trust: Reconciling the Two' [2013] *Trusts & Trustees* 1, 3.

[120] Waters, 'Reconciling the Two' (n 119) 5.

[121] Keith Mason, 'Deconstructing Constructive Trusts in Australia' (2010) 4 *Journal of Equity* 1, 45.

[122] RP Austin, 'Constructive Trusts' in PD Finn (ed), *Essays in Equity* (London, Law Book Co Ltd, 1985) 240.

[123] Bryan, 'Constructive Trusts' (n 5) 235.

[124] Joe Campbell, 'When and Why a Bribe is Held on a Constructive Trust: The Method of Reasoning Towards an Equitable Remedy' (2015) 39 *Australian Bar Review* 320, 325–29.

[125] *Muschinski v Dodds* (n 19) 450.

And further:[126]

> [Even] [i]f 'institution' is understood as connoting a relationship which arises and exists under the law independently of any order of a court, and 'remedy' is defined as referring to the actual establishment of a relationship by such an order … any perceived dichotomy between the two notions tend to prove ephemeral upon closer examination … Where an equity court would retrospectively impose a constructive trust by way of equitable remedy, its availability as such a remedy provides the basis for, and governs the content of, its existence *inter partes* independently of any formal order declaring or enforcing it. In this more limited sense, the constructive trust is also properly seen as both 'remedy' and 'institution' … there can be no true dichotomy between the two notions.

Later, by suggesting that 'the constructive trust has not outgrown its formative stages as an equitable remedy' in Australia, Deane J implicitly took the view that all constructive trusts were 'remedial'.[127] A similar view is proffered by Hang Wu Tang, who relies on Deane J's exposition to argue that 'the terminology of "institutional constructive trust" should be abandoned in Singapore'.[128]

It would be a distortion of the law to deconstruct constructive trusts in this way. Whatever the historical position may have been, it is an accurate observation of the modern law that no discretion as to goal and content is exercised in relation to the award of replicative constructive trusts. The fact that the law deems the parties' primary rights and duties as worthy of being enforced negates the need for courts to exercise discretion as to the goal of the remedy, and the content of the remedy is determined simply by direct reference to those rights and duties. Allowing even a residual possibility of considering afresh the goal and content of replicative constructive trusts on a case-by-case basis is not only unnecessary, but is also liable to cause contradictions and confusion. Moreover, it would detract from the full meaning of having *rights* at law. Since courts are prepared to say, in the context of the doctrine in *Rochefoucauld v Boustead* and secret trusts, that informally declared trusts will be enforced as constructive trusts, then beneficiaries under such trusts have rights enforceable as against their trustees which are similar in this respect to rights of beneficiaries under any—in particular, express—trusts. To hold that courts may yet exercise discretion to deprive beneficiaries under such constructive trusts of their rights would suggest that courts may also do so in relation to beneficiaries under any trust. This would in turn cast doubt as to whether beneficiaries have rights at all.

11.3.2. The Way Forward

It has been seen that the presence of remedial discretion and retrospectivity in the award of constructive trusts do not necessarily cause uncertainty or reflect a lack of proper principle. The question therefore arises: what is the nub of the matter which really troubles English jurists? The answer seems to be: the *ability* to exercise unconstrained or unbridled discretion. English courts are perfectly comfortable with exercising remedial discretion where the goal of the remedy constrains the exercise of such discretion, as proprietary estoppel

[126] ibid 451.
[127] ibid.
[128] Hang Wu Tang, 'The Constructive Trust in Singapore' (2010) 22 *Singapore Academy of Law Journal* 136 [11].

indicates, but not where the discretion is 'at large'. By reference to the language used in this book, English courts take no issue with replicative or reflective constructive trusts, but are opposed to those imposed as transformative remedies.

In attempting to avoid the exercise of such unbridled discretion, the temptation has been to exaggerate the amount of discretion involved in the imposition of transformative constructive trusts. For example, Birks writes that the remedial constructive trust device entails that 'flexibility is superabundant',[129] and criticises the use of such 'strong remedial discretion' for making the management of litigation impossible, depriving citizens of their dignity, and destroying the legitimacy of judicial authority.[130] Likewise, Lord Neuberger has observed extra-judicially that the device 'displays equity at its flexible flabby worst' and therefore criticises its use as being 'unprincipled, incoherent and impractical', which 'renders the law unpredictable'[131] because it contravenes principles of precedent and predictability.[132]

These exaggerations are unfortunate because they fail to recognise the fact that the discretion involved in the imposition of transformative constructive trusts is not *inevitably* unconstrained. In other words, simply because transformative constructive trusts provide courts with the *ability to* exercise unbridled discretion, this does not entail that such discretion must be exercised where these trusts are awarded.

In all the jurisdictions surveyed with the exception of Malaysia, courts have rejected Lord Denning's 'constructive trust of a new model' which can be imposed 'whenever justice and good conscience require it',[133] since using this as the *sole* criterion would entail that discretion is constrained by *no other consideration whatsoever.*[134] Instead, the courts have highlighted the need for an incremental development of the law, emphasising that they will be 'informed by the situations where constructive trusts have been recognized in the past.'[135] This indicates that, although transformative constructive trusts *allow for* the exercise of discretion as to the goal of the remedy, the doctrine of precedent provides a control mechanism which militates against the concerns of an unbridled exercise of discretion. It is therefore inaccurate to say that the sole criterion when imposing remedial constructive trusts is to ask whether their imposition 'would be contrary to any ordinary notion of fairness',[136] since due attention has to be paid to precedent.

This analysis has significant implications for the future development of the law. In relation to English law, courts and commentators ought to move away from asking *whether* discretion ought to be exercised in the imposition of constructive trusts, and instead focus on how best to *constrain* the exercise of remedial discretion. The crucial question is this: ought the law recognise transformative constructive trusts which provide the *possibility* for courts to depart from precedent, although this is very *unlikely* to occur? Put in this way, it is not immediately obvious that the answer ought to be a resounding 'no', since allowing for the ability to award transformative constructive trusts may provide a desirable balance between certainty and flexibility in the award of proprietary remedies.

129 Birks 'Rights, Wrongs, and Remedies' (n 116) 36–37.
130 ibid 23.
131 Neuberger, 'The Remedial Constructive Trust' (n 8) [6].
132 ibid [28].
133 *Hussey v Palmer* (n 97) 1290.
134 See, eg, *Muschinski v Dodds* (n 19) 452; *Pettkus v Becker* (n 62).
135 *Soulos v Korkontzilas* (n 63) [34]. See too *Baumgartner v Baumgartner* (n 46) 87.
136 *Angove's Pty Ltd* (n 103) [27].

As for the other Commonwealth jurisdictions, it is worth pausing to consider and appreciate the legitimate concerns which English courts have expressed concerning the exercise of unbridled discretion in relation to the imposition of constructive trusts. Certainty and predictability are core pillars of a fair and just legal system. It would therefore be undesirable to impose constructive trusts simply based on 'justice and good conscience'. The imposition of transformative constructive trusts does not exempt judges from expositing their reasons for doing so, and it is on the basis of such expositions that the doctrine of precedent can ensure certainty and predictability in the imposition of transformative constructive trusts.

PART C

12

Mutual Wills

The mutual wills doctrine has been part of English law since the eighteenth century.[1] Nevertheless, it remains difficult to define its operation, the legal principles involved, and its underlying rationale(s). These difficulties have caused many to doubt the usefulness and coherence of the doctrine. At the time of writing, the Law Commission is undertaking a review of the law concerning wills, with one of the four key areas to be reviewed being mutual wills.[2] This appears to be a response to the perceived undesirability of the doctrine. For instance, Mummery LJ said in *Olins v Walters*[3] that the doctrine 'continues to be a source of contention for the families of those who have invoked it. The likelihood is that in future even fewer people will opt for such an arrangement and even more will be warned against the risks involved'. Commentators have also suggested that mutual wills agreements are not 'sensible',[4] and should be 'avoided',[5] or even 'abolished'.[6]

This chapter examines the present understanding of the mutual wills doctrine and notes its shortcomings, particularly in relation to explaining the doctrine's rationale. It then demonstrates that the doctrine falls to be considered within the non-contract-based, bilateral events category of constructive trusts. It makes a distinction between two types of fact-pattern encompassed by the doctrine, and establishes that they respectively reflect QI and AI situations and can be explained by way of the norms which underpin those situations. The way in which this re-analysis affects our understanding of the inner workings of the doctrine will be explored. Finally, it discusses a number of lessons which emerge from this re-analysis.

12.1. The Present Understanding

In a typical mutual wills case, two individuals come to an agreement that the first to die (A) will leave his property to the survivor (B), with B promising to leave whatever is left at

[1] *Dufour v Pereira* (1769) Dick 419, 21 ER 332, reported more fully in F Hargrave, *Juridical Arguments and Collections*, vol II (London, GG & J Robinson, 1799) 304, 309.

[2] See www.lawcom.gov.uk/project/wills/. The other areas the Law Commission proposes to review are testamentary capacity, formality requirements, and rectification.

[3] *Olins v Walters* [2008] EWCA Civ 782, [2009] Ch 212 [3].

[4] Roger Kerridge (assisted by AHR Brierley), *Parry and Kerridge: The Law of Succession*, 13th edn (London, Sweet & Maxwell, 2016) [6-42].

[5] Ruth Hughes, 'Mutual Wills' (2011) 3 *Private Client Business* 131, 136.

[6] Nicky Richardson, 'Legislation for Mutual Wills in New Zealand' (2010) 24 *Trust Law International* 99, 109.

his death to one or more ultimate beneficiaries, C. In a rarer type of arrangement, A and B agree to make respective wills which benefit C directly. In both cases, B also promises not to revoke his will after A's death, this being indicated by an intention to create legally binding obligations.[7] When A dies and the property is left to B or C as the case may be, a constructive trust[8] binds B to carry out the agreement. Any subsequent volunteer recipient of B's property, such as his personal representative, executor, or heir,[9] is likewise bound to fulfil the mutual wills agreement. The constructive trust arises notwithstanding the informality of the agreement, that is to say, despite the fact that the arrangement may not appear in B's will as would normally be required by the Wills Act 1837, s 9,[10] and despite non-compliance with the Law of Property Act 1925, s 53(1)(b)[11] where it affects interests in land. As Mummery LJ observed in *Fry v Densham-Smith*,[12] 'if and when [the doctrine] applies, absolute beneficial testamentary dispositions ... do not take effect in accordance with their terms'.

12.1.1. Distinguishing Features of the Doctrine

There are two features of mutual wills which distinguishes it from the other doctrines explored in this book. First, the constructive trust binds not only A's property but also B's *own* property.[13] Secondly, B's promise is not to hold some property on trust immediately upon A's death, but to make a *testamentary* disposition in a particular form. These features pose tricky issues for a proper explanation of the doctrine, in particular during B's lifetime after A's death. How is it possible to reconcile B's apparent freedom to make use of property in his hands with the fact that he has trust obligations in relation to the property?

12.1.2. Attempted Explanations

Three possible approaches have been suggested, but none are satisfactory. The first takes the view that B's obligation is 'floating': it is suspended during his lifetime and 'crystallises' either upon B's death or when he makes gifts or settlements which are 'calculated

[7] *Birmingham v Renfrew* (1936) 57 CLR 666, 675; *Re Cleaver (deceased)* [1981] 1 WLR 939 (Ch) 947; *Re Goodchild (deceased)* [1997] 1 WLR 1216 (CA) 1225; *Osborne v Estate of Osborne* [2001] VSCA 228 [15]; *Birch v Curtis* [2002] EWHC 1158 (Ch), [2002] 2 FLR 847 [60].

[8] *Birmingham v Renfrew* (n 7) 680, 683; *Re Cleaver* (n 7) 947; *Re Newey (deceased)* [1994] 2 NZLR 590; *Re Dale (deceased)* [1994] Ch 31 (Ch) 46–47; *Manitoba University v Sanderman* (1998) 155 DLR (4th) 40; *Healey v Brown* [2002] EWHC (Ch) 1405, [2002] WTLR 849 (Ch) [8]; *Osenton v Osenton* [2004] EWHC 1055 (Ch) [33]; *Olins v Walters* (n 3) [39]; *Charles v Fraser* [2010] EWHC Civ 2154 (Ch) [59]; *Shovelar v Lane* [2011] EWCA Civ 802, [2012] 1 WLR 637 [37].

It is interesting to note that this categorisation of the trust has not been challenged by commentators who (wrongly) argue in other contexts (in the context of the doctrine in *Rochefoucauld v Boustead*, see Chapter 4, S 4.1.1.; in the context of secret trusts, see Chapter 5, S 5.1.) that trust which are based on the parties' intentions must always be express trusts.

[9] *Dufour v Pereira* (in Hargrave, n 1) 309, decided long before the Land Transfer Act 1897 made the concept of common law 'heir' obsolete.

[10] Among its requirements, a will must be put in writing and witnessed by two others to be valid.

[11] '[A] declaration of trust respecting any land ... must be manifested and proved by some writing signed by some person who is able to declare such a trust'.

[12] *Fry v Densham-Smith* [2010] EWCA Civ 1410, [2011] WTLR 387 [31]. See also *Olins v Walters* (n 3) [40].

[13] See *Re Goodchild* (n 7) 1224.

to defeat the intention of the [agreement]'.[14] This approach does not explain the nature of B's duties and C's rights during B's lifetime. By virtue of what right can B deal with his estate? How does C have a right against a recipient to whom B has left his estate contrary to the mutual wills agreement? Another problem with the 'floating trust' approach is that it envisages a trust which lacks certainty of subject-matter,[15] contrary to that which is required for the validity of any trust.[16] Others have suggested that the 'floating trust' should be given legal effect in the same way as floating charges are given effect.[17] However, it is difficult to reconcile this analysis with the policy underlying the Bills of Sale Act (1878) Amendment Act 1882, which prevents an individual from granting a floating charge over all his personal chattels.[18] Indeed, 'there is all the difference between a trust and a charge, in their inception'.[19]

The second approach treats mutual wills as *sui generis* or anomalous.[20] Based on the view that the doctrine is closely related to contractual actions,[21] its perceived anomaly lies in allowing C, a third party, to enforce a contract between A and B. However, the mutual wills doctrine is an equitable doctrine and, at least in the modern law, has nothing to do with claims in contract law.[22] Moreover, to write off the doctrine as *sui generis* is an act of despair which should be avoided until and unless other alternative explanations have been explored and found wanting.

A third approach treats the courts as imposing a remedial constructive trust, where judges are 'shaping the remedy to meet the circumstances'.[23] On this analysis, the mutual wills doctrine allows courts to impose transformative constructive trusts through the exercise of discretion as to both goal and content of the appropriate remedy. There is little to commend this approach. It has been seen in Chapter 11[24] that English courts have distanced themselves from the possibility of imposing transformative constructive trusts.

14 *Birmingham v Renfrew* (n 7) 689. This analysis has been cited in many English cases, eg in *Re Goodchild* (n 7) 225; *Re Cleaver* (n 7) 947; *Healey v Brown* (n 8); *Birch v Curtis* (n 7).

15 Peter Luxton, '*Walters v Olin* [*sic*]: Uncertainty of Subject Matter—An Insoluble Problem in Mutual Wills?' (2009) 73 *Conveyancer and Property Lawyer* 498 at 503–04.

16 *Knight v Knight* (1840) 3 Beav 148, 49 ER 58.

17 *Barns v Barns* (2003) 214 CLR 169 [152]. See too Christine J Davis, 'Floating Rights' (2002) 61 *CLJ* 423, 429.

18 See Louise Gullifer, *Goode on Legal Problems of Credit and Security*, 5th edn (London, Sweet & Maxwell, 2013) [4-01].

19 *Re Lehman Brothers* [2009] EWHC 3228 (Ch), [2010] 2 BCLC 301 [178].

20 *Re Goodchild* (n 7) 1230; TG Youdan, 'The Mutual Wills Doctrine' (1979) 29 *University of Toronto Law Journal* 390, 401; Henry Legge and Alastair Norris, 'Contract and Conscience: The Decline of the Mutual Will' [1998] 6 *Private Client Business* 332, 336; Rosalind Croucher, 'Mutual Wills: Contemporary Reflections on an Old Doctrine' (2005) 19 *Melbourne University Law Review* 390; AJ Oakley, *Parker and Mellows: The Modern Law of Trusts*, 9th edn (London, Sweet & Maxwell, 2008) [10-331].

21 The case of *Healey v Brown* (n 8) is often cited in support of this proposition. In that case David Donaldson QC, sitting as a deputy High Court judge, held that compliance with the Law of Property (Miscellaneous Provisions) Act 1989, s 2(1) is a prerequisite for the mutual wills doctrine to apply. However, this cannot be sustained as a matter of principle and consistency. It is indisputable that the mutual wills doctrine gives rise to constructive trusts, not merely contractual damages; and s 2(5) of the 1989 Act provides that 'nothing in this section affects the creation or operation of … constructive trusts'.

22 This point will be discussed in detail in S 12.4.1.

23 C Rickett, 'A Rare Case of Mutual Wills and its Implications' (1982) 8 *Adelaide Law Review* 178, 196. See too, eg, *Healey v Brown* (n 8) [24]; *Re Newey* (n 8) 593; Robert Burgess, 'A Fresh Look aAt Mutual Wills' (1970) 34 *Conveyencer and Property Lawyer* 230, 246; AHR Brierley, 'Mutual Wills—Blackpool Illuminations' (1995) 58 *MLR* 95, 99; Croucher, 'Mutual Wills' (n 20) 409.

24 See Chapter 11, S 11.3.1.

Moreover, in the mutual wills context constructive trusts do not appear to be imposed by way of discretion; and even if they were, an explanation for the pre-conditions for doing so is lacking. Furthermore, this approach does not identify the source and extent of B's and C's duties and rights; it merely addresses the consequences of B's breach of the agreement. Therefore, it fails to explain why, for instance, C's interest does not lapse if he predeceases B but dies after A.[25]

12.2. A Re-Analysis

In a recent article in the *Law Quarterly Review*,[26] I surveyed the various possible factual permutations which have triggered an application of the mutual wills doctrine in English and other Commonwealth courts. The conclusion reached in that article was that the mutual wills doctrine is triggered by the elements of B's promise and A's reliance.[27] B must promise to make a testamentary disposition either to A or C, and A must act in reliance on B's promise.

Identifying B's promise and A's reliance as the triggering events allows the mutual wills doctrine to be re-analysed in a way which is consistent with the structure of the law of constructive trusts proposed in this book. As we have seen in Chapter 3,[28] the doctrines which fall within the non-contract-based, bilateral events category of constructive trusts reflect these triggering events. Upon closer analysis, a distinction can be drawn between QI and AI situations within the mutual wills doctrine. This reflects a distinction between cases where B receives property from A pursuant to the parties' agreement, and cases where B does not do so.

12.2.1. B Receives Property from A

In the majority of cases, mutual wills agreements contemplate that B will receive property from A at A's death. It is clear that when A dies B is subject to certain duties and C obtains certain corresponding rights. However, the specific assets in B's hands may well alter during the course of his lifetime. It is therefore necessary to make a conceptual distinction between property in B's hands at the time of A's death (which, by definition, includes property acquired from A), and property which B may amass afterwards.

12.2.1.1. At A's Death

At the time of A's death, it may be tempting to analyse B's obligations as relating to two distinct sets of property, one belonging (formerly) to A and another to B. This would, however, misrepresent the true subject-matter of the parties' agreement, which is a *fund*.

[25] *Re Hagger* [1930] 2 Ch 190 (Ch).
[26] Ying Khai Liew, 'The Ambit of the Mutual Wills Doctrine' (2016) 132 *LQR* 664.
[27] ibid s IV.
[28] See Chapter 3, S 3.2.1.

A fund is 'a set of properties, the identity of which fund or set continues despite a change in the items of property that it comprises'.[29] A fund exists only when certain assets are demarcated, for example by a declaration of trust, by an executor, or to be treated as security.[30] In specific relation to an interest in a *trust* fund, Roy Goode writes:[31]

> The essential characteristic is that an asset or collection of assets is transferred to a trustee (or declared by a settlor to be held by himself as trustee on stated trusts) to manage on behalf of the beneficiaries, with power to change the assets within the limits, if any, set by the trust instrument or by law.

In the mutual wills context, this concept of a fund provides the only accurate explanation of the subject-matter of the parties' agreement, insofar as the property in B's hands at the point of A's death is concerned.[32] First, B's promise usually relates not to specifically defined property, but it is to leave 'whatever is left' at his death to C.[33] This indicates that the subject-matter of the agreement is a fund, since the parties do not intend to create rights and duties in relation to specific assets, but in relation to their combined assets *as a singular entity*. During B's lifetime, the assets are treated not as individual 'things', but as a singular collection of 'wealth',[34] since the parties are only concerned with specific assets as things at the time of B's death when the trust ends.

Secondly, the parties do not intend C to obtain any interest in specific assets during B's lifetime. This reflects the nature of a beneficiary's interest in a trust fund.[35] It is only when a breach occurs that a beneficiary may elect to enforce a proprietary interest in specific assets in the fund,[36] and this is also consistent with judicial statements in the mutual wills context that C may prevent certain dispositions from being made by B during his lifetime which are calculated to defeat the agreement.[37]

Thirdly, like a beneficiary of a trust fund, C has a right to his due share in accretions to the fund,[38] expressly stipulated to be at B's death. Fourthly, the subject-matter of the mutual wills agreement reflects other features of a trust fund, namely that it does not comprise *merely* B's assets, and that it is clearly demarcated, that is, at A's death. Fifthly, as in the case

[29] JE Penner, 'Duty and Liability in Respect of Funds' in John Lowry and Loukas Mistelis (eds), *Commercial Law: Perspectives and Practice* (London, LexisNexis Butterworths, 2006) [12-13], developing an idea propounded by Roy Goode (see Roy Goode, 'The Right to Trace and its Impact in Commercial Transactions, Part I' (1976) 92 *LQR* 360, 384; Roy Goode, *Commercial Law*, 2nd edn (London, Penguin, 1995) 66–67).

[30] Penner, 'Duty and Liability' (n 29) [12-14].

[31] R Goode, 'The Right to Trace and its Impact in Commercial Transactions, Part II' (1976) 92 *LQR* 528, 529.

[32] Notably, Lord Camden observed in *Dufour v Pereira* (in Hargrave, n 1) 308 that '[t]he property of both is put into a common fund, and every devise is the joint devise of both'.

[33] If the parties specifically identify the property or interest that B will leave to C at B's death, then there are three possibilities. If that property or interest was transferred from A to B upon A's death, then the case falls within the secret trusts doctrine, with the result that B obtains a life interest and C obtains an interest in remainder: see *Ottaway v Norman* [1972] Ch 698 (Ch). If the specified property or interest formerly belonged partly to A and partly to B, as in, eg, *Re Hagger* (n 25), then the specification relates to a 'fund' after all, and the analysis discussed in the text would be applicable. If the specified property or interest was not formerly A's at all, but was acquired by B on his own accord, then the analysis explained in S 12.2.2. will apply.

[34] For the distinction between things as 'things' and as 'wealth', see Bernard Rudden, 'Things as Thing and Things as Wealth' (1994) 14 *OJLS* 81.

[35] See, eg, Goode, 'Part II' (n 31) 530; Penner, 'Duty and Liability' (n 29) [12-16].

[36] Penner, 'Duty and Liability' (n 29) [12-16].

[37] See n 14 above.

[38] Goode, 'Part II' (n 31) 530.

of a trust fund, a power is imposed by law[39] which allows B to make changes to the specific assets comprising the fund.

Once the subject-matter of the parties' agreement is correctly identified as a fund, it becomes clear that the facts reflect a QI situation. By his promise, B promises to qualify the interest he will take *in the fund*. At the time the promise is made, B does not yet have the fund in his hands: it is acquired by B if and only if A completes his act of reliance by leaving his property at his death to B. By acting in reliance, A confers an advantage on B in relation to the acquisition of the fund. The relevant advantage B obtains lies not merely in the acquisition of 'A's property' (although this is certainly so), leaving it necessary to find a separate explanation for the rights and duties arising over 'B's property'. Instead, it materialises in the form of a fund in B's hands. Stated in the reverse, without A's reliance, B would not only fail to acquire A's property, but would also never obtain the fund in question. Therefore, upon A's death, a fund is constituted in B's hands, over which a constructive trust attaches to qualify the interest B acquires in relation to it in accordance with B's promise.

It might be objected that a trust fund of an express trust always begins with capital provided by the settlor only, and does not include property belonging to the trustee. However, nothing prevents A and B *as settlors* from creating an express trust with B holding the trust fund on trust for C's benefit. The same can also be said in relation to mutual wills: B, in his capacity analogous to an express trustee, promises to hold the fund on trust, and A and B, in their capacity analogous to joint settlors of an express trust, together supply the assets which constitute the fund in B's hands.

12.2.1.2. After A's Death

It is more difficult to determine the appropriate analysis in relation to property B amasses on his own account after A's death, that is, any accretion to B's estate which is not a traceable proceed of the assets in B's hands at the time of A's death. One major difficulty is that no case specifically affirms that such 'after-acquired' property is capable of being bound;[40] and although it is often presumed that it is so bound,[41] this view is not unanimous.[42] If such 'after-acquired' property *is* bound, an explanation is required.

It might be thought that an explanation can be found in the equitable maxim 'equity considers as done that which ought to be done'.[43] This relies on the line of authorities which provides that, where valuable consideration is given,[44] equity will enforce a declaration of

[39] See S 12.3.1.1.

[40] See Alexandra Braun, 'Revocability of Mutual Wills' in Kenneth GC Reid, Marius J de Waal, and Reinhard Zimmermann (eds), *Exploring the Law of Succession: Studies National, Historical and Comparative* (Edinburgh, Edinburgh University Press, 2007) fn 64. Note, though, that in *Re Gillespie* (1968) 69 DLR (2d) 368 [18], Stark J in the Ontario High Court construed the parties in that case as having agreed to *preclude* such after-acquired property from being subject to the trust.

[41] See, eg, LA Sheridan, 'The Floating Trust: Mutual Wills' (1977) 15 *Alberta Law Review* 211, 235; John McGhee (ed), *Snell's Equity*, 33rd edn (London, Sweet & Maxwell, 2016) [24-036].

[42] See Siôn Hudson and Brian Sloan, 'Testamentary Freedom: Mutual Wills Might Let You Down' in W Barr (ed), *Modern Studies in Property Law, Vol 8* (Oxford, Hart Publishing, 2015) 166.

[43] *Palette Shoes Pty Ltd v Krohn* (1937) 58 CLR 1, 16.

[44] The future property doctrine is discussed in Chapter 8. One argument made there is that it is necessary only for the contract to have been made for value; it is not necessary for consideration to have passed before the future property falls into possession (See Chapter 8, S 8.3.1.).

trust over future property as a contract to assign the property,[45] and a constructive trust attaches to the property immediately the property is acquired. However, this explanation attracts a number of insurmountable difficulties. First, the mutual wills doctrine is not based on a contractual analysis of the parties' agreement.[46] Secondly, this cannot account for any after-acquired property subject to the trust which is not land or a unique chattel, for instance B's salaries or pension pay-outs, since an order of specific performance is generally not available against such assets.[47] Thirdly, it is A, not C, who provides the consideration, therefore making it difficult to justify the imposition of a constructive trust in C's favour.[48]

One plausible analysis is to extend the 'fund' analysis to cover after-acquired property. This is a possibility if we take B's contribution to the trust fund as being 'her estate' instead of merely 'her assets at the time of A's death'. That is to say, the fund is taken to comprise properties received from A as well as B's own *estate*, the latter of which includes after-acquired property. The great attraction of this explanation is the consistency it achieves in the law's approach to mutual wills arrangements which involve B receiving property from A.

Treating B's 'estate' as a proprietary entity in this manner is, however, not free from controversy. In the first place, nowhere else in English law is one's estate treated as an entity of property capable of subjecting its owner to inter vivos obligations.[49] The closest idea to this conception can be found in the civilian 'patrimony', which is the sum total of one's assets minus liabilities.[50] Even so, this concept is neither here nor there for the purposes of the present discussion. It is most commonly employed for the purpose of explaining why each person is liable to his own creditors,[51] and how a civilian 'trustee' administers and manages another's 'patrimony' and is therefore not liable to the latter's creditors.[52] It tends not to be used to the effect that one may subject oneself to inter vivos obligations in relation to one's own patrimony.[53]

[45] *Ellison v Ellison* (1802) 6 Ves Jun 656, 31 ER 1243; *Holroyd v Marshall* (1862) 10 HLC 191, 210; 11 ER 999, 1006; *Tailby v Official Receiver* (1888) 13 App Cas 523 (HL) 530; *Re Lind* [1915] 2 Ch 345 (CA). See also *Williams v Inland Revenue Commissioners* [1965] NZLR 395.

[46] See S 12.4.1.

[47] *Sky Petroleum Ltd v VIP Petroleum Ltd* [1974] 1 WLR 576 (Ch) 578; *R Griggs Group Ltd v Evans* [2005] Ch 153 (Ch) [36].

It was argued in Chapter 8, S 8.3.3. that, contrary to some suggestions, it is necessary for the contract to be specifically enforceable for a constructive trust to arise over gifts or assignments of future property.

[48] Graham Virgo, *The Principles of Equity and Trusts* (Oxford, OUP, 2012) 154–55.

[49] Penner, 'Duty and Liability' (n 29) [12-14]; FH Lawson and Bernard Rudden, *The Law of Property*, 3rd edn (Oxford, OUP, 2002) 171. Although, of course, one's estate can be made the subject-matter of a testamentary disposition.

[50] Lionel Smith, 'Trust and Patrimony' (2008) 38 *Revue Générale de Droit* 379, 383; although it has been suggested that this concept is helpful in an English law context: Lawson and Rudden, *The Law of Property* (n 49) 46. In this regard, see the English case of *Mannox v Greener* (1872) LR 14 Eq 456 (Ct Ch), where the language of 'patrimony' was employed.

[51] Magda Raczynska, 'Parallels between the Civilian Separate Patrimony, Real Subrogation and the Idea of Property in a Trust Fund' in Lionel Smith (ed), *The Worlds of the Trust* (Cambridge, CUP, 2013) 454, 456–57 text to fn 17.

[52] George Gretton, 'Up There in the *Begriffshimmel*?' in Smith, *The Worlds of the Trust* (n 53) 531ff; Raczynska, 'Parallels' (n 51) 454–55, fns 6 and 7, text to fn 8; Ross G Anderson, 'Words and Concepts: Trust and Patrimony' in Andrew Burrows, David Johnston QC, and Reinhard Zimmermann (eds), *Judge and Jurist: Essays in Memory of Lord Rodger of Earlsferry* (Oxford, OUP, 2013) 347, 351–58.

[53] As Raczynska, 'Parallels' (n 51) 472 argues, a civilian patrimony is not an entity to which a proprietary interest can be asserted.

Moreover, an objection might be made to the analysis on policy grounds. In the context of the law of assignment,[54] courts have suggested that the assignment by an individual of his entire estate, both real and personal, present and future, is unenforceable as being contrary to public policy, since it renders him destitute or a quasi-slave of the assignee.[55] The same might be said about the present analysis. However, those statements made in the assignment context are strictly obiter, and so the issue remains an open one. Moreover, the fact that B remains capable of making use of the capital assets of the mutual wills fund during his lifetime militates against that policy concern.

The plausibility of this argument is supported by the fact that it does not entail the creation of inter vivos obligations over B's own estate *alone*, but a *fund* which includes both B's estate as well as contributions from A. The fact that A, too, contributes to the fund means that there is a clear demarcation[56] as to what properties make up the fund, as in the case of any ordinary trust fund.

Alternatively, the property B acquires after A's death could be analysed as an AI situation. On this approach, such property is not treated as being part of the trust fund; instead, as in the case of proprietary estoppel, B is treated as absolute owner of any after-acquired property, and C potentially gains a right to that property due to A's detrimental reliance on B's promise to leave the property to C. This places the analysis of B's after-acquired property within the discussion immediately below concerning the situation where B does not receive property from A. It is argued there that, on that analysis, if a court deems that a constructive trust is not an award proportionate to A's detrimental reliance, then C would have no claim, since monetary compensation would be awarded in favour of A or A's estate. This is, however, not necessarily a cause for concern, since it would appear intuitive that B should be free to dispose of property he acquires on his own account if A's detrimental reliance was relatively minor—for instance if A was destitute at the time of his death. The availability of judicial discretion to test the appropriateness of a constructive trust award in C's favour against the degree of A's detrimental reliance in relation to B's after-acquired property is therefore a plausible development of this area of law.

12.2.2. B Does not Receive Property from A

In a less common category of mutual wills cases, B does not receive any property from A. The most well-known case of this sort is *Re Dale*,[57] where it was held that the doctrine can apply where A and B agree to make respective wills which benefit C *directly*.[58] A variation of this situation is where, pursuant to the supposition that B will be the first to die, B makes a will leaving his estate to A absolutely and A makes a will leaving his estate to C absolutely. A then dies first which triggers a substitutionary gift in B's will in C's (or another's) favour. So, too, if

[54] See AG Guest and Ying Khai Liew, *Guest on the Law of Assignment*, 2nd edn (London, Sweet & Maxwell, 2015) [4-21].

[55] *Re Clarke* (1887) 36 Ch D 348 (CA) 354, 355; *Tailby v Official Receiver* (n 45) 530, 535; *King v Michael Faraday and Partners Ltd* [1939] 2 KB 753 (KB); *Syrett v Egerton* [1957] 1 WLR 1130 (Div Ct).

[56] Penner, 'Duty and Liability' (n 29) [12-14].

[57] *Re Dale* (n 8).

[58] To the same effect is the case where the agreement contemplates that A will make a testamentary disposition to C1, and B will make a testamentary disposition to C2: see *Olins v Walters* (n 3) [38].

(i) A relies on B's promise by acting in a way other than making a testamentary disposition in B's favour; or (ii) the parties agree that A will make a testamentary disposition of Property 1 to B, and B will make a testamentary disposition of Property 2 to C, where Properties 1 and 2 are distinct assets which do not together make up a fund. In all these cases, B does not receive any property from A pursuant to the parties' mutual wills agreement.

It is clear that these cases can only be analysed as reflecting an AI situation. B does not promise to take a qualified interest in property yet to be acquired; instead, his promise relates to his *own* property. Moreover, A's reliance consists of acts which do not confer any advantage on B in relation to the acquisition of the property to which B's promise relates.

While it might not be immediately obvious, some support for the AI analysis of the relevant mutual wills cases can be gleaned from case law.

12.2.2.1. Re Dale

Re Dale appears to be the only reported case where B does not receive property from A. In that case, a husband (A) and wife (B) entered into a mutual wills agreement where each executed identical wills leaving their estate directly to their son and daughter (Cs) equally. A died without revoking his will, but B made a fresh will altering the proportions that Cs were to obtain. A preliminary issue arose as to whether B must have received property from A for the mutual wills doctrine to apply. Morritt J held that 'such mutual benefit is a sufficient but not a necessary condition'.[59] B was compelled to perform his part of the agreement.

On close inspection, counsel framed the preliminary issue narrowly. It was assumed that B would incur no obligation at all if the mutual wills doctrine did not operate. Thus the only question was whether a benefit received from A was required for B to be duty-bound.[60] In giving a negative answer, the judgment goes so far as to hold that B did in fact incur a duty where A did not transfer anything to B. Notably, in the course of his judgment, Morritt J justified his conclusion by observing that 'certain cases of proprietary estoppel may be regarded as species of constructive trust, but in those cases the factor which gives rise to its imposition is not the receipt of property'.[61] Analytically, this is a crucial statement. It indicates that Morritt J recognised that a constructive trust is imposed *through proprietary estoppel* where B's promise relates to property he owns absolutely. This exemplifies the AI analysis, and indicates that the case was treated differently from other typical mutual wills cases where B receives property from A.

It seems that Morritt J did not think it necessary to draw an explicit distinction between QI and AI situations because he thought that the overarching aim of the mutual wills doctrine was simply 'to prevent [A] from being defrauded'.[62] Such 'fraud' would occur if B were permitted to renege on the arrangement, because A had performed his part of the bargain 'on the faith of the promise of [B]'.[63] However, the idea of 'fraud' as a justification for the imposition of a constructive trust is confusing and imprecise.[64] In particular, it fails

[59] *Re Dale* (n 8) 43.

[60] ibid 33.

[61] ibid 47.

[62] ibid 49. Indeed, Morritt J (*Re Dale* (n 8) 42) thought that the 'essence of the decision' in *Dufour v Pereira* (in Hargrave, n 1) related to A's fraud. See further the text following n 162 below.

[63] *Re Dale* (n 8) 48–49.

[64] See the discussion in the context of the doctrine in *Rochefoucauld v Boustead* in Chapter 4, S 4.4.

to explain why B should be bound to give effect to his promise when, in general, a promise does not necessarily give rise to a trust even if the promisee gives consideration or acts in reliance on the promise. It also fails fully to explain the significance of A's testamentary disposition. In contrast, analysing the case as an AI situation explains the constructive trust which arises upon A's death as being a proportionate response to A's detrimental reliance on B's promise. In *Re Dale*, A left all his real and personal property—valued at £18,500—by will to C. Moreover, A left his will unchanged until his death, and thereby gave up his freedom to make alternative testamentary dispositions. There is no doubt that a proportionate response would have been to impose a constructive trust in order to give effect to A's expectation, thus explaining the decision in that case.

12.3. Explaining the Mutual Wills Doctrine

The discussion thus far has identified two distinct analyses which make up the mutual wills doctrine. Where B does not receive property from A, B promises to give away property which he owns absolutely, and a court has the ability to award a remedy which is proportionate to the detriment A suffers in relying on B's promise. B will often, but will not necessarily, be bound to perform his promise through the imposition of a constructive trust. On the other hand, where B receives property from A, B promises to take a qualified interest in the trust fund yet to be acquired, and upon acquiring the fund a constructive trust is invariably imposed that binds B to carry out his promise. It was also seen that both analyses provide plausible explanations for B's obligations over property he acquires on his own account after A's death. The question dealt with in this section is how this re-analysis explains the inner workings of the mutual wills doctrine.

12.3.1. B Receives Property from A

12.3.1.1. An Orthodox Explanation

Unlike the 'floating trust' analysis which entails 'a floating obligation, suspended, so to speak, during the lifetime of [B] [which] descend[s] upon the assets at [her] death and crystallize[s] into a trust',[65] the analysis of B as having acquired a fund implies that a constructive trust arises upon B's receipt of the fund, and that the rights and duties under the trust also arise at that point.[66] The existence of a fund means that there is a manager—a trustee—who holds the assets which constitute the fund.[67] Explained by way of orthodox principles, B immediately becomes a trustee under a constructive trust for the benefit of C upon acquiring the fund at A's death.

[65] *Birmingham v Renfrew* (n 7) 689.

[66] *Olins v Walters* (n 3) [42]. As Lewison J observed in *Thomas and Agnes Carvel Foundation v Carvel* [2007] EWHC 1314 (Ch), [2008] Ch 395 [27], the trust is brought into effect upon A's, and not B's, death.

[67] Lawson and Rudden, *The Law of Property* (n 49) 171.

As for the content of B's obligations under the trust, this is determined by the content of B's promise. By promising to leave 'whatever is left' at B's death to C, B implicitly accepts that the traceable proceeds of any asset in the fund in his hands will be held upon the same trust. This is because the subject-matter in B's hands is treated as a fund, which entails that B has the power to sell and replace individual items in the fund.[68]

Moreover, the parties also agree that (i) B will not have an absolute interest in the fund, (ii) B will have latitude to use the capital assets, and (iii) C will not have an absolute interest in the fund during B's lifetime. The first point is deduced from the fact that B has an obligation to make a testamentary disposition of the fund to C; the second is reflected by the fact that the parties are interested in determining the specific assets to be left to C only at the time of B's death; and the third follows from the fact that the parties' agreement is inconsistent with an intention to allow C to exercise his *Saunders v Vautier*[69] rights to collapse the trust for himself during B's lifetime.[70] The upshot is that, through interpretation[71] or by necessary implication[72] of the parties' agreement, they intend that the fund will be held for B for *life* and C in *remainder*,[73] and that B should have a *general, personal power* by which he may appoint the capital assets in favour of anyone including herself.

12.3.1.2. Explaining 'Crystallisation'

This analysis accounts for the so-called 'crystallising' of C's rights, both when B makes dispositions calculated to defeat the agreement and when B dies, without attracting the conceptual difficulties inherent in the idea of a 'floating trust'. Writing in relation to rights under a trust fund, Roy Goode observes:[74]

> the beneficiaries ... cannot bring an end to the management functions prescribed by the trust instrument, so as to have the fund distributed among themselves, except where so provided by the trust instrument or where all of them, being *sui juris* and collectively entitled to the fund, terminate the trust.

Because the 'trust instrument'—that is, the mutual wills agreement—provides that B will make a testamentary disposition to C, the prescribed event which brings the trust to an end is B's death, and this allows C to call for distribution of the trust assets. During B's lifetime, C may not unilaterally exercise his *Saunders v Vautier* rights to collapse the trust for herself because B has a life interest in the fund. Thus, in *Olins v Walters*[75] where the dispute concerned C's interest during B's lifetime in what was formerly A's property which was left to B pursuant to a mutual wills agreement, the Court of Appeal merely made a declaration[76]

[68] ibid.

[69] *Saunders v Vautier* (1841) 4 Beav 115, 49 ER 282.

[70] *Gartside v Inland Revenue Commissioners* [1968] AC 553 (HL) 606.

[71] A technique used in *Barclays Bank Ltd v Quistclose Investments Ltd* [1970] AC 567 (HL) 580. See discussion in Chapter 13, S 13.2.2.

[72] See Geraint Thomas, *Thomas on Powers*, 2nd edn (Oxford, OUP, 2012) [3-01], [3-46].

[73] See Sheridan, 'The Floating Trust' (n 41) 211; JE Penner, *The Law of Trusts*, Core Text Series, 10th edn (Oxford, OUP, 2016) [7.52].

[74] Goode, 'Part II' (n 31) 530.

[75] *Olins v Walters* (n 3).

[76] ibid [23].

that the trust was immediately binding on B in relation to that property: there was no hint that C was able immediately to demand the transfer of the property.[77]

In relation to rights under a trust fund, James Penner has also written that 'when certain events occur—the most obvious example being a breach of trust—the beneficiary may elect to enforce a direct proprietary interest in individual items of the fund'.[78] This explains C's rights during B's lifetime. Because C is a beneficiary under the constructive trust, it is clear that B owes C, and not any potential objects of the power, a duty not to misuse his power.[79] One of the incidents of that duty is that B must not exercise his power in such a way that would amount to a fraud on a power, as this would constitute a wrong against C.[80] The typical facts concerning the doctrine of a fraud on a power involve the donee of the power making what appears to be a prima facie legitimate appointment, but in fact doing so to allow the appointee to make use of the property in a way which runs counter to the terms on which the power was granted. However, judicial statements have not limited that doctrine to such facts, the focus instead being on B's motive or intention in exercising the power. Thus, in *Vatcher v Paull*,[81] Lord Parker famously observed that in this context 'fraud' 'merely means that the power has been exercised for a purpose, or with an intention, beyond the scope of or not justified by the instrument creating the power'. It is crucial that there is 'at least, a deliberate defeating of what the donor of the power authorized and intended'[82]—an exercise of power with an 'ulterior object to be accomplished'.[83] An execution of a power for a corrupt purpose or a purpose foreign to the power is fraudulent and void.[84]

These statements explain why, in the mutual wills context, courts have focused on B's motive or intention where he makes an *inter vivos* disposition out of the fund. For instance, in *Healey v Brown*,[85] the transfer of a flat by a father (B) to himself and his son as joint tenants was held to run 'directly and fully counter to the intention of the mutual will compact that the flat should pass to [C] on [B's] own death'.

It is important to stress that B's power is a 'bare' power conferred on B in his personal capacity, and not a 'fiduciary power' conferred on his by virtue of his status *qua* trustee.[86] This means that C cannot complain if B exercises the power for his own enjoyment. Thus, to the question some commentators have posed as to whether B may spend part of the trust fund on a world cruise, the analysis here entails an affirmative answer,[87] provided that B does so without any intention of defeating the mutual wills agreement. Indeed, it is immaterial that B might exhaust the entirety of the trust fund, provided that B's dispositions do not amount to a fraud on a power.[88] This ought not to be disconcerting, given that the exercise

[77] Admittedly, a declaration was the remedy C asked for: *Olins v Walters* (n 3) [16]. But if C had wanted to collapse the trust and claim the property before B's death, this would surely not have been allowed, since this would have been inconsistent with the mutual wills agreement.

[78] Penner, 'Duty and Liability' (n 29) [12-16].

[79] *Mettoy Pension Trustees Ltd v Evans* [1990] 1 WLR 1587 (Ch) 1613.

[80] ibid.

[81] *Vatcher v Paull* [1915] AC 372 (PC) 378.

[82] *Re Dick* [1953] Ch 343 (CA) 360.

[83] *Duke of Portland v Topham* (1864) 11 HLC 32, 55; 11 ER 1242, 1251.

[84] *Cloutte v Storey* [1911] 1 Ch 18 (CA). See *Thomas on Powers* (n 72) [9-21]–[9-36].

[85] *Healey v Brown* (n 8) [14].

[86] *Thomas on Powers* (n 72) [1-50].

[87] As suggested by Davis, 'Floating Rights' (n 17) 425 and fn 25.

[88] *Barns v Barns* (n 17) [152].

of any power of appointment necessarily diminishes the interest of the beneficiary of the gift over in default.[89] Nevertheless, it remains the case that B cannot make any appointment with the motive of defeating the mutual wills agreement, because the application of the fraud on a power doctrine does not depend on the donee of the power being a fiduciary.[90]

12.3.1.3. Protecting B

It might be thought to be unnecessary for B to have a life interest in the fund: B could hold the fund for C absolutely, subject to a general power in B's favour. However, the analysis set out above is to be preferred, as it provides adequate protection to B in at least two aspects.

First, it remains possible for B and C collectively to collapse the trust by exercising their *Saunders v Vautier* rights.[91] In view of the fact that much could potentially change in B's and C's circumstances after A's death, this possibility is crucial. Suppose that C is comfortably well off, but B remarries and has another child (X). C may wish to allow B to reallocate his testamentary dispositions in order to make provision for X. The proposed analysis makes this possible. This does not mean, however, that C has an all-or-nothing choice, in that he must either choose to keep the trust intact *or* collapse the trust with B and C as joint tenants, no more and no less. Instead, C is free to secure an informal promise from B that B will dispose of the fund in a pre-determined form before agreeing to exercise their collective *Saunders v Vautier* rights in B's favour. For instance, C may make it a condition that B will make a testamentary disposition of the fund in favour of both C and X in equal shares. Because *this* promise by B is to the effect that B will qualify the interests he obtains in the fund after B's and C's *Saunders v Vautier* rights have been exercised in B's favour, a constructive trust would arise to compel B to hold the fund in favour of C and X.[92]

Secondly, the trust fund will very often include a family home, and the parties would normally intend for B to live in it during his lifetime. The Trusts of Land and Appointment of Trustees Act 1996, however, provides only for beneficiaries (as opposed to objects of a power) to have a right to occupy trust land, subject to certain conditions.[93] As a beneficiary under the trust, B's right to occupy the family home can easily be accounted for. As the 1996 Act provides, among the matters trustees are to consider when deciding upon which of two or more beneficiaries are entitled to occupy the land, they are to look to 'the intentions of the person or persons … who created the trust'.[94] In the mutual wills context, this allows effect to be given to A's and B's intentions as expressed in their mutual wills agreement.

12.3.1.4. Remedies

Mutual wills disputes characteristically come to light only after the death of both parties, and so it is largely a matter of speculation what remedies are available to C if B makes (or attempts to make) a disposition with an improper motive during his lifetime. In what is

[89] See, eg, *Re Ryder* [1914] 1 Ch 865 (Ch).

[90] See, eg, *Lane v Page* (1754) Amb 233, 27 ER 155; *Re Crawshay (deceased)* [1948] Ch 123 (CA); *Re Dick* (n 82).

[91] *Stephenson v Barclays Bank* [1975] 1 WLR 88 (Ch).

[92] In a highly similar vein to the facts and decision in *De Bruyne v De Bruyne* [2010] EWCA Civ 519, [2010] 2 FLR 1240 and *Ottaway v Norman* (n 33).

[93] Trusts of Land and Appointment of Trustees Act 1996, ss 12, 13.

[94] ibid, s 13(4)(a).

probably the only decided case where B was alive and denying the mutual wills agreement,[95] C merely asked for and was granted a declaration that the arrangement amounted to an effective mutual wills agreement.[96] It remains unclear, therefore, whether remedies traditionally available to a beneficiary following an unauthorised disposition of trust property are available to C. It is submitted that C, as a beneficiary under the trust, is able to invoke the assistance of a court in order to ensure B's proper exercise of his powers,[97] for instance by requesting an injunction to prevent a purported disposition made with an improper motive. Of course, in practice C would rarely have the necessary foreknowledge to prevent such dispositions. Nevertheless, because a disposition amounting to a fraud on a power renders the transaction void, orthodox principles dictate that C may assert a proprietary claim against B or a third party recipient (X) pursuant to the evidentiary process of tracing and/or following, or may alternatively bring a personal claim for substitutive performance or reparation.

Consider first the possible claims against B. Where a trustee uses trust assets (money, for example) to purchase a new asset without authority, the beneficiary is normally able to trace into that new asset and either assert an equitable ownership over that asset or enforce an equitable charge or lien for the repayment of the value of the original trust asset dissipated.[98] In the mutual wills context, the analysis would depend on whether assets acquired by B after A's death are considered as part of the trust fund.[99] If they are, then all the property owned by B will constitute the trust fund. Therefore, there is no need to make a claim for equitable ownership against the new asset, since any traceable proceed coming into B's hands immediately forms part of that fund. Similarly, obtaining an equitable charge or lien would merely mean that the monetary value of the new asset is restored to the trust fund out of the trust fund itself, and the claim would be superfluous. If, however, the property B acquires after A's death is considered not to be part of the trust fund, then C might wish to enforce an equitable charge or lien against traceable proceeds to compel B to repay the value of the original trust asset out of B's after-acquired property.

The same analysis would apply in relation to a substitutive performance or reparation claim against B. If B's after-acquired property is analysed as part of the trust fund, then such claims are superfluous, since B would be restoring or compensating the trust fund with money from the trust fund. But if B's after-acquired property is deemed not to be part of the fund, then B may be compelled to restore the trust fund or compensate for losses out of B's after-acquired property.

Consider next the possible actions C could have against X, a volunteer recipient of dispositions made by B pursuant to a fraud on a power. In line with orthodox principles,[100] C would have no claim if X were a bona fide purchaser for value without notice of B's fraud; but C would be able to follow or trace, and then claim the trust property or its proceeds in X's hands if X were a volunteer. Alternatively, it may be that X is a purchaser for value but does not act in good faith or has notice of the fraud. In such a case, X would be liable to a proprietary claim by C; and the extent to which X will be personally liable would depend

95 *Olins v Walters* (n 3) [4].
96 ibid [16].
97 Goode, 'Part II' (n 31) 530.
98 *Foskett v McKeown* [2001] 1 AC 102 (HL) 131.
99 See discussion in S 12.2.1.2.
100 *Re Diplock* [1948] Ch 465 (CA).

on whether X had sufficient knowledge[101] of B's fraud on a power while the trust assets or traceable proceeds remained in his hands, a question which would be determined according to the law concerning knowing receipt.[102] Finally, X would incur a personal liability if he dishonestly assisted in B's fraudulent exercise of his power.[103]

12.3.2. B Does not Receive Property from A

12.3.2.1. An Orthodox Explanation

Being the only orthodox doctrine by which an owner of property might be compelled to fulfil an informal promise to give away an interest in property which he owns absolutely, the doctrine of proprietary estoppel is capable of explaining mutual wills agreements which reflect AI situations.

As we have seen in Chapter 7, proprietary estoppel relates to a primary duty to act reliably in relation to one's induced assumptions. If a property owner fulfils his promise to cede an interest in his property to another, the primary duty is fulfilled and no claim in proprietary interest arises. In the mutual wills context, if B leaves his property to C in accordance with his agreement with A, C has no cause of complaint. But there are two ways in which B may breach his primary duty, which brings proprietary estoppel into the picture. Most obviously, B may amend his testamentary disposition after A's death, for example by executing[104] a new will which directs some or all of the property subject to his promise to a different recipient. Alternatively, B may deal directly with the property subject to the mutual wills agreement in a way which constitutes a breach, such as by making a disposition contrary to the agreement, or executing a charge over the property which undermines the reliability of his induced assumption.

Where a breach occurs, all the ingredients of a proprietary estoppel claim—promise or assurance, reliance, and detriment—are fulfilled. Although A has now died, the content and nature of B's promise indicate that A's substantive right is not one which is personal to A,[105] and therefore any potential proprietary estoppel claim against B does not disappear with A's death.[106] And because B's promise was to the effect that C would obtain the benefit of B's testamentary disposition, there is good reason to think that, when B commits a breach of

[101] *Westdeutsche Landesbank Girozentrale v Islington LBC* [1996] AC 669 (HL) 707.

[102] See *Baden, Delvaux v Société Générale pour Favoriser le Développement du Commerce et de l'Industrie en France SA* [1993] 1 WLR 509 (Ch); *Bank of Credit & Commerce International (Overseas) Ltd v Akindele* [2001] Ch 437 (CA); *Crédit Agricole Corporation and Investment Bank v Papadimitriou* [2015] UKPC 13, [2015] 1 WLR 4265 [33].

[103] See *Royal Brunei Airlines Sdn Bhd v Tan* [1995] 2 AC 378 (PC); *Barlow Clowes International Ltd (in liquidation) v Eurotrust International Ltd* [2005] UKPC 37, [2006] 1 WLR 1476.

[104] It is sufficient for B to indicate that he will carry out a transaction in the future which is tantamount to a breach: *Bradbury v Taylor* [2012] EWCA Civ 1208, [2013] WTLR 29.

[105] Ben McFarlane, *The Law of Proprietary Estoppel* (Oxford, OUP, 2014) [8-162]ff.

[106] The contractual parallel is that any contract which does not contain 'an implied condition of the continued existence of the life of the contractor' (*Taylor v Caldwell* (1863) 3 B & S 826, 836; 122 ER 309, 313) may be breached by one party after the death of the other, which gives the latter's executors or estate the right to pursue a claim for breach against the former. See, too, the observation in Simon Gardner, 'Reliance-Based Constructive Trusts' in Charles Mitchell (ed), *Constructive and Resulting Trusts* (Oxford, Hart Publishing, 2010) 66. Moreover, the maxim *action personalis moritur cum persona* 'never extend[s] to personal actions founded on any obligation, debt, covenant, or other duty to be performed' (*Wheatley v Lane* (1668) 1 Wms Saund 216a, 85 ER 228), but is instead 'always understood of a tort' only (*Sollers v Lawrence* (1743) Willes 413, 421; 125 ER 1243, 1247).

his primary duty, C obtains an 'equity by estoppel' against B. This 'equity' requires liquidation by a court. Pursuant to this, a proprietary or personal remedy may be awarded.

Depending on whether C's case is brought during B's lifetime or after B has died, different remedies may be imposed. In the former case, the court may award an injunction to prevent or undo the effects of an act by B such as a disposition contrary to the agreement. In the case where B makes a new will contrary to the agreement, it may well be that a mandatory injunction is awarded to compel B to make another will which complies with the parties' agreement.[107] If C's claim is brought after B has died, then a court may award a constructive trust in order to compel B (or anyone who is in no better position than B) to carry out B's promise.

Since the 'equity' is 'capable of binding B's successors in title',[108] the proprietary effect of such an award is backdated 'by virtue of some doctrine of relation back'[109] to the time of B's breach. So, for example, if in breach of the mutual wills agreement B executes a new will in favour of X and then dies, X as a volunteer will similarly be bound by the constructive trust in favour of C.

In all cases, if the court deems that a proportionate response to A's detriment would be to award compensatory damages, then these would be awarded for the benefit of A's estate, since it was A who personally incurred detrimental reliance.

12.3.2.2. Potential Objections

For this analysis to work, it is necessary to accept that a third party (C) may successfully claim in proprietary estoppel based on another's (A's) detrimental reliance, and that proprietary estoppel can apply where B's promise does not relate to land. It has been seen in Chapter 7[110] that there is in principle no objection to these features of proprietary estoppel.

Two other potential objections require noting. First, it might be thought to be problematic that B's promise may relate to after-acquired property, that is, property B acquires after reaching the agreement with A. This does not appear to be an issue, however, since if A has completed his acts of reliance (at A's death in the mutual wills context), a proprietary estoppel claim can be made against B as soon as B acquires the asset in question.[111] A related objection may be that proprietary estoppel requires A's expectation to relate to specific items of property,[112] and it is difficult to determine, at the time the agreement is made, what specific items of property B may acquire after A's death. However, in *Re Basham*,[113] where B

[107] This finds support in *Ottaway v Norman* (n 33), where Brightman J held, obiter, in the context of secret trusts, that nothing in principle prevents the court from compelling one to keep his promise to make a will in favour of another.

[108] The Land Registration Act 2002, s 116(a) provides that an 'equity by estoppel … has effect from the time the equity arises as an interest capable of binding successors in title'. This section did not aim to create a new rule, but meant merely to confirm the existing state of the law: Law Commission, *Land Registration for the Twenty-First Century: A Conveyancing Revolution* (Law Com No. 271, 2001) [5-30]–[5-31].

[109] Kevin Gray and Susan Francis Gray, *Elements of Land Law*, 5th edn (Oxford, OUP, 2009) [9.2.89]. See discussion in Chapter 7, S 7.2.5.2.

[110] See Chapter 7, S 7.4.3.1.

[111] *Watson v Goldsbrough* [1986] 1 EGLR 265 (CA). See Sean Wilken QC and Karim Ghaly, *Wilken and Ghaly: The Law of Waiver, Variation, and* Estoppel, 3rd edn (Oxford, OUP, 2012) [11-130].

[112] *Layton v Martin* [1986] 2 FLR 227 (Ch) 238.

[113] *Re Basham (deceased)* [1986] 1 WLR 1498 (Ch). See discussion in *Wilken and Ghaly* (n 111) [11-131]–[11-132].

promised to leave to A all of B's property in his will, A succeeded in a proprietary estoppel claim against B even though B's assets remained unspecified until B's death. Similarly, in *Thorner v Major*,[114] a proprietary estoppel claim was successful where the parties 'knew that the extent of the farm was liable to fluctuate'. It is therefore possible to say that, in principle, non-specification of items in a testamentary context is no bar to a proprietary estoppel claim.

Secondly, it may be objected that the constructive trust which arises to bind B in the mutual wills context appears not to be awarded through an exercise of remedial discretion, but is awarded invariably. In reply, it can be said that the dearth of authorities dealing with cases where B does not receive any property from A provides no support for the proposition that no remedial discretion is exercised. But the proposed analysis would remain plausible even if there were a large number of cases in which a constructive trust award is made on facts which reflect an AI situation. Because in mutual wills cases A's reliance usually consists of the making of a testamentary disposition, it is difficult to conceive of a situation whereby a court might deem it disproportionate to bind B to his promise. Were B allow to resile from his promise, the detriment which A would incur from committing to a particular form of testamentary disposition is quite obviously substantial, which would justify a constructive trust award. However, this is less obviously the case where A's reliance consists of inter vivos actions, for example, where A sells property or makes a gift in reliance on B's promise to leave B's estate to C at B's death. Remedial discretion in such a case is crucial, since a court would then be able to determine the appropriate remedy according to the degree of detriment A suffered. So, it would hardly be objectionable to deny C the benefit of a constructive trust where, for instance, A relied on B's promise by making an inter vivos donation of £100 to a charity.

12.4. Lessons

The award of constructive trusts in all mutual wills cases to date creates a deceptive impression that the cases are united by a single principle. The reality is that different types of agreement give rise to different types of claim. In cases where B does not receive property from A, C's claim depends on showing that B's breach of a primary duty to act reliably in relation to induced assumptions has caused compensable loss; in cases where B receives property from A, B is invariably bound to his promise through a constructive trust which replicates A's and B's primary rights and duties. The paucity of cases reflecting AI situations means that courts have not found occasion to clarify what goes on in such cases and how they differ from the more common cases reflecting QI situations. Nevertheless, distinguishing the two classes of case enables us to understand them more clearly.

It also follows from the distinction between the analyses that mutual wills cases are underpinned by two distinct rationales. Consistent with the discussion in Chapter 4,[115] the QI situations concern preventing the taking of an advantage; and as the discussion in Chapter 7[116] indicates, the AI situations concern compensating for harm caused. That the

[114] *Thorner v Major* [2009] UKHL 18, [2009] 1 WLR 776 [62].
[115] See Chapter 4, S 4.3.4.
[116] See Chapter 7, S 7.3.2.

'mutual wills' doctrine reflects an amalgamation of two distinct analyses and rationales is not surprising at all. Because both classes of case commonly involve a mutuality of wills, they can be described as falling within the 'mutual wills' label.[117] Moreover, the constructive trust response is usually the appropriate remedy even in the AI situations. Indeed, the courts have not found it necessary to distinguish between the two cases because they might both loosely be described as preventing A from being 'defrauded'. Nevertheless, analytical clarity calls for a recognition of their different underlying bases.

This analysis provides a number of important lessons for our understanding of the mutual wills doctrine. This section explores a number of these lessons.

12.4.1. 'Contract at Law'?

It has been suggested that mutual wills situations which reflect the QI situations are of a different breed from those doctrines discussed within this sub-category[118] because, unlike those doctrines, there is an additional requirement for there to be a 'contract at law' for the mutual wills doctrine to operate.[119] The question thus arises as to what that phrase means. Although a mutual wills agreement was described as a 'contract' from as long ago as the first reported mutual wills case of *Dufour v Pereira*,[120] the use of the phrase 'contract at law' is relatively more modern, and seems to find its first mention in *Re Dale*.[121] The difference between the two phrases is potentially significant. A description of the agreement as a 'contract' does not imply anything beyond the fact that the testators have 'bound [themselves] to an obligation … in such terms as to render it enforceable in equity'.[122] Where they have done so, '[w]hether one calls it a "contract", "an agreement", "an undertaking" or "legally enforceable promise" is merely a matter of nomenclature.'[123] Requiring a 'contract *at law*', on the other hand, suggests something more specific. It might lead one to assume that the enforceability of the agreement *at common law* is a prerequisite for the operation of the doctrine—that the fulfilment of the requirements such as the sufficiency of consideration is a precondition.[124] It also implies that a mutual wills agreement, if it involves a 'disposition of an interest in land', is invalid unless it complies with the formality requirements of the Law of Property (Miscellaneous Provisions) Act 1989, s 2(1).[125]

It is submitted that the phrase 'contract at law' does not in fact indicate a requirement that an agreement should amount to a contract enforceable at common law for the mutual

[117] See, eg, the loose definition of 'the doctrine of mutual wills' in *Re Dale* (n 8) 37.

[118] Viz those discussed in Chs 4, 5, and 6.

[119] See, eg, Ben McFarlane, 'Constructive Trusts Arising on a Receipt of Property *Sub Conditione*' (2004) 120 *LQR* 667, 688.

[120] *Dufour v Pereira* (1769) Dick 419, 21 ER 332; also reported in Hargrave (n 1) 304.

[121] *Re Dale* (n 8).

[122] *Osborne v Estate of Osborne* (n 7) 816.

[123] ibid 815.

[124] *Re Dale* (n 8) 37. See also *Dufour v Pereira* (in Hargrave, n 1) 310; *Lord Walpole v Lord Orford* (1797) 3 Ves Jun 402, 417; 30 ER 1076, 1083.

[125] *Healey v Brown* (n 8) [19]–[20]. This sub-section provides that '[a] contract for the sale or other disposition of an interest in land can only be made in writing and only by incorporating all the terms which the parties have expressly agreed in one document or, where contracts are exchanged, in each.'

wills doctrine to operate. This view is consistent with numerous judicial statements.[126] It has been said that the doctrine does not involve making a claim for contractual relief such as specific performance because C 'is not even a party to the contract';[127] that its principles are not precisely the same as those which apply to contractual disputes;[128] and that it arises from the parties' course of conduct and not the contract itself and therefore '[a] contract made without formality is enough'.[129] Indeed, in *Olins v Walters*,[130] the Court of Appeal applied the doctrine where the relevant agreement was held not to be certain enough to amount to a contract enforceable at common law. Moreover, since a mutual wills agreement can be made orally[131] or be inferred from the circumstances of a case,[132] then surely it is contemplated that the formality requirement of the 1989 Act has no relevance to the mutual wills doctrine. In this regard, the judgment of David Donaldson QC, sitting as a Deputy High Court judge in *Healey v Brown*,[133] which held that compliance with s 2(1) of the 1989 Act is a prerequisite for the doctrine to apply, cannot be sustained as a matter of principle and consistency.[134] After all, it is indisputable that the mutual wills doctrine gives rise to constructive trusts, not merely contractual damages; and s 2(5) of the Act provides that 'nothing in this section affects the creation or operation of … constructive trusts.'[135]

The distinction between contractual principles and the mutual wills doctrine can also be seen in relation to the Wills Act 1837, s 18, which provides that 'a will shall be revoked by the testator's marriage.' Under common law contractual principles, where parties enter into a covenant not to revoke their wills, damages may not be recovered against a party who revokes his will in line with this provision. As the Court of Appeal held in *Re Marsland*,[136] 'the covenant by the testator not to revoke or alter the earlier will does not amount to a covenant by him not to marry again.' In the mutual wills context, however, B's marriage after A's death does not negate his obligation under the constructive trust.[137] Thus, in *Re Green*,[138] although B's will was statutorily revoked by his second marriage, Vaisey J nevertheless compelled him to carry out his promise under a previous mutual wills agreement.

[126] *cf* the views of some commentators, eg Christine Davis, 'Mutual Wills; Formalities; Constructive Trusts' [2003] *Conveyancer and Property Lawyer* 238, 239; McFarlane, '*Sub Conditione*' (n 119) 688; Braun, 'Revocability of Mutual Wills' (n 40) 221.

[127] *Olins v Walters* (n 3) [36]. See also *Re Dale* (n 8) 38.

[128] *Re Hobley (deceased)* (*The Times*, 16 June 1997).

[129] *Lewis v Cotton* [2001] 2 NZLR 21 [44], [55].

[130] *Olins v Walters* (n 3). See especially counsel's submission at [24] which the Court of Appeal rejected at [35].

[131] *Charles v Fraser* (n 8) [59].

[132] *Fry v Densham-Smith* (n 12) [33].

[133] *Healey v Brown* (n 8) [19]–[20].

[134] Note also that in *Birmingham v Renfrew* (n 7) 680, Latham CJ held that the constructive trust imposed by way of the mutual wills doctrine is unaffected by any otherwise applicable formality requirement. Although his Honour referred specifically to the constructive trust exception in the Law of Property Act 1925, s 53, the same exception would likewise apply to the Law of Property (Miscellaneous Provisions) Act 1989 by virtue of s 2(5).

[135] See also Luxton, '*Walters v Olin* [*sic*]' (n 15) 402; Mark Pawlowski and James Brown, 'Problems with Mutual Wills—A Study of Probate Practice' (2012) 6 *Conveyancer and Property Lawyer* 467, 472–73.

[136] *Re Marsland* [1939] Ch 820 (CA) 826.

[137] See *Parker and Mellows* (n 20) [10-325] text to fn 812; David Hayton, Paul Matthews and Charles Mitchell, *Underhill and Hayton: Law Relating to Trusts and Trustees*, 19th edn (London, LexisNexis Butterworths, 2016) [8.239] fn 1.

[138] *Re Green (deceased)* [1951] Ch 148 (Ch) 155. This was the only case where this issue arose directly in point.

This difference in approach indicates that the mutual wills doctrine is conceptually distinct from contractual principles. A statutory revocation will release B from any *contractual* liability for breach of contract, since it is a policy concern under contract law to discourage the contractual restraint of marriage. In contrast, the mutual wills doctrine is concerned either with preventing B from taking an advantage or with compensating A for loss caused by B's unreliability, regardless of how B reneges on his promise.

Since the fulfilment of common law contractual principles is not a prerequisite for the mutual wills doctrine to operate, the phrase 'contract at law' is best understood simply to mean that the parties must have made an agreement *amounting to* a binding legal contract: they must intend to create legally binding obligations. This is consistent with the nature of equity, which looks to the substance of the agreement rather than the form in which it appears. As Lord Camden observed of the mutual wills doctrine, '[t]he actions of men here are stripped of their legal cloathing [*sic*], and appear in their first naked simplicity.'[139]

Such an understanding of the phrase has one distinct advantage in relation to the *standard* equity demands for a mutual wills agreement to be binding. In the domestic arena where the mutual wills doctrine operates, incidences of parties entering into agreements are very common; yet, the parties involved seldom intend to subject themselves to the sanction of a court of justice[140] and thus to be legally bound. With a fair amount of diligence, it is of course possible to spell out the precise threshold of the certainty of intention required for the mutual wills doctrine to operate. But such a technical and potentially arbitrary effort is unnecessary given that the *substance* of a legally binding contract already provides practical guidelines. Thus, there are different presumptions which operate in domestic and commercial contexts for establishing an 'intention to create legal relations' for the purposes of legal contracts,[141] and the same presumptions are helpful in the mutual wills context to preclude the doctrine from operating where the arrangement merely reflects an honorary engagement,[142] mutual expectations or desires,[143] coincidences,[144] and where any other evidence negates the inference of the relevant agreement.[145] The method by which courts scrutinise and interpret the terms of legal contracts is also useful for determining whether 'the terms of the mutual engagement … are sufficiently certain that the court can see its way to enforce them'[146] in the mutual wills context. It is therefore helpful to draw assistance from contractual principles, but at the same time crucial not to lose sight of the basal concern, which is to establish 'the existence of a legal obligation of a nature which *equity* would enforce.'[147]

[139] *Dufour v Pereira* (in Hargrave, n 1) 310.

[140] On the dichotomy of intending the sanction to be 'the authority of a Court of Justice' and 'the conscience of the devisee', see *M'Cormick v Grogan* (1867) 1 IR Eq 313, 328; *Re Snowden (deceased)* [1979] Ch 528, 537.

[141] See, eg, *Edwards v Skyways Ltd* [1964] 1 WLR 349 (QB).

[142] *Dufour v Pereira* (in Hargrave, n 1) 276; *Lord Walpole v Lord Orford* (n 124) 3 Ves Jun 420, 30 ER 1085.

[143] *Re Goodchild* (n 7) 1225; *Charles v Fraser* (n 8) [59]; *Osenton v Osenton* (n 8) [33].

[144] *Healey v Brown* (n 8) [9].

[145] *Re Oldham* [1925] Ch 75 (Ch).

[146] *Lewis v Cotton* (n 129) [55], paraphrasing *Re Oldham* (n 145) 86.

[147] *Osborne v Estate of Osborne* (n 7) [18] (emphasis added).

12.4.2. Subsuming the QI Situations within the AI Situations?

The dichotomy between QI and AI situations indicates that it is possible to treat cases which reflect the QI situations by way of the analysis which applies to AI situations. If B purports to qualify his interest in property yet to be acquired, it is logically possible to treat B as the absolute owner of that property when it is acquired, and to analyse the case as an AI situation. The reverse, however, is not permissible: if B's promise relates to property he already owns absolutely, B's promise cannot be treated as purporting to qualify an interest in a property acquired with A's participation.[148]

It follows that it might be asked whether *all* mutual wills cases should be analysed as AI situations. On this approach, even in cases where B receives property from A, the fund B obtains would be treated as being acquired of B's own accord, and A's act of transferring property to B would be considered an act of reliance which, if B does not perform his promise, will constitute a detriment for which B must compensate. In favour of this approach, it might be suggested that it is presently:[149]

> normatively questionable ... that the parties are able *conclusively* to decide for themselves what property is subject to a mutual wills arrangement without judicial intervention, while the property forming the subject of an estoppel representation might ultimately be considered a disproportionate remedy when a claim is litigated.

It is submitted that this analysis should be resisted. In the first place, it cannot explain and justify the crucial role which the parties' agreement plays. If A transfers property to B pursuant to an agreement which leads B to acquire a trust fund to be held for C's benefit, enforcing the agreement entails holding B to his promise, no more and no less. Analysing the case as an AI situation would add an unnecessary, superficial layer of reasoning: that B will be held to his promise *provided that this proportionately compensates for A's detrimental reliance*. This would attribute too little importance to the parties' agreement. It is only where A does not transfer property to B that the compensatory aim provides a justification for holding B to his promise in relation to property he owns absolutely, where a constructive trust award is deemed to be the appropriate response.

It can also be observed that the mutual wills doctrine, like many other constructive trust doctrines,[150] is concerned with identifying the true nature of the parties' dealings. This can be seen from the fact that 'fraud', which is often used to justify the imposition of a constructive trust in the mutual wills context,[151] is in fact merely a *description* of the state of affairs which the constructive trust prevents.[152] The true nature of B's promise in the case where A transfers property to B is precisely to qualify the interest in the trust fund that B obtains, according to the parties' agreement. If B's promise is then treated as relating to property he owns absolutely, this introduces an element of fiction into what has hitherto been recognised as an agreement-based doctrine. This is not to deny that there could be advantages in

[148] This point was made in relation to proprietary estoppel in Chapter 7, S 7.4.3.
[149] Hudson and Sloan, 'Testamentary Freedom' (n 42) 170.
[150] See, eg, in relation to the doctrine in *Rochefoucauld v Boustead*, Chapter 4, S 4.5.1.2.3.
[151] See, eg, *Dufour v Pereira* (in Hargrave, n 1) 310; *Re Dale* (n 8) 42; *Olins v Walters* (n 3) [38].
[152] See Chapter 4, S 4.4.2.4.

treating all mutual wills cases as AI situations;[153] however, to do so would be tantamount to overhauling most of what presently constitutes the mutual wills doctrine, which is uncalled for.

12.4.3. Secret Trusts as a Fallback?

On a number of occasions it has been suggested that the secret trusts doctrine may provide a fallback where a mutual wills claim is unsuccessful. Thus, in *Healey v Brown*,[154] David Donaldson QC said that, in cases where a mutual wills claim fails, an award may nevertheless be justified 'by reference to the separate case-law on so-called secret trusts'. On this analysis, where A transfers property to B pursuant to a mutual wills agreement but the agreement cannot be enforced by way of the mutual wills doctrine due, for example, to an insufficient intention to create legally binding and irrevocable obligations, the suggestion is that B can be compelled to hold (only) *A*'s property on trust for C by way of the secret trusts doctrine.

It is suggested that this possibility ought to be rejected. Consider the fact that the parties' intentions are solely determined with reference to their agreement. Apart from that agreement, there are no enforceable intentions, since the mutual wills agreement indicates that the parties' intentions are interdependent. That is to say, they do not have individual, independent intentions which merely happen to coincide at a point in time. Because B's intention is formed with the knowledge that *both* parties' estates will be affected, the agreement is wholly irrelevant to a consideration of what he *might* have promised if the subject-matter of the agreement comprised only A's estate. Similarly, the transfer of A's property to B is done in reliance on B's promise, and so it is impossible to conclude that A would have dealt with his property in the same way if B's promise was different from that which he actually promised to do. Therefore, an intention in relation to *A's property alone* cannot be derived from the parties' agreement which was reached in relation to what B would do with 'whatever is left' at his death.

This conclusion is fortified by the fact that B's promise relates to a fund and not to specific property. B's promise to qualify his interest in a fund is distinct from, and unrelated to, a promise to qualify his interest in specific assets which constitute the fund. Because in the mutual wills doctrine there is no requirement of segregation or separate accounting in relation to what was formerly A's property, it seems wrong even to speak of B's obligations as relating to 'A's property'. Thus, it cannot be suggested that B's acquisition of 'A's property' is qualified by a promise to hold it on trust for C. This would not only fail to take into account the true nature of B's promise, but would also fail to reflect the fact that B's obligation in the mutual wills doctrine differs from the obligation which arises in the secret trusts context.

All these considerations point to the fact that the distinction between mutual wills and secret trusts lies in the different *types* of agreement they enforce, and not in the different *degrees* of their reach—ie whether they cover 'A's property' only or 'A's and B's property'. The parties are, of course, free to choose one type of agreement or another; but a different

[153] Hudson and Sloan, 'Testamentary Freedom' (n 42) 171.
[154] *Healey v Brown* (n 8) [28].

type of agreement cannot be inferred from the agreement which they actually attempted to make.[155]

12.4.4. Abolishing the Mutual Wills Doctrine?

In recent times, many commentators have concluded that mutual wills agreements are not 'sensible',[156] and thus should be 'avoided'[157] or even 'abolished'.[158] In view of the Law Commission's ongoing review of the mutual wills doctrine, it is not implausible that a recommendation might be made to abolish the mutual wills doctrine completely.

It is submitted, however, that such a move would be undesirable. It is impossible to make a principled distinction between the mutual wills doctrine and other related constructive trust doctrines. This point is best made by observing that many situations which fall within the mutual wills doctrine can also be analysed in terms of other doctrines falling within the non-contract-based, bilateral events category of constructive trusts, and therefore it would be a messy—and certainly arbitrary—task to refuse to give legal effect only to mutual wills agreements.

In relation to QI situations, consider the following three cases. In the first case, A and B come to an informal inter vivos agreement that A will transfer land to B, with B promising to leave 'whatever is left' at his death to C. In the second case, an informal inter vivos agreement is reached that A will transfer land to B, with B promising to hold all the property at A's time of death for herself for life and for C in remainder, with B having a general power of appointment during his lifetime. In the third case, a testator, A, comes to an informal agreement with B that, if A leaves a specific property to B absolutely in A's will, B will leave 'whatever is left' of that property at his death to C. Although atypical, these three cases potentially engage the mutual wills doctrine. As to the first case, it has been recognised that the mutual wills doctrine is applicable if the agreement entails an inter vivos transfer of property from A to B, with B promising to make a particular testamentary disposition.[159] As to the second case, B's promise explicitly states what is normally implicit within B's promise in the typical mutual wills case.[160] In the third case, since parties to a mutual wills agreement have the freedom to define the specific properties which will be subject to the agreement,[161] it is arguably possible for the agreement to relate only to A's property in the manner set out above. But at the same time, the first two cases can be analysed as falling within the ambit of the rule in *Rochefoucauld v Boustead*,[162] and the third as falling within the ambit

[155] Although certain obiter statements in *Re Goodchild* (n 7), namely at 1224 and 1229–30, might seem to suggest that a secret trusts agreement can indeed be derived from a failed mutual wills agreement, the ultimate result in that case is consistent with the point made in the text. The finding that there was lacking a sufficiently firm agreement between the parties to engage the mutual wills doctrine lead to the result that B (and hence his 'heir' as his successor in title) was not bound by *any* constructive trust. This can be explained on the basis that the Court of Appeal was looking for a particular *type* of agreement; its absence meant that only one conclusion was appropriate—that B was free to dispose all of the property he owned.

[156] *Parry and Kerridge* (n 4) [6-42].

[157] Hughes, 'Mutual Wills' (n 5) 136. See too Braun, 'Revocability of Mutual Wills' (n 40) 221 fn 65.

[158] Richardson, 'Legislation for Mutual Wills (n 6) 109.

[159] *Lewis v Cotton* (n 129) [45]–[46].

[160] See S 12.3.1.1.

[161] See Liew, 'The Ambit' (n 26) s II.2.

[162] *De Bruyne v Dr Bruyne* (n 92) indicates that the doctrine can apply to three-party cases.

of the secret trusts doctrine.[163] So even if the mutual wills doctrine were abolished, relief in these cases could still be obtained through the other constructive trust doctrines. Moreover, because the QI doctrines aim to prevent an advantage from being taken by B in specific situations, a principled distinction cannot be drawn between an advantage conferred by A in an inter vivos context and an advantage conferred by A in a testamentary context, nor between cases where B's promise relates only to A's property and those where it relates to a fund consisting of A's and B's property. Like cases should be treated alike.

Consider next cases reflecting AI situations. A striking similarity exists between mutual wills cases and a number of proprietary estoppel cases:[164] they all involve B promising to make a particular form of testamentary disposition of property he owns absolutely. Abolishing the mutual wills doctrine would therefore not prevent the law from providing compensation for detrimental reliance incurred by A as a result of such a promise by B. It would also be impossible to draw a principled distinction in terms of the nature of A's reliance. Why should the law refuse to provide compensation if A's reliance takes the form of a testamentary disposition to C, as opposed to the more common proprietary estoppel cases where A provides services to B? After all, there would be a stronger argument for compensating A in the former case since A would no longer be alive to undo what has been done.[165]

The upshot is that the mutual wills doctrine cannot cleanly be hived off from other doctrines such as the doctrine in *Rochefoucauld v Boustead*, secret trusts, and proprietary estoppel, in order to justify abolishing the mutual wills doctrine. Instead, it is submitted that it would be better for the Law Commission to recognise and clarify the distinct bases which underly the two types of case within the mutual wills doctrine, as set out in this chapter. Recognising this renewed understanding not only allays the concerns which judges and commentators have expressed about the doctrine, but also indicates how the doctrine works alongside and consistently with other equitable doctrines in order to provide compensation for reliance losses or to prevent an undue advantage from being taken. So long as it continues to be possible to make wills without legal advice, there will be a variety of arrangements testators might attempt to enter, and these will need to be addressed in a way which is consistent with how courts approach the other related doctrines.

12.4.5. The Breadth of the QI Situations

Finally, the mutual wills doctrine provides an important lesson for the doctrines reflecting QI situations within the non-contract-based, bilateral events category of constructive trusts. This is that the analysis which underpins those doctrines is not confined to cases where B promises to perform his promise immediately upon acquisition of property, and where B's promise relates to specific property—both of which are common features of the doctrine in *Rochefoucauld v Boustead* and secret trusts. Instead, through a *firm* promise,

[163] Specifically, *Ottaway n Norman* (n 33).

[164] See, eg, *Wayling v Jones* (1995) 69 P & CR 170 (CA); *Gillett v Holt* [2001] Ch 210 (CA); *Jennings v Rice* [2002] EWCA Civ 159, [2003] 1 FCR 501.

[165] On this point, *cf Thorner v Major* (n 114) [63], where Lord Walker suggested that it is inappropriate to rely on mutual wills authorities in relation to proprietary estoppel because mutual wills 'are arguably a special case'. This chapter suggests the contrary insofar as AI situations are concerned.

it is also possible for B to qualify his interest in a fund. When B promises to hold a fund on trust for C, and A relies by transferring property to B to constitute that fund, a constructive trust binds B to his promise in relation to the fund. C's right in the fund crystallises when the pre-agreed event occurs, and also if and when B acts inconsistently with his promise. Whether B's promise relates to specific property or to a fund is a matter of construction of B's promise.

In principle, the analysis is not confined to testamentary arrangements. Suppose B informally but irrevocably promises that, when A transfers land to B, B will hold A's land as well as a plot of B's own land as a fund, upon the terms that B will have use of the fund for five years, at the end of which B will transfer 'whatever is left' to C. It is suggested that such a case would be treated in line with the mutual wills cases which reflect QI situations: upon A's reliance, a constructive trust would be imposed on *both* pieces of land as a fund to compel B to make good the entirety of his promise. The same would be the case if B's promise was to give 'both plots of land, or the proceeds of investments thereof' to C at the end of five years: B's promise would relate to a fund and not to specific property. These examples suggest another characteristic of the QI doctrines: if the subject-matter of B's promise is a fund, it does not matter how the properties comprising the fund are defined—whether by reference to properties at B's death or by express identification of the items comprising the fund. All that is necessary is that B firmly promises to treat the properties as a fund rather than individual items, and that he also evinces an intention not to revoke the arrangement.

13

The *Quistclose* Doctrine

The *Quistclose* doctrine[1] has by-and-large been treated in practice as a *sui generis* doctrine, which applies to commercial, inter vivos arrangements involving money. This restrictive understanding of the *Quistclose* doctrine causes little concern when it is applied to typical factual matrices. However, it may be asked whether, in fact, the doctrine has a wider application than that which is commonly assumed. A number of important and related questions arise: can the doctrine be applied in other non-typical factual scenarios; does the basis on which the doctrine rests also explain other equitable doctrines, so that our understanding of one doctrine may inform the analysis of another; what is the principle on which the doctrine is based; what does this tell us about the nature of the trust enforced; what degree of intention to create a trust is necessary; how does the doctrine relate to the borrower's insolvency?

This chapter examines the present understanding of the *Quistclose* doctrine and notes that its application is often (though erroneously) thought to be restricted to a certain factual ambit. In particular, there is nothing inherent within the doctrine which precludes its application from cases in which the underlying trust cannot be enforced as an express trust due to the parties' non-compliance with certain formality requirements. It then explains how the *Quistclose* doctrine and the doctrine in *Rochefoucauld v Boustead* can be aligned such that, where an express trust cannot be enforced through an operation of the *Quistclose* doctrine, the doctrine may nevertheless be understood as allowing for the imposition of constructive trusts which arise to prevent an advantage from being taken. This means that the *Quistclose* doctrine is capable of falling within the non-contract-based, bilateral events category of constructive trusts. Finally, it explores a number of lessons which emerge from this analysis.

13.1. The Present Understanding

In *Barclays Bank Ltd v Quistclose Investments Ltd*,[2] A loaned money to B for B to pay off dividends which B had declared and was unable to meet. The loan was accompanied by a letter indicating that the loan money 'will only be used to meet the dividend'.[3] The money

[1] Although the phrase 'the *Quistclose* trust' is often used, it seems better to refer to the subject as 'the *Quistclose* doctrine'. The term 'doctrine' indicates more precisely the subject-matter of the present discussion—a set of norms—rather than simply a type of trust. In the following discussion, the phrase 'the *Quistclose* trust' will be used only when quoting verbatim from other sources.

[2] *Barclays Bank Ltd v Quistclose Investments Ltd* [1970] AC 567 (HL).

[3] ibid 579.

had not yet been applied for the stated purpose and remained in a separate account in Barclays Bank when B went into voluntary liquidation. The House of Lords decided that B held the money on trust for A, and therefore A was entitled to the return of the money.

The unique equitable doctrine[4] reflected by this case is described in *Underhill and Hayton* as follows: '[a] loan arrangement may commence as a trust of the money loaned to enable [B] only to carry out a particular purpose resulting, if the purpose is performed, in a pure debtor-creditor relationship excluding any trust, but in the event of non-performance of the purpose [A] can rely on the loaned money being held on trust for [A]'.[5]

According to an analysis propounded by Sir Peter Millett QC (as he then was) in 1985,[6] the operation of the *Quistclose* doctrine can be explained using orthodox trust principles. In a *Quistclose* arrangement, B may, or may not, apply the loaned money pursuant to the stated purpose. As the judgment in *Quistclose* indicates, if B does not so apply the money, and it becomes clear that he is unable to so anymore, it is A, not B's creditors (X), who is entitled to the money. B therefore does not hold the money on trust for X. Neither does B take the money absolutely, since his use of the money is restricted by the purpose: if B is to use the money at all, he must do so *exclusively* pursuant to the agreed purpose. This indicates that the beneficial interest of the property vests in A until and unless B applies the money for the agreed purpose.[7] Thus, when B receives the money from A, B holds it on trust for A, subject to a power in B's favour to apply the money according to the agreed purpose. If, however, B carries out the purpose, the money vests absolutely in X, and the relationship between A and B becomes one of debtor-creditor.

The discussion will proceed on the basis that the foregoing analysis propounded by Millett QC accurately explains the *Quistclose* doctrine. There are two compelling reasons for adopting the analysis. First, it has strength of authority: since Lord Millett reiterated this analysis in the House of Lords in *Twinsectra Ltd v Yardley*,[8] it has been unquestionably applied by the lower courts in England.[9] Secondly, this analysis is the least controversial of the possible explanations of the doctrine.[10] Other attempts have been made to explain the doctrine on the basis that it creates a primary purpose trust which, if it fails, triggers a secondary trust for A's benefit;[11] that B holds the beneficial interest in suspense pending application of the money;[12] that it recognises a novel private purpose trust;[13] and that B obtains

[4] Note that the label 'the *Quistclose* doctrine' does not imply that the doctrine arose for the first time in the *Quistclose* case, since many cases prior to that decision also apply the same principle underlying the doctrine (see, eg, cases discussed in PJ Millett, 'The *Quistclose* Trust: Who can Enforce It?' (1985) 101 *LQR* 269, 270–74). Rather, the label indicates that that case provided the first modern statement of the doctrine the highest authority, and also contains the first serious attempt rationalising the underlying basis of the doctrine.

[5] David Hayton, Paul Matthews and Charles Mitchell, *Underhill and Hayton: Law Relating to Trusts and Trustees*, 19th edn (London, LexisNexis Butterworths, 2016) [1.30].

[6] Millett, 'The *Quistclose* Trust' (n 4).

[7] The agreement may, of course, provide that A does not have the right to collapse the trust within a reasonable amount of time in order to give B the opportunity to apply the property for X.

[8] *Twinsectra Ltd v Yardley* [2002] UKHL 12, [2002] 2 AC 164.

[9] Similarly, Australian courts take the view that the *Quistclose* doctrine represents an application of orthodox trust principles. See, eg, *Re Australian Elizabethan Theatre Trust* (1991) 30 FCR 491, 502; *Compass Resources Ltd v Sherman* [2010] WASC 41 [74]; *Raulfs v Fishy Bite Pte Ltd* [2012] NSWCA 135 [50]; *Salvo v New Tel Ltd* [2005] NSWCA 281 [77]; *Legal Services Board v Gillespie-Jones* [2013] JCA 35 [112].

[10] See especially James Penner, 'Lord Millett's Analysis' in William Swadling (ed), *The Quistclose Trust: Critical Essays* (Oxford, Hart Publishing, 2004).

[11] *Barclays Bank v Quistclose* (n 2).

[12] *Re Northern Developments (Holdings) Ltd* (CA, 6 October 1978).

[13] Noted in Penner, 'Lord Millett's Analysis' (n 10) 41 text to fn 5.

the entire beneficial ownership subject only to a contractual obligation in favour of A.[14] A counterpart argument to the last of the aforementioned is that the *Quistclose* doctrine is an exceptional example of a proprietary restitutionary response to unjust enrichment in respect of failure of consideration.[15] Each of these views has been convincingly criticised,[16] however, and need not be considered any further for the purposes of our present discussion.

13.1.1. Triggering Events and the Nature of the Trust

It is accepted that the doctrine requires (i) a transfer of property from A to B, (ii) based on an agreement that it will be used exclusively for a stated purpose. In addition, however, it is commonly assumed that three other events also need to be present. First, it has been claimed that the property in question must be money, and not any other asset such as land, goods, or intellectual property.[17] Secondly, the arrangement between the parties must be a commercial agreement.[18] Thirdly, the agreement between A and B must be an inter vivos agreement. The third of these follows from the argument that *Quistclose* arrangements can be enforced as express trusts, as discussed below. Since it has never been suggested that a *Quistclose* arrangement is unenforceable due to the informality of the arrangement, and because informal declarations of testamentary trusts are not enforceable as express trusts,[19] it follows that the arrangement must be inter vivos.

A cursory survey of the case law and academic discussion reveals that the three additional events are often explicitly or implicitly taken to define the boundaries of the *Quistclose* doctrine. While not necessarily denying that *a* trust may be imposed where one or more of these additional events are not met, an assumption is made that the trust would not arise *through an application of the Quistclose doctrine*. This implies that a commercial, inter vivos transfer of money for an exclusive purpose gives rise to a novel set of concerns which cannot properly be addressed using any other existing equitable doctrine.[20] This perception is reflected by the fact that the *Quistclose* doctrine has been developed independently from other equitable doctrines.

[14] Robert Chambers, *Resulting Trusts* (Oxford, OUP, 1997) Ch 3.

[15] See ibid 148–49; Andrew Burrows, *The Law of Restitution*, 3rd edn (Oxford, OUP, 2010) 400–01.

[16] See, respectively, *Twinsectra v Yardley* (n 8) [79] (on the primary/secondary trust analysis); Millett, 'The *Quistclose* Trust' (n 4) 282 (on the 'suspense' analysis); William Swadling, 'Orthodoxy' in Swadling, *The Quistclose Trust* (n 10) and *Re Australian Elizabethan Theatre Trust* (n 9) 502 (on the novel purpose trust analysis); *Twinsectra v Yardley* (n 8) [94]–[99] and Lusina Ho and P St J Smart, 'Re-interpreting the *Quistclose* Trust: A Critique of Chambers' Analysis' (2001) 21 *OJLS* 267 (on the contractual analysis).

On the 'counterpart argument' mentioned in the text above, see Charles Mitchell, Paul Mitchell and Stephen Watterson, *Goff & Jones: The Law of Unjust Enrichment*, 8th edn (London, Sweet & Maxwell, 2016) [38-24] fn 72, which notes that Lord Millett's analysis in *Twinsectra* renders that argument otiose.

[17] Robert Chambers, 'Restrictions on the Use of Money' in Swadling, *The Quistclose Trust* (n 10) 77. This is implicitly suggested in other trusts texts: see, eg, Penner, 'Lord Millett's Analysis' (n 10) 41; John McGhee (ed), *Snell's Equity*, 33rd edn (London, Sweet & Maxwell, 2016) [25-033]–[25-034]; *Underhill and Hayton* (n 5) [1.30]–[1.37].

[18] Implicitly suggested by Lord Millett in *Twinsectra v Yardley* (n 8) [99]. See too Lord Millett, 'Foreword' in Swadling, *The Quistclose Trust* (n 10).

[19] Declarations of testamentary trusts must comply with the Wills Act 1837, s 9 to be legally enforceable as express trusts.

[20] So, for example, this often leads to the misguided tendency of defining the whole purpose of the *Quistclose* doctrine as affording A priority in B's insolvency: see S 13.3.2.

Upon receipt of the money and pending his application of it for the stated purpose, B holds the money on trust for A. The nature of the trust remains an open question. Two views have garnered significant support. The first, propounded by Millett QC, is that B holds the property by way of an express trust.[21] To enforce the trust as an express trust, A must have had an intention to create a trust[22] over the money for the benefit of himself.[23] A must also *properly* manifest his intention to create a trust. This involves complying with any formality requirements which may be relevant, since non-compliance precludes the enforcement of the intended arrangement *qua* an express trust. Signed writing is required only for the enforcement of inter vivos express trusts concerning land[24] and testamentary express trusts;[25] inter vivos trust arrangements which do not concern land can be enforced *qua* express trusts even though they are orally declared. Because the *Quistclose* doctrine has typically been applied to inter vivos arrangements involving money, formality requirements have not prevented an analysis of *Quistclose* arrangements as express trusts. In addition, a settlor may unilaterally create an express trust,[26] and so on the express trust analysis the agreement between the parties to a *Quistclose* arrangement is relevant insofar as it reflects A's intention to create a trust. B's assent to the arrangement is indicative of A's intention.

The second view, propounded by Lord Millett in *Twinsectra v Yardley*,[27] is that the trust is a resulting trust. In his Lordship's words, '[A] pays the money to [B] by way of loan, but he does not part with the entire beneficial interest in the money, and in so far as he does not it is held on a resulting trust for [A] from the outset'.[28] Resulting trusts, unlike express trusts, arise by operation of law and thus can be imposed despite the informality of an arrangement. The imposition of a resulting trust turns on showing, by way of presumption or actual evidence,[29] that the property A transfers to B is not meant to be at B's free disposal—that A has a negative intention, an absence of intention to benefit B.[30] It is unnecessary for the enforcement of an arrangement *qua* a resulting trust to adduce evidence of the parties' positive intention that B will hold the property on trust, but such evidence supports the finding of a resulting trust, since a positive intention would indicate that the property is

[21] Millett, 'The *Quistclose* Trust' (n 4). As James Penner observes, 'the ascertainment of A's genuine intentions' is a common theme running through Millett's article: Penner, 'Lord Millett's Analysis' (n 10) 51 fn 31.

[22] *Knight v Knight* (1840) 3 Beav 148, 49 ER 58.

[23] This is implicit in Millett, 'The *Quistclose* Trust' (n 4) 288.

[24] The Law of Property Act 1925, s 53(1)(b) provides that 'all declarations … of trusts or confidences of any lands … shall be manifested and proved by some writing signed by the party who is by law enabled to declare such trust'.

[25] The Wills Act 1897, s 9 provides that a valid will must be made 'in writing and signed by the testator, in the presence of two or more attesting witnesses present at the same time.'

[26] *Fletcher v Fletcher* (1844) 4 Hare 67, 67 ER 564; *Mallott v Wilson* [1903] 2 Ch 494 (Ch); *Re Kayford Ltd* [1975] 1 All ER 604 (Ch) 607; *Re Goldcorp Exchange Ltd* [1995] 1 AC 74 (PC) 100. See Chapter 1, S 1.2.1.

While Australian courts have suggested that the *Quistclose* trust is a specific example of an express trust created by the *mutual* intention of A and B (see *Re Australian Elizabethan Theatre Trust* (n 9) 502), the better view is that an express trust can unilaterally be *created* by A, and that B's state of mind in receiving the property from A determines the duties which are imposed on B: see Jamie Glister, 'Mutual Intention and Quistclose Trusts' (2012) 6 *Journal of Equity* 221; Ying Khai Liew and Charles Mitchell, 'The Creation of Express Trusts' (forthcoming 2018).

[27] See *Twinsectra v Yardley* (n 8) [92].

[28] ibid [100].

[29] See *Vandervell v IRC* [1967] 2 AC 291 (HL) 313, 315; Robert Chambers, 'Is There a Presumption of Resulting Trust?' in Charles Mitchell (ed), *Constructive and Resulting Trusts* (Oxford, Hart Publishing, 2010).

[30] Chambers, *Resulting Trusts* (n 14). See Chapter 1, S 1.2.2.

not meant to be at B's free disposal.[31] The parties' agreement, and hence B's assent to the arrangement, is indicative of the central element of the resulting trust—A's negative intention. Another feature of a resulting trust is that A is always the beneficiary under that trust. The term 'resulting' originated from the Latin word '*resalire*', which means 'to jump back'; hence the resulting trust invariably *returns* the beneficial ownership of the trust property to A because A was the previous owner of the property prior to the transfer to B.[32]

13.1.2. Wider Applications

Since the cases which have shaped the *Quistclose* doctrine have concerned the return of money to A in an inter vivos commercial context, there seems to be little cause for concern so long as courts consistently impose *a* trust for A's benefit where B fails to apply the money for the agreed purpose. However, it is also necessary to avoid making 'subtle distinctions … between "true" *Quistclose* trusts and trusts which are merely analogous to them'.[33] A careful examination reveals that the doctrine can be applied beyond its traditionally perceived limits.

First, consider an informal *Quistclose* arrangement. Suppose A transfers land to B based on an oral agreement that B is to use the land solely for the purpose of raising a mortgage in his own name. Soon after acquiring the land from A, but before raising the mortgage, B dies. Or suppose A executes a will naming a company, B, legatee of £100,000. B is eventually heavily indebted to a creditor, X. On A's deathbed, A and B's sole director reach an informal agreement that B will use the £100,000 exclusively to repay X, failing which the money will revert to A's estate and thence to fall into residue. A dies without executing a revised will to reflect the arrangement, and B becomes insolvent soon after. In principle, there is no reason why the *Quistclose* doctrine would not apply in these cases despite the informality of the arrangements: a transfer of property is made from A to B which is conditional upon an exclusive purpose, and a trust ought to arise for A's benefit upon B's receipt of the property. The failure to apply the property thus ought to result in the return of the property to A in precisely the same way as in the typical factual scenario.[34]

Next, consider a *Quistclose* arrangement with a different pattern from the typical scenario. Suppose A transfers money to B pursuant to an agreement that B will use the money exclusively to repay B's creditor, X, and failing which the money will vest absolutely in C. It would follow from the resulting trust analysis that this situation falls outside the ambit of the *Quistclose* doctrine because the arrangement does not contemplate the *return* of the beneficial interest in the money to A. However, because the *Quistclose* doctrine is concerned with resolving arrangements involving property transferred pursuant to an exclusive purpose,[35] it appears immaterial that the parties intend C (instead of A) to take the money

[31] Chambers, *Resulting Trusts* (n 14) 34. Chambers' analysis was expressly adopted by Lord Millett in *Twinsectra v Yardley* (n 8) [92].

[32] See *Goff & Jones* (n 16) [38-07].

[33] *Twinsectra v Yardley* (n 8) [99].

[34] This conclusion is reinforced by extrapolating from equity's willingness to enforce informal inter vivos trust arrangements through an application of the doctrine in *Rochefoucauld v Boustead* (discussed in Chapter 4) and to enforce *testamentary* trust arrangements through the secret trusts doctrine (discussed in Chapter 5).

[35] See, eg, *Twinsectra v Yardley* (n 8) [69], [70]–[71]; Millett, 'The *Quistclose* Trust' (n 4) 269.

if B fails to apply the money as agreed. In principle, an application of the doctrine ought to compel B to hold the money on trust for the benefit of C, subject to a power in B's favour to apply the money for the purpose of repaying X.

Lastly, consider a *Quistclose* arrangement which features both an element of informality and a unique pattern. Suppose an irrevocable discretionary trust of both capital and income of shares is held for the benefit of a class of potential beneficiaries (As), which includes a number of minors. Collectively they agree that their trustee should exercise his discretion in favour of B (also a member of As) pursuant to B's promise to use the shares exclusively for the purpose of repaying X, one of B's creditors, and failing which the money will vest in C, another member of As.[36] They also agree that B's power to apply the shares for the stated purpose will be revocable by C, and that C will receive the dividends while the shares remain in B's hands. The trustee of the discretionary trust duly transfers the shares to B absolutely, thus terminating the discretionary trust. In principle, the *Quistclose* doctrine ought to compel B to hold the shares on trust for C, subject to a power in B's favour to apply the shares for the stated purpose. Yet, the trust can neither be analysed as a resulting trust nor an express trust. It cannot be a resulting trust because the beneficial interest in the shares is not returned to As or As' original trustee, but is held for the benefit of C.[37] It is also not an express trust: since not all As were *sui juris*, they could not have exercised their *Saunders v Vautier*[38] rights to collapse the discretionary trust for themselves as joint tenants and then collectively created a new (express) trust.

If, as argued, the *Quistclose* doctrine can apply in these scenarios, a proper understanding of the doctrine must be broad enough to take these situations into account.

13.2. A Re-Analysis

There is a high degree of similarity between the *Quistclose* doctrine and the doctrine in *Rochefoucauld v Boustead*. This section observes that the same material events are capable of triggering the operation of both doctrines. It then notes how the responses of both doctrines may be aligned. This latter point consists of two sub-arguments. The first is that, on the present understanding, the *Quistclose* doctrine is better understood as providing for the enforcement of express, as opposed to resulting, trusts. The second is that, where the trust cannot be enforced as an express trust, the doctrine may nevertheless give rise to a constructive trust for the same reasons as constructive trusts arise by way of the doctrine in *Rochefoucauld v Bosutead*.

13.2.1. The Doctrine in *Rochefoucauld v Boustead*

It is seldom thought that there is anything of significance shared by the *Quistclose* doctrine and the doctrine in *Rochefoucauld v Boustead*. This perception appears to be rooted in the

[36] These facts are an adaptation of the facts of *De Bruyne v De Bruyne* [2010] EWCA Civ 519, [2010] 2 FLR 1240.

[37] If the arrangement failed to name a beneficiary in default of B's exercise of the power, the property would either vest in B absolutely, be held on trust for X, or be treated as *bona vacantia*, depending on As' intention.

[38] *Saunders v Vautier* (1841) 4 Beav 115, 49 ER 282.

way these doctrines have historically developed. In relation to the *Quistclose* doctrine, the cases which have applied the doctrine since the first reported case of *Toovey v Milne*[39] have usually involved the enforcement by way of trust of an arrangement concerning money advanced for a particular purpose, usually (but not invariably) for the payment of one's creditors.[40] On the other hand, the doctrine in *Rochefoucauld v Boustead* reflected an application of the maxim that a statute may not be used as an 'instrument of fraud', a phrase that is likely to have originated from Lord Eldon's decision in *Mestaer v Gillespie*.[41] Despite being historically developed to deal with different factual scenarios, however, both doctrines can be understood as sharing the same basis: they both respond to similar causative events and yield similar responses in certain situations.

An in-depth discussion of the doctrine in *Rochefoucauld v Boustead* can be found in Chapter 4. For the purposes of the present discussion, a number of points bear repeating. The doctrine is triggered by an *agreement* between A and B. Thus, in *Rochefoucauld*, it was the agreement between A and B which led the court to hold that the '[land] was ... conveyed [to B] upon trust for [A], and that [B] ... [was] denying the trust and relying upon the form of conveyance and the statute, in order to keep the land himself'.[42] Similarly, in *Bannister*, the court held that it was essential to find a 'bargain' or 'agreement' which 'include[s] a stipulation under which some sufficiently defined beneficial interest in the property was to be taken by another'.[43] And in *De Bruyne*, the court 'concentrate[d] ... on the circumstances in which [B] came to acquire the property [that is, pursuant to the agreement between As and B] in order to provide the justification for the imposition of a trust'.[44]

However, it is not any agreement reached between A and B which engages the doctrine: the agreement must exhibit three crucial features. First, the transfer of property to B must be made *on the basis of* the agreement. If the relevant agreement is not secured before the transfer of the property, the doctrine does not apply.[45] Secondly, the agreement must *induce* A to transfer his property—the very property to which B's promise relates—to B. B's promise need not be a 'but for' cause of A's transfer of property, but it must have affected A's decision to transfer the property in some way: B's promise must be *a cause* of A's transfer of property for the agreement to be the *basis* upon which A acts.[46] Thirdly, the agreement must reflect a QI situation: B's promise to act as trustee must relate to property that he does not yet own, so that he promises to qualify the interest which he will obtain in the property.[47]

It was also seen in Chapter 4[48] that, contrary to suggestions by certain academics, the doctrine in *Rochefoucauld v Boustead* gives rise to trusts which are constructive in nature.

[39] *Toovey v Milne* (1819) 2 B & Ald 683, 106 ER 514.

[40] See Millett, 'The *Quistclose* Trust' (n 4) 270ff.

[41] *Mestaer v Gillespie* (1805) 11 Ves Jun 621, 32 ER 1230; Mark Pawlowski, 'Fraud, Legal Formality and Equity' (2001) 23 *Liverpool Law Review* 79, 79 fn 1. See also TG Youdan, 'Formalities for Trusts of Land, and the Doctrine in *Rochefoucauld v Boustead*' (1984) 43 *CLJ* 306.

[42] *Rochefoucauld v Boustead* [1897] 1 Ch 196 (CA) 206.

[43] *Bannister v Bannister* [1948] 2 All ER 133 (CA) 136.

[44] *De Bruyne v De Bruyne* (n 37) [51].

[45] See Chapter 4, S 4.5.1.1.2.

[46] See Chapter 4, S 4.2.2.2.

[47] See Chapter 3, S 3.2.1.1.

[48] See Chapter 4, S 4.1.

13.2.2. Agreement

The doctrine in *Rochefoucauld v Boustead* requires that the parties must in essence[49] agree that B will hold the acquired property on trust. In relation to the *Quistclose* doctrine, the parties must intend that B will use A's property exclusively for a specific purpose. On the face of it, it appears the *Quistclose* doctrine does not respond to any intention to create a trust. But upon closer inspection, the 'exclusive purpose' clause is not significant as an end in itself.[50] This can be seen from the fact that the *Quistclose* doctrine does not provide for the direct enforcement of such a clause so that B is compelled to apply the property for the stated purpose. Indeed, it would be impossible to enforce the clause directly in some cases such as *Twinsectra*,[51] where the purpose is expressed in ambiguous terms. Instead, the focus is on what is implied from the fact that B must use A's property 'exclusively' for the stated purpose: it is taken to indicate a positive intention that the money is to be returned to A if it is not applied for the stated purpose. As Lord Wilberforce observed in *Barclays Bank v Quistclose*, 'by process simply of interpretation, … if, for any reason the [purpose] could not be [attained], the money was to be returned to [A]: the word "only" or "exclusively" can have no other meaning or effect'.[52] Since A can only demand the return of the property if B holds the property on trust for A upon receiving it,[53] in effect the *Quistclose* doctrine is concerned with enforcing that which is left unsaid but unmistakably intended by the parties: that the property is transferred to B *on trust* for A pending application for the stated purpose.[54] As succinctly observed in *Re Holiday Promotions (Europe) Ltd*,[55] 'the decision in *Quistclose* does not undermine the basic proposition of trust law that you need to find an intention to create a trust, or at least an intention to do something that can only be given effect by the creation of a trust'. Thus, both doctrines require an (express or implied) intention that B will hold the property on trust.

The case of *Re Duke of Marlborough*[56] exemplifies this point. A, the Duchess of Marlborough, assigned a leasehold to B, the Duke, absolutely for the latter to raise a mortgage in his sole name. The parties orally agreed that B would later re-convey the equity of redemption to A. B died after raising the mortgage but before carrying out the re-conveyance. Stirling J decided that A was entitled to the equity of redemption despite the informal nature of the agreement. He also observed that, '[i]f [B] had in his lifetime refused to convey … he could not have set up the statute … [and B's creditors], as claiming under him, is in no better

[49] It is unnecessary that the agreement 'should include any express stipulation that [B] is in so many words to hold as trustee': *Bannister v Bannister* (n 44) 136.

[50] *cf* the decision of the Malaysian Federal Court in *PECD Berhad (in liquidation) v AmTrustee Berhad* [2014] 1 MLJ 91 (Federal Court, Malaysia), www.kehakiman.gov.my/directory/judgment/file/02_f_%C3%A2%E2%82%AC%E2%80%9C_59-08-2012_W.pdf, where the 'specific purpose clause' was enforced. This decision is criticised in Ying Khai Liew and Weng Tchung Low, 'The *Quistclose* Doctrine: Resurrection of the Primary Trust?' (2014) 25 *King's Law Journal* 8, republished in [2014] 6 *Malayan Law Journal* i–xiii.

[51] The purpose in that case was simply the 'acquisition of property': *Twinsectra v Yardley* (n 8) [9].

[52] *Barclays Bank v Quistclose* (n 2) 580.

[53] See main text from n 6 above.

[54] See *Challinor v Juliet Bellis & Co* [2015] EWCA Civ 59, [2016] WTLR 43 [56].

[55] *Re Holiday Promotions (Europe) Ltd* [1996] BCC 671, 674. See too *Challinor v Juliet Bellis & Co* (n 55) [56]: 'There must be an intention to create a trust on the part of [A].' A may manifest his intention to B, or to another person: *Challinor v Juliet Bellis & Co* (n 55) [61].

[56] *Re Duke of Marlborough* [1894] 2 Ch 133 (Ch).

position'.[57] This result can be explained on the basis of the *Quistclose* doctrine, because the parties' agreement that the transfer of the leasehold to B was to be subject to the exclusive purpose of raising a mortgage indicated A's intention to create a trust for herself. The result can also be explained on the basis of the doctrine in *Rochefoucauld v Boustead* since the parties had agreed, prior to the transfer to B, that B was to hold the leasehold on trust for A. Both analyses are therefore consistent inter se: they both aim to give effect to a positive intention to create a trust as gleaned from the parties' agreement. That is, the transfer of the leasehold to B for an exclusive purpose precisely revealed an intention that B will hold the lease on trust for A pending its application for the stated purpose.

The similarities between the doctrines in relation to their material events do not end there: the relevant agreement which triggers the operation of the *Quistclose* doctrine can be seen to share the same features of an agreement which triggers the doctrine in *Rochefoucauld v Boustead*. First, the agreement concerning B's use of the property is always the *basis* upon which A transfers the property to B. So, for example, if A transfers the property to B where B is unaware of, or disagrees to, any restriction placed on his use of the property, it would be impossible to say that a trust relationship was intended.[58] Secondly, the intention to create a trust, gleaned from the parties' agreement, always *induces* A to transfer the property to B. This is because, if A can be shown to have been indifferent as to whether B's application of the property was restricted, A would have essentially intended for the property to 'be at the free disposal of [B] and may be used as part of his cash-flow'.[59] Thirdly, the *Quistclose* doctrine operates only in QI situations, affecting property which B does not yet own when the parties enter their agreement. In particular, B cannot be treated as having declared himself as trustee after receiving the property absolutely from A: an application of the *Quistclose* doctrine imposes a trust from the moment B acquires the property, which means that B is never the absolute owner of the property.

In an earlier discussion,[60] it was noted that the *Quistclose* doctrine is often thought to be confined to a particular type of property (money), a particular context (commercial and inter vivos), and/or a particular pattern (the return of the property to A). The reason why these events-based restrictions ought to be rejected now emerges: they are inconsistent with the reality that the *Quistclose* doctrine responds to and enforces an intention *to create a trust*. So, just as in the case of the QI situations within the non-contract-based, bilateral events category of constructive trusts, the *Quistclose* doctrine is capable of applying in cases involving informal testamentary arrangements, informal inter vivos arrangements concerning land, and where the arrangement is that B will hold the property on trust not for A but for C, a third party volunteer. There is no reason in principle why the applicability of the *Quistclose* doctrine should otherwise be restricted.

13.2.3. Nature of the Trust

In general terms, the *Quistclose* doctrine and the doctrine in *Rochefoucauld v Boustead* both elicit the same legal response—the enforcement of the agreement that B will hold the

57 ibid 146.
58 *Twinsectra v Yardley* (n 8) [69].
59 ibid [71].
60 See main text to and following n 17 above.

property on trust. Because A would already have transferred the property to B, the only outstanding act is for B to fulfil his promise; thus, the legal response can also be said to enforce B's promise[61] to hold the acquired property on trust for A or C, as the case may be. However, there appears to be a difference in the nature of the trust enforced. While the doctrine in *Rochefoucauld v Boustead* gives rise to a constructive trust, the prevailing understanding of the *Quistclose* doctrine is that B holds the property either on an express trust or a resulting trust. Upon closer inspection, however, this difference can be reconciled.

13.2.3.1. The Quistclose *Doctrine: Express Trusts*

It is necessary first to consider the nature of the trust enforced in the *Quistclose* doctrine. As we have seen in Chapter 1,[62] express trusts and resulting trusts respond to A's intention in fundamentally different ways. Express trusts focus on A's positive, properly manifested intention to create a trust; resulting trusts focus on A's negative intention—that the property is not meant to be B's beneficially. Following Lord Millett's view in *Twinsectra v Yardley*[63] that the *Quistclose* doctrine gives rise to a resulting trust, the judicial trend in English law has been to prefer this analysis.[64] However, although it is often the case that A's positive intention to retain the beneficial interest in the property corresponds precisely to his lack of intention to give B the beneficial interest in the property, the distinction between the two types of trust is not illusory.

There are two principled reasons why the express trust analysis should be preferred. The first relates to the facilitative nature of the express trust device. Through an express trust, the law allows one legitimately to expect that his properly manifested intention to create a trust will be given legal effect. The fact that the law provides this facility indicates that equity prefers to enforce a positive manifestation of intention wherever possible,[65] since a declaration of an express trust by an owner of property is the clearest way in which a positive intention to create a trust can be manifested. This in turn advances 'the liberal vision of the institution of property'.[66] As Simon Gardner explains, '[l]iberalism argues that everyone should be permitted the largest possible degree of autonomy ... [A property owner's] autonomy is ... maximized if we accord him the greatest possible freedom as to how he may intentionally give [his property] away. The law provides the vehicle of the express trust in order to permit this'.[67] Preferring the resulting trust analysis over the express trust would be to ignore A's positive intention at the expense of giving effect to what A did *not* intend. Analytically, this would curb A's autonomy to decide what he wants done with his property.[68]

[61] See discussion in Chapter 4, S 4.2.2.

[62] See Chapter 1, SS 1.2.1. and 1.2.2.

[63] *Twinsectra v Yardley* (n 8) [100].

[64] See, eg, *Dubey v Revenue and Customs Commissioners* [2006] EWHC 3272 (Ch), [2008] BCC 22 [33]; *Templeton Insurance Ltd v Penningtons Solicitors LLP* [2006] EWHC 685 (Ch), [2007] WTLR 1103 [18]. *Bank of Cyprus UK Ltd v Menelaou* [2015] UKSC 66, [2016] AC 176 [137] is to the same effect.

cf the position in Australia, where the express trust analysis is the dominant view: see, eg, *Re Australian Elizabethan Theatre Trust* (n 9) 500; *Walsh Bay Developments Pty Ltd v Federal Commissioner of Taxation* (1995) 130 ALR 415, 425; *Roxborough v Rothmans of Pall Mall Australia Ltd* (1999) 167 ALR 326, 346; *George v Webb* [2011] NSWSC 1608 [271], [282]; *Legal Services Board v Gillespie-Jones* (n 9) [115]. But contrast *Salvo v New Tel Ltd* (n 9) [47]; *Raulfs v Fishy Bite Pte Ltd* (n 9) [43].

[65] It is 'possible' to do so if and when, inter alia, A complies with any relevant formality requirements.

[66] Simon Gardner, *An Introduction to the Law of Trusts*, Clarendon Law Series, 3rd edn (Oxford, OUP, 2011) 31.

[67] ibid 32.

[68] The same point was made in relation to the doctrine in *Rochefoucauld v Boustead* in Ch, 4 S 4.5.1.2.

The second reason is that the express trust analysis encourages judges to take the parties' intention seriously. This point has been thoroughly dealt with by James Penner. A resulting trust analysis artificially glosses over the parties' positive intention concerning B's use of the property;[69] it leads to 'an unwillingness to explore [the parties' positive intentions] and draw the appropriate inferences'.[70] Without basing the enforcement of the arrangement on A's positive intention, courts are in effect exercising a broad discretion to find a trust, which causes uncertainty in the law.[71] Most worryingly, the resulting trust approach 'amounts to an invitation to the courts to impose a trust wherever a purpose is stated'.[72] It was seen earlier[73] that the *exclusivity* of the agreed purpose is that which indicates a positive intention to create a trust. Diminishing the importance of the element of exclusivity may, in some cases, *cause B to be subjected to even though A does not positively intend for B to hold the property on trust.* It is therefore only appropriate that judges should carefully investigate whether a positive intention to create a trust can be found before imposing a trust of any sort, and the express trust analysis encourages such a judicial attitude.

13.2.3.2. The Quistclose *Doctrine: Constructive Trusts*

In situations where an express trust can be enforced, little else needs to be said, since equity's preference should be to enforce a positive manifestation of intention, given the facilitative nature of the express trust device.[74]

However, it has been observed that the *Quistclose* doctrine is applicable even where the subject-matter is land and/or the relevant agreement is made in a testamentary context, and where the relevant formality requirements for the creation or enforcement of an express trust are not fulfilled. It follows that there are potentially situations in which the *Quistclose* doctrine would apply, but which do not lead to the enforcement of express trusts.[75]

In these cases, the facts may still potentially give rise to a constructive trust. It is here where the responses of the *Quistclose* doctrine and the doctrine in *Rochefoucauld v Boustead* align. Where before receiving A's property B agrees to hold it on trust for A or C (pending application for the exclusive purpose in the *Quistclose* context), and where A transfers the property in question to B being induced by B's promise to do so, a constructive trust would arise to compel B to perform his promise, preventing him from taking an advantage for himself contrary to the parties' agreement.[76] Given the alignment between the

[69] Penner, 'Lord Millett's Analysis' (n 10) 52.

[70] ibid 64.

[71] ibid 56.

[72] ibid 54.

[73] See main text following n 52 above.

[74] See main text to n 68 above.

[75] A *Quistclose* arrangement is also unable to be enforced as an express trust where a purported group of settlors, 'As', are unable properly to declare an express trust where, for instance, a number of As are not *sui juris*, as the third example in S 13.1.2. indicates. In such a case, a constructive trust would nevertheless compel B to carry out the agreement, since B had promised to hold the property he will receive on trust for C, and this promise induced A to transfer their collective interest in the property to B.

[76] It must be emphasised that the constructive trust analysis proposed aligns the *Quistclose* doctrine with the principle underlying the doctrine in *Rochefoucauld v Boustead*. It is not based on the nebulous notion of B's 'unconscionability' as some commentators have suggested: see, eg, CEF Rickett, 'Trusts and Insolvency: The Nature and Place of the Quistclose Trust' in Donovan WM Waters (ed), *Equity, Fiduciaries and Trusts* (Toronto, Carswell, 1993) 340; Craig Rotherham, *Proprietary Remedies in Context* (Oxford, Hart Publishing, 2002) 160; Michael Smolyansky, 'Reining in the *Quistclose* Trust: A Response to *Twinsectra v Yardley*' (2010) 16 *Trusts & Trustees* 538, 567–68.

two doctrines in these cases, it follows that, at least where a constructive trust arises, the *Quistclose* doctrine falls to be considered as a QI situation within the non-contract-based, bilateral events category of constructive trusts.

An application of the constructive trust analysis in a *Quistclose* situation entails the notion of a 'constructive trust coupled with a power'—that B holds the property on a constructive trust for A, subject to a power to apply the property for the stated purpose. It might be objected that there is no authority that such a notion exists in the law. In truth, however, it is analytically sound. Consider a slight variation to the facts of *Re Duke of Marlborough*[77]—that B, who was in doubt as to his legal position, sought a court's declaration to determine the beneficial ownership of the leasehold. A declaration would undoubtedly be made to the effect that B holds the lease on a constructive trust for A, subject to a power in B's favour to raise a mortgage in his own name. Consider also a slight variation to the facts of *Rochefoucauld v Boustead*[78]—that the parties' agreement included an additional term allowing B to make use of the rental income generated by the land exclusively for the repayment of B's creditor, X. The arrangement would have given rise to a constructive trust in A's favour, subject to a power in B's favour to apply the income for the stated purpose. Moreover, in *Twinsectra v Yardley*, Lord Millett countenanced the notion of a 'resulting trust ... with a mandate to the transferee to apply the money for the stated purpose'.[79] This indicates that trusts arising by operation of law—particularly one arising from the moment of B's acquisition of the relevant property—can be coupled with a power in B's favour. Therefore, there is no conceptual difficulty with the notion of a 'constructive trust coupled with a power'.

13.3. Lessons

The foregoing analysis indicates that the present understanding of the *Quistclose* doctrine is too narrow. By recognising that the *Quistclose* doctrine shares similar events and responses as the doctrine in *Rochefoucauld v Boustead*, a more refined understanding of the *Quistclose* doctrine emerges, which indicates a wider basis than that which is normally presupposed. The most obvious lesson which emerges from this wider understanding is that, in situations where the *Quistclose* doctrine operates but where an express trust cannot be enforced, the doctrine may nevertheless lead to the imposition of a constructive trust. The constructive trust can be understood as having the aim of preventing the taking of an advantage, which is the same aim which underlies the QI doctrines within the non-contract-based, bilateral events category of constructive trusts.

This section observes three other lessons gained from this wider understanding. The first concerns the proper analysis where *Quistclose* arrangements make a distinction between income and capital of the property in question. The second considers the impact of the *Quistclose* doctrine in the context of B's insolvency. The third notes how courts ought to deal with the element of intention.

77 *Re Duke of Marlborough* (n 57). For the facts of the case, see text following n 57 above.

78 *Rochefoucauld v Boustead* (n 43). The facts of the case are set out in Chapter 7, S 4.1.2.1.

79 *Twinsectra v Yardley* (n 8) [92].

13.3.1. Income and Capital

It has been a common feature of the cases concerning the doctrine in *Rochefoucauld v Boustead* and the *Quistclose* doctrine that the relevant arrangement does not distinguish between the capital and income of the relevant property. However, nothing in principle prevents the parties from doing so. For example, an agreement might be reached whereby A transfers land to B for B to use the rental income exclusively for a stated purpose, and to return the land to A at a stated time. Alternatively, the parties may contemplate that B will apply the land for the stated purpose, but must account for its rental income to A until such time as the land is so applied.

In resolving such cases, it is necessary to determine what the parties positively intended, regardless of whether the arrangement gives rise to an express trust or a constructive trust. First, if B has the power to apply the capital for the stated purpose, then prior to exercising the power, B would hold any income generated from the property on trust for A, because A is the beneficiary under the trust pending B's exercise of power. Once the property is applied for the stated purpose, then the trust comes to an end. Secondly, B may have the power to apply a less-than-absolute interest in the capital for the stated purpose. For example, A may transfer land to B exclusively for B to raise a mortgage. Here, upon acquiring the property from A, B would hold it on trust for A; if and when B exercises the power, the remaining interest in the property will still be subject to a trust in A's favour. So, in the example, if B exercises the power to raise a mortgage, B would still hold the equity of redemption on trust for A.[80] Thirdly, if the parties contemplate that B's power should cover only the *income* of the property, then B's application of the income according to the stated purpose will not affect the underlying trust of the capital held in A's favour; and pending the said application, B will, of course, hold any income generated by the property on trust for A.

13.3.2. The Insolvency Context

The typical facts in which the *Quistclose* doctrine has been applied has led the doctrine to be understood as a means of distributing assets in the context of insolvency. Thus, in *Twinsectra*, Lord Millett said that 'the whole purpose of the arrangements ... is to prevent [A's] money from passing to [B]'s trustee in bankruptcy in the event of his insolvency'.[81] It has also been said that 'a "true" *Quistclose* trust is characterised by [A] retaining some form of security over the property'.[82] Relatedly, the doctrine is sometimes criticised as conferring on A an undeserved advantage in B's insolvency;[83] at other times it has been lauded as a flex-

[80] See *Re Duke of Marlborough* (n 57), discussed in the main text following n 57 above. See also *Coolbrew Pty Ltd v Westpac Banking Corp* [2014] NSWSC 1108 [49].

[81] *Twinsectra v Yardley* (n 8) [82].

[82] JA Glister, 'The Nature of *Quistclose* Trusts: Classification and Reconciliation' (2004) 63 *CLJ* 632, 634. See also Michael Bridge, 'The *Quistclose* Trust in a World of Secured Transactions' (1992) 12 *OJLS* 333; William MC Gummow, 'Equity: Too Successful?' (2003) 77 *Australian Law Journal* 30, 37; Ewan McKendrick, 'Commerce' in Swadling, *The Quistclose Trust* (n 10) 150.

[83] See, eg, Swadling, 'Orthodoxy' (n 16).

ible tool which takes into consideration 'the overriding commercial objective of conditional payment arrangements'.[84] There have also been suggestions that the doctrine should only be applied after an evaluation is undertaken as to whether it would produce 'a just and commendable decision' as between A and B's general creditors.[85]

It is submitted that the *Quistclose* doctrine ought not to be conceived of as a security device or means of gaining priority in the context of B's insolvency. Instead, the better view is that the priority afforded to A is merely the side effect of the parties' intention to create a trust, and not the *reason* for which a trust arises. This analysis holds true whether we are dealing with express trusts or constructive trusts under the *Quistclose* doctrine. In the first place, the operation of the doctrine is not limited to cases where B becomes insolvent. Even where B is insolvent, his insolvency is irrelevant: the trust responds to the parties' positive intention, and arises prior to (and continues to exist despite) B's insolvency. This can be illustrated by observing the typical case relating to the doctrine in *Rochefoucauld v Boustead*, where A transfers land to B based on the informal agreement that B will hold it on trust for A. If B becomes insolvent, there is no question that A, as beneficiary under a constructive trust, will have 'priority' in B's bankruptcy insofar as the land is concerned. The basis of the constructive trust—and the reason A has preference in B's bankruptcy—is sourced in the prior agreement between the parties. It is perverse to suggest that the *reason* the constructive trust arises is to provide A with priority in B's bankruptcy.

13.3.3. The Role of Intention

As a matter of commercial efficacy, it would, of course, be undesirable if a loan of money from A to B creates a trust in A's favour whenever B reveals some purpose for which he intends to use the property.[86] In a usual loan arrangement, B is contractually bound to repay A; the contract generally indicates that the property is at B's free disposal, and it creates a debtor-creditor relationship between A and B. This ought properly to be the default position between the parties.[87] However, the existence of a contractual debt does not necessarily preclude the existence of a trust,[88] and the line at which the trust relationship begins depends on the intention of the parties.[89]

Where a typical express trust is created, the settlor's intention to create a trust arrangement is normally unambiguous. Similarly, in the typical case applying the doctrine in *Rochefoucauld v Boustead*, the parties' intention to create a trust arrangement is often clearly expressed. In contrast, *Quistclose* arrangements require a degree of judicial interpretation in order to ascertain that the parties intend to create a trust. That is to say, on the face of the agreement the parties simply make provision for B's use of the property to be restricted to an exclusive purpose, but courts interpret such an agreement as evincing an intention

[84] Gerard McCormack, 'Conditional Payments and Insolvency' (1994) 9 *Denning Law Journal* 93, 115.

[85] William Goodhart and Gareth Jones, 'The Infiltration of Equitable Doctrine into English Commercial Law' (1980) 34 *MLR* 489, 494.

[86] *Twinsectra v Yardley* (n 8) [73].

[87] JE Penner, *The Law of Trusts*, Core Text Series, 10th edn (Oxford, OUP, 2016) [9.47].

[88] *Barclays Bank v Quistclose* (n 2) 581–82.

[89] *Twinsectra v Yardley* (n 8) [69].

that B will hold the property on trust for A pending application for the stated purpose.[90] The process of judicial interpretation inevitably allows scope for diverging emphases to be placed on the parties' intention to create a trust.

It is submitted that the aim of this process of interpretation should not merely be to determine whether the parties did not intended the property to be at B's free disposal.[91] Instead, as the foregoing analysis indicates, the overriding concern in every case should be to discover whether the parties positively intended for B to hold the property on trust pending its application for the stated purpose. Focusing on the parties' positive intention to create a trust relationship affects how the courts ought to interpret the agreement between the parties. In particular, the requirements that the stated purpose must be defined with sufficient certainty, and that the purpose should be 'exclusive', ought to be treated as part of the overarching aim of discovering whether there was a positive intention to create a trust.[92] It follows that the mere use of the word 'exclusive' may not give rise to a trust relationship if, from the circumstances, the courts objectively determine that a trust relationship was not intended.[93] It also follows that a trust relationship is not necessarily precluded if the stated purpose is not defined to minute precision, so long as there exists sufficient evidence that a trust relationship was in fact intended: in such a case, even if the power fails for want of conceptual certainty, this would not affect the underlying trust in favour of A where a sufficiently certain intention to create a trust is found.

It is unfortunate that, in line with the post-*Twinsectra* trend, the Supreme Court has indicated a willingness to enforce a trust based simply on A's negative intention. In *Bank of Cyprus UK Ltd v Menelaou*,[94] one point which arose for consideration was whether the owners of a property which was to be sold had the full beneficial interest in the sale proceeds. The property was subject to a charge in favour of a bank, and the sale proceeds were received by the owners' solicitor. Lord Carnwath was content to find that the bank was a beneficiary under a trust arising by operation of the *Quistclose* doctrine simply on the basis that 'there [was] nothing to suggest that the money was treated as freely at the disposal of the [owners]'.[95] This was despite the fact that nothing in the bank's letters of communication indicated that it would obtain a beneficial interest in the money pending its application for the purchase of another property in which the bank would obtain a charge. Such an approach risks imposing a trust in situations where it is not clear that commercial parties have intended a trust relationship to arise. Encouragingly, however, a different trend appears to be emerging in the lower courts. So, for instance, in *Challinor v Juliet Bellis & Co*,[96] Briggs LJ emphasised the need for there to be 'an intention to create a trust on the part of the transferor' before the *Quistclose* doctrine will arise. It is to be hoped that this latter approach will be followed by future courts.

[90] See main text following n 52 above.

[91] *cf Twinsectra v Yardley* (n 8) [74].

[92] This was precisely the approach taken by Beech J in *Compass Resources Ltd* v Sherman (n 9) [66]–[67]. He rejected the submission that an agreement to use the loaned funds for an exclusive purpose was itself sufficient to create a trust; what was needed was an intention that the monies should not become part of B's general assets and only be used for the particular purpose. See also *George v Webb* (n 66) [195].

[93] See *Tito v Waddell (No 2)* [1977] Ch 106 (CA) 211. See too *Challinor v Juliet Bellis & Co* (n 55) [58].

[94] *Bank of Cyprus UK Ltd v Menelaou* [2015] UKSC 66, [2016] AC 176.

[95] ibid [137].

[96] *Challinor v Juliet Bellis & Co* (n 55) [56].

14

The 'Common Intention Constructive Trusts'

It is a well-worn criticism that the English law of constructive trusts in the context of family homes purchased otherwise than by married couples and those in a civil partnership is in a state of flux. Despite having wrestled for over 40 years with the 'common intention constructive trust' (CICT)[1] device to provide an equitable division when the relationships of cohabitants break down, serious questions remain over the legitimacy of the exercise of judicial discretion. This is caused particularly by the judicial willingness to infer and even impute intention in order to reflect context-specific policy considerations, which upsets consistency and certainty in the law.

This chapter explains that, on the English courts' understanding of the CICT, it is imposed as a replicative remedy, but that there are insurmountable inconsistencies between this understanding and how the CICT is applied in practice. It then suggests that a better approach is to analyse the CICT as a reflective remedy. This places the CICT within the same conceptual space as proprietary estoppel. Finally, the case is made for the assimilation of CICT and proprietary estoppel.

14.1. The Present Understanding

The touchstone of the CICT is the concept of a 'common intention'—an 'agreement, arrangement or understanding reached between [the parties] that the property is to be shared beneficially.'[2] There are two stages to the process by which courts determine whether the parties have the relevant 'common intention'. First, courts determine whether there is a 'common intention' at all that A will acquire a share of B's beneficial interest (the 'acquisition' stage). The intention can be shown by evidence of express discussion or be inferred from the

[1] It is sometimes thought that certain QI doctrines falling within the non-contract-based, bilateral events category of constructive trusts can be described as 'common intention constructive trusts' because they are based on an agreement between the parties, which by definition evince a 'common intention' (see, eg, in relation to the doctrine in *Pallant v Morgan*, Chapter 6, S 6.1.4.). This temptation should be avoided in view of the fact that the 'CICT' is used as a term of art to describe the constructive trusts arising in the domestic shared homes context. Moreover, it is also inaccurate to say that those QI doctrines respond to a 'common intention'. It is not the mere fact that A and B share an intention, but that B's promise and A's reliance arises in a specific manner, which triggers those constructive trusts (see Chapter 3, S 3.2.1.1. for an overview of this point).

[2] *Lloyds Bank v Rosset* [1991] 1 AC 107 (HL).

parties' conduct, but it may not be imputed.[3] Second, if such an intention is adjudged to exist, courts then consider the proportion each party is to have in the property (the 'quantification' stage). A 'common intention' may be imputed at this second stage in the absence of express or inferred intention.[4] Where B is the sole legal owner, the starting point is that B owns the entire beneficial interest in the property; where A and B are legal co-owners, their 'beneficial ownership [is presumed to] be joint, so that it is held in equal shares'.[5] The burden of proof is on the party (A) who disputes his presumed beneficial interest.[6]

It has been suggested that the acquisition stage is irrelevant where the parties are legal co-owners, based on the logic that 'the parties already share the beneficial interest, and the question is [merely] what their interests are and whether their interests have changed'.[7] However, the material question at the acquisition stage in every case is not merely whether A should acquire a share *in the property*, but whether A should acquire *a portion of B's prima facie share*.[8] In legal co-ownership cases, the parties' presumed starting point of equal shares is not based on the parties' 'common intention' but a conclusion of law based on the maxims that 'equity follows the law' and 'equality is equity'.[9] Therefore, it remains necessary to determine whether the parties had a 'common intention' at all that A should acquire a portion of B's prima facie 50% share.

The way in which courts presently approach the subject is on the basis that the CICT is imposed as a replicative remedy.[10] Judges have repeatedly emphasised that their primary concern is 'to ascertain the parties' actual shared intentions',[11] independent of B's commission of any breach of any duty. The role of the courts is perceived to be purely declaratory: they simply recognise and enforce the parties' primary rights and duties. The operative event is said to be the parties' intentions. This explains the judicial reluctance to impute intention at the acquisition stage: judges are unwilling to make B liable where there was in fact no actual agreement to that effect.

The same approach is also detected at the quantification stage. Even from the first decided case which considered the CICT, the House of Lords eschewed any jurisdiction to exercise substantive remedial discretion;[12] and the same approach is taken today. Thus, judges refuse to impose a remedy 'contrary to what the evidence shows that [the parties] actually intended' in relation to quantification.[13] Even where intention is imputed at the quantification stage,[14]

> the court is not concerned with some form of redistributive justice. Thus it is irrelevant that it may be thought a 'fair' outcome for a woman who has endured years of abusive conduct by her

[3] *Jones v Kernott* [2011] UKSC 53, [2012] 1 AC 776 [31].

[4] ibid.

[5] *Stack v Dowden* [2007] UKHL 17, [2007] 2 AC 432 [109].

As will be discussed in S 14.2.2., the current law fails to explain how 'joint' beneficial ownership is severed such that the parties hold their interest in 'equal shares'.

[6] *Stack v Dowden* (n 5) [68].

[7] *Jones v Kernott* (n 3) [47].

[8] Simon Gardner and Katharine Davidson, 'The Supreme Court on Family Homes' (2012) 128 *LQR* 178, 181.

[9] *Stack v Dowden* (n 5) [109].

[10] A similar point is made in Terence Etherton, 'Constructive Trusts and Proprietary Estoppel: The Search for Clarity and Principle' [2009] *Conveyancer and Property Lawyer* 104, 115.

[11] *Jones v Kernott* (n 3) [31], [46]. See also *Gissing v Gissing* [1971] AC 886 (HL) 898; *Stack v Dowden* (n 5) [37].

[12] *Pettitt v Pettitt* [1970] AC 777 (HL), holding that the Married Women's Property Act 1882, s 17 did not confer jurisdiction for the exercise of substantive remedial discretion.

[13] *Jones v Kernott* (n 3) [47].

[14] *Graham-York v York* [2015] EWCA Civ 72 [2015] FLR 528 [22]. See too *Stack v Dowden* (n 5) [61].

> partner to be allotted a substantial interest in his property on his death. The plight of [the claimant] attracts sympathy, but it does not enable the court to redistribute property interests in a manner which right-minded people might think amount to appropriate compensation. [The claimant] is 'entitled' to the share which the court considers fair having regard to the whole course of dealing between them in relation to the property. It is these last words, which I have emphasised, which supply the confines of the enquiry as to fairness.

This reflects an understanding of the CICT as a replicative remedy: the reluctance to exercise discretion indicates an approach whereby the remedy is logically limited to enforcing the parties' primary rights and duties. Courts claim that the process of imputation—an exercise which allows the exercise of judicial discretion—is merely a 'fallback position' based on necessity. Where no actual intention is found at the quantification stage, 'the court has a duty to come to a conclusion on the dispute put before it',[15] hence the need to impute. As Lord Neuberger has described it, the ability to impute is only 'a small chink of darkness': 'it merely fills the gap, where there is one, as to how the beneficial interest under that institutional trust are [*sic*] to be assigned.'[16]

14.2. Deficiencies

Upon closer scrutiny, the analysis of the CICT as a replicative remedy is riddled with inconsistencies. This is indicated by difficulties in relation to imputation, severance, and policy considerations. These indicate that the reality is that the CICT does not give effect to A's primary rights. There is therefore a disparity between what judges claim to be doing and what they actually do in practice.

14.2.1. Imputation

Imputation is the process of attributing to the parties an intention they never had.[17] A remedy based on imputed intention can hardly be analysed as enforcing a pre-existing primary relationship which arose in response to the parties' intentions.

14.2.1.1. The Acquisition Stage

At the acquisition stage, short of evidence of an express discussion between the parties,[18] the parties' intentions can only be inferred from all the facts of the case.[19] An inferred intention 'is objectively deduced to be the subjective actual intention of the parties, in the light of their actions and statements.'[20] The refusal to impute intention at this stage gives

[15] *Jones v Kernott* (n 3) [47].
[16] Lord Neuberger, 'The Remedial Constructive Trust—Fact or Fiction', speech at the Banking Services and Finance Law Association Conference, Queenstown, 10 August 2014 www.supremecourt.uk/docs/speech-140810.pdf [18]–[19].
[17] *Stack v Dowden* (n 5) [126].
[18] *Lloyds Bank v Rosset* (n 2) 132.
[19] *Stack v Dowden* (n 5) [69].
[20] ibid [126].

the appearance of judges searching for the true, actual intentions of the parties. However, due to the multifariousness of interactions between the parties, judges can essentially 'cherry pick' specific episodes over the course of their relationship to infer a 'common intention'.[21] 'Nearly any case [can] be made "special"'.[22] Considering that a fine—often indistinguishable—line exists between a 'candid' and 'sophisticated' claimant,[23] a 'sympathetic' and non-sympathetic judge,[24] and words spoken 'in earnest' and 'in dalliance',[25] the ability to infer intention often allows for the exercise of judicial discretion, albeit masquerading as an evidential inquiry. Inference then becomes very much like imputation. This is a far cry from the way in which courts treat an agreement in the QI doctrines. Thus, in relation to the doctrine in *Rochefoucauld v Boustead*, judges insist that there must be a bargain that includes 'a stipulation under which some sufficiently defined beneficial interest in the property was to be taken by another';[26] and in relation to the doctrine in *Pallant v Morgan* B must give 'an assurance' to A as opposed to merely extending 'a friendly gesture'.[27]

Another difficulty at the acquisition stage concerns the requirement to establish A's detrimental reliance.[28] Where there is an express 'common intention', A's detrimental reliance can arise from his financial contribution to the house or other actions; if the 'common intention' is inferred from the parties' conduct, then that very conduct would also count as detrimental reliance.[29] Given that express 'common intention' is a 'rarer class of case',[30] in practice determining 'common intention' and detrimental reliance is conflated in the process of inferring intention. However, this conflation unjustifiably allows courts to infer a 'common intention' from A's conduct alone,[31] *to the exclusion of* a proper investigation into whether a '*common* intention' (properly so-called) exists on the facts. Insofar as courts are capable of doing so, it provides an avenue for imputing intentions through the back door.

Conflating 'common intention' and detrimental reliance fails to distinguish between three different situations which ought to yield distinct outcomes on a proper analysis. In the first case, B gives the relevant assurance to A, but A does not subsequently rely on B's assurance. Here, A's claim ought to fail at the acquisition stage, since he would not have demonstrated that he has acted 'in pursuance of some … understanding that … [he] had an interest.'[32] In the second case, B does not give the relevant assurance, but A's actions are referable to a mistaken belief. Here, A ought to be subject to the 'demanding criteria' of the 'acquiescence principle' of proprietary estoppel,[33] based on the 'five

[21] Martin Dixon, 'The Never-Ending Story—Co-Ownership after *Stack v Dowden*' [2007] *Conveyancer and Property Lawyer* 456, 459.
[22] ibid 459.
[23] *Gissing v Gissing* (n 11) 897.
[24] ibid.
[25] *Hammond v Mitchell* [1991] 1 WLR 1127 (Fam) 1139.
[26] *Bannister v Bannister* [1948] 2 All ER 133 (CA) 136.
[27] *Pallant v Morgan* [1953] Ch 43 (Ch) 46.
[28] *Grant v Edwards* [1986] Ch 638 (CA), 646–47.
[29] ibid 647.
[30] ibid.
[31] This appears to be the approach taken in, eg, *James v Thomas* [2007] EWCA Civ 1212 [27] and *Morris v Morris* [2008] EWCA Civ 257 [26], where the Court of Appeal, in considering whether to infer a 'common intention', looked to A's conduct.
[32] *Grant v Edwards* (n 28) 648. See also *Hyett v Stanley* [2003] EWCA Civ 942 [19].
[33] Ben McFarlane, *The Law of Proprietary Estoppel* (Oxford, OUP, 2014) [1-08], discussed in depth at [2-04]–[2-50].

probanda'[34] of *Willmott v Barber*.[35] In the third case, there is no evidence whatsoever of B making assurances and A relying on any mistaken belief, and a judge nevertheless infers a 'common intention' and detrimental reliance from the parties' words and actions. This is identical to imputing intention, 'since there can be no point in the court investigating whether [A] has relied to her detriment on a fictional common intention that the court has invented.'[36] It is fundamentally questionable whether the imposition of a constructive trust in this case is justified, given that A's lack of reliance would be fatal to his claim under *any* doctrine within the non-contract-based, bilateral events category of constructive trusts. If A takes it upon himself to commit to a certain course of action when there is no evidence that B intends for A to acquire property thereby, surely A takes a risk that his efforts will go uncompensated.[37]

14.2.1.2. The Quantification Stage

At the quantification stage, while judges claim that actual—express or inferred—intention is paramount,[38] in practice it is extremely rare for parties in a familial context to have formed any actual intentions concerning their respective beneficial shares.[39] Moreover, judges can easily sidestep such intention, either by holding that the agreement did not apply to the events which transpired,[40] or by holding that any discussion concerning quantification was not 'exact'[41] enough, thereby warranting imputation.[42] The upshot is that in the majority of cases courts impute intentions when quantifying the parties' shares. The ability to vary the size of the parties' respective beneficial shares strongly indicates that the remedy imposed does not merely enforce the parties' primary rights and duties, but instead reflects the exercise of remedial discretion.

Indeed, the Supreme Court's analysis of imputation as merely a 'fallback position' based on necessity at the quantification stage[43] does not withstand scrutiny. Consider the doctrine in *Pallant v Morgan* where, in the absence of a firm agreement concerning apportionment, the parties hold the beneficial interest in the property in equal shares, 'presumably on the basis that equality is equity'.[44] Similarly, where joint tenants sever their interests but they do not reach an agreement as to the specific share each is to obtain, the property will be held in equal shares.[45] One would have thought that the same approach would apply in relation to the CICT: where a common intention exists at the acquisition stage but there is lacking

[34] *Taylors Fashions Ltd v Liverpool Victoria Trustees Co Ltd* [1982] QB 133 (Ch) 145.
[35] *Willmott v Barber* (1880) 15 Ch D 96, 105–06.
[36] Charles Mitchell, *Hayton and Mitchell: Commentary and Cases on the Law of Trusts and Equitable Remedies*, 13th edn (London, Sweet & Maxwell, 2010) [15-30].
[37] *Cobbe v Yeoman's Row Management Ltd* [2008] UKHL 55, [2008] 1 WLR 1752.
[38] See main text following n 12 above.
[39] For a rare example, see *Williamson v Sheikh* [2008] EWCA Civ 990.
[40] *Gallarotti v Sebastianelli* [2012] EWCA Civ 865, [2012] 2 FLR 1231 [23].
[41] *Jones v Kernott* (n 3) [47].
[42] See discussion in James Lee, 'And the Waters Begin to Subside: Imputing Intention under *Jones v Kernott*' [2012] *Conveyancer and Property Lawyer* 421, 426.
[43] See main text to nn 39–41 above.
[44] *Holiday Inns Inc v Broadhead* (Ch, 19 December 1969), as reported in *Banner Homes Group plc v Luff Developments Ltd* [2000] Ch 372 (CA) 389–93, 390.
[45] *Goodman v Gallant* [1986] Fam 106 (CA); *Hunter v Babbage* [1994] 2 FLR 806 (Ch).

an actual agreement concerning the proportion each is to take, A should obtain half of B's equitable interest in the property by default. On this approach, the result ought to be that, where B is the sole legal owner, A would obtain a 50% beneficial interest in the property, and where the parties are legal co-owners, A would obtain 75%.[46] The point here is that it is in fact *unnecessary* for courts to impute intention in order to resolve a dispute. The ability to vary the parties' respective beneficial interests can therefore only be explained as an exercise of remedial discretion masquerading as a rule based on necessity.

14.2.1.3. Attempts to Minimise the Difficulty

There have been two significant judicial attempts to contain the difficulties raised by the process of imputation for the analysis of the CICT as a replicative remedy. First, the majority in *Jones* attempted to play down the distinction between inference and imputation.[47] In their joint judgment,[48] Lord Walker and Baroness Hale cited with approval Nick Piska's observation[49] that the two concepts present a 'distinction without a difference'. Piska's argument is based on the obvious inability of a judge to step into the minds of the parties in order to determine their subjective intentions; from this he concludes that inference and imputation are substantively similar, since *both* are concerned with drawing objective conclusions concerning the parties' intentions from the facts. This argument is fallacious. Inference involves objectively concluding from the parties' words or actions that the parties reasonably led each other to form an (actual) common intention.[50] In contrast, imputation involves attributing an intention to the parties *despite* concluding from the facts that the parties could *not* reasonably have led each other to form that intention.[51] The yardstick for inferring intention is the facts of the case—the parties' words or actions; the yardstick for imputing intention is a norm—that of 'fairness'.[52] Conceptually,[53] therefore, imputation is clearly different from inference.

Secondly, a 'new'[54] constraint was introduced in *Stack*: the CICT applies only in the 'domestic consumer context'.[55] The joint judgment of Lord Walker and Baroness Hale in *Jones* confirmed that different rules applied to the 'domestic' and 'business' context.[56] Presumably one concern was that inferring or imputing intention would destabilise business transactions. Yet, the 'domestic/business' distinction is inherently ambiguous,[57] causing

[46] The parties start out being joint tenants in equity (*Jones v Kernott* (n 3) [51]), and upon severance each party has a 50% share (*Goodman v Gallant* (n 45); *Hunter v Babbage* (n 45)). The default apportionment rule would thus give A half of B's 50% share (ie 25%), which, when added to A's own 50% share, gives A a total of 75% share in the property.

[47] *Jones v Kernott* (n 3) [34], [65]–[66].

[48] ibid [34].

[49] Nick Piska, 'Intention, Fairness and the Presumption of Resulting Trust after *Stack v Dowden*' (2008) 71 *MLR* 120, 127–28.

[50] *Gissing v Gissing* (n 11) 906.

[51] *Stack v Dowden* (n 5) [126].

[52] *Oxley v Hiscock* [2004] EWCA Civ 546, [2005] Fam 211 [69]; *Jones v Kernott* (n 3) [51].

[53] 'Conceptually', because in practice judges in fact exercise discretion, comparable to that exercised in imputing intention, when they infer intention: see main text at 18–27 above.

[54] Etherton, 'Constructive Trusts and Proprietary Estoppel' (n 10) 110.

[55] *Stack v Dowden* (n 5) [58], [60], [69]. See also *Jones v Kernott* (n 3) [31].

[56] *Jones v Kernott* (n 3) [31].

[57] See, however, Man Yip, 'The Commercial Context in Trust Law' [2016] *Conveyancer and Property Lawyer* 347.

uncertainty, for instance, in cases where the actual and anticipated use of the property differs, where the property is used for both 'domestic' and 'business' purposes,[58] where the property is used merely as a holiday[59] or secondary home, where the parties are involved in a culturally Chinese type of sexual (but not familial) relationship,[60] and so on. In fact, the Court of Appeal has, post-*Jones*, analysed cases relating to investment properties[61] and properties bought by business associates[62] in CICT terms. Clearly, courts have been unsuccessful in defining precisely what amounts to 'domestic' cases, and consequently have not found success in confining the difficulties inherent in imputation to the 'core' family homes situation. This is an obvious cause for concern.

14.2.2. Severance

Since legal co-owners are presumed to hold as joint tenants,[63] the CICT can only be said to replicate A's primary rights if the event which severs their equitable joint tenancy can be identified. The reason for this is obvious: the CICT operates to give each beneficial owner a *share* in the property. It is trite law that severance occurs only through specific methods such as written notice,[64] operating on one's share, mutual agreement, course of dealing,[65] or the murder of a joint tenant.[66]

It is difficult to see how any of these methods of severance occurs in the CICT context. In particular, given that 'common intention' can be inferred where none actually existed, '[a]n uncommunicated declaration … cannot operate as a severance.'[67] The only remaining plausible explanation is that severance occurs by court order. If so, then the CICT is certainly not a replicative remedy, since the court would not *simply* be enforcing the parties' primary relationship, but would be severing the joint tenancy pursuant to an exercise of discretion.

14.2.3. Policy

It is a well-rehearsed observation that the CICT responds to the 'continued failure' of Parliament to intervene in the non-marital context.[68] The desire to achieve parity in the courts' exercise of their discretionary jurisdiction regardless of whether the parties are

[58] The foregoing two examples are discussed in Etherton, 'Constructive Trusts and Proprietary Estoppel' (n 10) 111.
[59] See Etherton, 'Constructive Trusts and Proprietary Estoppel' (n 10) 111.
[60] *Favor Easy Management Ltd v Wu* [2012] EWCA Civ 1464. See discussion in Man Yip and James Lee, '"Less Than Straightforward" People, Facts and Trusts: Reflections on Context: *Favor Easy Management Ltd v Wu*' [2013] *Conveyancer and Property Lawyer* 431.
[61] *Geary v Rankine* [2012] EWCA Civ 555, [2012] 2 FLR 1409 [18].
[62] *Gallarotti v Sebastianelli* (n 40) [6].
[63] *Stack v Dowden* (n 5) [109].
[64] The Law of Property Act 1925, s 36(2).
[65] *Williams v Hensman* (1861) 1 John & H 546, 557–58; 70 ER 862, 867.
[66] The Forfeiture Act 1982, s 1.
[67] *Burgess v Rawnsley* [1975] Ch 429 (CA) 448.
[68] *Jones v Kernott* (n 3) [78].

married is, of course, understandable. However, difficulties arise in squaring the policy considerations which courts take into account when dealing with the cohabitation context[69] with the supposed imposition of the CICT as a replicative remedy. When constructive trusts are awarded as replicative remedies, courts are concerned solely with identifying whether pre-trial events trigger the parties' primary rights and duties. For instance, in relation to the QI doctrines within the non-contract-based, bilateral events category of constructive trusts, courts are concerned with whether A's reliance and B's promise arise in a specific way on the facts.[70] If they do, then the parties are in a pre-trial relationship which consists of their primary rights and duties, and a constructive trust remedy is awarded simply to replicative those rights and duties. Conversely, in awarding the CICT, courts take policy considerations *at trial* to be more important than ascertaining whether the parties had a pre-existing primary legal relationship.

The policy considerations specific to the cohabitation context have also resulted in a willingness by courts to assess A's reliance by looking at the whole course of the parties' relationship. This approach is vastly different from the QI doctrines, where A's reliance is always fulfilled before B acquires the property in question, in order for A's acts to have led B to acquire an advantage in relation to the acquisition.[71]

Moreover, a fundamental clash of norms can be detected. In relation to the QI doctrines, one of equity's primary concerns is the '[respect] for genuine intentions ... out of a libertarian respect for autonomy'.[72] Courts wish to reflect the same concern in the CICT by using the conceptual touchstone of 'common intention'. Yet, the willingness directly or indirectly to impute a 'common intention' indicates the contrary—a *lack* of respect for the parties' autonomy. It is difficult to justify suppressing *this* policy concern in favour of those which are more commonly rehearsed in this area of law.[73]

14.3. The CICT as a Reflective Remedy

In view of the difficulties with the present approach, a better understanding of what the courts are doing can be found in analysing the CICT as a reflective remedy, awarded to give effect to the parties' secondary rights and duties.

As explained in Chapter 7,[74] reflective remedies provide for the exercise of judicial discretion to tailor the content of the remedy to achieve a particular goal. Such remedial flexibility can be squared with the courts' willingness to impute intentions at the quantification stage. The yardstick for imputation, being 'fair[ness] having regard to the whole course of dealing',[75] can (tentatively)[76] be understood as the remedial goal which guides the courts'

[69] *Stack v Dowden* (n 5) [69].
[70] See Chapter 3, S 3.2.1.1. for an overview of this point.
[71] See, eg, Chapter 4, S 4.2.2.
[72] Gardner and Davidson, 'The Supreme Court' (n 8) 182. This is particularly reflected in that a firm agreement is necessary for such constructive trusts to arise: see text to n 27 above.
[73] eg *Stack v Dowden* (n 5) [69].
[74] See Chapter 7, S 7.1.4.
[75] *Oxley v Hiscock* (n 52) [69]; *Jones v Kernott* (n 3) [51].
[76] Tentatively, because the goal can be refined: see main text following n 110 below.

exercise of remedial discretion in determining the appropriate content of the remedy in a particular case.[77]

Moreover, unlike the QI doctrines within the non-contract-based, bilateral events category of constructive trusts, courts have held that 'the common intention may be formed at any time before, during or after the acquisition of the property'.[78] This is consistent with an understanding of the CICT as a reflective remedy, where the remedy ultimately has nothing to do with enforcing an agreement between the parties per se, but something else—the putting right of the consequences of B's breach of duty.

14.3.1. Elements to be Pleaded and Proved

In order to analyse the CICT as a reflective remedy, it is necessary to demonstrate that successful CICT cases give rise to the elements necessary to be pleaded and proved in relation to reflective remedies, namely a primary duty, breach, loss, and causation. In this regard, the doctrine of proprietary estoppel is instructive, since it is the only equitable doctrine which enforces B's secondary duty in order to allow A informally to acquire proprietary rights. While this re-analysis cannot be said to provide a perfect fit for every case in which a CICT is successfully claimed, it leads to a better understanding of the law, and also provides a far better justification for the exercise of judicial discretion than the current approach.

14.3.1.1. Primary Duty

To analyse the CICT as a reflective remedy, it must be possible to identify the primary duty which B breaches. The primary duty breached in the context of proprietary estoppel can be adopted: B has a 'duty to ensure the reliability of induced assumptions'.[79] This explains Lord Diplock's words in *Gissing v Gissing*[80] that it is necessary for B to be found 'by his words or conduct [to have] induced [A] to act to his own detriment in the reasonable belief that by so acting he was acquiring a beneficial interest in the land.' More specifically, B must have induced A to assume that A will obtain a portion of B's *prima facie* share.[81] This does not impose a duty on B to fulfil his promise by transferring to A an interest from the very moment such assumptions are induced; rather, B's duty is to act reliably in relation to such assumptions. If prior to A's acting in reliance B informs A that B will no longer fulfil the assumption, or if B fulfils the assumption, that duty is discharged.[82]

Since A's assumption can be induced through acquiescence or promise,[83] courts can avoid distorting the 'common intention' concept to facilitate the imposition of a constructive trust. It also becomes unnecessary to find or invent the element of mutuality which '*common* intention' evokes: it suffices that A's assumption was induced *by B*. This does not

[77] Notably, in contrast to the CICT, *inter partes* 'fairness' does not allow courts to exercise remedial discretion in relation to the QI doctrines within the non-contract-based, bilateral events category of constructive trusts.
[78] *James v Thomas* (n 31) [19]. See also *Jones v Kernott* (n 3).
[79] See Chapter 7, S 7.1.3.
[80] *Gissing v Gissing* (n 11) 905.
[81] See main text following n 6 above.
[82] Discussed in relation to proprietary estoppel in Chapter 7, S 7.1.3.
[83] McFarlane, *The Law of Proprietary Estoppel* (n 33) Ch 2.

distort the present law. In cases where an *express* 'common intention' has been found to exist, B would to the same extent be found to have induced A's assumptions; in cases where a 'common intention' has been *inferred*, the often fictitious 'intention' can likewise more realistically be re-analysed as an inducement of A's assumptions by B.

14.3.1.2. Breach

It is necessary for B to have breached his primary duty. Such a breach occurs when B deals with the property inconsistently with the induced assumption—when it becomes clear that B cannot, will not, and/or has not transfer(red) to A the beneficial interest which A expects. This will be so, for instance, where B unilaterally acts on his whole (in sole-name cases) or half (in joint-names cases) beneficial interest to the exclusion of A, such as by mortgaging, selling, or letting the property. Assuming that A has acted in reliance on the induced assumptions,[84] this is the earliest point when B can be said to have acted unreliably in relation to his induced assumptions.

It might be asked whether it is possible at all for B to avoid the breach by discharging his primary duty. In most of the decided cases, the parties do not explicitly state the moment at which A is to acquire part of B's beneficial interest.[85] The most obvious way that B can avoid the breach would be to secure A his expected interest *as soon as practicable*. If B fails to do so, that failure constitutes a wrong, even though it might not be B's fault. The seemingly strict nature of the wrong should not be surprising. The fact that B incurs a primary duty is the result of B's inducement of A's assumption in the first place. Having created the occasion for A to act in reliance, B is not in complete ignorance of the state of affairs he created; therefore, B cannot complain if he is held liable for failing to ensure he acts reliably, thereby causing A harm, even though he may not be at fault for doing so.[86]

It may be objected that B will often be unaware that he has a duty to transfer a share of his beneficial interest to A at all. There are two possible ways this objection might be read. First, this objection might refer to the courts' present ability to infer intention even though B is in fact unaware that a 'common intention' ever existed. In reply, it is submitted that the current law is, to that extent, misguided, since this is tantamount to *imputing* intention at the acquisition stage in the absence of any *actual* 'common intention'. A different reading of this objection may point to the fact that B's inducement might not consist of a 'one-off' act such as the making of a promise, but through a sequence of events over time, such that B is unaware of precisely when an induced assumption has in fact occurred. In reply, it can be noted that B does not need to be subjectively aware that he has induced A's assumption at all, since B need not be at fault to commit a breach. So long as B had in fact objectively induced A's assumptions, any unilateral action which excludes A is a breach of B's primary duty.

[84] As to which see S 14.3.1.4.

[85] This is similar to proprietary estoppel cases where B promises that A will have a 'home for life' (*Campbell v Griffin* [2001] EWCA Civ 990, [2001] WTLR 981), or that a hotel will 'all be [A's] one day' (*Wayling v Jones* (1995) 69 P & CR 170 (CA)), or that a farm is 'going to be [A's]' (*Gillett v Holt* [2001] Ch 210 (CA)). Contrast proprietary estoppel cases where B's promise is that A would inherit B's property *at B's death*: see, eg, *Jennings v Rice* [2002] EWCA Civ 159, [2003] 1 FCR 501; *Thorner v Major* [2009] UKHL 18, [2009] 1 WLR 776. This point is discussed in Chapter 7, S 7.1.5.

[86] The same analysis was made in relation to proprietary estoppel in Chapter 7, S 7.2.2.1.

It might be further objected that, even if B wishes to fulfil his primary duty by formally declaring a trust (in sole-name cases) or disposing part of his beneficial interest (in joint-names cases) in A's favour, it may not be clear what proportion of B's interest A ought to be given. This scenario is highly unlikely in practice. Nevertheless, B has two options. He could seek the court's guidance on the matter; alternatively, drawing an analogy from the doctrine in *Pallant v Morgan*,[87] B could transfer a half-share of his beneficial interest to A as a rule of thumb. The latter option would not prevent A from suing B for a larger share on the basis that some outstanding 'harm' is yet to be compensated for, but it would be extremely difficult for A to succeed on this point.

14.3.1.3. Loss

The requirement for A to establish *detrimental* reliance in order to obtain a CICT[88] indicates that A must have suffered loss or harm due to B's breach. As discussed in Chapter 7,[89] it is not simply A's costs in terms of time, money, and effort which needs to be demonstrated, but a net harm which A ultimately suffers, all things considered. It is this loss for which the CICT compensates.

14.3.1.4. Causation

B's breach must have caused A's harm for which compensation is sought. The element of causation can be squared with the requirement to establish detrimental *reliance* in order to obtain a CICT.[90] As Mustill LJ observed in *Grant v Edwards*,[91] 'the court must decide whether [A's] conduct is referable to the bargain, promise or intention.' There has been a dearth of authorities concerning the requisite causal link, with conflicting tests emerging from fleeting judicial considerations of this point. A 'but for' or 'sole cause' test emerges from *Morris v Morris*,[92] while an 'a cause' test is detected in *James v Thomas*.[93] This uncertainty leaves it open to courts to develop the causal test in line with proprietary estoppel, where the precise test depends on whether the claim is based on B's acquiescence or promise.[94]

14.3.1.5. Discretion as to Content

Once B breaches his primary duty which causes A to suffer detrimental reliance, A obtains an unliquidated secondary right to compensation, the content of which must be liquidated by a court. This provides an explanation for the courts' oft-found exercise of judicial discretion in CICT cases to determine the parties' respective shares in the property according to what is 'fair'.[95] This exercise of discretion to determine the appropriate content of the remedy can be contrasted with the QI doctrines within the non-contract-based, bilateral

[87] See main text to n 44 above.
[88] *Grant v Edwards* (n 28) 646–47.
[89] See Chapter 7, S 7.1.6.
[90] Elizabeth Cooke, *Land Law*, Clarendon Law Series, 2nd edn (Oxford, OUP, 2012) 93.
[91] *Grant v Edwards* (n 28) 652.
[92] *Morris v Morris* (n 31) [27].
[93] *James v Thomas* (n 31) [27].
[94] McFarlane, *The Law of Proprietary Estoppel* (n 33) Ch 3.
[95] *Oxley v Hiscock* (n 52) [69]; *Jones v Kernott* (n 3) [51].

events category of constructive trusts, where in the absence of an express agreement as to the parties' respective shares, the parties invariably hold the beneficial interest in the property in equal shares.[96]

This analysis of the CICT as a reflective remedy also allows judges to deviate from any express agreement between the parties concerning their respective. Although the Supreme Court has advised against this,[97] in practice courts are willing to sidestep the express agreement in favour of imposing what they deem to be a 'fair' share.[98] Moreover, if 'fairness' is the yardstick, then courts can easily conclude that an express agreement between the parties is 'unfair'. As David Hayton observes, '[i]f [A]'s detrimental conduct on a scale of one to 100 only registers 10 she should not necessarily obtain a promised half share'.[99]

14.3.2. Benefits of the Renewed Approach

There are a number of significant benefits in analysing the CICT as a reflective remedy. First, it better explains the discretion which courts presently exercise by unjustifiably stretching the 'common intention' concept. On the renewed approach, judges are understood as exercising the remedial discretion inherent in liquidating A's secondary right to compensation. '[I]f reasonable expectation induced by [B] can be accepted as forming the first limb of the [CICT] doctrine, we can jettison the subtleties of intentions, promises and their implicit contents. The crucial issue then turns on the circumstances in which [A]'s expectations will be enforced.'[100]

Secondly, the renewed approach is more conceptually coherent. It encourages a move away from the touchstone of 'common intention', and thus discourages the fictitious imposition of an actual agreement where none exists. In its stead, courts are encouraged to address the questions of whether B has induced A's assumption through B's words or actions, and whether A has detrimentally relied on this. Importantly, the renewed approach removes the need forcefully to align the CICT with the QI doctrines within the non-contract-based, bilateral events category, since they are analysed as performing different functions. It nevertheless remains possible, on the renewed approach, to maintain the present view that courts will not generally override the parties' actual intentions at the quantification stage.[101] The explanation lies not in treating this as indicating that courts are responding to primary rights, but by analogising this to the courts' approach in 'bargain' cases in proprietary estoppel—those where B makes a promise to cede an interest to A in return for a defined quid pro quo—where A's expectation interest is almost always protected.[102]

Thirdly, the renewed approach renders it unnecessary artificially to constrain the ambit of this area of law to the 'domestic consumer context'[103] in order to take into account contextual policy concerns. Instead, these policy considerations can be factored into the

[96] See main text to n 44 above.

[97] *Jones v Kernott* (n 3) [47].

[98] See main text following n 39 above.

[99] David Hayton, 'Constructive Trusts of Homes—A Bold Approach' (1993) 109 *LQR* 485, 487 fn 12. See also the suggestion by Browne-Wilkinson V-C to the same effect in *Grant v Edwards* (n 28) 657–58.

[100] John Eekelaar, 'A Woman's Place—A Conflict between Law and Social Values' [1987] *Conveyancer and Property Lawyer* 93, 100.

[101] *Stack v Dowden* (n 5) [61].

[102] Susan Bright and Ben McFarlane, 'Proprietary Estoppel and Property Rights' (2005) 64 *CLJ* 449, 458–60.

[103] See n 55 above.

exercise of discretion to determine the appropriate content of the awarded remedy. Indeed, policy concerns which are particular to *any* relationship, 'domestic' or 'commercial', can be accommodated within the renewed framework.

Finally, the renewed approach suggests a solution to the severance problem in legal co-ownership cases.[104] It explains severance as occurring by a 'course of dealing sufficient to intimate that the interests of all were mutually treated as constituting a tenancy in common'.[105] On this view, severance occurs when B induces A's assumption that A will obtain a portion of B's beneficial interest *and* when A acts in reliance—actions which are manifestly inconsistent with survivorship. Both inducement and reliance must have occurred for severance to take effect, since *both* parties must have dealt with their interests in the property as if they are interests in common and are not joint.[106] It follows that B is able to renege on the induced assumption before A has detrimentally relied on it, leaving the joint tenancy intact. It also follows that, if B's inducement and A's reliance are complete and a court ultimately decides to award monetary damages, then the parties will share the already-severed beneficial interest in the property in equal shares.[107] This appears to provide a plausible explanation as to what judges are trying to do when they apply the 'equality is equity' maxim[108] to joint-names cases, while avoiding the pitfalls of analytical inconsistency.

14.4. Going Further: The CICT as a Specific Application of Proprietary Estoppel

If we accept that the CICT can be understood as a reflective remedy, and if we further accept the parallel of this approach with proprietary estoppel, then there are two conclusions which we can draw. A more conservative view would be to conclude that the CICT reflects an AI situation within the non-contract-based, bilateral events category of constructive trusts. On this view, CICT and proprietary estoppel share the same conceptual space, but both doctrines remain distinct. A different view is that the CICT is but a specific application of proprietary estoppel. Given the similarities between the analysis of CICT proposed in this chapter and proprietary estoppel, the latter conclusion is plausible.

Some commentators have raised objections against such a conclusion, and their concerns require evaluation.

The most common objection relates to the difference in the nature of the remedies. It has been argued[109] that the CICT leads only to a constructive trust award, unlike proprietary estoppel where a monetary award is possible. While this is descriptively accurate, there is little by way of substance to the distinction in the present context. It is already commonplace for A to plead both the CICT and proprietary estoppel as alternative claims in family

[104] See discussion in S 14.2.2.
[105] *Williams v Hensman* (n 65) 558.
[106] *Gore and Snell v Carpenter* (1990) 60 P & CR 456 (Ch) 462.
[107] *Goodman v Gallant* (n 45); *Hunter v Babbage* (n 45).
[108] *Stack v Dowden* (n 5) [109]. See n 9 above.
[109] John Mee, 'The Limits of Proprietary Estoppel: *Thorner v Major*' (2009) 21 *Child and Family Law Quarterly* 367; Simon Gardner, 'Family Property Today' (2008) 124 *LQR* 422, 436–37; Patricia Ferguson, 'Constructive Trusts—A Note of Caution' (1993) 109 *LQR* 114, 120–23.

homes cases. Assimilating the CICT within proprietary estoppel does not deprive A, since a judge can award a constructive trust or a lesser remedy depending on the merits of the case. This would certainly encourage a more efficacious legal system.

A related objection is that the CICT and proprietary estoppel have irreconcilably different 'goals', the former being that of 'fairness'[110] and the latter being that of compensation. However, upon closer inspection, 'fairness' is too imprecise a yardstick, since it is liable to afford unbridled discretion to the courts.[111] Rather, 'compensation' provides a more refined yardstick: not only is it 'fair' to compensate A for harm caused by B's induced assumptions, it also aligns the current law on family homes with the well-established doctrine of proprietary estoppel.

Another objection points to the inability of proprietary estoppel to account for the way in which courts presently infer 'common intention' at the acquisition stage. Thus, John Mee argues that the courts' willingness to infer a 'common intention' from A's financial contribution to the acquisition of the property does not amount to a 'representation' for the purposes of proprietary estoppel.[112] Simon Gardner too argues that A often cannot properly be said to have suffered detrimental reliance in the CICT context, since there can be no *reliance* on an invented intention.[113] In reply, it is observed, first, that a 'representation' by B is not necessary on the approach proposed in this chapter: A's assumption can also be induced by acquiescence. Secondly, it seems strange to conclude from the differences between proprietary estoppel and the CICT that both doctrines ought to be kept separate. Given the courts' repeated refusal to impute 'common intention' at the acquisition stage, it is sensible to conclude instead that A ought *not* to obtain a remedy if he can only rely on fictitious intention. A more acceptable conclusion is that A ought only to obtain a remedy where he suffers harm caused by the unreliability of B's induced assumptions that he will obtain a portion of B's beneficial interest in the property.

A final objection is that remedies which give effect to secondary rights are different from the CICT because the former only has prospective effect.[114] The argument is that a prospective remedy works to A's disadvantage A if B deals with a third party (X) prior to a court order, since A would not have any rights enforceable against X.[115] There are two possible replies. First, given the artificiality of 'common intention' in the present law, judges already have discretion to determine when precisely A's proprietary right arises 'prior to the court order'. In this regard, the renewed approach proposed in this chapter ought to be commended for removing a fiction, and for recognising that it is ultimately judicial discretion at play. Secondly, as the Land Registration Act 2002, s 116(a)[116] confirms,[117] A's equity

[110] See main text to n 75 above.

[111] The difficulties with imposing constructive trusts whenever 'justice and good conscience' (*Hussey v Palmer* [1972] 1 WLR 1286 (CA) 1289) demand it are discussed in Chapter 11.

[112] John Mee, *The Property Rights of Cohabitees* (Oxford, Hart Publishing, 1999) 169.

[113] Gardner, 'Family Property Today' (n 109) 436.

[114] David Hayton, 'Equitable Rights of Cohabitees' [1990] *Conveyancer and Property Lawyer* 370, 372; Ferguson, 'Constructive Trusts' (n 109) 121; Hayton, 'Constructive Trusts of Homes' (n 99) 487.

[115] Ferguson, 'Constructive Trusts' (n 109) 121, 126–27.

[116] An 'equity by estoppel … has effect from the time the equity arises as an interest capable of binding successors in title'.

[117] Law Commission, *Land Registration for the Twenty-First Century: A Conveyancing Revolution* (Law Com No. 271, 2001) [5-30]–[5-31].

by estoppel is proprietary in nature and capable of binding X.[118] The renewed approach reveals the mechanics of the remedy: A obtains an equity by estoppel—an unliquidated secondary right—when B breaches his primary duty; this is liquidated at the date of judgment. Where a proprietary remedy is awarded, its proprietary effect is backdated, 'by virtue of some doctrine of relation back',[119] to the time of B's breach; where a merely personal remedy is awarded, A has no proprietary right against X, since A's equity by estoppel was, after all, merely '*capable of*' binding X. Since A obtains an 'equity by estoppel' only when B commits a breach, A therefore only has priority over X where B deals with X post-breach (and where a proprietary remedy is ultimately awarded). So, for example, A obtains no right against X if B deals with X before A incurs detrimental reliance.

[118] See, eg, *Re Sharpe (a bankrupt)* [1980] 1 WLR 219 (Ch) 223; *Re Basham (deceased)* [1986] 1 WLR 1498 (Ch) 1504; *Sen v Headley* [1991] Ch 425 (CA) 440; *Birmingham Midshires Mortgage Services Ltd v Sabherwal* (2000) 80 P & CR 167 (CA) [24]; *Lloyd v Dugdale* [2002] 2 P & CR 167 (CA) [38]–[39]. As Cooke, *Land Law* (n 90) 104 notes, s 116 'brings the estoppel claimant into line with the constructive trust claimant.'

[119] Kevin Gray and Susan Francis Gray, *Elements of Land Law*, 5th edn (Oxford, OUP, 2009) [9.2.89]. See discussion in Chapter 7, S 7.2.5.2.

15

Donatio Mortis Causa

Like the mutual wills doctrine, *donatio* (or '*donationes*' in the plural form) *mortis causa* ('DMC') finds its historical origins in Roman Law.[1] It is a doctrine which is notoriously difficult to conceptualise, but this difficulty is not simply a problem faced by modern law. As Jackson LJ has observed, '[e]ven Roman jurists found the concept of DMC perplexing, since it had some of the characteristics of a legacy and some of the characteristics of a gift inter vivos.'[2] In modern times, Nourse LJ has famously and categorically stated in *Sen v Headley*,[3] '[l]et it be agreed that the doctrine is anomalous.'

This chapter examines the requirements for a valid DMC. It then explains how, upon closer analysis, the doctrine can be understood as being an application of orthodox trust principles. Just like the mutual wills doctrine, DMC cuts across two categories of constructive trusts, although the categories are not identical. In some DMC cases, the facts fall to be analysed as a QI situation within the non-contract-based, bilateral events category of constructive trusts; others reflect an AI situation within the unilateral events category of constructive trusts. This chapter concludes by noting a number of lessons this renewed analysis provides: it reveals certain crucial but often hidden criteria for the doctrine to apply; it allows DMC to be understood as a doctrine firmly consistent with English law principles; and it allays the oft-rehearsed concern that DMC allows testators to sidestep the formality requirements for the creation of valid wills.

15.1. Requirements

The classic statement of the requirements for a valid DMC is found in the following words of Lord Russell CJ in *Cain v Moon*:[4]

> for an effectual donatio mortis causa three things must combine: first, the gift or donation must have been made in contemplation, though not necessarily in expectation, of death; secondly, there must have been delivery to the donee of the subject-matter of the gift; and, thirdly, the gift must be made under such circumstances as shew that the thing is to revert to the donor in case he should recover. This last requirement is sometimes put somewhat differently, and it is said that the gift must be made under circumstances shewing that it is to take effect only if the death of the donor follows ...

[1] See Andrew Borkowski, *Deathbed Gifts: The Law of Donatio Mortis Causa* (Oxford, OUP, 1999) Ch 1.
[2] *King v Dubrey* [2015] EWCA Civ 581, [2016] Ch 221 [37].
[3] *Sen v Headley* [1991] Ch 425 (CA) 440.
[4] *Cain v Moon* [1896] 2 QB 283 (QB) 286.

The phrase 'gift or donation' requires qualification. Although most cases involve gifts properly so-called, ie transfers from A to B intended for B's absolute enjoyment at A's death, a valid DMC can also arise where B's enjoyment of the property is intended to be subject to him fulfilling certain conditions,[5] or where A transfers property to B to be held on trust for C.[6] The latter two variations are rarely found in the DMC case law. Hence the discussion which follows will generally refer to A making a 'gift' to B, in line with the language commonly adopted to describe DMC transactions; however, this should not be read to exclude conditional transfers and transfers on trust.

These three requirements for a valid DMC as set out in *Cain v Moon* call for closer consideration, since each component is crucial for a proper understanding of the doctrine.

15.1.1. Contemplation of Death

First, the gift from A to B must be made in contemplation of A's death. The word 'contemplation' might suggest that A's death must be the motivation or reason behind the gift, but there is no trace in the cases that courts are concerned with A's subjective motivations. Instead, the function of the 'contemplation' requirement appears to be to provide a limit as to the *types* of death upon which A can hinge the gift's condition. Specifically, A's death must be caused by a 'specific reason' or a 'known cause', as opposed to death from A 'approaching the end of his natural life span.'[7]

In the usual case, A contemplates death from a serious illness,[8] but his death may also be contemplated from other events such as a planned dangerous operation or a dangerous journey about to be embarked upon.[9] It is not necessary for the transfer to be made in *expectation* of immediate death.[10] This widens the scope of potential events which may qualify, since death need not be an inevitable[11] or even probable consequence of the contemplated event. It is simply necessary for death to be a *possible* consequence of the event, so that it can be said that A *contemplates* death.

Some cases also appear to impose a time constraint between the transfer being made and the event under contemplation: they suggest that the event must be 'impending'[12] or 'in the near future'.[13] Since DMC commonly arises where gifts are made on A's deathbed, this issue of timing has never explicitly arisen for consideration.[14] However, it is difficult to see why the doctrine should turn on the precise moment at which the contemplated event occurs,

[5] See, eg, *Blount v Burrow* (1792) 4 Bro CC 722, 9 ER 784; *Hills v Hills* (1841) 8 M & W 40, 151 ER 1095; *Re Ward* [1946] 2 All ER 206 (Ch) 207.

[6] See, eg, *Drury v Smith* (1717) 1 P Wms 404, 24 ER 446.

[7] *King v Dubrey* (n 2) [55]–[56], overruling *Re Bogusz* [2013] EWHC 1449 (Ch), [2014] Ch 271. See too *Re Craven's Estate* [1937] 1 Ch 423 (Ch) 426; *Smallcombe v Elder's Trustee and Executor Co Ltd* [1963] WAR 3, 4-5.

[8] See, eg, *Wilkes v Allington* [1931] 2 Ch 104 (Ch); *Birch v Treasury Solicitor* [1951] 1 Ch 298 (Ch); *Sen v Headley* (n 3).

[9] *King v Dubrey* (n 2) [68].

[10] See, eg, *Duffield v Elwes* (1827) 1 Bli NS 497, 4 ER 959; *Wilkes v Allington* (n 8) 110.

[11] *King v Dubrey* (n 2) [55].

[12] *Re Craven's Estate* (n 7) 426.

[13] *King v Dubrey* (n 2) [55].

[14] Note, however, that '[i]n some earlier cases, as long as six years elapsed between the gift and the death': Peter Sparkes, 'Death-Bed Gifts of Land' (1992) 43 *Northern Ireland Legal Quarterly* 35, 35 fn 6.

all things being equal. Once it is accepted that DMC is not confined to deathbed gifts,[15] then a donor with the foresight to contemplate a certain dangerous event to be undertaken some time in the future ought not to be treated differently from a donor who scrambles to make a transfer closer in time to such an event. Instead, it is better to understand the relevant statements as simply hinting at the need for A's death to be caused by a specific reason, since the timing of such an event's occurrence would be determinable in advance. Thus, the contemplated event should be a 'premature death', that is, something other than 'some peril … which afflicts the generality of mankind [such as] the dangers of crossing the road or travelling in an ordinary aircraft flight or on a normal motor-car trip'.[16]

15.1.2. Delivery

The second requirement is that of delivery. This requirement has been described as 'the heart of the law of *donatio*'[17] and 'the essential circumstance'[18] of the doctrine. For a proper understanding of what this requirement entails, two central questions require examination: what constitutes delivery, and when should delivery occur?

15.1.2.1. 'Dominion'

In *Cant v Gregory*,[19] Lord Esher MR said: 'The delivery in a *donatio mortis causa* must be such a delivery as to pass the thing out of the dominion of the dying person and put it into the dominion of the person to whom it was given.'[20] In *King v Dubrey*, Jackson LJ explained:[21]

> From a review of the cases I conclude that 'dominion' means physical possession of (a) the subject matter or (b) some means of accessing the subject matter (such as the key to a box) or (c) documents evidencing entitlement to possession of the subject matter.

As the following discussion indicates, however, Jackson LJ's analysis leaves much to be desired, as possession is but one of four elements which need to be present before there is a transfer of dominion. Apart from possession (of a chattel, or, in the case of a chose in action, of its indicia), A must intend to dispose of the property; A must intend no longer to interfere with the property; and A must in fact practically (as opposed to theoretically) be unable to deal with the property. Only when these four elements are present will the requirement of delivery be fulfilled.

[15] See, eg, *Walter v Hodge* (1818) 2 Swans 92, 100; 36 ER 549, 552; *King v Dubrey* (n 2) [55].
[16] Robert Megarry, (1965) 81 *LQR* 21, 24.
[17] Borkowski, *Deathbed Gifts* (n 1) 63.
[18] *Tate v Hilbert* (1793) 4 Bro CC 286, 293; 29 ER 895, 898, a phrase which is used to summarise Lord Hardwicke's view in *Ward v Turner* (1752) Dick 170, 21 ER 234.
[19] *Cant v Gregory* (1894) 10 TLR 584 (CA) 585.
[20] Delivery may also be made to B's agent: see, eg, *Farquharson v Cave* (1846) 2 Coll 356, 367–68; 63 ER 768, 774.
[21] *King v Dubrey* (n 2) [59].

15.1.2.1.1. Possession

The first element is that a present and immediate[22] transfer of possession must take place 'in point of fact'.[23] As *Staniland v Willott*[24] indicates, possession may be transferred where B properly obtains legal title to the property from A. However, the vast majority of cases do not involve a perfect transfer of legal title: the doctrine may arise even though there is an incomplete inter vivos gift,[25] since 'a transfer, *or* something that amounts to a transfer'[26] is enough. Where the property is a chattel, putting it in B's possession is clearly sufficient to transfer possession. However, 'mere symbolic delivery will not suffice',[27] since this does not indicate that A intends to give up control of the property. Instead, what is necessary, at a minimum, is for B to obtain possession of the property's indicia of title.[28]

In the context of DMC, indicia means 'some physical thing the possession of which should be required in order to get at the property'.[29] Where the property is a chose in action, the indicia is usually 'a document essential to its recovery'[30]—something needed in an action on the chose.[31] For instance, a bank book would be the indicia of money in a bank account,[32] but bank statements would not suffice.[33] For certificated shares, a share certificate is the indicia.[34] In the case of unregistered land, the indicia is the title deeds to the land,[35] since its production is normally required for a transfer of legal title. Providing a means of accessing the property or indicia of title is also sufficient. For instance, it suffices to deliver a key which allows access to a chattel,[36] or a key granting B access to documents which form the indicia.[37] It has even been held to be sufficient for A to hand B a key to a trunk which contains the key to a safe deposit box wherein the property is stored.[38]

[22] *Hawkins v Blewitt* (1798) 2 Esp 662, 664; 170 ER 489, 490.

[23] *Irons v Smallpiece* (1819) 2 B & Ald 551, 553; 106 ER 467, 468.

[24] *Staniland v Willott* (1852) 3 Mac & G 664, 42 ER 416. Pursuant to a DMC arrangement, A effectuated a transfer to B of the legal title to shares.

[25] *Re Dillon* (1890) 44 Ch D 76 (CA) 82.

[26] *Ward v Turner* (n 18) Dick 173, 21 ER 235 (emphasis added).

[27] *Birch v Treasury Solicitor* (n 8) 308. See too *Gardner v Parker* (1818) 3 Madd 184, 185; 56 ER 478, 478.

[28] See, eg, *Snellgrove v Baily* (1744) 3 Atk 214, 26 ER 924; *Duffield v Elwes* (n 10); *Birch v Treasury Solicitor* (n 8); *Re Beaumont* [1902] 1 Ch 889 (Ch) 895; *Sen v Headley* (n 3) 438.

[29] *Re Wasserberg* [1915] 1 Ch 195 (Ch) 204.

[30] *Delgoffe v Fader* [1939] 1 Ch 922 (Ch) 928. Nicholas Roberts, '*Donationes Mortis Causa* in a Dematerialised World' [2013] *Conveyancer and Property* Lawyer 113, 121 suggests that, in practice, the test for whether a particular document is an indicia of title is to ask 'whether special, reasonably formal, steps have to be taken to account for its absence if it goes missing'.

[31] John Ross Martyn and Nicholas Caddick QC, *Williams, Mortimer & Sunnucks: Executors, Administrators and Probate*, 20th edn (London, Sweet & Maxwell, 2015) [42-13]. See too Borkowski, *Deathbed Gifts* (n 1) 86.

[32] *Birch v Treasury Solicitor* (n 8).

[33] *Tawil v Public Trustee of NSW* (1998) NSWSC 520.

[34] Although there are contradictory authorities (In *Staniland v Willott* (n 24) DMC arose in relation to certificated shares, but in *Re Weston* [1902] 1 Ch 680 (Ch) DMC was held not to apply), the production of share certificates is normally necessary for one's legal title to be registered, and as such they properly form the relevant indicia of certificated shares: see Borkowski, *Deathbed Gifts* (n 1) 100–02.

[35] *Sen v Headley* (n 3) 437. It would appear that transferring possession of the indicia to unregistered land is sufficient; it is irrelevant that B may retain the keys (and thereby possession) of the house, provided that the other elements necessary for a proper transfer of dominion have been met: see *Sen v Headley* (n 3) 438.

[36] See, eg, *Jones v Selby* (1710) Prec Ch 300, 24 ER 143; *Bunn v Markham* (1816) 7 Taunt 224, 129 ER 90.

[37] See, eg, *Sen v Headley* (n 3).

[38] *Re Lillingston* [1952] 2 All ER 184 (Ch) 191: 'it does not matter in how many boxes the subject of a gift may be contained or that each, except the last, contains a key which opens the next, so long as the scope of the gift is made clear.'

The fact that B must at a minimum possess the indicia of title indicates that some properties are less suited than others to be made the subject matter of a DMC. This is because not every property has an indicia of title. Two clear examples which Nicholas Roberts cites are registered land and uncertificated shares held via the CREST system,[39] in relation to which there are no documents the production of which is essential for any dealing with the legal title to these properties. In relation to such properties, the only way in which the requirement of delivery can be fulfilled is for A to effectuate an outright transfer of the legal title of the property to B.

15.1.2.1.2. Intention to Dispose

In addition to giving B possession of the property or indicia of title, it is also necessary for A to intend to dispose of the property. In *Reddel v Dobree*,[40] A delivered to B a cash-box and told B that it was to be hers after A died, but also that A wanted access to the cash-box every three months while he was alive. Shadwell VC held that the arrangement did not amount to a DMC: A had merely put B 'in possession of the box [while] retaining to himself the absolute power over its contents'.[41] Certainly, requiring A to have an intention to dispose does not mean that B's power to deal with the property must be *presently exercisable*, since the exercise of such power must be made conditional upon A's death;[42] however, A must intend presently to grant B the conditional power to deal with the property.

More often than not, A would only transfer possession to B where A intends to dispose of the property. However, this is not always the case, and keeping these elements distinct is particularly crucial where the facts are atypical. One such situation is where there is more than one equally viable means of accessing the property, and B is given possession only of one of those means. As Dillon LJ said in *Woodard v Woodard*,[43] 'If there are several keys to a box and the donor retains one, one would naturally ask "Why is he retaining it?" and "Did he intend to make an immediate gift? Did he intend to part with dominion?"' In such a case, the transfer of possession may or may not be coupled with an intention to dispose of the property.

Another atypical situation is where possession is given to B, who then returns the property to A for safekeeping. Such facts arose in *Re Hawkins* in relation to an envelope of bank notes, and PO Lawrence J held on the facts of that case that there was a valid DMC because A 'had no intention of resuming dominion over the subject matter of his gift.'[44]

Yet another atypical situation is where A attempts to subject more than one property to a DMC. In *Solicitor to the Treasury v Lewis*, for example, A expressed an intention to give all her property to B at A's death, and Stirling J held that this was not a valid DMC because A could not have meant immediately 'to divest herself of everything'; instead, A was held to intend 'during her life to retain a power of disposition.'[45]

Finally, the distinction between possession and intention to dispose is crucial to understand cases where an agent is involved. So, in *Birch v Treasury Solicitor*, the Court of Appeal

[39] Roberts, '*Donationes Mortis Causa*' (n 30) 116, 121.
[40] *Reddel v Dobree* (1839) 10 Sim 244, 59 ER 607.
[41] ibid 10 Sim 251, 59 ER 610. See too *Re Wasserberg* (n 29) 201.
[42] See S 15.1.3.
[43] *Woodard v Woodard* [1992] RTR 35 (CA) 40.
[44] *Re Hawkins* [1924] 2 Ch 47 (Ch) 52.
[45] *Solicitor to the Treasury v Lewis* [1900] 2 Ch 812 (Ch) 818.

held that it was possible for a valid DMC to arise in B's favour where A transfers possession to X in X's initial capacity as A's agent, where X then later holds as agent for B in line with A's intention to dispose of the property to B.[46]

15.1.2.1.3. Intention Not to Deal

Because B's ability to deal with A's property is *conditional*, A remains entitled[47] to alter or deal with his property until the condition—A's death—is fulfilled. The possibility of A doing so is, however, contrary to the requirement for A to make a *present* gift to B.[48] Therefore, it is necessary for A also to have an intention not to interfere with the property after possession is transferred.[49] This aspect of delivery is best explained by Farwell J in *Re Craven's Estate*, where he said:[50]

> the reason for imposing as a condition of a valid donatio that [A] must part with dominion over the subject-matter ... [is] ... to ensure that, [A] must put it out of his power between the date of the donation and the date of the death to alter the subject-matter of the gift and substitute other chattels or property for it. Otherwise ... [A] might at any time between the donatio and the gift deal with it as he or she pleased.

As will be seen below,[51] this element is crucial for understanding the underlying basis of DMC: A's intention no longer to alter or to deal with the property corroborates with a finality of intention to give the property to B.

15.1.2.1.4. Practical Inability to Deal

The final element of a transfer of 'dominion' is that A must practically, as opposed to theoretically, put it out of his ability to deal with the property after possession is transferred. This element is focused on what A might actually have done with the property *in reality*. This is seen in *Re Wasserberg*, where Sergeant J held that there was sufficient delivery where A handed to B a key which provided access to a locked box at his bank which contained certain bonds, because 'there was ... a corresponding *deprivation of [A]'s facilities for dealing with them*.'[52]

The clearest case in which the distinction is made between A's *practical* and *theoretical* ability to interfere with his property is *Sen v Headley*.[53] A was in hospital, suffering from

[46] *Birch v Treasury Solicitor* (n 8) 304.

[47] Where B obtains the legal title, this entitlement arises due to the fact that B holds the property on trust for A for life (see main text following n 102 below). Where B obtains mere possession, this entitlement arises because A remains the legal owner of the property.

[48] *Jones v Selby* (n 36) Prec Ch 303, 24 ER 144.

[49] In *Re Bogusz* (n 7) [37], Jonathan Gaunt QC, sitting as a deputy judge of the High Court, held that, pending A's death, A would be entitled to enjoy rental income generated by A's land which is subject to a DMC because the gift is not effective until A's death. This, the deputy judge said, was 'no different in principle from [A] continuing to enjoy his own house by living in it' (*Re Bogusz* (n 7) [37]). In the light of the present discussion, this observation is clearly wrong. The fact that A is entitled to rental income—an entitlement arising by virtue of A being a beneficiary of a trust (see SS 15.2.1.1. and 15.2.2.1.)—does not detract from the fact that delivery—including an intention not to interfere with the property by living in it—is a prerequisite for DMC to apply.

[50] *Re Craven's Estate* (n 7) 427.

[51] See main text following n 159 below.

[52] *Re Wasserberg* (n 29) 203 (emphasis added).

[53] *Sen v Headley* (n 3).

inoperable pancreatic cancer and was told that his condition would inexorably deteriorate.[54] Three days before A's death, he purported to make a DMC of his house to B, informing her (B) that he had placed in her bag the keys to a steel box which contained the title deeds.[55] The Court of Appeal upheld the DMC. In the course of the judgment, Nourse LJ had to consider whether the fact that A retained his own set of keys to the house, thereby retaining possession of it, would cause the DMC to fail. Holding that it did not, his Lordship said: 'the benefits which thereby accrued to him [through retaining the keys] were wholly theoretical … there could have been no practical possibility of his ever returning home … [B] was in effective control of it.'[56] This indicates that it is essential for A to put it out of his practical ability to deal, alter, or interfere with the property.

The modern[57] law of DMC was initially developed to deal with gifts of chattels[58] where one on his deathbed had no opportunity to make a will;[59] and because DMC still commonly arises in such a context, the practical inability of A to deal with the property is usually taken for granted. However, it is now clear that DMC may arise outside the deathbed context, for instance where A is planning to embark on a dangerous journey or risky procedure in the future.[60] Such cases outside the deathbed context raise two questions.

First, would DMC never apply in these situations where A retains one practical means of accessing the property? This may be a relevant question where, for instance, A gives B but one of a number of keys which provides access to the property, while retaining the remaining means of access.[61] It is suggested that DMC would not apply in such cases:[62] since A is not confined to his deathbed, A retains the practical ability to interfere with the property. The case of *Woodard v Woodard*[63] is indicative of this approach. In upholding a DMC, the Court of Appeal held on the facts that it was inconsequential that A, who was in hospital suffering from leukaemia, retained a second set of keys to the car, 'which he could not anyhow use unless circumstances arose in the way of his recovery which would anyhow operate to revoke the gift.'[64] This indicates that, had A not been on his deathbed, it would have been possible for him to make use of the car with his own set of keys, and therefore DMC would not have applied. Similarly, in *Bunn v Markham*,[65] an alleged gift of (among other things) bank notes contained in a chest belonging to A without delivery of the keys to B was held not to be a valid DMC. The failure to transfer possession was certainly central to this decision; but Dallas J also went on to observe that it was not a valid DMC because '[i]f [A] had chosen to take out the bank-notes the next day, and dispose of them to another,

[54] ibid 430–31. B was initially diagnosed in Hammersmith Hospital, and went home to die, but collapsed on the floor and was admitted to Ealing Hospital where the DMC was made before his death there.
[55] *Sen v Headley* (n 3) 431.
[56] ibid 438–39.
[57] ie post-Statute of Frauds 1677: see n 151 below.
[58] It was only in *Snellgrove v Baily* (n 28) that DMC was held to be capable of arising over choses in action of which delivery was insufficient to pass the legal title: Borkowski, *Deathbed Gifts* (n 1) 14.
[59] *Hedges v Hedges* (1708) Prec Ch 269, 269; 24 ER 130, 130.
[60] See main text following n 8 above.
[61] *Woodard v Woodard* (n 43) 40.
[62] ibid.
[63] ibid.
[64] ibid 40.
[65] *Bunn v Markham* (n 36).

it was competent for him so to do.'[66] This indicates that A's practical ability to deal with the property by virtue of retaining a means of access will defeat a purported DMC.

Secondly, would DMC never apply in these non-deathbed situations because A will always be able practically to deal *in equity* with the property even though possession of the property or indicia has been transferred to B? In *Sen v Headley*, Nourse LJ answered this in the negative, observing that 'it has never been suggested that [A]'s continuing ability to [constitute himself a trustee for a third party or assign a chose in action] amounts to a retention of dominion over the chose in action.'[67] Perhaps the best explanation runs thus: it is practically more likely that one will interfere or deal with his property where he has a means of accessing it as compared to dealing merely with its equitable interest. As such, unless there is evidence that A intends to deal with the equitable interest in the property, this ability is considered to be 'theoretical' for the purposes of DMC, thus fulfilling the requirement for a transfer of dominion. Of course, if later A in fact deals with the equitable interest in such a way, then that act will suffice as revocation of the gift.[68]

15.1.2.2. Timing

It has been seen that delivery entails a transfer of dominion, a concept which embodies four separate elements. The present discussion relates to the timing aspect of delivery. It is said that there must be a *present* delivery. This means that delivery must occur during B's lifetime:[69] in particular, delivery (as opposed to the gift itself) must not be conditional upon A's death. Thus, in *Re Johnson*,[70] where A said 'If I die, [the key to a box] will be sent to you', it was held that there was no present delivery.

The element of 'present-ness' in relation to delivery is to be distinguished from the conditional nature of the third requirement, to be discussed below,[71] namely A's intention that the gift will take effect absolutely only at A's death. As Eldon LC famously said, a DMC 'is a gift *in praesenti*, to take effect *in futuro*'.[72] Requiring a present act of delivery, including a present intention to give,[73] allows DMC to be distinguished from a future gift.[74] Although a DMC is ambulatory until A's death, the requirement of a present delivery avoids the arrangement from amounting to a nuncupative (oral) will which, by virtue of the Wills Act 1837, s 9, is invalid.[75]

An interesting issue arises as to the relationship between the A's transfer of possession and A's intention to dispose from the perspective of timing. It has been said that transfer of possession need not be simultaneous with A's having an intention to make a conditional gift to B. So, in *Re Stoneham*, PO Lawrence J said that there is in principle 'no distinction between a delivery antecedent to the gift and a delivery concurrent with or

[66] ibid 7 Taunt 233, 129 ER 93.
[67] *Sen v Headley* (n 3) 438.
[68] Revocation is discussed in the main text following n 89 below.
[69] The gift fails if delivery is not made during B's lifetime: *Hardy v Baker* (1738) West T Hard 519, 25 ER 1063.
[70] *Re Johnson* [1904-07] All ER Rep 539 (Ch) 541.
[71] See S 15.1.3.
[72] *Jones v Selby* (n 36) Prec Ch 303, 24 ER 144.
[73] See S 15.1.2.1.
[74] *Re Ward* (n 5) 207. The validity of future gifts is discussed in Chapter 8.
[75] See *Ward v Turner* (n 18) Dick 173, 21 ER 235.

subsequent to the gift.'[76] A transfer of possession concurrent with or subsequent to an intention to make a gift is unproblematic: DMC cases usually reflect either one of these patterns. But in relation to an antecedent transfer of possession, the judge said that DMC can arise 'where chattels have been delivered to [B] before the gift as bailee *or in any other capacity*, so long as they are actually in his possession at the time of the gift to the knowledge of [A].'[77] Insofar as an antecedent delivery is made to B as bailee, this statement is uncontroversial. For instance, in both *Woodard v Woodard*[78] and *Sen v Headley*,[79] B had possession of a key (respectively to a car and to title deeds to unregistered land) as bailee before A expressed the relevant intention to make a gift of the property to B upon B's death, and a DMC arose in both cases. However, it is difficult to accept that a DMC would arise *regardless of* the capacity in which B takes the antecedent delivery. In particular, DMC would surely not apply if a chattel was delivered to B pursuant to an intention by A to make an absolute gift,[80] with A afterwards attempting to make the gift conditional upon A's death. That is to say, a later intention to make a gift conditional upon A's death is only effective if it gives B *more* than what B was entitled to through the antecedent delivery: the later intention cannot *reduce* B's existing right in the property.[81]

15.1.3. Conditional upon Death

Thirdly, the gift must be made conditional upon A's death. This requirement is crucial for distinguishing DMC from purported inter vivos gifts, since an intention to make a gift prior to A's death is mutually exclusive with an intention that the gift take effect upon A's death. Maintaining this distinction is important for at least two reasons. First, what would fail as an inter vivos gift may yet fulfil the requirements for a valid DMC.[82] Secondly, it explains why, unlike inter vivos gifts, DMC will not operate if B does not survive A.[83]

The key to determining whether or not A's gift meets this third requirement turns entirely on A's intention. As Farewell J said in *Re Craven's Estate*,[84] there must be 'a clear intention to give, but to give only if the donor dies.' Such an intention is clearly shown when A uses words to that effect; however this is not always necessary. Where the gift is made when A is severely ill, as often is the case, courts have shown a willingness to imply that the gift is conditional upon A's death.[85] Indeed, in *Duffield v Elwes*,[86] where A was so ill that he could hardly speak, the conditional nature of the gift was held to be expressed merely 'by a look

[76] *Re Stoneham* [1919] 1 Ch 149 (Ch) 153–54.

[77] ibid 154 (emphasis added). See too *Sen v Headley* (n 3) 289, where it was said that an 'antecedent delivery … to the defendant to hold it in a different capacity, the capacity in which she held it being changed by what took place subsequently when the donatio mortis causa was effected, was a sufficient delivery to satisfy the rule requiring delivery in gifts of chattels.'

[78] *Woodard v Woodard* (n 43).

[79] *Sen v Headley* (n 3).

[80] *Re Cole* [1964] Ch 175 (CA).

[81] This distinction is crucial for rationalising DMC: see discussion in the main text following n 121 below.

[82] *Hedges v Hedges* (n 59) Prec Ch 270, 24 ER 130; *Edwards v Jones* (1836) 1 My & C 226, 40 ER 361.

[83] *Delgoffe v Fader* (n 30) 927.

[84] *Re Craven's Estate* (n 7) 426.

[85] See, eg, *Gardner v Parker* (n 27); *Re Lillington* (n 38); *Wilkes v Allington* (n 8).

[86] *Duffield v Elwes* (n 10) 1 Bli NS 533, 4 ER 972.

[rather] than a word'. And as *Woodard v Woodard*[87] might suggest, evidence of A's intention may even be drawn from whether or not A retains items which relate to (but do not form part of) the property in question, for example the log book or extra set of keys to a car.

Consistent with the requirement that the gift must be made in contemplation of death caused by a specific reason or a known cause,[88] the gift cannot simply be conditional upon death from old age or the normal vicissitudes of life. Instead, it must be conditional upon the specific reason or cause contemplated. But there is a proviso: DMC remains operative '[i]f a man, in contemplation of death … in fact dies from some [supervening] cause other than the disorder which was present to his mind when he made the gift'.[89]

If and when the contemplated risk of death ends, for example where A recovers from his sickness,[90] the gift is revoked. The conditional nature of the gift also entails that A may expressly revoke the gift through actions amounting to a resumption of dominion,[91] or by giving notice to B. As discussed below,[92] cases where A retains the legal title to the property fall within the unilateral events category of constructive trusts; and consistently with this analysis in these cases it might also be suggested that A may revoke the gift unilaterally without communicating to B the intention to revoke, so long as the intention to revoke is objectively and properly manifested in some way.

15.2. A Re-Analysis

In *King v Dubrey*,[93] Jackson LJ confessed 'to some mystification as to why the common law has adopted the doctrine of DMC at all. The doctrine obviously served a useful purpose in the social conditions prevailing under the later Roman Empire. But it serves little useful purpose today, save possibly as a means of validating death bed gifts.'[94] Contrary to Jackson LJ's sceptical approach, it is submitted that the doctrine can satisfactorily be explained and convincingly justified. It appears that one of the main reasons why DMC has eluded a proper explanation is the failure to distinguish between two types of case in which the doctrine arises, namely cases where legal title to the property passes from A to B pursuant to delivery, and those where A retains legal title to the property. As will be seen, although both cases have to satisfy the same requirements for the doctrine to apply, they create different rights and duties in the parties. Drawing a distinction between these two types of case allows DMC to be understood by way of orthodox analyses.

[87] *Woodard v Woodard* (n 43) 40.

[88] See S 15.1.1.

[89] *Wilkes v Allington* (n 8) 110. *cf* the obiter statement at *King v Dubrey* (n 2) [57] that DMC 'comes to an end if [A] fails to succumb to the death which was anticipated when he made the DMC.' This appears to be *per incuriam* the higher authority of *Wilkes*.

[90] *Staniland v Willott* (n 24). See too *Woodard v Woodard* (n 43) 40, discussed in the main text following n 63 above.

[91] *Bunn v Markham* (n 36) 7 Taunt 231, 129 ER 92–93. But a mere resumption of possession of the property for safekeeping alone does not amount to a revocation: *Re Hawkins* (n 44).

[92] See S 15.2.2.3.

[93] *King v Dubrey* (n 2) [53].

[94] Note, however, that a little later on, his Lordship observed: 'I do not say that DMC is only available when [A] is on his deathbed': *King v Dubrey* (n 2) [55].

15.2.1. B Has the Legal Title

It was seen previously[95] that DMC may operate where the legal title of the property in question is transferred from A to B. This may occur where legal title to the property passes by actual or constructive delivery of certain documents,[96] or where a proper transfer of legal title is effectuated, for instance where A's shares are effectively registered in B's name,[97] or where money in A's bank account is put into the joint names of A and B.[98]

15.2.1.1. An Orthodox Explanation

A hint of the appropriate analysis to be adopted in cases of this kind can be gleaned from *Staniland v Willott.*[99] In that case B obtained the legal title to A's shares, but A then recovered from the illness in relation to which death was contemplated. Truro LC observed that one of the questions which had to be resolved was 'whether, [A] not having died, [B] had *continued* to possess those shares as a trustee for [A], and ought to be decreed to retransfer them.'[100] This sentence indicates that a trust had arisen before A's recovery, that is, when the shares were transferred to B. Such a trust does not arise merely from the time of A's death or recovery.[101]

In line with this, such cases can be understood by way of an orthodox explanation. Where the requirements for a valid DMC are fulfilled, the parties are taken, through a process of interpretation,[102] to intend to create a trust in the following way: upon obtaining the legal title, B holds the property on trust for A for life, B in remainder, with B's interest being contingent[103] upon A's not recovering from or surviving the contemplated cause of death. Thus, B's interest immediately becomes absolute if A dies from the contemplated cause,[104] but it is extinguished otherwise.[105] In addition, A is also a donee of a general power of appointment during his lifetime which is exercisable at any time. Thus, A can revoke the gift prior to the contemplated event of death. So, where A resumes dominion or gives notice to B,[106] A will have exercised the power in favour of himself, thus bringing the trust to an end.

[95] See main text following n 24 above. It was also noted there that such facts are uncommon.

[96] See Borkowski, *Deathbed Gifts* (n 1) 55.

[97] *Staniland v Willott* (n 24).

[98] *Re Korvine's Trust* [1921] 1 Ch 343 (Ch).

[99] *Staniland v Willott* (n 24).

[100] ibid 3 Mac & G 668, 42 ER 417 (emphasis added). His Lordship answered this question in the affirmative.

[101] Robert Chambers, 'Conditional Gifts' in Norman Palmer and Ewan McKendrick (eds), *Interests in Goods*, 2nd edn (London, LLP, 1998) 456.

[102] That is to say, although the parties do not in so many words say that a trust etc is to arise, this is the only interpretation which can be given to their words. This technique of interpreting the parties' agreement has been encountered in our discussion of the *Quistclose* doctrine: see Chapter 13, main text following n 51. Note also that specific terms need not be used to create a trust, if in essence that is what the parties meant: see *Paul v Constance* [1977] 1 WLR 527 (CA).

[103] In contrast to a vested estate 'when there is an immediate fixed right of present or future enjoyment', 'an estate is contingent when a right of enjoyment is to accrue on an event which is dubious and uncertain': *Pearson v IRC* [1981] AC 753 (HL) 772, quoting Richard Preston, *An Elementary Treatise on Estates: With Preliminary Observation of the Quality of Estates* (London, J & WT Clarke, 1820) 89.

[104] See *Re Beaumont* (n 28) 892–93.

[105] Thus, in *Staniland v Willott* (n 24), the gift was revoked when A recovered from the contemplated illness, even though A then became a lunatic, and would have been unable to exercise a power of appointment.

[106] See main text following n 90 above.

Certain modifications to this trust structure are necessary where the gift is made conditional upon B fulfilling certain conditions, and where A transfers property to B to be held on trust for C.[107] In the former case, B's interest is additionally subject to a condition subsequent, the fulfilment of which is necessary to avoid B's actual enjoyment of an existing interest (which arises at A's death) from being negatived and destroyed.[108] In the latter case, it is C, instead of B, who is the contingent remainderman, all else remaining the same.

15.2.1.2. Nature of the Trust

The next matter to be resolved concerns the nature of the trust. On the basis of the orthodox explanation, the trust may either be analysed as express or constructive in nature,[109] depending primarily on whether gifts by way of DMC fall to be analysed as inter vivos or testamentary gifts,[110] and secondarily on the nature of the property given. Valid and enforceable inter vivos express declarations of trust do not require compliance with any formality requirements except where the subject matter is an interest relating to land;[111] and so if gifts by way of DMC are inter vivos gifts, the trust which arises is an express trust in all cases except where land is concerned, in relation to which the trust is constructive in nature. On the other hand, since by definition gifts by way of DMC do not comply with the formality requirements for the creation of express testamentary trusts,[112] then the trust is constructive in nature if gifts by way of DMC fall to be analysed as testamentary gifts. Hence the nature of the trust turns on whether gifts by way of DMC are inter vivos or testamentary in nature.

It is well-known that Buckley J in *Re Beaumont*[113] expressed the view that gifts by way of DMC are of 'an amphibious nature, being … neither entirely inter vivos nor testamentary.' However, such an analysis is not satisfactory, given that the categories 'inter vivos' and 'testamentary' are mutually exclusive. Some cases have suggested that the gifts are testamentary because they are in 'the nature of a legacy',[114] or they '[differ] in nothing from a will',[115] or that they raise '[questions] of administration'.[116] However, upon closer inspection, those cases either prove to be unreliable authorities,[117] or they do not ultimately commit to such a view.[118] Other cases suggest that these gifts are inter vivos in nature, and there are good

[107] See main text to n 5 and n 6 above.

[108] See David Hayton, Paul Matthews and Charles Mitchell, *Underhill and Hayton: Law Relating to Trusts and Trustees*, 19th edn (London, LexisNexis Butterworths, 2016) [8-95].

[109] Chambers, 'Conditional Gifts' (n 101) 457 suggests that in *Staniland v Willott* (n 24) the trust fell to be analysed as an express trust, but nowhere in the judgment does this categorisation appear.

[110] It is sometimes suggested that it rarely matters whichever way the classification is made (see, eg, Chambers, 'Conditional Gifts' (n 101) 453), but as we will see, it affects how we explain and justify the DMC doctrine.

[111] The Law of Property Act 1925, s 53(1)(b).

[112] The Wills Act 1837, s 9.

[113] *Re Beaumont* (n 28) 892.

[114] *Delgoffe v Fader* (n 30) 927; *Smith v Casen* (unreported; cited in *Drury v Smith* (n 6)).

[115] *Jones v Selby* (n 36) Prec Ch 303, 24 ER 144.

[116] *Re Craven's Estate* (n 7) 429–30.

[117] The judgment of *Smith v Casen* is unreported, and appears only as a memorandum at the end of the report of *Drury v Smith* (n 6). *Jones v Selby* (n 36) is an old case which does no more than assert the proposition. *Delgoffe v Fader* (n 30), although being a judgment of the Court of Appeal, also merely asserts the proposition without any hint of elaboration.

[118] In *Re Craven's Estate* (n 7) 429, Farwell J also said that a DMC gift does not 'purely' raise a question of administration.

reasons to subscribe to this view. In particular, this view explains why A must effectuate delivery during A's lifetime,[119] and it is also consistent with the courts' reluctance to enforce such gifts as nuncupative wills in contravention of the Wills Act 1837.[120]

If it is accepted that gifts by way of DMC are inter vivos gifts, then in DMC cases where A transfers legal title of the property to B, the trust which is enforced is an express trust, except in the case where an interest in land is involved, where the trust is a constructive trust due to the lack of compliance with the relevant formality requirement.

15.2.1.3. Categorising the Constructive Trust

Where an express trust is enforced, it is A's unilateral and proper manifestation of intention as settlor which triggers the express trust.[121] Where the trust is constructive in nature, the question arises: where do these trusts fit within the structure of constructive trusts?

The first matter is to determine whether they fall within the 'bilateral events' or 'unilateral events' category of constructive trusts. The key to resolving this question is to observe that it is in fact necessary for the trust to exist that B has knowledge of the conditional nature of the gift *before* he obtains legal title to A's property. Although this point has never been explicitly considered by the courts, it is wholly consistent with common sense. The point can be made by observing that, if B has no knowledge of the conditional nature of the gift when obtaining the legal title to the property, B would be at liberty to assume that the gift is an outright gift from A and that he is receiving an unencumbered interest when A transferred the legal title to him.[122] If it is then permissible for communication concerning the conditional nature of the gift to be made to B *after* legal title has been transferred to him, this would unduly prejudice B.[123] In particular, where B deals with the property during A's lifetime before being aware of his trusteeship, B may yet find himself in breach of trust.[124]

In addition to prior communication, it seems necessary further for B to *agree* to take the gift conditionally. This is because, if B expresses his refusal to take the gift conditionally and yet A nevertheless goes ahead with the transfer of the legal title to B, it can hardly be said that A intends for the gift to be conditional upon A's death.

The preceding discussion indicates that the constructive trusts which arise in the DMC situation under discussion fall within the non-contract-based, bilateral events category of constructive trusts. Within this category, it is clear that they reflect a QI situation, since by virtue of his prior agreement, B becomes a trustee of A's property immediately legal title is acquired. Therefore, the constructive trust can be explained by virtue of the 'norm against taking an advantage':[125] the trust compels B to carry out his promise to hold on trust for

[119] *Re Korvine's Trust* (n 98); *Ward v Turner* (n 18).

[120] See, eg, *Drury v Smith* (n 6); *Re Ward* (n 5). See too Mark Pawlowski, 'Death-Bed Gifts' (1994) 144 *New Law Journal* 48; Megarry, *LQR* (n 16) 22; Borkowski, *Deathbed Gifts* (n 1) 25.

[121] See discussion in Chapter 1, S 1.2.1.

[122] The fact that B can so assume is reinforced by the Law of Property Act 1925, s 60(3) which abolishes the presumption of resulting trust where an interest in land is voluntarily transferred: see too *Lohia v Lohia* [2001] EWCA Civ 1691 and *Ali v Khan* [2002] EWCA Civ 974, [2009] WTLR 187.

[123] Analogously, fully secret trusts only take effect if A's intention to create such a trust is communicated to B during A's lifetime, that is, before the property in question is acquired by B: *Moss v Cooper* (1861) 1 J & H 352, 366; 70 ER 782, 788; *Re Boyes* [1884] LR 26 Ch D 531 (Ch) 536.

[124] See main text to n 81 above.

[125] This norm was explained in Chapter 4, S 4.3.4.

A on terms which we have explained earlier;[126] and this is to ensure that B does not take an advantage for himself that the parties have intended ought not to be taken by B for his own enjoyment.

In fact, this analysis aligns the DMC situation under discussion closely with the *Quistclose* doctrine.[127] In both contexts the parties' arrangements normally give rise to express trusts, and in both contexts constructive trusts nevertheless become relevant where the necessary formality requirements are not complied with. Where the trusts are constructive in nature, they arise in response to B's promise to take only a contingent interest in the land which A transfers to B, and to A's reliance on that promise by effectuating the transfer.

15.2.2. A Has the Legal Title

In contrast to the DMC situation discussed above, the vast majority of cases do not involve a transfer of legal title to B. In such cases, the gift 'leaves the whole title in [A], unless the event occurs [that is, death] which is to divest him.'[128] A different analysis is required in this situation.

15.2.2.1. An Orthodox Explanation

It is at least clear from the cases that, when A dies from the contemplated cause, there is a trust in B's favour which is exercisable against A's legal personal representative.[129] The question arises as to when such a trust first arises. In *Sen v Headley*,[130] Nourse LJ asserted that Lord Eldon in *Duffield v Elwes*[131] had held that 'a trust to perfect the gift … arose by operation of law *on the death of [A]*'. Upon closer inspection of *Duffield*, however, nothing in Lord Eldon's judgment suggests that the trust *first* arose at that point; all his Lordship does say[132] is that A's personal representative is under a trust obligation in B's favour after A's death. Indeed, it is difficult to see why a trust would arise *only* as between A's personal representative and B given that the DMC gift was not initiated by either of them; moreover, there is otherwise no connection between those two parties. The better view is that A's personal representative is under a trust obligation because he steps into A's shoes: it is because A was a trustee in B's favour during his lifetime that A's personal representative is obliged to honour the trust.

It is submitted that, when the requirements for a valid DMC are fulfilled, a trust is created, the structure of which is identical to that arising in cases where B obtains legal title, with the one exception that it is A, not B, who is the trustee. Thus, A holds the property on trust for himself for life, B in remainder, with B's interest being contingent upon A's not recovering from or surviving the contemplated cause of death. A is also a donee of a general

[126] See S 15.2.1.1.
[127] This doctrine is discussed in Chapter 13.
[128] *Edward v Jones* (1836) 1 My & C 226, 235; 40 ER 361, 365.
[129] *Re Beaumont* (n 28) 894; *Delgoffe v Fader* (n 30) 928.
[130] *Sen v Headley* (n 3) 435 (emphasis added).
[131] *Duffield v Elwes* (n 10).
[132] ibid 1 Bli NS 531, 4 ER 971.

power of appointment during his lifetime which is exercisable at any time. Thus, A can revoke the gift prior to the contemplated event of death by resumption of dominion or by giving notice to B.

Certain modifications to this trust structure are necessary in certain situations. Where A makes the gift conditional upon B fulfilling certain conditions, the trust structure remains the same but with the addition of B being subject to a condition subsequent. But the analysis is different where A intends B to hold the property on trust for C.[133] Here, the trust structure remains the same (viz A holds on trust for A for life and B in contingent remainder, with A having a general power of appointment), but with the additional feature that, if and when B receives the property, B becomes a trustee for C based on A's and B's agreement to that effect.

15.2.2.1.1. Bailment?

It is necessary briefly to address an alternative explanation suggested by Robert Chambers that a DMC arrangement which leaves the legal title in A's hands can be explained 'as a bailment to [B] which becomes ownership if the condition is satisfied.'[134] Bailment fails fully to explain the DMC situation under consideration. First, because bailment 'is an exclusively common law notion',[135] it does not properly justify the fact that B is a beneficiary under a trust which arises when A dies. Equity's involvement suggests that the relevant arrangement gives rise to a trust as discussed previously. Secondly, 'it is strictly not a case of bailment at all since [B] is under no contractual obligation to return the property'.[136] Finally, at least in cases which involve B obtaining only the indicia of title, it is clear that B does not *become* owner of the property upon A's death, since the assistance of A's personal representative is necessary for this to occur.[137] This leaves outstanding the question of why A's personal representative is under an obligation to provide such assistance; and the best explanation of that obligation is found in the fact that during A's lifetime he was a trustee, rather than a bailor.

15.2.2.2. Nature of the Trust

It is clear that the trust is not express in nature. This is because equity will not perfect an imperfect gift by giving effect to a purported but failed attempt to make a gift by way of an express trust.[138] Thus, the cases have identified the trust as arising 'by operation of law'.[139]

[133] See main text to n 5 and n 6 above.

[134] Chambers, 'Conditional Gifts' (n 101) 431. More specifically, Chambers suggests that cases which involve B obtaining only the indicia of title creates a bailment of the indicia, with B requiring the assistance of A's personal representative after A's death for B to obtain any interest in the property (Chambers, 'Conditional Gifts' (n 101) 454); whereas cases which involve B obtaining possession of a chattel may be explained either as a bailment or as a form of conditional ownership (Chambers, 'Conditional Gifts' (n 101) 455).

[135] Michael Bridge, Louise Gullifer, Gerard McMeel et al, *The Law of Personal Property* (London, Sweet & Maxwell, 2013) [2-067].

[136] Borkowski, *Deathbed Gifts* (n 1) 106.

[137] See main text following n 129 above.

[138] See *Moore v Moore* (1874) LR 18 Eq 474, 483; Sparkes, 'Death-Bed Gifts of Land' (n 14) 43. This is the same reason for which the trust enforced in relation to the rule in *Re Rose* is not an express trust: see discussion in Chapter 9, S 9.2.1.

[139] *Duffield v Elwes* (n 10) 1 Bli NS 543, 4 ER 976; *Re Dillon* (n 25) 82; *Sen v Headley* (n 3) 435; *Re Beaumont* (n 28) 893.

It is certainly not a resulting trust since it does not involve returning the beneficial interest in the property to its previous owner. There is no doubt, therefore, that the trust is a constructive trust.

15.2.2.3. Categorising the Constructive Trust

Where do these trusts fit within the structure of constructive trusts? The first matter is to determine whether they fall within the 'bilateral events' or 'unilateral events' category of constructive trusts. In relation to this matter, it is observable that the agreement of—and, indeed, communication to—B of the conditional nature of the gift is not essential for DMC to operate in the situation under consideration. Certainly, in most cases, B will be aware of this when A delivers the property or indicia to B; however, it is neither necessary for B to be aware of nor accept the delivery.[140] And while the cases have all involved, at a minimum, communication to B of the conditional nature of the gift during A's lifetime, this is strictly speaking unnecessary. Since the situation under consideration does not involve B obtaining the legal title to A's property during A's lifetime, a secret intention by A to make a gift by way of DMC to B which is discovered post-mortem simply gives B more than what B obtains when B takes possession of the property or its indicia; and as discussed earlier,[141] this is entirely permissible. Indeed, even if B were aware of the delivery during A's lifetime without being cognisant of A's intention to make a conditional gift to him, there is no risk of B harbouring the false assumption that B has obtained the unencumbered interest in the property and that he is free to deal with it at will.[142]

The preceding discussion entails that the DMC situation under discussion falls within the unilateral events category of constructive trusts, since A's actions alone are sufficient to give rise to the trust. It also reflects an AI situation, since the constructive trust arises in relation to property belonging to A. This aligns the DMC situation under discussion closely with the rule in *Re Rose*.

15.2.2.4. Rationale

In fact, it is possible to explain the DMC situation under discussion by way of the rationale which underpins the rule in *Re Rose*. These DMC situations advance the liberal vision of the institution of property by allowing A maximal freedom in the disposition of his assets *in the specific situation where the gift is made conditional upon a contemplated death*. It does so by giving effect to A's intention to give away his property where he successfully complies with the requirements for a valid DMC. In doing so, DMC—like the rule in *Re Rose*—reflects the ideas of consistency and finality, the former referring to the fact that A's actions are taken to

[140] As in *Sen v Headley* (n 3) 431, where the keys to the steel box which contained the title deeds to the property were slipped into B's handbag without B noticing.

[141] See main text following n 76 above.

[142] *cf* the position in relation to the DMC situation where B obtains the legal title from A during A's lifetime: see main text following n 121 above.

Of course, the discussion in the text is predicated upon the assumption that, where delivery of a chattel is involved, A does not express an intention to make an absolute gift of the property to B when delivery is made. Otherwise the case would fall to be considered as one where B obtains the legal title from A during A's lifetime, since delivery coupled with an objective intention to make an absolute gift passes the legal title to a chattel: *Re Cole* (n 80).

be consistent with his intentions unless a contrary intention is shown, and the latter relating to the fact that A's intention to effectuate a transfer of property is taken to be conclusive despite the fact that legal title to the property is not yet vested in B.[143]

The above proposition requires careful examination, since the obvious differences between the doctrines raise two difficult questions: why does A's death have a central role to play in relation to DMC but not in relation to the rule in *Re Rose*; and why is it sufficient in the DMC context that delivery occurs, and not that A should do everything in his power to transfer the legal title to B?

In relation to the rule in *Re Rose*, it was observed in Chapter 9[144] that it is not only necessary for A to do everything in his power to effectuate a transfer, but that B must also be put in a position to complete the transfer without A's assistance. The reason for this, it was seen, is that requiring A's assistance to complete B's title would contravene the maxim that equity will not assist a volunteer.[145] Although B is a 'volunteer' in the sense that he does not provide consideration in return for A's gift, the maxim is not contravened so long as the assistance *of A* is not required. In *Re Dillon*, Lindley LJ said that 'the principle of not assisting a volunteer to perfect an incomplete gift does not apply to a *donatio mortis causa*.'[146] However, technically speaking, DMC does not contravene this maxim, since 'the question [is never] what [A] can be compelled to do, but what [B] ... can call upon the representatives ... of [A] to do'.[147] Nevertheless, as earlier observed,[148] this does not fully explain why A's personal representatives *ought* to be held as trustee for B's benefit. A more convincing explanation is required.

It is apt to begin with the words of Eldon LC in *Duffield v Elwes*:[149]

> [T]he question is this, whether the act of [A] being, *as far as the act of [A] itself is to be viewed*, complete, the persons who represent [A] ... are not bound to complete that which, *as far as the act of [A] is concerned* in the question, was incomplete.

This indicates that what counts as a 'complete' act so as to compel equity to make perfect what would otherwise be an imperfect gift depends on the context in which the question arises. As to what that context may be, the words of Cowper LC in *Hedges v Hedges*,[150] the first reported case on the modern law of DMC,[151] are relevant. His Lordship said, speaking of the doctrine:[152]

> where a man lies in extremity, or being surprized with sickness, and not having an opportunity of making his will; but lest he should die before he could make it, he gives with his own hands his goods to his friends about him: this, if he dies, shall operate as a legacy; but if he recovers, then does the property thereof revert to him.

[143] For a discussion of these points in relation to the rule in *Re Rose*, see Chapter 9, S 9.3.3.
[144] See Chapter 9, S 9.1.2.
[145] *Mascall v Mascall* (1985) 50 P & CR 119 (CA) 126.
[146] *Re Dillon* (n 25) 83.
[147] *Duffield v Elwes* (n 10) 1 Bli NS 530, 4 ER 971.
[148] See main text from n 137 above.
[149] *Duffield v Elwes* (n 10) 1 Bli NS 530, 4 ER 971 (emphases added).
[150] *Hedges v Hedges* (n 59).
[151] Borkowski, *Deathbed Gifts* (n 1) 10. The 'modern' law of DMC is taken to begin from the passing of the Statute of Frauds 1677, which first imposed formality requirements for the making of a valid will.
[152] *Hedges v Hedges* (n 59) Prec Ch 269–70, 24 ER 130 (emphases omitted).

There are two key ideas in this passage. The first is that A's death is central to the rationale of the doctrine. Death is, of course, inevitable; and gifts which are conditional simply on the eventuality of death are testamentary in nature, properly so-called, and therefore must comply with the relevant formality requirements for a valid will[153] to be effective gifts.[154] However, *in the context* where A contemplates death from a specific reason,[155] equity takes compassion on such donors,[156] reflecting the desire to 'satisfy a deep felt need of mankind.'[157] The second key idea reflected by Cowper LC's words is that DMC is concerned with A's freedom to dispose of his property. The doctrine gives effect to the substance of an intention to dispose without being hindered by the formalities or practicalities involved in the making of a will (or, indeed, a declaration of trust).

Certainly, the law has moved on since *Hedges v Hedges*, and it is clear that DMC can now also arise even though A is not on his deathbed[158] and therefore has the opportunity to—but does not—make a will before dying. It is also clear that A does not need to have done everything in his power to transfer property to B for DMC to operate.[159] Nevertheless, equity's compassion can be understood as translating—in the DMC situation under consideration—to a *concession* which is made to donors who have not done enough to engage the rule in *Re Rose*, but who *do* fulfil the requirements for a valid DMC and therefore fall within the specific context in question. That is to say, in view of the seriousness and piteousness of death from a specific reason, equity gives effect to the substance of A's unilateral intention to make a gift conditional upon that contemplated cause of death without insisting that A should have done everything in his power to effectuate a transfer of that property, *provided that A indicates an intention no longer to exercise his right to deal with the property in question*. Through delivery and thereby precluding himself practically from dealing with the property, A's intention to make a conditional gift of that property to B can be ascertained, and this is given effect to by the doctrine. In doing so, DMC recognises that A's actions are taken to be consistent with his intentions unless a contrary intention is shown: hence an express revocation or a resumption of dominion by A during his lifetime would undo the gift. The finality of A's actions is also recognised: despite the fact that legal title to the property is not vested in B either when the conditional gift is created or at A's death, A's fulfilment of the requirements of a valid DMC indicates his conclusive intention to make a contingent gift, and equity gives effect to the gift when the contingency is fulfilled.

[153] Wills Act 1837, s 9.

[154] For the same reason, as already observed, DMC does not operate where B merely contemplates his natural death: see S 15.1.1.

[155] As Buckley J observed in *Re Beaumont* (n 28) 892–93, '[i]n order to make the gift valid it must be made so as to take complete effect on the donor's death.' Thus, DMC would not apply where a gift is made conditional upon a condition other than A's death from a specific reason: in such cases, short of an express declaration of trust or an outright transfer of the property to B, it remains necessary for A to fulfil the requirements of the rule in *Re Rose* for the gift to be effective.

[156] See Peter Luxton, 'In Search of Perfection: The *Re Rose* Rule Rationale' [2012] *Conveyancer and Property Lawyer* 70, 72 fn 28.

[157] PV Baker, 'Land as a *Donatio Mortis Causa*' (1993) 109 *LQR* 19, 19.

[158] See *King v Dubrey* (n 2) [55].

[159] *Duffield v Elwes* (n 10) 1 Bli NS 530, 4 ER 971. See too *Veal v Veal* (1859) 27 Beav 303, 307–08; 54 ER 118, 120.

15.2.3. Lessons

The analysis of DMC proposed above distinguishes between two types of case: where legal title to the property passes from A to B, and those where A retains legal title to the property. This distinction provides two valuable lessons. The first, which relates to how we understand and justify the doctrine itself, concerns how we might resolve the tension (or, indeed, perceived conflict) between the Wills Act 1837 and DMC. The second, which relates to the bigger picture of constructive trusts, concerns how DMC can be aligned with other constructive trust doctrines.

15.2.3.1. The Wills Act

The relationship between DMC and the statutory formality requirements for the creation of a valid will[160] has proved to be a cause of concern for judges dealing with DMC cases. For instance, in *Sen v Headley*,[161] Nourse LJ declared that '[e]very [DMC] gift is a circumvention of the Wills Act 1837' and therefore that 'the doctrine is anomalous'; and in *King v Dubrey*,[162] Jackson LJ cautioned that 'courts must not allow DMC to be used as a device in order to validate ineffective wills.' Certainly, if DMC gifts are viewed as testamentary gifts, the concern that the doctrine unduly treads into the territory of the Wills Act is warranted; but as discussed earlier,[163] the better view is that they are inter vivos gifts.

But perhaps the deeper concern is that to allow DMC gifts is, *in substance*, to allow for the Wills Act to be sidestepped. Certainly, if DMC operates simply whenever a gift is made conditional upon A's death, there is cause for concern. However, it has been seen that, unlike testamentary gifts properly so-called, DMC requires a gift to be made conditional upon a death from a specific reason, and that a transfer of dominion must be made during A's lifetime. The former requirement ensures that DMC operates within confined boundaries and the latter requirement 'avoids ... the dangers of attaching to mere nuncupative legacies [*sic*] which were guarded against by the ... Wills Act'.[164]

Nevertheless, there remains a valid concern that, unlike wills, gifts by way of DMC can be proven by relying on parol evidence. As Jackson LJ observed in *King v Dubrey*:[165]

> What [A] says to those who are ministering to him in the last hours of his/her life may be a less reliable expression of his/her wishes than a carefully drawn will. The will may have been prepared with the assistance of a solicitor and in the absence of the beneficiaries. There are no such safeguards during a deathbed conversation. The words contained in a will are there for all to see. There may be much scope for disagreement about what [A] said to those visiting or caring for him in the last hours of his life.

It would appear, post-*King*, that a new approach is taken towards what counts as evidence sufficient to prove that a purported DMC gift was made by A 'in contemplation of death'. While it certainly remains unnecessary that A should be on his deathbed and therefore has

[160] The Statute of Frauds 1677, s 5 and its modern iteration in the Wills Act 1837, s 9.
[161] *Sen v Headley* (n 3) 440.
[162] *King v Dubrey* (n 2) [52].
[163] See S 15.2.1.2.
[164] *Re Wasserberg* (n 29) 204.
[165] *King v Dubrey* (n 2) [53].

no opportunity to make a will, it seems that, where it was open to A during his lifetime to make a valid will which gave the property to B but such a will was not made, courts will be sceptical that a gift by way of DMC was made.[166] Such an approach is to be welcomed, and encourages prospective donors to comply with the Wills Act and thereby availing themselves the safeguards provide by the formality requirements.

15.2.3.2. DMC and Other Constructive Trust Doctrines

There have been two passing suggestions that DMC can be rationalised consistently with certain constructive trust doctrines. In *Sen v Headley*, Nourse LJ observed, citing proprietary estoppel and the common intention constructive trust as examples, that '[i]n general it may be said that the constructive trust has been a ready means of developing our property law in modern times and that the process is a continuing one.'[167] And Robert Chambers writes that, 'where the donor is dead and no longer able to perfect the gift himself or herself the constructive trust can arise in favour of a pure donee, as it does in cases of secret trusts or mutual wills.'[168]

It is submitted that these statements, without more, are unhelpful, at least for the purposes of attaining a structured understanding of constructive trusts. In relation to Nourse LJ's statement, we have seen that proprietary estoppel[169] and the 'common intention constructive trust'[170] are doctrines which are best analysed as allowing for the imposition of constructive trusts as reflective remedies, which come with the judicial ability to exercise remedial discretion as to content. In contrast, constructive trusts arising in the DMC context are imposed as replicative remedies without the exercise of discretion.

In relation to Chambers' statement, the common ground shared by DMC, secret trusts, and mutual wills—namely that they are closely connected to the donor's or testator's death—is neither here nor there in relation to unearthing the underlying rationales of these doctrines. As the discussion above has indicated, a more helpful approach draws a distinction between DMC cases which involve B obtaining the legal title to the property in question and those which do not. The former cases which involve the imposition of constructive trusts are similar to secret trusts and the *Quistclose* doctrine, in that they arise in response to B's promise to qualify the interest he will obtain in A's property and A's reliance on B's promise by transferring the legal title to B. The latter cases can be viewed alongside the rule in *Re Rose*, whereby A's unilateral actions confirm a firm intention to make a gift, which equity recognises and enforces, thereby giving A maximal freedom in the disposition of his assets.

[166] ibid [68]–[70].
[167] *Sen v Headley* (n 3) 440.
[168] Chambers, 'Conditional Gifts' (n 101) 455.
[169] See Chapter 7.
[170] See Chapter 14.

16

Conclusion

In 1969, Edmund Davies LJ said that 'English law provides no clear and all-embracing definition of a constructive trust. Its boundaries have been left perhaps deliberately vague, so as not to restrict the court by technicalities in deciding what the justice of a particular case may demand.'[1] Unlike express and resulting trusts, constructive trusts are not underpinned by a single rationale. However, this lack of unity does not entail that constructive trusts ought to be left vague, or that the best which can be said of them is that they respond to the demands of 'justice'. The analysis provided in this book suggests that a structured understanding of constructive trusts is not out of reach. In general terms, constructive trusts can be understood as arising (i) where a positive intention cannot be enforced as an express trust, either because an intention to create a trust is not properly manifested, or because an intention to make a gift or enter into a contract is inconsistent with an intention to create an express trust, (ii) in response to wrongs, either where errant fiduciaries make a personal gain or where one fails to act reliably in relation to induced assumptions that an interest in one's property will be given away to another, or (iii) in response to a court's exercise of discretion as to the appropriate goal and content of the imposed remedy. Through a structured approach to the law of constructive trusts, our understanding is advanced not only in relation to individual doctrines which give rise to constructive trusts, but also in relation to the different ways in which a particular doctrine may inform our understanding of other seemingly distinct doctrines.

This concluding chapter does three things. It explains why certain doctrines which are sometimes said to give rise to constructive trusts have been excluded from the scope of this book. It observes the lessons which can be learnt when different categories of doctrines within the structure of the law of constructive trusts are compared and contrasted. Finally, it concludes with some observations from the historical context of the law of trusts.

16.1. Scope

This book has discussed 13 substantive doctrines which give rise to constructive trusts: the doctrine in *Rochefoucauld v Boustead*, secret trusts, the doctrine in *Pallant v Morgan*, proprietary estoppel, specifically enforceable contracts of sale, assignments and trusts of future property, the rule in *Re Rose*, errant fiduciary gains, the 'remedial constructive trust', mutual wills, *Quistclose* trusts, the 'common intention constructive trust', and *donatio mortis*

[1] *Carl Zeiss Stiftung v Herbert Smith & Co (No. 2)* [1969] 2 Ch 276 (CA) 300.

causa. Owing to the fact that the categories of constructive trusts are not closed, this list of 13 doctrines is not exhaustive: new situations may emerge in the future which call for the imposition of constructive trusts. Be that as it may, it might be thought that the present law contains other well-established constructive trust doctrines, but which are not discussed in this book. Their omission requires explanation.

16.1.1. Personal Liabilities

The first group of omitted situations is said to relate to 'constructive trusts', but upon closer inspection those situations involve no *trusts* being imposed at all, but simply give rise to personal liabilities.

16.1.1.1. Liability as a 'Constructive Trustee'

There are three doctrines where one is said to be liable to account as a 'constructive trustee', namely dishonest assistance, knowing receipt, and trusteeship *de son tort*. In relation to these doctrines,[2] Millett LJ has observed:[3]

> Equity has always given relief against fraud by making any person sufficiently implicated in the fraud accountable in equity. In such a case he is traditionally though I think unfortunately described as a constructive trustee and said to be 'liable to account as constructive trustee'. Such a person is not in fact a trustee at all, even though he may be liable to account as if he were. He never assumes the position of a trustee, and if he receives the trust property at all it is adversely to the plaintiff by an unlawful transaction which is impugned by the plaintiff. In such a case the expressions 'constructive trust' and 'constructive trustee' are misleading, for there is no trust and usually no possibility of a proprietary remedy; they are "nothing more than a formula for equitable relief."[4]

Unlike the subject-matter under discussion in this book—constructive *trusts*—these doctrines impose only a personal liability on the part of the 'constructive trustee'.[5] This personal liability to account is to be distinguished from a trustee's duty, properly so-called.[6] Hence, liability as a trustee *de son tort*[7] or a dishonest assistant[8] does not require the receipt of any trust property by the 'trustee', and a knowing recipient's liability persists although the received property has been dissipated.[9] Certainly, if a trustee *de son tort*, dishonest assistant,

[2] Although Millett LJ did not explicitly identify these doctrines in this passage, other judges have made this observation. In relation to dishonest assistance and knowing receipt, see, eg, *NBA Brothers Ltd v Lloyds Bank International (Guernsey) Ltd* [2005] EWHC 405 (Ch), [2005] ILPr 37 [70]. In relation to trusteeship *de son tort*, see, eg, *Jasmine Trustees Ltd v Wells & Hind (a firm)* [2007] EWHC 38 (Ch), [2008] Ch 194 [42].

[3] *Paragon Finance plc v DB Thakerar & Co* [1999] 1 All ER 400 (CA) 409.

[4] *Selangor United Rubber Estates Ltd v Cradock (No. 3)* [1968] 1 WLR 1555 (Ch) 1582.

[5] See *Williams v Central Bank of Nigeria* [2014] UKSC 10, [2014] AC 1189.

[6] JE Penner, 'Distinguishing Fiduciary, Trust, and Accounting Relationships' (2014) 8 *Journal of Equity* 202.

[7] It is necessary only for the 'trustee' to '[take] upon himself to intermeddle with trust matters or to do acts characteristic of the office of trustee': *Mara v Browne* [1896] 1 Ch 199 (CA) 209. See too *Taylor v Davies* [1920] AC 636 (PC) 651.

[8] 'Liability as an accessory is not dependent upon receipt of trust property. It arises even though no trust property has reached the hands of the accessory': *Royal Brunei Airlines Sdn Bhd v Tan* [1995] 2 AC 278 (HL) 382. See too *Novoship (UK) Ltd v Mikhaylyuk* [2014] EWCA Civ 908, [2015] QB 499.

[9] In practice, liability under knowing receipt 'is needed precisely where the recipient has not retained the [trust] property': *Ultraframe (UK) Ltd v Fielding* [2005] EWHC 1638 (Ch), [2006] FSR 17 [1577].

or knowing recipient receives trust property or its traceable proceeds, then from the moment of receipt he is liable to a proprietary claim by the beneficiaries of the trust.[10] This liability, however, relates to the fact that the recipient is a volunteer instead of a bona fide purchaser for value without notice of the received property;[11] the liability is independent of the aforementioned doctrines.

16.1.1.2. 'Subject To' Cases

A fourth doctrine also falls within the first group of omitted situations, namely cases where a vendor sells property to a purchaser 'subject to' the purchaser's recognition of a third party's personal rights. In these cases, the purchaser is compelled to fulfil his agreement.[12] Courts have described equity as intervening by imposing a 'constructive trust'.[13] In truth, however, a *trust*, properly so-called, is not involved at all: the phrase 'constructive trust' is not used in this context to reflect the conferral of a (proprietary) beneficial interest on the third party, but is used merely as a label which is not indicative of the substance of the remedy.[14]

16.1.2. Situations Better Analysed as Express or Resulting Trusts

The second group of omitted situations is inherently controversial. Ambiguity arises not merely as to whether the trusts imposed in these doctrines ought to be labelled 'constructive' or resulting', but also in relation to whether a trust arises at all, and if so, what events trigger the trusts. The primary reason for omitting these situations, however, is not merely due to their controversy or ambiguity, but because it is better to analyse them as giving rise to express or resulting trusts. Since the aim of this book has been to make sense of constructive trusts, the inclusion of these situations would threaten to obscure the conceptual divisions between constructive trusts and other types of trusts. For this reason, they have been omitted.

16.1.2.1. Revesting of Title following Rescission

First, consider the retrospective revesting of title to property in the context of equitable 'fraud',[15] that is, where a partly or fully executed contract is rescinded in equity. It is clear

[10] *Ultraframe (UK) Ltd* (n 9) [1518]; *Independent Trustee Services Ltd v GP Noble Trustees Ltd* [2012] EWCA Civ 195, [2013] Ch 91 [111].

[11] The nature of this liability is discussed in S 16.2.3.

[12] See, eg, the judgment of Lord Denning MR in *Binions v Evans* [1972] Ch 359 (CA); *Ashburn Anstalt v WJ Arnold & Co* [1989] Ch 1 (CA); *Lyus v Prowsa Developments Ltd* [1982] 1 WLR 1044 (Ch); *Chattey v Farndale Holdings Inc* (1998) 75 P & CR 298 (CA).

[13] See, eg, *Binions v Evans* (n 12) 368; *Lyus v Prowsa Developments Ltd* (n 12) 1053; *Ashburn Anstalt* (n 12) 26; *Chattey v Farndale Holdings Inc* (n 12) 317.

[14] See Ben McFarlane, 'Constructive Trusts Arising on a Receipt of Property *Sub Conditione*' (2004) 120 *LQR* 667, 679–82; Simon Gardner, 'Reliance-Based Constructive Trusts' in Charles Mitchell (ed), *Constructive and Resulting Trusts* (Oxford, Hart Publishing, 2010) 89–90.

It is, however, possible to explain the 'subject to' cases by way of the same rationale which underpins the QI doctrines within the non-contract-based, bilateral events category: see S 16.2.1.2.

[15] *Westdeutsche Landesbank Girozentrale v Islington LBC* [1996] AC 669 (HL) 708, 716.

that a trust arises from the moment a claimant exercises his power to rescind a contract. While in Australia it seems that the trust is a 'discretionarily' imposed 'remedial constructive trust',[16] English courts have rejected such an analysis.[17] Yet, it is unclear what type of trust it is in English law, with judges having suggested that rescission gives rise to a 'constructive (resulting) trust', a 'constructive trust', and a 'resulting trust'.[18] A related issue is the underlying rationale for this revesting rule. Understood as a proprietary remedy for unjust enrichment,[19] the trust is restitutionary.[20] On this view, it makes better sense to label these trusts as resulting trusts. This is because resulting trusts are always restitutionary in nature,[21] and can be analysed as arising due to the transferor's lack of intention to benefit the transferee in circumstances where the contract is voidable.

16.1.2.2. Mistaken Payments

The same can be said about trusts imposed to reverse mistaken payments. In *Chase Manhattan Bank NA v Israel-British Bank (London) Ltd*[22] a trust arose to reverse a mistaken payment; and it is well known that Lord Browne-Wilkinson in *Westdeutsche*[23] rejected Goulding J's reasoning in *Chase Manhattan*. However, the primary objection to the decision in *Chase Manhattan* relates to the law of unjust enrichment and not the law of trusts: the point of departure related to whether the mere fact of a mistaken payment ought to give the payor an immediate proprietary interest in the payment.[24] Strictly speaking, *Chase Manhattan* remains good law,[25] the decision never having been overruled. The question therefore arises as to what the nature of the trust was. It is generally assumed that the trust was constructive in nature. However, as Chambers notes, Goulding J 'refused to call it constructive when invited to do so'.[26] Instead, the judge relied on Viscount Haldane LC's judgment in *Sinclair v Brougham*[27] to fortify his decision, and upon close inspection Viscount Haldane LC was of the opinion that a mistaken payment gives rise to a resulting trust.[28]

[16] *Grimaldi v Chameleon Mining NL (No. 2)* [2012] FCAFC 6 [277]. See too Lord Browne-Wilkinson's suggestion in *Westdeutsche* (n 15) 716 that a constructive trust is imposed. His Lordship noted, however, that clear authority for this was difficult to find; and this was reiterated by Rimer J in *Shalson v Russo* [2003] EWHC 1637 (Ch), [2005] Ch 281 (Ch) [111].

[17] *El Ajou v Dollar Land Holdings plc* [1993] BCC 698 (Ch) 713.

[18] All three references are found in Potter LJ's judgment in *Twinsectra Ltd v Yardley* [1999] Lloyd's Rep Bank 438 (CA) [99]. The trust was also described as a resulting trust by Millett J in *El Ajou* (n 17) 713, and as a constructive trust in *Papamichael v National Westminster Bank* [2003] EWHC 164 (Comm), [2003] 1 Lloyd's Rep 341 and *Bailey v Angove's PTY Ltd* [2016] UKSC 47, [2016] 1 WLR 3179 [50].

[19] See, eg, Charles Mitchell, Paul Mitchell, and Stephen Watterson, *Goff & Jones: The Law Of Unjust Enrichment*, 9th edn (London, Sweet & Maxwell, 2016) [40-17]; Andrew Burrows, *The Law of Restitution*, 3rd edn (Oxford, OUP, 2010) 712.

[20] *Twinsectra Ltd v Yardley* (n 18) [99].

[21] See Robert Chambers, *Resulting Trusts* (Oxford, OUP, 1997) 104; *Goff & Jones* (n 19) [38-44].

[22] *Chase Manhattan Bank NA v Israel-British Bank (London) Ltd* [1981] Ch 105 (Ch).

[23] *Westdeutsche* (n 15) 714–15.

[24] *Goff & Jones* (n 19) [37-26] notes that 'there is no theory which can explain when [proprietary remedies awarded for unjust enrichment] should be awarded in a way that reconciles the results in all of the cases.'

[25] ibid [38-34] fn 113, citing *Commerzbank Aktiengesellschaft v IMB Morgan plc* [2004] EWHC 2771 (Ch), [2005] 2 All ER (Comm) 564 [36] and *Re Farepak Food and Gifts Ltd (in administration)* [2006] EWHC 3272 (Ch), [2008] BCC 22 [39]–[40].

[26] Chambers, *Resulting Trusts* (n 21) 228.

[27] *Sinclair v Brougham* [1914) AC 398 (HL) 419–20.

[28] ibid 421.

Because resulting trusts are restitutionary in effect, classifying the trust as a resulting trust places the *Chase Manhattan* trust—and, indeed, any trust imposed to reverse an unjust enrichment[29]—in its rightful conceptual space, and avoids unduly interfering with the domain of constructive trusts.[30]

16.1.2.3. Tracing-Related Claims

A more difficult issue arises as to a beneficiary's potential proprietary claims in relation to trust property or its traceable proceeds where there has been a breach of trust. Such claims may be made against an errant trustee or a third party volunteer, depending on who holds the property or traceable proceeds when the claim is made.

First, consider the potential claims of a beneficiary under an express trust against an errant trustee. There are two situations which may give rise to such a claim. The trustee might improperly take physical possession of a trust asset, or he might substitute trust property for another and keep the traceable proceeds for himself in breach of trust.[31] The former situation does not involve constructive trusts: the beneficiary's equitable right is not interrupted and persists in the trust asset, and that right is enforceable against the errant trustee.[32] But, the latter situation has been said to involve constructive trusts. In *Re EVTR Ltd*,[33] Dillon LJ observed:

> if a person who is a trustee receives money or property because of, or in respect of, trust property, he will hold what he receives as a constructive trustee[34] on the trusts of the original trust property.[35]

[29] See, eg, David Hayton, Paul Matthews and Charles Mitchell, *Underhill and Hayton: Law Relating to Trusts and Trustees*, 19th edn (London, LexisNexis Butterworths, 2016) [32-6].

[30] *Goff & Jones* (n 19) [38-44]. Indeed, classifying the trust as resulting in nature is capable of providing a better explanation than those given by Lord Browne-Wilkinson in *Westdeutsche* (n 15) 714 for why *Chase Manhattan* (n 22) was wrongly decided. Thus, Lord Millett, writing extrajudicially, notes of *Chase Manhattan* that 'the fact that the transferor intended to part with the beneficial interest was inconsistent with the existence of a resulting trust': see PJ Millett, 'Restitution and Constructive Trusts' (1998) 114 *LQR* 399, 412–13.

[31] Where trust property is used exclusively to acquire the traceable property, the beneficiary has a claim in relation to the entire traceable property. Where the traceable property is acquired partly with trust property and party with the trustee's own property or property which the trustee misappropriates from another innocent source, the beneficiary's claim is to a proportionate share in the traceable property: *Foskett v McKeown* [2001] 1 AC 102 (HL) 130–31.

[32] Ben McFarlane and Charles Mitchell, *Hayton and Mitchell: Text, Cases and Materials on the Law of Trusts and Equitable Remedies*, 14th edn (London, Sweet & Maxwell, 2015) [12-105].

[33] *Re EVTR Ltd* (1987) 3 BCC 389 (CA) 393. See too *Boscawen v Bajwa* [1996] 1 WLR 328 (CA) 334–35: 'If the plaintiff succeeds in tracing his property, whether in its original or in some changed form, into the hands of the defendant, … he is entitled to a remedy … if he seeks a proprietary remedy he must usually prove that the property to which he lays claim is still in the ownership of the defendant. If he succeeds in doing this the court will treat the defendant as holding the property on constructive trust for the plaintiff and will order the defendant to transfer it in specie to the plaintiff.'

[34] Read in the context of his Lordship's judgment, Dillon LJ here meant that the trust property was held on a (proprietary) constructive *trust*, as opposed to the personal liability of a 'constructive trustee' (the latter of which is discussed in S 16.1. above).

[35] It might be thought that the trusteeship of the trustee in relation to these traceable proceeds does not arise unless the beneficiary exercises his power 'to adopt the investment and to hold it as trust property': *Wright v Morgan* [1926] AC 788 (PC) 798. However, adopting a transaction does not entail a positive act; rather, it is passive: it is simply the withholding of the beneficiary's right to complain: PJ Millett, 'Equity's Place in the Law of Commerce' (1998) 114 *LQR* 214, 226. Thus, the better view is that trustee duties arise in relation to these traceable proceeds unless the beneficiary chooses to falsify the transaction. Only if he complains will the trustee be forced to 'keep the investment himself [and to become] debtor to the trust for the money which has been applied in its purchase': *Wright v Morgan* (n 35) 798.

However, in apparent contradiction, his Lordship then went on to hold that such moneys or properties 'are subject to the *same trusts* as the original [trust money]'.[36]

There seems to be no reason why it is necessary to invoke constructive trusts at all in this situation. As *Underhill & Hayton* notes,[37] the source of the beneficiary's rights is similar to the case where an authorised investment is made: it is 'the settlor's intention, agreed to by the trustee, to create such rights in their favour, the trustee being under an obligation always to act in the beneficiaries' best interests.'[38] That is to say, courts are concerned simply with enforcing the trustee's primary obligation to carry out his express trusteeship. To reflect this fact, the traceable property is best analysed as being held subject to the original express trust.

It also follows from this analysis that, if the original trust is a constructive or resulting trust, then a trustee who takes physical possession of a trust asset or its traceable proceeds would hold the property to the order of the original constructive[39] or resulting[40] trust, as the case may be. The source of the beneficiary's right would depend on the source of the original trust; there is no need to rely on any special constructive trust doctrine to explain the beneficiary's right. In short, the trustee's duties over the trust asset or traceable proceeds is simply 'an implication of the stewardship he has over the property … His obligation … would be exactly the same as his obligation in respect of the original property.'[41]

The beneficiary's position vis-a-vis third party volunteers is less straightforward. Again, we need to distinguish between cases where the original trust property is in the hands of a volunteer, and cases where the volunteer substitutes the trust property for traceable proceeds.

Four distinct analyses may explain the former case. The first analysis mirrors that discussed above in relation to a beneficiary's claim against an errant trustee. That is, the volunteer holds the trust property to the order of the original trust.[42] The persistence of the beneficiary's right against the volunteer is the result of the application of two rules. In relation to the errant trustee is the rule *nemo dat quod non habet*,[43] that is, no one can give what he does not have. Because the volunteer is not a bona fide purchaser for value of the legal interest in the trust property without notice, the beneficiary's right is not overreached. The other rule is that, as between mere equitable claimants, the first in time prevails.[44] This analysis reflects a Hohfeldian view of property rights. As Lionel Smith explains:[45]

> [Hohfeld] argued that the only rights that exist are rights against people, and he saw proprietary rights as aggregations of personal rights; so the right against a particular transferee that he

[36] *Re EVTR Ltd* (n 33) 393 (emphasis added).

[37] *Underhill and Hayton* (n 29) [90.9].

[38] The trustee's duty is, of course, liable to being falsified by the beneficiary: see n 35 above.

[39] See Simon Gardner, *An Introduction to the Law of Trusts*, Clarendon Law Series, 3rd edn (Oxford, OUP, 2011) 35 fn 51; Lionel Smith, 'Unravelling Proprietary Restitution' (2004) 40 *Canadian Business Law Journal* 317, 330 fn 38.

[40] Chambers, *Resulting Trusts* (n 21) 106.

[41] Smith, 'Unravelling' (n 39) 330.

[42] See, eg, *Foskett v McKeown* (n 31) 108–09; Smith, 'Unravelling' (n 39) 321; Charles Mitchell and Stephen Watterson, 'Remedies for Knowing Receipt' in Charles Mitchell (ed), *Constructive and Resulting Trusts* (Oxford, Hart Publishing, 2010) 116. *cf Peffer v Rigg* [1977] 1 WLR 285 (Ch) 294.

[43] Gardner, *Law of Trusts* (n 39) 309.

[44] *Underhill and Hayton* (n 29) [99.14].

[45] Smith, 'Unravelling' (n 39) 326.

> retransfer a thing owned by another was a right that a was always in the bundle, before the transfer. In other words, the source of the transferee's obligations whatever was the source of the original proprietary right.

As evidence of the fact that the source of the volunteer's obligation is the original trust, it may be noted that, if the original trust was a bare trust, then the beneficiary can call for the property directly, instead of compelling the volunteer merely to reconstitute the trust property to a trustee.[46]

In the context of a breach of an express trust, it has recently been suggested by Lloyd LJ in *Independent Trustee Services Ltd v GP Noble Trustees Ltd*[47] that a volunteer holds the trust property on a constructive trust. According to his Lordship:[48]

> Since the trust arises from the asset having been extracted, in breach of trust, from a fund held on express trusts, it seems correct to characterise the trust as a constructive trust, rather than an express trust.

The reasoning appears to be as follows: a breach of trust entails a wrongdoing; trusts imposed in the context of wrongdoing can only arise by operation of law;[49] and since as between constructive and resulting trusts only the former are imposed in relation to wrongdoing, the trust is necessarily constructive in nature. However, this appears to be a misanalysis. The volunteer may well be innocent, in which case the rationale of wrongdoing does not apply to trust property in *his* hands. Moreover, as discussed above, a trustee of an express trust does not automatically hold by way of a constructive trust whenever he physically misappropriates trust property or keeps for himself traceable property, even though doing so constitutes a wrongdoing.

Another potential objection to labelling a volunteer as holding trust property to the order of the original express trust is that the volunteer is not simply substituted for the trustee of the express trust, and therefore labelling an innocent volunteer as a trustee of a constructive trust reflects the fact that the volunteer does not take over all the duties of the express trustee.[50] The source of this contention, it seems, is that the volunteer is likely to be unaware of his trusteeship, and therefore it is inapposite to label his relationship with the beneficiary as an 'express trust'. However, it is clearly possible for one to become a trustee of an expressly declared trust even if he is unaware of the trust, for example where the settlor declares a trust and transfers the trust property to the trustee without the trustee's knowledge.[51] Obviously, until the trustee consents to taking office, he would not take on the full range of duties contemplated under the declaration of trust.[52] Nevertheless, if the trust relationship between the ignorant trustee and the beneficiary is to be given a label which has the aim of explaining the *source* of the trust relationship, then there is no objection to saying that the ignorant trustee is a trustee of an 'express trust', since the source of his trusteeship is the settlor's proper manifestation of intention to declare a trust. The same analysis

[46] Donovan DM Waters, Mark Gillen, and Lionel Smith, *Waters' Law of Trusts in Canada*, 4th edn (Toronto, Carswell, 2012) 1341.
[47] *Independent Trustee Services Ltd* (n 10) [80].
[48] ibid.
[49] Smith, 'Unravelling' (n 39) 321.
[50] Gardner, *Law of Trusts* (n 39) 309–10.
[51] See Ying Khai Liew and Charles Mitchell, 'The Creation of Express Trusts' (forthcoming 2018).
[52] ibid.

applies to an innocent volunteer recipient of trust property: although he may be unaware of the tainted origins of the property, the *source* of his obligation is to be found in the nature of the original trust of which the trustee breached.

The other three possible analyses of a beneficiary's right in relation to trust property in the hands of a volunteer also apply in relation to traceable proceeds which the innocent volunteer substitutes for trust property. The first of these is that the volunteer has committed a non-wrongful interference with the beneficiary's property.[53] The second is that the volunteer commits a strict liability wrong, analogous to conversion at common law.[54] The third is based on unjust enrichment: a trust arises in order to prevent the volunteer from being unjustly enriched at the beneficiary's expense.[55] Whatever the merits of these analyses, it is clear that they all recognise that the trust imposed upon the volunteer is restitutionary in nature.[56] On these analyses, then, it is again better to label the trust as a resulting trust[57] in order to recognise its restitutionary effect, and to avoid such claims from interfering with the conceptual space of constructive trust.

16.1.2.4. Theft

Finally, it has been said that a constructive trust arises in the context of theft, compelling the thief to hold the property for the benefit of the victim.[58] It is apt to distinguish between the victim's right to the stolen property and its traceable proceeds.

There are significant difficulties in analysing a thief as holding the stolen property itself on constructive trust—or, indeed, on trust at all—both as a matter of precedent and in principle. As Chambers notes, no English or Commonwealth court has found a trust to arise in relation to stolen property; the cases always involve traceable proceeds of stolen property.[59] As a matter of principle, the theft of a victim's property does not entail a transfer of the victim's property right to the thief.[60] While it may be *possible* to impose a trust on the thief's possessory title,[61] this is analytically unnecessary. 'So long as the victim retains legal title, her or his claim against the thief is … simply the enforcement of a right acquired before the theft'.[62]

[53] Peter Birks, 'Misnomer' in WR Cornish, Richard Nolan, J O'Sullivan et al, *Restitution: Past, Present & Future* (Oxford, Hart Publishing, 1998) 24; Smith, 'Unravelling' (n 39) 326, 330.

[54] This is suggested in *Hayton & Mitchell* (n 32) [12-115]. See also Mitchell and Watterson, 'Remedies for Knowing Receipt' (n 42) 116 fn 5. As *Underhill and Hayton* (n 29) [99.62] notes, however, this analysis has never provided the basis for which such cases have been decided.

[55] Peter Birks, 'Property and Unjust Enrichment: Categorical Truths' [1997] *New Zealand Law Review* 623, 661. *Hayton & Mitchell* (n 54) [12-115]; *Underhill and Hayton* (n 29) [99.63]; Mitchell and Watterson, 'Remedies for Knowing Receipt' (n 42) 116 fn 5; Burrows, *The Law of Restitution* (n 19) Ch 6.

[56] See, in particular, in relation to the first of these analyses, Birks 'Misnomer' (n 53) 24.

[57] Hence, as *Waters' Law of Trusts in Canada* (n 46) 1341 fn 31 notes in relation to the trust which arises in relation to traceable proceeds in a volunteer's hands, '[i]t is usually understood as a constructive trust but it may be best understood as a resulting trust'. This develops the analysis propounded in Chambers, *Resulting Trusts* (n 21) 106–07 that 'a resulting trust should arise over the substitute in accordance with the ordinary principle that it arises in favour of a contributor to the purchase price.'

[58] *Westdeutsche* (n 15) 716; *Armstrong DLW GmbH v Winnington Networks Ltd* [2012] EWHC 10 (Ch), [2013] Ch 156 [127]–[129]; *Black v S Freedman & Co Ltd* (1910) 12 CLR 105; *Bailey v Angove's PTY Ltd* (n 18) [50].

[59] Robert Chambers, 'Trust and Theft' in Elise Bant and Matthew Harding (eds), *Exploring Private Law* (Cambridge, CUP, 2010) 228.

[60] *Shalson v Russo* (n 16) [110]; *Hayton & Mitchell* (n 32) [15-198].

[61] Chambers, 'Trust and Theft' (n 59) 229.

[62] ibid 235.

In contrast, the victim's original property right can only be protected by means of the imposition of a trust on traceable proceeds of the stolen property, since the substitute is distinct from the original property. It is therefore relevant to ask whether the trust is constructive or resulting in nature. Chambers observes[63] that it is certainly possible to say that the thief commits a wrongdoing in substituting the stolen property for the traceable property, the wrong of which triggers a constructive trust. However, it is also possible to analyse the trust as a purchase money resulting trust, with '[p]roof of the misappropriation provid[ing] the necessary evidence that the victim did not intend to make a gift.'[64] The resulting trust analysis appears to be the better option. In particular, it recognises the fact that there is no legally material difference between the case where a thief substitutes stolen property for traceable property, and the case where a thief transfers the stolen property to an innocent volunteer's account before it is substituted by the volunteer for traceable property,[65] or indeed the case where an innocent volunteer finds money lost by a 'victim' and exchanges it for other property.[66] In all these cases, the victim's claim depends less upon whether the person who makes the exchange does so innocently or wrongfully,[67] and more on the victim's lack of intention to make a gift to the legal title holder of the traceable property. This is similar to the case discussed above[68] where trust property is transferred in breach of trust to an innocent volunteer, who then substitutes it for traceable property: the beneficiary's claim relates not to the fact that the volunteer is *innocent*, but to the fact that he is a *volunteer*, that is, that the beneficiary did not intend to make a gift to him. There is no reason in principle why the law should treat differently cases where the original property is stolen property, and where it is property transferred in breach of trust.

16.1.3. Doubtful Doctrines

The final group of omitted situations includes the forfeiture rule and breach of confidence. These situations are sometimes thought of as falling within the domain of constructive trusts. However, they are omitted from the scope of this book because it is ultimately doubtful whether constructive trusts do in fact arise in these situations, and moreover it is far from clear whether they ought to be imposed at all.

16.1.3.1. Forfeiture Rule

It has long been established that one who kills another is prevented from benefitting from property which the killer would otherwise have enjoyed as a result of the victim's death.[69] By virtue of the Forfeiture Act 1982, s 1 this rule of public policy is identified[70] as the

[63] ibid 238.

[64] ibid 239.

[65] *Heperi Pty Ltd v Belle* [2009] NSWCA 252, discussed in Chambers, 'Trust and Theft' (n 59) 241ff.

[66] Birks, 'Categorical Truths' (n 55) 661.

[67] In the case where the thief makes the substitution, 'the [wrongdoer] has done the [victim] a wrong, but this is merely incidental to the resulting trust': Chambers, *Resulting Trusts* (n 21) 108.

[68] See main text to and from n 53 above.

[69] See *Cleaver v Mutual Reserve Fund Life Association* [1892] 1 QB 147 (CA) 153.

[70] 'Section 1(1) Forfeiture Act 1986 defines the forfeiture rule as "the rule of public policy which in certain circumstances precludes a person who has unlawfully killed another from acquiring a benefit in consequence of the killing." That seems to me to be a statement by way of identification and not one which purports to codify the rule or set it out in full, for which one must look to the decided cases': *Henderson v Wilcox* [2015] EWHC 3469 (Ch), [2016] 4 WLR 14 [9].

'forfeiture rule'. This rule may apply, for example, where the killer is a legatee under the victim's will, or entitled to the victim's property by operation of intestacy rules, or where the killer and the victim were joint tenants of property and hence the killer stands to gain by operation of the doctrine of survivorship.

According to the Estates of Deceased Persons (Forfeiture Rule and Law of Succession) Act 2011,[71] the forfeiture rule operates by deeming that the killer predeceased the victim. One might have thought that the killer is therefore *never* able to benefit from his crime, and not that the killer obtains the benefit but holds in on constructive trust. After all, no English court has held that the forfeiture rule gives rise to a constructive trust. However, other Commonwealth jurisdictions[72] have suggested that the constructive trust analysis is appropriate. Moreover, Ian Williams has observed that the scope of the 2011 Act is not comprehensive: '[i]t applies only to testate and intestate succession, ignoring other circumstances in which the forfeiture rule applies. The coverage of testate succession is also limited.'[73] As a result, it might be arguable that there are situations in which a constructive trust analysis of the forfeiture rule would apply under English law.[74]

It is unnecessary for the present purposes conclusively to resolve the question of whether the constructive trust analysis provides a better explanation for the forfeiture rule. What matters is that there are compelling arguments against the constructive trust analysis to justify omitting the rule from the scope of this book. In this regard, Williams' comprehensive analysis of the 'constructive trust model' of the forfeiture rule is instructive.[75] A number of points he makes merit observation. First, it is commonly suggested that the constructive trust analysis is meritorious since it can be applied flexibly and in such a way as to reflect the testamentary intentions of the victim. However, these reasons do not withstand scrutiny: it is doubtful whether constructive trusts allow for such flexibility; moreover, the forfeiture rule is not a rule relating to testamentary intentions at all. Secondly, it is commonly argued that the constructive trust analysis is the only analysis consistent with express statutory provisions such as the Administration of Estates Act 1925 which seems to provide that the killer obtains title to property he is otherwise entitled to. However, nothing dictates that the relevant statutory provisions ought to be read literally; moreover, the statute is to be read against the background of the common law. Thirdly, the constructive trust analysis would pose 'difficulties for the coherence of the law', as it would raise 'difficult questions about the place of that trust in wider trusts doctrine.'[76] These difficulties strongly indicate that it is at best doubtful whether the forfeiture rule falls within the domain of constructive trusts, and is therefore omitted from the scope of this book.

[71] This Act makes certain amendments to the Wills Act 1837 and Administration of Estates Act 1925.

[72] See, eg, *Rasmanis v Jurewitsch* (1969) 70 SR (NSW) 407; *Rosenfeldt v Olson* [1985] 2 WWR 502; *Schobelt v Barber* (1966) 60 DLR (2nd) 519; *Re Pechar* [1969] NZLR 574.

[73] Ian Williams, 'How Does the Forfeiture Rule Work?' in Birke Häcker and Charles Mitchell, *Current Issues in Succession Law* (Oxford, Hart Publishing, 2016) 52.

See, however, *Re K* [1985] Ch 85 (Ch) 100, where Vinelott J observed that, where the killer and the victim were joint tenants, a constructive trust does not arise in English law; instead, 'the beneficial interest [is treated] as vesting in the [victim] and the [killer] as tenants in common.'

[74] See, eg, Roger Kerridge and AHR Brierley, *Parry and Kerridge: The Law of Succession*, 12th edn (London, Sweet and Maxwell, 2009) [14-83].

[75] Williams, 'Forfeiture Rule' (n 73) 56ff.

[76] ibid 61.

16.1.3.2. *Breach of Confidence*

Although there is no English case which has imposed constructive trusts in relation to profits made by means of breach of confidence, a number of English judges have mooted in favour of such an approach.[77] Other Commonwealth jurisdictions have also made similar suggestions.[78]

Upon closer inspection, it is highly doubtful whether situations of breach of confidence fall within the domain of constructive trusts at all.[79] In the first place, in many cases a breach of confidence amounts also to a breach of fiduciary duty, and any trust arising therefrom is more easily explained as a response to the breach of fiduciary duty.[80]

Moreover, there is little by way of authority and principle to support the conclusion that breach of confidence, as a standalone doctrine, triggers a constructive trust. By way of authority, the observation of Sales J (as his Lordship then was) in *Vercoe v Rutland Fund Management Ltd* is apposite:[81]

> The law relating to breach of confidence covers a very wide range of different factual situations, and it is unsurprising that the strength of the arguments in favour of any particular remedy or set of remedies in respect of a particular breach of confidence varies across that range. Sometimes the nature of the obligation of confidence may be closely similar to a fiduciary obligation … in which case it may be appropriate for remedies to be available similar to those in respect of a breach of fiduciary duty; sometimes the nature of the obligation may be closely similar to the obligations which protect forms of intellectual property … in which case it may be appropriate for remedies to be fashioned equivalent to those available in that context; sometimes … the obligation may spring from a contract, or arise in circumstances closely similar to a contractual relationship, in which case the appropriate remedy (in the absence of exceptional circumstances) is likely to be similar to those available for breach of contract; in yet other cases, e.g. where the law of confidence is used to address use of private information obtained by a stranger, a relevant analogy may be drawn from the law of tort.

It might be thought that the decision of the Canadian Supreme Court in *LAC Minerals Ltd v International Corona Resources Ltd*[82] supports the constructive trust analysis; but upon closer inspection the trust imposed in that case was a *remedial*—that is, a transformative—constructive trust. As we have observed in Chapter 11,[83] a 'remedial constructive trust' can potentially be imposed in any case, 'whatever the field of private law involved'.[84] This means that there is nothing inherent in cases of breach of confidence which entails that the constructive trust will arise.

[77] See, eg, *Attorney General v Guardian Newspapers (No. 2)* [1990] 1 AC 109 (HL) 288; *Ocular Sciences Ltd v Aspect Vision Care Ltd* [1997] RPC 289 (Ch) 416; *United Pan-Europe Communications NV v Deutsche Bank AG* [2000] 2 BCLC 461 (CA).

[78] See, eg, *LAC Minerals Ltd v Int Corona Resources Ltd* [1989] 2 SCR 574. See too *ABC v Lenah Game Meats* [2001] HCA 63 [102], [311].

[79] See, generally, Matthew Conaglen, 'Thinking about Proprietary Remedies for Breach of Confidence' [2008] *Intellectual Property Quarterly* 82.

[80] See, eg, John McGhee (ed), *Snell's Equity*, 33rd edn (London, Sweet & Maxwell, 2016) [9-023].

[81] *Vercoe v Rutland Fund Management Ltd* [2010] EWHC 424 (Ch), [2010] Bus LR D141 [344].

[82] *LAC Minerals* (n 78).

[83] See Chapter 11, S 11.2.2.2.

[84] Donovan Waters, 'The Constructive Trust: Two Theses—England and Wales, and Canada' http://archive.is/5neoh.

By way of principle, there is nothing which *logically* dictates that a constructive trust ought to be imposed on gains made by way of breach of confidence, as opposed only to a personal duty to account for such profits.[85] Therefore, at most the relevance of constructive trusts in relation to breach of confidence is doubtful, and therefore this situation is omitted from the scope of this book.

16.2. Comparing and Contrasting Different Categories

In Chapter 3,[86] a schematic of the structure of the law of constructive trusts was produced. To facilitate the discussion in this section which compares one category with another, the same structure is reproduced in Figure 3 below, but with each category being re-labelled by a letter.

	BILATERAL		UNILATERAL	COURT-BASED
	NON-CONTRACT-BASED	CONTRACT-BASED		
Replicative Constructive Trusts	[A]	[C]	[D]	—
Reflective Constructive Trusts	[B]	—	[E]	
Transformative Constructive Trusts	—			[F]

Figure 3: The structure of the law of constructive trusts, each category being represented by a letter

16.2.1. Categories [A] and [B]

There are two important lessons which can be learnt by comparing the core doctrines falling within categories [A] and [B]. The first concerns their causative events; the second concerns the remedial aspect.

[85] See, eg, *Hayton and Mitchell* (n 32) [15-189].

[86] The same schematic was set out twice. Fig 1 in Chapter 3, S 3.1. identified where the 'core' constructive trust doctrines were located within the structure, and Fig 2 in Chapter 3, S 3.5. providing the locations of both 'core' and 'non-core' doctrines.

16.2.1.1. Causative Events

It is often thought that there is little which distinguishes the doctrines falling within categories [A] and [B]. Thus, judges[87] and commentators[88] often emphasise the similarities between these doctrines; likewise, it is common practice for counsel to run arguments based on both groups of doctrines in tandem without clearly distinguishing between them.[89]

Certainly, the way in which the elements of promise and reliance feature in these categories are functionally similar in many ways. In relation to B's promise, it is the means by which B's intention is communicated to A which enables A to act in reliance. Moreover, it provides an event by which courts can ascertain B's intention objectively, consistent with other areas of private law.[90] In addition, it allows courts to determine B's original intention, ignoring any later change of mind after A's reliance is complete. Finally, it also provides the maximum extent of the remedy which may be imposed on B.

Similarities can also be detected in relation to A's reliance. This element indicates that B's promise was operative, in the sense that A's course of conduct was induced by B's promise. It also forms part of the justification for why the law provides relief by way of these doctrines: since a mere promise is unenforceable[91] and equity will not assist a volunteer,[92] A's reliance goes some way to explain why equity is justified in intervening at all.

Upon closer examination, however, significant differences emerge, primarily due to the fundamental distinction between QI and AI situations. The distinction bears repeating. In QI situations, the property in relation to which obligations under a constructive trust arise

[87] For example, in *Samad v Thompson* [2008] EWHC 2809 (Ch), [2008] NPC 125 [128]–[129] it was observed that the doctrine in *Rochefoucauld v Boustead* overlaps with proprietary estoppel to a considerable degree; in *Healey v Brown* [2002] EWHC (Ch) 1405, [2002] WTLR 849 (Ch) [25]–[29] the logic of proprietary estoppel formed part of the reasoning which led to a secret trust being imposed; in *Banner Homes Group plc v Luff Developments Ltd* [2000] Ch 372 (CA) 397 the doctrine in *Pallant v Morgan* was said to have much in common with proprietary estoppel.

[88] For an observation that the doctrine in *Rochefoucauld v Boustead* and proprietary estoppel operate in similar circumstances, see Christine Davis, 'The Inheritance Tax and Capital Gains Tax Consequences of Informal Transfers of Rights in Land' (2006) 4 *British Tax Review* 458, 462. For an argument that secret trusts and proprietary estoppel cover the same ground, see Mark Pawlowski, 'Revocable Gifts and Estoppel' (2012) 28 *Trusts and Trustees* 64. For the argument that proprietary estoppel provides the better basis for deciding cases which fall within the doctrine in *Pallant v Morgan*, see Nicholas Hopkins, 'The *Pallant v Morgan* "Equity"?' [2002] *Conveyancer and Property Lawyer* 35. And in Gardner, 'Reliance-Based Constructive Trusts' (n 14) the argument is made that the QI doctrines and proprietary estoppel all achieve the same aim of remedying A's reliance loss.

[89] See, eg, *Webster v Ashcroft* [2011] EWHC 3848 (Ch), [2012] 1 WLR 1309 for an overlap between secret trusts and proprietary estoppel; *Crossco No. 4 Unlimited v Jolan Ltd* [2011] EWHC 803 (Ch), [2011] NPC 38 [256]ff for an overlap between the doctrine in *Pallant v Morgan* and proprietary estoppel.

[90] See Robert Stevens, 'Rights Restricting Remedies' in Andrew Robertson and Michael Tilbury (eds), *Divergences in Private Law* (Oxford, Hart Publishing, 2016) 164: 'The meaning of promises, just as with words in general, is not determined by the subjective intent of those who use them, and both as a matter of morality and law we are bound by the promises for which we are responsible, regardless of whether we subjectively intended to make them. Promises, as actions in the world, do not take place in our heads. We cannot just will them to be.'

[91] 'The breaking of a promise, without more, is morally reprehensible, but not unconscionable in the sense that equity will necessarily prevent its occurrence or remedy the consequent loss': *Commonwealth of Australia v Verwayen* (1990) 170 CLR 394, 416. See also, eg, *Cobbe v Yeoman's Row Management Ltd* [2008] UKHL 55, [2008] 1 WLR 1752 [92]; *Walton v Walton* (CA 14 April, 1994): 'if there had been nothing more than the promise, [the defendant] would have been free to change her mind'.

[92] *Milroy v Lord* (1862) 4 De GF & J 264, 45 ER 1185; Jeffrey Hackney, *Understanding Equity and Trusts* (London, Fontana Press, 1987) 118.

is not previously owned by B; in AI situations a constructive trust arises in relation to property which B already owns. The fact that the former situations, and not the latter, involve an *acquisition* of property by B is central to understanding the key differences between the two categories.

Consider first the element of B's promise. In category [A] B's promise always relates to property yet to be acquired, since it is by promising that he indicates his intention to take only a qualified interest in that property when acquired. In category [B], on the other hand, B promises that he will cede an interest in property he already owns absolutely. An obvious distinction is therefore that category [A] doctrines are concerned with pre-acquisition promises while category [B] is concerned with post-acquisition[93] promises.[94] As Chadwick LJ observed of the doctrine in *Pallant v Morgan* in *Banner Homes group plc v Luff Developments Ltd*, '[i]t is the pre-acquisition arrangement which colours the subsequent acquisition by the defendant and leads to his being treated as a trustee if he seeks to act inconsistently with it.'[95]

The relevance of the fact of acquisition to the distinction between the QI and AI doctrines extends also to the element of A's reliance. Thus, the nature of A's reliance differs according to the category in question. In category [A], A must rely in such a way that confers a relevant advantage: he must participate[96] in B's acquisition of the property to which B's promise relates by increasing B's opportunity of acquiring it. In contrast, the nature of A's reliance in category [B] has nothing to do with B's acquisition of the property to which B's promise relates. This follows from the fact that B's promise relates to property which he already owns absolutely.

Because the nature of A's reliance differs between the two groups of doctrines, it also follows that the notion of 'reasonable reliance'[97] is relevant only to category [B] and not to category [A]. In the former category, this concept protects B and reflects the fact 'that [A] has some responsibility for his or her well-being and cannot expect [B] to be responsible for detriment arising from *any* action [A] takes in reliance on [B]'s … promise'.[98] In category [A], however, once it is shown that B's promise led A to act in reliance in such a way that B obtains an advantage in relation to his acquisition, it is no defence for B to show that A's reliance was 'unreasonable'. For instance, it will not help B's case to argue that it was

[93] There is a minor proviso, namely that a pre-acquisition promise which is relied upon post-acquisition triggers the operation of proprietary estoppel: see Chapter 7, S 7.4.2.

[94] It might be tempting to surmise from this that category [A] relates to a promise to create a *trust* whereas category [B] relates to a promise to make a *gift*. This sort of distinction is, however, unnecessarily confusing, since the categories of 'trust' and 'gift' are not mutually exclusive. For example, on one view a trust is 'essentially a gift, projected on the plane of time and so subjected to a management regime': Bernard Rudden, 'Book Review' (1981) 44 *MLR* 610. It is important, rather, to focus on the material distinction—that of whether the promise relates to property B owns absolutely, or property he does not yet own.

[95] *Banner Homes* (n 87) 397. See also *Cobbe* (n 91) [33]. Similarly, in *Crossco* (n 89) [363]–[364], Morgan J observed that 'there can be an important difference between a case of a pre-acquisition arrangement and a post-acquisition arrangement.'

[96] 'Participation' here refers to the fact that A transfers the property to B or confers an opportunity upon B to acquire the property in question.

[97] See, eg, *Thorner v Major* [2009] UKHL 18, [2009] 1 WLR 776 [29]; *Thompson v Foy* [2009] EWHC 1076 (Ch), [2010] 1 P & CR 16.

[98] Ben McFarlane, *The Law of Proprietary Estoppel* (Oxford, OUP, 2014) [3-20].

unreasonable for A to have trusted B to carry out B's promise, or that a reasonable person in A's position would have ensured an express trust was properly declared instead of transferring property to B on the basis of an informal agreement.

Another difference arises in relation to the timing of A's reliance. In category [A], A's act of reliance is always completed prior to B's acquisition of the property. This is necessarily so, since only then can A's reliance lead to B obtaining an advantage in relation to the acquisition of the property. Thus, B's acquisition represents a clear 'cut-off point' up to which the parties' actions are measured. Indeed, B always has ample opportunity to revoke his promise and to inform A of this before the acquisition, and surely he ought to do so if he does not wish to keep his promise. Absent such a revocation, B will always acquire the property *on the basis of* his promise. Furthermore, A would have had the option to refuse to rely on B's promise; and his decision to act serves to confirm the fact that B's promise forms the basis of A's reliance and B's acquisition. In contrast, A's reliance in category [B] has nothing to do with conferring on B an opportunity to acquire the property to which B's promise relates. Therefore, A's actions up to the date of judgment are potentially relevant to the assessment of the appropriate remedy.

16.2.1.2. Remedies Beyond Constructive Trusts

The second lesson is that the rationales which underlie the doctrines falling within categories [A] and [B] are capable of explaining remedies other than constructive trusts.

In relation to category [B], the discussion in Chapter 7[99] has explained that courts may impose a constructive trust or some lesser remedy in order to compensate A for the loss he suffers due to B acting unreliably.

In relation to category [A], it can be observed that parties may enter into arrangements which involve B promising to qualify his interest in the property he receives from A by way of ceding some non-proprietary interest to C. For instance, in the 'subject to' cases, a vendor (A) sells property to a purchaser (B) subject to B's recognition of a third party's (C's) personal right. Even here, courts compel B to carry out his promise if A relies in the appropriate way, albeit through imposing a personal remedy. Thus, in *Binions v Evans*,[100] B was compelled to give effect to a contractual licence;[101] in *Lyus v Prowsa Developments Ltd*[102] B was compelled to build a house on a plot of land on B's acquired estate and to sell it to C; and in *Chattey v Farndale Holdings Inc*[103] B was compelled to recognise a purchaser's lien over money deposited by C to purchase flats on the land.

A number of points can be made in relation to these cases. First, although courts have described equity's intervention by way of an imposition of a 'constructive trust',[104] that phrase is not used in this context to reflect the conferral of a proprietary beneficial

[99] See Chapter 7, S 7.1.1.

[100] See the judgment of Lord Denning MR in *Binions v Evans* (n 12). Megaw and Stephenson LJJ found for C on a different basis.

[101] This was approved in *Ashburn Anstalt* (n 12).

[102] *Lyus v Prowsa Developments Ltd* (n 12).

[103] *Chattey v Farndale Holdings Inc* (n 12).

[104] See, eg, *Binions v Evans* (n 12) 368; *Lyus v Prowsa Developments Ltd* (n 12) 1053; *Ashburn Anstalt* (n 12) 26; *Chattey v Farndale Holdings Inc* (n 12) 317.

interest on C.[105] Instead, B is simply compelled to give effect to his promise, whatever its content may be.[106] The phrase 'constructive trust' is not indicative of the substance of the imposed remedy.

Secondly, it is neither necessary nor sufficient for B to have acknowledged or agreed to give effect to a pre-existing personal obligation owed by A to C: B must qualify his interest in the property by promising to confer 'fresh rights on third parties who may be entitled to the benefit of the incumbrances'.[107] For instance, in *Lyus*,[108] C contracted with V, a vendor, to buy V's land after a house was built on it. Before fulfilling the contract, V became insolvent. A, V's bank and mortgagee, sold the land to B. Because A had a legal charge prior in date to C's contract, A had no pre-existing obligation towards C.[109] However, A decided to sell the land subject to C's contractual rights anyway. Dillon J held that C had an enforceable right against B.[110] Very often such a promise is embodied in the contract between A and B. However, provided that B makes the promise to A, it does not matter whether it is referred to in the parties' contract.[111] Instead, consistently with category [A], these cases can be understood as responding to B's promise to take a qualified interest; and the courts bind B to the entirety of his promise by conferring on C a right which corresponds precisely to the right which B promises to cede to him.

Thirdly, it is also necessary for A to have relied on B's promise. Its importance can be detected in the factors which the courts take into account when determining whether B has undertaken to recognise a 'fresh right'. According to Nicholas Hopkins,[112] these factors are: where A risks liability to C unless C is granted a right against B;[113] where B pays less than the market value for the property;[114] and the absence of any other reason for the inclusion of the 'subject to' clause.[115] It can be seen from these factors that B will be taken to have made a promise to grant a 'fresh right' only where A relies on B to carry out his promise. The element of reliance is fulfilled where the property is transferred; it is unnecessary for A to have acted because he owed C a pre-existing obligation.[116]

Fourthly, consistent with the analysis in Chapter 4,[117] B's promise does not need to be a 'but for' cause of his acquisition of A's property; it is simply necessary that B's promise induces A to transfer the property *on the basis* of B's promise to confer a right on C. This can be tested by examining whether B could have struck out the term without A objecting to it. If so, then A did not rely on B's promise, since the term would have been inserted without A having given it any thought at all. As the Court of Appeal noted in *Ashburn Anstalt*,[118]

[105] See McFarlane, '*Sub Conditione*' (n 14) 679–82; Gardner, 'Reliance-Based Constructive Trusts' (n 14) 89–90.

[106] See also *Ryan v Starr* [2005] NSWSC 170 [97]; Nicholas Hopkins, *The Informal Acquisition of Rights in Land*, Modern Legal Studies (London, Sweet & Maxwell, 2000) 57.

[107] *Lyus v Prowsa Developments Ltd* (n 12) 1051, affirmed in *Ashburn Anstalt* (n 12) 25. See also *Lloyd v Dugdale* [2001] EWCA Civ 1754, [2002] 2 P & CR 13 [52].

[108] *Lyus v Prowsa Developments Ltd* (n 12).

[109] ibid 1053.

[110] ibid.

[111] ibid 1048.

[112] Hopkins, *The Informal Acquisition of Rights in Land* (n 106) 50–51.

[113] See, eg, *Binions v Evans* (n 12), as explained in *Lyus v Prowsa Developments Ltd* (n 12) 1051.

[114] See, eg, *Binions v Evans* (n 12).

[115] See, eg, *Lyus v Prowsa Developments Ltd* (n 12) 1053.

[116] *Ashburn Anstalt* (n 12) 24.

[117] See Chapter 4, S 4.2.2.2.

[118] *Ashburn Anstalt* (n 12) 25–26.

'[t]he mere fact that the land is expressed to be conveyed "subject to" a contract does not necessarily imply that [B] is to be under an obligation, not otherwise existing, to give effect to the provisions of the contract.'

Finally, the 'subject to' cases indicate that the underlying rationale of the doctrines falling within category [A] is not limited to cases where the property in B's hands is subjected to a (proprietary) constructive trust. Because B will always be bound to carry out the entirety of his promise in relation to the acquired property, the appropriate remedy, whether proprietary or personal in nature, will be determined by the content of B's promise.

16.2.2. Categories [A] and [C]

It is a unique feature of categories [A] and [C] that they each involve the identification of common rationales which underpin seemingly distinct core doctrines. It might therefore be asked whether in these categories the law should completely abandon the 'nominally distinct doctrines' in favour of a direct recognition of their respective underlying common rationale.[119]

In order to answer this question, it is first necessary to consider why distinct doctrines exist within each of those categories. One plausible answer is that each doctrine has been developed to deal with a specific factual scenario. Thus, within category [A], the label 'the doctrine in *Rochefoucauld v Boustead*' reflects an application of the underlying rationale in an inter vivos context; the label 'secret trusts' reflects a testamentary context; and 'the doctrine in *Pallant v Morgan*' reflects an application of the rationale where A is not the transferor of the property in question. Within category [C], 'specifically enforceable contracts of sale' and the 'future property' doctrines indicate the application of the underlying doctrine to contracts relating to the transfer of presently-owned property and expectancies respectively.

The gist of the matter, therefore, is whether there is any useful purpose in distinguishing between the different factual scenarios within each category. It is suggested that it is indeed useful to do so in relation to category [A] but not in relation to category [C]. Take the latter first. The analysis in Chapter 8[120] has suggested that the requirements of the two doctrines are indistinguishable. If this is correct, then there is no need to maintain the distinction between the doctrines, since absolutely nothing turns on the 'present-ness' or 'future-ness' of the subject-matter of the contract.

In relation to category [A], however, the different factual scenarios affect how courts determine whether the underlying rationale applies. For example, each doctrine relates to the lack of compliance with a different formality requirement, and so the contextual application of the underlying rationale is important. Moreover, the different factual contexts in which the elements of promise and reliance arise in these doctrines have an important bearing on how courts assess whether these elements are fulfilled. By maintaining the distinction between the doctrines, courts can ensure that the underlying rationale is applied in the best possible way to the facts which give rise to it. And where a novel case arises for consideration, the application of the rationale can be extended by analogy with the established

[119] Gardner, 'Reliance-Based Constructive Trusts' (n 14) 80.
Note that the question pursued here is different from that relating to whether the proper analysis of a particular doctrine ought to be affected by the label used, an issue pursued below in the main text following n 131 below.

[120] See Chapter 8, S 8.3.

doctrines; or alternatively, a wholly new set of facts may be identified by a new label as and when necessary in order to inform future applications of the rationale on similar facts.

16.2.3. Categories [A] and [D]

One underlying thesis of this book is that each type of trust—express, constructive, and resulting—has a unique role to play in the law of trusts.[121] The relationship between the three types of trusts in relation to the element of intention has troubled some judges and commentators. For example, it might seem inexplicable for the law to give effect to purported arrangements which fall short of enforceable express trusts or incomplete transfers of legal title as constructive trusts, in particular for the benefit of volunteers. Where property has passed pursuant to an agreement which cannot be enforced as an express trust, it might also be thought that only a resulting trust ought to be imposed to return the parties to their status quo. As categories [A] and [D] indicate, however, far from intruding on the domain of express and resulting trusts, the fact that constructive trusts arise in these categories in fact support the underlying aims of express and resulting trusts.

Take first the relationship between express and constructive trusts. Although it is true that express trusts are created by the settlor's unilateral intention, it is also trite that, where the settlor and trustee are different individuals, it is necessary for a trustee to consent to act as trustee before personal rights and corresponding duties which are created by the settlor can come into existence.[122] By accepting office, the trustee agrees to qualify his interest in the property he obtains from the settlor. Certainly, this is not the primary reason why the law enforces express trusts: their rationale relates to the settlor's unilateral freedom to deal with his own property by making use of the express trust facility.[123] Nevertheless, it remains true that the enforcement of express trusts have the desirable *effect* of ensuring that a trustee takes only a qualified interest in the property according to the terms of the trust which he consents to carry out. But if an arrangement cannot be enforced as an express trust, it may remain necessary to enforce the parties' agreement in order to ensure that the recipient of property takes only a qualified interest in it. Otherwise, the law will be responding to form (or, more precisely, the lack of form) over substance, and it is the very essence of express trusts that they exist to give effect to the substance of an agreement despite the appearance of legal title at common law. This explains why constructive trusts falling within category [A] arise despite the non-enforceability of the parties' arrangement as express trusts.

Consider next the relationship between constructive and resulting trusts. Resulting trusts provide a default position in the law which ensures that one does not effectively transfer away property unless there is a clear indication that such alienation of property was intended.[124] They give effect to substance over form by recognising a property owner's lack of intention to benefit the recipient despite a successful transfer of legal title to the recipient. This position is further enhanced by the imposition of constructive trusts in category [D]: if a property owner has a firm enough intention to benefit the recipient, this should not

[121] See, in particular, Chapter 1, S 1.2.
[122] Liew and Mitchell, 'The Creation of Express Trusts' (n 51).
[123] See Chapter 1, S 1.2.1.
[124] See Chapter 1, S 1.2.2.2.

be impeded by an unsuccessful transfer of legal title. In this way, constructive and resulting trusts can be understood as working alongside each other without friction.

16.2.4. Categories [B] and [E]

The idea that constructive trusts may be awarded in response to a breach of a primary right might be thought to be a difficult proposition to accept. The most common remedy imposed where a wrong is committed is compensatory damages, which is a personal remedy. Moreover, it might be thought that, in principle, a wrong affects both the wrongdoer and the victim only, which would suggest that a personal remedy is all that is needed to make things right as between them. Such views have affected how certain judges and commentators have rationalised constructive trusts imposed in relation to doctrines falling within categories [B] and [E], namely proprietary estoppel and gains made in breach of fiduciary duty. These views have led to the adoption of certain strategies in order to avoid the perceived concerns. For example, these constructive trusts have been characterised as not responding to a wrong at all but either imposed to enforce primary rights and duties, or not in response to duties at all but mere liabilities.

As the discussion of those doctrines has indicated, however, these are mischaracterisations which mislead a proper analysis. Categories [B] and [E] demonstrate that it is possible for one to exercise one's power as an owner of property or as a fiduciary in an undesirable way such that it causes harm to another or leads to a personal gain being made. The compensatory or disgorgement aim of the imposed remedy may, in certain circumstances, justify a court's exercise of its remedial discretion in relation to the appropriate content of the remedy which leads to the imposition of a constructive trust.

Three important lessons can be drawn from recognising that these constructive trusts respond to a wrong. First, the ability to exercise discretion in relation to the award of a constructive trust in response to a wrong does not entail that the trust falls within category [F]. Unlike transformative constructive trusts, a constructive trust awarded in response to a wrong does not provide for the exercise of discretion as to the goal of the remedy, and this is an important factor which limits the discretion of the court. Secondly, apart from a lack of discretion as to goal, the doctrine of precedent may also be deployed as a mechanism to control the judicial exercise of remedial discretion. This cautions against denying that constructive trusts are imposed in response to a wrong simply because the courts do not appear to exercise discretion on a case-by-case basis. Finally, and most importantly, the selection of a constructive trust remedy as a response to a wrong requires explicit and proper justification. Given the proprietary effects of a constructive trust, the reasons for its imposition over other, lesser remedies must properly be enunciated. Understanding these constructive trusts as responding to a wrong entails recognising that a remedial choice is being made. It is crucial for courts to make explicit the policy reasons behind such a choice.

16.2.5. Categories [A] and [E]

In relation to the point last made, a comparison between categories [A] and [E] indicates that there is a crucial distinction between justifications based on the parties' agreement and those not so based. Simply because an agreement between the parties may be found in the chain of events leading to a constructive trust's imposition does not mean that it is always appropriate to analyse the constructive trust as being triggered or justified by reference to that agreement. So, for instance, doctrines falling within category [A] can properly be said to be 'agreement-based', since the agreement is the basis on which one party acts, and the constructive trust imposed on the other party arises precisely to compel him to carry out his part of the agreement. Conversely, in relation to category [E], simply because fiduciary relationships are commonly created by express agreement does not entail that a constructive trust imposed on gains made in breach of fiduciary duty can be justified simply on the basis of that agreement.

The temptation to justify the imposition of constructive trusts by reference to the parties' agreement whenever one is found may be due to a general unease, characteristic of English courts, over the exercise of judicial discretion to vary property rights. Consider again category [E]. One rationale which has been put forward for those constructive trusts is that the fiduciary, when taking office, agrees that any gain he makes in office will be attributed to his principal. This explanation appears to sidestep the need to characterise the imposition of a constructive trust as a product of the exercise of judicial discretion at all: if it were based on the parties' agreement, then it simply gives effect to that agreement, no more and no less. The same tendency to rely on the parties' agreement was also seen in Chapter 14 in relation to the 'common intention constructive trust' which courts claim to arise simply in response to a 'common intention'—an agreement—between the parties. Upon closer inspection, however, explaining the constructive trusts in these two contexts on the basis of the parties' agreement requires courts to manufacture the *terms* which the constructive trusts purportedly give effect to. In the context of category [E], it is unlikely that the parties would have even thought about the possibility that the fiduciary would receive bribes, let alone how those bribes ought to be held by the fiduciary. In the context of the 'common intention constructive trust', in all but the rarest of cases the parties would not have considered what is to be done with the beneficial interest in their family home. Explaining the constructive trusts by reference to the parties' agreement therefore involves an element of fiction, and fails to explain the true reason for which they are imposed. Conversely, recognising the wrong-based nature of the doctrines does not necessarily entail the widespread exercise of judicial discretion, this being curtailed by the goal of the remedy as well as the doctrine of precedent. More importantly, it highlights the need to give proper, policy-based justifications for the imposition of the constructive trusts.

16.2.6. Categories [B] and [D]

It is trite that ownership of property provides the owner with unique opportunities to deal directly with, or in relation to, property one owns. In particular, one may commit oneself to giving away an interest in one's property. Short of entering a contract to do so, such commitments may either be coupled with acts which indicate a finality of intention to transfer legal title to the property to another, or cause another party to act in detrimental reliance. Categories [B] and [D] indicate how a constructive trust might arise in relation to the exercise of power by a property owner.

Because both categories involve an owner committing to give away property to another, there is a temptation to collapse both categories into one. As we have seen, this was precisely the error which the Court of Appeal fell into in *Pennington v Waine*,[125] where the Court misanalysed the case as one falling within category [D] when it ought properly to have been decided as a category [B] case. Such an unstructured understanding promotes an unhelpfully reductionist approach—that constructive trusts in these categories simply respond to 'unconscionable' behaviour—and risks masking the different reasons why they arise. The distinction between the two categories compels us to recognise the different ways in which a property owner may deal with his property and the distinct legal consequences which may attach to different acts by a property owner. In particular, a distinction must be drawn between constructive trusts imposed in the interests of finality and certainty on the one hand, and of compensating for the unreliability of induced assumptions on the other.

16.3. The Historical Context

Given the rich history of the law of trusts, it is fitting to conclude by observing how the analysis proffered in this book may have, historically, informed the enforcement of trusts arrangements. This specifically relates to the doctrines which fall within category [A], that is, those reflecting QI situations within the non-contract-based, bilateral events category of constructive trusts.

Although not everything is known about the beginnings of the law of trusts (originally, uses), two things are certain. First, the very first use arrangements which were enforced by the Court of Chancery were not express uses. One could not create a use merely because he wanted to, given that there was no facilitative device available for an owner of property to create a use. Secondly, the very first use arrangements involved a *transfer* of property from A to B which constituted B as the *feoffee*, as opposed to cases where A declared *himself* as *feoffee* for the benefit of another. As FW Maitland and Francis Montague note,[126] '[i]n the second half of the fourteenth century many causes were conspiring to induce the landholders of England to convey their lands to friends, who, while becoming the legal owners of those lands, would, nevertheless, be bound by an honourable understanding as to the uses to which their ownership should be put.'

The willingness of the Chancellor to enforce these arrangements was undoubtedly based on the principles of 'Conscience, Good Faith, Honesty and Equity', as derived from the prerogative of Grace that was delegated to him.[127] This suggests that, before the facility of the express use was made available in English law, the enforcement of use arrangements

[125] *Pennington v Waine* [2002] EWCA Civ 227, [2002] 1 WLR 2075, discussed in Chapter 9, S 9.1.4.1.

[126] Frederic William Maitland and Francis C Montague, *A Sketch of English Legal History* (New Jersey, The Lawbook Exchange, 2010) 122–23.

[127] George Spence, *The Equitable Jurisdiction of the Court of Chancery* (Philadelphia, Lea and Blanchard, 1846) 407–08.

was not primarily focused on what A did but what B promised:[128] B was bound to give effect to the arrangement because *he* acquired A's property on the basis of his promise and therefore *his* conscience was affected. Adopting the terminology used in this book, the first arrangements which were enforced in the Court of Chancery were 'constructive trusts' which reflected a QI situation: B was bound because his promise to qualify his interest in the property had induced A's transfer of the property to him. It is perhaps for this reason that the courts later described equity's intervention as aiming to prevent B from acting in an 'unconscionable' or 'fraudulent' manner.

Undoubtedly, the Court of Chancery acted based on precedent. As George Spence writes,[129] '[n]othing is recorded as having been delivered judicially from the bench which can warrant the supposition that the private opinion or conscience of the judge ... independent of principle and precedent, was a legitimate ground of decision.' Due to the Court's consistent response of enforcing such arrangements, the express use facility eventually emerged. In essence, it became possible for A to rely on the courts' enforcement of such arrangements without having to rely merely on B's honesty and good faith.[130] This shift of focus from B's integrity to A's employment of the express use facility was also embraced by the courts. For instance, the courts were soon willing to enforce A's intention directly where he had properly declared an express use. At least two developments in the law of trusts reflect this shift. First, given the focus on A's intention, A no longer needed to secure B's promise; hence the maxim 'a trust will not fail for the want of a trustee': express trusts could generally be carried out provided that *anyone* was willing to act as trustee. Secondly, once the facility of the express trust had been well-entrenched in the law, A could also declare *himself* as trustee of his own property for the benefit of C. Of course, such self-declared trusts did not involve any transfer of property, and so did not reflect a QI situation. Nevertheless, it remains clear that they grew out of trust arrangements which were enforced against recipients of transferred property.[131]

This historical relevance of constructive trusts also provides two other lessons. First, the mere fact that a certain phenomenon is (or is not) given a particular label ought not to dictate how we rationalise the substance of the phenomenon. The first uses which were enforced historically were most certainly not given the label 'constructive uses' or 'constructive trusts'; but this does not detract from the fact that the concern which motivated the enforcement of the first uses is similar to that which underlies certain QI doctrines which are now said to give rise to 'constructive trusts'. The same attitude ought properly to inform our approach towards other constructive trust doctrines. For example, the doctrine of proprietary estoppel ought to be understood for how it is applied in substance, without being misled by the technical meaning of 'estoppel'.[132] To take another example, simply because constructive trusts are best understood as remedies does not entail that all constructive trusts fall to be considered within the '*remedial* constructive trusts' doctrine, by which courts

[128] This is also seen in that B who would not keep faith was imprisoned by the Chancellor: Maitland and Montague, *A Sketch of English Legal History* (n 126) 123.

[129] Spence, *The Equitable Jurisdiction* (n 127) 415.

[130] See Gardner, 'Reliance-Based Constructive Trusts' (n 14) 84–85.

[131] Indeed, it is only by recognising this fact that it becomes clear why one who declares himself as trustee is treated as playing two roles—one *qua* 'settlor' and another *qua* 'trustee'.

[132] Lord Scott fell into this precise error in *Cobbe* (n 91) [28].

exercise wide-ranging discretion to determine both the goal and content of the appropriate remedy to be imposed in any particular case.[133] Consistent with equity's general approach, a proper understanding of constructive trusts ought properly to focus on the substance of the various doctrines rather than the form or label by which they are known.

The second lesson is that the majority of constructive trusts are not imposed *simply* to correct or prevent an undesirable state of affairs such as the perpetration of 'fraud' or 'unconscionable' conduct. Instead, many constructive trust doctrines respond to rights and duties which are intentionally created. All too often the active roles of the parties to a constructive trust are downplayed. For instance, Lord Browne-Wilkinson famously said in *Westdeustche Landesbank Girozentrale v Islington LBC*[134] that constructive trusts are 'imposed by law against the intentions of the trustee'. Similarly, Lionel Smith has written that obligations under a constructive trust are 'not voluntarily undertaken'.[135] A related worry is that certain constructive trust doctrines allow parties intentionally to subvert certain statutory formality requirements, turning those formality provisions into 'optional' rules in practice.[136] However, the courts generally do not appear to be concerned with the possibility of parties deliberately effectuating informal agreements which may be enforced as constructive trusts; and this can be explained by the historical context of the law of trusts. The first uses enforced by the Chancellor suggest that, short of creating an express trust, it remains possible for parties purposefully and intentionally to enter into transactions which give rise to a constructive trust relationship. The same is the case in relation to many of the doctrines discussed in this book. Appreciating the different ways in which constructive trusts respond to different acts of the parties allows us to take a significant step towards attaining a proper, structured understanding of the law of constructive trusts.

[133] See Chapter 11, S 11.2.2.2.
[134] *Westdeutsche* (n 15) 708.
[135] Smith, 'Unravelling' (n 39) 323.
[136] See, eg, McFarlane, '*Sub Conditione*' (n 14) 695 fn 154; Gardner, 'Reliance-Based Constructive Trusts' (n 14) 86–87.

INDEX

Introductory Note

References such as '178–79' indicate (not necessarily continuous) discussion of a topic across a range of pages. Wherever possible in the case of topics with many references, these have either been divided into sub-topics or only the most significant discussions of the topic are listed. Because the entire work is about 'constructive trusts', the use of this term (and certain others which occur constantly throughout the book) as an entry point has been restricted. Information will be found under the corresponding detailed topics.

www.ingramcontent.com/pod-product-compliance
Ingram Content Group UK Ltd.
Pitfield, Milton Keynes, MK11 3LW, UK
UKHW051449290926
15471UKWH00008B/1102